LATIN AMERICAN HISTORY: SELECT PROBLEMS

Identity, Integration, and Nationhood

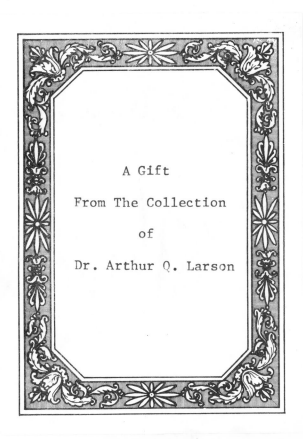

VOLUME EDITOR

Fredrick B. Pike

UNIVERSITY OF NOTRE DAME

THE EDITORS

William V. D'Antonio
UNIVERSITY OF NOTRE DAME

Charles Gibson
UNIVERSITY OF MICHIGAN

J. León Helguera
VANDERBILT UNIVERSITY

Peggy K. Korn
SWARTHMORE COLLEGE

J. H. Parry
HARVARD UNIVERSITY

John Leddy Phelan
UNIVERSITY OF WISCONSIN

Fredrick B. Pike
UNIVERSITY OF NOTRE DAME

Kalman H. Silvert
FORD FOUNDATION

Thomas E. Skidmore
UNIVERSITY OF WISCONSIN

Robert Freeman Smith
UNIVERSITY OF CONNECTICUT

Alfred C. Stepan
RAND CORPORATION

John Womack, Jr.
HARVARD UNIVERSITY

Under the General Editorship of John Morton Blum, Yale University

Latin American History:
Select Problems

Identity, Integration, and Nationhood

HARCOURT, BRACE & WORLD, INC.

New York / Chicago / San Francisco / Atlanta

PREFACE

The area most commonly known today as Latin America has consistently puzzled and perplexed outsiders. The Spaniards who arrived with the Columbus expeditions did not know what to make of the region and were undecided whether to settle there or to abandon it and continue the search for a new route to Asia in the hope of establishing permanent colonies there. Even before their resolution to remain had been bolstered by the discovery of precious metals, they had begun to debate how the area should be governed. Differences of opinion were particularly sharp in regard to the treatment of native populations. The often cruel conduct of the conquerors suggests that most of them basically accepted the philosophy of imperialism advanced by certain Spanish theologians who believed in the innate inferiority of the natives. Other Spaniards held more humanistic views, however, and somehow the Indians, although greatly reduced in number, did manage to survive, particularly in those areas that would become the republics of Mexico, Guatemala, Ecuador, Peru, Bolivia, and Paraguay.

Outsiders such as the first Spanish explorers and conquerors are not the only observers to have been puzzled by Latin America. Throughout their history, the Latin Americans themselves appear to have been perplexed about their lands and their national characters. The descendants of the conquerors—whether creoles (those of pure Spanish ancestry) or mestizos (those of mixed Spanish-Indian background)—who made their permanent homes in the New World continued through the centuries to be as divided in their opinions concerning the capabilities of the surviving Indians, the potential of the mixed bloods, and the means for incorporating non-Spanish groups into society as were the conquerors, early colonial administrators, and Spanish theologians. To this day in those areas of Latin America that actually are best described as Indo-America, fundamental agreement has not been achieved in interpreting the contemporary reality and future destiny.

In New Spain (Mexico), ambivalence of attitude toward the Indian and his place in society was evident at the inception of the country's independence movement. Some leaders within the movement wished to preserve the rigidly stratified, hierarchical colonial social structure in which skin color and ethnic background had figured among the many criteria for determining a person's status. Others wished to develop a somewhat more open society and frequently proclaimed the natural rights of all men. Even these more liberal Mexicans evidenced both doubt and fear, however, when they considered the future role in society of Indians and mestizos who had long been the victims of exploitation and discrimination. Sorely divided over whether to identify with the colonial past or with the intellectually exciting but socially dangerous models and institutions of liberal and economically progressive European nations and the United States, the men who won Mexican independence took almost no significant steps toward assimilating the Indian and marginal masses into an integrated nation.

Once Peru achieved its independence from Spain, intellectuals and political leaders continued the debate, begun in early colonial times, over the relative merits of the Spanish and Inca cultures. Not until the middle of the twentieth century did the intensity of this polemic begin to abate as national leaders sought a compromise position. Substantial differences still remained, however, in the ways that Peruvians assessed the qualities of the various ethnic and cultural elements that made up the national population; as a result, no widely shared consensus emerged as to what is the true identity and destiny of the land. Nor were effective steps taken toward integration; the vast Indian masses remained outside any meaningful participation in the national existence.

In Argentina, disagreement over the relative merits and vices of the native, creole elements and of the immigrants who swarmed into the country in the second half of the nineteenth century prevented the achievement of widely shared values, of a sense of identity, and of socio-politico-economic integration, all of which are prerequisites of genuine nationhood. As in other parts of Latin America, the differences separating contending cultural groups were often exaggerated by passionate polemicists who saw good only in one group, evil and vice in all others. Seldom basing their assertions on objective, empirical investigation, the polemicists have been inspired largely by myth and fantasy.

Colombia, not presented with the challenge of assimilating large masses of Indians or immigrants, encountered other obstacles in the quest for integration and identity. In addition to being divided by some of the most formidable geographic barriers in the western hemisphere and separated by almost unbreachable social walls, Colombians were deeply embroiled in the Liberal–Conservative controversy. Tending to regard themselves first as either Liberals or Conservatives, depending upon the set of social, political, intellectual, and philosophical values with which they identified, then as residents of a particular city or region, and finally as Colombians, the people of this strife-torn country made little progress in the nineteenth century toward transforming their land into a nation.

In Brazil, perhaps even more than in Colombia, regional diversities, imbalances, and animosities prevented the country, at least until the 1930's, from progressing consistently toward national unification. In contrast to their Hispanic American neighbors, however, Brazilians were able to prevent the division of their vast national territory into several countries. Their success in retaining some degree of unity in the face of striking diversity was threatened by the nineteenth-century dispute over slavery which pitted the slaveowning North against the free South. Ultimately, the Brazilian genius for compromise overcame this source of divisiveness; and the peaceful abolition of slavery, despite the glum reactions of a few die-hard opponents, touched off widespread celebrations and evoked a sense of national accomplishment and pride. Nonetheless, Brazilians remained in fundamental disagreement as to what type of role and what degree of participation in national life should be permitted the freedmen. Thus, abolition in some ways intensified the problem of integration. To this day the problem has not been resolved, despite the exaggerated claims, so frequently heard, that Brazil has achieved a true racial democracy.

Throughout the first century of their independence and beyond, most Latin American countries were characterized by cultural heterogeneity, by lack of social, political, and economic integration, and by fundamental disagreement over what models, values, and systems to identify with in struggling toward unity and nationhood. Because widely shared values among a homogeneous population were lacking, political structures were often relatively unimportant. They were mere forms, lacking in organic development and substance, imported heedlessly from other countries that had already achieved relatively homogeneous populations and modern nation-state status. When introduced into Latin America, these models functioned, if at all, only for the very small percentage of the population that was politicized. To the great masses, unassimilated and nonparticipating in a rigidly organized class structure based in part on cultural-racial discrimination, political forms were meaningless; more often than not they were mere masks, hiding the true faces of the countries.

In the twentieth century, various Latin American countries have resorted to social revolution in the attempt to achieve integration and establish a consensus on identity and national destiny. The Revolution that erupted in Mexico in 1910 at first meant all things to all men. Slowly, wider and wider support began to crystallize around a set of values that were progressively and pragmatically being better defined. The Revolution also led to important measures for incorporating Indian masses into society. As a result, Mexico came to be, in the appraisal of some political scientists and sociologists, the first true nation in Latin America.

Earlier in the twentieth century, Argentina, rather than Mexico, seemed preeminent in the drive for nationhood, but it began to falter in the 1930's, and the regime of Juan Domingo Perón was unable to restore its momentum. Although traditional and conservative, as well as highly opportunistic, in many of his approaches, Perón presided over a movement that unleashed forces of revolutionary change; in the long run, however, his attempt to mold a cohesive entity out of a divided land through a combination of traditional and revolutionary expedients failed. The Perón era left a legacy of intensified social hatreds, regional rivalries, political tensions, and cultural and ideological hostility. As a result, Argentina in the post-Perón era has seemed farther than ever from achieving nationhood.

When the Cuban Revolution began in the 1950's, ideological divisiveness and lack of agreement concerning the models that should be utilized in creating an integrated nation at first seriously obstructed its progress. Even after the elements farthest to the left gained control over the movement, they frequently differed fundamentally in their choice of goals and means. Whether or not Fidel Castro had by the mid-1960's begun to succeed in establishing a sufficient degree of national self-awareness and consensus among the majority of citizens to render Cuba a true nation is a question that will long be debated. Undoubtedly, the Cuban Revolution had at least given a sense of participation to many people who previously had been only marginally incorporated into the national existence. In so doing, the Revolution vastly extended the politicization and social mobilization of the island's populace.

In Venezuela and Chile, encouraging signs of progress toward social integration and more widespread consensus regarding national values were apparent in the mid-1960's. These two countries may be able to resolve their problems of identity and integration through peaceful, evolutionary means. Perhaps some other Latin American countries will also be able to deal effectively with these issues using peaceful means, even though in 1952 Bolivia found it necessary to turn to revolutionary procedures; but quite clearly, Venezuela and Chile are in many ways unique. For them, obstacles to nationhood have been far less imposing than for many of their sister republics. They both emerged from the colonial period with comparatively homogeneous populations and with geographic barriers to integration that were decidedly less formidable than in such countries as Peru, Bolivia, Colombia, and Mexico. In the nineteenth century, Chile established a system able to confer considerable political legitimacy on its governors, while Venezuelan society became increasingly open and racially tolerant. Part of their success during this period may perhaps be attributed to the fact that neither country was confronted, as were Argentina, Uruguay, and southern Brazil, with the challenge of absorbing vast numbers of immigrants with alien cultural patterns. The relatively successful experiences of Venezuela and Chile in the drive toward identity, integration, and nationhood have been atypical in the overall Latin American scene. Chapters describing these experiences would have made this book seem more optimistic; unfortunately, considerations of space made it necessary to omit them as special cases.

In 1900, the difficulties of Latin America did not seem overwhelming, in part because the area's population of approximately 60 million inhabitants was increasing at the annual rate of only 1.3 per cent. The political, social, and economic structures in the various countries, disorganized and unintegrated as they usually were, nevertheless were capable of extending minimal services to the slowly expanding populace and of caring for some of their most pressing needs. These results were often achieved through paternalistic and charitable devices that, combined with the foreign capital that poured into the area, were remarkably successful in sustaining the established order.

By the end of the 1960's, the Latin American populace had risen to some 260 million and was increasing at an annual rate of about 3 per cent. This meant that masses of new people had to be absorbed into structures that previously had scarcely been capable of accommodating even limited numbers. Furthermore, this process of integration had to be carried out quickly; for the new masses, more politically aware and socially conscious owing to the worldwide communications revolution, seemed less patient than in the past. However, the social systems in many of the Latin American republics were ill adapted to the task of rapid integration and politicization. Without ever having achieved agreement on the acceptable and proper values, rights and duties, hopes and aspirations, or scope and extent of citizenship, many countries of Latin America were at a loss as to how to proceed toward assimilating new citizens in unprecedented numbers. Their problems stemmed largely from the fact that they had failed to resolve their crises of national identity and remained unintegrated groups of differing, often hostile, cultures and subcultures.

Political stability and economic progress can be regarded as altogether worthwhile and beneficial in countries that have achieved social and regional integration, widespread agreement on values, and a sense of identity and destiny. In Latin America, where with the possible exception of Mexico and Cuba, the countries have not yet become nations,* political stability and economic progress sometimes serve as a veneer, temporarily masking long unresolved and increasingly explosive conflicts over identity, integration, and destiny. Political stability and economic progress can actually impede national integration by allowing regional imbalances to increase and by widening the gulf between different social, cultural, ethnic, and functional-interest groups.

In developing their particular topics, the twelve chapters of this book focus, in their selection of reading materials and in their introductions, on the factors that have been most in evidence as Latin America's republics have struggled toward the elusive goal of identity, integration, and nation-

---

* Some observers contend that Brazil has developed into a true nation. This contention is skillfully advanced by Charles Wagley in *An Introduction to Brazil* (New York: Columbia University Press, 1963, third printing). The special nature of Chilean and Venezuelan development has been alluded to above.

hood. These factors would seem collectively to point the way toward an understanding of the meaning of the frequently tortuous political, economic, and social history of Latin America, as well as its relations with the United States and the rest of the world.

The editor acknowledges with deep appreciation the advice and assistance of Thomas F. McGann of the University of Texas and Lewis Hanke of the University of California, Irvine.

F. B. P.

CONTENTS

II

The Problem of Conflicting
Spanish Imperial Ideologies
in the Sixteenth Century
John Leddy Phelan

III

The Problem of the Impact
of Spanish Culture
on the Indigenous American Population
Charles Gibson

IV

The Problem of the Roots of Revolution:
Society and Intellectual Ferment
in Mexico on the Eve of Independence

Peggy K. Korn

V

The Death
of Brazilian Slavery, 1866–88

Thomas E. Skidmore

VI

The Problem of Identity
and National Destiny
in Peru and Argentina
Fredrick B. Pike

VII

The Problem of Liberalism
Versus Conservatism in Colombia: 1849–85

J. León Helguera

VIII

The Continuing Problem of Brazilian Integration: The Monarchical and Republican Periods

Alfred C. Stepan

IX

The Mexican Revolution, 1910–40: Genesis of a Modern State

John Womack, Jr.

X

Peronism in Argentina:
A Rightist Reaction
to the Social Problem of Latin America
Kalman H. Silvert

XI

The Cuban Revolution:
A Leftist Reaction
to the Social Problems of Latin America
Robert Freeman Smith

XII

The Problem of Population Growth in Latin America

William V. D'Antonio

LATIN AMERICAN HISTORY: SELECT PROBLEMS

Identity, Integration, and Nationhood

I

The Problem of Discovery:
A New World?

J. H. Parry

CHRONOLOGY

INTRODUCTION

The creation of a Spanish empire in the Americas was a product of disappointment, a *pis aller*. Columbus, whatever his original intentions may have been, returned to Spain in 1493 convinced that he had landed in or near the eastern extremities of Asia. Quinsay, the Great Khan's capital, he said, was only ten days' sail from Hispaniola. The implications of such an announcement were not only commercial but political, strategic, religious. European Christendom in the fifteenth century was isolated and confined. Its bastions against Islam were falling, its territory shrinking. The possibility of contact with civilized non-Muslim peoples or, better still, with Christian communities living on the eastern flank of Islam suggested sympathy, reassurance, even military support. Long-lived Christian traditions, such as that of St. Thomas in India, moreover, appealed to those who sought an ideal of Christian perfection, lost in Europe, which had existed long ago and might be found again surviving far away. A practicable sea route to Asia not only promised an immensely valuable trade in silk and spices; it also evoked a wide range of cherished dreams.

Columbus's claims were not altogether implausible. There was nothing fantastic, at least in theory, about a proposal to reach the East by sailing west. In practice, it would be a question of winds and currents, above all of distance. Columbus's own geographical calculations, as later appeared, were wildly wrong, but, given his premises, they had a perverse consistency. They were supported by—or, with a little ingenuity, could be reconciled with—respectable and respected authorities. Natural features of the Antillean scene—aromatic trees, brightly colored birds, even crocodiles—which recalled ancient accounts of India were eagerly seized on. The people, it is true, did not immediately suggest the fabled East. Though they had golden trinkets, they did not go dressed in silk; many, indeed, wore no clothes. But what of that? Nicolò de'Conti had reported primitive peoples in some of the Asian islands. If the Caribs ate their neighbors, so, according to Conti, did the Bataks of Sumatra. The Greater Antilles were, in a primitive fashion, populous and productive; though not themselves part of a civilized and powerful kingdom, they might well lie on the outskirts of one. Ferdinand and Isabella were sufficiently impressed by Columbus's report to undertake a considerable outlay in money and diplomatic effort. They insisted on the inclusion, in one of the bulls (*Dudum siquidem*) which they secured from Alexander VI, of an explicit reference to India. As soon as preparations could be made, they sent Columbus off again in command of a formidable fleet and company, with the double task of settling and exploiting Hispaniola with its gold "mines" and of pursuing the search for Cipangu and Cathay.

Thus early, there appeared in Spanish policy in the "Indies" an ambiguity which was never fully resolved. Columbus's naive insistence, on his second voyage, that Cuba actually *was* Cathay or Mangi [1] carried little conviction. Phrases such as "new world," "new country," "hitherto unknown continent," soon began to appear, notably in Peter Martyr's well-informed letters. Their use implied belief that the true Indies lay farther west. This belief did not cause officials, investors, and would-be adventurers to dismiss Asia from their calculations, but it did force them to consider whether the interests of the Crown and its subjects, and the cause of true religion, would best be served by systematic conquest, settlement, and exploitation of the new discoveries for their own sake; or whether the discoveries should be regarded primarily as bases and ports of call in a maritime drive to reach the commercial centers of the East. The obvious ideal was to combine the two projects; but with the resources available, this was not easy. They called for different types of men and different kinds of skill and effort. Settlers or conquerors were best attracted by the prospect of immediate plunder or free land and labor; only a few of the most imaginative among them— Balboa, for example, and notably Cortés—were to show any constructive interest in the search for India and the Spicery. The professional explorers, navigators, and cosmographers—many of them not Spaniards—with an outlook more scientific and more worldwide were for long-range exploring and the search for Asia; but even among their number, some chose to turn conquistador. Columbus's pilot Juan de la Cosa, one of the most eminent hydrographers of his day, took to slaving and died of a poisoned arrow in Urabá. The Crown inclined first one way, then the other, as fresh reports came in and as succeeding monarchs or their ministers were moved, either by the need for immediate revenue or by the hope of long-range commercial profit.

The social and economic circumstances of late medieval Spain produced many would-be conquistadors, and the Caribbean offered the sort of opportunity they welcomed. Adventurers—fighting men by inclination if not by profession—were willing enough to try their luck in the Indies with their own weapons and, if need be, at their own expense. They could hope to obtain, by barter or by force, gold grains and trinkets in the islands or pearls off Cumaná. If they survived the initial hardships and escaped their rivals' knives, they could create territorial fiefs, employing cowed natives to pan gold and grow food. The system of *encomienda*,[2] organized by Ovando as

---

[1] Cipangu, Cathay, Mangi: Marco Polo's names for Japan, North China, and South China, respectively.

[2] The entrusting of Indian laborers to Spanish settlers, who in turn assumed responsibilities for Christianizing and protecting their wards.

governor of Hispaniola, made this possible. As a last resort, adventurers could always kidnap a shipload of "wild" natives for sale as slaves; many expeditions covered their expenses in this way. This entailed heavy cost in death and suffering to the native Indians but little cost to the Crown, which drew a share of the profits. Ovando was left in no doubt by Ferdinand's officials that his function was not to organize discovery but to produce revenue, and in this he achieved considerable success.

Attempts to reach Asia required well-equipped, well-armed, well-manned fleets. Competent ocean navigators were few, suitable ships not readily available in Spain.[3] The fleets would have to carry trade goods and specie for making purchases. Heavy capital investment would be required, and this, as the Portuguese discovered in organizing their trade to India, involved the participation of the great German and Italian commercial and banking houses. These shrewd investors would not risk their money in Spanish expeditions merely on vague assurances that the Spice Islands lay just around the corner. More precise information would be needed about the extent of the Spanish discoveries and their position in relation to Asia. Much more exploration would be necessary, at royal expense.

Amerigo Vespucci's voyages of 1499 and 1501, and his written accounts of them, established beyond doubt the existence of a large continental land mass, which in northern Europe—though not in Spain—soon came to be called America. The coastline Vespucci explored could be interpreted as the east coast of the great tongue of land which in the standard Ptolemaic maps stretched south from Cathay toward Terra Australis. If so, the only possible opening must lie far to the south, leading by way of the "Cape of Catigara" into Ptolemy's Great Gulf and so to the Golden Chersonese and India. If, on the other hand, as Vespucci himself seemed to think, the continent was one hitherto quite unknown to Europeans, then it must be separated from Asia by a sea passage somewhere west of the Antilles. Vespucci was a dedicated explorer, moved by genuine scientific curiosity—a type much rarer in the great age of discovery than is commonly supposed. He was also in a position to influence policy: When the King convened conferences in 1505 at Toro and in 1508 at Burgos to discuss (among other matters) prospects in the Indies, on both occasions Vespucci was the principal expert adviser on overseas affairs.

The *junta* of Toro recommended that Vespucci and Vicente Yáñez

---

[3] They were not always available for the routine Atlantic crossing. A revealing instance: In 1513, when the great fleet intended to carry Pedrarias Dávila to his government in Darien was being assembled, Vicente Yáñez Pinzón was sent to Portugal to buy caravels, and King Ferdinand formally asked the king of Portugal to suspend, for this purpose, Portuguese laws forbidding the sale of such vessels to foreigners. Manuel Serrano y Sanz, *Orígenes de la dominación española en América* (Madrid: Nueva Biblioteca de Autores Españoles, Editorial Bailly-Baillière, 1918), p. 323.

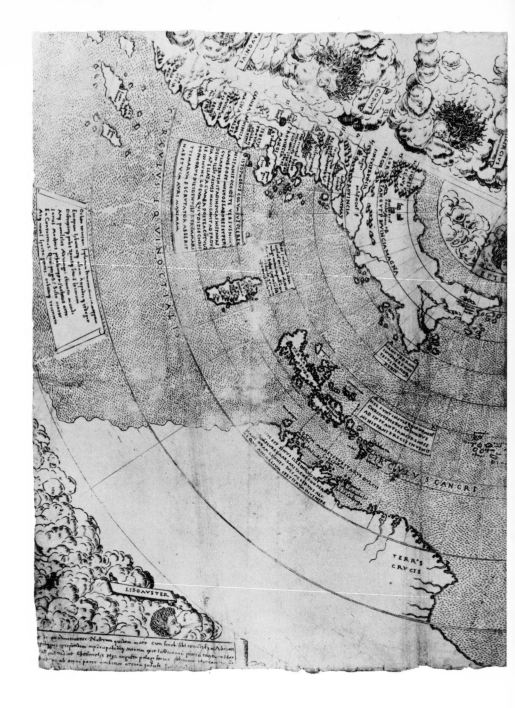

The earliest printed map to show any part of the New World, drawn by G. M. Contarini and engraved by Francesco Rosselli at Florence in 1506. It shows, in the center, the islands discovered by Columbus; to the south, "Terra Crucis," the continent of South America; to the west, the island of "Zimpangu," Japan; and to the north, the "lands discovered by the Portuguese," Newfoundland and Labrador, shown as a great easterly promontory of the mainland of Asia. *British Museum.*

Pinzón should fit out a fleet to search for a route to the Spice Islands,[4] but
the disturbed political situation resulting from Isabella's death prevented
its dispatch. The junta of Burgos (at which Vespucci was formally nominated Piloto Mayor, in charge of hydrography and the training of navigators) made two separate proposals, one for maritime discovery, the other
for territorial conquest. The first proposal led to a fleet being equipped at
royal expense and sent off under the joint command of Pinzón and Juan
Díaz de Solís to search for the Spicery. It sailed through the northern Caribbean, calling at Santo Domingo on the way out, and probably entered the
Gulf of Mexico,[5] but of course found no passage leading farther west. The
other proposal was to authorize the first formal occupation of mainland
territory; it resulted in the expeditions of Ojeda and Nicuesa to the coast
immediately east and west of the Gulf of Urabá in what is now Colombia.
These expeditions, undertaken in 1509 at private expense, were not intended
for maritime exploration—the coast there was already known to be continuous—nor even for settlement in the full sense; they were concerned with
taking possession, with prospecting for gold, and (though this was not explicitly stated) with slaving. Both expeditions were disasters; most of the
participants died or were killed by Indians. Ironically, however, whereas the
royally sponsored exploring expedition, led by able captains, achieved nothing, the private expeditions of conquest, led by bunglers, had a sequel significant for the progress of discovery. Thanks to the energy of Vasco Núñez
de Balboa, a small band of survivors from the Ojeda expedition succeeded
in establishing themselves on the Darien coast. Under Balboa's vigorous
leadership, their settlement took root. The local Indians possessed worked
gold, raised abundant crops, and were amenable. From them Balboa learned
of the proximity—only a few days' march—of the coast of the other ocean,
the South Sea. Soon he was writing to the King proposing exploration,
promising oriental wealth, and demanding substantial reinforcements.

By the time of Vespucci's death in 1512, hopes of finding an open seaway
through the western Caribbean, though not abandoned, had receded. The
other possibility raised by Vespucci's 1501 voyage, that a passage might be
found in the far south leading to Ptolemy's Great Gulf, remained in mind.
Juan Díaz de Solís was sent to investigate in 1515; he reached the Río de
la Plata and died there, killed by Indians. Four years later Magellan would
follow him south and go on to win a Pyrrhic victory over the sea. Meanwhile, Balboa's reports suggested still a third possibility: If Tierra Firme
could not be circumvented, it could be surmounted, and exploration pursued in ships built on the farther coast. Balboa himself, however, as the

<hr>

[4] Manuel de la Puente y Olea, *Los trabajos geográficos de la casa de contratación*
(Sevilla: Escuela Tipográfica y Librería Salesianas, 1900), pp. 29–34.
[5] Carl O. Sauer, *The Early Spanish Main* (Berkeley: University of California Press,
1966), p. 167.

first New World conquistador to achieve leadership through personal ascendancy rather than through royal appointment, was suspect. The famous expedition of 1513, in which he actually sighted the Pacific and proved how narrow an isthmus separated the two oceans, came too late to prevent his supersession. In 1513 the King, or his minister Juan de Fonseca, took Darien in hand as a major royal enterprise. An experienced officer of high military and social rank was to take charge. He was to go out in a powerful fleet, with a numerous and well-armed following. The instructions issued to Pedrarias Dávila summarize clearly the official rules of the time on conquest, settlement, and civil administration; on native policy, the distribution of encomiendas, and the circumstances in which resistant natives might be enslaved; on trade, the collection of gold, and the sharing of profits. On Balboa's dream of Pacific exploration they are silent.[6] Pedrarias, in any event, was not the man for it. Cunning, brutal, and lazy, he was interested in little save plunder. His government was almost wholly destructive. He granted permission to Balboa to build ships on the Pacific in order to get that formidable warrior out of the way; Balboa was thwarted at every turn, and in 1519 Pedrarias had him executed.[7]

The year 1519 was momentous in the history of the Indies. Magellan left Spain in that year on his great expedition, which showed that an all-sea westward route to Asia was practicable if scarcely economic, which revealed that the South Pacific was no mere gulf but an ocean wider than the Atlantic, which established a Spanish post in the Moluccas, and which sailed around the world. In 1519, also, Hernán Cortés—arrogating to himself, as Balboa had done, an independent command to which he had no title—left Cuba for the conquest of Mexico. At last, it must have appeared, the divergent strands of empire were beginning to draw together. Mexico was something quite new in Spanish experience, an immensely greater population, a far more sophisticated culture and economy than any so far encountered in America; at last, a territory seriously comparable with the kingdoms of the East, a situation inviting systematic campaigns of conquest in place of random marauding.

A prospect as vast and diverse as Mexico might have been expected to occupy Cortés's whole attention; in fact, however, it appealed to his imagination as only part of a whole world of beckoning opportunity. The tale of Mexico's conquest has been told many times and needs no repetition. The brief extracts from Cortés's letters reprinted here represent three conclusions which Cortés reached on the immediate morrow of conquest,

---

[6] Serrano y Sanz, *op. cit.*, p. 279 (text of Pedrarias's instructions).

[7] Balboa's plan of Pacific navigation, or at least its coastal aspect, was adopted by other independent captains. Gil González Dávila later explored well beyond the Gulf of Fonseca; his voyage was fully reported by Peter Martyr. Pascual de Andagoya sailed south from Panama and brought back the first report of Peru.

which he presented to the Emperor with characteristic clarity, courage, and tact, and to which he clung with great tenacity. Ruined Tenochtitlán, though associated with a bloodstained pagan past, must be restored, in Christianized, Hispanicized form, to provide a living heart for the kingdom of New Spain. The system of encomienda, though associated with heartless devastation in the islands and the isthmus, and though notoriously disliked by the Emperor on political and humane grounds, must, with safeguards, be retained; otherwise there would be no settlement. New Spain, finally, must not divert Spanish attention from the maritime drive to the true Indies, the Spicery; on the contrary, it must be made the base for redoubled effort.

Two successes, then, and one failure. The little bush harbors of Tehuantepec could not seriously be expected to build ships capable of crossing the Pacific. The Spaniards in the Moluccas could not be supported effectively from Mexico (nor, indeed, despite strenuous efforts, from Spain). There was no safe and convenient strait. Sebastian Cabot's expedition in 1525, of which Peter Martyr had high hopes, was a failure. By 1527 Charles V had decided that Spain must abandon the Spicery, and in the Treaty of Saragossa in 1529 he sold out to the Portuguese. His decision caused angry remonstrance in Spain and presumably disappointed Cortés, though by that time Cortés was no longer much listened to at court. In the Emperor's eyes, he had had his reward.

Fresh developments in the Indies soon distracted Spanish attention from the commercial prospects of the East. In the 1530's a second and greater native empire was discovered in South America, conquered, and laid under tribute. None of the conquistadors of Peru or their backers showed any interest in Asia. In the 1540's immensely productive silver veins were found in both New Spain and Peru. Within a decade or so, a stream of bullion was flowing into Spain beside which the pepper profits of Portugal seemed insignificant. By the middle of the century, to all appearances, the crucial decision had been made. The overseas interest of Spain was to be concentrated on an empire of territorial dominion, tribute, and mineral exploitation in the New World, not on an empire of commercial profit in the Old.

READINGS

1. Columbus in the Bahamas

The log Columbus kept day by day on his first transatlantic voyage has disappeared, probably because it was treated as a secret paper; but a condensed version was made from an imperfect copy, years later, by the Dominican missionary and historian Bartolomé de las Casas. The following extract from this version illustrates Columbus's determination to find evidences of Asia in the West Indies.

There are here very extensive lagoons, and by them and around them there are wonderful woods, and here and in the whole island all is as green and the vegetation is as that of Andalusia in April. The singing of little birds is such that it seems that a man could never wish to leave this place; the flocks of parrots darken the sun, and there are large and small birds of so many different kinds and so unlike ours, that it is a marvel. There are, moreover, trees of a thousand types, all with their various fruits and all scented, so that it is a wonder. I am the saddest man in the world because I do not recognise them, for I am very sure that all are of some value, and I am bringing specimens of them and also of the herbs. As I was thus going round one of these lagoons, I saw a snake, which we killed, and I am bringing its skin to Your Highnesses. When it saw us, it threw itself into the lagoon and we went in after it, for the water was not very deep, until we killed it with our spears. It is seven palms in length; I believe that there are many similar snakes here in these lagoons. Here I recognised the aloe, and to-morrow I am resolved to have ten quintals brought to the ship, since they tell me that it is very valuable. Further, going in search of very good water, we arrived at a village near here, half a league from where I am anchored. The inhabitants, when they saw us, all fled and left their houses and hid their clothing and whatever they had in the undergrowth. I did not allow anything to be taken, even the value of a pin. Afterwards, some of the men among them came towards us and one came quite close. I gave him some hawks' bells and some little glass beads, and he was well content and very joyful. And that this friendly feeling might grow stronger and to make some request of them, I asked him for water; and, after I had returned to the ship, they came presently to the beach with their gourds full, and were delighted to give it to us, and I commanded that another

SOURCE: "Columbus in the Bahamas" from *The Journal of Christopher Columbus*, translated by Cecil Jane, revised by L. A. Vigneras (London: Hakluyt Society, 1960), pp. 40–41.

string of small glass beads should be given to them, and they said that they would come here to-morrow. I was anxious to fill all the ships' casks with water here; accordingly, if the weather permit, I shall presently set out to go round the island, until I have had speech with this king and have seen whether I can obtain from him the gold which I hear that he wears. After that I wish to leave for another very large island, which I believe must be Cipangu, according to the signs which these Indians whom I have with me make; they call it "Colba." They say that there are ships and many very good sailors there. Beyond this island, there is another which they call "Bofio," which they say is also very large. The others, which lie between them, we shall see in passing, and according to whether I shall find a quantity of gold or spices, I shall decide what is to be done. But I am still determined to proceed to the mainland and to the city of Quinsay and to give the letters of Your Highnesses to the Grand Khan, and to request a reply and return with it.

2. *Peter Martyr*
on Columbus's First Voyage

Peter Martyr d'Anghiera was an Italian ecclesiastic and diplomat, resident for most of his life at the Castilian court. He was a well-informed *amateur* of geographical discovery, and met and questioned many of the New World discoverers, whose achievements he described in letters to ecclesiastical dignitaries in Italy, including several successive Popes. Martyr gathered these letters together and published them by installments, the complete series of eight "Decades" appearing at Alcalá in 1530 under the title *De orbe novo*. The work is the first history of events in the New World and is contemporary with them. The passages quoted here, dealing with Columbus's claim to have reached Asia, are good examples of Martyr's style of shrewd and detached comment.

Upon seeing strangers approaching, the natives collected and fled into the depths of the forests like timid hares pursued by hounds. The Spaniards followed them, but only succeeded in capturing one woman, whom they took on board their ships, where they gave her plenty of food and wine and clothes (for both sexes lived absolutely naked and in a state of nature); afterwards this woman, who knew where the fugitives were concealed, returned to her people, to whom she showed her ornaments, prais-

SOURCE: "Columbus's First Voyage" from Peter Martyr d'Anghiera, *De orbe novo*, translated and edited by Francis A. MacNutt, 2 vols. (New York: G. P. Putnam's Sons, 1912), 1, pp. 61, 64–65.

ing the liberality of the Spaniards; upon which they all returned to the coast, convinced that the newcomers were descended from heaven. They swam out to the ships, bringing gold, of which they had a small quantity, which they exchanged gladly for trifles of glass or pottery. For a needle, a bell, a fragment of mirror, or any such thing, they gladly gave in exchange whatever gold was asked of them, or all that they had about them.

.   .   .

The islanders set some value on gold and wear it in the form of fine leaves, fixed in the lobes of their ears and their nostrils. As soon as our compatriots were certain that they had no commercial relations with other peoples and no other coasts than those of their own islands, they asked them by signs whence they procured the gold. As nearly as could be conjectured, the natives obtain gold from the sands of the rivers which flow down from the high mountains. This process was not a difficult one. Before beating it into leaves, they form it into ingots; but none was found in that part of the island where the Spaniards had landed. It was shortly afterwards discovered, for when the Spaniards left that locality and landed at another point to obtain fresh water and to fish, they discovered a river of which the stones contained flakes of gold.

With the exception of three kinds of rabbits, no quadruped is found in these islands. There are serpents, but they are not dangerous. Wild geese, turtle-doves, ducks of a larger size than ours, with plumage as white as that of a swan, and red heads, exist. The Spaniards brought back with them some forty parrots, some green, others yellow, and some having vermilion collars like the parrakeets of India, as described by Pliny; and all of them have the most brilliant plumage. Their wings are green or yellow, but mixed with bluish or purple feathers, presenting a variety which enchants the eye. I have wished, most illustrious Prince, to give you these details about the parrots; and although the opinion of Columbus seems to be contradictory to the theories of the ancients concerning the size of the globe and its circumnavigation, the birds and many other objects brought thence seem to indicate that these islands do belong, be it by proximity or by their products, to India; particularly when one recalls what Aristotle, at the end of his treatise *De Coelo et Mundo,* and Seneca, and other learned cosmographers have always affirmed, that India was only separated from the west coast of Spain by a very small expanse of sea.

Mastic, aloes, cotton, and similar products flourish in abundance. Silky kinds of cotton grow upon trees as in China; also rough-coated berries of different colours more pungent to the taste than Caucasian pepper; and twigs cut from the trees, which in their form resemble cinnamon, but in taste, odour, and the outer bark, resemble ginger.

Happy at having discovered this unknown land, and to have found indications of a hitherto unknown continent, Columbus resolved to take advantage of favouring winds and the approach of spring to return to Europe. . . .

3. *The Bull* Dudum Siquidem

In 1493, after Columbus's return, the Spanish monarchs induced Pope Alexander VI to issue a series of bulls confirming the Spanish claim to the new discoveries and to future discoveries in the same area. *Inter caetera* asserted the Spanish right to explore, settle, trade, and proselytize anywhere west of a line drawn from north to south down the middle of the Atlantic; *Dudum siquidem* stated specifically that this right was to be recognized in any part of Asia (including India) which the Spaniards might reach by a western route.

Alexander, bishop, servant of the servants of God, to the illustrious sovereigns, his very dear son in Christ, Ferdinand, king, and his very dear daughter in Christ, Isabella, queen of Castile, Leon, Aragon, and Granada, health and apostolic benediction.

A short while ago of our own accord, and out of our certain knowledge, and fullness of our apostolic power, we gave, conveyed, and assigned forever to you and your heirs and successors, kings of Castile and Leon, all islands and mainlands whatsoever, discovered and to be discovered, toward the west and south, that were not under the actual temporal dominion of any Christian lords. Moreover, we invested therewith you and your aforesaid heirs and successors, and appointed and deputed you as lords of them with full and free power, authority, and jurisdiction of every kind, as more fully appears in our letters given to that effect, the terms whereof we wish to be understood as if they were inserted word for word in these presents. But since it may happen that your envoys and captains, or vassals, while voyaging toward the west or south, might bring their ships to land in eastern regions and there discover islands and mainlands that belonged or belong to India, with the desire moreover to bestow gracious favors upon you, through our similar accord, knowledge, and fullness of power, by apostolic authority and by tenor of these presents, in all and through all, just as if in the aforesaid letters full and express mention had been made thereof, we do in like manner amplify and extend our aforesaid gift, grant, assignment, and letters, with all and singular the clauses contained in the said letters, to all islands and mainlands whatsoever, found and to be found, discovered and to be discovered, that are or may be or

SOURCE: "The Bull *Dudum Siquidem*" from *European Treaties Bearing on the History of the United States*, edited by Frances G. Davenport, 4 vols. (Washington, D.C.: Carnegie Institution, 1917–37), 1, p. 82.

may seem to be in the route of navigation or travel toward the west or south, whether they be in western parts, or in the regions of the south and east and of India. We grant to you and your aforesaid heirs and successors full and free power through your own authority, exercised through yourselves or through another or others, freely to take corporal possession of the said islands and countries and to hold them forever. . . .

4. *Peter Martyr*
on Columbus's Second Voyage

The Admiral selected an elevation near the port as the site for a town; and, within a few days, some houses and a church were built, as well as could be done in so short a time. And there, on the feast of the Three Kings (for when treating of this country one must speak of a new world, so distant is it and so devoid of civilisation and religion) the Holy Sacrifice was celebrated by thirteen priests.

· · ·

During this time the Admiral despatched some thirty of his men in different directions to explore the district of Cipangu, which is still called Cibao. This is a mountainous region covered with rocks and occupying the centre of the island, where, the natives explained by signs, gold is obtained in abundance. . . . Columbus gave them to understand that he was very willing to give them what they asked, if they would bring him gold. Upon hearing this promise the natives turned their backs and ran to the neighbouring river, returning soon afterwards with hands full of gold. One old man only asked a little bell in return for two grains of gold weighing an ounce. Seeing that the Spaniards admired the size of these grains, and quite amazed at their astonishment, he explained to them by signs that they were of no value; after which, taking in his hands four stones, of which the smallest was the size of a nut and the largest as big as an orange, he told them that in his country, which was half a day's journey distant, one found here and there ingots of gold quite as large. He added that his neighbours did not even take the trouble to pick them up. It is now known that the islanders set no value on gold as such; they only prize it when it has been worked by a craftsman into some form which pleases them.

· · ·

SOURCE: "Columbus's Second Voyage" from Peter Martyr Anghieri, *De orbe novo*, translated and edited by Francis A. MacNutt, 2 vols. (New York: G. P. Putnam's Sons, 1912), 1, pp. 83, 88–90, 91–92.

Having carefully examined the region of Cibao, Columbus returned on the calends of April, the day after Easter, to Isabella; this being the name he had given to the new city. Confiding the government of Isabella and the entire island to his brother and one Pedro Margarita, an old royal courtier, Columbus made preparations for exploring the island which lies only seventy miles from Hispaniola, and which he believed to be a continent. He had not forgotten the royal instructions, which urged him to visit the new coasts, without delay, lest some other sovereign might take possession of them. For the King of Portugal made no secret of his intention also to discover unknown islands.

.   .   .

Leaving Hispaniola, the Admiral sailed with three vessels in the direction of the land he had taken for an island on his first voyage, and had named Juana. He arrived, after a brief voyage, and named the first coast he touched Alpha and Omega, because he thought that there our East ended when the sun set in that island, and our West began when the sun rose. It is indeed proven that on the west side India begins beyond the Ganges, and ends on the east side. It is not without cause that cosmographers have left the boundaries of Ganges India undetermined. There are not wanting those among them who think that the coasts of Spain do not lie very distant from the shores of India.

The natives called this country Cuba. Within sight of it, the Admiral discovered at the extremity of Hispaniola a very commodious harbour formed by a bend in the island. He called this harbour, which is barely twenty leagues distant from Cuba, San Nicholas.

Columbus covered this distance, and desiring to skirt the south coast of Cuba, he laid his course to the west; the farther he advanced the more extensive did the coast become, but bending towards the south, he first discovered, to the left of Cuba, an island called by the natives Jamaica, of which he reports that it is longer and broader than Sicily. It is composed of one sole mountain, which rises in imperceptible gradations from the coasts to the centre, sloping so gently that in mounting it, the ascent is scarcely noticeable. Both the coast country and the interior of Jamaica are extremely fertile and populous. According to the report of their neighbours, the natives of this island have a keener intelligence and are cleverer in mechanical arts, as well as more warlike than others. And indeed, each time the Admiral sought to land in any place, they assembled in armed bands, threatening him, and not hesitating to offer battle. As they were always conquered, they ended by making peace with him. Leaving Jamaica to one side, the Admiral sailed to the west for seventy days with favourable winds. He expected to arrive in the part of the world underneath us just near the Golden Chersonese, which is situated to the east of Persia.

He thought, as a matter of fact, that of the twelve hours of the sun's course of which we are ignorant he would have only lost two.

It is known that the ancients have only followed the sun during the half of its course, since they only knew that part of the globe which lies between Cadiz and the Ganges, or even to the Golden Chersonese.

.   .   .

While the Admiral was carefully examining the character of these places, coasting along the shore of Cuba, he first discovered, not far from Alpha (that is from the end of it), a harbour sufficient for many ships. . . . A landing was made, but no people were found; nevertheless there were wooden spits arranged about the fire, on which hung fish, altogether of about a hundred pounds' weight, and alongside lay two serpents eight feet long.[1] . . . The Spaniards rested there to eat, and were pleased to find the fish, which had cost them nothing, much to their taste; but they did not touch the serpents. They report that these latter were in no wise different from the crocodiles of the Nile, except in point of size. According to Pliny, crocodiles as long as eighteen cubits have been found; while the largest in Cuba do not exceed eight feet.

5. *Vespucci on the New Continent*

Amerigo Vespucci was almost certainly the first explorer-geographer to make up his mind that South America was a separate, hitherto unknown continent. His exploits and opinions, set out in a garbled form in contemporary printed pamphlets of doubtful attribution, appear more clearly in manuscript letters subsequently discovered and more certainly attributable to him. Relevant passages from the letters are quoted here.

[FROM SEVILLE, 1500, DESCRIBING THE 1499 VOYAGE]

We found the land [1] heavily covered with trees which were most amazing not only in height but in their greenness, since they are never denuded of all their leaves. They had a fragrant smell, being all aromatic, and gave forth such tonic odors that we were greatly invigorated.

We followed the edge of the land in the small boats to see whether we could discover a place to jump ashore. What a world of shallows it

---

[1] [Presumably iguanas.]

[1] [The Guiana coast.]
SOURCE: "The 1499 Voyage" from Frederick J. Pohl, *Amerigo Vespucci, Pilot Major* (New York: Columbia University Press, 1944), p. 77.

was! We rowed hard all day until nightfall, but were prevented from penetrating inland not only by the shallowness but by the density of the forest through which we could never find so much as a chimney opening. We decided, therefore, to return to the ships, and attempt a landing in some other region. We observed one remarkable fact in this part of the ocean. Always when we approached within twenty-five leagues of the coast, we found the water fresh like that of a river and drank of it and filled all our empty casks. Having rejoined the ships, we raised anchor and set sail. We pointed our prows southward, since it was my intention to see whether I could turn a headland that Ptolemy calls the Cape of Catigara, which connects with the Sinus Magnus. In my opinion we were not a great distance from it, according to computed longitude and latitude, as hereinafter stated.

Sailing southward, we saw two most tremendous rivers [2] issuing from the land, one coming from the west and flowing to the east, and having a width of four leagues, which is sixteen miles. The other flowed from south to north, and was three leagues, or twelve miles, wide.

[FROM LISBON, 1502, DESCRIBING THE 1501 VOYAGE]

The last letter written to Your Excellency was from the coast of Guinea from a place which is called Cape Verde. In it you learned of the beginning of my voyage. By this present letter you will be informed in brief of the middle and end of my voyage and of what has happened up to now.

We departed from the above-mentioned Cape Verde very easily, having taken in everything necessary, such as water and wood and other requirements essential for putting to sea across the ocean wastes in search of new land. We sailed on the wind within half a point of southwest, so that in sixty-four days we arrived at a new land which, for many reasons that are enumerated in what follows, we observed to be a continent. . . . We ran the course of that land for about eight hundred leagues, always in the direction of southwest one-quarter west. . . .

We found the land thickly inhabited. I noted there the wonders of God and of nature, of which I determined to inform Your Excellency, as I have done of my other voyages. . . .

We coursed so far in those seas that we entered the Torrid Zone and passed south of the equinoctial line and the Tropic of Capricorn, until the South Pole stood above my horizon at fifty degrees, which was my latitude

---

[2] [The Amazon and the Pará.]
SOURCE: "The 1501 Voyage" from Frederick J. Pohl, *Amerigo Vespucci, Pilot Major* (New York: Columbia University Press, 1944), pp. 130–31.

from the equator. We navigated in the Southern Hemisphere for nine months and twenty-seven days, never seeing the Arctic Pole or even Ursa Major and Minor; but opposite them many very bright and beautiful constellations were disclosed to me which always remain invisible in this Northern Hemisphere. There I noted the wonderful order of their motions and their magnitudes, measuring the diameters of their circuits and mapping out their relative positions with geometrical figures. I noted other great motions of the heavens, which would be a tedious matter to write about.

.   .   .

To conclude, I was on the side of the antipodes; my navigation extended through one-quarter of the world; my zenith direction there made a right angle, at the center of the earth, with the zenith direction of the inhabitants of this Northern Hemisphere in the latitude of forty degrees. This must suffice.

6. *First Rumors of the South Sea*

Most of Balboa's letters, including that describing his discovery of the Pacific, have disappeared. This extract is from an earlier letter to the King describing the process of settlement and discovery in Darien and announcing—with evident excitement—the receipt of Indian reports of the existence of another ocean.

[PART OF BALBOA'S LETTER TO THE KING FROM DARIEN, JANUARY 20, 1513]

The Indians say that the other sea is three days' journey from there [Comogre]. The chiefs and Indians of the province of Comogre all tell us such tales, of pieces of gold heaped up in the houses of the chiefs on the coast of the other sea, that we are almost beside ourselves with the thought of it. They say that great quantities of gold, in large nuggets, are found in all the rivers of the other coast. They say that Indians of that coast come by river in canoes to the house of the Cacique Comogre, bringing smelted gold in large ingots. The gold is paid for with cotton garments and good-looking slaves of both sexes. They do not eat these captives, as the Río Grande Indians do; I am told, indeed, that these people from the

SOURCE: "Balboa's Letter to the King" translated from Ángel de Altolaguirre y Duvale, *Vasco Núñez de Balboa* (Madrid: Imprenta del Patronato de Huérfanos de Intendencia e Intervención Militares, 1914), pp. 19–20. Translated by the chapter editor.

other coast are good people and peaceably inclined. They say that the other sea is safe for navigation in canoes, because it is always calm and never dangerous like the sea on this side. I believe there are many islands off that coast. They say that pearls are fished there, in great quantities and very large. The chiefs wear necklaces of them, and so do all the people. . . . Since Our Lord has been pleased to make Your Royal Highness master of this great country, the opportunity should not be neglected. If Your Highness will be pleased to send me men, I will undertake, God willing, to make such discoveries and find such riches that Your Highness could conquer half the world.

[Peter Martyr on Balboa]

Our Vasco Balboa is seen to have changed from a ferocious Goliath into an Elias. He was an Antaeus; he has been transformed into Hercules the conqueror of monsters. From being foolhardy, he has become obedient and entirely worthy of royal honours and favour. Such are the events made known to us by letters from him and the colonists of Darien, and by verbal reports of people who have returned from those regions.

Perhaps you may desire, Most Holy Father, to know what my sentiments are respecting these events. My opinion is a simple one. It is evident from the military style in which Vasco and his men report their deeds that their statements must be true. Spain need no longer plough up the ground to the depth of the infernal regions or open great roads or pierce mountains at the cost of labour and the risk of a thousand dangers, in order to draw wealth from the earth. She will find riches on the surface, in shallow diggings; she will find them in the sun-dried banks of rivers; it will suffice to merely sift the earth. Pearls will be gathered with little effort. Cosmographers unanimously recognise that venerable antiquity received no such benefit from nature, because never before did man, starting from the known world, penetrate to those unknown regions. It is true the natives are contented with a little or nothing, and are not hospitable; moreover, we have more than sufficiently demonstrated that they receive ungraciously strangers who come amongst them, and only consent to negotiate with them, after they have been conquered. . . .

It is not therefore astonishing that these immense tracts of country should be abandoned and unknown; but the Christian religion, of which you are the head, will embrace its vast extent.

source: "Peter Martyr on Balboa" from Peter Martyr Anghieri, *De orbe novo*, translated and edited by Francis A. MacNutt, 2 vols. (New York: G. P. Putnam's Sons, 1912), 1, pp. 314–15.

7. Magellan's Geographical Ideas

There are two good contemporary accounts of Magellan's voyage: that of Pigafetta, who sailed on the voyage and wrote a lively and dramatic record of it, but whose geography was somewhat muddled; and that of Maximilian, the young son of the archbishop of Salzburg, who was a pupil of Peter Martyr, and who wrote, apparently as an exercise, a very lucid account based on interviews with the survivors. Note Maximilian's reference to the roaring of the sea, suggesting that Tierra del Fuego was an island and not (as most contemporaries supposed) part of Terra Australis.

[FROM THE LETTER OF MAXIMILIAN OF TRANSYLVANIA, 1522]

Ferdinand Magellan, a distinguished Portuguese, who, for many years had explored the coasts of the whole of the East as Admiral, took a great hatred to his king, whom he complained of as being most ungrateful to him, and came to Caesar. Christopher Haro, too, my own father-in-law's brother, who had traded for many years in the East by means of his agents, he himself staying in Ulyssipone, commonly called Lisbon, and who had lastly traded with the Chinese, so that he has great practice in such things, having also been unjustly treated by the King of Portugal, came also home to Spain. And they both showed Caesar that though it was not yet quite sure whether Malacca was within the confines of the Spaniards or the Portuguese, because, as yet, nothing of the longitude had been clearly proved, yet that it was quite plain that the Great Gulf and the people of Sinae lay within the Spanish boundary. This, too, was held to be most certain, that the islands which they call the Moluccas, in which all the spices are produced, and are thence exported to Malacca, lay within the Spanish western division, and that it was possible to sail there; and that spices could be brought thence to Spain more easily, and at less expense and cheaper, as they came direct from their native place.

Their course would be this, to sail westward, coasting the southern hemisphere [till they came] to the East. The thing seemed almost impossible and useless, not because it was thought a difficult thing to go from the west right to the east under the hemisphere, but because it was uncertain whether ingenious nature, which has done nothing without the greatest foresight, had not so dissevered the east from the west, partly by

SOURCE: "The Letter of Maximilian" from *The First Voyage Round the World by Magellan, Translated from the Accounts of Pigafetta and Other Contemporary Writers* by Lord Stanley of Alderley (London: Hakluyt Society, 1874), pp. 186–89, 194–98.

sea and partly by land, as to make it impossible to arrive there by either land or sea travelling. For it had not then been discovered whether that great region which is called Terra Firma did separate the western sea from the eastern; it was clear enough that that continent, in its southern part, trended southwards and afterwards westwards. It was clear, also, that two regions had been discovered in the North, one of which they called Regio Bacalearum (Cod-fish Land),[1] from a new kind of fish; and the other Terra Florida. And if these two were united to that Terra Firma, it was impossible to get to the east by going from the west, as nothing had ever been discovered of any channel through this land, though it had been sought for most diligently and with great labour. And they considered it a very doubtful and most dangerous enterprise to go through the limits of the Portuguese, and so to the east. For which reason it seemed to Caesar and to his counsellors that these men were promising a thing from which much was to be hoped, but still of great difficulty. When they were both brought to an audience on a certain day, Magellan offered to go himself, but Christopher offered to fit out a fleet at his own expense and that of his friends, but only if it were allowed to sail under the authority and protection of Caesar. Whilst they both persisted rather obstinately in their offers, Caesar himself equipped a fleet of five ships, and appointed Magellan its admiral. Their orders were, to sail southwards along the coast of Terra Firma till they found either its termination or some channel through which they might reach the spice-bearing Moluccas. So Magellan set sail on the 10th of August, 1519, with five ships from Seville. A few days after he reached the Fortunate Islands, which are now sometimes called the Canaries. Thence they arrived at the Islands of the Hesperides, from which they took a south-western course towards that continent which we mentioned before; and after some days' fair sailing they sighted a promontory, to which the name of Santa Maria has been given. Here Juan Ruy Diaz Solis had been eaten, with some of his companions, by the anthropophagi, whom the Indians call cannibals, whilst, by order of Ferdinand the Catholic, he was exploring the coast of this continent with a fleet. Sailing thence, our men coasted in an unbroken course along the coasts of this continent, which extend a very long way south, and tend a little west, so that they crossed the Tropic of Capricorn by many degrees. I think that this continent should be called that of the Southern Pole. But it was not so easy as I have said; for not till the last day of March of the following year did they reach a bay, to which they gave the name of Saint Julian. Here they found the Antarctic Pole star 49⅓ degrees above their horizon, both by the altitude and declination of the sun from the Equinoctial, and also by the altitude of the Antarctic (Pole star) itself. This star our sailors

[1] Newfoundland.

generally make use of more than of any other. They state also that the longitude was 56 deg. west of the Fortunate Isles. For, as the ancient cosmographers, and specially Ptolemy, reckoned the longitude from the Fortunate Islands eastward to Catigara at 180 deg., so our men, sailing as far as they could westward also, began to reckon another 180 deg. westward to Catigara, as was right. Yet our sailors seem to me rather to be mistaken in the calculation of the longitudes than to have fixed them with any certainty, because in so long a voyage, and being so distant from the land, they cannot fix and determine any marks or signs for the longitude. Still I think that these accounts, whatever they be, should not be cast aside, but rather accepted till more certain information be discovered.

This Gulf of Saint Julian seemed very great, and had the appearance of a channel. Wherefore Admiral Magellan ordered two ships to explore the Gulf and anchored the rest outside. After two days, information was brought to him that the Gulf was full of shoals, and did not extend far inland.

·   ·   ·

As soon as ever Magellan saw the storminess of the sea and the rigour of the winter mitigated, he set sail from the gulf of St. Julian on the 24th of August. And, as before, he followed the course of the coast southwards for many days. A promontory was at last sighted, which they called Santa Cruz, when a severe storm, springing from the east, suddenly caught them, and one of the five ships was cast on shore, the men being all saved, with the merchandise and equipment, except one Ethiopian slave, who was caught and drowned by the waves. After this the land seemed to bear a little east and south, and this they began to coast along as usual, and on the 26th of November certain inlets of the sea were discovered, which had the appearance of a strait. Magellan entered them forthwith with the whole fleet, and when he saw other and again other bays, he gave orders that they should be all carefully examined from the ships, to see if anywhere a passage might be discovered; and said that he would himself wait at the mouth of the strait till the fifth day, to hear what might happen.

One of the ships, which Alvarus Meschito, his nephew, commanded, was carried back by the tide to the sea, to the very place where they entered the gulf. But when the Spaniards perceived that they were far away from the other ships, they made a plot to return home, put Alvarus, their captain, in irons, bent their course northwards, and were at last carried to the coast of Aethiopia [Guinea], and, having victualled there, they reached Spain eight months after they had deserted the rest. There they compel Alvarus to stand his trial in chains, for having, by his counsel and advice, induced his uncle Magellan to practise such harshness on the Spaniards.

But when Magellan had waited for this ship some days longer than the time fixed, another returned, which had discovered nothing but a bay full of shoals and shingle, and very lofty cliffs. The third ship, however, re-ported that the largest bay had the appearance of a strait, as in three days' sail they had found no way out; but the farther they had gone the nar-rower the sea was, and they had not been able to sound the depth of it in many places by any length of line, and that they had also noticed that the tide was rather stronger than the ebb, and that so they were persuaded that a passage was open in that direction to some other sea. He made up his mind to sail through it. This channel, which they did not then know to be a channel, was at one place three Italian miles wide, at another two, sometimes ten, and sometimes five, and pointed a little westward. The altitude of the southern pole was found to be 52 deg., and the longitude to be the same, as at St. Julian's Bay. The month of November was upon them, the night was rather more than five hours long, and they had never seen any human beings on the shore.

But one night a great number of fires were seen, mostly on their left hand, from which they guessed that they had been seen by the natives of the region. But Magellan, seeing that the country was rocky, and also stark with eternal cold, thought it useless to waste many days in examining it; and so, with only three ships, he continued on his course along the channel, until, on the twenty-second day after he had entered it, he sailed out upon another wide and vast sea. The length of the channel they attest to be nearly a hundred Spanish miles.

There is no doubt that the land which they had upon their right was the continent of which we have spoken, but they think that the land on the left was not a mainland, but islands, because sometimes on that side they heard on a still farther coast the beating and roaring of the sea.

Magellan saw that the continent stretched northwards again in a straight line; wherefore, leaving that huge continent on the right hand, he ordered them to sail through that vast and mighty sea (which I do not think had ever seen either our or any one else's ships) in the direction whence the wind called Corus generally blows—that is, 'twixt north and west—so that he might, by going through west to east, again arrive at the torrid zone; for he thought that it was proved sufficiently clearly that the Moluccas were in the most remote east, and could not be far from the equator. They kept this course uninterruptedly, nor did they ever depart from it, except when rough weather or violent winds compelled them to diverge; and then they had in this manner been carried for forty days by a strong and gen-erally favourable wind, and had seen nothing but sea, and everywhere sea—when they had almost reached the tropic of Capricorn once more, two islands were sighted, but small and barren.[2] These they found uninhabited when they tried to land; still, they stopped there two days for their health's

[2] Probably Clipperton and Clarion.

sake, and general recruiting of their bodies, for there was very fair fishing there. They named these the Unfortunate Islands by common consent. Then they again set sail thence, following their original course and direction of sailing. And when, for three months and twenty days, they had been sailing over this ocean with great good fortune, and had traversed an immense part of the sea—more vast than mind of man can conceive, for they had been driven almost continuously by a very strong wind—they were now at last arrived on this side of the equinoctial line, and at last they saw an island, called, as they learnt afterwards, Inuagana by the natives. When they had approached nearer, they discovered the altitude of the Arctic pole to be 11 deg. The longitude they thought to be 158 deg. west of Gades. Then they saw other and still more islands, so that they knew they had arrived at some vast archipelago.

.   .   .

Our men, having taken in water in Acaca, sailed towards Selani; here a storm took them, so that they could not bring the ships to that island, but were driven to another island called Massaua, where lives a king of [the?] three islands, after that they arrived at Subuth.³ This is an excellent and large island, and, having made a treaty with its chieftain, they landed immediately to perform divine service, according to the manner of Christians, for it was the feast of the resurrection of Him who was our salvation.

[PETER MARTYR ON MAGELLAN'S VOYAGE]

Leaving this archipelago ¹ on the left, our fleet of five ships took the opposite direction from that followed by the Portuguese ships. Out beyond the land we call our continent and whose extremity belongs to the Portuguese, advancing as we have already described more than fifty degrees towards the antarctic pole,—I do not give the precise figures, for the calculations differ somewhat,—the Spaniards sailing west, as the Portuguese had sailed east, arrived east of the Moluccas, which lie not far from the country where Ptolemy placed Gatigara and the great gulf, the gateway to China. What shall I say of the great gulf and Gatigara? The Spaniards claim they did not find them where Ptolemy placed them; but I do not insist on this point, for perhaps I shall speak later more fully concerning it.

Let us return to the tour of the world. We have here, therefore, another

---

³ Maximilian appears to make no distinction between the Marianas and the Philippines. Subuth is Cebu.

¹ [The Cape Verde Islands.]
SOURCE: "Peter Martyr on Magellan's Voyage" from Peter Martyr Anghieri, *De orbe novo*, translated and edited by Francis A. MacNutt, 2 vols. (New York: G. P. Putnam's Sons, 1912), 2, pp. 168–69.

route leading to the Golden Chersonesus and just opposite to that discovered by the Portuguese. The *Victoria,* that Queen of Argonauts, returned by the first route, passing in view of the Golden Chersonesus and following the track of the Portuguese.

.   .   .

It is planned to profit by an undertaking so well begun. What will finally be decided, what treaty may be signed with the Portuguese, who claim to have been seriously injured by this voyage, I shall later make known to you. The Portuguese affirm that the Moluccas lie within the limits assigned to them by the division made by Pope Alexander VI., between the kings of Castile and Portugal, and they point out that villages, districts, and farms carry their produce to the markets of the Moluccas, Calicut, and Cochin, and that everywhere peasants bring to the towns and fortresses, whatever they produce and cultivate. We claim, on the contrary, that the Moluccas were usurped by the Portuguese, since they lie outside the line drawn from pole to pole separating the east from the west.

8. *Hernán Cortés on the Settlement of Mexico and the Search for the Spicery*

Cortés's five dispatches to the Emperor Charles V were designed to secure royal approval of a successful, but initially highly irregular, enterprise; naturally, they contain some special pleading and some exaggeration. In the main, however, they consist of detailed, matter-of-fact narrative and description; lucid analysis of a very complex situation; and clear and imaginative advice on how New Spain was to be settled, administered, and used as a base for further advance towards the East. On this last proposal, Cortés was warmly supported by the influential Peter Martyr, now an old man, greatly respected, and serving as Councillor of the Indies.

[FROM THE THIRD LETTER, 1522]

I had obtained a short time ago information of another sea to the south, and had learned that, in two or three different directions, it was twelve or fourteen days' journey from here. I was very much concerned because it seemed to me that in discovering it a great and signal service would be rendered to Your Majesty, especially as all who have any knowledge or experience of the navigation in the Indies have held it to be

SOURCE: "The Third Letter" from *Letters of Cortés,* translated and edited by Francis A. MacNutt, 2 vols. (New York: G. P. Putnam's Sons, 1908), 2, pp. 132–33, 135–36, 147–48.

certain that, with the discovery of the South Sea in these parts, many islands rich in gold, pearls, precious stones, spices, and other unknown and admirable things would be discovered: and this has been and is affirmed by persons of learning and experience in the science of cosmography. With this desire, and wishing to render Your Majesty this most singular and admirable service, I dispatched four Spaniards, two through certain provinces, and the other two through certain others; and, having first informed myself of the routes they were to take, and giving them guides from amongst our friends, they departed. I ordered them not to stop until they had reached the sea, and, upon discovering it, to take actual and corporeal possession of it in the name of Your Majesty.

The first travelled about one hundred and thirty leagues through many beautiful and fair provinces without encountering any hindrance, and arrived at the sea, and took possession of it, in sign of which they placed crosses on the coast of it. Some days afterwards, they returned with an account of the said discovery, and informed me very minutely of everything, bringing me some of the natives of the said sea [coast] and also very good samples from the gold mines, which they found in some of those provinces through which they passed; I send these, with the other samples of gold, to Your Majesty. The other two Spaniards were somewhat longer, because they travelled about one hundred and fifty leagues through other parts until they reached the sea, of which they likewise took possession. They brought me a full description of the coast, and, with them, came some natives of it. I received them and the others graciously, and they, having been informed of Your Majesty's great power, and given some presents, returned very contented to their country.

•   •   •

Having taken measures for the accomplishment of these two conquests, and having heard of the good success of them, and seeing how I had already peopled three towns with Spaniards and that a number of them still remained with me in this city, I debated where to establish another town within the circuit of the lakes; for it was needed for the greater security and peace of all these parts. Considering also that the city of Temixtitan, which was a thing so renowned and had made itself so important and memorable, it seemed to us that it was well to rebuild it, for it was all destroyed. I distributed the lots to those who offered themselves as householders, and I appointed the alcaldes and municipal officers in the name of Your Majesty, as is customary in your kingdoms; and, while the houses were being built, we agreed to continue living in this city of Cuyoacan, where we are at present. In the four or five months since the rebuilding of the said city of Temixtitan was begun it is already very beautiful, and Your Majesty may believe that each day it will become nobler, so that as it was before the head and mistress of all these provinces, so it will be henceforward; it is being and will be so built that the Spaniards will be perfectly strong and safe, and supreme lords of the natives, secure from any fear of being assailed by them.

. . .

In one of my letters, I told Your Majesty that the natives of these parts were much more capable than those of the other islands, appearing to be as intelligent and as reasonable as is ordinarily considered sufficient; wherefor it appeared wrong to oblige them to serve the Spaniards as those of the other islands do, though without some assistance, the conquerors and settlers of these parts would on the other hand be unable to maintain themselves. In order not to force the Indians to help the Spaniards, it seemed to me that Your Majesty might order that as compensation the latter should receive assistance from the incomes which here belong to Your Majesty for their provisions and sustenance; respecting this Your Majesty may provide what seems profitable to your service, according to the more extensive relation which I have made to Your Majesty. Seeing the many and continual outlays of Your Majesty, and that we ought rather to augment your rents by all possible means than to be an occasion of further expenses, and considering also the long time we have spent in the wars, and the necessities and debts caused thereby, and the delay attendant upon Your Majesty's decision in this case, and above all the many importunities of Your Majesty's officials and of all the Spaniards from which it was impossible to excuse myself, I found myself almost forced to place the chiefs and natives of these parts amongst the Spaniards, to recompense them for the services they have rendered to Your Majesty. Until something else is ordered or this confirmed, the said chiefs and natives serve and give each Spaniard to whom they are allotted the needful for his subsistence. This step was taken with the approbation of intelligent persons, who have had, and have, great experience of the country, for there was nothing else possible not only for the maintenance of the Spaniards but also for the preservation and good treatment of the Indian, as is shown in the more extensive relation which the procurators who now go from this New Spain will make to Your Majesty. The plantations and farms of Your Majesty have been established in the best and most convenient provinces and cities.

[FROM THE FOURTH LETTER, 1524]

In the last account, and also in this, I have mentioned to Your Majesty that I had begun to build four ships on the South Sea, and, as

SOURCE: "The Fourth Letter" from *Letters of Cortés*, translated and edited by Francis A. MacNutt, 2 vols. (New York: G. P. Putnam's Sons, 1908), 2, pp. 199–200, 202–03, 207–09.

some time has passed since they were begun, it may seem to Your Royal Highness that I have been slow in finishing them; but I now give Your Sacred Majesty the cause, which is that the port on the South Sea where these ships are building, is two hundred leagues, and even more, from the ports on the North Sea where all material which arrives in this New Spain is delivered, and there are very steep mountain passes in some parts, and in others great rivers, over which everything required for the said ships must be carried, as nothing can be obtained elsewhere. Another thing also happened, which was that when I had got together the sails, cordage, nails, anchors, tar, tallow, tow, bitumen, oil, and everything else required, and stored them in a house in that port, it took fire and everything was burned, except the anchors, which could not burn. I have now again begun, as a ship arrived from Castile, four months since, bringing me everything necessary for the ships; as, foreseeing the possibility of what had happened, I had already ordered material to be sent. And I certify to Your Caesarian Majesty that the ships cost me to-day, before launching them on the water, more than eight thousand *pesos* of gold, without the extra outlays, but now—our Lord be praised—they are in such a condition that, between the Feast of the Holy Ghost and that of St. John in June, they will be ready for navigation if the tar does not fail me, for I have not been able to replace that which was burned, though I have ordered more to be sent me. I attach more importance to these ships than I can say, for I am positive that—God willing—I shall discover for Your Majesty more kingdoms and dominions than all those discovered up till now, and that, with His guidance, my projects may succeed according to my desires, and Your Highness will become the Sovereign of the World.

•   •   •

So well and quickly does work go on in these parts, that many of the houses are finished and others are well advanced, for there is an abundance of stone, lime, wood, and bricks which the natives make, so that the houses are mostly large and good, and Your Sacred Majesty may believe that, within five years, this will be the most nobly populated city which exists in all the civilised world, and will have the finest buildings.

The town where the Spaniards have settled is distinct from that of the natives, for an arm of water separates us, although there are bridges of wood which connect them. There are two great native markets, one in their quarter and one in the Spanish quarter, where every sort of provisions can be bought; for the people come from all over the country to sell, and there is no scarcity as sometimes happened in the days of its prosperity. It is true that now there are no jewels of gold, silver, or feather work and other rich things, as there used to be, although some small miserable pieces of gold and silver appear, but not as formerly.

•   •   •

In the past chapters, Most Powerful Lord, I have told Your Excellency to what points I had sent people, both by sea and land, believing that, with God's guidance, Your Majesty would be well served by them; and, as I always take great care and bethink me of all possible means to carry out my desires for the advancement of the royal service of Your Majesty, it seemed to me that it remained only to explore the coast from Panuco to the coast of Florida, which was discovered by Juan Ponce de Leon, and from there to follow the coast of Florida towards the north as far as the Bacallaos. For it is believed absolutely that there is a strait on that coast which leads to the South Sea, and if it should be found according to a certain drawing which I have of that coast, it must lead very near to where the Archipelago was discovered by Magellanes under Your Highness's commands. And should it please God, our Lord, that the said strait be found there, it would open a good and short passage from the spiceries to these dominions of Your Majesty quite two-thirds shorter than that which is at present followed, and which will be free from risks and dangers to the ships; for they would then always go and come through the dominions of Your Majesty having facilities for repairs in any port they choose to enter. I thought over to myself the great service which would be rendered to Your Majesty, though I am quite wasted and exhausted by all I have done, and spent in the expeditions I have fitted out by land and sea and in providing ammunition and artillery in this city, and in many other expenses and outlays which daily occur; for all our provisions are expensive and of such excessive prices that, although the country is rich, the income I obtain does not correspond to the outlays, costs, and expenses which I have—yet repeating all I have said before, and setting all personal interest aside, I have determined to prepare three caravels and a brigantine, of which the cost will reach more than ten thousand *pesos* of gold which I swear to Your Majesty I shall have to borrow. I add this new service to those I have already rendered, for I hold it to be the most important, hoping as I do to find the strait; and even if this should not be found, certainly many good and rich countries will be discovered, where Your Caesarian Majesty will be served, and other dominions in considerable number will be brought under Your Imperial Crown. If there be no such strait, then it will be useful that this be known, so that other means may be discovered by which Your Caesarian Majesty may draw profits from the Spicelands and other countries bordering on them. Thus I hold myself at Your Majesty's service, very happy if you will so command me, and, in the absence of the strait, I hope to conquer these countries at less expense than anyone else; but I pray the Lord, nevertheless, that my armada may attain the object I pursue, which is to discover the strait, for that would be the happiest of all results. Of this I am well convinced, because, to the royal good fortune of Your Majesty, nothing can be denied, and diligence and good preparation and zeal will not be wanting on my part to achieve it.

I likewise expect to send the ships I have built on the South Sea, which vessels—our Lord being willing—will sail down the coast at the end of July of this year 1524 in search of the same strait; for if it exists it cannot escape both those who go by the South Sea and those who go by the North; for the South Sea Expedition will go till they either find it or reach the country discovered by Magellanes, and those of the North, as I have already said, until they reach the Bacallaos. Thus on one side or the other we cannot fail to discover the secret. I certify to Your Majesty that, judging by my information, I should have obtained greater returns and rendered greater service to Your Majesty by sending these ships to the countries up the coast of the South Sea, but, as I am informed of Your Majesty's desire to discover this strait, and of the greater service your royal crown would thereby receive, I ignore all other profits and interests to follow this other expedition. May our Lord grant it as it best pleases Him, and may Your Majesty's desire be satisfied, and my desire to serve be likewise gratified.

[Peter Martyr on Cortés's Search for the Spicery]

Let it be remembered that the Moluccas, where spices grow, are partly situated under the equator. Taken altogether, these islands occupy but an insignificant space in the universe, and the equatorial line circles the entire globe. May not other islands, therefore, exist, as well as the Moluccas, equally favoured by climate and fructified by the sun's rays, so as to produce spices? And why may not such countries have remained unknown until the present time, if such was the will of Divine Providence? Do we not likewise know that there exist numerous parts of the ocean and the continent, unheard of until our time? The southern coasts of the empire of Temistitan are not more than twelve degrees from the equator, so there would be nothing astonishing were we now to discover what was heretofore unknown, and were these discoveries to augment the fortune of our Emperor who was the pupil of Your Holiness. I would repeat this to all who are resolved only to believe what they understand, and I would do this in the name of Your Holiness, who has not only wisely pondered the secrets of Nature, the universal mother, but has also studied divine science.

I am, moreover, swayed by another argument. Cortés has accomplished such great things that I cannot believe him to be so wanting in common

SOURCE: "Cortés's Search for the Spicery" from Peter Martyr Anghieri, *De orbe novo*, translated and edited by Francis A. MacNutt, 2 vols. (New York: G. P. Putnam's Sons, 1912), 2, p. 200.

sense as to undertake, blindly, at his own cost, such an important enterprise as the construction in the South Sea of four ships, fitted out for the discovery of those countries, did he not possess some certitude or at least some probability of success.

9. *Peter Martyr on Cabot's Search*
for the Spicery

John Cabot had made his famous North Atlantic voyages in the service of Henry VII of England, but his son Sebastian, finding English interest in discovery waning after Henry VII's death, moved to Spain, where he followed his father's trade, and eventually became Pilot Major, in succession to Vespucci and Solís. In 1526 he commanded an expedition to search for a shorter and more convenient route to the Pacific than Magellan had found; but although (as this extract shows) high hopes were entertained of this venture, its only practical achievement was the exploration of a long stretch of the Río de la Plata.

Perhaps we are not far from the realisation of our desires. In fact, we hope that Sebastian Cabot, the discoverer of the country of Bacallaos, will return more quickly and under better auspices than the *Victory*, the only one out of five vessels to return to Spain with a cargo of cloves, after encircling the world. About the calends of September the India Council, in response to his solicitation authorised him to undertake the voyage of exploration. I have told this story in its proper place. Cabot had asked from the imperial treasury the equipment of a fleet of four ships, completely furnished and provided with cannon. He said he had found partners at Hispalis,—otherwise called Seville,—a great port whence ships sail for India. Animated by the hope of large profits, his partners had themselves proposed to furnish him with the sum of ten thousand ducats for the expenses of the fleet; and at the ides of September we sent Cabot back so that he might settle his business with these men, each of whom will have a proportionate part of the profit if, as it is hoped, the undertaking succeeds.

It remains for me, Most Illustrious Prince, to show by some reasonable arguments why I am right in saying that Cabot should come back more quickly than did the *Victory*, and why we believe that the expedition will be fortunate; otherwise you may accuse me of presumption for indulging

SOURCE: "Cabot's Search for the Spicery" from Peter Martyr Anghieri, *De orbe novo*, translated and edited by Francis A. MacNutt, 2 vols. (New York: G. P. Putnam's Sons, 1912), 2, pp. 288–91.

in prophecy. Cabot should start next August, in 1525. His departure will not take place sooner, because he cannot provide what is required for such a great undertaking before that date, nor would the season be propitious for sailing before that epoch. For he must go towards the equator when our summer draws to its close and the days diminish in length. He must, in fact, not only cross the Tropic of Cancer and the equator, but he must follow a direct line across the Tropic of Capricorn to the fifty-fourth degree towards the antarctic pole, where the Strait of Magellan opens. The opening of this route cost dear, and caused the deaths of many people. Cabot will not have to creep from coast to coast, nor stop, nor double back on his track, as Magellan had to do, who for three years endured cruel fatigues and bitter calamities during his voyage. He lost four out of five ships of his squadron and most of his companions, and he himself perished. I have dilated on this point in the description of the voyage around the world, which I dedicated to Pope Adrian. Cabot will, therefore, take less time on his voyage, since the regions he will traverse and which were so long unknown, are now very well known.

I must, however, sum up the arguments which enable me to hope that Cabot will start under better auspices and end more happily. At the period when northern peoples have the shortest days, Cabot will have the longest. He will thus easily follow the coasts until after passing the tortuous Strait of Magellan, near the constellation of Argo. He will guide the prows of his ships to the right behind the new continent, of which I have spoken so fully in my first Decades addressed to your uncle, Ascanio, and to the Popes Leo and Adrian. He will again cross the Tropic of Capricorn and return to the equator. In the course of this voyage he will discover numberless islands scattered through the immensity of the ocean.

Learn now why we hope that Cabot will collect great wealth. After losing many men, Magellan's vessels sailed through the strait they sought, and passed by all the islands they discovered right and left as well as those they beheld in the distance, without stopping. Their one desire was to reach the Moluccas towards which they continued their course. All other islands were passed by in their hurried voyage, although they landed on a number to take provisions of wood and water and to trade for necessaries of life; their stop was never long.

Magellan, nevertheless, profited as best he could by these stops to inform himself by means of signs and gestures concerning the products of each island he touched, and he thus learned that in many places the sands were mixed with gold. In others, valuable cinnamon-trees, resembling pomegranates, were pointed out to him. Fragments of this precious bark have been presented to me, as Maino and Gillino will witness. He also obtained considerable information concerning the large pearls and other precious stones. He intended to revisit and examine these islands another

time; for the moment he thought only of the Moluccas. And while he revolved great thoughts in his mind, a cruel destiny made him the victim
of nude and barbarous people. I have related this story in its proper place.
If, therefore, during this rapid voyage never before accomplished by man,
such valuable information was collected concerning the excellence of these
islands, what may not be expected from the trading relations which will
be gradually opened with the islanders? It is necessary to proceed gently,
without violence, or the least outrage, and these peoples will yield to kindness and gifts.

The ten thousand ducats Cabot's partners must furnish him for this
enterprise will be spent, first in furnishing him with supplies for two years,
next for paying the wages of one hundred and fifty men of the crew, and
the remainder for purchasing such merchandise as is known to please the
islanders. They will willingly exchange their natural products, of which
they think little, for our merchandise, which they do not know; in fact
they do not use money,—the cause of so many misfortunes,—and every
nation regards as precious those articles which are foreign to it. When
these islands shall have been visited and carefully examined, Cabot will
follow the south coast of the new continent, landing at the new colonies
of Panama and Nata, stations established at the extremity of Castilla del
Oro. Whoever may be governor then will notify us of the success of the
enterprise.

The advisability of replacing most of the governors is just now under
consideration, especially those who have not conquered the provinces they
administer; for it is feared that long enjoyment of power may make them
insolent. Different treatment is accorded to the governors who have conquered the countries where they rule.

As soon as we learn of his fleet's departure, we will pray God that Cabot
may succeed and bring his undertaking to a happy termination.

10. *The Treaty of Saragossa*

The long rivalry between Spain and Portugal in the field of oceanic
exploration was punctuated by three major treaties: Alcaçovas (1479),
which confirmed the Canaries to Spain, West Africa, Madeira, and the
Azores to Portugal; Tordesillas (1694), which superseded the bull *Inter
caetera* and established an agreed Atlantic demarcation, leaving (as
later appeared) Brazil to Portugal, the rest of the Americas to Spain;
and Saragossa (1529), in which the Spanish government agreed, for a
money consideration, to leave the spice-producing Moluccas to the

source: "The Treaty of Saragossa" from *European Treaties Bearing on the History
of the United States*, edited by Frances G. Davenport, 4 vols. (Washington, D.C.:
Carnegie Institution, 1917–37), 1, pp. 187–88.

Portuguese. For practical purposes, this agreement confined Spanish expansion to America and ended Spanish interest in Asiatic trade and settlement until López de Legazpi revived it by his settlement in the Philippines in 1565.

1. First, the said Grand Chancellor, the Bishop of Osma, and the Commander-in-chief of Calatrava, attorneys of the said emperor and sovereign of Castile, declared that they, in his name, and by virtue of their said power of attorney, would sell and in fact did sell from this day and for all time, to the said King of Portugal, for him and all the successors to the crown of his kingdoms, all right, action, dominion, ownership, and possession, or quasi-possession, and all rights of navigation, traffic, and trade in any manner whatsoever, that the said Emperor and King of Castile declares that he holds and could hold howsoever and in whatsoever manner in the said Moluccas, the islands, places, lands, and seas, as will be declared hereafter; this, with the declarations, limitations, conditions, and clauses contained and stated hereunder, for the sum of three hundred and fifty thousand ducats of gold, paid in the current money, of gold or silver, each ducat being valued in Castile at three hundred and seventy-five *maravedis*.

. . .

2. *Item*, it is covenanted and agreed by the said attorneys, in the names of their said constituents, that, in order to ascertain what islands, places, lands, seas, and their rights and jurisdiction, are sold henceforth and forever by the said Emperor and King of Castile, by this contract under the aforesaid condition, to the said King of Portugal, a line must be determined from pole to pole, that is to say, from north to south, by a semicircle extending northeast by east nineteen degrees from Molucca, to which number of degrees correspond almost seventeen degrees on the equinoctial, amounting to two hundred and ninety-seven and one-half leagues east of the islands of Molucca, allowing seventeen and one-half leagues to an equinoctial degree.

CONCLUSION

The initial settlements in Spanish America had been incidents in a race to reach the East. As the extent, the populousness, and the wealth of the new Indies were revealed, their development became an urgent concern of Spanish policy, and Spain's interest in a western route to Asia correspondingly declined. The delimitation of areas of influence, the strategic withdrawal from Asia at a price, seemed in retrospect to be sensible as well as unavoidable. Yet the interwoven stories of European penetration in the East and the West Indies were not so easily to be separated, nor colonial-Spanish ambitions in Asia so easily diverted. The Treaty of Saragossa, backed by Portuguese pugnacity, kept Spaniards away from the Moluccas; but the Portuguese made no effective protest when Miguel López de Legazpi landed in the Philippines in 1565 and in 1571 founded the city of Manila. Manila, through the Chinese junks which traded there and the Portuguese ships which came from Macao, became a unique back door to the closed, self-sufficient, xenophobic half-world of late Ming China, linking a society in which silver was in high demand with one in which it was cheap and plentiful. The ships which carried silver from Acapulco to Manila returned with silk, porcelain, jewelry, and drugs, some for sale in Mexico, some for transshipment to Peru (whence much of the silver came), some for re-export to Europe. At its height the trade equaled in value the official transatlantic trade of Seville. In the middle decades of the seventeenth century a number of factors, of which governmental restriction was one, combined to reduce the trade to little more than the volume which Mexico itself could absorb; but this volume was still considerable. The Manila galleons maintained their hazardous but profitable sailings down to 1815—a lasting reminder of the world-encircling ambitions of Columbus and Cortés.

In another and more general sense, the stories of the East and West Indies were connected. In the course of the seventeenth century the Portuguese monopoly of European-Asian trade was invaded, and the volume of that trade greatly increased, by Dutch, English, French, and other European trading companies. Since few European goods were salable in the East, the companies exported silver to pay for their purchases of silk, spices, calicoes, and (later) coffee and tea. Much of this silver came directly or indirectly from America. Supplies of American silver could not, of course, always be assured, especially in the middle decades of the seventeenth century, when levels of production declined, and English and Dutch traders were driven to acquire silver—some of it of Japanese origin—by means of the "country trades." But in general, Spanish America was the principal source of the silver available in Europe for eastern trade. Some of it was coined in northern Europe as ducatoons, rix-dollars, or thalers; but throughout much of the seventeenth century and the whole of the eighteenth, Spanish or Mexican piastres, pieces of eight, were the coins most commonly used and most readily accepted in business dealings between Europeans and Asians throughout the East. The piastres flowed to the East not only across the Pacific and through Manila but also across the Atlantic and round the Cape, having played their part in European commerce on the way. Without this flow of silver, the successes of the East India companies would have been difficult, perhaps impossible. Columbus, Balboa, Cortés were intuitively right, in ways they could not have dreamed of. The exploitation of the New World was a necessary condition of the eastward spread of European trade and influence in the Old.

BIBLIOGRAPHY

A general discussion of discovery and its interpretations is found in J. H. Parry, *The Age of Reconnaissance* (London: Weidenfeld & Nicholson, 1963). Boise Penrose, *Travel and Discovery in the Renaissance* (Cambridge, Mass.: Harvard University Press, 1955) is a good narrative of voyages with a comprehensive survey of the literature.

On the legacy of the classical geographers, the definitive work is J. Oliver Thomson, *History of Ancient Geography* (London: Cambridge University Press, 1948). The best English version of Ptolemy is Edward L. Stevenson, ed., *The Geography of Claudius Ptolemy* (New York: N.Y. Public Library, 1932). On medieval geographical knowledge the standard work is C. Raymond Beazley, *The Dawn of Modern Geography*, 3 vols. (London: Oxford University Press, 1896–1906). A briefer and more up-to-date survey is George H. T. Kimble, *Geography in the Middle Ages* (London: Methuen, 1938).

The lure of the East and its fascination for fifteenth-century Europeans is described in Francis M. Rogers, *The Quest for Eastern Christians: Travels and Rumor in the Age of Discovery* (Minneapolis: University of Minnesota Press, 1962). Donald F. Lach, *Asia in the Making of Europe*, Vol. 1 (Chicago: University of Chicago Press, 1965), is a monumental survey of the literature and also contains an excellent chapter on the spice trade.

Of the enormous and often controversial literature on Columbus, the best and most convincing account is Samuel E. Morison, *Admiral of the Ocean Sea*, 2 vols. (Boston: Little, Brown, 1942). It has the special merit of concentrating on Columbus's achievements as a seaman. George E. Nunn, *The Geographical Conceptions of Columbus* (New York: American Geographical Society, 1924) is a useful technical study. Carl O. Sauer, *The Early Spanish Main* (Berkeley: University of California Press, 1966) traces the story of Caribbean discovery, with profound geographical as well as historical insight, from 1492 to 1519.

A good though perhaps too laudatory book on Vespucci is Frederick J. Pohl, *Amerigo Vespucci, Pilot Major* (New York: Columbia University Press, 1944). An excellent life of Balboa is Kathleen Romoli, *Balboa of Darien* (Garden City, N.Y.: Doubleday, 1953). The standard work on Magellan and his achievement is Jean Denucé, *Magellan; la Question des Moluques et la Première Circumnavigation du Globe* (Brussels: Académie Royale de Belgique, 1911). A more popular biography in English is Charles McKew Parr, *Ferdinand Magellan, Circumnavigator* (New York: T. Y. Crowell, 1964). There is room for a good modern study of Cortés; his intense interest in the route to Asia has never been adequately studied. On his principal exploit, the conquest of Mexico, William H. Prescott's great work, *The Conquest of Mexico*, though written more than a hundred years ago, has never been surpassed. An abridged version is available in paperback, edited by C. H. Gardiner (Chicago: University of Chicago Press, 1966).

II

The Problem of Conflicting Spanish Imperial Ideologies in the Sixteenth Century

John Leddy Phelan

CHRONOLOGY

1516–56	Charles V rules Spain
1519–21	Conquest of the Aztecs by Cortés
1521–1720	Encomienda
1521–40	Epidemics among the Indians
1535–51	Administration of Viceroy Antonio de Mendoza
1550–51	Valladolid debate between Las Casas and Sepúlveda
1551–64	Administration of Viceroy Luis de Velasco
1556–98	Philip II rules Spain
1563	Arrival of Visitor-General Valderrama
1576–80	Epidemics among the Indians
1595–96	Mendieta's *Historia eclesiástica indiana* completed; epidemics among the Indians

INTRODUCTION

In building an empire in the New World, Spain exercised its conscience as well as its sword. As the conquest progressed, Spanish theologians and scholars attempted to define what means ought to be employed to secure the new empire and what ultimate purposes it ought to serve. Three principal approaches or patterns of ideas emerged. The work of Juan Ginés de Sepúlveda (1490–1573) is perhaps the outstanding example of one pattern, this-worldly humanism. Bartolomé de las Casas (1475–1566) expressed a second approach that was largely derived from Thomas Aquinas and Roman and canon law. A third pattern of ideas found its most eloquent spokesman in the Franciscan chronicler Friar Gerónimo de Mendieta (1525–1604), who was dazzled by the mystical idea that the Indians' conversion could begin the millennial kingdom preceding the end of the world.

Famous already as an Aristotelian scholar, Sepúlveda consistently based his vision of Spain's new empire on Aristotle's axiom that all lower forms of created life should be subject to higher forms. From this central premise of natural slavery, Sepúlveda took a metaphysical leap and concluded that the Indians as a race were grossly inferior to the Spaniards. The Indians were barbarians, not simply in the vulgar sense that their human sacrifices, cannabalism, and other practices were barbaric, but in the original Greco-Roman meaning of the word as well: They lacked the *humanitas* of the Christian and Roman civilization of Spain—that quality of mind and spirit that makes a given people competent to achieve civilization.

Several conclusions followed from these basic considerations. By virtue of its cultural superiority, the Spanish nation had the right and the duty to assume the legal guardianship of the Indian race. The Spaniards were obligated not only to Christianize their wards but also to Hispanicize them. The Indians should be made to work for the Spaniards so that in time they might acquire the good customs and social organization of their guardians. The eventual goal of Spain's wardship was to raise the Indians gradually to the higher level of Spanish humanitas.

Sepúlveda seems ethnocentric today, but he was a passionate and sincere Spanish nationalist. Deeply moved by the glittering exploits of the Spain in which he lived, he was contemptuous of the cultural achievements of the Indians. He once observed that in wisdom, intelligence, virtue, and humanitas the Indians were as inferior to the Spaniards as infants were to adults and women were to men (see page 48). Sepúlveda was one of the first defenders of modern imperialism. He invented a central justification for imperialism (reformulated by Rudyard Kipling as "taking up the

white man's burden") that was to be invoked endlessly from the sixteenth
to the twentieth centuries.

Both Las Casas and Mendieta challenged Sepúlveda's attempt to apply
the Aristotelian doctrine of natural slavery to the Indians. In the course of
a formal debate convoked in Valladolid in 1550–51 to advise the Crown
on Indian policy, Las Casas argued that the concept of natural slavery
could not be applied to any race as such; it could be applied only to a few
deformed individuals. Las Casas based himself squarely on Aquinas's interpretation of Aristotle; Sepúlveda, in contrast, followed the interpretation
of the poet Dante. Fifty years after Aquinas, Dante had extended the
category of natural slavery to include whole races in order to justify the
right of the Roman people to rule the world. Sepúlveda's aim was to establish the right of the Spanish nation to govern the Indies, and he naturally
followed Dante's lead. In fact, Sepúlveda saw the Spaniards as constituting
a new Roman empire, an image that was congenial both to his classical
tastes and to his militant Spanish nationalism.

Bartolomé de las Casas found his inspiration, not in classical antiquity
or in Spanish nationalism, but in the ideological traditions of the Dominican order to which he belonged. Francisco de Vitoria, *prima* professor of theology at the University of Salamanca and a somewhat older
Dominican contemporary of Las Casas, was the first to articulate an
essentially ecclesiastical and juridical justification of the conquest. His
frame of reference was that all nations and all peoples belonged to one
world community that was based on natural law and the law of nations,
the *jus gentium* of Roman jurisprudence. The Spaniards might preach
the gospel to the Indians, but they must also respect the political sovereignty and property rights that the Indian nations and their citizens
possessed by virtue of their membership in the world community of
peoples.

Vitoria and Las Casas were in fact endeavoring to replace an Augustinian with a Thomistic view. During the first decades of discovery and
conquest, Spanish actions were largely inspired by the view, long identified
with St. Augustine, that only membership in the Church guaranteed the
personal, political, and economic rights of individuals. The prevailing
belief was that those who remained outside the pale of Christianity were
without social rights when they came in contact with a Christian people.
In the 1520's and 1530's, however, partly as a consequence of a drastic
decline of the Indian population in the Antilles and partly as a reaction
to the conquest of Mexico, a change of attitude occurred. The Dominicans
and other members of the regular clergy vigorously protested the inhumane
treatment accorded the Indians and attempted to awaken the conscience
of the new imperialism. The most eloquent and tireless spokesman in this
campaign of protest was Las Casas himself.

Aquinas, the great theologian of the Dominican order, had provided his sixteenth-century successors with a veritable arsenal of arguments with which to challenge the Augustinian view of the proper relation among the peoples of the world. Aquinas was emphatic in denying that the Pope possessed temporal jurisdiction over infidels. Hence, mere infidelity was no justification for depriving pagans of their social rights, which were derived from natural law and the law of nations; the Pope could exercise temporal sovereignty in pagan lands only in order to further strictly spiritual ends.

These Thomistic views were fundamental to the thinking of both Vitoria and Las Casas. Las Casas held that the preaching of the gospel was the sole basis of Spanish sovereignty; only after the Indians had been baptized could the Spanish Crown begin to exercise some political jurisdiction over them. Furthermore, the Spaniards had no authority over the pagans unless they willfully obstructed the preaching of the gospel; accordingly, the Spaniards were constrained to choose a method to convert the Indians that would not alienate them. Las Casas was not a pacifist of the kind that opposes all war per se, but he bitterly denounced Sepúlveda's use of the "just war" doctrine because he believed military action would prejudice the Indians against voluntary acceptance of the

Bartolomé de las Casas (1475–1566). *Pan American Union.*

True Faith. His ideal was conversion by means of persuasion and reason; warlike measures prevented the operation of free will and the use of reason.

Las Casas spent more than four decades tirelessly defending the principle that the personal, economic, and political rights of the Indians were founded in natural law and the law of nations and must be respected by the Spaniards. Yet he could not deny that the Spanish kings, to whom he directed his appeals, in fact exercised political jurisdiction over the Indies. He extricated himself from this dilemma by asserting that Pope Alexander VI in his celebrated donation had made the Spanish kings "emperors of the Indies" in order to promote the spiritual welfare of the natives.[1] The imperial authority granted did not conflict with local political jurisdictions of preconquest origins; rather, the two jurisdictions complemented each other. Las Casas had in mind the contemporary situation in Germany, where the sovereignty of the Holy Roman Emperor complemented but did not eradicate the sovereignties of the secular and ecclesiastical princes of the separate German states. Las Casas's view of sovereignty in the Indies was pluralist, in short, while Sepúlveda's was unitary.

Gerónimo de Mendieta many years later challenged the Aristotelian theories of slavery Sepúlveda had expressed during the Valladolid debate. Whatever relevance the doctrine of the "gentile philosopher" may have had in antiquity, Mendieta contended, had disappeared with the coming of the Christian ideal of the equality of all men. Aristotle's natural slavery had given way to St. Paul's doctrine that Greek and Jew (and, Mendieta pointedly added, Spaniard and Indian) were equal in the sight of God.

Mendieta shared with Las Casas the conviction that Spanish rule in the New World flowed exclusively from Spain's evangelical obligation. But Mendieta's approach is more difficult to understand today than the legalism of Las Casas or the secular humanism of Sepúlveda. Mendieta was a Franciscan mystic, heir to a rich mystical tradition that went back to St. Francis himself. He thought in symbolic, figurative, and at times poetic terms, rather than in the more formal logical terms of his fellow theologians. For Mendieta the Bible was to be interpreted symbolically through the ancient method of exegesis. Sepúlveda was a humanist scholar, Las Casas a lawyer-lobbyist at the royal Court. Mendieta, who actually

---

[1] Shortly after Columbus's first voyage, Pope Alexander VI issued three bulls (usually referred to as the Donation of Alexander VI), in which he divided Africa, America, and Asia between Spain and Portugal. It is not at all clear from the text of the bulls whether the Pope was merely dividing the world between the two Iberian powers for missionary purposes or actually transferring sovereignty of the newly discovered lands to the crowns of Spain and Portugal.

spent all of his adult life in Mexico, was a missionary caring for the souls of the Indians in his parish.

Mendieta was not alone in interpreting the discovery and conquest of the New World as an apocalyptic event: Columbus held the same view. Yet nowhere in the writings of Mendieta's contemporaries can we find a formulation of the proposition that the New World represented a specific step in mankind's passage to the end of the world that is as systematic or eloquent as his own. All Christians believed that before the Last Judgment there would be a millennial kingdom in which man would achieve angelic perfection. Mendieta passionately believed that together the Franciscan friars and the Indians could create the most perfect form of Christianity ever practiced on this earth and that this would be the millennial kingdom prophesied in the Apocalypse of St. John.

Mendieta idealized the Indians; more precisely, he "franciscanized" them, stressing their meekness, their docility, and their contentment with poverty. St. Francis and the Franciscans after him had regarded avarice as the deadliest of the seven deadly sins. They idealized the life of poverty, which they identified with the Primitive Apostolic Church before the Emperor Constantine (311–37), as the most perfect fulfillment of Christian asceticism. Thus, Mendieta naturally saw contentment with poverty as a common bond uniting Franciscan and Indian. The Indians became for him children of God who would inherit the earth.

The vineyard of terrestrial perfection that the friars and the Indians were beginning to build in the New World was ravished well before the end of the sixteenth century. Mendieta placed all the blame on the avarice of the Spanish colonists, whose only concern, he claimed, was to live off the sweat and blood of the Indians. He saw the colonists as the slaves of Mammon, literally engaged in a diabolical conspiracy. And Mendieta became overwhelmed by what he regarded as the parallels between the histories of the Old Testament Jews and the Indians. The preconquest period was the Egyptian slavery of the Indians, that is, the bondage of idolatry. Hernán Cortés was the new Moses who liberated the natives from slavery and led them to the Promised Land of the Church. The period 1524–64 was the golden age of the Indian Church, just as the time between Moses and the destruction of Jerusalem by the Babylonians was the golden age of the Jewish people. And the period between 1564 and 1596 was the Babylonian captivity of the Indian Church or the great Time of Troubles before the end of the world prophesied in the Apocalypse. Likening himself to the prophet Jeremiah, Mendieta predicted the ultimate fall of Spain's monarchy if her kings did not deliver the Indians from bondage.

Mendieta's description of the Time of Troubles that had deluged the Indian Church is a Franciscan image of the Apocalypse. It is the final battle between the city of God and the city of the Devil, between the lambs of poverty and the wolves of greed on the eve of the establishment of the millennial kingdom. His apocalyptic pessimism must be interpreted as a reflection of the larger crisis through which the Spanish Empire was passing in the time of Philip II. Spain herself was beginning to show signs of collapsing under the strain of the herculean obligations that she had assumed. In Mexico, the Indian population was declining rapidly. The Crown's partiality toward the secular clergy in Mexico over the regular clergy (to which branch Mendieta belonged) also contributed to his mood of gloom, for he was deeply moved by the misfortunes and sufferings of his Indian flock, whom he loved out of a sense of Christian compassion.

READINGS

1. *Sepúlveda*

In the following passages, Sepúlveda applies Aristotle's doctrine of
natural slavery to the Indians and strikes a note of ardent Spanish
nationalism, at the same time downgrading Indian civilization. He
concludes with an explanation of his concept of the "just war."

You should remember that authority and power are not only of
one kind but of several varieties, since in one way and with one kind of law
the father commands his children, in another the husband commands his
wife, in another the master commands his servants, in another the judge
commands the citizens, in another the king commands the peoples and
human beings confined to his authority. . . . Although each jurisdiction
may appear different, they all go back to a single principle, as the wise men
teach. That is, the perfect should command and rule over the imperfect,
the excellent over its opposite. . . .

And thus we see that among inanimate objects, the more perfect directs
and dominates, and the less perfect obeys its command. This principle is
even clearer and more obvious among animals, where the mind rules like a
mistress and the body submits like a servant. In the same way the rational
part of the soul rules and directs the irrational part, which submits and
obeys. All of this derives from divine and natural law, both of which demand that the perfect and most powerful rule over the imperfect and the
weaker. . . .

The man rules over the woman, the adult over the child, the father over
his children. That is to say, the most powerful and most perfect rule over
the weakest and most imperfect. This same relationship exists among men,
there being some who by nature are masters and others who by nature are
slaves. Those who surpass the rest in prudence and intelligence, although

SOURCE: "Sepúlveda" translated from Juan Ginés de Sepúlveda, *Democrates alter de
justis belli causis apud Indos*, edited by Marcelino Menéndez y Pelayo, in *Boletín de la
Real Academia de la Historia* (Madrid, 1892), 21, pp. 291, 293, 305–09, 313–15, 331–33.
This edition, which contains the original Latin text and a Spanish translation, represents
the first publication of Sepúlveda's treatise, which he wrote around 1547, although it
circulated in manuscript during the sixteenth century. A second edition was published
in 1941 by Fondo de Cultura Económica in Mexico City. I would like to express my
appreciation to James Lauer, who while a graduate student at the University of Wisconsin very helpfully made an initial draft of the translations in this chapter. I assume
sole responsibility for the final draft.—JLP

47

not in physical strength, are by nature the masters. On the other hand, those who are dim-witted and mentally lazy, although they may be physically strong enough to fulfill all the necessary tasks, are by nature slaves. It is just and useful that it be this way. We even see it sanctioned in divine law itself, for it is written in the Book of Proverbs: "He who is stupid will serve the wise man." And so it is with the barbarous and inhumane peoples [the Indians] who have no civil life and peaceful customs. It will always be just and in conformity with natural law that such people submit to the rule of more cultured and humane princes and nations. Thanks to their virtues and the practical wisdom of their laws, the latter can destroy barbarism and educate these [inferior] people to a more humane and virtuous life. And if the latter reject such rule, it can be imposed upon them by force of arms. Such a war will be just according to natural law.

.   .   .

One may believe as certain and undeniable, since it is affirmed by the wisest authors, that it is just and natural that prudent, upright, and humane men should rule over those who are not. On this basis the Romans established their legitimate and just rule over many nations, according to St. Augustine in several passages of his work, *The City of God*, which St. Thomas [Aquinas] collected and cited in his work, *De regimine principum*. Such being the case, you can well understand . . . if you know the customs and nature of the two peoples, that with perfect right the Spaniards rule over these barbarians of the New World and the adjacent islands, who in wisdom, intelligence, virtue, and *humanitas* are as inferior to the Spaniards as infants to adults and women to men. There is as much difference between them as there is between cruel, wild peoples and the most merciful of peoples, between the most monstrously intemperate peoples and those who are temperate and moderate in their pleasures, that is to say, between apes and men.

You do not expect me to make a lengthy commemoration of the judgment and talent of the Spaniards. . . . And who can ignore the other virtues of our people, their fortitude, their humanity, their love of justice and religion? I speak only of our princes and those who by their energy and industriousness have shown that they are worthy of administering the commonwealth. I refer in general terms only to those Spaniards who have received a liberal education. If some of them are wicked and unjust, that is no reason to denigrate the glory of their race, which should be judged by the actions of its cultivated and noble men and by its customs and public institutions, rather than by the actions of depraved persons who are similar to slaves. More than any other country, this country [Spain] hates and detests depraved individuals, even those who have certain of the virtues that are common to nearly all classes of our people, like courage and the martial spirit for which the Spanish legions have always provided examples that exceed all human credibility. . . . And I would like to emphasize the absence of gluttony and lasciviousness among the Spaniards. Is there any nation in Europe that can compare with Spain in frugality and sobriety? Although recently I have seen the intrusion of luxury at the tables of the great as a result of commerce with foreigners, men of good will condemn this innovation, [and] it is to be hoped that in a short time the pristine and natural frugality of national customs may be restored. . . . How deeply rooted is the Christian religion in the souls of the Spaniards, even among those who live amidst the tumult of battle! I have observed many outstanding examples. The most notable among them, it appears to me, occurred after the sacking of Rome during the papacy of Clement VII [1527]. There was scarcely a single Spaniard among those who died from the plague who did not order all the goods he had stolen from the Roman citizens returned in his last will and testament. Not a single other nation that I know of fulfilled this Christian duty, and there were many more Italians and Germans than Spaniards there. I followed the army and noted everything down scrupulously. . . . And what will I say of the gentleness and humanity of our soldiers, who even in battle, after the attainment of victory, expressed great concern and care in saving the greatest possible number of the conquered, protecting them against the cruelty of their allies [the Germans and Italians]?

Now compare these natural qualities of judgment, talent, magnanimity, temperance, humanity, and religion with those of these pitiful men [the Indians], in whom you will scarcely find any vestiges of humanness. These people possess neither science nor even an alphabet, nor do they preserve any monuments of their history except for some obscure and vague reminiscences depicted in certain paintings, nor do they have written laws, but barbarous institutions and customs.[1] In regard to their virtues, how much restraint or gentleness are you to expect of men who are devoted to all kinds of intemperate acts and abominable lewdness, including the eating of human flesh? And you must realize that prior to the arrival of the Christians, they did not live in that peaceful kingdom of Saturn that the poets imagine, but on the contrary they made war against one another continually and fiercely, with such fury that victory was of no meaning if they did not satiate their monstrous hunger with the flesh of their enemies. . . . These Indians are so cowardly and timid that they could scarcely resist the mere presence of our soldiers. Many times thousands upon thousands of them scattered, fleeing like women before a very few Spaniards, who amounted to fewer than a hundred.

.   .   .

---

[1] [Sepúlveda bases these generalizations on incorrect and inadequate information about the character of Indian societies.]

In regard to those [of the Aztec and other Indian civilizations] who inhabit New Spain and the province of Mexico, I have already said that they consider themselves the most civilized people [in the New World]. They boast of their political and social institutions, because they have rationally planned cities and nonhereditary kings who are elected by popular suffrage, and they carry on commerce among themselves in the manner of civilized people. But . . . I dissent from such an opinion. On the contrary, in those same institutions there is proof of the coarseness, barbarism, and innate servility of these men. Natural necessity encourages the building of houses, some rational manner of life, and some sort of commerce. Such an argument merely proves that they are neither bears nor monkeys and that they are not totally irrational. But on the other hand, they have established their commonwealth in such a manner that no one individually owns anything, neither a house nor a field that one may dispose of or leave to his heirs in his will, because everything is controlled by their lords, who are incorrectly called kings. They live more at the mercy of their king's will than of their own. They are the slaves of his will and caprice, and they are not the masters of their fate. The fact that this condition is not the result of coercion but is voluntary and spontaneous is a certain sign of the servile and base spirit of these barbarians. They had distributed their fields and farms in such a way that one third belonged to the king, another third belonged to the religious cult, and only a third part was reserved for the benefit of everyone; but all of this they did in such a way that they themselves cultivated the royal and religious lands. They lived as servants of the king and at his mercy, paying extremely large tributes. When a father died, all his inheritance, if the king did not decide otherwise, passed in its entirety to the oldest son, with the result that many of the younger sons would either die of starvation or subject themselves to an even more rigorous servitude. They would turn to the petty kings for help and would ask them for a field on the condition that they not only pay feudal tribute but also promise themselves as slave labor when it was necessary. And if this kind of servitude and barbaric commonwealth had not been suitable to their temperament and nature, it would have been easy for them to take advantage of the death of a king, since the monarchy was not hereditary, in order to establish a state that was freer and more favorable to their interests. Their failure to do so confirms that they were born for servitude and not for the civil and liberal life. . . . Such are, in short, the character and customs of these barbarous, uncultivated, and inhumane little men. We know that they were thus before the coming of the Spaniards. Until now we have not mentioned their impious religion and their abominable sacrifices, in which they worship the Devil as God, to whom they thought of offering no better tribute than human hearts. . . . Interpreting their religion in an ignorant and barbarous manner, they sacrificed human victims by removing the hearts from the chests. They placed these hearts on their abominable altars. With this ritual they believed that they had appeased their gods. They also ate the flesh of the sacrificed men. . . .

How are we to doubt that these people, so uncultivated, so barbarous, and so contaminated with such impiety and lewdness, have not been justly conquered by so excellent, pious, and supremely just a king as Ferdinand the Catholic was and the Emperor Charles now is, the kings of a most humane and excellent nation rich in all varieties of virtue?

.   .   .

War against these barbarians can be justified not only on the basis of their paganism but even more so because of their abominable licentiousness, their prodigious sacrifice of human victims, the extreme harm that they inflicted on innocent persons, their horrible banquets of human flesh, and the impious cult of their idols. Since the evangelical law of the New Testament is more perfect and more gentle than the Mosaic law of the Old Testament (for the latter was a law of fear and the former is a law of grace, gentleness, and clemency), so also [since the birth of Christ] wars are now waged with more mercy and clemency. Their purpose is not so much to punish as to correct evils. What is more appropriate and beneficial for these barbarians than to become subject to the rule of those whose wisdom, virtue, and religion have converted them from barbarians into civilized men (insofar as they are capable of becoming so), from being torpid and licentious to becoming upright and moral, from being impious servants of the Devil to becoming believers in the true God? They have already begun to receive the Christian religion, thanks to the prudent diligence of the Emperor Charles, an excellent and religious prince. They have already been provided with teachers learned in both the sciences and letters and, what is more important, with teachers of religion and good customs.

For numerous and grave reasons these barbarians are obligated to accept the rule of the Spaniards according to natural law. For them it ought to be even more advantageous than for the Spaniards, since virtue, humanity, and the true religion are more valuable than gold or silver. And if they refuse our rule, they may be compelled by force of arms to accept it. Such a war will be just according to natural law. . . . Such a war would be far more just than even the war that the Romans waged against all the nations of the world in order to force them to submit to their rule [for the following reasons]. The Christian religion is better and truer than the religion of the Romans. In addition, the genius, wisdom, humanity, fortitude, courage, and virtue of the Spaniards are as superior to those same qualities among those pitiful little men [the Indians] as were those of the Romans vis-à-vis the peoples whom they conquered. And the justice of this war becomes even more evident when you consider that the Sovereign Pontiff, who represents Christ, has authorized it.

2. *Las Casas*

> The following are selections from a treatise Las Casas published in Seville in 1552.

PROPOSITION I

The Roman Pontiff, canonically chosen vicar of Jesus Christ and successor of St. Peter, has the authority and the power of Christ himself, the Son of God, over all men in the world, believers or infidels, insofar as it is necessary to guide and direct men to the end of the eternal life and to remove any impediments to this goal. Although the Pontiff uses and ought to use such power in a special fashion with the infidels, who have never entered into holy baptism of the holy Church, especially those who never heard tidings of Christ nor of His faith, he uses another kind of authority with Christians and those who at one time were Christian.

PROPOSITION II

St. Peter and his successors had and have a necessary duty by the injunctions of God to adopt measures with the greatest care that the gospel and faith of Jesus Christ may be preached to all men throughout the whole world, and in my opinion it is unlikely that anyone will resist the preaching of the gospel and the Christian doctrine.

PROPOSITION IV

. . . For the conversion of the infidels the Christian kings are very necessary for the Church; with their secular power, armed forces, and temporal wealth, they may help, protect, preserve, and defend the ecclesiastical and spiritual ministers. . . .

PROPOSITION VII

In order to avoid confusion, the vicar of Christ with his divine authority can and has wisely and justly divided the kingdoms and provinces of all the infidels, of whatever infidelity or sect they may be, among the Chris-

SOURCE: "Las Casas" translated from Bartolomé de las Casas, *Aquí se contienen treinta proposiciones muy jurídicas* (Seville, 1552). For a recent edition, see Bartolomé de las Casas, *Tratados*, 2 vols. (Mexico: Fondo de Cultura Económica, 1965), 1, pp. 461–99.

tian princes, charging and entrusting those princes with the task of spreading the holy faith, the expansion of the universal Church and the Christian religion, and the conversion and health of their souls as the ultimate end.

Proposition VIII

This division, commission, or concession was not made (nor is it made, nor should the Sovereign Pontiff in the future make it) primarily or ultimately to concede grace or to increase the power of Christian states and to bestow on these princes honor, titles, and riches, but primarily and ultimately for the spread of the divine worship, the glory of God, and the conversion and salvation of the infidels, which is the purpose and final intention of the King of kings and the Master of masters, Jesus Christ. He imposed a most dangerous duty and office upon the Christian princes, about which they will have to give the most meticulous account before divine judgment at the end of their lives. Thus, the said division and grant is more for the well-being and profit of the infidels than of the Christian princes.

Proposition IX

It is a just and worthy thing that the primary reward of Christian kings for the services they render to God and the welfare of the universal Mother Church in their royal persons does not consist in worldly and earthly things—to which kings should not aspire, for they are transitory and of little value—but in co-reigning with Christ in heaven. . . . The Supreme Pontiff may concede and donate to Christian princes compensation in the kingdoms of the infidels in order to fulfill the purpose for which he originally entrusted those kingdoms to them. This is a just thing, which does not notably harm or damage the rights of those kings, princes, and notable individuals among the infidels.

Proposition X

Among the infidels who have distant kingdoms that have never heard the tidings of Christ or received the faith, there are true kings and princes. Their sovereignty, dignity, and royal preeminence derive from natural law and the law of nations. . . . Therefore, with the coming of Jesus Christ to such domains, their honors, royal preeminence, and so on, do not disappear either in fact or in right.

Proposition XI

The opinion contrary to that of the preceding proposition is erroneous and most pernicious. He who persistently defends it will fall into formal heresy. It is likewise most impious and iniquitous and has been the cause of innumerable thefts, violent disturbances, tyrannies, massacres, larcenies, irreparable damages, the gravest sins, infamy, stench, and hatred against the name of Christ and the Christian religion. . . .

PROPOSITION XII

The said infidels, monarchs or subjects, are not deprived of their domains, dignities, or other property by any sin of idolatry or any other sin, regardless of how grave or abominable it may be. . . .

PROPOSITION XIII

Infidels, especially those whose paganism is a simple denial, cannot be punished by any judge in the world for the sin of idolatry or for any other sin they committed during their infidelity, regardless of how enormous, extensive, or abominable such sins may have been, until they voluntarily receive the sacrament of holy Baptism. The only exceptions are those infidels who maliciously obstruct the preaching of the gospel and who refuse to desist after they have been sufficiently warned.

PROPOSITION XIV

The Sovereign Pontiff, Alexander VI, during whose reign the vast new world that we call the West Indies was discovered, had the duty by divine injunction to select a Christian king to whom he could entrust the task of preaching the gospel in those lands. That Christian king was also to have the responsibility of establishing and spreading the divine cult and the universal Church in all the kingdoms of the Indies. . . . In compensation for this undertaking, the Pope granted him the dignity and the imperial crown of [universal] sovereignty over all the kingdoms of the New World.

PROPOSITION XV

The kings of Castile and León, Ferdinand and Isabella, the Catholic kings, possessed more outstanding virtues than all the other Christian princes. For this reason, the Pope entrusted this task to them rather than to any other Christian prince. . . . Among their notable virtues there are two in particular. First, inheriting from their royal ancestors the obligation to reconquer all of the Spanish kingdoms from the grip of the tyrannical Muslim enemies of our holy Catholic faith, with their own royal persons and at a heavy expense they reconquered the great kingdom of Granada and at long last restored it to Christ and the universal Church. Secondly, at their own expense and upon their own initiative they sponsored an expedition commanded by the eminent Christopher Columbus, whom they honored and exalted with the title of First Admiral of the Indies, and he discovered the vast and extensive Indies.

Proposition XVI

The Roman Pontiff, vicar of Jesus Christ, whose divine authority extends over all the kingdoms of heaven and earth, could justly invest the kings of Castile and León with the supreme and sovereign empire and dominion over the entire realm of the Indies, making them emperors over many kings. . . . If the vicar of Christ were to see that this was not advantageous for the spiritual well-being of Christianity, he could without doubt, by the same divine authority, annul or abolish the office of emperor of the Indies, or he could transfer it to another prince, as one Pope did when he transferred the imperial crown from the Greeks to the Germans [at the coronation of Charlemagne in 800]. With the same authority, the Apostolic See could prohibit, under penalty of excommunication, all other Christian kings from going to the Indies without the permission and authorization of the kings of Castile. If they do the contrary, they sin mortally and incur excommunication.

Proposition XVII

The kings of Castile and León are true princes, sovereign and universal lords and emperors over many kings. The rights over all that great empire and the universal jurisdiction over all the Indies belong to them by the authority, concession, and donation of the said Holy Apostolic See and thus by divine authority. This and no other is the juridical basis upon which all their title is founded and established.

Proposition XIX

All the kings and princes, cities, communities, and towns of those Indies are obliged to recognize the kings of Castile as universal and sovereign lords and emperors in the said manner, after having received by their own free will our holy faith and the sacred baptism. If before baptism they do not wish to accept [the imperial sovereignty of Castile], they cannot be punished by any judge or justice.

Proposition XX

The kings of Castile are obligated by the Apostolic See and also by divine law to procure, to provide, and to send with all diligence qualified ministers to preach the faith everywhere, calling and inviting the people in the Indies to come to the wedding and banquet of Christ. . . .

PROPOSITION XXII

The kings of Castile are obliged by divine law to ensure that the faith of Jesus Christ be preached in the same manner that He, the Son of God, established for His Church. [This method and this method only] was literally and without any change or diminution followed by His apostles, and the universal Church has made it customary law, enshrining it in its decrees and canons. The holy doctors expostulated and glorified it in their books. The gospel should be preached peacefully, with love, charity, sweetness, and affection, with meekness and good example. The infidels, especially the Indians (who by nature are very gentle, humble, and peaceful), should be persuaded by gifts and presents, and nothing should be taken away from them. And thus they will regard the God of the Christians as a good, gentle, and just God. Hence they will want to be His subjects and to receive His Catholic faith and holy doctrine.

PROPOSITION XXIII

To conquer them first by war is contrary to the law, gentle yoke, light load, and sweetness of Jesus Christ. It is the same approach that Mohammed and the Romans followed when they disturbed and plundered the world. It is the same manner that the Turks and Moors have adopted today. . . . Therefore it is iniquitous, tyrannical, and infamous to the sweet name of Christ, causing infinite new blasphemies against the true God and against the Christian religion. And we have abundant evidence of the damage that this warlike approach has done and is still doing in the Indies. Since the Indians regard our God as the most cruel, unjust, and pitiless god of all, the conversion of the Indians has been hindered, and it has become impossible to convert infinite numbers of infidels. . . .

PROPOSITION XXV

The kings of Castile have prohibited wars against the Indians of the Indies from the time that the First Admiral [Columbus] discovered them, but the Spaniards never honored, observed, or fulfilled these orders and instructions that the kings issued. . . .

PROPOSITION XXVI

Since our kings never sanctioned just wars against the innocent Indians . . . we affirm that all such wars that have taken place in the Indies since their discovery have been, are, and will be unjust, iniquitous, and tyrannical. . . .

PROPOSITION **XXVII**

The kings of Castile are obliged by divine law to establish a government and administration over the native peoples of the Indies that will preserve their just laws and good customs and abolish the evil ones, which are very few. . . . Whatever defects their society may have had can be removed and corrected with the preaching and the spread of the gospel. . . .

PROPOSITION **XXVIII**

The Devil could invent no worse pestilence to destroy all that world and to kill all the people there . . . than the *repartimiento* and *encomienda*, the institution used to distribute and entrust Indians to the Spaniards.[1] This was like entrusting the Indians to a gang of devils or delivering herds of cattle to hungry wolves. The encomienda or repartimiento was the most cruel sort of tyranny that can be imagined, and it is most worthy of infernal damnation. The Indians were prevented from receiving the Christian faith and religion. The wretched and tyrannical Spanish encomenderos worked the Indians night and day in the mines and in other personal services. They collected unbelievable tributes. The encomenderos forced the Indians to carry burdens on their backs for a hundred and two hundred leagues, as if they were less than beasts. They persecuted and expelled from the Indian villages the preachers of the faith. . . . And I solemnly affirm, as God is my witness, that so long as these encomiendas remain, all the authority of the kings, even if they were resident in the Indies, will not be enough to prevent all the Indians from perishing.

3. *Mendieta*

In the following passages, Mendieta describes the mission of the universal monarchy of the Spanish Hapsburgs, "franciscanizes" the Indians in interpreting their character, and conjures up the image of a terrestrial paradise that seems to him a real possibility. He concludes on a pessimistic note, saying that this terrestrial paradise was destroyed by the greed of the Spanish colonists.

---

[1] [The encomienda was an institution in which the Crown distributed the Indian population among the Spanish colonists, who in turn collected a yearly tribute from the Indians assigned to them. Although the individual *encomenderos* were obligated to provide protection to their Indian wards, the system was subject to many abuses. Repartimiento refers to the actual distribution of the Indians among the encomenderos.]
SOURCE: "Mendieta" translated from Gerónimo de Mendieta, *Historia eclesiástica indiana*, edited by Joaquín García Icazbalceta (Mexico, 1870), pp. 17–18, 24–26, 448–49, 451, 556, 559–60, 561. A second edition was published by Editorial Salvador Chávez Hayhoe in 1945.

With respect to our Christian princes of the New Testament . . .
who does not know how very devoutly and piously the very religious emperors Constantine, Theodosius, Justin, Justinian, and Charlemagne venerated and treated the things of God? Moreover, their empires flourished,
and they themselves won celestial immortality because of the marvelous
virtues and deeds that they accomplished through the favor of God. And
if these and other examples (which are too numerous to list) confirm the
law of God that says He will glorify and exalt those who solicit His divine
honor and glory, with so much more reason we can say that in our own
times this law of God applies to our Catholic rulers [Ferdinand and Isa-
bella]. They . . . took pains in the care and reverence of the divine cult
and in fulfilling the task of spreading the Christian religion. They devoted their whole lives and income to remedying necessities, building
churches, reforming the estates [the clergy, the nobles, and the com-
moners], administering justice to their vassals, abolishing abuses in the
religious brotherhoods . . . and finally by purifying the observance of
Christian life by establishing the Holy Inquisition. Thus, God richly rewarded them on this earth, and in heaven He also made them glorious
kings. He endowed them with grace and strength so that they might subject and reduce to the obedience of the Church all the visible multitudes
of Lucifer. This prince of hell, we know . . . raised up a three-pronged
army of deceived and perverted people and has supported them since the
founding of the Church. The three prongs are the Jews (treachery), the
Muslims (falsehood), and idolatry (blindness); he also fostered among the
Christians a fourth prong, the heretics (malice). . . . In order to oppose
and defeat the three very powerful enemy armies that have ensnared and
conquered a major part of the world, it seems that God has chosen our
Catholic kings as his special leaders. In the case of the Jews, our kings
banished from the kingdoms of Spain the rites and ceremonies of the
old law, which had been tolerated up to their time. Moreover, they expelled the Muslims from the city and the kingdom of Granada, previously
under their control. In this way they cleansed all Spain of the impurity
with which for so many years those two sects had contaminated it in dishonor and offense to our Christian religion. It is understandable that,
for their most holy zeal and for these heroic feats, they deserved what
followed. Scarcely was the war with the Muslims concluded when God
put in their hands the conquest and conversion of the infinite number of
idolatrous peoples [of the New World]. . . . I am convinced that as the
Catholic kings were granted the task of beginning to extirpate the three
diabolical squadrons mentioned above, as well as the fourth squadron of
the heretics, for whom the cure and medicine is the Holy Inquisition, it
is also the will of Providence that Ferdinand and Isabella's royal successors
complete this task. Just as Ferdinand and Isabella have cleansed Spain

of these wicked sects, so also their royal successors will complete their worldwide destruction, and they will bring about the final conversion of all the peoples of the world to the bosom of the Church.

[MENDIETA'S EXEGESIS OF A PARABLE FROM LUKE 14]

As the hour of the supper approached (which symbolizes the end of the world), a certain man sent his servant out into the streets to invite the guests to the banquet. They excused themselves, each with a different pretext. It was therefore necessary to send the servant out a second time to the squares and streets to bring the poor, the weak, and the crippled so that they might be seated in the empty chairs at the supper. Yet there was still room for more guests, and so the host dispatched his servant for a third time to the highways and the hedgerows. He ordered his servant to compel people to come to the supper so that his house might be filled. We well know (if we wish to consider the matter) that this business and task of searching, calling, and procuring souls for heaven is of such importance that our Almighty God . . . has done nothing else (in our way of speaking) during the almost seven thousand years since He created the first man. By means of His illuminations, warnings, and punishments; by His servants, the patriarchs and prophets; by His own son in person, and later by the apostles, martyrs, preachers, and saints, God has been calling all the peoples of the earth to hasten to prepare themselves to enter and to enjoy that everlasting feast. This vocation of God will not cease until the number of the predestined is reached, which according to the vision of St. John must include all nations, all languages, and all peoples. Although the servant in the parable . . . symbolizes the preachers who announce the word of God and preach the holy gospel, with even more propriety . . . we can say that the Pope symbolizes the servant [referring to the Pope's delegation of missionary activity to the kings] . . . because to be sent by the king is the same as to be sent by the Pope. What the Pontiff does through the king is as if the Pontiff himself did it. Thus, the parable in the Holy Gospel about the servant being sent to call people for the banquet of the Lord has now come to pass literally in the person of the king of Spain. The hour of the banquet stands for the approaching end of the world. . . . And it should be emphasized that the three types of invitations issued by the servant in the parable coincide with the differences between those three nations. . . . In the case of the Jews, who are acquainted with the Holy Scriptures, they will sin only out of pure malice. Hence, it is enough that the preacher simply inform them of the truth of the word of God. This is an adequate summons for this nation. Thus, in the parable, the first invitation was simply to tell the guests that they might come to the supper, that is, that the Messiah had arrived and that the prophecies were coming to pass. In the case of the Muslims, who can sin out of some (although gross) ignorance of the truth of the law of the Scriptures (for their knowledge has been perverted with the blind errors of the false prophet Mohammed), it is necessary that the priests not only preach to them the word of Christian truth but also persuade them with examples of the good life and with good works. The preachers must demonstrate to the Muslims that they are motivated by pure zeal to save their souls. . . . Therefore, the host ordered his servant in the second invitation to go out and lead the guests to the supper. . . . In the case of the Indian Gentiles, on the other hand, who not only are ignorant of the Truth but who also are likely to sin in matters of the faith and in observing the commandments of God out of sheer weakness, for they are very weak, for them the mere preaching of the gospel will not suffice, nor will the verification of the doctrine by the good example of the ministers, nor even good treatment on the part of the Spaniards. . . . For this reason, God said to His servant in reference to the Gentiles, "Give them no choice but to come in." He did not mean that the Gentiles should be compelled by harsh treatment (as some are, which only shocks and alienates them); He meant that the Gentiles should be compelled in the sense of being guided by the power and the authority of fathers, who have the right to discipline their children for committing evil and harmful actions and to reward them for good and beneficial deeds, especially in respect to all those matters relating to the obligations necessary for eternal salvation.

[MENDIETA'S FRANCISCAN VISION]

Some of the Indians, especially the old people and more often the women than the men, are of such simplicity and purity that they do not know how to sin. Our confessors, who are more perplexed by some of these Indians than they are by notorious sinners, search for some shred of sin by which they can grant them the benefit of absolution. And this difficulty does not arise because the Indians are stupid or ignorant, for they are well versed in the law of God. They answer well all the questions, even the trifles, that they are asked. The fact is, because of their simple and good nature they do not know how to hold a grudge, to say an unkind thing of anyone else, to complain even of mischievous boys, or to forget to fulfill one particle of the obligation that the Church has imposed on them. And in this case I do not speak from hearsay but from my own experience.

.   .   .

And thus I mean that they [the Indians] are made to be pupils, not teachers, parishioners, not priests; and for this they are the best in the world. Their disposition is so good for this purpose that I, a poor, useless good-for-nothing . . . could rule with little help from associates a province of fifty thousand Indians organized and arranged in such good Christianity that it seemed as if the whole province were a monastery. And it was just like the island of Antillia [1] of the ancients, which some say is enchanted and which is located not far from Madeira. In our own times it has been seen from afar, but it disappears as one approaches it. In Antillia there is an abundance of all temporal goods, and the people spend their time marching in processions and praising God with hymns and spiritual canticles. . . . It would be equally appropriate to ask of Our Lord that the Indians be organized and distributed in islands like that of Antillia; for then they would live virtuously and peacefully serving God, as in a terrestrial paradise. At the end of their lives, they would go to heaven, and thus they would avoid all those temptations for which many of us go to hell.

. . .

Not only can I not conclude my history with a psalm of praise, but on the contrary . . . this is indeed the right time for me to sit down with Jeremiah and to relate and bewail the miserable fall and the catastrophes of our Indian Church with tears, sighs, and laments that would reach to heaven itself (as Jeremiah did over the destruction of the city of Jerusalem). For this task I could use the very words and sentences of that prophet. . . . In the ecclesiastical sphere, the first bishops in each see were saintly men similar to the prelates of the Primitive Church. In the temporal realm, there were Christian and pious governors, true fathers of the Indians and of the whole commonwealth. After Don Hernán Cortés, Marqués del Valle, they were Don Sebastián Ramírez de Fuenleal (the worthy bishop of Cuenca), Don Antonio de Mendoza, and Don Luis de Velasco, at whose death [1564] the golden age ended and the men who were the flower of New Spain began to fall from their high estate.[2] At this time the high wall of very saintly laws, *cédulas*, and commands that the fortunate and invincible Emperor Charles V and his good governors had constructed for the defense, aid, and protection of the vineyard of the Lord began to crumble. The Emperor well knew that the vineyard was surrounded by wild animals and beasts of prey who were eager to seize, ravish, and destroy

---

[1] [Antillia was a legendary island in medieval folklore that was supposed to exist somewhere in the Atlantic. It is in fact the origin of the other name for the West Indies, the Antilles.]

[2] [Sebastián Ramírez de Fuenleal was president of the second *audiencia* (1530–35); Antonio de Mendoza was Viceroy of Mexico (1535–51), and so was Luis de Velasco (1551–61).]

it; but a little door was opened in the wall with the arrival of a *visitador* [Valderrama] who came to increase the tributes [of the Indians] and to shout for money and more money,[3] and suddenly the wild beast of unbridled avarice and the wild boar entered the vineyard. Every day they increased—so rapidly that they have now occupied and seized the whole vineyard. The wall has been torn down so that all kinds of animals of prey can enter. Not only have the fruits of the Indians' Christianity and the branches of their temporal prosperity disappeared, but even the few stocks of the vine that are still left are sick, lean, worm-infested, sterile, and profitless. The vineyard has turned into an uncultivated pasture, just as Judas Maccabeus and his companions found Mount Zion and the holy city of Jerusalem profaned by the Gentiles and covered with ashes. They cast off their garments, threw themselves on the ground, and uttered a loud lament, as we also ought to do. . . . Great evil, evil of evils, numberless and indescribable! And all this proceeds from having allowed the wild beast of avarice, who like the beast of the Apocalypse has made himself adored as the lord of the whole world, to ravish and destroy the vineyard. The beast has blinded all men by making them put hope and happiness in black money, as if there were no other god in whom men could trust and hope.

[3] [A visitador, or visitor-general, was a special agent sent from Spain to investigate abuses and recommend reforms. A clash between the audiencia and Viceroy Velasco prompted the mission of Licenciado Valderrama, who accused the friars of abusing their authority. He raised the tribute tax imposed on the Indians.]

CONCLUSION

Sepúlveda, Las Casas, and Mendieta did not speak only for themselves. Each was the spokesman for a series of interests, all of which were deeply involved in the pattern of events shaping the character of the Spanish empire overseas.

Sepúlveda's lofty phrases invoking the Aristotelian doctrine of natural slavery and stressing the moral obligation of the Spaniards to raise the "inferior" Indian civilization to the "higher" level of Spanish humanitas were arguments that struck a responsive chord among the Spanish colonists. His Aristotelian humanism was used to rationalize the hunger of the colonists for a cheap and abundant supply of Indian labor.

Las Casas' Thomistic appeal to the sanctity of natural law and the law of nations provided what was in effect a smoke screen behind which the Crown could restrict the economic power of the colonists. The governments of Charles V and Philip II were acutely aware that if the encomenderos were given unrestricted control over Indian labor, they might develop autonomous political aspirations at variance with the centralizing objectives of the Hapsburg monarchy. Hence, the Crown lent a sympathetic ear to the thunderings of Las Casas, much to the discomfort of the colonists.

And Mendieta, for all his genuine mystical piety, was the spokesman for the pro-Indian party among the Franciscans. Their enemies among the royal bureaucrats and secular clergy accused the friars of wanting to create their own empire, virtually independent of royal and episcopal supervision.

The idealistic statements about the universal monarchy of the Spanish Hapsburgs contained in these selections never completely shaped the complex reality of actual events. Yet each of these ideologies represented real, if sometimes contradictory, tendencies in Spanish imperial policy. Sepúlveda's principle that the Indians should be placed under the guardianship of the Spaniards, for example, was incorporated in the *Recopilación de las leyes de los reynos de las Indias*, published in 1681. In that digest of colonial legislation, the Indians received the status of minors, though their rights were to be paternalistically protected by royal and ecclesiastical authorities. The Dominican emphasis on natural law and the law of nations found in the works of Las Casas similarly affected reality, contributing mightily to the defense of Indian property rights all during the colonial regime. And the Christian humanitarianism and idealism, the dedication of the missionaries and the ideal of the Christian brotherhood of man, that we see so clearly stated in the pages of Mendieta were also a profound influence on the conquest. Avarice and cruelty did constitute other tendencies in the conquest, but no revolution, including the Spanish conquest of America, has ever enjoyed the miracle of an immaculate conception.

BIBLIOGRAPHY

Gibson, Charles. *Spain in America* (New York: Harper & Row, 1966), Chapters 1–7. An authoritative overview of Spanish colonial policy.

Hanke, Lewis. *The Spanish Struggle for Justice in the Conquest of America* (Philadelphia: University of Pennsylvania Press, 1959). A standard account of the ideological aspect of the conquest, focusing on Las Casas.

Kubler, George. *Mexican Architecture in the Sixteenth Century* (New Haven, Conn.: Yale University Press, 1948). The introduction is a concise analysis of the ideological aspects of the missionary enterprise in Mexico.

Mendieta, Gerónimo de. *The Ecclesiastical History of Mexico* (Washington, D.C.: Academy of American Franciscan History, 1969). An English translation of the standard Franciscan chronicle.

Motolinía, Toribio de. *A History of the Indians of New Spain*. One English translation by the Academy of American Franciscan History (Washington, D.C., 1951) and the other by the Cortés Society (Berkeley, Calif., 1950). A moving account of the missionary enterprise in Mexico, written by one of the early Franciscan missionaries.

O'Gorman, Edmundo. *The Invention of America* (Bloomington: Indiana University Press, 1961). A stimulating and original discussion of the ideological birth pangs of the discovery of America.

Parry, J. H. *The Spanish Seaborne Empire* (New York: Alfred A. Knopf, 1966). An authoritative overview of Spanish colonial policy.

———. *The Spanish Theory of Empire* (London: Cambridge University Press, 1940). A suggestive analysis.

Phelan, John Leddy. *The Millennial Kingdom of the Franciscans in the New World*, rev. ed. (Berkeley: University of California Press, 1969). A consideration of the ideological aspects of the conquest, focusing on the contribution of the Franciscan friar Gerónimo de Mendieta.

Ricard, Robert. *The Spiritual Conquest of Mexico* (Berkeley: University of California Press, 1966). An English translation of a classic work on the missionary enterprise in Mexico.

Scott, J. B. *The Spanish Origin of International Law* (London: Oxford University Press, 1924). A classic account of Vitoria's contribution.

Simpson, Lesley Byrd. *Many Mexicos*, 4th rev. ed. (Berkeley: University of California Press, 1966), Chapters 3–10. Readable and concise summary of the social and institutional background of early colonial Mexico.

The Problem of the Impact
of Spanish Culture
on the Indigenous American
Population

Charles Gibson

CHRONOLOGY

1492   First contacts between Spaniards and Indians in the West Indies

1511   Sermon by Antonio de Montesinos in Santo Domingo against the harsh treatment of Indians

1512   Laws of Burgos, permitting encomienda

1519   Beginning of the conquest of Mexico by Hernán Cortés

1523   Beginning of the conquest of Guatemala by Pedro de Alvarado

1524   Arrival of twelve "apostolic" Franciscans in Mexico

1531   Departure of Francisco de Pizarro from Panama for the conquest of Peru

1537   Bartolomé de las Casas' experiment for peaceful colonization in Verapaz, Guatemala

1542   New Laws enacted for good treatment of Indians and abolition of encomienda

1545   Partial revocation of New Laws and restoration of encomienda

1572   Execution of Túpac Amaru I, the "last" Inca ruler

1610   Founding of Santa Fe, New Mexico

1680   Pueblo revolt in New Mexico

1681   Publication of the *Recopilación de las leyes de los reynos de las Indias*

1692   Indian-mestizo riots in Mexico City

1720   Formal abolition of encomienda

1779   Outbreak of rebellion of Túpac Amaru II in Peru

1782   Founding of Santa Barbara mission, California

INTRODUCTION

American Indian civilizations had their beginnings more than twenty thousand, and perhaps more than fifty thousand, years ago in Mongoloid migrations from Siberia. The migrations themselves continued for many centuries, and Indian society, also migratory at first, changed slowly. In the periodization of American prehistory, the longest eras occur first, while successive stages occupy progressively shorter time spans. The portion that we know least well is the one in which the most gradual change took place, equivalent to perhaps ninety per cent of the total time. Our most abundant information applies to the Aztec and Inca empires, the histories of which do not antedate the thirteenth century A.D.

By the late fifteenth century, most peoples of the regions that were to become Spanish America had progressed beyond a condition of nomadic hunting to village living and an economy based on agriculture. In some areas these steps had been taken several thousand years before, and intermediate civilizations antecedent to the Aztec and Inca had already risen, flourished, and collapsed. In Mexico, Peru, and many other parts of America a community organization supported by agriculture and trade formed the local foundation on which larger political states could be, and were, established. The Aztec and Inca empires may be thought of as the last in the sequence of native superstructures resting on this base.[1]

During the first fifty years after the discovery of America by Columbus, Spain overthrew and displaced the native American superstructures. Indian organizations were wholly eliminated at the uppermost level and severely curtailed at intermediate levels. The new colonial government, like its Indian predecessors, rested on local community foundations, but it introduced more disruption than earlier empires, for Spaniards were alien overlords and their relation to Indian society tended to be exploitative in new ways. The immediate transition from native rule to Spanish rule was accomplished principally by military conquest. The great native empires in particular felt the direct attack of Spanish arms and were taken over by the invaders. Almost everywhere, force, whether applied or threatened, marked the beginnings of Spanish control. And the fundamental fact governing subsequent relations between the two peoples was that Indians were subordinated to Spaniards.

Conquest had a direct impact on Indian society in the loss of life and the physical destruction that accompanied the warfare. The Spanish cam-

---

[1] Pedro Armillas, "Cronología y periodificación de la historia de la América precolumbina," in *Journal of World History*, 3 (1956), pp. 463–503.

paigns in America are notorious among all wars of history for their excesses, and while it is possible to argue that some of the written record exaggerates their destructiveness, their status in the history of European expansion as extreme examples of aggressive action seems firmly established.[2] But it should be noted that warfare was by no means unknown in aboriginal America and that many Indians found in the Spanish invasions an opportunity to join with the conquistadors in battles against their own Indian enemies. Thus the military aspect of conquest, though it uniformly resulted in Spanish victory, could be construed by the Indians at the time as an additional element in the furtherance of their own wars. Indian records of conquest express a variety of conditions and attitudes: helplessness, local patriotism, material deprivation, supernaturalism, opportunism, matter-of-fact acceptance of the event.

Though the conquistadors tended to employ militarism without consideration or scruple, the use of force came to be justified in Hispanic imperial theory as a means to Christianization.[3] In practice, in the New World, friars did follow the conquistadors, and the period of militarism gave way to a period of intensive proselytism. The work of conversion was aided by the appeal of the Christian message and acts of humility by individual friars, but it also depended partly on force, for it was attended by destruction of idols and temples, execution of recalcitrants, and punishment.[4] The initial Indian response to Christianity included some cases of defiance, but the larger part of Indian society, following the example of its leaders, accepted the new religion within the first generation after the conquests. Accustomed to mass labor of different kinds, the Indian population readily acceded to demands for construction labor on the huge new churches and other ecclesiastical buildings.[5] It is likely that Indian peoples were in some degree already disillusioned with the pagan deities who had so manifestly failed them. Christianity offered an alternative faith under novel conditions, as well as a further means for demonstrating ideological commitment, or submission, to the winning side.

The ecclesiastical organization in the colony followed standard Spanish forms. In its relation to the Indians it depended also on the surviving native towns, which provided the jurisdictional structure for a colonial parochial organization. Friars further extended the pattern of Indian set-

[2] Rómulo D. Carbia, *Historia de la leyenda negra hispano-americana* (Madrid: Consejo de la Hispanidad, 1944).

[3] Lewis Hanke, *The Spanish Struggle for Justice in the Conquest of America* (Philadelphia: University of Pennsylvania Press, 1949), pp. 33, 120.

[4] Wigberto Jiménez Moreno, "The Indians of America and Christianity," in *History of Religion in the New World* (Washington, D.C.: The Secretary of the Conference on the History of Religion in the New World During Colonial Times, 1958), p. 83.

[5] George Kubler, *Mexican Architecture of the Sixteenth Century*, 2 vols. (New Haven, Conn.: Yale University Press, 1948), 1, pp. 134–38.

tlement by combining small units into composite towns and by assembling remote families into new *congregaciones*.[6] By the late sixteenth century the established colonial church was employing this revised form of settlement for the collection of tithes and fees, for the support of clergy, and for the staffing of minor positions in the ecclesiastical hierarchy. Though Indians were forbidden to take orders as priests, they served everywhere as sacristans and musicians and lay missionary aides. The typical Indian town received a church, a new Christian name, and a patron saint, and its inhabitants, under ecclesiastical tutelage, established sodalities and celebrated fiestas that combined the community's religious and secular life. Thus, the ecclesiastical arm of the Spanish state tended in some ways to reinforce an existing Indian communality.

The Indians' religion of the late sixteenth and early seventeenth centuries nevertheless fell short of original missionary goals, chiefly because the associated elements of Indian belief, lore, cosmology, and ritual were never fully eradicated. Indian Christianity existed side by side with, or in some degree of compromise with, persistent elements of paganism. The overall situation was not new in the history of Christianity, but its particular features in Indian America were new, and despite occasional periods of revived missionary campaigning they continued through colonial times.

In the secular sphere, Indians were most useful to Spaniards as laborers, and various colonial institutions were designed to organize the society for work and to apportion workers among Spanish colonial employers. Such apportionment was called *repartimiento*, but its principal institutional form in the early colonial period was given the name *encomienda*, for this signified a relationship of entrustment rather than simple allocation. Conquistadors and other Spanish colonists were rewarded with grants of encomienda, which permitted them to employ designated groups of Indians, commonly an entire town or a portion of a town, as laborers and tribute payers. Within certain limits, encomiendas were inheritable by the sons and grandsons of the original colonial grantees, and in some cases they persisted for generations.[7] The derivatively feudal device of encomienda allowed for much gross exploitation of Indian society by individual Spaniards, whose tribute demands and abuses in labor exaction became notorious. Spanish colonists were legally forbidden to make slaves of Indians save under very special circumstances, but in the extreme cases the assertion that encomienda was a legalized form of slavery is not an exaggeration.

It remains true that encomienda was a relatively short-lived institution in the central areas of the colonies. The Crown legislated against it, partly

---

[6] Howard F. Cline, "Civil Congregations of the Indians in New Spain, 1598–1606," in *Hispanic American Historical Review*, 29 (1949), pp. 349–69.

[7] Silvio Zavala, *La encomienda indiana* (Madrid: Imprenta Helénica, 1935).

because its exploitative character ran counter to the Christian and humanitarian goals of Spanish imperialism, but more practically because the *encomendero* class in America threatened to become a powerful aristocracy in opposition to royal authority. As encomiendas were abolished in the middle and late sixteenth century, a larger fraction of Indian society came under direct royal control. Indians outside of encomienda paid tributes to royal officials rather than to private encomenderos. Their labor was apportioned in a new and more organized system of repartimiento that assigned them to short-term but recurrent periods of work for private employers in agriculture, mining, construction, and other occupations. The new repartimiento included a wage payment, but it was a forced labor system, and Indian communities experienced much difficulty in filling their quotas. In the peripheral areas of the colonies encomiendas tended to survive longer, and the original abuses either continued unchanged or were modified in the direction of the repartimiento.

The Indian population meanwhile underwent a severe decline. This decline was absolute in the West Indies, where Indian society was totally extinguished by about 1550, and in parts of the mainland coast, where the process required somewhat more time. In central Mexico, the foremost modern studies indicate a depopulation of more than ninety per cent in the hundred years following the conquest.[8] The subject has not been examined so precisely for other areas, but there can be little doubt that population loss occurred everywhere. It affected the history of encomienda, for encomenderos could profit from their grants only as long as they controlled large numbers of Indians. It also encouraged the importation of Negro slaves; heavy Negro concentrations developed in the regions where Indian populations could no longer serve the labor need.

Depopulation meant both a quantitative reduction in the size of Indian society and a loss of vigor in the individual communities. In the middle of the sixteenth century, Indian towns responded in some spirit of affirmation to the lay and ecclesiastical programs of political Hispanicization by reorganizing their municipal governments in a *cabildo* form, by holding local elections, and by maintaining Indian *gobernadores, alcaldes,* and *regidores.* Staffing the positions and preserving the forms of Hispanic municipal life became more difficult as the populations declined. The high Indian death rate meant abandonment of lands, both private and communal, and Spanish colonists, now more numerous, readily preempted the sparsely populated or vacant properties.[9] The Indians' capacity to resist Spanish pressures was much reduced. The colonists, amassing great tracts

---

[8] Sherburne F. Cook and Woodrow Borah, *The Indian Population of Central Mexico, 1531–1610* (Berkeley: University of California Press, 1960).

[9] Lesley Byrd Simpson, *Exploitation of Land in Central Mexico in the Sixteenth Century* (Berkeley: University of California Press, 1952).

of land as plantations, haciendas, or ranches, were in a position to force the communities to yield more land and to submit to their bidding in other ways. Under stress, community life became disunited. An individual or group might choose to capitulate to an *hacendado* for a price, alienating the community in the process. Indian towns were especially weak in times of drought or poor harvests. Indians moved from the towns to the haciendas, improving their own private positions through wage advances in the system of peonage but leaving the communities still more depopulated and vulnerable. In the standard Spanish American conflict between the Indian town and the hacienda, the latter steadily gained ground. Colonial courts upheld Indian possession in particular instances, but the results of legal victories were likely to be only temporary, and the amount of land actually returned to Indian communities after white appropriation was infinitesimal.

A similar and related loss of energy on the Spanish side affected those colonial institutions that were designed to civilize or educate the Indian in Hispanic terms. The original impulse had been partly Christian and partly humanistic. In the sixteenth century a few Spaniards made efforts to teach natives, and some exceptional Indians had learned to read and write and even to converse in Latin. But this original promise was not fulfilled. Schools for Indians were virtually nonexistent in the developed colony. The elements of Hispanic civilization that Indians adopted were restricted to a few domestic animals, a small number of household effects, and some articles of dress and diet. Of course, the extent and tempo of acculturation varied with circumstances and opportunity. The Indians of the upper classes and those living in cities changed the most, while rural dwellers and those lower on the social scale tended to retain their Indian ways. The great achievements of the preconquest peoples in architecture, sculpture, feather art, astronomy, and calendrical computation had become things entirely of the past by the seventeenth century. The degradation of Indian society was evident everywhere in its low status, its extreme poverty, its attitude of fatalism, and its inclination to drunkenness. Whites of the seventeenth and eighteenth centuries almost unanimously regarded Indians as sullen and uncooperative people. "Fear cannot stimulate, respect induce, nor punishment compel them," wrote Antonio de Ulloa, a judgment that suggests the complete stolidity with which Indian society showed itself to whites.

A quite different reaction appeared among Indians located beyond the frontiers of Spanish settlement. These were peoples of a simpler native culture, and Spaniards ordinarily assumed them to be hostile. A basic difference between Indians who were incorporated into the Spanish colonial regime and those who remained outside was that the former were sedentary inhabitants of communities, whereas the latter were wholly or partly nomadic. This distinction goes far toward explaining the effective geographical limits of Spanish colonization. In the early period, the Spaniards' motives for expanding these limits depended mainly on the need for pacifying the mining areas and the routes to them. In the seventeenth century, a principal objective was Christian conversion, for the role of the missionary orders within the colony had by this time been much reduced, and they were able to continue an active proselytization only on the frontiers. In the eighteenth century, the key purpose became imperial and strategic, for rival European powers were now intruding upon Spanish claims. In all three centuries, Indian peoples at or beyond the frontiers were to some degree successful in resisting Spanish pressures, partly because of their fierce guerrilla tactics, partly because Spaniards no longer made the effort that they had made in the great conquests. Frontier Indians who were ultimately brought within the sphere of colonial life commonly occupied the position of mission dwellers in areas that remained remote from the Spanish colonial centers.

The Bourbon reforms of the late eighteenth century in the Spanish colony had as a secondary and derivative purpose the elevation of the Indian standard of living. But this was not achieved in the colonial period. In some areas, by the late eighteenth century, a population still called Indian had become ethnically mixed with white and Negro. Royal legislation had always tended to place Indians in a special category and to offer them protection from other elements of colonial society. Such laws became more difficult to enforce when an individual's status as either Indian or mestizo was in doubt. Moreover, the protective legislation was more characteristic of the Hapsburg sixteenth century than of the Bourbon eighteenth, and while it remained as written statute, it became increasingly unrealistic in colonial life. Liberal legislation of the independence and post-independence periods, which was in part an extension of the reform movement of the eighteenth century, sought to remove Indians from their special legal category—by eliminating tribute, by declaring all classes to be equal in citizenship, and in other ways. But the essential subordination of Indian to white society survived this legislation and persisted as a continuing legacy.

READINGS

1. *The Conquest in Guatemala* (c. 1524)

Reality and fantasy mingle in this Indian relation of an episode in the Spanish conquest of Guatemala. The narrative records that armed native resistance was broken, but it also provides some imaginative details that have the effect of rendering defeat less humiliating.

In the year 1524, the *adelantado* [1] Don Pedro de Alvarado arrived in this region after having conquered Mexico and all those lands. He came to the town of Xetulul Hunbatz and conquered the land. Don Pedro de Alvarado Tunadiú [2] arrived at the town of Xetulul and stayed three months, conquering all the coast.

At the end of this time the people of Xetulul sent a message to the town of Lahunqueh, saying that the Spaniards were coming to conquer. Galel Atzih Vinac Tierán, who was the *cacique* [chief] of the town of Lahunqueh, sent a message to the people of Chi Gumarcaah, telling them also that the Spaniards were coming to conquer so that they could be warned and could prepare themselves. He sent another message to the cacique of the town of Sakpoliah, named Galel Rokché Zaknoy Isuy. Still another message he sent to the caciques of Chi Gumarcaah. The messenger was named Ucalechih. He was the one who took the news to the King.

The king of Chi Gumarcaah sent out a great captain named Tecún-Tecum, grandson of the cacique Quicab. This captain brought many people from many towns, amounting in all to ten thousand Indians, with their bows and arrows, slings, spears, and other weapons. Captain Tecum, before going out from his town in front of the caciques, demonstrated his valor and his spirit, and he put on his wings for flight. He had plumage on his two arms and legs. He wore a crown, and on his chest he had a large emerald like a mirror. He had another on his forehead and another at his back. He was very elegant. This captain flew like an eagle. He was a great chief and a great animal spirit.

Adelantado Tunadiú came to sleep at a place called Palahunoh. Before

---

[1] [The office of adelantado was frequently given to conquistadors and governors, especially in frontier areas.]

[2] [Tunadiú or Tonatiuh (Sun) was the Indian name given to Alvarado.]

SOURCE: "The Conquest in Guatemala" translated from "Títulos de los antiguos nuestros antepasados, los que ganaron estas tierras de Otzoyá antes que viniera la fe de Jesucristo entre ellos, en el año de mil y trescientos," in *La sociedad económica de Guatemala*, 4, Nos. 34–36 (1876). Except where noted otherwise, the translations in this chapter are by the chapter editor.

he arrived, thirteen chiefs went with more than five thousand Indians to a place called Cuabah. There they made a huge stone rampart so that the Spaniards could not pass, and they dug many large pits and trenches, closing off the entrances and obstructing the route by which the Spaniards would enter. The Spaniards were halted three months in Palahunoh because they were unable to approach the large number of Indians.

Then an Indian captain made up as an eagle went out from the town of Ah Xepach with three thousand Indians to fight with the Spaniards. They went out at midnight, and the captain who was made up as an eagle went to kill Adelantado Tunadiú. But he could not kill him because a white girl defended him. While they were making their approach and as soon as they saw this girl, they fell to the ground and were unable to get up. Immediately they saw many birds without legs, and the birds surrounded the girl.

The Indians tried to kill the girl, and the legless birds defended her and pecked their eyes out.

The Indians were not able to kill Tunadiú or the girl, and they went back and sent another Indian captain, made up as a lightning bolt, named Ixquín Ahpalotz Utzakibalhá, called Nehaib. This Nehaib went as a lightning bolt to where the Spaniards were and sought to kill the adelantado. As soon as he arrived he saw a white dove above the Spaniards, defending them. When the dove returned a second time, the captain's vision was destroyed, and he fell to the ground and could not get up. Three times the captain rushed at the Spaniards as a lightning bolt, and each time his eyes were blinded and he fell to the ground. And when the captain realized that he was unable to get near the Spaniards, he went back and told the caciques of Chi Gumarcaah that these two captains had gone to try to kill Tunadiú, and he told about the girl and the legless birds and the dove who defended the Spaniards.

Then Adelantado Don Pedro de Alvarado came with all his soldiers and made his entrance at Chuaraal. They brought two hundred Tlaxcalan Indians, and they filled the pits and trenches that the Indians of Chuaraal had made. Thereupon the Spaniards killed the Indians of Chuaraal. Three thousand was the number that the Spaniards killed. From Xetulul they brought two hundred Indians who were tied up, and those of Chuaraal whom they did not kill they also tied up and tortured so that they would tell them where they had their gold.

The Indians who were being mistreated implored the Spaniards not to torture them further, saying that a large amount of gold, silver, diamonds, and emeralds was held by the captains Nehaib Ixquín, Nehaib as eagle and lion. Then they gave themselves up to the Spaniards and remained with them, and this Captain Nehaib invited all the Spanish soldiers to eat and gave them native birds and eggs.

Another day the great captain named Tecum addressed the Spaniards, saying that he was extremely upset because they had killed three thousand of his valiant soldiers. As soon as the Spaniards heard this, they rose up and saw that he had brought with him Captain Ixquín Nehaib. The Spaniards began to fight with Captain Tecum. The adelantado asked Captain Tecum if he wished to make peace, and Captain Tecum said he did not, but rather he wanted to test the courage of the Spaniards.

The Spaniards began to fight with the ten thousand Indians brought by Captain Tecum. But they soon separated, and only after they were half a league apart did they come together again to fight. They fought for three hours, and the Spaniards killed many Indians. Those whom they killed were without number. No Spaniards died. Only the Indians whom Captain Tecum had brought were killed. Quantities of blood flowed from the bodies of all the Indians whom the Spaniards killed. This occurred in Pachah.

Then Captain Tecum rose in flight, for he had become an eagle, covered with feathers that grew by themselves—they were not artificial. He had wings growing from his body, and he wore three crowns, one of gold, another of pearls, and another of diamonds and emeralds. Captain Tecum came with the intention of killing Tunadiú, who was on horseback. He rushed at the horse in order to attack the adelantado, and he cut off the horse's head with his sword. It was not a metal sword but one of native style, and the captain did this by casting a spell.

When he saw that he had killed the horse rather than the adelantado, he started to fly upward so that he could come down on the adelantado from above and kill him. But the adelantado waited for him with his lance and ran him through in the middle of his body.

Two hairless dogs came up and snatched at this Indian in order to tear him to pieces. But the adelantado, seeing that he was very elegant and that he wore the three crowns of gold, silver, diamonds, emeralds, and pearls, protected his body from the dogs and stood looking at him very slowly. He was covered with beautiful quetzals and feathers, and it is for this that the town of Quetzaltenango was named, because the death of Captain Tecum occurred here.

Then the adelantado summoned all his soldiers to see the beauty of the Indian quetzal. The adelantado told his soldiers that he had never seen any other Indian so elegant and noble or covered with such beautiful quetzal feathers. He said that he had not seen this in Mexico or in Tlaxcala or in any other region that they had conquered. And for this reason the adelantado said that the town would be named Quetzaltenango, and it remained afterward with this name.

The other Indians fled when they saw that the Spaniards had killed their captain. Then Adelantado Don Pedro de Alvarado, seeing that the soldiers of Captain Tecum were fleeing, ordered that they had to die too. The Spanish soldiers went after the Indians and attacked them and killed them all, so that none remained.

2. Christianization in Mexico (1540)

The Indian acceptance of Christianity in central Mexico is here described by a Franciscan missionary in a spirit of warm Christian sympathy and faith. Encouraged by the early native response, Motolinía thought that the labor of conversion had been essentially completed by 1540.

When the land had been conquered and allotted by the Spaniards, the friars of Saint Francis who were there at the time began to go about among the Indians and converse with them, at first only in the places where they had a house of the Order, as was the case in Mexico, Tetzcoco, Tlaxcallan, and Huexotzinco;[1] for the few friars who were there at first were divided among those provinces. In each of these and in those in which the Order later had houses (there are nearly forty in this year of 1540) there was so much to tell that not all the paper in New Spain would suffice. Pursuing the brevity which is pleasing to all, I shall recount what I saw and knew and what happened in the towns where I lived and visited. Although I may say or relate something about a province, it will be of the time when I lived there; others may write of the same province and tell quite truthfully of other things that happened there, and they may be more striking and better written than what is told here, and yet it may all be accepted without contradiction.

The town to which the friars first went out to teach was Cuautitlán, four leagues from Mexico. They went also to Tepotzotlán. This they did because there was much disturbance in Mexico, and because among the sons of lords who were being taught in the House of God there were the young lords of these two towns, nephews or grandsons of Moteuczuma and among the most important members of the school. Out of deference to them the friars began to teach in these two towns, and to baptize the children. The teaching of the Faith was always continued there and these young lords were always the leaders in all good Christian practices, as were also the towns subject to them, and their neighbors.

[1] [Towns in central Mexico, including their surrounding areas.]
SOURCE: "Christianization in Mexico" from Motolinía (Toribio de Benavente), *Motolinía's History of the Indians of New Spain*, translated by Elizabeth A. Foster (Berkeley, Calif.: Cortés Society, 1950), Documents and Narratives Concerning the Discovery and Conquest of Latin America, n.s., No. 4, pp. 124–25, 127–28, 131–33. Reprinted by permission of the Cortés Society.

In the first year that the friars came to this land the Indians of Mexico and Tlatilolco began to assemble, those of one parish or district on one day and those of another parish on another day, and the friars went to these meetings to teach them and to baptize the children. Shortly afterward they all assembled on Sundays and feast days, the people of each section in the center where they had their old halls, for as yet there were no churches. The Spaniards also, for some three years, held their Masses and sermons in one of these halls, which served as a church; it now houses the mint. Almost no burials were made there, but the dead were buried in the old church of Saint Francis, until later they began to build churches. For five years the Mexicans were very indifferent, either because the Spaniards had their hands full and because of the building of the city of Mexico, or because the elder Mexicans had little enthusiasm. After five years many of them woke up and built churches, and now they are very frequent attendants at the daily Masses and receive the sacraments devoutly.

.   .   .

The first two years the friars did not go out very much from the town where they had their residence, both because they knew very little of the country and of the language, and because they had plenty to attend to where they lived. The third year the people in Tetzcoco began to assemble daily to learn the catechism, and a great many also came to be baptized; as the province of Tetzcoco is very populous, the friars, both inside and outside of the monastery, were unable to keep up with the work or to help others, for many people were baptized from Tetzcoco, Huexotzinco, Coatlichan, and Coatepec. Here in Coatepec they began to build a church and made great haste to finish it because it was the first church outside of the monasteries. It was called Santa María de Jesús. After having gone about for several days among the towns under the jurisdiction of Tetzcoco, which are numerous and among the most populous in New Spain, they went on to other towns. As they did not know the country very well, when they set out to visit one town people would come out from other towns to ask them to go with them to preach the word of God, and they often came across other little villages and would find the people assembled, waiting with a meal all prepared and begging the friars to eat and to teach them. At other times they went to places where they made up by fasting for the abundance they had had elsewhere. Among the places to which they went were Otompa, Tepepolco, and Tollantzinco, which had no resident friars for a good many years after that.

Among these, Tepepolco did very well and kept growing and progressing in the knowledge of the Faith. The first time that friars came to this place was one afternoon—I omit any account of the reception which the Indians gave them—and as the inhabitants were all assembled the friars began to teach them and in the space of three or four hours many of the people, before they left, knew how to cross themselves and repeat the Pater Noster. The next day in the morning a great many people came, and when the friars had taught them and preached to them as much as was suitable for a people who knew nothing and had never heard of God nor received His word, they took aside the lord and the principal men of the town and repeated to them how God in heaven was the true Lord, creator of heaven and earth, and who the devil was whom they adored and honored, and how he deceived them, and other things of the sort. They said it so effectively that the Indians at once and in the presence of the friars destroyed and broke all their idols and burned their teocallis.

This town of Tepepolco is built on a high hill where there was one of the big and splendid temples of the devil, which they then tore down. As the town is big and has many others subject to it, it had big teocallis or temples of the devil, and this is the general rule by which you can tell whether a town is big or small—whether it has many teocallis.

. . .

Many come to be baptized, not only on Sundays and on the days indicated for baptism, but every day, children and adults, the sick and the well, from all districts. When the friars go about making visits the Indians come out to meet them with their children in their arms and carrying the sick on their backs; even decrepit old people they bring out to be baptized. Many, after they have been baptized, leave their many wives and marry only one. When they come to be baptized some beg for it, others insist, others ask for it kneeling, others raising and clasping their hands, moaning and crouching, others demand and receive it weeping and sighing.

In Mexico a son of Moteuczuma, who was the great lord of Mexico, asked to be baptized, and because this son was ill we went to his house, which was near where the church of St. Hypolitus now stands. Mexico was conquered on this saint's day and for that reason a great festival is celebrated on that day in all New Spain and Hypolitus is considered the special patron of this land. They brought the sick man out in a chair to be baptized, and as the priest was performing the exorcism, when he said the words *Ne te lateat Satanas* not only the sick man but also the chair in which he was sitting began to tremble so violently that, in the opinion of all of those who were present, it seemed that the devil was going out of him. This scene was witnessed by Rodrigo de Paz, who was at that time *alguacil mayor* [2] (because he was acting as godfather the Indian was baptized with the name of Rodrigo de Paz), and other officials of his Majesty.

In Tetzcoco as a baptized woman was going along with an unbaptized child on her back (that being the way they carry children in this country)

[2] [Chief constable.]

and passing at night through the courtyard of the teocallis, which are the houses of the devil, the devil came out to her and seized the child, trying to take it from the mother, who was terrified because the child was not yet baptized nor signed with the cross. She cried aloud: "Jesus! Jesus!" and the devil at once let go of the child; but as soon as she ceased to speak the name of Jesus the devil tried again to take the infant. This happened three times, until she got out of that fearful place. The very next morning she brought the child to be baptized in order that no such peril might befall him again, and so it was done. It is very striking now to see the children that come every day to be baptized, especially here in Tlaxcallan. There are days when we have to perform the baptismal service four or five times. Counting those who come on Sundays, there are weeks when we baptize three hundred children, and sometimes we baptize four or five hundred, taking in the children within the radius of a league. And if ever, out of carelessness or because of some obstacle, we fail to visit the towns two or three leagues away, there are so many to be baptized later that it is a marvel.

Also many have come, and still do come, from a distance to be baptized, bringing their wives and children, the sick and the well, the lame, the blind and the deaf, dragging along and suffering great hardships and hunger, for these people are very poor.

In many parts of this country they bathed newborn children on the eighth or tenth day and then, if the child was a boy, they put a tiny shield in his left hand and an arrow in his right hand; if it was a girl, they gave her a tiny broom. This ceremony seemed to be a sort of symbol of baptism and meant that the baptized were to fight against the enemies of the soul and to sweep and clean their souls and consciences so that, by baptism, Christ might enter.

I calculate the number of the baptized in two ways: first by the towns and provinces which have been baptized, and second by the number of the priests who have administered the sacrament. There are at present in New Spain about sixty Franciscan priests, for few of the other priests have done much baptizing. Although some have, I do not know what the number may be. Besides the sixty priests I speak of, more than twenty others must have returned to Spain, some of whom baptized numerous Indians before they went away. There were more than twenty others, now dead, who also baptized many, especially our father, Fray Martín de Valencia, the first prelate in this land who represented the Pope, and Fray García de Cisneros and Fray Juan Caro, an honorable old man who introduced and first taught in this land the Castilian tongue and part singing, a very difficult task. There were also Fray Juan de Perpiñán and Fray Francisco de Valencia, each of whom must have baptized over one hundred thousand persons. From the sixty who are here in this year of 1536

I subtract twenty who have not baptized, because they are new to the country and do not know the language. For the forty who remain I would estimate one hundred thousand or more baptisms each, for there are some of them who have baptized nearly three hundred thousand, others two hundred thousand and one hundred and fifty thousand, and others much smaller numbers; so that including those baptized by the priests now dead or returned to Spain, there must have been baptized up to the present day nearly five millions.

By towns and provinces I calculate as follows: Mexico and its dependent towns, Xochimilco with the towns of the fresh-water lake, Tlalmanalco and Chalco, Cuauhnahuac with Eecapitztlan, and Cuauhquechollan and Chietla, over a million; Tetzcoco, Otompa, Tepepolco, and Tollantzinco, Cuautitlán, Tollan, Xilotepec with their provinces and towns, more than another million; Tlaxcallan, Puebla, Cholollan, Huexotzinco, Calpa, Tepeyacac, Zacatlán, Hueytlalpán, more than another million; the towns along the South Sea,[3] more than another million. And since this report was copied, over five hundred thousand more have been baptized, for in this past Lent of 1537,[4] in the province of Tepeyacac alone there have been baptized by actual count over sixty thousand souls. So that, in my opinion and truthfully, there must have been baptized in the time I mention—a matter of fifteen years—more than nine million Indians.

3. *Exploitation by Local Officials in Peru* (1666)

> Local officials called *corregidores*, whose jurisdictions were called *corregimientos*, habitually profited from their positions by distributing mules, textiles, and other goods to Indians at exorbitant prices. In this document the royal court (*audiencia*) at Lima seeks, unsuccessfully, to exercise control, and in so doing it provides a commentary on local exploitation practices and on disobedience of the law.

The president and judges of this royal audiencia, governing these kingdoms of Peru, Tierra Firme,[1] and Chile, in the absence of a viceroy, etc.:

---

[3] [The Pacific Ocean.]

[4] [Motolinía evidently prepared different passages of this text over a period of several years; hence the different dates mentioned in this account.]

[1] [The name Tierra Firme was given to the northern coast of South America.]

SOURCE: "Exploitation by Local Officials in Peru" translated from Guillermo Lohmann Villena, *El corregidor de indios en el Perú bajo los Austrias* (Madrid: Ediciones Cultura Hispánica, 1957), Appendix VI, pp. 569–73.

In repeated cédulas, His Majesty (whom God preserve) has ruled that we are to watch over the welfare of the Indians. They are to be supported and favored, freed from the oppressions from which they now suffer, and treated as vassals of the Crown, for that is what they are. With persuasive words, His Majesty has appealed to the consciences of ministers and others, especially in his most recent order on the conference for righting Indian wrongs. It is notorious, and all experience has shown, that despite the laws, cédulas, and ordinances in their favor, the principal cause of the Indians' suffering is the excessive behavior of the corregidores appointed for the provinces of this kingdom. This results from their greed for silver during the ordinary year of their tenure, not to mention the additional year that may be granted them. So extreme is this greed that it is now quite acceptable, not prohibited or regarded as bad, for them to employ all available means for molesting the miserable Indians so that they may make more profit. Such heavy burdens are imposed upon the natives that they run away from their towns, neglect their Christian obligations, and cross over into the frontier provinces to mingle with the infidels. The result is that not enough are left to meet the labor obligations, which therefore fall with increased severity upon the few that remain. Indeed, some of them become so desperate that they kill themselves and their children. And there are many other undesirable consequences, not readily summarized in a brief space.

And although the viceroys, and most recently Viceroy Conde de Santisteban, with his Christian zeal and ability and prudence, sought to control these very serious conditions . . . our experience is that nothing has sufficed. Rather, it appears that everything that is ordered in favor of the Indians redounds to injure them, and this in an ever increasing way, while the corregidores' greed remains unsatisfied. It makes any pious person sad to hear that over a period of two years a given corregimiento is worth fifty thousand pesos or that another is worth seventy thousand. And it is said that there have been corregimientos worth one hundred thousand pesos in illegal income squeezed in blood from the Indians. Having considered all this and having discussed it with full attention and consultation, as is proper in a matter so important for the service of God our Lord and His Majesty, and in the belief that unless a remedy is speedily forthcoming total ruin will be threatened, we have determined to strike at the root of the problem. Therefore, when orders to new corregidores are given, and before any new appointee receives his orders, he is to be summoned before this Royal Governmental Tribunal, and the following is to be put to him:

1. He should understand that the corregimiento to which he is being appointed is for one year only and that the addition of the second year, common as the practice may have been, remains and should remain com-

pletely at the discretion of this government. The fact that an office is assigned, or may be assigned, to another person is not to be taken as a sign of disfavor toward an incumbent officeholder, since the office was given to him for one year, and he accepted it under this condition.

2. When corregidores have taken the oath to observe the ordinances and royal cédulas and governmental provisions and to refrain from commercial transactions while holding office, the proper form has not been followed. Hence, they have felt able to disobey without scruple, saying that they did not swear or that they swore without attention or making other excuses. To prevent this and to ensure a proper form, the oaths will now be administered before this governmental tribunal in the presence of its members, where there is to be a cross, or where the cross worn by a person of a military order may be used. The corregidores are to swear clearly and expressly not only to observe the cédulas, royal ordinances, and governmental provisions in general but also, in all good faith, to observe particularly and completely the rules that follow.

3. Neither in person nor through any other party nor in any other way is a corregidor to introduce mules into his district, in small or large number, nor is he to have any connection or relationship, contract, dependency, or interests—close or distant—with the persons who do introduce them. And he will understand that in addition to the punishment for perjury, if this is involved, and the punishments for breaking other laws relating to business transactions, the mules introduced by any of these means are to cease to be his and to become crown property. And a third of the income derived from their sale is to go to the person who gives sufficient proof that he was the one who made the public or secret accusation against the corregidor.

4. In the same way, the corregidor is to swear that he will not introduce any wine in his district, in small or large quantities, by himself or through any other person, nor will he authorize the sale of wine to Indians. . . .

5. With the same penalties and declaration, he is to swear that he will not introduce Spanish or native clothing into his district, nor for this purpose will he buy any in this city or elsewhere, in cash or on account. And he will allow the merchants and peddlers who do introduce such goods to sell and bargain freely. And he will do them no harm or injury, nor will he allow anyone else to do so, directly or indirectly through another person or in any way.

6. If there are textile workshops and looms in his district, he will swear that he will not ask the owners or other interested parties or anyone to give him a share or to weave any cloth in his interest, in great or small amount. And even though they may offer it to him of their own free will, he is not to accept it, whether as a gift or in partnership or in concession or in any other arrangement. . . . And the owner who gives him such a

share, or any administrator or foreman who does so, without manifesting and declaring what he is doing either in person or by letter to this government will have his workshop closed, and his Indians will be reassigned to such other person as may be convenient. And if any workshops are operating without the license of the government, he will proceed to close them and to execute the penalties against those who hold or possess them.

7. Also he is to swear that he will not buy, in person or through intermediaries, any cattle or other animals, but will leave all such transactions freely to particular individuals of his district or to those whose business this is, inside or outside the district, under the same penalties.

8. Also he will swear that he will not make any transactions involving any kind of clothing, wool, yarn, or sleeping mats but will allow the Indians, men or women, to work freely and sell to anyone they wish.

9. He is to swear in the same way with respect to transactions involving bread, meat, jerked beef, corn, and other foodstuffs. He will leave the trade in these goods wholly to the Indians and to particular persons, without intruding in any way or using such foodstuffs for himself or for any second party. Nor will he permit his aides, servants, or agents to do this; rather, he will forbid them and punish them in an exemplary way.

10. If any of these rules is broken, and if the corregidor himself or any intermediary distributes or delivers any mules, wine, yarn, or goods on trust to any Indians, in addition to the other penalties the sale will be nullified, and the goods distributed or sold will remain with the Indian involved, who will not be obliged to pay anything for them. . . .

4. Deculturation in Quito (c. 1745)

After two centuries of Spanish rule, the outstanding traits of Indian society appeared to be stupidity, torpor, and drunkenness. A traveling Spaniard comments on what he has seen of this society in Ecuador.

It is no easy task to exhibit a true picture of the customs and inclinations of the Indians, and precisely display their genius and real turn of mind; for if considered as part of the human species, the narrow limits of their understanding seem to clash with the dignity of the soul; and such is their stupidity, that in certain particulars one can scarce forbear entertaining an idea that they are really beasts, and even destitute of that in-

SOURCE: "Deculturation in Quito" from Jorge Juan and Antonio de Ulloa, *A Voyage to South America*, translated by John Adams, 2 vols. (London: J. Stockdale, 1806), 1, pp. 402–06, 408–10. Originally published as Jorge Juan and Antonio de Ulloa, *Relación histórica del viaje a la América meridional*, 4 vols. (Madrid, 1748).

stinct we observe in the brute creation. While in other respects, a more comprehensive judgment, better-digested schemes, and conducted with greater subtilty, are not to be found than among these people. This disparity may mislead the most discerning person: for should he form his judgment from their first actions, he must necessarily conclude them to be a people of the greatest penetration and vivacity. But when he reflects on their rudeness, the absurdity of their opinions, and their beastly manner of living, his ideas must take a different turn, and represent them in a degree little above brutes.

Such is the disposition of the Indians, that if their indifference to temporal things did not extend itself also to the eternal, they might be said to equal the happiness of the golden age, of which the ancient poets have given such inchanting descriptions. They possess a tranquillity immutable, either by fortunate or unfortunate events. In their mean apparel they are as contented as the monarch clothed with the most splendid inventions of luxury; and so far are they from entertaining a desire for better or more comfortable clothing, that they give themselves no manner of concern about lengthening their own, though half their bodies continue naked. They shew the like disregard for riches; and even that authority or grandeur within their reach is so little the object of their ambition, that to all appearance it is the same thing to an Indian, whether he be created an alcalde, or forced to perform the office of a common executioner.

And thus reciprocal esteem among them is neither heightened nor lessened by such circumstances. The same moderation appears in their food, never desiring more than what suffices; and they enjoy their coarse simple diet with the same complacency as others do their well-furnished tables. Nor do I indeed question but if they had their choice of either, they would prefer the latter; but at the same time they shew so little concern for the enjoyments of life, as nearly approaches to a total contempt of them: in short, the most simple, mean, and easiest preparation seems best adapted to their humour.

Nothing can move them, or alter their minds; even interest here loses all its power; it being common for them to decline doing some little act of service, though offered a very considerable reward. Fear cannot stimulate, respect induce, nor punishment compel them. They are indeed of a very singular turn; proof against every attempt to rouse them from their natural indolence, in which they seem to look down with contempt on the wisest of mortals: so firmly bigoted to their own gross ignorance, that the wisest measures to improve their understanding have been rendered abortive; so fond of their simplicity and indolence, that all the efforts and attention of the most vigilant have miscarried. But in order to give a clearer idea of their tempers, we shall relate some particular instances of their genius and customs; as otherwise it will be impossible to draw their true character.

The Indians are in general remarkably slow, but very persevering; and this has given rise to a proverb, when any thing of little value in itself requires a great deal of time and patience, that it is "only fit to be done by an Indian." In weaving carpets, curtains, quilts, and other stuffs, being unacquainted with any better method, at passing the woof they have the patience every time to count the threads one by one; so that two or three years is requisite to finish a single piece. This slowness undoubtedly is not entirely to be attributed to the genius of the nation; it flows, in some measure, from the want of a method better adapted to dispatch. And perhaps with proper instructions they would make considerable progresses, as they readily comprehend whatever is shewn them relating to mechanicks: of this the antiquities still remaining, in the province of Quito, and over all Peru, are undeniable testimonies. . . . This indifference and dilatoriness of the Indians is blended with sloth, its natural companion; and their sloth is of such a nature, that neither their own interest, nor their duty to their masters, can prevail on them to undertake any work. Whatever therefore is of absolute necessity to be done, the care of it is left to the Indian women. These spin, and make the half-shirts and drawers, which constitute the whole apparel of their husbands. They cook the matalotage, or food, universally used among them; they grind the barley, for machca, roast the maize for the camcha, and brew the chicha; in the meantime, unless the master has been fortunate enough to get the better of the husband's sloth, and taken him to work, he sits squatting on his hams (being the usual posture of all the Indians), and looks on his wife while she is doing the necessary work of the family; but, unless to drink, he never moves from the fireside, till obliged to come to table, or wait on his acquaintance. The only domestic service they do, is to plough their chacarita, or little spot of land, in order to its being sown; but the latter, together with the rest of the culture, makes another part, which is also done by the wife and children. When they are once settled in the above posture, no reward can make them stir; so that if a traveller has lost his way, and happens to come to any of these cottages, they hide themselves, and charge their wives to say that they are not at home; when the whole labour consists in accompanying the traveller a quarter of a league, or perhaps less, to put him in his way: and for this small service, he would get a rial, or half a rial at least. Should the passenger alight and enter the cottage, the Indian would still be safe; for, having no light but what comes through a hole in the door, he could not be discovered: and even if he should see the Indian, neither entreaties nor offers would prevail on the slothful wretch to stir a step with him. And it is the same if they are to be employed in any other business.

That the Indians may perform the works appointed by their masters, and for which they are properly paid, it will be of little signification to shew them their task; the master must have his eye continually upon them: for whenever he turns his back, the Indian immediately leaves off working. The only thing in which they shew a lively sensation and alacrity, is for parties of pleasure, rejoicings, entertainments, and especially dancings. But in all these the liquor must circulate briskly, which seems to be their supreme enjoyment. With this they begin the day, and continue drinking till they are entirely deprived both of sense and motion.

Such is their propensity to intemperance, that they are not restrained by any dignity of character; the cacique and the alcalde never fail to be of the company, at all entertainments; and drink like the rest, till the chicha has quite overcome them. It is worth notice, that the Indian women, whether maids or married, and also the young men before they are of an age to contract matrimony, entirely abstain from this vice; it being a maxim among them, that drunkenness is only the privilege of masters of families, as being persons who, when they are unable to take care of themselves, have others to take care of them.

. . .

Their habitations, as may be imagined, are very small; consisting of a little cottage, in the middle of which is their fire-place. Here both they and the animals they breed, live promiscuously. They have a particular fondness for dogs; and never are without three or four little curs in their hut: a hog or two, a little poultry, and cuyes, with some earthen ware, as pots, and jugs, and the cotton which their wives spin, constitute the whole inventory of an Indian's effects. Their beds consist of two or three sheepskins, without pillows or any thing else; and on these they sleep in their usual squatting posture: and as they never undress, appear always in the same garb.

Though the Indian women breed fowl and other domestic animals in their cottages, they never eat them: and even conceive such a fondness for them that they will not even sell them, much less kill them with their own hands; so that if a stranger, who is obliged to pass the night in one of their cottages, offers ever so much money for a fowl, they refuse to part with it, and he finds himself under the necessity of killing the fowl himself. At this his landlady shrieks, dissolves in tears, and wrings her hands, as if it had been an only son; till, seeing the mischief past remedy, she wipes her eyes, and quietly takes what the traveller offers her.

Many of them in their journeys take their whole family with them; the women carrying on their shoulders such children as are unable to walk. The cottages in the mean time are shut up; and there being no furniture to lose, a string, or thong of leather, serves for a lock: their animals, if the journey is to last for several days, they carry to the cottage of some neighbour or acquaintance: if otherwise, their curs are left guardians of the whole; and these discharge their trust with such care, that they will fly at any one, except their masters, who offers to come near the cottage. And here it is worth observing, that dogs bred by Spaniards and Mestizos have such a hatred to the Indians, that, if one of them approaches a house where he is not very well known, they fall upon him, and, if not called off, tear him to pieces: on the other hand, the dogs of Indian breed are animated with the same rage against the Spaniards and Mestizos; and, like the former, scent them at a distance.

The Indians, except those brought up in cities or towns, speak no language but their own, called Quichua, which was established by the Yncas, with an order for its being propagated all over the vast empire, that all their subjects might be able to understand each other; and therefore was distinguished by the name of the Yncas language. Some understand the Spanish, and speak it; yet very few have the good-nature to answer in it, though they know at the same time, that the person with whom they are conversing cannot understand them in Quichua. Nor is it of any consequence to desire and press them to explain themselves in Spanish, for this they absolutely refuse: whereas it is quite otherwise with the Indians born and bred in the towns; for, if spoken to in their own language, they are sure to answer in the Spanish.

5. *Disease in Lower California* (c. 1790)

Illness and death accompanied the Spaniards in their frontier expansion. The effects for mission Indians are here described for Lower California in the eighteenth century.

It is indisputable that the land of California has a very healthy climate. The air is pure, the sky beautiful, the atmosphere transparent and the night very clear. The salubrity of its climate is favorable, not only to the natives, but also to foreigners, and much more so to the Spaniards. The Indians, whose constitution is very ardent, have many wild fruits [*semillas*] which temper and cool their blood; such are the *pitahayas*, and even more efficacious some that they call *carambullos*, like plums, but very red and without stones, but I attribute the health which the unconverted Indians enjoy to the fact that their foods are very simple. Salt is not used, and as they are almost entirely fruits and herbs, they are very easily digested. They lack physicians, only the old men serve as such, but they never use blood-letting nor other drastic remedies. Add to this the many and continuous sweatbaths with which they keep their

SOURCE: "Disease in Lower California" from P. Luis Sales, O.P., *Observations on California*, translated by Charles N. Rudkin (Los Angeles: Dawson's Book Shop, 1956), pp. 53–62. Reprinted by permission of Dawson's Book Shop, Los Angeles.

circulations active. Although they are sometimes ill they always sleep on
the hard ground near the fire, smoke and all.

The races, wrestling matches, fights, and other voluntary exertions cause
many chest ailments and other mischances. It is certain also that from
time to time there have occurred severe epidemics of high fevers, small-
pox and French boils,[1] which have completely desolated the missions and
towns. The little diet control they have (since even if they were dying,
if fish or anything else were offered them they would not refuse it), the
exposure to inclement weather, and sticking close to the fire and smoke
even though the heat may be terrific, throwing themselves into the sea
when sick, and other follies which they practice, erroneously thinking to
rid themselves of their pains, are the reasons these epidemics kill them
off. The desertion of acquaintances and friends (since on seeing someone
sick they leave him and go elsewhere) causes them to die of starvation and
like wild animals. I myself have found in the country moribund persons
whom we then took to the mission and fed; they have lived many years.
When one falls sick they care for him a little while, but if he gets worse
they use to put a little pot of water beside his head and leave him. However there are other areas where the wife holds her husband in her arms,
watching his every movement, until he expires.

What afflicts these unfortunate people now is the French disease,[2]
which has been introduced with such force and violence that since it
exterminated the nation of the Pericúes (which was very widespread and
inhabited the southern part of this province, and of whom not a single
one is left, their lands depopulated and deserted) it has penetrated into
the northern parts and in the same way has finished off the pueblos.
Those in which the Indians were counted by thousands now have about
a hundred, and where there were six or seven hundred persons they hardly
amount to thirty, for which reason the missionaries can never fulfill their
aspirations. Some are of the opinion that this French disease is endemic,
based on the fact that the most remote heathen (and I have seen many)
show it. But I have also noticed that this is a mistake, because it is not
ulcers that they show but tumors that appear in the groin and then disappear. But that which shows up only in the converted pueblos are
malignant ulcers which make them useless for work, which are promptly
transmitted, and which end up with almost all infected. That of the
heathen hardly spreads at all and sometimes it leaves them without the
application of any remedies at all, but of the Christians, no matter how
many remedies are used, few are those who are cured. This has led me
to believe that what the unconverted suffer from is not the French

---

[1] [Buboes, a symptom of syphilis.]
[2] [*El gálico*, or syphilis.]

disease, since that would cause pain in their bodies and would leave them no ability to race and dance, as they do continuously.

Others judge that the troops, whose life and irregularities in this province are licentious enough and give the conquest a very bad name, introduced this disease, since only in the towns where the soldiers live is this sickness observed, they being the first to suffer from it, from which it would appear that perhaps by their affairs with the Indian women and theirs with others this very contagious disease has been propagated.

Most people say that the original cause of this misfortune was an uprising that the Indians made against the Spaniards and the missionary fathers of this province, and that God sent this punishment for their evil deeds. I will set forth what establishes this from authentic papers in the archives at the mission of San José at Cape San Lucas, which I have seen and examined for myself. Two uprisings have been substantiated among those Indians called Pericúes, who inhabit the southern part. One took place in the year 1734 and the other in the year 1740. In the first they killed Father Nícolas Tamaral of the expelled Company and in the second the servants and the people of the China ship, which was anchored at that port and mission. In these uprisings they showed themselves very barbarous, for they laid waste and burned everything. Two years after the last uprising, that is in the year 1742, there began among them an epidemic so strange and so terrible that it seemed to be a punishment from heaven. The sick could not be tolerated by the others because of the multitude of pustules that came out all over the body. At the mission alone five hundred people died. This sickness lasted two years and a half. From this mission it spread to that of Santiago, from there to Todos Santos. Even while the epidemic continued in the south, it suddenly broke out in the north in the farthest mission, which was then San Ignacio, and spread from there to infect the other missions. This pestilence was as widespread as the uprising of the Indians had been, and it is a marvel that the epidemic never reached the unconverted Indians of the north and that only those died who were accomplices in the atrocities, while those who did not join in were cured by lemon juice, orange drinks and bathing in sea water; these same remedies applied to the evil-doers acted like poison and they died in two days.

In 1748 there began another epidemic, of measles, of which an enormous number died, and in 1768 another, much more contagious, broke out, in which only a few malignant pustules appeared. This epidemic put an end to most of the Indians. They became all swollen and died in two days. And when they [the pustules] broke they emitted such a stench that others had to go away because they could not bear it. There was no one, large or small, who did not experience this scourge. But it was clearly seen that the whole nation of the Pericúes, which was the most rebellious and intractable and which even then was meditating the complete destruction of all, was itself wiped out and in the year 1789 there remained scarcely two Indians of that race, which had counted thousands of souls. This epidemic began in October of the year 1788 and in that month they had rebelled, apostatized from the faith, revolted against the Spaniards and killed the missionaries. And even as they were showing themselves to be the enemies of religion the epidemic attacked them. Because that department was left completely depopulated arrangements were made to send people from the north to its towns, but all encountered the same misfortune, and even when the astrologers of Spain and France were observing the transit of Venus and had set up their tents at this mission [San José del Cabo] the same misfortune happened to all of them and one French gentleman, a member of the Royal Academy of Paris, died. Also it is worth noting that in the middle of their rebellion the galleon from the Philippines arrived in the year 1735, anchored in the port of the mission as was the custom every year, and the Indians trapped all the sick from the crew and killed them, but directly afterward the malefactors caught the same disease and died. All these circumstances make it clear that this epidemic was a punishment from heaven but, be that as it may, from the pustules which afflicted the Indians were developed putrid ulcers which appeared on the genital parts, and this sickness it is that has spread throughout all this province, although, as I have said, it does not attack the unconverted Indians, but we see that they are to be made Christians, which then and until recently was an impossibility. This is the origin of that sickness which here is called *gálico*.

Epidemic small-pox has been experienced only twice and then because it was brought in by families from Sonora who were already infected and entered this province with it. In fact in 1781 (a year memorable for unhappy California because missions and Indian *rancherías* were wiped out) there entered the port of Loreto a bark which brought families from Sonora, infected with the small-pox. Through the Commandant's lack of precaution they went into the town, and immediately it spread like lightning through all the missions, not excepting the most distant ones, and caused havoc which only those who have seen it can believe. The towns and missions were, as it were, deserted, and bodies were seen in the roads, but what the missionaries suffered and how they labored will be told in its place. The lack of proper care among the heathen during this epidemic, the lack of food, and the many silly things they did, [such as] throwing themselves into the sea at the onset of the disease, were the causes of the high mortality. In truth what results can small-pox be expected to have when as soon as they discover the pustules or ulcers some wash themselves with fresh water, some cast themselves into mud-holes, others into the fire, and still others set about burning the pustules with live coals? They attribute these deaths to the gachupines, as they call the Spaniards. A missionary father tried inoculating them for the small-pox, since he was going to be left without Indians, and he had such good success that hardly more than three or four died. This was at the mission of San Ignacio and I was present.

As for the remedies which have been tried here I can assure you that some are very efficacious. The juice of the *cardón* is an antidote for the ulcers of the French disease, but it cannot be borne because it is so painful. The chameleon, cooked in a pot over a slow fire until three-fourths of the water is boiled away, has the same effect as mercury ointment, but a regulated diet is necessary. The roots of the *chocuit*, a plant that grows in swamps, is efficacious for all sorts of ulcers, and there are other herbs that are useful. If from the beginning some intelligent persons had applied themselves to making a careful investigation of these herbs surely a curious book of great utility could have been written. If the many labors and unavoidable obligations of a missionary on the heathen frontier did not take up the greater part of the day, somewhat more might be added here, describing the form, color, distribution, and other facts about these herbs.

In some of the missions already converted are seen Indians with lung trouble and some who are weakly, and it is to be noted generally that because they eat only herbs while they are heathen they enjoy less good health after becoming Christians, when they are given wheat to eat, which no doubt arises from the new mode of living, from the labor, and from the fact that they have not as much freedom. And so it is arranged that they do not suddenly quit their manner of living but that little by little one thing and then another is enforced upon them until they are living a Christian life. Then it should be pointed out that the Indians who are being converted and who receive baptism, although they may be from up to ten leagues away, never return to their territory to establish themselves in it unless a pueblo is founded there. All remain in the mission precinct in order to keep it populated and little by little to advance its territory.

6. *Degrees of Change* (1955)

In the following article, a modern anthropologist analyzes the history of white-Indian relations throughout Latin America. Original differences within Indian society are identified as factors influencing the way Indians and Europeans adjusted to each other in various regions.

SOURCE: "Degrees of Change" from Elman R. Service, "Indian-European Relations in Colonial Latin America," reproduced by permission of the American Anthropological Association from the *American Anthropologist*, 57 (June 1955), pp. 416–17, 422–23.

The degree to which aboriginal racial and cultural traits are retained in modern Latin America varies greatly from region to region. Southern South America, including most of Argentina and all of Uruguay, is a great expanse of almost purely European settlement. Costa Rica, some parts of coastal Brazil, and most of the Antilles are also largely non-Indian in both race and culture. Other parts of Latin America are populated primarily by descendants of an early mixture of Indians and Europeans who live in essentially European-style communities, retaining only a few discrete traits of aboriginal culture. Paraguay and much of interior rural Brazil are the best examples of this type; but some of western Argentina, middle Chile, lowland Peru, interior Central America, and parts of Venezuela and Colombia are also of this mixed Indian-European, or Mestizo, type of population. A third category is found most strikingly in the highlands of Bolivia, Peru, Ecuador, Mexico, and Guatemala, where there are huge rural populations of pure Indian descent. Despite their long submission to the national political systems and many important modifications in the organization of their cultures, they tend to retain certain elements of the aboriginal traditions as well as a rather distinctive ethos. I shall refer to these three kinds of regions as Euro-America, Mestizo-America, and Indo-America.

. . .

The European colonists were faced with truly remarkable cultural and demographic differences among the Indians they encountered in the New World. The inhabitants of the Mesoamerican and Andean highlands, the "high culture" areas, numbered in the millions and were densely settled, often in large communities or even cities. Their agriculture was intensive and stable, and the economy was controlled by highly organized theocratic states. In the lowland regions the population density was not nearly so great, nor were the villages large. Food production was based on slash-and-burn horticulture, so that the villages were not stable, although some of the lowland peoples in especially favorable areas, the so-called circum-Caribbean tribes, had achieved some intervillage confederations or realms and had developed incipient political and religious states. The Indians who sparsely populated the plains of Uruguay, Argentina, and northern Mexico depended on hunting and gathering. They lived a relatively nomadic life with no permanent social organization larger than the extended family.

It is suggestive that the regions of greatest European success in controlling the natives were in the highlands, where the Indians also have survived most completely as racial and cultural entities incorporated into the modern nations. Spanish culture was in many important structural aspects quite similar to these "high cultures," both being based on intensive agriculture and the exploitation of a huge class of agricultural laborers. Political and religious aspects of both cultures not only had local manifestations but also were organized into hierarchical bureaucracies. But the resemblance of Iberian culture to that of the Indians of the lowland areas was less, for the lowland horticulturalists lacked a developed economic, political, and religious state. Iberian culture was even more distinct from that of the marginal hunters and gleaners. A logical suggestion, then, might be: The more alike the conquerors and conquered, the more simple and easy the adjustment will be, other things being equal. The less difficult and disruptive the adjustment, the more likely are the conquered people to survive, preserving at least the local basis of their native social organization and cultural forms.

This proposition possibly contributes to our general understanding of the situation in Latin America, but we need in addition a fuller analysis of the interplay of specific factors and some sort of a test of the relative importance of these factors. From the point of view of the needs of the Europeans, certain attributes of Indian culture were more significant than others. Of course single features such as presence or absence of intensive agriculture, a certain population density, stability and size of communities, specialization of labor, public works, kinds of political and religious state institutions, and so on, do not arise independently of each other. The present attempt to establish a priority of one factor over another is not to deny their real interrelationship but merely to suggest that certain of them had more direct relevance to the actions of the conquerors than others.

The varying characteristics of native culture which influenced the actions of the colonists must be judged largely in terms of their effect on the means used in the subjugation and control of the natives as a labor force, for this was the primary need which governed the actions of the Europeans. All the different kinds of encomiendas were used explicitly to gain such control. Once the brief initial period of ransacking the Indian treasurehouses was over, control of Indians was requisite first for tribute in food, and second for handicrafts for trade. When mining began, and trade was increased, an even larger labor force was essential.

If Indians were to be exploited for tribute and labor the technology of the society would have to be adequate to the production of surpluses in food above the needs of the food producers. Here would seem to be one of the most significant differences between the highland cultures and those of the lowlands. In the Andes and in Mexico native agriculture was sufficiently intensive and efficient to support both the Spaniards and a native labor corps which could engage in petty manufacturing, mining, and transportation, as it had previously supported native nonagricultural classes of bureaucrats and artisans and part-time labor on public works. Furthermore, the highland production supported a dense population and large-sized communities, which meant not only that a sufficient percentage of the population was available for work but also that the sheer size of the labor force was very great within one small area. The lowland horticultural peoples, on the other hand, did not consistently produce a sufficient surplus for a permanent labor force, nor was the basic population so numerous. It should go without saying that the marginal tribes offered much less.

.   .   .

A multifamily village culture, lacking state institutions, is much less a barrier to change at the family level, for contact and control must be direct and personal. When the Indians were controlled and put to work as villages, the community organization was very quickly altered. But village institutions are suprafamilial. Their function is to integrate the families for greater cooperation and proficiency in production and in warfare. They also take over certain familial functions of economics, politics, education, and religion and thus make the family a dependent part of a larger unit, although the functions of the family in these matters are not entirely superseded. A change in village organization may alter all these interfamilial relations, but the residual, purely familial aspects of the culture are less directly affected and can survive longer.

As we have seen, in the tropical forest areas of European control, the native village organization did not protect the Indian families for very long. Since the Indians could escape easily the Europeans had to enslave them as individuals. Even in areas where the villages came more easily under European control, as in Paraguay, native production was so inadequate that the Indians were finally put to work on the Europeans' estates under European direction. After the families were stripped of their village organization, their assimilation was rapid.

The kind of acculturation which occurred in the Jesuit missions was quite different. It appears that the change at the level of village institutions was rapid, but that the fundamentals of family life were not importantly altered, even after 150 years, for after the expulsion of the Jesuits most of the Indians were able to survive in the remote jungles. I have visited some of these Indians in northern Paraguay and in the Mexican Sierra Madre Occidental, and suggest that they seem more "deculturated" than acculturated, so simple is their social and political life compared to their aboriginal state. If this is so in other areas as well, it may possibly be due to the nature of mission acculturation. The full expression of aboriginal community culture was lost in the missions, while that of the family was not. Today, because these natives live scattered in marginal areas, they have never fully recovered their village culture. The typical suprafamilial organization is the composite band, a simple compounding of families for rather ephemeral and expedient purposes, so that a complex of extended relationship bonds has no chance to crystallize. There are often no local exogamous marriage rules, and a true village organization can hardly be said to exist.

The vaunted success of the Jesuits in controlling and acculturating the natives deserves a further comment. They had little difficulty in adjusting the Indians to the missions and, conversely, the Indians had little difficulty later in readjusting to an independent existence, because of some unusual circumstances. Most of the Indians were sheltered in the missions as individuals and single families, much as refugees might be cared for in a modern "DP" camp. The communities of the Indian refugees no longer existed, and the missions represented a *substitute* for the native organization. Therefore, it cannot be said that the mission system was an acculturative influence on village institutions. The success of the Jesuits in imposing the Catholic religion was likewise not exactly a case of "acculturation." The Indians of the missions had no state religion to be changed; the Jesuits merely *added* Catholicism as a cultural overlay, just as the teaching of European instrumental music did not first involve a change or destruction of a native music, for these Indians had none. Aspects of some of these cultural overlays penetrated the familial culture, but the Indian family held its own in most other respects.

A thorough and final cultural assimilation takes place when familial institutions are changed. When the marriage customs, intrafamilial division of labor, family religious practices, relations of husband and wife and parents and children are significantly altered, each new individual, the ultimate pinpoint repository of the cultural heritage, is changed in all important respects. This also occurs, of course, as single members of a primitive society are made to give up their "old ways" and adjust themselves individually to the invading system. Familial and individual assimilation of this sort occurred to some extent in all three areas of Latin America; among the marginal Indians, however, it was the only way in which acculturation could take place. It did not occur so frequently as among the village Indians because, although marginal (i.e., familial) culture is the most vulnerable, the marginal peoples were able to escape control more easily. It follows, nevertheless, that this kind of acculturation should become more frequent as the invading culture becomes more pervasive and the alternative of retreat becomes less and less feasible. Thus the rate of assimilation (and destruction) of the heretofore independent tribal Indians of Latin America has increased greatly in recent years as modern civilization has so rapidly expanded its range and intensified its influence.

CONCLUSION

The conquests have always received a preponderant attention in the history of Spanish-Indian relations, and the presence or absence of conquest has emerged as a crucial point of distinction between Spanish and other European colonizations in America. Yet it is clear from the foregoing readings that Spanish-Indian relations were complicated by many factors besides conquest. The Indian societies that were wiped out were not directly destroyed by conquest. The attributes of the conquered societies that enabled them to survive were frequently the very attributes that had induced Spaniards to conquer them in the first place.

The pressures that the Spaniards brought to bear on the Indians varied from time to time and from place to place. Conquest, conversion, encomienda, repartimiento, and corregimiento rule brought institutionalized forms of stress, each making a distinct series of demands. Indian society confronted not one but many crises. We have emphasized the problems of the Indian community or village, because this was ordinarily the largest social unit that survived the conquest and the largest that was called upon to make an adjustment to Spanish colonization. The community struggled to preserve its lands, to maintain its government, to pay its tribute, to feed its people, to provide laborers, and to achieve other goals necessary for survival under colonial conditions. But the community was made up of lesser units, and the interests of the whole and the parts did not always correspond. Thus, an Indian governor might sell out independently to Spaniards who wanted more land or more tribute or more laborers. Indian classes, families, and individuals confronted separate situations. In an economy in which surpluses went to Spaniards, Indian society was disunited, and its parts, subjected to different kinds of choice, reacted differently. And community life was much weaker in some areas than in others.

It remains true that Indian society survived to a greater degree under Spanish colonial government than under the colonial government of any other European power in America. There can be no doubt that this survival was due in part to the legislation of the Crown and the labors of the missionary clergy. Both the Church and the civil government acted in particular ways to reinforce and protect the Indian communities. But this is only a partial explanation. Ecclesiastical and civil authorities might themselves be exploitative. Protection and benevolence were limited in time, location, and applicability. Where Indian society survived, it perhaps did so more as a result of its internal structure and character than because of any external efforts to preserve it.

BIBLIOGRAPHY

Armillas, Pedro. *Program of the History of American Indians,* 2 vols. (Washington, D.C.: Pan American Union, 1958–60). Comprehensive scheme of Indian history.

Canals Frau, Salvador. *Las civilizaciones prehispánicas de América* (Buenos Aires: Editorial Sudamericana, 1955). Survey of pre-Spanish civilizations.

Chamberlain, Robert S. *The Conquest and Colonization of Honduras, 1502–1550* (Washington, D.C.: Carnegie Institution, 1953). Scholarly treatment of the subject.

———. *The Conquest and Colonization of Yucatan, 1517–1550* (Washington, D.C.: Carnegie Institution, 1948). Best account of early Yucatan.

Cook, Sherburne F., and Woodrow Borah. *The Indian Population of Central Mexico, 1531–1610* (Berkeley: University of California Press, 1960). Summarizes and expands earlier work by the same authors on Indian demography.

Fisher, Lillian Estelle. *The Last Inca Revolt, 1780–1783* (Norman: University of Oklahoma Press, 1965). Details on rebellion of Túpac Amaru II.

Garcilaso de la Vega, El Inca. *Royal Commentaries of the Incas and General History of Peru,* translated by Harold V. Livermore, 2 vols. (Austin: University of Texas Press, 1966). Classic work by the Peruvian mestizo.

Gibson, Charles. *The Aztecs under Spanish Rule* (Stanford, Calif.: Stanford University Press, 1964). Indian-Spanish relations in the Valley of Mexico in the colonial period.

Hanke, Lewis. *The Spanish Struggle for Justice in the Conquest of America* (Philadelphia: University of Pennsylvania Press, 1949). Spain's effort to deal justly with Indians.

Haring, Clarence H. *The Spanish Empire in America* (New York: Oxford University Press, 1947). Detailed analysis of Spanish imperialism.

Las Casas, Bartolomé de. *Del único modo de atraer a todos los pueblos a la verdadera religión* (Mexico: Fondo de Cultura Económica, 1942). Las Casas on peaceful relations between Spaniards and Indians.

Lohmann Villena, Guillermo. *El corregidor de indios en el Perú bajo los Austrias* (Madrid: Ediciones Cultura Hispánica, 1957). The main political official in Spanish government over Indians.

Powell, Philip W. *Soldiers, Indians, and Silver* (Berkeley: University of California Press, 1952). The north Mexican frontier in the sixteenth century.

Prescott, William H. *History of the Conquest of Mexico,* abridged ed., edited by C. H. Gardiner (Chicago: University of Chicago Press,

1966). First published in 1843, this remains the classic account in English.

————. *History of the Conquest of Peru* (New York: Heritage Press, 1957). First published in 1847, this is also a classic, though the subject was less attractive than the conquest of Mexico to Prescott himself.

Ricard, Robert. *La "Conquête Spirituelle" du Mexique* (Paris: Institut d'Ethnologie, 1933). Mexican missionary history in the sixteenth century.

Simpson, Lesley Byrd. *The Encomienda in New Spain* (Berkeley: University of California Press, 1950). Sixteenth-century *encomienda* in the West Indies and Mexico.

Spicer, Edward H. *Cycles of Conquest* (Tucson: University of Arizona Press, 1962). White-Indian relations in northern Mexico and the borderlands.

Steward, Julian H., ed. *Handbook of South American Indians*, 7 vols. (Washington, D.C.: U.S. Government Printing Office, 1946–59). Articles on Indians of South America of all periods.

Tibesar, Antonine. *Franciscan Beginnings in Colonial Peru* (Washington, D.C.: Academy of American Franciscan History, 1953). Early Franciscan missionary labors in Peru.

Wauchope, Robert, ed. *Handbook of Middle American Indians*, 13 vols. (Austin: University of Texas Press, 1964–   ). Compendium of current knowledge on Indians of Middle America.

Wolf, Eric. *Sons of the Shaking Earth* (Chicago: University of Chicago Press, 1959). Interpretative history of Middle American Indians from earliest times to the present.

Zavala, Silvio. *La encomienda indiana* (Madrid: Imprenta Helénica, 1935). Basic analytic treatment.

IV

The Problem of the Roots of Revolution: Society and Intellectual Ferment in Mexico on the Eve of Independence

Peggy K. Korn

CHRONOLOGY

1759–88 Charles III rules Spain

1767 Jesuits expelled from Mexico

1768 Alzate's *Diario Literario*

1771(?) Representation of the Ayuntamiento of Mexico City

1776 American Revolution

1786 Intendency system introduced in Mexico

1788–95 Alzate's *Gaceta de Literatura de México*

1788–1808 Charles IV rules Spain

1789 French Revolution

1799 Manuel Abad y Queipo's "Representation Concerning the Personal Immunity of the Clergy"; Death of Alzate

1803 Alexander von Humboldt visits Mexico

1808 Napoleon's armies invade Spain; Spaniards in Mexico depose Viceroy José de Iturrigaray

1808–13 Joseph Bonaparte attempts to rule Spain

1810 Proclamation of the Spanish Regency calling for election of deputies to the Spanish Cortes ordered published in Mexico (May 7)
Miguel Hidalgo gives the *"grito* of Dolores"; Mexican Revolution begins (September 16)

1811 Report of the Consulado of Mexico

1812 The Spanish Cortes promulgates a liberal constitution

1813 José María Morelos declares Mexico independent of Spain

1814–33 Ferdinand VII rules Spain

1814 Ferdinand quashes the Spanish constitution

1815 Death of Morelos; Vicente Guerrero and Guadalupe Victoria carry on the revolution

1820–21 In Spain, an abortive attempt to reinstate the Constitution of 1812

1821 Guerrero and Agustín Iturbide proclaim the Plan of Iguala; the viceroy, Juan O'Donoju, concurs in Mexican independence

INTRODUCTION

Causation is never easy to ascertain; yet the urge to understand the "why" of an event remains irresistible. So it is with the Mexican Revolution of 1810. Historians have long recognized the need for a clearer explanation of the origins of that bloody uprising. Some have gone beyond a simple listing of background conditions, such as the external ones of Spanish weakness and involvement in European wars and the internal introduction of revolutionary ideas, in an attempt to assign priority to one or another set of these causes. Most recently, however, dissatisfied with the inadequacies of past evaluations, a number of scholars have been concerned with gaining a better understanding of the *interrelationships* of the numerous roots of revolution.

Within this trend, studies of social change and intellectual ferment in Mexico in the latter part of the eighteenth century have provided some important, if tentative, answers to longstanding questions concerning the origins of the Revolution of 1810.[1] These works give evidence that there existed within Mexico a set of conditions tending to undermine previously established notions of how society should be ordered and to promote the setting of revolutionary goals. Certainly these studies lay to rest the old assertion that all Mexicans were somnolent until pressures built up by the French Revolution and Napoleon's invasion of Spain set off an explosive chain reaction in that part of Spanish America. Historians now know that prior to active political revolt certain small but influential segments of Mexican society ardently sought social and economic reform, became increasingly alienated from the existing regime, and came to serve as heralds of the revolution.

Although a more intricate picture of the Mexican milieu is now presented, it is at the same time a far clearer one than heretofore. For our purposes, two aspects of this scene are particularly important. First, there is evidence of a gradually evolving intellectual ambience within Mexico that welcomed change and ensured a ready but selective adaptation of enlightened and revolutionary ideas as they arrived from Europe and from other regions of the western hemisphere. Second, and contrary to a number of older accounts, there is a newer view of Mexican society that makes obsolete the assertion that an absolute dichotomy existed between a class of European Spaniards supporting governmental policies and a class of

---

[1] See the selective bibliography at the end of the chapter. Other pertinent works are cited in the footnotes that follow.

creoles [2] intent on subverting them; factional groupings are now recognized to have been much more complex.

The readings in this chapter, dated from the 1770's to 1811, corroborate the newer viewpoints. Two were written by creoles, two by European Spaniards. The viewpoints expressed in them may be considered representative of the states of mind of four influential, elite segments of society in Mexico. All express dissatisfaction with the existing state of affairs, all criticize current economic and social arrangements, all criticize the government, and all appear certain that the existing order is moribund. Yet, while some insist that governmental policies are destroying the traditional order, others complain that these same policies are perpetuating it. Thus, while some object to measures that they feel subvert the old order, others demand action designed to do just that. There is little agreement on the nature of the fundamental principles of the political system. No two of these readings reveal identical concepts of the Spanish role in Mexico.

The attitudes of the creoles and the European Spaniards who wrote these papers tend to cross class lines. Even when the authors discuss Americans and European Spaniards as if they were cohesive and distinct classes, what they say is often modified by the divergent attitudes they exhibit. For example, the majority of the *regidores* (councilmen) of the Cabildo or Ayuntamiento of Mexico City who drew up Reading 1 were creoles who declared themselves proud of their Spanish ancestry while, as we shall see, the author of Reading 2, José Antonio Alzate y Ramírez, was a creole who took pride in a different heritage.

The regidores reveal themselves as men of aristocratic mien and vast pretension. The Mexican historian Lucas Alamán observed that fifteen of the councilmen held perpetual and inherited positions originally purchased by their fathers from the Crown. He wrote, "They were old *mayorazgos* [propertyholders in perpetuity] of very little education in general, and the majority of them of ruined fortunes." [3] Six additional, honorary regidores, however, were chosen biennially from among the distinguished merchants, landowners, and lawyers of the capital. Thus, the Ayuntamiento in this period represented both propertied and professional elements of creole society. The combination is discernible in its Representation, included here.

This document exudes a strong sense of *criollismo*, a feeling of pride in Spanish heritage compounded with a sense of belonging to the soil of Mexico (and of it belonging to them). It was an outlook they shared with

---

[2] While the term "creole" as used in Spanish America is often defined as a native American of Spanish descent, as used in Mexico in this period it also included Mexicans of (usually unacknowledged) mixed Spanish and Indian descent. For example, the author of Reading 2, José Antonio Alzate y Ramírez, was a creole having both Spanish and Indian forebears.

[3] Alamán, *Historia de México*, 5 vols. (Mexico: Lara, 1849), 1, p. 57.

many of the wealthier, landed creoles, the *hacendados* referred to by another Mexican historian, Manuel Orozco y Berra, as "the semi-feudal *señores*." [4] Many of the regidores and hacendados claimed descent through pure Spanish bloodlines from the conquistadors. It was an improbable ancestry for most of them, since, as the conquistador-historian Bernal Díaz del Castillo, among others, had made clear, and as the anti-creole authors of Reading 4 pointedly reiterated, the legitimate offspring of the first Spaniards in Mexico were few and not prolific. Nevertheless, these creoles would insist (in 1808) that the fruits of the conquest were theirs by right of inheritance, that their conquistador forebears had left to them the legacy of a right to preeminence over the other cabildos of Mexico. The old order venerated by the regidores was static, hierarchical, and regulated by creole aristocrats, the natural nobility of the Kingdom of New Spain.[5]

A sense of pride also permeated the writings of José Antonio Alzate y Ramírez, although his pride in the main stemmed from an outsized esteem of his own intellectual ability. Alexander von Humboldt, the European savant and scientist who visited New Spain in 1803, did not entirely concur in Alzate's self-evaluation. Humboldt, an astute commentator, wrote that, while Alzate was one of the three distinguished creoles who by their astronomical observations "did honor to their country towards the end of the last century," he was also "the least informed of them. Alzate, [although] a correspondent of the Academy of Sciences of Paris, was an observer of little accuracy. Of a frequently impetuous temperament, he devoted himself to too many pursuits at one time." [6]

Humboldt judged Alzate's enthusiasm and his influence on his fellow Mexicans to have been much greater than his mental rigor: "He had the very genuine merit of having excited his compatriots to the study of the physical sciences. The *Gaceta de Literatura*, which he published for a long time in Mexico, contributed singularly to give encouragement and stimulation to Mexican youth." [7] Alzate is significant here because, in seeking to awaken young creoles to new ways of considering old problems, he attempted to revolutionize current habits of thought.

Such scientifically minded creoles were few in Mexico, but they grew more numerous and very much more articulate throughout the latter part of the eighteenth century. As early as the 1740's, a handful of young Mexican-born Jesuits had voiced concerns and views of the kind evidenced

---

[4] Manuel Orozco y Berra, *Historia de la dominación española en México*, 4 vols. (Mexico: Biblioteca Historia Mexicana de Obras Inéditos, 1938).

[5] This was the official designation given to the viceroyalty often, and more popularly, known as Mexico.

[6] Alexander von Humboldt, *Essai Politique sur le Royaume de la Nouvelle-Espagne*, 5 vols. (Paris: Chez F. Schoell, 1811), 2, p. 19.

[7] *Ibid.*

in Alzate's writings. By the 1760's, similar sentiments and interests were common to a number of creoles engaged in the professions, among them teachers, lawyers, journalists, secular and regular clergymen, doctors of medicine, and lesser bureaucrats. In general, these men were more educated and less propertied than the semi-feudal señores. They also differed from most of the regidores in that they lacked assured positions. Within this group, then, were to be found the creoles whose plight was described by the councilmen of Mexico City: Raised and educated as an elite, trained to be leaders in their own society, they were frustrated by exclusion from high state and church positions.[8]

Yet Alzate and other intellectuals went beyond the concern with governmental appointments expressed by the Ayuntamiento to a serious consideration of the broader economic and social problems of Mexico. Alzate, like his enlightened contemporaries in Europe, was enamored of the idea of abetting material progress by disseminating principles and pieces of useful knowledge. In his literary gazette he included notes from all over on economics, the physical sciences, mathematics, medicine, agriculture, history, and jurisprudence. He sought to provide his fellow Mexicans with factual and practical information that, once assimilated and properly applied, he felt would ensure the creation of a paradise on earth. Thus, while the regidores invoked a golden past, Alzate looked to an idyllic future.

He insisted that dependence on ancient authorities, especially on Aristotle, was responsible for "that profound and shameful lethargy that holds [Mexicans] deadened in perpetual inactivity," [9] that education by the still-prevalent scholastic method was at the root of all Mexico's afflictions. Alzate, who had been ordained a priest, found his true calling as a missionary to the unenlightened. He appeared certain that he need only rout the forces of obscurantism in order to allow Mexicans through their own efforts to return their land to its natural state of abundance and health.

Alzate was critical of the state of affairs at present and in the recent—the Spanish—past. Condemning the old order, he looked back to a still older order. He was prominent among those creoles who found in the greatest of the pre-Hispanic Indian civilizations their own classical antiquity.[10] In eulogizing the achievement of high states of culture by the ancient indigenous peoples, he implicitly denied the validity of the civiliz-

[8] See Reading 1, pp. 108, 110, 113.

[9] See p. 119.

[10] For others, see John Leddy Phelan, "Neo-Aztecism in the Eighteenth Century and the Genesis of Mexican Nationalism," in *Culture in History· Essays in Honor of Paul Radin*, edited by Stanley Diamond (New York: Columbia University Press, 1960), pp. 760–71.

ing mission of the Spanish. Thus he opened to question the legitimacy of Spanish rule in America, which, as the writers of Reading 4 take for granted, was based on an early shouldering by Spain of the white man's burden. In short, the past, present, and future that were of interest to Alzate were Mexican. He did not state where the Indians of his own day fit into his utopian expectations. Yet consideration of the faith he expresses in the natural goodness of human nature, at least within Mexico, leads to the conclusion that he considered the Indians, too, capable of being educated to the point of entering national life at some future time.

He urged activism upon creoles and stressed the need for change, positive that it would be for the better. In one sense, Alzate's faith in the salutary effects of change was not far removed from that of the Bourbon government. Changes that took place in eighteenth-century Spain, many of them under governmental aegis, have been described as revolutionary. Although these changes were carried out within the fabric of the old order, at least one historian considers them a factor in undermining the state of mind supporting the old order.[11] Revolution or no, economic and political institutions had in fact undergone considerable redirection. For example, in order to strengthen central government the Crown had striven to abbreviate the authority of the old, semiautonomous corporations, including that of the Church and of the merchant guilds. It is not surprising, therefore, that the two remaining documents in this chapter, written by European Spaniards in Mexico by members of these corporations, include criticisms of innovations made by the Government.

Reading 3 was written in 1799 by a priest, Manuel Abad y Queipo, then vicar to the Bishop Antonio de San Miguel of Michoacán, later bishop-elect of that province. In his Representation, Abad y Queipo warned the Crown against enforcing royal ordinances placing a direct tax on clerical investments and restricting clerical *fueros* (privileges) in general. Social unrest was increasing, he argued; the Church must remain strong in order to continue to function successfully as the one institution capable of mediating between the government and the people.

While Abad y Queipo as a priest opposed certain innovations, especially the taxing of the clergy, as an enlightened and objective observer he desired others. He urged general political reform: "America," he wrote elsewhere, "can no longer be governed by the maxims of Philip II." [12] Furthermore, much like Alzate, he expressed confidence in Mexican potential. To realize this potential, he argued, the Crown must institute

[11] See Richard Herr, *The Eighteenth Century Revolution in Spain* (Princeton, N.J.: Princeton University Press, 1958).

[12] "Representación al arzobispo virrey . . . el 18 de agosto de 1809," in *Documentos para la Guerra de Independencia de México, 1808 a 1821*, edited by Juan Hernández y Dávalos, 6 vols. (Mexico: Sandoval, 1877), 2, pp. 894–95.

economic and social reforms. Unlike the creole journalist, Abad y Queipo looked to the Spanish government to remedy Mexican ills. He urged that a new order be imposed from above. His was a faith in enlightened monarchy buttressed by the traditional Spanish reliance on the fair-mindedness of the law-giving king. This self-styled Montesquieu of Mexico was certain that good laws would bring wealth, health, and happiness to New Spain, as well as increased revenue to the Spanish treasury.

Other European Spaniards, the merchants of the Consulado of Mexico City, were just as certain a decade later that such liberal notions were subverting the Empire. In Reading 4, they demand retreat from reform. In direct opposition to the dictum of Abad y Queipo, they counsel a return to the principles of His Most Catholic Majesty, arguing that only a show of imperial force would avert the loss of the colonies. They looked back with longing to their particular view of the old order, to the golden age of Hapsburg imperialism. Spain, they insisted, had an unfulfilled civilizing mission in America.

If the Consulado looked with a jaundiced eye on the political abilities of Americans, its vision was unimpaired when it observed a new spirit of self-sufficiency among creoles. Even Mexicans such as the regidores of the capital, seeking high position *within* the Spanish administration, evinced a new spirit of self-consciousness, compounded of pride in the expanse and growing population of Mexico, optimism concerning its future, recognition of the depopulated and decadent state of the mother country, and perhaps above all a desire to demonstrate that "We are a nation as great as any in the world. Even this is to claim too little; permit us, Your Majesty, to say that we [the creoles] have distinguished ourselves above all." [13]

In short, self-proclaimed creole intellectuals, officeholders, and semi-feudal señores, whatever their differences, expressed in common a sense of *conciencia de sí*, of Mexican particularism. Though they differed in their views of the proper place in society of the other inhabitants of Mexico (Indians, Negroes, and "castes," or mestizos), though the Ayuntamiento wanted only to dominate them and Alzate apparently wanted to educate them, yet they acknowledged these people as fellow inhabitants of Mexico.

It is interesting to note that the readings also reveal transition in the creole concept of "nation." The Ayuntamiento used the word "nation" in a somewhat traditional sense: The Mexican creoles, they implied, constituted a nation within the Spanish Empire. Yet in the same period, ministers of Charles III disavowed this old notion of imperial identity. Members of the Royal Council declared that they hoped to integrate the

[13] See p. 114.

Indies into the Spanish nation-state. Henceforth Mexico was to be neither kingdom nor colony, but an intrinsic part of a *"solo cuerpo de Nación."* [14]

This idea of the nation as the natural polity was in vogue among the European *philosophes*; Alzate and other creoles followed the fashion, thereby intensifying and restricting the concept of nation entertained by the Ayuntamiento. Their nation, too, was composed solely of men born on the soil of Mexico, but their national feeling could not, like the older sense of imperial identity, be made to cross the ocean.

"Nation" was but part of a larger political vocabulary coming into use and boding ill for Spanish domination. Even the regidores appealed to such an anti-imperial governing principle as that of "right reason" and placed a new emphasis on the right of native peoples (by which they meant creoles) according to "the law of nations." Alzate was more radical, as early as 1768 sprinkling his short-lived *Diario Literario* with such dangerous catchwords as "tyranny" and "liberty." The viceroy, in suspending the periodical for containing "propositions offensive to the Law and the Nation," [15] aired additional notions associated with theories tending, at the least, to limit monarchy and silenced Alzate only temporarily. In his *Gaceta de Literatura,* published from 1788 to 1795, Alzate combined potentially revolutionary notions with the new sense of national identity. For example, he declared public utility to be the supreme law, individual reason to be the ultimate authority, and the duty of the individual to be to engage in all forms of civic activity. It was but a step to the logical conclusion, reached by some creoles in 1810, that the nation was the supreme political entity and that sovereignty resided solely in its citizens. As the Consulado predicted in 1811, rebellious Mexicans would assume "the airs and trappings of a sovereign people." [16]

[14] Cited by Richard Konetzke, "La condición legal de los criollos y las causas de la independencia," in *Estudios Americanos,* 2 (1950), p. 45.

[15] Edict of Marqués de Croix, Mexico, May 15, 1768. Reprinted in *El Nacionalismo en la prensa mexicana del siglo XVIII,* edited by Xavier Tavera Alfaro (Mexico: Club de Periodistas, 1963), p. 7.

[16] See p. 128.

READINGS

1. A Representation of the Ayuntamiento
of Mexico City (1771)

In the following document, the councilmen inform the Crown that
they speak for the Kingdom of New Spain and desire to defend Spanish
Americans against the slanderous report, made by an unidentified
peninsular Spanish official serving in New Spain, that creoles are inferior to Europeans and incapable of holding public office.

We have reflected for days, not without the greatest grief, that
the kind gestures and provisions of Your Majesty in favor of the Spanish
Americans have become rarer than ever, not only in secular positions but
in ecclesiastic, where until now we have received attention. We have
observed this but contained our sorrow within the most respectful silence,
and we would never have broken it even if we had never received another
benefice from Your Majesty, who is incomparable in recognizing us, your
vassals. [Yet we have news that some minister or prelate has slandered
the Spanish Americans, and so we are now compelled to present a re-
joinder.[1]]

This is not the first time that malevolence has attacked the reputation of
the Americans in order to make them appear inept for all types of honors.
Since the discovery of America, a war has been waged against the native
Indians. In spite of the evidence, even their rationality is questioned.
With no less injustice, it is claimed that those of us born of European
parents on this soil scarcely have sufficient powers of reason to be considered men.

. . .

He who made the report proposed to obtain Your Majesty's assent
that Spanish Americans not attain any but lower government posts in
order to make sure that Europeans will always be placed in the highest
positions of honor. This is to say that we shall be excluded, in the ecclesiastical realm, from being bishops and high dignitaries of the Church

---

[1] [Bracketed summaries of omitted material have been supplied by the chapter editor.]
SOURCE: "A Representation of the Ayuntamiento of Mexico City" translated from
Documentos para la Guerra de Independencia de México, 1808 a 1821, edited by Juan
Hernández y Dávalos, 6 vols. (Mexico: Sandoval, 1877), 1, pp. 427–55. All translations
in this chapter are by the chapter editor. There is some question of whether this repre-
sentation was written, as Hernández y Dávalos states, in 1771, or six years later, in 1777.

and, in the secular sphere, from being military officers and governors and from holding the highest positions in town councils. This is to try to overturn the law of nations! It is the road not only to the loss of America but also to the ruin of the state. It is, in a word, the greatest and most enormous injustice, one that a person with less animosity would not have dared propose to Your Majesty.

. . .

In regard to the provision of honorific posts, the European Spaniards have to be considered foreigners in these parts. . . . This is what the Europeans are by birth, but not by civil right, in America. But civil right has not the power of natural inclinations, and we have to be aware of these inclinations in the sons of Old Spain, no matter how they think of themselves as civilly no strangers in New Spain. Among natural inclinations are included, with good reason, the love that men have for the soil on which they were born and the lack of affection for all other. These two motives are the most solid principles that argue for the employment of the native and against that of the foreigner.

. . .

Even if they do not consider themselves civilly foreigners in the Indies, it is obvious that they were not born here. In Old Spain they have their houses, their parents, their brothers, and whatever is capable of arousing ambition in a man. When they are exiled to this distance to fill a public office, their nature does not change, and their impulses do not deaden. For these reasons, in these regions they do not forget their own. They consider how to help their families (if not to enrich them). They think of themselves as transients in America. Their only concern is to return as rich men to the quietude of their land and homes.

So experience teaches each day. It is inevitable if the public offices are conferred on those who were not born in the regions where they serve.

. . .

There are public offices, such as all the *alcaldes mayores* of the kingdom, that have no pay assigned to them. How, then, will these men repay the onerous financial obligations incurred in taking office? . . . The Indies are very abundant in gold and silver for ambitious men unscrupulous in acquiring them. They will be urged on by necessity, annoyed by creditors, and besieged by the judge, to whom people have come to make them pay. They will see that they can frequently find means to escape the pinch. They will grant favors that shortly decline into bribes. They will sell justice. Their concern for their own interest will lead to the ruin of all that the public entrusted to them.

It is also inevitable that merit is exaggerated when seen through the spectacles of greater affection. From this it follows that a prelate with many European familiars, however numerous, considers them deserving above many others the first benefices that are within his power to bestow. Our students moan, oppressed by the weight of years and by the burdens of the academy and of clerical administration. They obtain the highest qualification in their studies, the best degrees in the university. They distinguish themselves in instructing the villagers. They do not cease to strive for better positions, nor do they avoid competition.[2] Yet, after all, they finish the contest with no other reward than praise for their performance, and the awards go to a familiar. Many of these Europeans are just starting out. They have not proved their fitness in any public contest. They have not taught in the Indies or served in any of the churches. In some cases (and it is the rule), they have never before entered a contest.

· · ·

The European comes to govern people he does not know, to administer laws he has not studied, to regulate customs he does not understand, and to treat with people whom he has never seen, and to do these he usually comes surrounded by retainers equally inexpert. He comes full of European principles inadaptable to these lands. Here, we Spaniards do not set ourselves apart from the Europeans; the miserable Indians are of another condition. On one hand, they are a group weaker and worthier of attention, and on the other, they are the ones making up the bulk of the kingdom and all the sinews of it. They are the object of the pious concern of Your Majesty's government. They require different rules from those prescribed for Spaniards. Nevertheless, the new arrival tries to implant his ideas, to establish his principles. In this endeavor, he miserably loses time until disillusionment opens his eyes. What can be expected of his government but errors and prejudices, one after another?

· · ·

The Spanish Americans are capable of the highest offices. They do not yield in intelligence, application, conduct, or honor to any of the other nations of the world. So impartial authors whose criticism the literary world respects have confessed. So experience proves each day, except to those who willfully close their eyes to plain truths. But hopeful, capable, useful, and worthy men of this kind are nevertheless reported to be dissuaded from improvement, abased, and abandoned. So says the informant, who claims that "they are worthy of nothing else than to be submissive and subjugated. They are serfs, detested by foreigners."

[Americans will decrease in number if they have no way of supporting families. Ordinary commercial jobs are not for them, for trade nearly always has to be transacted from Europe by Europeans. Manual labor is

---

[2] [The Law of the Indies (*Recopilación de leyes de los reynos de las Indias*) of 1681, following the ruling of the Council of Trent, decreed that bishops hold public competitions to select candidates for vacant parish benefices (Lib. I, tit. 6, ley 24).]

incompatible with the luster of their birth, nor does it suffice in the Indies for a decent subsistence; for, since the best manufactures are carried from Europe, where they are made cheaper than the Americans can make them, we can never support ourselves by manufacturing in the Indies.]

The principal basis on which we Spanish Americans can count to meet our obligations is the rents or salaries of public office. If the door to them is closed to us, we must live an obscure life. Unable to contract illustrious alliances, the sons that we shall have will augment the common people, or we will find ourselves reduced to the necessity of celibacy and perhaps forced to embrace the religious or secular ecclesiastical state, in order to rely on charity from a Mass. Gone will be the principle of increasing, or even of honestly conserving, the population of America.

Nor will the fate of Europe be better. Many European nations have already reflected on the depopulation experienced by Spain since the conquest of America. It is so harmful that the greatest political theorists have urged means to remedy it—and these are certainly not to employ European Spaniards in the public posts of the Indies. This practice is the origin of the great depopulation of Spain. . . . This adverse effect on Spain, although lamented by our best political thinkers, seems an enjoyable spectacle to malevolent foreigners.

We have always considered ourselves sons of Your Majesty, just like the natives of Old Spain. Old and New Spain are like two estates. They are two wives of Your Majesty. Each one has her dowry in the honorific posts of your government, paid with the income produced by both. We have never complained that the sons of Old Spain take advantage of the dowry of their mother, but it seems fitting that ours be left to us.

· · ·

It is indispensable that we be sent some ministers from Europe. But must all those who come be given the highest positions? Must all the governors that Your Majesty places in the provinces and towns of this region of America be born and raised in Old Spain as today they are? Are we never to have, as at present we do not have in all the continent of this kingdom, an archbishop or bishop that was born here? Is it necessary that the magistrates of these lands be, as they are today, mostly Europeans? That even the chairs of the choirs of our cathedrals be scarcely occupied by our natives? That in the management of the income that this New Spain produces for Your Majesty, only rarely do we see among many employees one of our country? That in the military offices our requests are paid so little attention that only in the militias do our volunteers generally secure a place? Even then their positions are not the best.

· · ·

It does not seem that either the equity or the attention that we, your vassals of these regions, owe Your Majesty can tolerate this. . . . Our crime must be very grave for us to suffer the punishment of eternal ignominy by being excluded from the highest offices and by receiving little attention in the others. What then is this crime that, contaminating such vast regions as those of America, has called down such an enormous punishment on all these individuals? . . .

What will the rest of the world say of America? What concept will the nations form from the attention Your Majesty pays to the cultivation of the Spanish Americans? Will they not conclude that these most ample domains of Your Majesty are full of carcasses useless to society and think them more a burden than an adornment to the state? . . . Show the world that we are not useless carcasses, but men suited for all offices, even the highest, that in nothing are the men of the Old World superior to us, that Your Majesty exceeds the other monarchs not only in the vast extension of lands and in the number of individuals inhabiting them but also in the abundance of vassals who are as loyal, as generous, as able, and as useful as those gloried in by the most cultured state of the world. Let the world know that we of the Indies are apt for counsel, useful for war, experienced in the management of finances, fit for governing churches, towns, provinces, and even entire kingdoms. . . .

Thus will Your Majesty be more glorious, for the honor of children is the glory of their parents. Thus your dominion over these regions will be even more secure. Enemies would not hesitate to invade them, knowing them to be full only of pasteboard men. But they would give it much thought if they concluded from the prodigious multitude of subjects Your Majesty has in these lands that they would find here many generous vassals, all capable of resisting any foreign encroachment with decision, tenacity, loyalty, and their lives.

.   .   .

It is understood that we do not speak of the Indians taken in war or of those whose ancestors were conquered by our arms, but of the Spaniards, of us who are born in these lands. We originate pure in all lines from men who came from Old Spain to these regions to conquer, to settle, to do business, or to serve in some government post. The Indians, whether by descent, by divine punishment, by their condition as individuals of a subjugated nation, or perhaps by their lack of culture, even after two centuries of conquest are born in misery, raised in rusticity, and driven by punishment, and they can support themselves only by the hardest work. They live without shame, without honor, and without hope. Degraded and fallen in spirit, they are abased in character. All judicious authors say so; after long observation and much travel they have given the Indians the epithet in their books of "defeated ones." A poor understanding or perhaps a too hasty reading of these writings has caused errors in copying these expressions by men wanting to apply them to the Spanish Americans as well as to the Indians. In order to commit such injustice, one must refuse to give ear to the cries of reason. . . .

America has a large number of Spaniards, all as pure as those of Old Spain. . . . Interbreeding has been claimed of the early Spanish settlers in order to deny our purity of lineage. There were very strong arguments against it. Interbreeding did not occur except because of the attraction of beauty or other natural gifts, because of wealth, or because of the desire for honor. None of these motives has been strong enough to drag down Spanish settlers into mating with Indian women and producing mestizo sons. Generally speaking, and with only rare exceptions, the mestizos are positively of a disagreeable aspect, very bad color, rough features, and notable slovenliness of dress when not naked, and none are clean. They lack culture and rationality, have great aversion to Spaniards, and even refuse to talk to them. They are very poor and live in huts with walls of mud or branches, roofs of straw, and floors of nothing but what the soil naturally provides. They eat in the greatest misery and slovenliness. If they dress, it is no better than the way in which they eat. They have no beds to rest in, but cover themselves with a palm mat or animal skin. The little they need for such poor furnishings, they get by very hard work; a description of it would touch the limits of hyperbole.

Above all, the Spaniard, had he interbred with an Indian woman, would see his sons lacking the honor of being Spaniards and even excluded from enjoying the privileges conceded to Indians. The same thing, and with greater reason, could be said of interbreeding with Negroes, mulattoes, or the other castes originating from them. Thus, there is no way mixed bloods may be considered equal. These mixtures are much less common than malevolence paints them.

There was some interbreeding of Spaniards with Indians in the early days of the conquest, but it was with the royal families of the indigenous nations, and their descendants are among the highest grandees of Spain. They are considered Spanish citizens of pure blood.

· · ·

But what if Spanish Americans are to be perpetually subordinated to Europeans? It would be as if humanity, the law of nations, and right reason permitted this absolute and perpetual subordination of native peoples, this entire exclusion from the highest honors, and this subjugation to foreigners. It is indeed a cunning misrepresentation of the sentiments of humanity and of tenderness of heart that advocates so inhuman a principle. It is pernicious to society and contrary to the interests and honor of a nation making up the greater part of the monarchy.

· · ·

Spain has needed no army to maintain loyalty in these dominions, whose extension is sufficient to embrace many of the greatest kingdoms of Europe.

.   .   .

When has the loyalty of the Spanish Americans faltered, weakened, flagged, or wavered? In this region of America there has never been a rebellion offending the fidelity owed to Your Majesty. It is true that sometimes some movements of the common people have been noted. These risings are always very reprehensible and are directed against the ministers of Your Majesty. But they have never been undertaken to break the yoke of obedience to the sovereign. And, after all, these were popular movements; no nation of the world has been without them. In America they have been very rare compared to Europe. They have been solely of the lowest common people. The Spaniards of this kingdom have participated in none of them. . . .

Rather, there has been scarcely any project of magnitude conducive to the government, felicity, and quietude of the public and to the authority of Your Majesty in these lands that was not due to our zeal and solicitude. [We have raised militias, held a *cabildo abierto*, or municipal council open to all notables of the city, and offered personal help and housing when troops arrived from abroad. The Mexican militias were of help in "the commotions attending the expulsion of the Jesuits" (1767). Now that war with Britain threatens, even artisans volunteer for military service.]

In loyalty and service we are distinguished. We are a nation as great as any in the world. Even this is to claim too little; permit us, Your Majesty, to say that we have distinguished ourselves above all. To the merit of other peoples has been added the attraction of reward. Without it, has the generous impulse of our obligation alone moved us? Without reward? Yes, Sire. . . . It cannot be your wish to allow the honor of an entire nation such as America to be trampled underfoot. . . .

May God guard the Royal Catholic Person of Your Majesty for many years.

2. Excerpts from the Gaceta de Literatura

of José Antonio Alzate y Ramírez

José Antonio Alzate y Ramírez (1738–99) was a first-generation creole on his father's side and a great-nephew of Sor Juana Inés de la Cruz,

SOURCE: "Excerpts from the *Gaceta de Literatura*" translated from José Antonio Alzate y Ramírez, *Gacetas de Literatura de México*, 4 vols. (Puebla, Mexico: Office of the Hospital of San Pedro, in charge of the citizen Manuel Buen Abad, 1831), 1, pp. 1–4.

the poet and prodigy of Mexico's baroque era, on his mother's side. He attended the Jesuit Colegio de San Ildefonso in Mexico City. From 1788 to 1795 he edited 115 issues of the *Gaceta de Literatura*, a monthly of six to eight pages that, though not widely read, was influential.

[PROLOGUE OF THE AUTHOR, 1788]

The outpouring of periodical literary productions is so great that if they were to be categorized in terms of the cities in which they are published, the simple alphabet could not contain them. With such abundance elsewhere, is it not strange that in the metropolis of the New World, where rare talents—the particular productions of the three kingdoms [1]— are found, a vacuum exists that a Mexican spokesman could fill with brilliance? . . .

One sees the well-justified esteem that the *Gaceta de México* acquires from day to day because its author, complying with the requirements of exactitude, tells us about happenings of the time that would remain in obscurity if he did not publish them. The palpable utility of this enterprise, in which its author has experienced inexplicable fatigue, mutterings, and the other inconveniences that are felt by an author and that do not come to the notice of readers, has moved me to publish the present gazette, restricted to literature. Through it I will attempt to disseminate reports and dissertations concerning the progress of trade and navigation by extracting, copying, or translating what is useful. The progress of the arts will not be the least appreciable object to which my ideas are directed. Natural history, which holds such portents for our America, will be a major concern.

The lives and deeds of men who have shed glory on our Hispano-American nation—ought they to remain in obscurity? Not at all. They will be spoken of with ingenuity, without hiding what is useful in their accomplishments, but perhaps glossing over or remaining silent concerning that which men should ignore.

The geography of New Spain is so unknown that one scarcely recognizes the true relationship of its principal places to one another. It will become clear when they are discussed in documents that, if not admitting of a geometric demonstration, will be approximately correct. Not the least of the objects of my efforts will be the diaries of voyages, which are so instructive either about the customs of inhabitants or about natural products.

---

[1] [That is, New Spain, New Galicia, and Guatemala, all under the jurisdiction of the Viceroy of Mexico.]

Shall I omit the discoveries that have taken place in Europe in experimental physics, mathematics, medicine, chemistry, and agriculture? Objects of such interest ought to be my first concern, since my duty is to be useful to my native land. Jurisprudence, designed to conserve the rights of men, to conserve their tranquility (inestimable treasure), will be found among my investigations. Those deeds worthy of serving as a model, those determinations of our wise tribunals, will be expounded upon to enlighten those whose profession obliges them to be so informed. What utility has not resulted from the periodical of jurisprudence published in Paris? How many, recognizing its transactions comparable or similar to those they intend to engage in, will abstain from a risky business when they see the outcome has been decided upon beforehand?

The few antiquities of the Mexican nation that remain will be described, and, if the costs of printing allow, illustrations will be published.

It is certain that few documents about the history of the Mexicans remain. This scarcity makes it necessary to conserve them. If not, in the short space of a century documents will seldom be found. Destruction is quick; loss of memory of deeds done is even quicker, especially since it cannot be verified that anyone is dedicated to conserving in writing the irreplaceable documents that serve as an index to discovering the genius, the character, and the customs of the Mexican nation. The writings of the learned Torquemada, of the great Sigüenza, of the collector Boturini, and of the renowned Clavijero are the only ones that in the past and present centuries supply us with historic accounts of what the Mexicans were. . . .[2]

Health and its restoration, those two poles of medicine, in Europe attain great advantage by means of the gazettes of health, welfare, and medicine circulated in various lands. They present to the public those particular cures, those methods, that are ordinarily a mystery to the members of a family, a town, and even some physicians. Thus they gain great advantages or much fame, because a resulting cure would remain forgotten if it were not publicized in such a work.

If we consider the utility to wealth: How great it will be when the present value of comestibles and other goods traded in each province is pointed out in a printed work! Then will the merchants have a sure guide to buying those things sold cheaply. And in this does not the public receive great benefit? This part of my plan is very vast, and, although it appears difficult of execution, I am confident of help from the person whose destiny and love for humanity will ensure all the necessary means. I dare to engulf

---

[2] [Carlos de Sigüenza y Góngora and Juan de Torquemada wrote in the seventeenth century, Benaduci Boturini and Francisco Javier Mariano Clavijero in the eighteenth. Alzate probably knew the first three through Clavijero's Storia Antica del Messico (Cesena: Biasini, 1780–81), wherein he praises their work.]

myself in an occupation that is greeted with a regard varying according to self-esteem and to the greatest motivation, the love of wealth.

To give news of works published in New Spain and to form an analysis and expound a short criticism so that readers may know in advance the character of the work is an annoying, inconvenient occupation, scarcely fitting for those who dedicate themselves to publishing their own productions; but if a judicious criticism is considered in Europe to be most useful for limiting the printing of useless works and for avoiding the loss of precious time to readers, why in America would it not be most advantageous?

.   .   .

I do not confide in my weak forces in order to sustain the level that I have proposed. I am satisfied that other people, whose humility is greater than their opinion of their own literature, will contribute to ensuring it, on seeing that a licit means to expound their ideas is presented to them. A work of the character of this one supplies them with an innocent conveyance to divulge that which they judge useful and would not be able to divulge in any other way. . . .

Available to them now is a means to send their productions to the editor without more expense, without more fatigue. These will be printed under their own names or as they desire, with the understanding that the *Gaceta de Literatura de México* is not begun in order to publish productions satisfying self-esteem, irreligion, vengeance, etc., etc. The characteristics that will enable the projected work to be carried out are submission to the authorities and the obligation to be useful to one's fellow men.

Happy will I be if the plan that I propose attains the innocent effect to which it is directed! Most happy if I am able to abandon the enterprise to other persons of greater wisdom and of felicitous execution, if I succeed in being one of their readers who is able to say: *Vires acquirit eundo* (It gains strength as it goes).

[DEDICATION OF AN ESSAY ON THE RUINS
OF XOCHICALCO, 1791]

Alzate dedicated this essay to the members of the Spanish politico-scientific expedition to America led by Alejandro Malaspina that was ostensibly engaged in discovering the secrets of nature, including the nature of the organization of Spanish American society, but was secretly gathering material on which to base political reform.

SOURCE: "Dedication of an Essay on the Ruins of Xochicalco" translated from José Antonio Alzate y Ramírez, *Gacetas de Literatura de México*, 4 vols (Puebla, Mexico: Office of the Hospital of San Pedro, in charge of the citizen Manuel Buen Abad, 1831), Supplement to Vol. 2.

The variety of terms in which up to now the Mexican Indians have been described, the excessive scorn with which some people, even our own [creoles], are accustomed to look upon them, and especially the black and vile colors with which foreign authors usually paint them to us moved me some years ago to investigate their origin and their habits and customs, and, in a word, everything concerning their arts, sciences, and so on. I desired to appraise the diverse judgments of the first mentioned, to rectify the injustice of the second, and ultimately to show all the world the ignorance and calumny of the last.

To this effect, in the *Gaceta de Literatura* Number 11, I treated of their origin. . . . In other issues, as occasion has permitted, I have tried to impart some competent reflections, according to my judgment, to persuade readers that the Mexican nation was not so little civilized as is commonly believed. Nevertheless, as these reflections could only make an impression on perfectly impartial men, I considered that it was necessary to add to them other more convincing and persuasive products, taken from old monuments left to us by this celebrated nation. Accordingly, I went to Xochicalco, where I had heard that one could find the ruins of an old palace.[1] I found in them a work of such precious architecture that I decided to give a complete description of it to the public. This is the subject of the present article.

For thousands of reasons I have thought, gentlemen, that it should be dedicated to you. Of these the principal ones are, first, your profound and fine education, which puts you in a position to judge their true merit; and second, the object of your expedition, which is not limited to surprising nature in the formation of its most admirable and portentious effects or to the vast extension of the natural sciences, but which also endeavors to collect all that information relative to the habits, customs, and arts of the towns through which you pass. Fortunate will I be if this short and informal *memoria* I publish will come to dissipate the false impressions that the sinister information that foreigners are generally accustomed to give in their works has created among literate men concerning the old Mexican Indians!

May the Lord protect for many years your lives, so important to the utility and progress of the natural sciences.

[1] [Xochicalco, in present-day southern Morelos, was probably built about 900 A.D. and was a fortress town covering more than six hundred acres. The "old palace" was undoubtedly what remained of the imposing fort, complete with walls and moats, built on a steep hill. See the chapter by William T. Sanders in *Prehistoric Settlement Patterns in the New World*, edited by Gordon R. Willey, Viking Fund Publications in Anthropology, 23 (1956).]

[News from Querétaro, 1791]

Some time ago a paper was sent to me by post from Querétaro. I would have enjoyed publishing it immediately, if certain circumstances had not obliged me to defer its publication until now.

It states that in the house of Don Marcos Ijar de Arenaza, four learned men—a secular ecclesiastic, a religious, a captain, and another gentleman named Don Antonio—met in order to divert themselves. The subject of their conversations, always informal and spontaneous, had long been either political news or some matter of erudition. But at the end of April of last year, one of these gentlemen proposed to the others the idea that the five of them should form a group or an academy to treat solely of one branch of literature. The idea appeared so fine to all of them that from then on they gave serious thought to the establishment of such a group. Naming a director, a secretary, and so on, these men resolved to busy themselves with poetry.

.   .   .

I cannot allow to pass in silence or fail to note that these gentlemen deserve much praise for the particular noble enterprise whereby they strive to fulfill their function as academicians and for having chosen to divert themselves by so pleasant and innocent a subject. It would be desirable in a court like Mexico,[1] where so many and such fertile talents abound, to arouse them by the influence of such a praiseworthy example from that profound and shameful lethargy that holds them deadened in perpetual inactivity. The most celebrated academies have originated in this type of private group. Since men are naturally inclined to imitation, it is incredible what utility this type of useful and agreeable occupation brings to the republic of letters.

3. *Manuel Abad y Queipo, "Representation Concerning the Personal Immunity of the Clergy" (1799)*

On behalf of the Bishop and Cathedral Chapter of Michoacán, Abad y Queipo wrote to the Crown to point out the importance of the clergy

---

[1] [Alzate here refers to Mexico City as the capital, or court, of the viceroyalty.]

SOURCE: "News from Querétaro" translated from José Antonio Alzate y Ramírez, *Gacetas de Literatura de México*, 4 vols. (Puebla, Mexico: Office of the Hospital of San Pedro, in charge of the citizen Manuel Buen Abad, 1831), 2, pp. 201–03.

SOURCE: "Abad y Queipo's Representation" translated from *Documentos para la Guerra de Independencia de México, 1808 a 1821*, edited by Juan Hernández y Dávalos, 6 vols. (Mexico: Sandoval, 1877), 2, pp. 823–52.

to royal government and, thus, the disservice done by the recent law limiting ecclesiastical privileges. This excerpt includes his report on the state of society in New Spain and his suggestions for laws "that would form the principal base of a liberal and beneficial government."

The population of New Spain is composed of approximately four and a half million inhabitants, who can be divided into three classes: Spaniards [including Spanish Americans], Indians, and "castes." [1] The Spaniards compose a tenth of the total population. They alone have nearly all the property and wealth of the kingdom. The other two classes, who compose nine tenths, can be divided into thirds: two of castes and one of pure Indians.[2] Indians and castes are employed in domestic service, agricultural work, the ordinary tasks in commerce, and the arts and crafts. That is to say, they are employees, servants, or day laborers for the Spanish class. Consequently, there results between the Indians and castes and the Spaniards that opposition of interests and feelings which is common in those who have nothing and in those who have everything, between workers and masters. There is envy, robbery, poor service on the part of some; scorn, usury, hardheartedness on the part of the others. These results are common to a degree everywhere. But in America they are more intense, because there are no gradations nor medians; all are rich or miserable, noble or worthless.

In effect, the two classes of Indians and castes are found in the greatest abasement and degradation. The skin color, ignorance, and misery of the Indians put them at an infinite distance from a Spaniard. The privileges conceded by law to the former benefit them little and in general harm them greatly. These people are forced by the law to live in a community circumscribed by a circle that forms a radius of 1680 feet. They have no individual property; they cultivate communal lands by compulsion and without immediate return. It is undoubtedly a heavy burden, made more hateful to them as the difficulty of availing themselves of urgently needed products increases from day to day. Their difficulties have

---

[1] [The census of 1793 estimated the population of New Spain at "5,200,000 souls." At the end of 1803, Humboldt estimated "5,800,000 inhabitants for the Kingdom of Mexico," adding that he thought his figure low. Of these, more than one million were creoles and seventy to eighty thousand were gachupines. "Castes," as used here, includes Negroes, mulattoes, and all peoples of mixed Spanish, Indian, and Negro descent. There is some evidence that Abad y Queipo overestimated the number of "pure Indians" and underestimated the number of castes.]

[2] [Humboldt found more than two and a half million Indians, and he discovered that the castes were almost as numerous as the Indians, rather than twice as numerous. In 1810, Navarro y Noriega stated that the Indians comprised sixty per cent of the population, castes only twenty-two per cent. Work remains to be done before we shall arrive at reliable population estimates for New Spain on the eve of independence.]

become insuperable because of the introduction of the new form of administration, the system of intendancies. Now no one is able to settle any matter without recourse to the *junta superior* of the Royal Treasury in Mexico City.

Legally prevented from cohabiting and intermixing with the castes, the Indians are deprived of the education and help they should receive through communication and contact with them and with other peoples. Isolated by their language and by their most useless and tyrannical native government, the customs, uses, and gross superstitutions are perpetuated that mysteriously maintain in each pueblo eight or ten old indians living lazily at the expense of the sweat of the others and dominating them with the hardest despotism. Unable by law to make a lasting agreement, to go into debt for more than five pesos, and to treat and contract, it is impossible for them to advance in that instruction which betters fortunes or to take a step forward to lift themselves from their misery. . . . This concurrence of causes maintains the Indians in a state truly apathetic, inert, and indifferent to the future and to nearly everything that does not arouse the gross passions of the moment.

As descendants of Negro slaves, the castes are declared scoundrels by law. They pay tribute, and, as the head count is so exact, the payment of tribute has come to be an indelible mark of their servitude.[3] Time cannot efface it, nor can the mixture of races in subsequent generations. There are many who by their color, physiognomy, and conduct could be elevated to the class of Spaniards, if there were not this impediment keeping them abased in the same class. This class, then, is worthless according to law. Its members are poor and dependent. They have no proper education, only retaining traces of habits and customs ascribable to their origin. In such circumstances, they should be abased in mind and dragged down by the strong passions of their impetuous and robust temperament. They are, indeed, guilty of excess. But it is a marvel that they are not much more guilty, that there are in this class good customs observable in many individuals.

Thus, the Indians and castes are governed directly by the territorial justices, who are more than a little responsible for the condition of these groups.[4] Formerly, the *alcaldes mayores* were considered not so much

[3] While the head count was more reliable at the end of the eighteenth century than it had previously been—and this in large measure was due to the administrative and fiscal reforms recommended and in part introduced by the Visitor-General José de Gálvez—yet, as Alexander von Humboldt realized in 1803 and as the obvious discrepancies visible in census figures of the period indicate, those figures were still far from "exact."

[4] Abad y Queipo is attacking a Bourbon reform, the new administrative system of intendancies, introduced in 1786 in Mexico. While he finds that the new territorial justices and subdelegates are more oppressive to the lower classes than were the old local

judges as merchants with an exclusive privilege to trade in their province. As officials, they had the power to enforce their monopolies. In a five-year period they often accrued from thirty thousand to two hundred thousand pesos. Their usurious and forced transactions caused great vexation. Yet despite all this, there were usually two favorable results: One, they administered justice with disinterest and rectitude in cases to which they were not party; the other, they promoted industry and agriculture where they deemed it important. The abuses of the alcaldes mayores were to be remedied by the subdelegates, who were forbidden to engage in all commerce. But as they were assigned no annual salary, the remedy was infinitely more harmful than the original evil. If they were to confine themselves to the business of adjudicating among miserable people who only litigate when a crime is committed, the subdelegates would perish of hunger. Necessity forces them to prostitute their offices, swindle the poor, and do business with criminals. For the same reason, it is extremely difficult for the intendants to find men suited to these posts. Only the unsuccessful or those who by their conduct and lack of talent cannot find other means to subsist seek these positions. In such circumstances, what beneficence, what protection can these ministers of the law dispense to the Indians and castes? By what means can these officials gain their good opinion and respect, when extortion and injustice are necessary to maintain themselves?

Rather, it is the priests and their assistants, dedicated only to the spiritual service and temporal aid of these miserable classes, who can gain by those ministrations and services their affection, gratitude, and respect. The clergy visit and counsel them in sickness and at work. They act as doctors . . . and as lawyers and intercessors with the justices and with those who bring suit against them. They also favor the poor when they are oppressed by the justices and the more powerful townsmen. In a word, the people do not, and cannot, have confidence in anyone but the priest or the superior magistrates, to whom appeal is very difficult.

In this state of affairs, what interest can unite these two classes with the first class and bind all three to the laws and the government? The first class has the greatest interest in the observance of the laws, for the laws assure it and protect its life, honor, property, and wealth against the insults of envy and the assaults of misery. But the other two classes have no belongings or honor or anything that can be envied. If a member of one of them be attacked, what appreciation has he of laws that only

officials, the alcaldes mayores (a group excoriated earlier by the Ayuntamiento of the capital), and while other royal officials, notably the Conde de Revillagigedo (viceroy of Mexico, 1788–94), shared his opinion, it must be remembered that Abad y Queipo is not an objective reporter but a cause-pleader here. The clergy, he is saying, are the most effective agents of government in the villages.

mete out punishments? What affection, what good will can these people have for the ministers of the law, whose authority is exercised only to send them to jail, to the pillory, to the frontier garrison, or to the gallows? What chains can bind these classes to the government, whose beneficent protection they are not capable of comprehending?

Can the fear of punishment suffice to keep the people in subordination to the laws and the government? Two classes, says a politician, make this resort useless: The powerful break the net; the miserable are caught in its mesh. If this maxim is true of Europe, it is much truer of America, where the people live in the open, without permanent domicile, nearly as vagabonds. Then let modern legislators come and point out a means, if they can find one, to hold these classes in subordination to the laws and the government, other than that of a religion preserved in the depth of their hearts by ministers preaching and advising from the pulpit and in the confessional. Therefore, they [the ministers] are the true custodians of the laws and the guarantors of their observance.

It appears opportune and in accord with the charge of the laws to suggest, for the supreme consideration of Your Majesty, remedies for these ills. After profound meditation based on a practical understanding of the character, temper, habits, and customs of these peoples, we think it most appropriate to raise them from their misery, suppress their vices, and tie them to the government by obedience and subordination to the laws. We do not intend to preempt the sovereign judgments of Your Majesty or the wise advice of your zealous ministers. We only wish to point out a state of affairs that is perhaps not as well known there as, naturally, it is here. If such measures as we propose should now be under consideration or adopted, we shall have the satisfaction of thinking as does Your Majesty. If they should not be adopted now, but are adopted sometime, it will double our future pleasure in having contributed to so important a step. . . . And in any case we give, Sire, a testimony of our good wishes for a felicitous outcome in this glorious enterprise of Your Majesty's.

We say, then, that of major importance is, first, general abolition of tributes in the two classes of Indians and castes. The second measure is abolition of the legal infamy affecting these castes; they should be declared honest and honored, capable of obtaining civil positions that do not require noble rank, if they should merit them for their good demeanor. The third is free division of all the unappropriated lands between Indians and castes. The fourth is free division of the communal lands of the Indians among the inhabitants of each village. The fifth is an agrarian law similar to that of Asturias and Galicia. There, by means of leases and transfers of twenty to thirty years and exemption from the royal *alcabala* or sales tax, the people will be permitted to work the uncultivated lands of the great proprietors. There will be just charges in adjudicating cases of discord. The reclaimed land must be enclosed. Everything will be done in order to keep intact the rights of private property. Over all these proceedings the intendants of the province will judge in the first instance; appeal will be to the *audiencia* of the district, as it is in all other civil business.

The sixth measure is free permission to all classes of Spaniards, castes, and Indians of other pueblos to live in Indian villages, to buy land in them, and to construct houses and buildings. The seventh is a sufficient salary for all the territorial judges, with the exception of the *alcaldes ordinarios*, who ought to fill their posts gratuitously as public obligations. If to these is added the free operation of the ordinary cotton and wool workshops, it will increase the impact of the other measures, which should allow people to take the first step toward happiness. Wholesale workshops are now permitted with special license of the viceroys or governors; but this licensing is an insuperable obstacle to the poor and ought to be stopped. So should all other tax burdens, except the charge of alcabala in the importation and exportation of articles.

We know that a proposition to abolish tributes in the present urgent circumstances of the Crown will cause surprise. But if in the arithmetic of royal finances there are cases in which three and two are not five, this is certainly one of them. And by close calculation it can be proved that the abolition of tributes and the other mentioned proposals, far from diminishing the royal finances, will augment them in less than ten years to triple or quadruple what the tributes produce today.

4. Report of the Consulado of Mexico (1811)

In this report, the merchant guild protests the decree of the Spanish Cortes of Cádiz of February 9, 1811, which declared equality between Spaniards and Americans in obtaining government office and in representation in the Cortes. It attempts to prove that the inhabitants of New Spain are incapable of fulfilling these political responsibilities.

Sire,

The Royal Tribunal of the Consulado of Mexico reports to Your Majesty with much detail and judgment the state of the diverse castes of inhab-

SOURCE: "Report of the Consulado of Mexico" translated from *Documentos para la Guerra de Independencia de México, 1808 a 1821*, edited by Juan Hernández y Dávalos, 6 vols. (Mexico: Sandoval, 1877), 2, pp. 450–66.

itants of New Spain, their quantity, civilization, disposition, customs, passions, desires, and patriotism. From this analysis it deduces the bitter truth concerning these remote provinces: They are not even nearly ready to equal the metropolis in order, form, and number of national representation. After discussing the injustice, grievances, dangers, and uselessness of allowing them the proposed representation, it indicates the most easy, simple, and appropriate plan, perhaps the only sure one, to reconcile American representation with the conservation of the Americas.

. . .

What then was the New World, its empires and its inhabitants? Half of the terraquious globe, the New World was a frightful desert, or a land barely occupied, unproductive and uncultured, in the hands of diverse tribes, wandering, barbarous, and employed in hunting and in war, without peace, serenity, communication, commerce, roads, agriculture, stock-raising, industry, or arts. They were preoccupied with the most rabid superstition, with rites and ceremonies insulting to reason and to nature, with laws malevolent, absurd, and mad, and with practices adding up to an abominable composite of all the errors and atrocities committed by peoples in every land and time.

Such, Sire, were the Indians, their empires, and the miserable beings that occupied them, submerged in a tender infancy, with all the appearances of vile automata, so that even respectable theologians whose opinion was very honored in the sixteenth century were persuaded that these beings had no rationality and that the Omnipotent had denied them qualities essential to man.

Such were the natives of the America . . . whom Divine Providence put under the protection of the magnanimous Spaniards, then the most powerful and illustrious nation of the cultured world. In vain do some foreigners, infatuated with the fanatic and hypocrite Las Casas, emulate him slavishly and bitterly accuse us of brutality in the conquest.

. . .

By the most marvelous metamorphosis that the centuries have known, the orangutan settlers [the Indians] of America were suddenly transformed, Sire, into domesticated men, subject to a mild government.

. . .

If happiness depended on following the exigencies of temper and inclination, nothing would compare with the pleasures and delights of the Indian. He is gifted with laziness and languor that cannot be described. His greatest gift is an absolutely frugal inclination concerning physical necessities. Removed from the superfluities, he sacrifices only a few days of resting a year and would never move if hunger or vice did not prod him. Stupid by constitution, without inventive talent or force of thought, abhorring the arts and trades, he does not lack a way of life. A drunkard by instinct, he satisfies this passion at little cost with very cheap beverages, and this depravity takes up a third of his life. Carnal, with a vice-ridden imagination, devoid of pure ideas about continence, chastity, or incest, he provides for his fleeting desires with the women whom he encounters closest to hand. He is as uncaring in Christian virtue as he is insensible to religious truths, so remorse does not disturb his soul or restrain his sinful appetites. Undiscerning about his duties to society and indifferent to all his fellow beings, he does not economize in the crimes that can bring him an immediate punishment. . . .

If this being, corrupted by the feebleness of his own powers, by his own inertia, by attachment to custom, or by the violent propensity to pleasure, has not perfected even his morals, it would be very unjust to blame legislation or the government. The government and legislation influence or work very slowly on morality and even more slowly on the emotions. . . .

The Indian does not at present carry his ideas, thought, interests, and will beyond his own reach or the range of his eyes. Disinterested in patriotic sentiments and in all social activity, he asks of public authority only an indulgent priest and a lazy subdelegate. He pays no attention to the doings of the intendant, the viceroy, the monarch, or even the nation. In his mind, all are simply a jumble of names. Three million Indians in this condition live presently in New Spain. . . .

There are two million castes; their lazy arms are employed in peonage, domestic service, trades, crafts, and the military. They are of the same condition, character, temperament, and negligence as the Indian, in spite of being reared and living in the shade of cities where they form the lowest class of the populace. With more opportunity to acquire money, with more money to pursue their vices, with more vices to destroy themselves, it is no wonder that they can be most lost and miserable. Incontinent inebriates, indolent, without shame, pleasantness, or fidelity, without notions of religion, morality, luxury, cleanliness, or decency, they appear more mechanical and slovenly than even the Indian himself. They are governed by the common law of the land. No direct imposition weighs on them; they are indirectly taxed only on what they drink! Their foodstuffs are not taxed. Their clothing is rags and the sun. They feign humility to the police. They pay no attention to the government; in turn, it counts on them neither for the immediate advantage of the state nor even for the perpetration of robberies. If the vigilance of the authorities and the exaction of tribute hinder the prosperity and civilization of the Indian, how is it that emancipation from this oppressive authority and exemption from contributions have the same effect on the castes? Is it through a defect of physical constitution caused by the climate, the food they eat, their general laxity, or their education, or is it due to another, unknown cause? The final result, at any rate, is that the castes have none of the qualities of the dignified citizen, none of the properties of vassals, none of the virtues demanded of townsmen, and none of the attributes signifying the civil and religious man.

A million whites, called Spanish Americans, show their superiority to the other five million natives more by their hereditary wealth, their careers, their luxury, their manners, and their refinement in vices than by substantial differences of temperament, sentiments, and propensities. According to experience, the multitude of whites sink themselves into the populace by squandering their patrimony. Spanish Americans occupy themselves in ruining the paternal house. They study when young under the direction of their elders and are placed in all the offices, public posts, and salaried positions of the state. They swell the professions and arts and console themselves, in the absence of wealth, with dreams and schemes of independence that would give them domination of the Americas. Destitute, adept at dreaming of the future, without reflection or judgment, with more indolence than ability, with more attachment to hypocrisy than to religion, with extreme ardor for all the delights, and without the restraint to stop themselves, the indigenous whites gamble, make love, and drink. In a few days they dissipate inheritances, dowries, and property that should support them all their lives. Later they curse at fortune, envy the thrifty, get angry at the denial of their pretensions, and sigh for a new order of things that will do them justice. . . .

In these six million inhabitants the European Spaniards do not bulk very large. Some of these seventy-five thousand men also degenerate because of the force of bad example, because of their way of life, or because of the rudeness of the country; nevertheless, this small and ill-bred family is the soul of the prosperity and opulence of the kingdom due to its undertakings in agriculture, mining, factories, and commerce. It enjoys the management of it nearly exclusively, not so much because of its energy or greed as because of the disinterest of the creoles. Man is a very incomprehensible being. The Europeans, knowing that they work for their ungrateful, spendthrift, and alienated sons, do not shirk financial anxieties, severe privations, or self-sacrifice in order to increase a patrimony that cost half a century and will be squandered in days. In the end this blindness, this show of fatherly affection, can be reproved neither for its origin nor for its consequences, for it always benefits the state and bestows on the European Spaniard the reputation of a loyal vassal, inseparably united to the metropolis by chains of nature, of recognition, and even of egoism.

Yes, Sire, egoism is part of this notable fidelity, because the European runs the risk of losing his life at the first cry of American insubordination. In the New World, "patrimony" is understood as "the love of the land in which one has been born." This truncated and mistaken definition causes hard feelings and resentment between Spaniards from overseas and natives. It is the root of the loyalty of some men and the aversion of others to the mother country.

.   .   .

New Spain is a remote province, seduced by the sum of its population and by its riches, made haughty by the abasement of the metropolis, pushed toward anarchy by corruption, stupidity, and imbecility, denuded of all decent sentiments, of all generous passions, of all political combinations, of all rational foresight. It is the abode of five million automatons, a million intractable vassals, and a hundred thousand citizens addicted to order.

.   .   .

It was proposed in the sovereign congress to grant the colonies of the conquest a representation proportionate to that of the conquering nation. This decision, a product of the talents and patriotism of the creoles, was sustained ardently by a faction and by its influence. What blindness hurls the white Americans into such straits? Is it their haste to die, their imprudence, their ill will toward the human species, or their dreams of self-government?

The Cortes would enfranchise five million drunkards, friends of robbery, bloodshed, and evil-doing, susceptible to all emotions of hate, libertinage, and looseness, dragged along mechanically by the furor of vengeance, and without an idea of shame or religion. Five million of these barbarians, united in bands spread over the area of New Spain, would take on the airs and trappings of sovereign people. They would be presided over by most perfidious chiefs, the men most excited and sanguine about independence, the fiercest, the greatest enemies of the motherland. These leaders would be assisted, urged on, and ordered about by a million lost whites, who are extremely vicious, superficial, artificial, and divorced from Christian piety and from political, moral, and natural notions of social welfare. What a cruel perspective! What road so short and so conducive to insurrection! Is this what the creole deputies seek? No, Sire, far from desiring it, they would not dare to live in the capital of the viceroyalty, anticipating such evil days, such scenes of death, horror, and weeping, expecting the victims to be of their own color and class.

.   .   .

What is there in common? What comparison fits, or what analogy may be found in the laws, situation, spirit, manners, exigencies, interests, institutions, habits, and regions of conquering Spain and of the conquered colonies? Would not the parallel between the Spaniard and the Indian be a comparison between a crowd of gibbon monkeys and an association or republic of urbane men?

CONCLUSION

In the late eighteenth century, a new spirit was abroad in Mexico, made manifest by the regidores of Mexico City *within* the old framework of thought concerning the relation of Mexico to the peninsula. Although blown up with creole pride, they spoke of "we Spaniards." In 1778, however, Alzate expressed himself within another ideological framework. He combined creole pride with concern for the populace of all New Spain and wrote of "we Mexicans."

Alzate served not only as an example of intellectual ferment but also as a champion of it. He was prominent among those who raised the cry for liberty of opinion that presaged the cry raised for political liberty in 1810 by members of that same Querétaro Literary Academy he so admired. One of them, Miguel Hidalgo y Costilla, when asked by what right he had taken upon himself the destiny of Mexico, revealed to what lengths civic activity may go when he replied that he was exercising the right that any citizen has when he sees his native land in danger. Hidalgo gave an eminently popular cast to current liberal notions. He declared slaves free, abolished tribute payments, and restored lands to the Indians—measures advocated earlier by his one-time friend and fellow cleric, Abad y Queipo. Hidalgo went beyond Alzate's concept of the nation to explicitly include as fellow citizens men of all ethnic backgrounds born in Mexico.

Dissatisfaction with existing governmental policy was voiced by members of the group that should have been its staunchest adherents, the European Spaniards. Conflict was evident not only among members of the governing group but also within the mind of the individual Spaniard. Abad y Queipo represented the dilemma of the enlightened peninsular who wanted to preserve certain privileges, notably those of the Church, and abolish others in the interest of economic, social, and political reform.

If Abad y Queipo was a product of the eighteenth-century revolution in the Spanish climate of opinion, the Consulado exemplified the conservative reaction to it. That previously powerful corporation blamed liberals such as Abad y Queipo for overturning the old imperial order and thus ensuring the loss of America. They insisted that liberal Spaniards share responsibility for the rejection of Spanish imperialism and the exaltation of Mexican nationality that permeated the creole revolt of 1810.

Further, these documents reveal that enlightened creoles, unlike enlightened gachupines, could not reconcile their desire for economic and social reform with the Spanish drain of Mexican wealth and with government imposed from overseas. They also shed light on related historical problems. For example, in 1778, a year *before* the French Revolution, Alzate used a vocabulary often attributed to the influence of that revolution. His writings, and others, indicate that an internal development of ideas occurred within Mexico in the latter part of the eighteenth century, that creoles had prepared for themselves an ambience receptive to concepts of Mexican liberty.

In short, these documents show how attitudes that undermined Spanish authority developed among widely varying segments of society in Mexico. They also indicate how intellectual ferment (initially directed against traditional methods of education) gave rise to concern with social and economic reform and, finally, to political activity. When revolution came, creoles had a ready-made ideology: the concept of a nation to call to arms. While creole society, like gachupín society, was far from monolithic in outlook, the regidores of the capital, the journalist Alzate, and the revolutionaries of 1810 had one thing in common: a concept of Mexican nationality, a patriotic attachment to the soil on which they were born.

Hidalgo and a small group of fellow creoles rose in the name of the nation, calling on all men born on Mexican soil to join them. For a brief period, the possibility existed that all Mexicans could unite, as Abad y Queipo had warned they might, in the cause of freedom from oppression by European Spaniards. The hope of unity died as Hidalgo's undisciplined mass of followers increasingly indulged in looting and bloodshed. The riotous nature of the revolt repelled the majority of creoles, including many of those adhering to Alzate-like liberal principles. They would neither join the rebels nor continue to look to Spain. The blandishments proffered to them by the Spanish Cortes in the form of American representation in that body and the liberal Constitution of 1812 they took instead as guides to the formulation of a Mexican congress and constitution.

Small bands of insurgents carried on the revolution. Hidalgo's successor as leader, the mestizo priest José Maria Morelos, declared Mexico independent in 1813, yet not until a new and more elitist unity was effected among elements of Mexican society was independence in fact achieved. In 1821, Vicente Guerrero, an insurgent leader, joined Agustín Iturbide, an Army officer representing the military, the hacendados, the mineowners, and the Church and, with the blessing of the liberal Spanish viceroy, Juan O'Donoju, formed a government that was to be dominated by elitist creole interests, liberal and conservative, for the greater part of a century. The continuance of a Consulado-like outlook among Spaniards helped to bring about the expulsion of all Spaniards from Mexico in 1828. No sector of influential society worked to include the Indian in the nation proper until the second decade of the twentieth century, when revolution again proposed to solve old problems while at the same time posing new ones.

BIBLIOGRAPHY

For the Spanish background in the late eighteenth century, see Richard Herr, *The Eighteenth Century Revolution in Spain* (Princeton, N.J.: Princeton University Press, 1958); Antonio Domínguez Ortiz, *La sociedad española en el siglo XVIII* (Madrid: Consejo Superior de Investigaciones Científicas, 1955); Jean Sarrailh, *L'Espagne Éclairée de la Seconde Moitié du XVIIIème Siecle* (Paris: Imprimaire Nationale, 1954); and H. R. Trevor-Roper, "The Spanish Enlightenment," in *Historical Essays* (New York: Harper & Row, 1966), pp. 260–72.

Particularly appropriate on the general Latin American background are Robert A. Humphreys, "The Fall of the Spanish American Empire," in *History*, n.s. 37 (1952), pp. 213–27; Robert A. Humphreys and John Lynch, eds., *The Origins of the Latin American Revolutions* (New York: Alfred A. Knopf, 1965); and Arthur P. Whitaker, ed., *Latin America and the Enlightenment*, 2nd ed. (Ithaca, N.Y.: Cornell University Press, 1961).

Social arrangements in Mexico in the late eighteenth century are discussed by Lyle N. McAlister, "Social Structure and Social Change in New Spain," in *Hispanic American Historical Review*, 43 (1963), pp. 349–70. See also his *The 'Fuero Militar' in New Spain, 1764–1800* (Gainesville: University of Florida Press, 1957); and María del Carmen Velázquez, *El estado de guerra en Nueva España, 1760–1808* (Mexico: Colegio de México, 1950), for discussion of the introduction of a new element, the military, into Mexican society. The Bourbon innovations and an indication of their effects are treated in H. I. Priestley, *José de Gálvez, Visitor-General of New Spain, 1765–1771* (Berkeley: University of California Press, 1916); and Clement Motten, *Mexican Silver and the Enlightenment* (Philadelphia: University of Pennsylvania Press, 1950).

Intellectual ferment within Mexico during this period can best be understood by reading a number of specialized studies. Among the most outstanding and most recent of these are: Pablo González Casanova, *La literatura perseguida en la crisis de la colonia* (Mexico: Colegio de México, 1958), and his *El misoneísmo y la modernidad cristiana en el siglo XVIII* (Mexico: Colegio de México, 1948); Luis González y González, "El optimismo nacionalista como factor de la independencia de México," in Silvio Zavala, ed., *Estudios de historiografía americana* (Mexico: Colegio de México, 1948), pp. 155–215; Gloria Grajales, *Nacionalismo incipiente en los historiadores coloniales* (Mexico: Universidad Nacional Autónoma, 1961); José Miranda, *Humboldt y México* (Mexico: Universidad Nacional Autónoma, 1962), and his *Las ideas y las instituciones políticas mexicanas* (Mexico: Instituto de Derecho Comparado, 1952), Vol. 1; Bernabé Navarro, *Cultura mexicana moderna en el siglo XVIII* (Mexico: Universidad Nacional Autónoma, 1964); Monelisa Lina Pérez-Marchand, *Dos etapas ideológicas del siglo XVIII en México a través de los papeles de la*

Inquisición (Mexico: Colegio de México, 1945); and Mario de la Cueva, *et al.*, *Major Trends in Mexican Philosophy*, translated by Robert Caponigri (Notre Dame, Ind.: University of Notre Dame Press, 1966), especially Rafael Moreno's chapter, "Modern Philosophy in New Spain," and Luis Villoro's chapter, "The Ideological Currents of the Epoch of Independence."

Xavier Tavera Alfaro, ed., *El nacionalismo en la prensa mexicana del siglo XVIII* (Mexico: Club de Periodistas de México, 1963), includes a number of extracts from the periodicals published by Alzate and others. Also concerning Alzate: Juan Hernández Luna, ed., *José Antonio Alzate* (Mexico: Secretaría de Educación Pública, 1945); Rafael Moreno, "Alzate, educador ilustrado," in *Historia Mexicana*, 2 (1953), pp. 371–89, and his "Creación de la nacionalidad mexicana," in *ibid.*, 12 (1963), pp. 531–51.

On Abad y Queipo, there is Lillian Estelle Fisher's *Champion of Reform: Manuel Abad y Queipo* (New York: Library Publishers, 1955). Two very recent monographs supply welcome additional information on the Church in Mexico: Michael B. Costeloe, *Church Wealth in Mexico: A Study of the "Juzgado de Capellanías" in the Archbishopric of Mexico, 1800–1856* (New York: Cambridge University Press, 1967); and N. M. Farriss, *Crown and Clergy in Colonial Mexico, 1759–1821: The Crisis of Ecclesiastical Privilege* (London: University of London Press, 1968).

For the initial phase of the Revolution of 1810, see Hugh Hamill, *The Hidalgo Revolt* (Gainesville: University of Florida Press, 1966). The best single recent work on that revolution as a whole is Luis Villoro, *La Revolución de Independencia* (Mexico: Universidad Nacional Autónoma, 1953).

V

The Death
of Brazilian Slavery,
1866–88

Thomas E. Skidmore

CHRONOLOGY

1807   Prohibition of slave trading from British ports and into British possessions

1815   Treaty between Britain and Portugal, prohibiting slave trade north of the Equator

1817   Treaty between Britain and Portugal, giving right to search suspected slave ships

1826   Treaty between Britain and Brazil (now independent), re-affirming right of search and promising total abolition of slave trade within three years

1831   Brazilian parliament sanctions treaty of 1826 and declares free any slaves subsequently imported (but this remains unenforced)

1850   Brazilian parliament passes Eusébio de Queiroz Law, fixing harsh penalties for involvement in slave trade

1852   Last year in which any slaves were landed in Brazil

1858   Gradual abolition decreed in Portugal's African colonies

1863   Emancipation Proclamation in the U.S.

1865   Thirteenth Amendment to U.S. Constitution, abolishing all slavery in the U.S.

1866   Emperor Dom Pedro II receives abolitionist appeal from French Abolitionist Society

1871   Law of the Free Womb (Rio Branco Law) passed, freeing all children subsequently born to slave mothers (September 28)

1884   All slaves in the provinces of Ceará and Amazonas manumitted

1885   Brazilian parliament passes the Sexagenarian Law, an amended version of the Dantas Bill, freeing all slaves over sixty (after three-year transition period)

1887   Brazilian Army publishes manifesto declaring it will not recapture runaway slaves

1888   Brazilian parliament passes the Golden Law, decreeing total abolition without compensation (May 13)

INTRODUCTION

No country in the New World had a more profound experiment with slavery than Brazil. Slave labor was inextricably connected with the growth of its economy and remained an important institution until total abolition came in 1888. In the final decades of slavery, after the slave trade had totally ended in 1852 (the date by which the law of 1850 had been effectively enforced), Brazilian writers and politicians engaged in a growing debate over the morality as well as the politics and economics of abolishing the "peculiar institution." Their analyses and arguments are the subject of this chapter.

From the time the land was discovered by the Portuguese in 1500, the Europeans in Brazil faced a labor problem. The Indians of the region, who were much less advanced than the Indians whom the Spanish encountered in the Andes and Middle America, at first furnished the manpower for a primitive barter economy in brazilwood (valuable for its qualities as a dye). By the middle of the sixteenth century, however, barter had already ceased to entice the Indians sufficiently, and the scattered Portuguese settlers began enslaving them in order to ensure the wood supply. The need for slaves became even more pressing when the Portuguese discovered the great profits to be gained in the Brazilian Northeast from growing sugar, the crop that was to form the backbone of the export economy until the end of the seventeenth century.

But the Brazilian Indians soon proved to be unsatisfactory for plantation labor. First, their background as a hunting and fishing people had given them no experience in the routine of regular field labor. Second, they quickly fell victim to the numerous European diseases against which they had no immunity. Third, the Church partially blocked the use of Indians as slaves. In Brazil, as in Spanish America, the Church sought with varying degrees of intensity to prevent the enslavement of the Indian. This intervention, motivated largely by theological concern over the Indian's status as a potential convert to Christianity (which was the regal and papal rationale for Iberian conquests in the New World), certainly did not keep the Indian totally free. Indeed, many of the Catholic orders themselves owned slaves in sixteenth-century Brazil. But the Church's sporadic attempts to protect the Indian—culminating in the abolition of all Indian slavery in the 1750's—did help force Portuguese planters to look elsewhere for their labor supply.

The logical place to look for better plantation laborers was black Africa. Even before the Spanish and the Portuguese came to America, they had successfully exploited African slaves on the plantations—primarily sugar plantations—of their Atlantic island possessions. Furthermore, the Portuguese African possessions offered an inviting supply of captives. The Portuguese began systematically importing enslaved Africans into Brazil about 1570 in a stream that was eventually to total three and a half million before the slave trade was suppressed in 1850.

Working the sugar plantations or *fazendas* was the first major task of Brazilian slaves. By the seventeenth century, the humid northeastern coast of Brazil had become the world's leading sugar producer, generating a per capita income for the area that has never been equaled since. This prosperity was based squarely on the Negro slave, who was aptly known as "the hands and feet of the planter." The handsome profits from Brazil's productive Northeast attracted foreign invaders—first the French and then the Dutch. The latter occupied the coast of Pernambuco from 1630 until their expulsion in 1654. Quickly appreciating the basis of Brazilian wealth, the Dutch for a time seriously considered a plan to conquer Angola, Brazil's "black mother," a dream that was never realized. The South, on the other hand—from the province of São Paulo southward—had a largely nonexport economy that did not require plantation labor, and this area continued to use primarily Indian rather than Negro slavery.

If the Brazilian economy had continued to derive its dynamics from the sugar plantations, Negro slavery never would have developed into the countrywide phenomenon that it became. But the geographical distribution of Negro slaves was shifted as a result of the discovery of gold and diamonds in central and western Brazil (what later became the states of Minas Gerais, Mato Grosso, and Goiás) at the end of the seventeenth century. A wild gold rush ensued. By 1730 the economic axis of the colony had moved to Minas Gerais, and a prosperous new society emerged—once again based on slavery. The fortunes to be made in gold and diamonds (Brazil was Europe's principal supplier of precious metals in the eighteenth century) put an enormous premium on the availability of Negro slaves, who performed all manual labor in the mines. The importation of enslaved Africans into Brazil rose steadily in the early eighteenth century, and many black hands already in Brazil were bid away to the mines from the decaying plantations of the Northeast.

In the second half of the century a familiar story was repeated in Brazil: the gradual exhaustion of a boom cycle. Earlier, the sugar boom had run its course, its decline accelerated by the competition of the more fertile lands and more efficient planters of the Caribbean. Now it was the turn of gold and diamonds. Worked-out mines, ghost towns, and retreat to subsistence agriculture became the hallmarks of the once-prosperous mine fields. By 1800 the Brazilian economy had entered a general recession.

When the Portuguese court arrived in Bahia in 1808 with its retinue of ten thousand refugees from the onslaught of Napoleon's armies, it found a Brazil still heavily dependent on Negro slave labor. By this time the proportion of slaves in the population was remarkably constant throughout Brazil. Unlike the situation in the United States, Brazilian slavery was a national institution, one that had penetrated every region of the country. Furthermore, the existence of Negro slavery over several centuries had been accompanied by the emergence of a relatively large class of free men of color, whereas in the United States even half-breeds had great difficulty escaping bondage. Miscegenation was widespread in both societies, but in North America there was little mobility out of slavery, unlike Brazil and most of the rest of Latin America. By 1800 free men of color (including both Negroes and mulattoes, which have long been considered separate social categories in Brazil) [1] represented approximately fifteen per cent of Brazil's total population. The census data for this period is scanty, but this figure is corroborated by other, more informal sources, such as travelers' accounts. Mobility out of slavery into the world of free men was frequent, and it is probably even understated in the official figures because of the Brazilian tendency to define color (especially for mulattoes) in terms of a man's position rather than his physical appearance. Many persons of notably mixed blood were, and still are, called "white."

The Brazilian slave economy had grown up by heavily importing slaves, not by depending on self-replenishment. Planters could count on the trade with Africa for ready replacement of infirm and aging slaves, and this was a disincentive to invest in the slaves' welfare or to encourage their breeding. When the slave trade was endangered in the first half of the nineteenth century, slaveowners naturally found reason to change their attitude toward the care of their human property. It was this relatively new attitude that impressed many travelers who commented on the benign treatment of slaves in Brazil in the middle of the nineteenth century. The relative cruelty of slaveowners in Brazil as compared to other slave societies, especially the United States, has remained a much-disputed topic ever since—and the dispute has generated distinctly more heat than light.

In general, the rigidity and harshness of Brazilian slavery tended to decrease in regions suffering economic decline, especially the Northeast and the old mining areas of Minas Gerais. Although these areas were in economic retreat by 1800, other regions soon experienced the next great agricultural boom of Brazilian history. In the 1830's and 1840's slave labor

---

[1] Throughout this chapter, "Negro" is used in the Brazilian sense, meaning a "black"; "mulatto" refers to a person with mixed blood. No such distinction is made in North American English; a mulatto, however light-skinned (unless he is light enough to "pass" for white), is referred to as a Negro. This difference in language reflects the difference in race relations explained above.

A slave market in Rio de Janeiro. A lithograph from a drawing by Moritz
Rugendas in his book *Malerische Reise in Brasilien*, 1835, *Zentralbibliothek
Zürich*.

was in great demand for the coffee plantations of the province of Rio de
Janeiro, southeastern Minas Gerais, and São Paulo. Just as sugar had
ruled in the seventeenth century and gold and diamonds in the eighteenth,
coffee became king in the nineteenth. By 1850 Brazil had become the
world's largest producer of the new drink that rapidly captured the fancy
of the prosperous inhabitants in the industrializing North Atlantic world.
Negro slave labor seemed as indispensable to the huge coffee plantations
as it had once been to the sugar plantations and the mines. But the coffee
boom differed from earlier ones in a basic respect: Now the end of the
African slave trade was imminent, and abolitionist opinion had grown
strong. For economic and social reasons, therefore, the coffee planters had
to think in terms of alternative sources of labor.

From the very beginning of the coffee cycle, there were voices urging
the abolition of slavery in Brazil. One of the earliest and most important
—much quoted by later abolitionists—was José Bonifácio Andrada e

Silva, a principal patriarch of Brazilian independence in 1822. The greatest enemies of Brazilian slavery in the first half of the century, however, were politicians and writers not in Brazil itself but in England. From the British Isles came growing pressure against continuation of the slave trade by the Portuguese and Brazilians. It was British intervention that proved most crucial in finally abolishing the trade in 1850.

Once the slave trade between Africa and Brazil had ended, domestic Brazilian political activity focused on extinguishing the institution of slavery within the Empire. The progress of the struggle was slow, however, and Brazil proved to be the last realm in the New World to arrive at formal abolition. But the delay should not lead to the conclusion that Brazilian slavery remained virulent to the end. Manumission and self-purchase of freedom had long been practiced and had given rise to a large population of free men of color. After 1871, the nation moved toward abolition step by step. Success in the Brazilian struggle against slavery was gradual rather than violent and sudden.

After the supply of slaves from Africa had been cut off, the defenders of slavery knew full well that the institution would die a natural death through the attrition of the remaining slave population. Indeed, this possibility was one of the principal arguments they used against the abolitionists. But history moved too fast for the "attritionist" solution to be tested. As Brazil's inglorious war with Paraguay (1865–70) drew to a close, a new generation of politicians and writers stepped forward to denounce the moral outrage and economic anachronism of slavery. The impatience and stridency of the politicians increased as the pressure generated by the abolitionists rose. The first victory for the movement was the so-called Law of the Free Womb (Rio Branco Law) of 1871, which declared free all children born of slave mothers. This law, however, was less effective than its advocates had hoped. The agitation for total abolition gathered momentum as the 1870's ended.

In the early 1880's the abolitionists merged their efforts by centralizing their finances and propaganda, especially in the cities of Rio de Janeiro and São Paulo. Pressure was brought to bear not only on the national Parliament in Rio but also on many provincial governments. The second legislative victory for the abolitionists came with the Sexagenarian Law of 1885, which freed all slaves over sixty years old. But the abolitionists were not satisfied for long with this half step. Despite the fact that natural attrition was rapidly depleting the remaining slave population, the campaign for total abolition grew in fervor, frequently erupting in street riots. The Parliament and the monarchy finally acted on May 13, 1888, when slavery was totally abolished by law. The arguments heard in the two decades preceding that final step are represented in the readings that follow.

READINGS

1. *Slavery on the Coffee Plantations*

Stanley J. Stein's study of one coffee-growing county in the province of Rio de Janeiro between 1850 and 1900 is based on a thorough investigation of contemporary sources, including plantation records, public documents, and "manuals" that gave the planter candid advice on how he could get maximum profit from his slave labor force. Emerging from Stein's book is a picture of Brazilian slavery, at least as it was practiced in the coffee country of Rio de Janeiro, as being much harsher than earlier historians (such as Brazil's Gilberto Freyre and certain foreign scholars who relied on travel literature) had indicated. Some of Stein's conclusions about the planters' practices and beliefs follow.

"Greater or lesser perfection . . . of discipline determines the greater or lesser degree of prosperity of agricultural establishments" [explained one of the manuals on the management of slaves]. Constant supervision and thorough control through discipline joined to swift, often brutal punishment were considered an absolute necessity on coffee plantations. Proper functioning of a fazenda varied directly with the steady application of the working force; in an epoch of little machinery, slave labor, or what Brazilians termed "organized labor," had to be guided carefully and supervised closely.

It seemed that apparently slow-witted slaves had to be driven to produce. In a day's work conscientious planters had to "look for a fugitive slave, consider punishing a second, decide to send a third to help a neighbor—check the weeding . . . complain about the escolha [low-grade coffee beans] . . . explain each morning in detail to a flock of slaves the nature of extremely simple tasks they were to accomplish, check each evening to see if they have been barely achieved." In their reasoning, the needs of production dovetailed with concepts of slave character. "Only with constantly exercised vigilance under military-like discipline" would slaves work hard and earnestly, was a widespread opinion. The Negro slave was "by nature the enemy of all regular work," the "passive partner" in the transaction that entrusted him to his owner at the time of purchase. His salary? The purchase price and food and clothing provided by his master.

source: "Slavery on the Coffee Plantations" from Stanley J. Stein, *Vassouras: A Brazilian Coffee County, 1850–1900* (Cambridge, Mass.: Harvard University Press, 1957), pp. 132–34. Reprinted by permission of Harvard University Press.

Those Brazilian planters who failed to find in the nature of their plantation economy sufficient justification for slavery could find support in the
writings of foreigners, both resident and transient. In 1839 planters were
informed, for example, that the Negro was a "man-child" with the mental
development of a white man fifteen or sixteen years of age. To the French
émigré Charles Auguste Taunay, the "physical and intellectual inferiority
of the Negro race, classified by every physiologist as the lowest of human
races, reduces it naturally as soon as it has contact and relations with other
races (especially the White race) to the lowest rung and to society's
simplest tasks. One searches in vain for examples of Negroes whose intelligence and works merit admiration." He felt that Negroes' inferiority
obliged them to live in a state of perpetual tutelage and that therefore it
was "indispensable that they be kept in a state of servitude, or near
servitude." Another Frenchman assured Brazilian slaveholders that the
Negro was intellectually inferior to the white because the Negro's cranium
was smaller and therefore he could not develop his "moral intelligence to a
comparable degree." In defense of these writers it must be noted that their
line of reasoning was akin to that of many Brazilian slaveholders who
taught their sons that Negroes were not humans but different beings
"forming a link in the chain of animated beings between ourselves and the
various species of brute animals." This conception of Negro inferiority was
generally universal, although some planters and town residents did not
share it. A description of a Parahyba Valley planter published shortly
before the abolition of slavery underscores the prevalence of prejudices,
the effect of routinism, and the absence of scientific knowledge. Though
a planter might be capable of displaying compassion and pity for whites,
toward his slaves he was "harsh and very cruel," for he refused to see
in them the "nature and dignity" of men. The slave was little more than
"an animated object, a tool, an instrument, a machine."

2. An American View
of Brazilian Slavery

One of the most interesting travel books about the Brazilian Empire
between the end of the slave traffic and the successive abolitionist laws
was written by the noted Harvard zoologist Louis Agassiz and his wife.
They visited Brazil in 1865 with a scientific expedition (which included
William James) that spent most of its time in the North gathering

SOURCE: "An American View of Brazilian Slavery" from Louis J. R. Agassiz and
Elizabeth Cary Agassiz, *A Journey in Brazil* (Boston: Ticknor and Fields, 1868), pp.
128–29.

scientific specimens. The following are Agassiz's notes on a conversation aboard a coastal steamer that carried the foreign scientists at a leisurely pace northward from Rio de Janeiro to the mouth of the Amazon.

July 30th.—Off Maceió. Last evening, when the rain was over and the moonlight tempted everyone on deck, we had a long conversation with our pleasant traveling companion, Mr. Sinimbu, senator from the province of Alagôas, on the aspect of slavery in Brazil. It seems to me that we may have something to learn here in our own perplexities respecting the position of the black race among us, for the Brazilians are trying gradually and by installments some of the experiments which are forced upon us without previous preparation. The absence of all restraint upon the free blacks, the fact that they are eligible to office, and that all professional careers are open to them, without prejudice on the ground of color, enables one to form some opinion as to their ability and capacity for development. Mr. Sinimbu tells us that here the result is on the whole in their favor; he says that the free blacks compare well in intelligence and activity with the Brazilians and Portuguese. But it must be remembered, in making the comparison with reference to our own country, that here they are brought into contact with a less energetic and powerful race than the Anglo-Saxon. Mr. Sinimbu believes that emancipation is to be accomplished in Brazil by a gradual process which has already begun. A large number of slaves are freed every year by the wills of their masters; a still larger number buy their own freedom annually; and as there is no longer any importation of blacks, the inevitable result of this must be the natural death of slavery. Unhappily, the process is a slow one, and in the meanwhile slavery is doing its evil work, debasing and enfeebling alike whites and blacks. The Brazilians themselves do not deny this, and one constantly hears them lament the necessity of sending their children away to be educated, on account of the injurious association with the house servants. In fact, although politically slavery has a more hopeful aspect here than elsewhere, the institution from a moral point of view has some of its most revolting characters in this country, and looks, if possible, more odious than it did in the States.

3. The French Abolitionists Appeal to Dom Pedro II (1866)

With the end of the slave trade in 1852, slavery seemed a dead issue in Brazil. However, the country's retention of slavery as an internal institution increasingly irritated the professional humanitarians of Europe who had taken the lead in forcing abolition in virtually all the European colonies except those of Spain (especially Cuba) and Portugal (the African possessions). Prominent French abolitionists, many of them members of the French Academy and all of them well aware of the enormous cultural prestige their country enjoyed in Brazil, addressed a direct appeal to the philosopher-king Dom Pedro II in July 1866.

To His Majesty, the Emperor of Brazil

Sir:

At a time when the Republic of the United States, victim of a long and bloody war, has just freed four million slaves, at a time when Spain seems ready to yield to the voice of humanity and justice, we take the liberty of directing to Your Majesty an ardent appeal on behalf of the slaves in your empire.

We know, Sir, and no one in Europe can be unaware, that Your Majesty is powerful in your empire. Your strength lies in your highly respected administration and in the sincere love of your people.

You have already abolished the [slave] trade, but that measure is incomplete. A word, a gesture of Your Majesty can bring to pass the liberation of two million men. You can offer an example, Sir, and you may rest assured that you will not be alone, because Brazil has never looked upon slavery as a divine institution.

Liberal voices are raised every year in the legislatures, in the press, and in the pulpit, asking for abolition. The number of slaves is less than that of free men; and almost a third already live in the cities, performing jobs or acting as servants, and it is easy to raise them to the position of wage-earners. Emigration will flow to your provinces once slavery has disappeared. The task of abolition, which should be adjusted to the prevailing

SOURCE: "The French Abolitionists Appeal to Dom Pedro II" translated from the reprint in *Revista do Instituto Histórico e Geográfico Brasileiro, Contribuições Para a Biografia de D. Pedro II*, Part 1, Tomo especial (Rio de Janeiro: Imprensa Nacional, 1925), pp. 418–19. Printed by permission of the Instituto. All translations in this chapter are by the chapter editor.

facts, interests, and conditions, seems less difficult in Brazil, where, moreover, habits are gentle and hearts are human and Christian.

We desire for Your Majesty, who is already celebrated in arms, letters, and the art of governing, a purer and more beautiful glory, and we permit ourselves to hope that Brazil will no longer continue to be the only Christian land infected by slavery.

4. *The Brazilian Reply:*

A *Commitment to Abolition* (1866)

> In reply to the appeal of the French abolitionists, the following letter was drafted by Dom Pedro II himself, although it was sent on August 22, 1866, over the signature of Martim Francisco Ribeiro de Andrada, as the Foreign Minister. Henceforth the Martim Francisco letter was cited by abolitionists at home and abroad as a solemn commitment on the part of the Imperial Government to carry out abolition. The great controversy was to come over the *manner* of abolition.

Gentlemen:

I have had the honor of informing His Majesty the Emperor of the letter in which you manifest your ardent hope for the abolition of slavery in Brazil.

Entrusted by His Majesty with answering you in his name and in the name of the Brazilian Government, I am happy to be able to assure you that your wishes have been received most sympathetically.

It was fitting, gentlemen, for you, whose noble voices are always raised on behalf of the great principles of humanity and justice, to make known the ardor with which you pursue an enterprise as great as it is difficult, and it is with the keenest satisfaction that the Brazilian Government noted your doing justice to the personal feelings of His Majesty the Emperor, the members of the Ministry, and the trend of public opinion in Brazil.

The emancipation of the slaves, a necessary consequence of the abolition of the trade, is nothing more than a matter of procedure and opportunity. When the painful circumstances in which the country finds itself [1]

[1] [The waging of the Paraguayan War.]
SOURCE: "The Brazilian Reply" translated from the reprint in *Revista do Instituto Histórico e Geográfico Brasileiro, Contribuiçoes Para a Biografia de D. Pedro II*, Part 1, Tomo especial (Rio de Janeiro: Imprensa Nacional, 1925), p. 419. Printed by permission of the Instituto.

permit, the Brazilian Government will consider to be an object of first importance the realization of what the spirit of Christianity has long since demanded of the civilized world. Accept, gentlemen, the assurance of my highest regard.

5. A Famous Romanticist Attacks the Rio Branco Bill

Less than a year after the reply to the French appeal, the Emperor's Cabinet further committed the Government to abolition by inserting in the annual Message from the Throne (May 1867) an appeal for an approach that would "respect present property" and avoid any "profound shock to our leading industry, agriculture." In 1871 a Conservative government, after finally gaining victory in the Paraguayan War, presented the Chamber of Deputies with the Rio Branco Bill (named for Viscount Rio Branco, the head of the Cabinet). The bill declared that any children born of slave mothers would be free (thus the bill was also called the Law of the Free Womb), although they would remain under the authority of the mother's master until the age of eight. A child's fate was then in the hands of the master, who could either grant him immediate liberty and thereby claim an indemnification from the Government (in six per cent thirty-year bonds), or retain the child under his authority (that is, in slavery) until the age of twenty-one. José de Alencar (1829–77), a Conservative deputy from the northeastern province of Ceará, famous novelist and playwright of Brazil's romantic movement, argued against passage of the bill.

Gentlemen, there are other methods of liberation that would not be fatal, but would be useful and advantageous for the country, and the Government ought to prefer these to the free womb. Such measures are: the emancipation of the vote, which is the slave of government; the emancipation of justice, which is the slave of caprice; the emancipation of the citizen, who is the slave of the national guard; and finally, gentlemen, the emancipation of the country, which is the slave of absolutism, the slave of the tyranny of personal government.

But these emancipations do not have the support of the proclamations of European philanthropy; they are vital necessities of the country and not obeisances to foreign opinion! These essential interests of the country do

SOURCE: "A Famous Romanticist Attacks the Rio Branco Bill" translated from *Anais do Parlamento Brasileiro, Camara dos Deputados*, Terceiro Ano da Décima-quarta Legislatura, Sessão de 1871 (Rio de Janeiro, 1871), 1, pp. 134–35, 139.

not have a French voice to say to someone, "Sir, by this act your name will acquire everlasting fame."

Let us resign ourselves, then, let the Brazilian nation be resigned, to live in repression until the suggestions of European philanthropy or the intervention of some foreign society insists on her liberty.

Meanwhile, gentlemen, in this battle which unfortunately has been joined in our country, civilization, Christianity, the cult of liberty, and true philanthropy are on our side. They fight for our cause. It is they who inspire in us this calm and firm conviction, which is not frightened by the threats of power and does not become irritated at the injustices of her imprudent friends.

You, the propagandists, the emancipators at all costs, will be nothing more than the envoys of revolution, the apostles of anarchy. You are the retrogrades who try to retard the progress of the country, wounding it in the heart and killing its leading industry, farming.

If you think not, let us compare matters. Look at what you want and look at what we want. You want emancipation as a vain ostentation. You sacrifice the essential interests of the country to whims of glory. You think that to liberate is merely to steal from captivity, and you forget that liberty given to these brutish masses is a fatal gift; it is the sacred fire given to the impetuosity and boldness of a new and savage Prometheus!

We want the redemption of our brothers, as Christ desired. It is not enough for you to tell the creature paralyzed in his intelligence and repressed in his conscience, "You are free, go, run through the fields like a wild beast!" . . .

No, gentlemen, it is necessary to enlighten the benumbed intelligence and elevate the humbled conscience, so that one day, when giving him his freedom, we may say, "You are men, you are citizens. We ransom you not only from captivity but also from the ignorance, the vice, the misery, the bestiality in which you lie!"

. . .

Compulsory freedom on the pretext of salvation or of arbitrary decision creates a dangerous weapon for the hate, intrigues, and ill will of small localities. And it must result in the violation of the citizen's home, the disruption of family harmony, and the plundering of the property that is supposed to be guaranteed.

This freedom of the womb, gentlemen, is unjust and barbarous. It is unjust because it concedes liberty to the offspring and denies it to the present generation, who have shown long service and dedication. It is barbarous because it condemns the innocent offspring to abandonment, which means misery and death.

Gentlemen, it is a recognized fact that moderation and mildness have always characterized the institution of slavery in our country and have done so even more in recent times. Our habits and the generous character of our race will continue to infuse this institution with a gentleness and solicitude that will virtually transform it into servitude.

Which of us, gentlemen, has not many times had the opportunity to see, in the bosom of the family, the loved and respected mother bending over the sickbed where a slave lies, moved not by petty and sordid interests but by the impulse of that sentiment of charity that is the glory of the Brazilian woman?

Very well, if with our impatience we stifle these generous sentiments, if we paralyze these benevolent sentiments, if we create antagonism between races that will always live together, one repaying the services of the other with its protection, do you not fear that this quality of moderation and charity may suddenly disappear? For my part, I confess that I tremble, and, thinking about how passions will transform men, I foresee a slaughter of innocents.

6. Report of the Parliamentary Commission Approving the Law of the Free Womb (Rio Branco Law, 1871)

The Rio Branco Bill was based on the draft drawn up three years earlier by the famous liberal Senator, José Thomaz Nabuco de Araujo, father of the abolitionist orator Joaquim Nabuco. The parliamentary commission appointed to study the Rio Branco Bill issued a favorable report in June 1871. Its language reflected the mood of prudence that predominated among the deputies. This report helped to pave the way for final approval of the bill, which became law on September 28, 1871.

One of the ills that oppresses us, impoverishes us, demoralizes us, and shows us as stagnant, if not backward, is this hateful, brutalizing spectacle [of slavery]; and, in turn, it contributes to the dishonor of work.

Work, which is the law of God and the penalty and reward of humanity, is the unavoidable obligation of every citizen. But it becomes unbalanced in countries that have slaves. There the slaves form the lowest class beneath the free class. The tasks entrusted to the slave caste become as debased

SOURCE: "Report of the Parliamentary Commission" translated from *Anais do Parlamento Brasileiro: Camara dos Deputados*, Terceiro Ano da Décima-quarta Legislatura, Sessão de 1871 (Rio de Janeiro, 1871), 2, pp. 221–22, 224–26.

as it is; while the aristocracy of free men consists in their not sullying themselves with contemptible labor. For the slave, it is manual labor; for the free man, it is exemption from it. This exemption subsequently breeds foolish haughtiness, unproductive laziness, and corrupt idleness. Once men are ennobled through equality, all work will become noble, and then and only then will intolerable distinctions cease.

From that hour the character of things will change. Slave labor is always imitative, crude, unfinished, slow, and barely profitable; free labor is enterprising, intelligent, clever, dynamic, creative, and ten times more profitable. Our trade, based on imperfect crops produced by slave labor, will languish with the passage of time compared with that of other countries, even though they may be less endowed by nature. With free labor and with the moral and physical customs of our society having been greatly improved, we will proudly compete with all nations, and perhaps in many instances we shall even vanquish them.

.   .   .

This idea of immediate and unconditional abolition, although it may be consistent with natural principles, would in practice be the same as the eruption of a destructive volcano, such would be the sudden disorder erupting in the midst of society.

.   .   .

We would convert the country into a den of evildoers, because a prematurely freed slave, lacking religion, scoffs at conscience; lacking discipline, he scoffs at men; lacking education, he does not know the advantages of civilization; lacking coercion or incentives, he becomes a vagabond; lacking work, he robs; lacking fear, he gets drunk; lacking morality, he plunges into every possible crime. We would create a sudden gap in the supply of labor as well as a radical and unforeseen change in its structure. We would not allow time for the conversion of labor. We would harm the nation, the farming class (the most important in Brazil), and the slave himself, for whom mass liberty without any transition would be a cruel gift because it would only bring him misfortunes. One cannot for a single moment countenance such dangerous rashness. Nor could the commission in any case advise immediate abolition based on indemnification given to the slaveowners by the state.

.   .   .

The commission concludes, therefore, that, with minor alterations, the proposal of the Government is worth your approval.

.   .   .

We are in a much better position than those countries that can be found in the same circumstances; these are seas whose reefs have already been noted on foreign maps by foreign experience. This teaches us that the

transition occurred spontaneously and smoothly where the legislation proceeded slowly and prudently, as happened in England, Sweden, Denmark,
the Spanish-speaking republics, Russia, Holland, and Portugal. Where
liberation was sudden, it was accompanied by a succession of disasters, as
happened in France. Where anachronistic resistance finally sought to dam
it up, as in the United States, an ocean of blood and calamities swept
it away.

7. Jeronymo Sodré Calls
for Total Abolition (1879)

The Law of the Free Womb soon proved to be less effective than its
most earnest supporters had hoped it would be, and the abolitionists
grimly and correctly asserted that death remained Brazil's greatest
emancipator. The fact that this law, enacted in 1871, could hardly
have had much effect before the early 1880's did not pacify the critics,
who had tired of the continuing national disgrace involved in the
gradualist solution. The first widely publicized call for immediate
abolition after 1871 came from Jeronymo Sodré, a professor in the
Faculty of Medicine in Bahia and a deputy to the Chamber of Deputies. Sodré's proposal launched the second phase of the legislative
struggle, which ended with the passage of the Dantas Bill (1885),
freeing all slaves over sixty. The asides from other deputies illustrate
the objections that his suggestion immediately aroused.

Sr. Jeronymo Sodré: I appeal to the humanitarianism of this venerable
chamber and of public authority. Would it not be much better for us, all
Liberals, to solve the great problem? To go beyond what the Conservatives did? They began the march, although it was denounced. We who
represent democratic ideas, we who want to liberate the citizen by means
of elections, votes, and education, need only announce to the country,
"In this country all Brazilians are citizens, all are free!"
Sr. Candido de Oliveira: It would be the ruin of Brazil and nothing more.
Sr. Marcolino Moura: The United States proved the contrary.

. . .

Sr. Jeronymo Sodré: Mr. President, I am not surprised at the position in
which I find myself in this illustrious assembly, and, if you are not frightened by the parallel, I would say that I find myself in the same circum-

SOURCE: "Jeronymo Sodré Calls for Total Abolition" translated from *Anais do Parlamento Brasileiro: Camara dos Deputados*, Primeiro Ano da Décima-sétima Legislatura,
Sessão de 1878 (Rio de Janeiro, 1879), 3, pp. 194–96.

stances as Wilberforce in the English parliament, gentlemen, when that
great humanitarian, supported by Pitt and Fox, first presented the slave
trade bill. Did that not produce turmoil?

There was the same displeasure, and the same commotion took place,
drowning out the voices of the speakers; there were the same considerations, ending up with the rejection of the bill by a large majority. But so
great was the force of the idea, so great was the enthusiasm, that Wilberforce later had the pleasure of seeing the realization of the ideas that he
had always held and that had created so much commotion!

Sr. Joaquim Nabuco: England indemnified.

Sr. Jeronymo Sodré: No one denies it. And I did not tell the Chamber that
I wished to disregard the right of property; on the contrary, I insist that
emancipation should take into consideration established rights, because
the opposite would be an offense against the privileges guaranteed by the
Constitution.

A deputy: The matter is one of indemnification.

Sr. Candido de Oliveira: With what funds? Only after discovering a Potosí.[1]

Sr. Jeronymo Sodré: We don't need a Potosí for such a purpose.

Every day here we talk about a current of European immigration, a
massive naturalization, and we discuss all these complicated problems of
modern societies. But, gentlemen, I ask you now in good conscience,
noble deputies, in each of whom I discern rich talents combined with
enlightenment, do you believe that immigration into this country can be
established as long as it continues to include the servile class, which destroys, ruins, and corrupts everything?

The noble deputy is wrong. In North America the slaves were in the
southern states. Everyone knows, however, that the great wave of immigration went at this time to New England—precisely the states of the
Union in which there was no servile class.

Above all, every one of us is afraid of this idea of emancipation. Well,
gentlemen, must we do ourselves the injustice of saying that we, a great
civilized American people, alone cannot do without such an institution?

.   .   .

And, gentlemen, let us have no doubts. On the day the American sun
gilds our mountains and illuminates our fertile plains without any longer
hearing the suffering cry of the miserable slave, in that hour, gentlemen,
we shall proudly be able to sit down, confident of our worth, at the great
sumptuous banquets of modern civilization.

---

[1] [The world's richest silver mine, discovered by the Spanish in southern Bolivia.]

8. *The Classic Abolitionist Argument:*

Joaquim Nabuco (1883)

Brazil's leading abolitionist was Joaquim Nabuco, grandson (on his mother's side) of a wealthy planter family in the northeastern province of Pernambuco. Entering Parliament as a deputy from Pernambuco in 1879, he made abolition the cornerstone of his early political career. Nabuco's handsome presence, striking eloquence, and impeccable social background made him an incomparable asset to the abolitionist movement, on whose unification in 1883 he exercised a powerful influence. In O *Abolicionismo* (published, ironically enough, in London in 1883), Nabuco skillfully combined humanitarian and practical arguments to make a powerful case for abolition, as the following passages illustrate.

By the law of September 28, 1871, slavery is limited to the lives of the slaves who were born before the law. But . . . every year slave women give their masters thousands of "twenty-one year slaves." . . . A slave born on September 27, 1871, can be a mother in 1911 of one of these innocent ones, who will thus remain in provisional captivity until 1932. That is the law and that is the period of slavery it still permits.

· · ·

It is said that slavery is mild among us and that the masters are good. The truth is, however, that all slavery is the same. And as for the kindness of the masters, this cannot go beyond the resignation of the slaves. Anyone who undertakes the labor of preparing statistics on crimes committed by slaves or against slaves or who attempts an inquiry into slavery and listens to the complaints of those who suffer under it will see that in Brazil today it is just as hard, just as barbarous and cruel, as it was in any other country of America. Slavery is like this by its very nature; and when it ceases to be so, it is not because the masters have become better but rather because the slaves have resigned themselves completely to the annihilation of their personalities.

As long as it exists, slavery includes every possible barbarity. It can be administered with relative mildness only when the slaves obey blindly and submit to everything. Their slightest reaction, however, awakens the sleep-

SOURCE: "The Classic Abolitionist Argument" translated from Joaquim Nabuco, O *Abolicionismo* (London: Abraham Kingdon, 1883), pp. 114–16, 133–34, 207, 252, 255–56.

ing monster in all its ferocity. The fact is that slavery can exist only through infusing absolute terror into the soul of man.

. . .

The abolitionists include all those who believe in a Brazil without slaves; all those who foresee the miracles of free labor; all those who regard slavery as a hateful vassalage imposed upon the entire nation by a few and in the interest of a few; all those who already feel suffocated by this noxious air breathed freely by slaves and masters; and all those who do not believe that once slavery disappears, the Brazilian will lie down to die, as did the Roman in the time of the Caesars because he had lost his liberty.

This means that we shall serve the highest interests of our country, her civilization, the future to which she is entitled, and the mission to which her place in America calls her. But between us and those who are blocking the path, which will conquer? Indeed, this is the very enigma of Brazil's national destiny. Slavery infiltrated fatalism into her bloodstream, and therefore she does nothing to take the command of her destiny away from the blind and indifferent forces that are silently guiding her.

. . .

We do not want to end slavery simply because it is illegitimate in view of the development of the moral concepts of cooperation and solidarity or simply because it is illegal in view of our legislation from the period of the slave traffic or simply because it is a violation of the public trust, expressed in treaties such as the Convention of 1826, laws such as that of November 7, solemn gestures such as the letter of Martim Francisco, the measures of the Conde d'Eu in Paraguay [who decreed the abolition of slavery in Paraguay while commanding the military occupation force there], and the promises of the statesmen responsible for the conduct of public affairs.

We certainly do want to end slavery for these reasons, but even more so for the following:

1. Because slavery, since it ruins the country economically, prevents its material progress, corrupts its character, demoralizes its member elements, saps its energy and resolution, and debases its politics. It accustoms it to servility, prevents immigration, dishonors manual labor, delays the appearance of industries, promotes bankruptcy, diverts capital from its natural course, keeps away machines, and arouses hate among classes. And it produces an illusory appearance of order, prosperity, and wealth, thus covering over the chasms of moral anarchy, misery, and destitution that darken our entire future from north to south.

2. Because slavery is an enormous burden that retards Brazil's growth in comparison with the other South American states that are without it; because, furthermore, this institution must perforce result in the dismem-

berment and ruin of the country; because the sum of its costs and the profits it loses us reduces to nil its supposed contribution and results in an enormous and continuing national loss; and because only after slavery has been totally abolished will the people begin to lead a normal life: Then a market for labor will exist, and individuals will assume their true roles, wealth will become legitimate, honor will cease being conventional, public order will be founded upon liberty, and liberty will no longer be a class privilege.

3. Because only with total emancipation can all the members of the community cooperate for the great work of a strong and respected common country. The members of this community are at present in conflict, some with each other and others with themselves: the slaves and those who are outside the body of society; the masters, who see themselves under attack as representatives of a doomed system; the enemies of slavery, because of their incompatibility with the latter; the inactive mass of the population, which is the victim of this monopoly on land and curse on labor; and Brazilians in general, whom slavery condemns to continue as they are, a nation of proletarians.

. . .

Let us compare the present-day Brazil of slavery with the ideal that we abolitionists uphold of a country where all may be free; a country where European immigration, attracted by the generosity of our institutions and the liberality of our regime, may constantly bring to the tropics a flow of lively, energetic, and healthy Caucasian blood, which we may absorb without danger, instead of this Chinese wave [1] with which large landowners hope to pervert and corrupt our race even further; and a country that may labor creatively for the benefit of humanity and the advancement of South America.

9. Proslavery Arguments
for Dom Pedro II (1884)

Those who opposed any far-reaching change in the slave system were as active as the abolitionists in trying to exploit the Emperor as an ally. An example of such attempts may be found in the open letters to the Emperor from a "faithful subject" that were published first in

[1] [Nabuco refers to a then-current proposal to import Chinese coolies, as was done in Peru.]

SOURCE: "Proslavery Arguments for Dom Pedro II" translated from A. Coelho Rodrigues, *Manual do Subdito Fiel ou Cartas de um Lavrador a Sua Majestade o Imperador Sobre a Questão do Elemento Servil* (Rio de Janeiro: Moreira & Maximino, 1884), pp. 6–7, 29–30, 72–74, 108.

the Rio press and later as a book in 1884. Although the letters appeared anonymously, there is little doubt that they were written by Antônio Coelho Rodrigues, a law professor and a Conservative deputy from the relatively backward northeastern province of Piauí. He believed that the law of 1871 would solve the problem in thirty years and would "bring about peacefully the precarious transition from slave labor to free labor, an extremely difficult and unexpected process."

Anyone who is looking for an apologia of slavery or a work of abolitionist propaganda should not waste time with this book, which is neither. It is not an apologia for slavery because no man among us today is capable of formulating one. The *Antislavery Conference* [an abolitionist periodical] would be even better able to say now what it said in 1867: "In Brazil, slavery has never found a party nor apologists, either in the press or in the tribune." Really, we have no newspapers or orators that truthfully deserve the title of slavery advocates. . . .

Anyone in doubt should compare the language of *Brazil* and the *Diario do Brazil*, considered by [abolitionist] propaganda to be slavery organs, with the language of [the U.S. proslavery papers] the *Columbia Telescope*, the *Squatter Sovereign*, and the *Richmond Enquirer*; or the language of Sr. Andrade Figueira, who is described as an intransigent, with that of the individuals who defended slavery in the great North American republic. A comparison on this question, made on any basis, puts us far above that unusual nation, which is so superior to us from many other points of view.

.   .   .

I live from my own labor and the labor of my slaves, whose lot is not inferior to that of the workers of the most advanced countries of Old Europe, according to the recent impartial admission of Senator Ottoni.

The English worker eats meat twice a week at most, and the French only once. Mine have it twice a day, and they have coffee in the morning as well as at night, and in the rainy season they receive clothing and medicine regularly and on time.

They were living, therefore, very satisfied with their situation, like the dog who is the companion of the wolf in the fable. And since happiness in this earthly world is more a matter of opinion than of reality, they could be considered happy in the life that they were living.

In truth, so they seemed. They were going along satisfied, greeting me happily when I went out on the job, and often they continued their work to the sound of songs whose words or melody could elicit a smile even from the serious mien of Your Imperial Majesty.

But the wolves came, and this time they were from the city. They whispered into their ears the new ideas from the Court. They told them of Your Majesty's wishes and of the hopes that European wise men have of seeing slavery abolished in Brazil, come what may, by the next centennial of the discovery of America.

Since then my slaves have begun to flee, that is, to desert me, in order not to wound the sensitivities of your supernumerary counselors from Rua Uruguayana and the Polytechnical School. [1] . . .

In spite of this I live to thank God, because it could be worse, as it was for a neighbor of mine, a father of eight young children and one as yet unborn, who was recently assassinated by his slaves to the sound of cheers for Your Majesty. They had no other motive than the certainty of pardon and the desire to try for the new life announced by the apostles of the Court, who proclaim themselves to be the instruments of your thought.

The news of this occurrence ran like an electric spark among us other *fazendeiros* [planters] . . . because, Sir, nothing so arouses disorder and encourages crime as the certainty of impunity. I offer as an example the repeated arbitrary acts of your ministers, who are always justified by precedent and never punished for their excesses.

.   .   .

Slavery in Brazil is a twin sister of monarchy in America. They are based on the same arguments: tradition, custom, and law.

Your government . . . will be able to obtain a law that tumultuously annuls slavery, thereby breaking with all customs and traditions. That done, your government will not be able to resist the inherent logic of sooner or later applying the same process to the monarchy that the monarchy now wants to apply to her sister.

The logic is republican, as intangible as it is dangerous, and it has a certain primitive momentum that is capable of making it jump in one leap the entire distance from Negro slave quarters to the Emperor's palace.

I am not speaking for myself. I would never direct a revolution, because I know that it is more perverse than Saturn [2] and that before it devours the children, it usually devours the father. But, Sir, not all your subjects are as loyal as I. Your fellow believers in today's official abolitionism will be the radicals of tomorrow.

[1] [The abolitionist merchants and professors.]
[2] [Coelho Rodrigues has apparently confused Saturn with Thyestes, another figure in Roman mythology, who unwittingly ate his own sons at a revenge banquet offered by his brother Atreus.]

10. *Minority Report Opposing the Bill*

to Liberate Sexagenarians (1884)

In 1884 the Cabinet, headed by Souza Dantas, a Liberal, introduced a new bill for gradual abolition that provided for the freeing of slaves over sixty. This measure was bitterly attacked by Antonio Alves de Souza Carvalho, who was from the northeastern province of Paraíba and was also a Liberal. Souza Carvalho's attack was published as a minority opinion in the report of the parliamentary commission that endorsed the proposal. After undergoing sharp modification, in part to provide a three-year transition period before sexagenarians were given their freedom, the bill was guided to adoption by a Conservative Cabinet in September 1885.

Both before and after the law of 1871, our government squandered enormous sums to attract European immigration, but it managed only to demonstrate its inability to endow this country with the laborers that are so badly needed to replace the present ones and to carry out many other essential services.

This lamentable failure should cause us to guard very carefully, like a great gem, the workers we still have. The humanitarian reformers who proceed in the opposite direction are greatly lacking in good sense.

.   .   .

In effect, the purpose of the proposal of July 15 of this year is precisely to destroy and liquidate what the law [of 1871] had very wisely preserved: It dispenses with the present work force and hastens abolition, showing complete disrespect for the principle of property and deeply shaking what is virtually our only industry—agriculture.

That proposal appears to me to be a kind of national suicide, a death sentence for the Constitution, spelling ruin for individuals and for the public treasury, bankruptcy for the State, and a great opportunity in this country for the doctrines of communism and their unlimited application. It is a gigantic and ill-considered step, to which the Government wants to commit us in order to make us into a present-day Egypt.

In fact, everyone knows that our treasury and our commerce, along with the members of all classes, survive and draw their sustenance and

SOURCE: "Minority Report Opposing the Bill to Liberate Sexagenarians" translated from *Camara dos Deputados, Projecto N. 48, Sessão de 4 de Agôsto de 1884: Parecer N. 48A; Formulado em Nome dos Commissões Reunidas de Orçamento e Justiça Civil, Acerca do Projecto de Emancipação dos Escravos Pelo Sr. Ruy Barbosa* (Rio de Janeiro, 1884), pp. 214–16.

resources from the results of slave labor, without which everything would collapse into paralysis and poverty.

But if we have the right to ruin ourselves at will, we do not have the right to defraud our creditors by willfully doing away with our means for paying them. If the State advocates and carries out the elimination of the means of national production—those who produce the revenues with which it pays the interest and amortization of the public debt—its action will resemble that of a farmer with creditors who thinks of freeing the slaves with whose labor he cultivates the land and obtains the means to fulfill his obligations and give a good account of himself. It is superfluous to explain how such behavior would be judged.

I cannot see any reasons in favor of the frivolous and insane idea of speeding up emancipation and thus ruining this country, except pure sentimentality, foolish vanity, or as a pretext for agitation, revolution, and social subversion. The latter will be capitalized upon by the feared anarchists, whom some propose to placate by the violent and dishonest exploitation of a large number of citizens, especially the most law-abiding, the most useful, and, to tell the truth, the only well-to-do class of Brazilians—the farmers.

In effect, these persecuted men, who consent to live and work among primitive people in the desert, are more useful and respectable than those whose only occupation is to wander in the city streets or regularly collect rents, interest on bonds, and dividends from stock companies.

To diminish any feelings of sentimentality, one might note the following:

．　．　．

The number of slaves that still exist in Brazil is nothing in comparison with the many millions who have existed and still exist in various parts of the globe.

The time it will take, without needing any law, for slavery to end among us naturally or to become so reduced in extent that it would be very easy and inexpensive to extinguish entirely without stealing property is insignificant for an institution so many centuries old, one that was known before the Flood and has always survived.

The few slaves we still have are accustomed to their fate, and it can be said with certainty that in general they will not profit from freedom, which will only make it possible for them to succumb to laziness and the vices that will make them unhappy.

In view of this, I believe that there are no grounds for the kind of emotionalism and impatience that is so harmful and fatal for our country.

The benefits that abolition is supposed to bring to the emancipated are far less in scale and importance than the evils that it could not fail **to bring to the State and all Brazilians.**

11. *Slaves Flee Their Masters* (1887)

After the passage of the Sexagenarian Law in 1885, the final stage of
the movement toward total emancipation began. The proslavery forces
found themselves surrounded by a breakdown in the whole system that
protected their human property, and increasingly the police and other
public authorities hesitated to carry out their traditional duty as the
hunters of fugitive slaves. More and more slaves, encouraged by abolitionist agitators, took matters into their own hands and simply fled
their masters. The following description of such slave escapes is based
on contemporary sources.

In 1887 the slaves began to protest directly. Their protest consisted, above all, in passive withdrawal. They left the fazendas, they fled
the slave quarters, they escaped the fields. . . . They were soon called
"migrants," in the ironic language of the abolitionists. The phenomenon
became most widespread, naturally, where the resistance to emancipation
was strongest—in the provinces of São Paulo, Minas Gerais, and Rio de
Janeiro.

Drawing on the newspapers of the period, oral testimony, and two
official reports, we can construct a succinct account of [the slave escapes in
São Paulo] that caused so much upheaval. Without having attacked any
persons or property, a group of slaves left Capivary and headed toward
Santos, thus having to go through Itú. They numbered more than one
hundred. On October 18, 1887, the *Diario Popular* noted that "a band
of fugitives already swollen in number has entered Itú and passed through
the city without encountering any resistance or committing any violence."

Nevertheless, they met a small police force, which was probably over-
confident because of the former passivity of the slaves. The *Provincia de
São Paulo* noted on the following day that "The slaves, who are from a
fazenda in Capivary, passed through Itú quite peacefully, and the only
occasion for conflict was the imprudence of an official who sent eight
soldiers to pursue and perhaps imprison more than sixty slaves."

Despite this intervention by force, the "migrants" continued toward
Santos, following the old road. Near Villa de Santo Amaro, in the vicinity
of São Paulo, they ran into another force (this time of cavalry) that the
government had sent in pursuit. Because it was raining, the soldiers could
not use their carbines. They therefore attacked the Negroes with swords

SOURCE: "Slaves Flee Their Masters" translated from Evaristo de Moraes, A Cam-
panha Abolicionista, 1879–1888 (Rio de Janeiro: Leite Ribeiro, 1924), pp. 304–07.
Printed by permission of Evaristo de Moraes Filho.

and horseback charges. The incident was grave. One soldier and one Negro died.

The government of São Paulo was frightened and asked the Central Government for the assistance of line troops. At the same time it sent in pursuit of the "migrants" a force of sixty enlisted men under the command of Army Captain Canto e Mello. The chief of police personally accompanied the force.

By now the Negroes were already resisting the soldiers in São Paulo, shouting, "Liberty or death!" "Long live liberty!" "Here no one surrenders. We prefer to die!" Finally the authorities gave up their offensive. They adopted a new plan: to encircle the "migrants" in the foothills of Cubatão on the way to Santos, thus taking up a defensive position. The strategy did not succeed. Shrewdly working their way through the woods, the fugitives from captivity succeeded in reaching their blessed Canaan, the high hills, from which they slowly descended in great numbers to Santos.

• • •

But it was not only in São Paulo that the movement assumed this character. In Minas Gerais the slaves also left the fazendas in bands and set out unopposed for Ouro Prêto, where they were to demand liberty and guarantees. In the province of Rio de Janeiro the principal exodus was in Campos. At the beginning of 1888 the fazendas belonging to Srs. Antonio Ferreia, Saturnino Braga, and Orbilio Bastos did not have a single slave. Others were much depleted.

12. *The Army Refuses to Hunt Runaway Slaves (1887)*

By June of 1887 more than one thousand fugitive slaves had gathered in Santos, waiting to flee northward to provinces that were already liberated. Under pressure from irate slaveowners, the Imperial Government sent a gunboat to the *paulista* port. Army detachments were also ordered to the interior of the country to recapture runaway slaves. But the Army was hesitant to assume the role of slavehunter (or *capitão de mato*—"killing captain"—as Brazil's freelance slavehunters were traditionally called), because abolitionist sentiment had deeply penetrated their ranks. The extent of this sentiment became public knowledge in October 1887, when the Military Club, an unofficial organization of Army officers, sent a memorandum to Princess Isabel, the interim monarch in the absence of her ailing father, Dom Pedro II.

SOURCE: "The Army Refuses to Hunt Runaway Slaves" translated from the reprint in R. Magalhães Júnior, *Deodoro: A Espada Contra o Império*, 2 vols. (São Paulo: Companhia Editora Nacional, 1957), pp. 317–18. Printed by permission of Companhia Editora Nacional.

Madame:

The officers of the Army and members of the Military Club request permission of Your Imperial Highness to direct to the Imperial Government a request that is, in fact, an entreaty. All those who are and will continue to be the most dedicated and loyal servants of His Majesty the Emperor and of his dynasty, all those who are the most sincere defenders of the institutions that govern us, and all those who will never fail to make the most courageous sacrifices for your welfare hope that in the case of Army detachments going into the interior with the unquestionable purpose of maintaining order, calming the population, and guaranteeing the sanctity of families, the Imperial Government will not permit the soldiers to be ordered to capture poor Negroes who have fled from slavery either because they have grown tired of suffering horrors or because a ray from the light of liberty has warmed their hearts and lit up their souls.

Madame, freedom is the greatest blessing we possess on earth; once an individual's right to act is violated, he is capable of doing anything to regain it. At any moment the man who was a coward may become a hero; he who before was inert, grows and spreads. Even though he be crushed by the weight of suffering and persecution, even though he be reduced to death, freedom is forever reborn from his ashes purer and more beautiful. Throughout the ages the violent techniques of persecution, which fortunately were not practiced among us, have never produced the desired effect. In vain thousands of men are confined in cold, guarded dungeons, where they die for lack of air and light. Sorrows flow across those ramparts, sufferings filter through those thick walls just as the rays of light filter through glass windows, and they emerge to tell the horrors of martyrdom!

In vain thousands of families are dragged off to endless deserts, where lichen grows and winds sweep the surface of the ice and kiss the steppes. Everything dies there, but the intense hate of the many doomed is brought back and sometimes lodges in the breasts of the persecutors themselves. Thus it is impossible, Madame, to crush the human being who wants to be free.

Therefore, in the name of the most sacred principles of humanity, in the name of human sympathy, in the name of civilization, in the name of Christian charity, in the name of the sufferings of His Highness the Emperor, your august father, whose feelings they believe they express and over whose absence they weep tears of nostalgia, in the name of your future and the future of your son, the members of the Military Club hope that the Imperial Government will not permit the officers and the enlisted men of the Army to be diverted from their noble mission. The Army does not wish the oppression of the black man by the white man, nor would it ever consent that the black man, brutalized by the horrors of slavery, should manage to guarantee his freedom by crushing the white man.

The Army must maintain order. But faced with men who flee calmly, silently, and peacefully, avoiding both slavery and battle and, when passing through cities, offering great examples of morality (the absence of which has often dishonored the most civilized of armies), the Brazilian Army hopes that the Imperial Government will grant it what it respectfully asks in the name of humanity and of the honor of the very flag it defends.

13. *Abolitionist Threats* (1887)

The momentum of abolitionist propaganda seemed irresistible during 1887. Total abolition had come three years earlier in two northern provinces, Ceará and Amazonas, and the city of São Paulo had raised a fund to pay for the liberation of all its slaves. During the legislative session of 1887, Affonso Celso Júnior, an ardently abolitionist Liberal deputy from Minas Gerais, introduced a bill calling for total abolition after a two-year transition period. José do Patrocínio wrote a passionate editorial in the *Gazeta da Tarde* in favor of the bill. The fact that Patrocínio, an intransigent abolitionist, was willing to accept a two-year transition period is further proof of the remarkably conciliatory atmosphere that continued to prevail despite the profound interests at stake.

Today no one in good faith can support slavery as a factor necessary for the economic life of our country, because the arguments that can be produced are flagrantly contradicted by the facts. By the spontaneous decision of the Brazilian people, the slave population has been reduced by two-thirds, and this reduction has in no way reduced the national wealth. On the contrary, the Minister of Finance has just pointed out in the Message from the Throne that government receipts have increased, and this can only come from the greater production and prosperity of the nation, in view of the fact that no direct tax has been imposed on the population.

The history of abolitionist victories around the world, including our own country, is consistent with the claim that we are making. Whenever slavery is struck down, this pruning of the black tree is accompanied by a kind of social rebirth, because the labor released from its fatal shadow can flourish and prosper.

SOURCE: "Abolitionist Threats" translated from the editorial in *Gazeta da Tarde*, May 5, 1887. Reprinted in Affonso Celso Júnior, *Oito Anos de Parlamento* (São Paulo: Melhoramentos, n. d.), pp. 131–32.

Everyone remembers that when the slave traffic was really extinguished, we entered a period of commercial and industrial activity that greatly profited the country and that might be considered the renaissance of our commerce and industry.

If the Imperial Government had then put its duty and the rights of all above the interests of petty political and oligarchical maneuverings, a redemption of the public spirit would have taken place, and now, instead of being a nation that is the scandal of America and of the civilized Old World, we would be one of the examples of human greatness and glory in our century.

We are much better blessed by nature than the United States, since we have greater mineral reserves and a soil of providential fertility. Furthermore, we have a vast area, which offers all climates for human adaptation. We have been able to fuse all races into a single native population, because Portuguese colonization assimilated the savage races instead of trying to destroy them, thus preparing us to resist the devastating invasion of race prejudice.

.   .   .

The proposal of Sr. Affonso Celso finds its best defense, aside from the talent of its proponent, in the history of the country. It is not a great leap in the dark that he wishes to carry out. It is a measured and safe step toward the future. In two years the more backward sectors of our agriculture could perfectly well arm themselves with the instruments necessary for the conversion of their labor force. The slaves, for their part, would have received a first baptism of liberty and would have begun to receive wages and guidance in the legal confirmation of their new position, and after the two years they would have had the necessary apprenticeship in free labor.

Slaveocracy, however, will not see with certainty that its hour has come and that this proposal is a friendly warning given by the aspirations of a majority of the Brazilian people. It will be blind once again, looking to its past like a worthless son to an inheritance from his parents, and perhaps it will not allow the Brazilian nation to celebrate proudly in 1889 the centenary of the Rights of Man by recognizing the legal equality of all Brazilians. Perhaps stubbornness is forcing us abolitionists to write in red letters the decree that is dictated to us by the unanimous voice of civilization.

14. A Conservative Minister Pleads
for Realism (1888)

On May 8, 1888, Rodrigo Augusto da Silva, Minister of Agriculture in the Conservative government organized by João Alfredo Correia de Oliveira to preside over the final step toward abolition, proposed to the Chamber of Deputies a bill of admirable simplicity. It contained two articles: "Slavery in Brazil is declared extinct" and "All provisions to the contrary are hereby revoked." Once again, as in 1871 and 1885, it was the Conservatives and not the Liberals who formed the government that managed to turn proposals into reality. The following excerpts are from a speech in which Silva defended his proposal and himself from the charge that he had betrayed his party's principles.

On the one hand we see agitation in favor of declaring the end of slavery in the country, and on the other hand we see that all the forces of resistance have been broken. What ought to be the course of action for any man in public life who is entrusted with the responsibility of government and is responsible for legality and order?

．　　．　　．

There is not a single respectable organ of the press . . . that is not engaged in the great crusade. I can recall the intervention of some, against which the action of the Government was ineffective, if not useless. The episcopate, with its holy word, has been speaking to the hearts of the faithful through eloquent sermons, which are anointed in love and piety and which suggest the manumission of slaves as the most beautiful commemorative offering for the jubilee of the Holy Father.[1] . . . Youth, during all of the noble festivals in their schools, are giving events a new aspect and attracting followers, including all of us who are fathers and admirers of these emissaries of our future greatness. On all important occasions in private family life and at all great public ceremonies, the freeing of slaves has become an obligatory climax. . . . All this supports the measure that we have had the honor to propose.

What is even more extraordinary is that those who are most interested in maintaining slave property are offering the most admirable examples of self-denial every day by unconditionally liberating their slaves. I can cite here the consistent opinion of the courts, which favor, as far as possible,

---

[1] [That is, the fiftieth anniversary of the ordination of Pope Leo XIII.]
SOURCE: "A Conservative Minister Pleads for Realism" translated from the reprint in Affonso Celso Júnior, *Oito Anos de Parlamento* (São Paulo: Melhoramentos, n.d.), pp. 137–38.

the most liberal solutions. There is also the attitude of classes and groups, which invariably distinguish themselves by obeying passively and which prove unresponsive to any suggestions that are more risky or compromising. Finally, I can cite the voice of the press, that great bastion of opinion, which is the principal factor in this reform.

Now, if we look at this movement, this peaceful agitation that is everywhere, can we who hold power cross our arms and let the revolution decree the liberation of the slaves? That would be a fatal error for our institutions, a precedent that might in any future upheaval neutralize the action of public authorities and deliver the direction of society to the rebelling populace.

15. *The Delirium of the "Golden Law"* (1888)

In May 1888, Rio was virtually taken over by the abolitionists. They crowded the halls leading to the chambers of Parliament, much to the disgust of the diehard opponents of abolition. The popular pressure could not be resisted, and Princess Isabel agreed to sign into law the Rodrigo Silva Bill, which Parliament had quickly passed. It fell to the Princess to sanction total abolition, since her father, Dom Pedro II, was still in Europe on an extended health cure. The following description of the signing appeared in O *País*, a Rio daily of abolitionist and republican sympathies.

Popular celebrations exploded yesterday in a way that we have very seldom witnessed. . . . The decree for immediate and unconditional abolition was to be signed, and for this purpose the Senate convened in special session. . . .

An hour before the Senate session began, the areas surrounding the building were filled with people who eagerly awaited the voting of the glorious law.

The Abolitionist Confederation, gallantly holding up its standards, represented the victors, who awaited the confirmation of the law for which they had battled so boldly. . . .

Outside as well as inside, the people were excited, restlessly shifting in waves, waiting for the moment when it would be announced that with the Princess Regent's signature slavery would disappear from Brazil.

The instant the first applause greeting the vote in the august assembly

SOURCE: "The Delirium of the 'Golden Law'" translated from O *País* (Rio de Janeiro), May 14, 1888.

was heard outside, enthusiastic cheers went up, accompanied by a great quantity of fireworks.

Whenever one of the senators or deputies who had most distinguished themselves in the abolitionist campaign appeared at a window, the people greeted him with a shout and continued their demonstrations. . . .

At three in the afternoon, with the courtyard, staircases, and adjoining rooms of the imperial palace all packed with onlookers eager to witness the solemn act of signing the redemptive law, Her Imperial Highness and her husband arrived.

Noisy ovations exploded from all the rooms that the crowd could invade.

Once the drapes were pulled aside, the people invaded the throne room, where Her Highness the Princess was.

After the Senate commission entered the room, Councillor Dantas, rapporteur for the commission, read the following speech, written by Councillor Affonso Celso:

> Madame: The special Senate commission, having fulfilled the duty of presenting for the sanction of Your Imperial Regent Highness the law that henceforth extinguishes slavery in our country, reverently asks permission of Your Imperial Highness, in the first place, to rejoice with Your Imperial Highness and all Brazilians at . . . the improvement in the health of His Highness the Emperor—the first representative of the nation and also the first among the staunchest defenders of the great and joyful event that has just taken place—and in the second place we ask to congratulate Your Imperial Highness for having taken upon herself the glory of signing the law that erases the nefarious dishonor from our laws, since it is now appropriate for you to confirm the decree that does not allow any more slaves to be born in the Empire of the Southern Cross. . . .

Entering the next room, Her Highness received from Dr. Luiz Pedro Drago the pen acquired with the sum raised by the popular donations to be used in the signing of the Golden Law.

Her Highness expressed her gratitude, but it was not possible for us to hear her words because of the crowd that filled the palace room.

Then the Regent received the document from the hands of Councillor João Alfredo, president of the Council, and signed it with that pen. . . .

The Abolitionist Confederation, represented by our colleague of the *Cidade do Rio*, José do Patrocínio, who spoke, offered Her Highness a beautiful bouquet of artificial violets and camellias with green and yellow ribbons, on which was inscribed: "*Libertas Alma Mater*—To Her Imperial Regent Highness—the Abolitionist Confederation—May 13, 1888."

As soon as the news of the signing of the decree was announced, the bands stationed in front of the palace played the national hymn, and festive demonstrations rose in fervor, prolonging themselves late into the night.

The enthusiasm of the people rapidly increased and spread, and at their request Her Highness the Imperial Princess appeared at one of the windows of the palace, where she was met with the resounding and unanimous greeting of the more than ten thousand people who filled the Largo do Paco Square.

16. *The Melancholy Aftermath of Abolition*

> Once abolition was enacted, the ex-slave became just another member of the illiterate mass, to which little thought had been given at any time. The failure of the abolitionists to take an interest in the fate of the ex-slaves was candidly admitted by Joaquim Nabuco in his classic autobiography, *Minha Formação* (*My Early Years*), published in 1900.

The movement against slavery in Brazil was humanitarian and social in character, rather than religious. For this reason, it did not have the moral profundity of the movement that grew up, for example, among the abolitionists of New England. It consisted of heterogeneous elements that were capable of destroying a social structure erected upon privilege and injustice, but were not capable of building a new edifice on other foundations. Therefore, its work naturally ended with the suppression of slavery. Its triumph was followed . . . by political accidents that even included revolutions, but not by any supplementary measures for the benefit of the freedmen, any great inner movement, any renovation of the public conscience, or any expansion of the noble instincts that had been lulled to sleep. Liberty alone and in itself is fertile, and in time a more unified society of broader ideas will grow up on the ruins of slavery. It is possible that this society will claim as its founding fathers those men whose only contribution was to end the oppression that once overshadowed birth. . . . The truth is, however, that the abolitionist current stopped on the day of abolition, and on the following day it receded.

17. *The Fate of the Ex-Slave in São Paulo*

> The most prosperous area of Brazil after abolition was São Paulo, which continued to experience a spurt of industrialization largely

SOURCE: "The Melancholy Aftermath of Abolition" translated from Joaquim Nabuco, *Minha Formação* (Rio de Janeiro: José Olympio, 1957), pp. 209–10.
SOURCE: "The Fate of the Ex-Slave in São Paulo" translated from Florestan Fernandes, A *Integração do Negro à Sociedade de Classes* (Rio de Janeiro: Centro Brasileiro de Pesquisas Educacionais, 1964), pp. 41–43. Printed by permission of the Centro.

financed by profits from coffee. Many new jobs opened up, but few went to ex-slaves. In fact, men of color generally found great difficulty in being assimilated into the dynamic economy of this region. This pattern has been studied by Florestan Fernandes of the University of São Paulo, who has directed a large-scale investigation of the last hundred years of race relations in the region from São Paulo southward. The following passages are from his massive study of the ex-slave in the rapidly industrializing economy of São Paulo.

The essential fact about the position of the Negroes and mulattoes in the new social and economic order is that they were excluded as a social group from the modern trends of capitalist expansion in São Paulo. The two poles of that socioeconomic process were the social circles of the dominant classes and the human masses transplanted from Europe. Negroes and mulattoes shared in the success brought by these developments only sporadically—whenever they could be taken for members of the "great families" or were accidentally caught up in the waves of prosperity that favored the marginally educated sectors of society and the migratory parts of the native population.

In interviews carried out as part of our research on this subject, it became clear that the whites interpreted the ex-slaves' situation in psychological terms: The mulattoes and Negroes "had no ambition," and therefore, unlike the European immigrants, they did not subject themselves to the stern discipline of saving in order to achieve capitalist accumulation, occupational mobility, and social ascension. The Negroes and mulattoes who were interviewed showed more realism, explaining that they had been convinced that they lacked the means to enter into the process of economic expansion in the form of competition with white nationals or with immigrants.

.   .   .

They took advantage of the gaps created by the sudden economic growth without any larger idea of benefiting from the positions created by the trends of the capitalist development then under way.

The explanation of this fact is apparently to be found in the particular psychosocial condition of the recently freed slave. The slave and the manumitted ex-slaves were prepared only for the economic and social roles that were vital for the slave society's own internal equilibrium. As for anything else, the prevailing trend was to prevent any development of organized social life among the slaves and the manumitted because of the constant fear of "black rebellion." As Perdigão Malheiro wrote [in 1866], the slave appeared as "a domestic enemy" and "a public enemy": "He is a volcano that constantly threatens society, a mine ready to explode at the least spark." For this reason, every form of organization or solidarity among the slaves was forbidden and destroyed, since there was a clear realization that only by imposing an atmosphere of *anomie* would it be possible to secure and perpetuate the submission of the slaves and the fundamental dependence of the manumitted. At the same time, a refined and severe system of supervision and punishment was maintained in order to guarantee the subservience of the slave and the security of the master and his family as well as the slaveocratic social order. The rigidity with which this entire system was set up in São Paulo is proved by the reports that accompanied the news of slave escapes. Since the whites were lost on isolated farms or lived in primitive cities and since they had precarious police protection, being almost everywhere a numerical minority, they could observe the laws meant to protect the slaves only at some risk to themselves. By every possible means they prevented any organization of the slaves or the manumitted, and they monopolized the use of violence as a mechanism of social control. The effect of all this was that the Negro and the mulatto emerged from the world of slavery without any preparation for organizing their lives or for integrating themselves normally into the predominant social order. Not only did they come out of slavery as morally and materially exploited beings, but the overwhelming majority were bereft of any means by which they could assert themselves as a separate social group or by which they could be rapidly integrated into the social groups open for their participation.

CONCLUSION

As the readings make clear, the debate in Brazil between the opponents and the proponents of slavery proceeded within a context very different from that which obtained in the United States prior to our Civil War.

First, in Brazil no significant attempt was made to defend slavery as justifiable in either moral or religious terms. Most of slavery's advocates admitted that it was immoral, but they argued that it was necessary to Brazil's continued existence. Second, no extensive "biological" justification of slavery or systematic theory of racial inferiority was ever elaborated. Third, slavery was recognized as a national problem, not a regional one. Although planters from prosperous São Paulo sometimes complained that abolitionists from the Northeast could afford to preach total abolition because their own decaying economy had little to lose, the entire political elite conceded that a decision of the national Congress would settle matters throughout the Empire.

In another respect, however, the Brazilian debate over slavery sounded much like the controversy in the United States. Many members of the Brazilian elite, especially the younger ones, opposed slavery because they thought it degraded their country in the eyes of "civilization." Abolition was for them, as it was for many antislavery leaders in North America, an indispensable step toward making their country a respectable member of the family of nations.

Brazil's solution to the problem of slavery was gradualist; the institution was undermined piecemeal by a series of scattered measures. The first step was the Law of the Free Womb in 1871. Then in 1884 the provinces of Ceará and Amazonas became the first provinces in which all slaves had been freed (by manumission). The next year Parliament passed a bill granting freedom to all slaves over sixty years old. The supporters of slavery fought fiercely against every concession, demanding liberal compensation in return for any further abolitionist legislation. They also ridiculed the abolitionists' preoccupation with the opinion of foreign humanitarians. During the remaining four years of slavery, there was an unceasing campaign led by representatives of the younger generation of the established elite, such as Joaquim Nabuco and Affonso Celso Júnior, along with black and mulatto orators such as José do Patrocínio and the distinguished engineer André Rebouças, who helped finance the abolitionist movement. In the end, slavery was undermined from every direction: Slaves fled their masters, the Army and the police refused to recapture them, and the courts began to ignore the claims of the owners. When Princess Isabel signed the Golden Law, she brought to a culmination the humanitarian movement that had succeeded in dominating Brazilian politics. She also ratified a process long under way: the replacement of slave labor by free labor.

Brazil's gradualist solution had the advantage of giving the planters—especially the owners of the more modern coffee plantations—ample time to adjust to the inevitable disappearance of forced labor. By the 1850's some of them were already discovering that European immigrants were more efficient and cheaper in the long run than slave labor. The abolitionists tried to mobilize the support of these planters by constantly pointing out that the much-needed immigrants could not be attracted as long as slavery remained.

Abolition in Brazil thus resulted from both humanitarian concern and hard-headed business calculations. Slavery was replaced by wage labor in the farms and homes of Brazil, just as it had been throughout the New World. The manner in which it was replaced, however, reflected Brazil's deep-seated conciliatory political tradition as well as her long-standing experience with a multiracial society of free men.

This is not to say that Brazil emerged from a slave-based economy with no negative heritage. Having solved the narrow legal problem of forced servitude, Brazil then faced the challenge—today still largely unmet—of assimilating the ex-slaves, along with the large mass of unskilled and illiterate workers, into a modern society of equal opportunity. But in dealing with this problem, the nation enjoys at least one advantage: Abolition came through the good offices of politics rather than the holocaust of civil war.

BIBLIOGRAPHY

Boxer, C. R. *Race Relations in the Portuguese Colonial Empire, 1415–1825* (London: Oxford University Press, 1963). Contests Freyre's claim that the Portuguese colonizers showed virtually no color prejudice.

Davis, David Brion. *The Problem of Slavery in Western Culture* (Ithaca, N.Y.: Cornell University Press, 1966). First volume of an ambitious comparative study that includes Brazil.

Freyre, Gilberto. *The Masters and the Slaves*, 2nd ed. (New York: Alfred A. Knopf, 1956), and *The Mansions and the Shanties* (New York: Alfred A. Knopf, 1963). Two important works by the most influential writer on Brazilian slavery.

Furtado, Celso. *The Economic Growth of Brazil* (Berkeley: University of California Press, 1963). Analyzes slavery as a factor in Brazil's economic history.

Graham, Richard. "Causes for the Abolition of Negro Slavery in Brazil: An Interpretive Essay," in *Hispanic American Historical Review*, 46 (May 1966). A recent reinterpretation, with an excellent bibliography.

Haring, C. H. *Empire in Brazil* (Cambridge, Mass.: Harvard University Press, 1958). Useful study of the political context of nineteenth-century Brazil.

Harris, Marvin. *Patterns of Race in the Americas* (New York: Walker, 1964). Criticizes Freyre and Tannenbaum for having neglected demographic factors in their comparisons of Latin and Anglo-Saxon America.

Mörner, Magnus. *Race Mixture in the History of Latin America* (Boston: Little, Brown, 1967). A useful survey treatment, with an extensive bibliography.

Nabuco, Carolina. *The Life of Joaquim Nabuco* (Stanford, Calif.: Stanford University Press, 1950). Biography of the famous abolitionist, written by his daughter.

Rodrigues, José Honório. *Brazil and Africa* (Berkeley: University of California Press, 1965). Provides much valuable information on the slave trade and miscegenation in Brazil.

Stein, Stanley. *Vassouras: A Brazilian Coffee County, 1850–1900* (Cambridge, Mass.: Harvard University Press, 1957). A meticulous study of one area of coffee plantation slavery.

Tannenbaum, Frank. *Slave and Citizen: The Negro in the Americas* (New York: Alfred A. Knopf, 1947). A pioneer comparative study that emphasizes law and religion as having limited the dehumanizing effects of slavery in Latin America.

VI

The Problem of Identity
and National Destiny
in Peru and Argentina

Fredrick B. Pike

CHRONOLOGY

Peru

1569–81   Viceroy Francisco de Toledo governs the kingdom of Peru. He suppresses Túpac Amaru I's Indian uprising and decrees the transfer of over one million Indians to new communities. To this day he stands as a symbol in the identity debate, praised by *hispanistas*, condemned by *indigenistas*.

1780   Túpac Amaru II leads an uprising in the sierra, demanding justice for the Indians. Degenerating into a race war, it plants terror of Indians in the hearts of coastal Peruvians.

1812   The population of the viceroyalty is estimated at: 178,000 Spaniards (creoles and peninsulares), living mainly on the coast; 955,000 Indians, nearly all of whom reside in the sierra; 287,000 mestizos, interspersed throughout the kingdom but concentrated in the sierra; 89,000 Negro slaves and 45,000 free Negroes and negroid castes, living almost exclusively on the coast.

1829–33   Mestizo Agustín Gamarra serves as president, suggesting that prejudices are more cultural than racial.

1854   Mestizo President Ramón Castilla abolishes Negro slavery and suppresses payment of Indian tribute.

1879–83   Peru and its ally, Bolivia, are defeated by Chile in the War of the Pacific. In the aftermath of defeat, intellectuals concern themselves over the plight of the Indian, convinced that if the natives had been assimilated, participating citizens, Peru could have crushed Chile.

1894   Manuel González Prada publishes *Páginas libres*, in which he denigrates white, coastal Peru, extols the Indian, and sees Peruvian progress as depending upon a violent Indian uprising.

1900–14   The modernization and mechanization of coastal agriculture begin. This widens the gulf between the coast and the sierra, where archaic agricultural methods and semifeudal practices prevail.

1921–23   A commission to investigate Indian violence in the sierra is appointed. The commission's report, recommending land reform, is ignored, because absentee owners of sierra estates (*gamonales*) dominate the National Congress.

1924   The Alianza Popular Revolucionario Americano (APRA) is founded by Víctor Raúl Haya de la Torre and other Peruvians in exile in Mexico. Although fundamentally concerned with middle-sector support, the APRA advances an indigenista program and hails González Prada as a precursor.

1928   José Carlos Mariátegui, after breaking with APRA intellectuals, publishes his indigenista, Marxist-influenced analysis of Peruvian history, *Siete ensayos de interpretación de la realidad peruana.* Shortly, Víctor Andrés Belaúnde replies in his *La realidad nacional,* stressing the importance of Spanish-Catholic traditions and thereby initiating one of Peru's most significant intellectual exchanges.

1932–33   Luis M. Sánchez Cerro, who prides himself on being a *cholo* and is the first candidate to campaign widely among Indian communities, is elected president, triumphing over Haya de la Torre. Within sixteen months Sánchez Cerro is assassinated, apparently as the result of an APRA plot. Peru is plunged into virtually an Aprista–anti-Aprista civil war, and the situation is complicated by the tendency of hispanistas to identify with Fascism and of indigenistas to identify with Communism and socialism.

1939–45   World War II market conditions result in a prosperity that diverts the attention of coastal Peruvians from the Indian and other social problems.

1948–56   Military dictator Manuel Odría launches lavish building programs in Lima but ignores provincial, rural, Indian Peru.

1963   Fernando Belaúnde Terry is elected to a six-year presidential term. The Cooperación Popular program is launched, encouraging skilled coastal Peruvians to establish contact with Indian communities of the sierra, estimated to number at least five thousand, and to aid them in initiating community development projects.

1964   An agrarian reform law is passed, promising to return lands illegally acquired by private owners in the sierra to Indian communities. Passage of the law reveals that gamonales have lost the political power they wielded in the 1920's.

1965   As land redistribution begins, Indian violence in the sierra tends to subside. Greater Lima has approximately two million inhabitants, nearly half of whom are migrants from rural, largely Indian communities. The total national population is about eleven million. Overall urban population is estimated at forty-eight per cent, compared to thirty-five per cent in 1940.

1966–67   Important progress is made on the *carretera marginal,* a highway along the eastern slopes of the Andes that is expected to link Peru with Colombia, Ecuador, and Bolivia and to open undeveloped areas to Indian migration, thus relieving pressure on coastal cities.

Argentina

1824–27   Bernardino Rivadavia, as governor of Buenos Aires province and would-be president of a united La Plata, attempts to suppress various privileges of the Catholic Church. Prominent Church leaders oppose Rivadavia, accusing him of trying to introduce the heresies of foreign lands.

1835–52   Dictator Juan Manuel de Rosas maintains friendly relations with many provincial *caudillos* but quickly alienates the *porteño* intelligentsia, many of whose members, including Domingo Faustino Sarmiento, find their way into exile. Ownership of large estates is consolidated in the hands of a few. Thus, when immigrants later begin to arrive, they will generally have to accept tenant-farmer status in rural Argentina. Many will prefer to remain in the greater Buenos Aires area.

1853   A constitution with many liberal political provisions is promulgated. In its omission of serious immigration restrictions, the charter reflects the influence of Juan Bautista Alberdi.

1875   Newly arriving immigrants number approximately sixty thousand.

1876   The first refrigerator ship reaches Buenos Aires, an event that will give impetus to the rise of a scientific cattle industry and augment the economic power of the landowning aristocrats (*estancieros*).

1884   Church leaders severely criticize the program of lay, public instruction, which excludes religious instruction, as contrary to Argentina's spiritual traditions. The Government responds by exiling the Bishop of Córdoba.

1885   Newly arriving immigrants number over 100,000.

1890   Immigrants number over 220,000.

1891   The Radical Civil Union (ultimately, the Radical party) is founded, its membership made up largely of immigrant-origin, urban groups. It assumes the role of opposition, violent and nonviolent, to the dominant Autonomist National party, which to a considerable extent represents the estancieros.

1894–96   A Socialist party is founded as extremist elements begin to infiltrate labor and intellectual circles. This intensifies the concern of creole aristocrats about foreign immigrants and their alien ideologies.

1900–10   Immigration again soars, after a decline in the 1890's occasioned by a serious Argentine depression, reaching 210,-000 in 1910.

1912   An honest electoral law is proclaimed, preparing the way for Radical party electoral triumphs and manifesting the moderation and compromising spirit of some aristocratic elements.

1914   In a total population of approximately eight million, men outnumber women by 518,000. The disproportion between the sexes is particularly striking in Buenos Aires, where it leads to widespread prostitution and frequent fighting among men for the attention of women. Provincial Argentines have come to view Buenos Aires as a turbulent, sinful city that is infecting national society. The allegedly erotic tango, a popular dance among lower-class porteños, is regarded as a symbol of the depravity caused in part by immigration.

1916   Radical party candidate Hipólito Irigoyen is elected president. Some traditionalists are alarmed by the political power of immigrant-origin, urban sectors.

1922–28   The presidency of Marcelo T. de Alvear produces a split in the ranks of Argentine Radicalism. One faction supports Alvear and seeks accommodations with the landowning aristocracy; another faction backs Irigoyen and proclaims intransigent opposition to traditionalist elements.

1930   Beset by problems of the worldwide depression, Irigoyen is forced to resign after beginning his second term. General José Félix Uriburu seizes the presidency and hopes to transform Argentina into a corporate state. Traditionalist, creole elitist elements appear to have triumphed. (For additional chronology of post-1930 events, see Chapter X.)

1936–43   An annual average of seventy thousand provincials arrive in the greater Buenos Aires locale from rural Argentina and Bolivia. This influx begins to alarm well-to-do sectors of porteño society. To a large extent, newly-arrived provincials constitute the *descamisados* (shirtless ones) who will be wooed by Juan and Eva Perón.

1960   The urban agglomeration of greater Buenos Aires, continuing to grow rapidly as the result of a rural-to-urban population shift, has approximately six million inhabitants. The national population of over twenty million is estimated to be sixty-nine per cent urban, in comparison to thirty-seven per cent in 1895.

INTRODUCTION

The individual, if he is to function effectively in society and develop his potential, requires a sense of identity. Loss of this sense results in symptoms of mental illness. Two authorities upon this matter have recently written:

> Identity is the nucleus of the individual's belief system, which serves, in turn, as his blueprint for relating to his physical and social environment. When it is lost, the individual finds it difficult to live with himself, or to adapt to the reality around him. If he is ever to function viably, he must find the answer to three related questions: (1) Who am I? (2) What is the nature of the society and of the world in which I live? (3) How can I relate to it? [1]

Nations, too, require a sense of identity if they are to proceed consistently toward the realization of their possibilities for cultural and economic development. And, just as an individual's sense of identity springs from the form and extent of his self-understanding, so a nation's sense of identity is determined largely by its understanding of its own history. Widely accepted historical interpretations, or agreement by the majority of a people as to who their heroes and who their villains have been, which events have been triumphs and which ones tragedies, can provide an indispensable glue for holding together disparate geographic and ethnic groups within a country.

In Peru, no standard historical interpretations of this kind exist. Rather, as Peru's greatest twentieth-century historian, Jorge Basadre, has said, the teaching and writing of history in his country have constituted a perpetual civil war.[2] The same statement is applicable to Argentina, although for different reasons. In Argentina, the discord has been caused primarily by differing interpretations over the role that nineteenth- and early twentieth-century immigration has played in shaping national destiny. In Peru, debate has centered upon the potential of the main ethnic groups—Spanish, Indian, and mestizo—that have comprised the population since the middle of the sixteenth century, when Spaniards began massive miscegenation with the Indians.

On the surface, it would appear unlikely that disagreement over the

---

[1] Walter Adams and Adrian Jaffe, "A Special Report on Government, the Universities, and International Affairs: A Crisis in Identity" (Washington, D.C.: prepared for the United States Advisory Commission on International Educational and Cultural Affairs, 1967), p. 1.

[2] Jorge Basadre, *Meditaciones sobre el destino histórico del Perú* (Lima: Ediciones Huascarán, 1947), p. 48.

potential of the white, predominantly Spanish-origin element in Peruvian society could be the occasion of continuing divisiveness. By 1940, Indians comprised an estimated 45.9 per cent of the Peruvian populace and mestizos 52.9 per cent. Taking into account the .5 per cent of the country's inhabitants who were Negro, Spanish-origin whites in Peru could scarcely have constituted one per cent of the population in 1940.[3] How, then, could disagreement over the abilities, historical accomplishments, and future potential of the Spanish-origin white Peruvians have produced the bitter disputes that have divided the country for generations and even centuries?

The answer must be sought partially in the social, intellectual, political, and economic influence and power which the Spanish-origin, white element of the Peruvian population has been able to exercise from colonial times to at least the early twentieth century. Moreover, a large number of Peruvian mestizos pass for white, consciously identify with the white group, and thereby vastly augment the effective power of that tiny minority at the apex of the social pyramid.

When these factors are taken into account, it is easier to understand how Basadre can write, with ample justification, that the main battles in Peru's incessant historiographical civil war have been fought between one group of teachers and writers (the *hispanistas*) bent upon venerating the Spaniards and contemptuously dismissing all those of different ethnic origins, and a second group (the *indigenistas*) dedicated to exalting the Indian and denigrating all other racial elements. For the first group, the Spaniards are heroes, and the conquest is a triumph of unmitigated glory. And Peru can never keep its rendezvous with destiny unless it builds upon the foundations of its Hispanic, colonial values and eschews the influence of native traditions. For the second school, the Indians alone are heroes, and the conquest is a tragedy. The future greatness of Peru, moreover, depends on the country's being guided by models that inhere in pre-Colombian civilization, especially in the communal, collectivist features of Inca life.

The passage of centuries has not served to raise appreciably the level of debate over the nature of the Indian and his preconquest empire. Since the arrival of the conquerors and their chroniclers, with the outstanding exception of a very few writers, most Peruvian historians have been guided by romantic attitudes and unfounded prejudices, glib exaggerations and superficial generalizations, and have given themselves over to uncritical exaltation or contemptuous denigration of Peru's aborigines and their historical feats.

[3] Center on Intercultural Formation (Cuernevaca, Mexico), *Study No. 1, Socio-Economic Data: Latin America in Maps, Charts, Tables,* compiled by Yvan Labell and Adriana Estrada (Mexico, D.F., 1963), p. 77.

Various chroniclers of the early conquest period found much to admire in the empire of Tahuantinsuyo, as the Inca confederation was called, and its citizens. One of the most reliable of all sixteenth-century chroniclers, Pedro Cieza de León, described the Indians as people of great intelligence and in many respects altogether admirable, because of their just customs and good laws.[4] A far more glowing account was presented by Juan Espinosa, a leading exponent of nineteenth-century liberalism in Peru, who described the Indian as "docile, sweet, kind, hospitable, loving, humble, religious, pure in his customs, obedient to duty and religion, industrious, able, hard-working, intelligent, quick to learn, patient, scientific in his knowledge of botany and medicine." The Indian, concluded Espinosa, "was happy because he was good before the arrival of those fierce men from Spain who corrupted him and his nature." [5]

On the other hand, the sixteenth-century chronicler Juan de Matienzo depicted the Indians of Peru as timid, fatalistic, indolent, and not endowed with intelligence equal to that of Spaniards.[6] And the nineteenth-century positivist Luis Carranza argued that the lowly estate in which Peru's Indian elements then found themselves was not owing to the harsh treatment they had received from the Spaniards but to the "psychological aberrations" that were characteristic of the "singular and curious" Indian race.[7]

Obviously in fundamental disagreement over the past and potential value of Indian civilization, the Peruvians have been just as divided in assessing the contribution of the Spaniards. Rafael Cubas, a rather typical hispanista, has asserted: "It is necessary to recognize as the very essence of Peru its Hispanic nature. This Hispanic nature should be loved and venerated as the reason for our present existence and the source of

---

[4] See Raúl Porras Barrenechea, *Los cronistas del Perú, 1528–1650* (Lima: Sanmartí Impresores, 1962), for a description of the attitudes of Cieza de León and other chroniclers toward the Indians.

[5] Juan Espinosa, *Diccionario para el pueblo: republicano, democrático, moral, política, y filosófico* (Lima: Imprenta del Pueblo, 1855), pp. 609–10. Translations of Spanish materials in the introduction are by the editor.

[6] See Raúl Porras Barrenechea, *Mito, tradición e historia del Perú* (Lima: Imprenta Santa María, 1951), pp. 47–48.

[7] Luis Carranza, *Artículos publicados por . . . segunda colección de artículos* (Lima, 1888), 2, pp. 49–51. In Chapter II of this book, John Phelan presents documents that reveal conflicting Spanish attitudes in regard to the Indians. In Peggy Korn's chapter (IV), Readings 1, 3, and 4 pertain to attitudes of officials in New Spain toward the Indian masses. In Charles Gibson's chapter (III), Reading 4 sets forth the attitudes of two eighteenth-century Spanish officials toward Ecuador's Indians.

Watching a demonstration of a new sewing machine in the Peruvian Alto Plano between Cuzco and Puño. *Dick Davis, Photo Researchers.*

our right to that existence; as the only foundation for our hopes of future development and salvation." [8]

An altogether different appraisal has been presented by one of Peru's better-known twentieth-century writers, Alberto Hidalgo: "I hate Spain because it has never done anything worthwhile for humanity. Nothing, absolutely nothing. In no order of activity has Spain contributed to the advance of the world. Its children lack inventiveness, imagination, and even intelligence. Spaniards are brutes by nature." [9]

In the 1920's and early 1930's, the Peruvian debates over identity and the true nature of national destiny reached a peak of intensity and bitterness. Luis E. Valcárcel insisted that only the Indian could redeem and regenerate Peru. He saw Peru's future in the imposition by the Indian of his allegedly collectivist civilization on the entire country. "European culture," he wrote, "has never truly affected the Indian. Peru is Indian and will be Indian. . . . The only true Peru is Indian Peru." [10] Another indigenista of the period wrote, "Peru will not emerge as a nation until power is transferred into the hands of the majority, the Indians of the sierra. Peru will not begin genuine political life until the socialist *serranos* [Indian inhabitants of the sierra] take the capital." [11] Reacting against these assertions, one group of Peru's hispanistas, increasingly influenced by Fascism, charged that a combination of "Jewry, Communism, and Protestantism" was trying to take advantage of the Indian issue in order to force alien forms of life and culture on the Peruvian people. Hispanistas at this time tended to dismiss all indigenista movements as Communist fronts. [12]

Indicative of the general level of the discussion was a polemic carried on between *El Comercio*, Lima's leading newspaper, and *La Sierra*, a journal published in Cuzco, the center of Andean Peru. *El Comercio*, speaking for coastal, Westernized Peru, asserted that the country would be better off without its sierra region. *La Sierra*, speaking for the overwhelmingly Indian masses of the Andes, the serranos, retorted: "When it comes to deciding if Peru would be more fortunate without the sierra or without the coast, it can be demonstrated that it would be much more fortunate without the coast." [13]

[8] Rafael Cubas, *Hacia una auténtica concepción de la realidad peruana* (Lima, 1955), p. 30.

[9] Alberto Hidalgo, *Diario de mi sentimiento, 1922–36* (Buenos Aires: Edición Privada, 1937), pp. 340–41.

[10] Luis E. Valcárcel, *Tempestad en los andes* (Lima: Editorial Minerva, 1927), p. 116.

[11] César Góngora P., "La geografía humana del Perú," in *Letras: Órgano de la Facultad de Letras de San Marcos*, primer cuatrimestre, 1936, p. 15.

[12] See *Revista de la Universidad Católica del Perú*, 13, Nos. 4–5 (July–August 1940), pp. 439–40.

[13] *La Sierra*, Año I, No. 5 (May 1927), editorial by J. Guillermo Guevara.

Happily, since the 1940's there has been an increasing tendency among Peruvian intellectuals and statesmen to look to *mestizaje,* the mixing and fusion of all Peru's racial groups and their respective cultural patterns, as the source of historical strengths and values and also as the basis for the country's future greatness. In this new intellectual ambience, the *cholo* or mestizo has found many champions, particularly the essayist-historian José Varallanos. "The cholo," writes Varallanos, "is the only true Peruvian. . . . The cholo is the new person, the mixture of the streams of blood and culture and habits, the man in whom the elements have combined in harmony. . . . He is the symbol of the original affinity among men." [14]

Optimistic about the future that he feels Peru will attain through mestizaje, Varallanos also sees positive features in the country's past:

> The colonial period does not afford just a history of disintegration, conflict, and mutual rejection. . . . Its great feature . . . is its historic work in favor of the harmonious creation that was achieved by the emergence of the cholo. . . . The colonial period prepared the way for the equilibrium, balancing, harmony, and fusion of Spanish and Indian elements in the cholo. . . .[15]

Until Peruvians can achieve wider agreement on the relative capacities and proper roles in society of different ethnic groups and cultures, they will not approach success in their quest for national identity. Luckily, their prejudices are based more on cultural than racial considerations. The discriminated-against Indian can look forward to acceptance and fair treatment if he "ceases to be an Indian," abandons the chewing of coca leaves,[16] and adopts the cultural outlooks, values, habits, dress, and language of the white or cholo, Westernized way of life. Cultural prejudice is less vicious and permanent than racial prejudice, for people can, and in Peru increasingly do, change their cultures quite rapidly.

The main issue in Argentina's search for identity and destiny has not revolved about the conflicts of Western and indigenous values. It is true that one of the country's most revered writers, Ricardo Rojas (1882–1957),

[14] José Varallanos, *El cholo y el Perú* (Buenos Aires: Imprenta López, 1962), pp. 209, 112.
[15] *Ibid.,* pp. 207–09.
[16] Coca leaves are the source of cocaine. Indians of Peru's central sierra often chew the leaves from the time of adolescence, finding in the practice a source of energy and a means of withstanding cold and hunger. Peruvians, even those who are medical doctors, disagree profoundly over the effects produced by this habit. Generally, those who are not favorably inclined toward the Indians contend that mastication of coca leaves results in permanent psychic, physiological, and even genetic damage. Those who incline toward the indigenista position assert that coca-leaf chewing is no more harmful than the chewing of gum or the drinking of tea or coffee.

as a relatively young man in 1910 asserted that the major struggle in Argentine life was between foreign or exotic elements, associated mainly with nineteenth-century European values, and Indian traditions.[17] By Indian traditions, however, Rojas meant particularly the style of life that had developed since the beginning of colonial times in interior, provincial Argentina, which was never so exposed to foreign fashions as the port city of Buenos Aires. And Rojas recognized the important contribution of the Spanish element in shaping the values and patterns of life in provincial Argentina.

Specifically, it was the *gaucho* traditions of rural Argentina that appealed to Rojas. He was impressed above all by the untrammeled individualism and the stubborn insistence upon freedom and self-determination that characterized the gaucho's style of life (a style that roughly resembled a combination of the patterns established on the United States frontier by trappers and adventurers, Indian fighters, and cowboys). Rojas saw the need for the Argentine republic to develop political institutions that would safeguard the precious provincial heritage of individual freedom.

An illustrious predecessor of Rojas, Domingo Faustino Sarmiento (1811–88, President of the Republic 1868–74), had also been a champion of political liberalism, but he saw nothing of value in the colonial, Spanish, Catholic values and traditions of interior Argentina. In fact, Sarmiento identified his country's rural traditions with barbarism.[18] It was the duty of the enlightened *porteños* of Buenos Aires, he believed, to introduce culture and civilization, based upon European and United States models then in vogue, into interior Argentina.

In many ways, the Argentine intellectual Juan Bautista Alberdi was less optimistic than his contemporary Sarmiento about the capabilities of the Argentine capital's mid-nineteenth-century population. He felt that true civilization, shaped by the progressive patterns of life then developing in Western Europe and the United States, could be introduced only by flooding Argentina with waves of immigrants from advanced countries.

By the 1880's, the flood of immigrants desired by Alberdi had become a reality. Between 1881 and 1890, 638,000 immigrants arrived. By 1910 an additional 1,440,000 had established their residence in Argentina. These figures become all the more dramatic when projected against the background of a total Argentine population that in 1869 was less than two million. A comparison with the United States also helps to underline the significance of immigration. The foreign-born in Argentina made up 25.5 per cent of the population in 1895, 30.3 per cent in 1914, and 15.7 per

---

[17] Ricardo Rojas, *Blasón de plata* (Buenos Aires: M. García, 1912).

[18] This was a central thesis which Sarmiento presented in his masterpiece, *Facundo: civilización i barbarie en la república Argentina*, first published in 1845.

cent in 1950. In the United States, the percentage of foreign-born in the total population was 14.4 in both 1890 and 1910, and 6.7 in 1950.[19]

While the French, Germans, Swiss, British, and Irish accounted for about twenty-one per cent of the immigrants arriving in Argentina between 1857 and 1958, Italians and Spaniards constituted forty-six and thirty-three per cent, respectively. Between 1881 and 1900, moreover, Italians outnumbered Spaniards by about three to one. Most of the immigrants settled in and around Buenos Aires and contributed to a process of rapid economic and social transformation. Meanwhile, rural, interior Argentina continued largely in its traditional ways of life. Many thoughtful provincial inhabitants grew apprehensive over the changes being wrought in Buenos Aires, and they even came to fear that Spanish, the pronunciation of which was already noticeably altering in Argentina, would soon be replaced as the national language by Italian.

In 1872, even before immigration had assumed truly massive proportions, José Hernández published an epic poem entitled *El Gaucho Martín Fierro*. This masterpiece challenged the views and prejudices of Sarmiento and Alberdi and glorified the traditions of interior, rural, gaucho Argentina, thus anticipating by some thirty years one of the central contentions that would be championed by Ricardo Rojas. The true national values, Hernández implied, were those of the countryside, and the republic must defend itself against the imposition of alien patterns and traditions. Argentina could only achieve its proud destiny by remaining true to its own unique way of life that had developed spontaneously, in isolation from foreign influence.

Early in the twentieth century, a new group of Argentine intellectuals, headed by the Hispanophile and arch-Catholic glorifier of colonial traditions Manuel Gálvez, gave new and more explicit expression to some of the ideas adumbrated by Hernández in his great poem. The new generation of intellectuals depicted a golden age of the past in which, under Hispanic Catholic influence, spiritual values had prevailed over the skepticism, immorality, and materialism allegedly associated with liberal capitalism as then practiced in Western Europe and the United States. The creole elements of Argentina, those men of Spanish origin who had lived in the land prior to the beginning of massive immigration in the 1880's, were called upon to achieve national unity by forcing their values and patterns of life upon the uncivilized immigrants.

Increasingly, as the twentieth century advanced, the glorifiers of tradition and the revilers of immigrant influence added a new concept to their message: authoritarianism. Influenced in part by Fascist ideology, they

[19] See Arthur P. Whitaker, *Argentina* (Englewood Cliffs, N.J.: Prentice-Hall, 1964), p. 54.

also pragmatically recognized the fact that only through heavy-handed methods could the purportedly enlightened creole leadership continue to force its way of life on the immigrant hordes who together with their off-spring were coming to constitute a majority.

Ricardo Rojas objected to the new direction being taken by the defenders of traditional Argentina. He saw in the Spanish colonial past not the authoritarianism that Gálvez associated with it, but rather a lively concern for individual freedom. Moreover, in 1924 Rojas rejected some of the ideas he had held in 1910 and conceded that European immigrants had made some laudable contributions to the formation of Argentina, precisely through strengthening the values of political liberalism and individual freedom that had been first introduced by Spain and then nourished by the gaucho.[20] In effect, Rojas was advancing a new type of nationalism that paid homage to the contributions of Spaniards, creoles, gauchos, and immigrants.

Rojas made little headway in winning widespread support for his pluralistic nationalism. More and more, the country split into two camps. The traditionalist camp identified itself with the Spanish, spiritual, Catholic colonial past, whose values were said to endure in the provinces, and preached the need for an authoritarian political structure. The other camp identified with the values said to be associated with the immigrant, condoned the obsession with material progress, preached anticlericalism, denied the existence of worthwhile traditions in Argentina prior to the liberal Constitution of 1853, and proclaimed, not always sincerely, the glories of liberal political institutions. For the first group, the country's great political hero was Juan Manuel de Rosas, who as a dictator from 1835 to 1852 had allegedly based his rule upon colonial, Catholic values while respecting rural, provincial traditions.[21] Intellectual heroes for this group included Hernández and Gálvez, and its basest villains and cultural traitors were Sarmiento and Alberdi. The second group, of course, singled out the same men in their reading of Argentine history, but they reversed the hero–villain status. Thus, there arose a situation not unlike the one that would exist in the United States if a deeply meaningful debate still raged as to whether George Washington or Benedict Arnold was the true national hero.

One hero, to be sure, both sides in the Argentine identity debate have tried to claim: the great Liberator, José de San Martín. Traditionalists

---

[20] See Ricardo Rojas, *Eurindia* (Buenos Aires: J. Roldán y Compañía, 1924).

[21] An important work defending Rosas as a champion of true Argentine values is Carlos Ibarguren, *Juan Manuel de Rosas: su vida, su tiempo, su drama* (Buenos Aires: Librería Argentina, 1930). A bitter denunciation of Rosas as a tyrant is José Manuel Estrada, *La política liberal bajo de la tiranía de Rosas* (Buenos Aires: Imprenta Americana, 1873).

point to the San Martín who was the stern disciplinarian and conservative monarchist. Defenders of the post-1853, immigrant values point to
the self-effacing San Martín who withdrew voluntarily from newly
liberated Chile, Peru, and Argentina in deference, so it is said, to the
principles of self-determination and civilian rather than military rule. Thus,
although San Martín is the great symbol of Argentine nationalism, he
means different things to different nationalists, and his figure serves as a
focal point for the exacerbated debates caused by Argentina's agonizing
division over its identity.

In the United States, where the turn-of-the-century surge of immigration contributed proportionately less to the overall population than it did
in Argentina, those already established in the land were able to impose
their standards on the new arrivals, and an enduring conflict did not develop. The situation was roughly comparable in Chile and Colombia,
where immigration was considerably less significant than in the United
States and less significant still than in Argentina. In Uruguay, on the
other hand, the minuscule native population was virtually submerged beneath waves of immigrants in the late nineteenth and early twentieth
centuries; these immigrants succeeded rather easily in imposing their
values upon the small republic.

In Argentina, the problem has been that the immigrants were too
numerous to be forced into the customs and value patterns of previously
established society, but were not powerful enough to impose their customs
and values upon the native sons. The resultant cultural heterogeneity
has made it difficult for Argentina to establish consistent national policy
in any sphere of activity. In Peru, a contrasting situation is found. National cohesiveness in that republic has been prevented by disagreement
over whether marginal Indian masses should be assimilated and over the
effects that such assimilation, if attempted, would have on the type of
society maintained for generations by white, Spanish-origin groups and
those who identify with them.

READINGS

Peru

1. *Socialism and the Indian*

José Carlos Mariátegui (1895–1930), whose ideology was a blend of
Marxian socialism and Peruvian traditions, agreed with most of his
fellow socialist indigenistas that the plight of the native was owing
exclusively to socioeconomic exploitation. As soon as this exploitation
ended, the Indian, in whose culture there allegedly still inhered the
socialist values of the Quechua-speaking pre-Columbian Inca confederation, would be ready to assume his proper place in guiding the
destinies of Peru. The following extracts are from Mariátegui's best-
known book, the first edition of which appeared in 1928.

The faith in the revival of the Indian is not based upon the conviction that the destiny of the Quechua land is to undergo material
Westernization. It is not the civilization or the alphabet of the white man
that will uplift the Indian soul. It is the mystique, the idea of the socialist
revolution. The hope of the Indian rests only in revolution. The same
mystique, the same idea are the decisive factors in the awakening of other
ancient peoples, of other ancient races lying dormant in decadence, such
as the Hindus and Chinese, among others. Today as never before, universal history tends to be ruled by the same laws. How could it be that
the Inca people, who developed the most advanced and harmonious
communist system in history, would be the only people insensitive to
worldwide sentiments? . . .

All of the theories concerning the Indian problem that ignore the fact
that it is a socioeconomic problem are futile, purely verbal, theoretical
exercises that are absolutely discredited. Nor are they redeemed by the
claim that they rest on good intentions. Almost all of these theories have

SOURCE: "Socialism and the Indian" translated from José Carlos Mariátegui, *Siete
ensayos de interpretación de la realidad peruana* (Lima: Biblioteca Amauta, 1943), pp.
25, 29. Translations of all material in the Peruvian section of this chapter are by the
chapter editor.

either hidden or distorted the real problem. Only socialist criticism un-
covers and clarifies the Indian problem. It searches for the causes of the
problem in the country's economy, not in the administrative, juridical, or
ecclesiastical processes, not in the duality or the plurality of races or the
cultural and moral conditions of those races. The Indian problem has its
roots in the nature of our economy, specifically in the system of land
ownership. Any attempt to solve the Indian problem with administrative
or police measures, or with educational reforms or protective laws, will
constitute only a superficial measure so long as feudal *gamonalismo* [1]
persists. . . .

The supposition that the Indian problem is an ethnic one derives its
strength from the most obsolete collection of imperialistic ideas. The
concept of the inferiority of some races was useful to white Westerners in
their work of expansion and conquest. To await the emancipation of the
Indians through a crossing of the native races with white immigrants is
an antisociological attitude, conceivable only in the rudimentary mind of
an importer of blooded livestock. The Asiatic people, to which the Indians
are in no manner inferior, have admirably assimilated Western culture
in its most dynamic and creative aspects without transfusions of European
blood. The concept of the degeneration of the Peruvian Indian is a cheap
invention of the lackeys of feudalism.

2. *Revolution and the Indian*

Hildebrando Castro Pozo (1890–1945), a leading student of Peruvian
Indian communities and a socialist activist, believed it necessary for
the Indian to reject the white man's tutelage and to initiate on his
own the process of Peruvian regeneration. The following selection is
from Castro Pozo's little-known novel *Renuevo de peruanidad*.

Who is the Indian? Is he a being capable of serving as an efficient
instrument in a renovating social revolution? . . . [Not only is he capable
of this, but] the Indian is the most valuable factor in our economic,
productive system and in our entire socioeconomic organization. . . .

[1] [Gamonalismo, referring to the exploitation of Indian peasants through a system
resting upon semifeudal land and labor usages, is described by Thomas R. Ford as
"the condition of inequality of the Indian with respect to the other social classes. . . .
[It] is colonialism and clericalism projected through a century of independent life; it
signifies spoliation . . . the connivance of . . . authorities, clergy, and landowners
in exploiting the Indians without conscience and without scruple." See Ford, *Man and
Land in Peru* (Gainesville: University of Florida Press, 1955), p. 111.]

SOURCE: "Revolution and the Indian" translated from Hildebrando Castro Pozo,
Renuevo de peruanidad (Lima: no publisher given, 1934), pp. 21–24, 26–28.

Studies of the Peruvian *ayllu* [1] prove that it is the least primitive social institution that exists in all our land. And the Indian who has crystallized and protected this institution is one of the most vital and transcendent specimens of *homo sapiens*. This conclusion is amply corroborated by history. . . .

And how can one close his eyes to the present reality? The Army, with the exception of fifty per cent of its officers, is composed of Indians; the great majority of coastal manual laborers, both in industry and agriculture, and all of the rural laborers of the sierra are Indians. In other words, the Indian constitutes the entirety of the economic-political base of the republic.

But of what does the Indian, so indispensable to the republic, complain?

He complains of having had to support and having still to support the whole system fashioned by gamonalismo, by the clergy and the autocratic bureaucracy. These groups have used their system for their own exclusive benefit and to increase their fortunes while depleting the Indian's energy and keeping him permanently in ignorance. The Indian complains about the plundering of his communal land, the ravishing of his daughter's virginity, and the theft of his wife's fidelity. He complains that his people are being castrated, assassinated, and enslaved. . . .

Of what else do the Indians complain? They have begun to grow bitter over not having been real men. Already they have a secret presentiment that they will someday become real men and that they will then be ashamed of having resorted to servile complaint. . . .

Only the Indians and their mestizo descendants, sensitive to their own ideals, can vindicate themselves. Vindication will not be accomplished by the slow and rusty machinery of education, as the lords of gamonalismo imagine. It will come about through a sudden blow, struck in manful posture, in the same way that man reaches out and takes what is essential for survival. . . .

---

[1] [Originating as a nomadic social cell based upon consanguinity, the ayllu had come to be, as the Inca civilization advanced to the sedentary stage, a tribal group located permanently on a carefully delimited area. In each ayllu, land was apportioned to the various interrelated families, while additional tracts were set aside for the support of the Inca ruler, his vast bureaucracy, and the priestly elite. Periodic redistribution of property was made in accordance with the changing number of members in the various families. Property ownership was thus semicommunal, with land being assigned in usufruct rather than in outright ownership. Furthermore, much of the labor on the ayllu was performed in common. According to Mariátegui, Castro Pozo, Valcárcel, and their partisans, twentieth-century Indian communities in the sierra still retained communal-socialistic land and labor systems. Moreover, the Indians were said still to be primarily motivated by collectivist ideals. Recently, anthropologists have challenged this viewpoint, still widely held among Peruvian intellectuals, claiming that fairly early in the twentieth century, the Indians began to lose their collectivist values and to undergo a process of individualization, in the course of which their main desire came to be the outright, fee-simple, private ownership of property.]

Our historical viewpoints proceed from two cultural sources. One source has been Western individualism. . . . The other cultural source is Inca (Quechua-Aymara) communalism, established in the deepest warp of our social and family instincts, which has survived five hundred years of oppression and tyrannical attempts to destroy¯it. Our social and family instincts, renewed with idealism and intuition, turn back now toward communalism, the most just system of economic and social equality among men.

3. *Industrialism and the Indian*

In the 1920's, at the flood tide of indigenista sentiment, Luis E. Valcárcel (1891–   ) extolled the Indians as the only true Peruvians. Twenty years later, the distinguished professor and prolific author seemed willing to accept the permanent place of Peru's Westernized population and called upon its members to initiate a peaceful process aimed at utilization of the Indians' vast potential.

The soul of the Indian has remained resolute and steadfast, completely closed to Spanish penetration. The spiritual landscape of Indian-sierra Peru, like the natural landscape, reveals only fleeting instances of Spanish influence. The Spaniard never gained complete possession of the Indian. Like the heroines of romantic literature, the Indian people were able to tell the Spaniards: "My body will be yours, but never my soul."

The Indians did not offer active resistance; but their attitude of the last four hundred years in developing an intense inactivity has constituted an imperceptible form of sabotage. Pretense, hypocrisy, rapaciousness, inactivity—these are some of the many manifestations of the defensive system of the Indian, through which he has accomplished his main objective, survival. With patience and perseverance, the Indians have overcome the worst crises. For four hundred years, while living in a state of profound introversion, they maintained intact, we scarcely know to what degree, their cultural heritage. As with the people of ancient China, the faith for the Indians has been that the invaders would pass on, that the conquest is only fleeting, and that what is important is to live, to survive, to persevere.

.   .   .

The process of transculturation, effected through Spanish colonization and the contemporary institutions surviving this colonization . . . has

SOURCE: "Industrialism and the Indian" translated from Luis E. Valcárcel, *Ruta cultural del Perú* (México, D.F.: Fondo de Cultura Económica, 1945), pp. 118, 228, 235, 236–37.

impoverished the Indian people. The Indians have lost many of their own
cultural traits without being able to absorb the new integrating elements
of Western culture. The Indian today is simply a shadow of the citizen
of the Tahuantinsuyo empire; and he is not even so much as a vague sketch
of the descendants of the man of Western civilization. But this is only
a temporary situation. This condition of the Indian soul will not endure.
Everything seems to indicate that the Indian is emerging from this darkness; and coastal Peru does not yet realize the significance of this awakening of five million people. . . .

Our country will emerge from its feudal, colonial, and agricultural
state; it will undergo industrialization. In order for this to transpire, there
is no need to increase our population by bringing foreign immigrants,
who have difficulty in establishing roots; it is only necessary to utilize the
five million Indian workers.

With the Indians we are not dealing with a decrepit, tired population,
overcome with disillusionment and the suffering caused by the great crisis
of Western culture; we are dealing with new men. . . . The miracle of
Peruvian transformation can be achieved through a ten-year plan that
will place these millions of Indians under the guidance of experts in industrial development.

Because of an instinctive terror, the populace of coastal Lima has not
been willing to acknowledge the tremendous potential of the Indian. But
today there are increasing pressures from abroad, especially the pressure
of international commerce, which awaits five million new consumers. . . .
These pressures are beginning to force Lima to recognize the urgency of
achieving national integration by equipping the Indian masses to become
a political, economic, and cultural factor in Peru.

DISPARAGEMENT OF THE INDIAN

4. *The Indian as a Machine*

Through his long career as a philosophy professor and political activist, Alejandro O. Deustua (1849–1945) was one of Peru's most popular and influential intellectuals. Despairing of the potential of the
ethnic components of Peru's population, for many years he urged
massive immigration of non-Latin whites as the only hope for his
country's future.

SOURCE: "The Indian as a Machine" translated from Alejandro O. Deustua, *La
cultura nacional*, 2nd ed. (Lima: Empresa Editora El Callao, 1937), pp. 66–68.

Those who have thought that the regeneration of the Indian is attainable have either been influenced by the desire to appear patriotic or else have not taken sufficient account of the magnitude of the educational program that such an endeavor would necessitate. An educational program of this type would require effective methods that no government concerned with Indian regeneration has yet had at its disposal. The complete failure of previously adopted programs is sufficient proof of this statement.

The problem of the moral resurrection of the Indian is concerned primarily with the question: Do there exist in the subconscious depths of the Indian, in a dormant stage, psychic forces that justify a belief in the possibility of resurrection? . . . Within the monotonous, rigidly routine life that experience has indicated and continues to indicate is the Indian's only mode of existence, do there exist any signs that suggest the possibility of redemption? We believe not. The poor and limited base of consciousness of the preconquest Indian does not indicate the presence of a free force endowed with that spontaneity that is necessary for redemptive conversion. The static imagination of the Indian lacks the power to effect the radical transformation that is necessary for moral progress. . . .

[Under these conditions] can we have confidence in the efficacy of education in bringing about a higher moral level in the consciousness of the Indian, thereby qualifying him to participate fruitfully in the evolution of the national conscience? We believe not.

That branch of pedagogy which is primarily concerned with the education of abnormal peoples has not yet discovered sufficiently efficacious methods for transforming a great mass of people burdened by the heavy weight of a lamentable tradition into an element of value to the nation. All that has been done in Mexico, whose resources are vastly superior to ours, has failed to redeem the Indian from the enslavement of his nature. Nor are the Mexican efforts likely to achieve this end in the future.

We believe that the enslavement of the consciousness of the Indian is irremediable. We do not believe in the capacity of the individual consciousness for indefinite progress. We agree with the hypothesis that each individual and each race acquire a certain psychic energy that is limited in its intensity; individuals and races can develop within the various epochs of their history only according to the potential of their psychic energy. What occurs in the individual man is repeated to a certain degree in society, even though it is not totally correct to speak of the inevitability of infancy, youth, and old age in the history of peoples. There are races that overcome certain inherent weaknesses, struggling mightily to surmount the limiting, conserving factors within their natures. Other races succumb readily and thus pass from a state of rigorous dynamism to one that is hopelessly static. Peru unhappily finds itself confronting this second situation. The country's misfortune is owing to the Indian race, which has reached the point of its psychic dissolution and which, because of the biological ridigity of its beings, who have definitely ended their evolutionary cycle, has not been able to transmit to the mestizo peoples the virtues that it exhibited in its period of progress.

It is painful to recognize this fact. But it is necessary to recognize it in order to consider the problem of Indian education in the proper light. It is worthwhile to utilize the mechanical aptitudes of the Indians; it is better still to protect and defend them against all types of exploiters and to instruct them in sanitary and hygienic habits, now so lacking among them. But educational efforts should not pass beyond these limits, sacrificing in what will necessarily be a vain endeavor resources that could be utilized advantageously in satisfying other urgent social needs. The Indian is no more than, and can never be more than, a machine.

IDENTIFICATION WITH THE SPANIARD AND
HISPANIC TRADITIONS

5. *The Spaniard*
and Integral Peruvianness

Víctor Andrés Belaúnde (1883–1966), one of his country's most distinguished writers, teachers, and diplomats, was regarded as a leading spokesman of progressive Catholicism in Peru. Although he advocated an integral "Peruvianness" based upon both Spanish and Indian elements, it is quite clear that he judged the Spanish to be by far the more important of Peru's two main ethnic-cultural components. The following extract is from the revised and expanded edition of Belaúnde's *Peruanidad;* the first edition appeared in Lima in 1942.

The focus in which one views Peruvian culture is determined by those factors that he considers to have inspired the formation of Peru as a spiritual entity. In this regard, there are four well-defined propositions:

1. The peninsularist or exclusively hispanista position, according to which our nationality is simply a prolongation of the culture of the Hispanic Peninsula.

SOURCE: "The Spaniard and Integral Peruvianness" translated from Víctor Andrés Belaúnde, *Peruanidad,* 2nd ed. (Lima: Ediciones Librería Studium, 1957), pp. 268–70.

2. The autochthonous position, which stresses principally the indigenous element of our culture. According to the proponents of this position, the Hispanic element has simply been superimposed and eventually will be absorbed and disappear as the primitive or Indian culture is further developed.

3. The fusionist position, the advocates of which see in the Peruvian nationality and culture the juxtaposition, and in some cases the fusion, of primitive elements with the principles and institutions of Western culture.

4. Finally, the position of integral Peruvianness, the proponents of which say that a living synthesis has been created through the assumption by the Hispanic-Catholic culture of the biological, ecological, and cultural elements of pre-Columbian Peru.

Advocates of the peninsularist position would consider our culture as no more than a calculated imitation of Spanish models. They would thereby ignore the creativity of this Hispanic culture, denying its tremendous capacity to assimilate and to incorporate indigenous elements in fashioning a new synthesis. It is precisely in the ability to create a new synthesis that the supreme merit and unmistakable originality of Spanish colonization are manifest. Thus the peninsularist interpretation, ostensibly Hispanophile in its viewpoint, is, because of its narrowness and exclusiveness, a denial of the grandeur and creativity of the Spanish spirit.

The advocates of the autochthonous position support a completely one-sided view of our reality. They entertain the impossible desire to reverse the tide of history. If they had their way, they would mutilate our present spiritual reality. They would condemn us to the ethical, mental, technical, and esthetic backwardness of pre-Columbian civilization. Because the great empire of Tahuantinsuyo that once maintained unity among the Indian tribes has now disappeared and cannot be revived, autochthonism as espoused today would lead logically to an exaltation of tribalism, to fetishism, and to the most backward forms of property ownership. The autochthonous position, in short, embodies attitudes that are hostile to our culture and national interests.

The fusionist position represents a false attempt to evaluate our cultural elements in terms of empirical and mechanistic criteria by regarding them as equal in worth. From a juxtaposition or fusion that is only material in scope there cannot result a spiritual or cultural national character. Lamentably, however, the fusionist position has been the one most widely accepted by our historians and sociologists. . . .

Only the theory of a living synthesis, as embodied in the position of integral Peruvianness, explains the phenomenon of transculturation. The history of our culture and of our national formation demonstrates the process in which the superior values of our culture, upon assuming the indigenous elements found in the land, created original cultural matrices by giving a new form to primitive elements. Thereby a new national spirit was brought into being. Transculturation is something more than mere juxtaposition or the mechanical fusion of two cultures. In true transculturation, values themselves are integrated and then transformed by superior values. Assumption by a higher culture of primitive elements is quite distinct from juxtaposition or fusion. In the process of assumption, the inferior culture does not disappear altogether; its worthwhile and permanent traits are assimilated and better illuminated by the superior culture. Only a process such as this can explain the originality of the Peruvian culture, which is not simply a reflection of Spanish culture but rather a new creation, a new synthesis in which the Hispanic-Catholic elements, without losing either their ecumenical features or their most typical and unique characteristics, assimilated the economic institutions, political structures, and esthetic elements of the new land.

6. *The Spaniard and His Cultural Dominance*

Like Belaúnde, Alberto Wagner de Reyna (1915–   ), a leading Peruvian diplomat and diplomatic historian, sees Spanish traditions as the essential ingredients in shaping his country's destiny. In disagreement with Valcárcel and all indigenistas, Wagner de Reyna feels that Indian culture was thoroughly transformed, even to the point of disappearing, by Spanish influence.

The Iberian culture assimilated certain Indian cultural traits. However, it incorporated these traits without fundamentally changing its Western character. . . . Spanish culture absorbed Indian contributions and made them its own, forming thereby a new and original mode of being. . . . In this great task, the Indian influence was merely a new breath of air in the Spanish sails; it is comparable to the German or barbarian influence in modern European civilizations. . . .

Indian cultural traits provided the matter and the Iberian Catholic culture supplied the form for our creole Westernism.[1] The most im-

---

[1] [Wagner de Reyna is using the terms "matter" and "form" largely in the sense in which they are employed in Aristotelian and Thomistic philosophy. According to this philosophical conception, everything that exists (except God, Who is pure form) is

SOURCE: "The Spaniard and His Cultural Dominance" translated from Alberto Wagner de Reyna, "Iberoamérica," in *Mercurio Peruano* (Lima), Año XIX, Vol. 26, No. 212 (November 1944), pp. 520–33.

portant component of a culture and a way of life is its form. Form dictates the characteristics of the final product, assigns the different ingredients to their proper places, and determines the hierarchy of values within the product as well as its true nature. Matter is the passive element that, in contributing such accidental qualities as color and constituency, individualizes and serves to support the form. Thus, the dignity of Hellenic-Christian culture has remained uncorrupted and permanent in its essence, but various accidental or superficial traits have imparted to it a new individuality. . . .

The Ibero-American culture is, in its past, present, and future significance, fundamentally Western, as Western as the Roman, French, or German cultures. It is a part of a branch of the Spanish culture, with certain added Indian-material traits, resulting from history, race, and ecology, which impart to it a unique character. . . .

Ibero-America, a culture born of tension as the West confronted the aborigines, is caught in a dialectical process between centripetal and centrifugal forces. It has a duty to justify itself as an original cultural force in the continent. It can only fulfill this duty if, conscious of its Hellenic-Christian form, it affirms its ecumenical spirituality and serves as the animating force for all the people of the continent.

7. *The Spaniard*
and the Dominance of His Religion

José de la Riva Agüero (1885–1944), one of Peru's finest historians, as a young man saw his country's future greatness and destiny in an ethnic and cultural fusion of Indian and Spanish elements. Later, he placed his trust exclusively in the Spanish style of life, which found its highest expression in Hispanic Catholicism. The following address, presented at the blessing of a new police school in 1934, is representative of the later period of his thinking.

While the influence of any religion may be great and advantageous, simply by reason of the fact that it is a religion, the influence of

constituted by substantial form and prime matter. Prime matter exists in potency; that is, potentially it is capable of becoming anything. What it does in fact become in essence or substance is determined by the substantial form that is united to it. Thus it is form, not matter, that determines the true essence, the substantial nature, of all things.]
    SOURCE: "The Spaniard and the Dominance of His Religion" translated from José de la Riva Agüero, *Por la verdad, la tradición y la patria* (Lima: Imprenta Torres Aguirre, 1938), 2, pp. 164–67.

our Catholic faith is by all odds the greatest. Even nonbelieving statesmen, attentive only to empirical norms, cannot fail to admire the Catholic
religion and the Church it has created as the most enduring and formidable example in history of order, prodigious wisdom, permanence, and
hierarchy. Most of us Peruvians descend physically and all of us descend
spiritually from the European, Roman, Mediterranean culture that Spain
introduced into our land. Catholicism, consubstantially united with the
Spanish culture, has shaped even our most inward values; it tempered the
cruelty that is a part of all conquests, and, with a spirit of generosity totally
lacking in other European conquests of the period, it established an
equality between conquerors and conquered; frequently it inspired our
great conquerors, in the highest spirit of honor and equity, to donate
even to the last penny their fortunes gained through military exploits so
that hospitals and charitable institutions might be established. . . .

We are not conservers; rather, we are restorers, for we plan to extend
and to purify everything of value that has inhered in our national traditions. To maintain that there are not traditions in Peru is an absurd
blasphemy, equivalent to asserting that there are no common interests or
inherited ideals and that we lack the body and soul of a fatherland. However pessimistic we might be, we could never advance such a monstrous
absurdity. . . .

Let us respect and protect the traditions of our fatherland and, above all,
the cardinal, supreme tradition of religion. Without its influence, sacrifice
would be discarded, morality would disappear, and we would fall into
materialistic hedonism with neither institutions nor individuals being
able to conserve decency or true values.

DISPARAGEMENT OF THE SPANIARD AND HISPANIC TRADITIONS

8. *The Spaniard and His Inimical Legacy*

In 1894, at the beginning of an illustrious career in teaching and
politics, Javier Prado y Ugarteche (1871–1921) published a scathing

SOURCE: "The Spaniard and His Inimical Legacy" translated from Alejandro
O. Deustua's review of Prado's *Estado social del Perú durante la dominación española:
estudio histórico-sociológico* (Lima, 1894), published in the newspaper *El Callao*,
March 28, 1894. A new edition of the Prado work containing the text of Deustua's
review was published in Lima by Librería e Imprente Gil in 1941.

indictment of the Spanish character and colonial traditions, attributing to them Peru's slow pace of development. In reviewing the book, Alejandro O. Deustua (see Reading 4) expressed complete accord with Prado's conclusions.

Like Javier Prado, we have believed that the inheritance received by the generations destined to form the Republic was very inadequate and inferior. Like him, we can now assert that the colonial period left a legacy thoroughly inimical to the attainment of unity and the development of a vigorous national life.

Politically, it bequeathed to us the vices of totalitarianism, the enemy of all social liberty. This and related vices have dried up the fountain of civic virtue and weakened the political structure with rivalries, suspicions, jealousies, and discords. . . .

From the colonial period we have received traditions of incorrigible bureaucratic abuses in public administration; bribery nourished by avarice and impunity that extended even to the highest officials; and, as Prado puts it, "a sick obsession with wealth, no matter how acquired, that became an all-pervasive and incurable disease." Finally, we have received a heterogeneous and decadent society.

What has been our inheritance in the economic order? As Prado explains it, "The immediate exploitation of our sources of wealth without long-term planning and with only immediate results in mind." In short, we have inherited a most pernicious system that in Peru has produced abominable and destructive habits persisting even to the present day because of the immutable law of psychological inheritance.

The colonial ecclesiastical heritage has left in our church officials an unbridled ambition to govern, even in the temporal order; an intransigent fanaticism, developed to the most refined point of cruelty by the Holy Office of the Inquisition; and a frightful lack of organization among the clergy, whose individual morals are weakened by the abundance of pleasures attaching to their positions. And in society in general, the ecclesiastical heritage has left us with a sensual love for the ceremonies of the cult that intoxicate the senses and render our people effeminate.

According to Prado . . . the clergy . . . who possessed the power to influence society through their example failed to take advantage of their opportunity. In three hundred years they could have employed their immense power to pour forth benefits for all sectors of the populace. But all they did during three hundred years was to abuse their power. As teachers, they suffocated the spirit of scientific investigation. As models of perfect men, they served only to weaken the ties of social morality. They poisoned the atmosphere with superstition, pride, wrath, impurity, and their terrible train of consequences. Cloaked in a primitive doctrine of charity and chastity, they proceeded actually to institute a policy of hatred, extermination, and profligacy. . . .

Under colonial influences, intelligence atrophied and the practical spirit of work and economy disappeared, along with concern for political rights. All that remained were absurd ideals, aggressiveness, hallucinatory fanaticism, and a reverential form of homage to the king and his government. Such was the spirit of the race to which the conquerors belonged. Such was the spirit that they imparted to the blood of our creoles.

IDENTIFICATION WITH MESTIZAJE IN THE QUEST FOR NATIONAL REALIZATION

9. A *Positive View* of *Peru's Two Cultures*

Manuel Solari Swayne is a well-known journalist in present-day Peru. His opinions reflect the tendency of contemporary Peruvian intellectuals to look for a compromise that will end the destructive indigenista–hispanista debate and provide for the emergence of a broad and pluralistic Peruvian nationalism.

It has been the custom to repeat glowing appraisals of the accomplishments of the various indigenous cultures of Peru. All of this seems very worthwhile to us, provided these appraisals rest upon scientific investigation and not mere supposition. . . . At the same time, it seems to us equally worthwhile to affirm all those positive values that inhered in the Hispanic spirit in Peru, provided once again that these values can be documented through historical research and do not rest merely upon supposition.

What we are absolutely not in accord with is that destructive attitude, unfortunately very prevalent, that finds it impossible to affirm an indigenous value without pointing to a Spanish defect, or vice versa. We cannot be in accord with this attitude because present-day Peru is the product of both roots, and we gain nothing by saying that Atahualpa

SOURCE: "A Positive View of Peru's Two Cultures" translated from Manuel Solari Swayne, "Los paises se levantan sobre afirmaciones," in *El Comercio* (Lima), March 24, 1964.

drank chicha from the skull of Huáscar or that Francisco Pizarro [1] came to our soil only to enslave the Indians and rob them of gold. . . .

We think, and we wish that all of our countrymen believed, that Peruvians are a mestizo people. And we believe that if we wish to destroy the prejudices and the complexes of racial inferiority and superiority that suffocate us, we should begin by exalting the eternal values that have enriched our country, both indigenous and Hispanic. . . .

Let the pseudo-hispanistas learn to accept the fact that the colonial period is finished, once and for all; and let the pseudo-indigenistas accept the ending of the Inca empire. Let us be careful not to weep excessively for the destruction of these two epochs in our history, lest with too many tears we drown ourselves. . . . Let us stop suffering for the evil perpetrated by our predecessors on Peruvian soil and think instead of the good that they accomplished.

10. *The Andes as the Cradle of a New Culture*

At the height of the indigenista–hispanista debate in 1929, José Uriel García (1891–   ) published a plea for moderation. Relatively ignored at the time, his book has in recent years come to be widely esteemed as an important explanation and justification of mestizaje.

Contemplating the situation from the vantage point of our Andes and from the intuitive knowledge of our Indian hearts, it is possible to appreciate the magnitude of the error committed by the hispanistas, who in referring to our colonial history consider it as the fruit of a single progenitor, the Spaniard, taken in this instance as an abstract being incapable of projecting himself into other forms of expression and acquiring a new consciousness and personality. The men on whose actions the hispanistas base their viewpoints are those who returned to Spain or settled in the locales that seemed most congenial and natural to them, the cities of our coastal desert. In the sierra, however, other Spaniards decided to make their home. These men, as Indianized Spaniards, soon . . . acquired a new orientation in life. . . . They became men of the

---

[1] [Atahualpa and Huáscar were rivals for control of the Inca confederation at the time the Spanish, led by Francisco Pizarro, undertook the conquest of Peru. Chicha is an alcoholic beverage made from maize.]

SOURCE: "The Andes as the Cradle of a New Culture" translated from José Uriel García, *El nuevo Indio: ensayos indianistas sobre la sierra surperuana*, 2nd ed. (Cuzco: H. G. Rozas Sucesores, Librería e Imprenta, 1937), pp. 86–87, 95, 97, 107–08, 109–10.

Andes, which is the same as saying that they became indigenous beings, destined from that time on to struggle with the Andes, which became their voluntary prison. . . . These historic Andes, where human values are largely those imposed by the Indian soul, enveloped the Spaniard and submerged him in their essence, at the same time developing in him a personality distinct from that which he brought from Spain. . . .

The process that occurred in the Andes produced a profound change in the soul of the Spanish immigrant. And at the same time the Indian in his own land became an immigrant from the conquered Inca confederation, an immigrant about to enter into a new sociological panorama. . . . The Spanish immigrant who penetrated into the Andes with the desire of remaining there forever ceased to be a stranger, because he discarded his bonds with his native land and severed his ties with his history. . . . Thus he lost his Spanish personality and took on an Indian personality. At the same time, the Indian, upon accepting the ideas, techniques, and science of the conqueror, entered a profoundly modified world, forming a new tradition and initiating a new historic life. . . . What emerged was a new people, a mestizo people. . . .

We do not refer to the physiological but rather to the spiritual mestizo. The question of blood and the crossing of seeds is far less important than the mingling and fusion of what is spiritual. More than a reproducer, man is a spiritual consciousness; and the spiritual consciousness of one man, when mingled with others, is strengthened in its creative force. The Spaniard who puts his heart in the land and makes himself Indian in his mode of life undergoes mestizaje, just as the Indian who flees from the Inca way of life and accepts a new style and feeling also undergoes mestizaje. . . .

The mestizo soul is the spiritual zone that the Indian, emerging from past centuries, begins to penetrate, elevating himself toward the complexity and the new problems, fears, and hopes of another way of life; and the mestizo soul is the spiritual zone that the other element from across the seas enters, becoming at first primitive and barbarous in order to be able to emerge later as a true American. Thus, it is psychologically impossible ever to recapture the pure Indian tradition of ancient times, just as it is impossible for a full-grown man to return to infancy. Art and all forms of American culture cannot return to the Indian-Incan simplicity but must derive their inspiration from the Indian-mestizo reality, which is far richer and far more immediate.

The mestizo soul, then, in spite of the disdain that commonly attaches to the term "mestizo," is the beginning of total Americanness. It is the germ of a new personality and not a physical-chemical substance that can be broken down into two atoms or two halves, the one European and the other Indian. It is the soul that infuses American life at the present moment; better said, it is the soul of the Andes, the soul of all the Andean regions of the continent, the soul toward which proceed both the Indian out of the dim recesses of the past and also all . . . who would enter into the American essence in order to be reincarnated and realized. . . .

When all Indians have become truly new Indians, they will then be fully capable of redeeming themselves. . . . And only then will they produce their true standards and values. . . . Thus, the process of mestizaje in America, generating a new spirit that advances toward the future, faces the grave challenge of infusing in all Indians this fresh and youthful soul and of making them thereby completely new Indians.

DISPARAGEMENT OF MESTIZAJE

11. *Race Mixture Viewed as a Source of Biological Deterioration*

Alejandro O. Deustua was as pessimistic about the mestizo as he was about Indian and Spanish components of the Peruvian populace (see Readings 4 and 8). Unable to anticipate worthwhile accomplishments by his country's allegedly inferior racial elements and having abandoned his earlier faith in immigration as a panacea, Deustua proposed a new formula for national salvation.

The problem of the crossing of races has greatly preoccupied those men who . . . believe that the prosperity of a nation depends principally on the purity of the race that forms it. Almost always, it has been thought that the mixing of races results in biological disequilibrium and moral ruin. . . . The mestizo problem is far more grave among us than in other countries. Engendered by the Indian in his period of moral dissolution and by the Spaniard in his era of decadence, the mestizo has inherited the defects of both without conserving the virtues of either. . . . The mixture has been fatal to our national culture. The disequilibrium produced by two antithetical natures has endured, and all of the progress of civilization has not been able to purify the Peruvian conscience of the infection produced by the germs of progenitors who were in complete decadence. . . .

SOURCE: "Race Mixture Viewed as a Source of Biological Deterioration" translated from Alejandro O. Deustua, *La cultura nacional*, 2nd ed. (Lima: Empresa Editora El Callao, 1937), pp. 76–77, 81–82.

Immigration . . . has been unable to effect the purification of the moral conscience that throughout the ages has remained basically unchanged in the mestizo, the heir of whites, Negroes, and Indians who had already lost their physiological and psychic strength in the state of society that existed after the conquest.

It is not the immigration of foreigners but the emigration of nationals that can produce, in the distant future, the required national regeneration. We must send young people, those least infected by the infirmity of the mestizo, to countries where public and private life offer sufficiently powerful examples to create new and indelible habits and norms, and then await the ultimate return of these temporary emigrants. Only in this way will it be possible to prevent the infection of good tendencies by bad examples.

Argentina

IDENTIFICATION WITH WHITE, MATERIALLY PROGRESSIVE WESTERN EUROPE AND WITH THE UNITED STATES IN THE ARGENTINE QUEST FOR NATIONAL REALIZATION

1. *The United States as a Model for South America*

Compared to Peru, Argentina has a population that is racially homogeneous; yet Argentine intellectuals have been almost as addicted as their Peruvian counterparts to discussing their country's problems and evolution in terms of "race." Juan Bautista Alberdi (1810–84) felt that Argentina could realize a worthwhile future only by eradicating its existing traditions, introducing foreign development models, and submerging what he saw as a racially inferior population beneath waves of white immigrants. The following essay originally appeared in 1858.

An economically sick society must be cured in the same manner that an individual cures the poverty that is caused by his own misconduct. A society recovers quickly and fully if it associates with those who have

SOURCE: "The United States as a Model for South America" translated from Juan Bautista Alberdi, *Escritos póstumos*, 16 vols. (Buenos Aires: Imprenta Europea, 1895), Vol. I: *Estudios económicos*, pp. 68, 71, 79, 100, 103, 113, 499, 522, 525. Translations of all material in the Argentine section of this chapter are principally the work of Thomas O'Dea, Department of Modern Languages, University of Notre Dame, and his wife, Marcia.

already mastered the intelligent habits of work and savings, the only source of wealth and the exclusive remedy for poverty. This is to say that South America can cure its economic malaise only by increasing its population through immigration from rich and productive European areas. With this outlook and with this result in mind, the fundamental institutions of the Spanish colonial period, which still linger in our midst, must be eradicated.

New constitutions should be formulated that will serve to attract the most industrious and frugal Europeans. South America will thus be enriched by the skills and habits of its immigrants. . . .

South America . . . was poor from the beginning, because it was conquered by a nation that in the course of eight centuries of holy war forgot or learned to ignore the fact that work is the only source of wealth, just as its absence is the only cause of poverty. . . . South America was burdened by a multitude of convents, heavy tithes, and the outstretched clerical hand that impeded agricultural progress; by love for fiestas and attendant vices and indulgences; by fear of work as a means of enrichment; by the cultivation of idleness as a desirable goal. All of these burdens of tradition have been the cause of poverty—that is, of impotence and dependency. . . .

At the time of its formation, South America, as a result of its Spanish origin and the colonial organization, received civilization, language, religion, temperament, and customs . . . peculiar to Spain, a way of life that was inimical to economic progress. . . . While North America was being populated by the most industrious and purest people from the most highly industrial nations of Europe, South America was being populated by nobles, military men, and priests, who brought with them their corresponding habits. . . .

South America is simultaneously rich and miserable. She is rich because of her soils and resources. She is poor due to the ways of her people. Wealth is properly the combination of the rich soil and the labor of men. Regardless of the wealth of their land, the people who live on it will be poor if they do not know how to extract the wealth through intelligent and energetic labor. To teach the people how to create wealth is to teach them to be both strong and free. Wealth is power and freedom. . . .

In economic matters, the great model for South America is North America. Wealth and liberty in North America antedated her independence. . . . Freedom and wealth emerged in the United States with the very first colony established by the English. . . . Thus, even the colonial regime in North America is a good model for the independent South American states. Above all, it is the present United States, not just the old and powerful states of Europe, that should be the model for South America, and the model in far more than just economic matters. . . .

In the United States, the land of liberty, wealth is the instrument and arm of freedom. Both are simultaneously produced and sustained. One arrives at freedom through wealth, and vice versa. Thus, one does not know which is greater, freedom or wealth. . . .

The power and greatness of the United States spring as much from her wealth as from her freedoms; the heights attained by her civilization are owing equally to her labor and industry and to her elections and free political debates.

South America is full of copiers of United States doctrines, laws, and books. What South Americans forget to imitate from their great model to the north are her industrialists, engineers, mariners, entrepreneurs, miners, fishermen, and farmers. In a word, what they do not imitate is her economic know-how, her habits of work, economy, and sobriety in social life—without which her liberties would be mere myths and abstractions.

ACCEPTANCE OF TRADITION AS AN INESCAPABLE FACTOR IN NATIONAL DESTINY

2. *Enduring Legacy of Provincial Argentina*

Joaquín V. González (1863–1923), a revered intellectual and founder of the University of La Plata, attested to the inescapable influence of past traditions and thus differed from Alberdi, who seemed to regard Argentina as a *tabula rasa* awaiting the impression of new cultural patterns. However much he abhorred many traditions associated with interior Argentina, González, writing in 1905, realized the part they must play in forging a viable and authentic national culture.

The spread of the Latin population over the American continent, inhabited before by a virgin race that lacked the historical and traditional consistency that maintained at least an intermittent harmony in the Old World, signifies a profound evolution in ideas, inclinations, beliefs, sentiments, art, and poetry. Although the intellectual level of the invading race was more elevated than that of the conquered race, this did not prevent a certain tension and rivalry, which brought about a mutual transformation of the two elements. . . .

SOURCE: "The Enduring Legacy of Provincial Argentina" translated from Joaquín V. González, *La tradición nacional*, 3rd ed. (Buenos Aires: Librería y Editorial la Facultad, 1930), pp. 51, 197–98, 208.

The social class born directly from the cultured families that immigrated to this country [beginning in colonial times], the class that was educated in schools and in the practices of civilization, conserved its natural superiority . . . and assumed the legitimate direction of public affairs and of the national culture. The remaining masses, taken up more with immediate personal goals than with mastery of the outer world, concerned with cattle raising and rural occupations in general and estranged from the civilizing influence of new ideas, maintained itself in isolation, leading a monotonous existence in the expanses of the pampas. In solitude and isolation, these masses assumed that somber and over-concentrated character that sporadically would explode, impelling them to seek to impose themselves upon the superior classes by dint of their crude strength and extraordinary cohesiveness. . . .

Each of the caudillos who, as though fascinated by an infernal power, led on the murderous masses, is a character shaped in the mold of the heroes of terror whom poets . . . such as Shakespeare in *Macbeth* . . . have immortalized; and each of the leaders who headed the civilized militia as it set out to find and tame those devastating torments in the midst of the immense and desolate pampas, pursuing the furies to their very lairs, is the hero of liberty, always ready even after innumerable victories to save the land anew from failure and conflagration.

The present generation, intoxicated by the harmonies of progress that each day present us with new and wonderful spectacles, has lost sight of those fateful furies that gripped the hearts of its fathers; and upon forgetting the past, this generation has interrupted the flow of the fatherland's tradition, covering the past with a heavy veil, as though through this deceit our traditions will disappear from society. . . . They are unfamiliar with an unavoidable law of human evolution according to which each epoch leaves its seeds within succeeding ones. Culture can attenuate and transform the effects of these seeds . . . but always certain facets of the past will reappear. . . . Those who would blot out memories of the past also forget that a people should conserve the traditions of its tyrants and sorrows, just as it conserves those of its heroes and triumphs. There is nothing that will so strengthen the fraternal bonds between men as the memory of a common misfortune.

When love for the nation is deeply rooted in the hearts of citizens, the scenes and the perpetrators of past miseries arise in the memories of all alike as a prophetic voice that, speaking from the depths of darkness, inspires the eternal sentiment of protest that should never fade; for this is the sentiment that strengthens civic virtue and liberty. Far from being relegated to oblivion, the memories of past misfortunes should be kept constantly before us, emphasizing by way of sinister contrast our resplendent national glories.

IDENTIFICATION WITH TRADITION AS A
POSITIVE FACTOR IN NATIONAL DESTINY

3. *The Spiritualization of Argentina*

Manuel Gálvez (1882–1963) looked to the traditions of Spanish,
provincial, Catholic Argentina for positive examples and models that
should guide the country toward its national destiny.

Our strong and beautiful Argentina lives these moments in her
supreme hour; the hour in which her best intellectuals and truest hearts
cry out for the spiritualization of the national conscience. . . . The
skeptical materialism of today is a recent thing, for it has appeared along
with the fever for riches and, as such, has arrived from Europe with the
immigrant. The conquering immigrant, through his enormous success in
acquiring wealth, has introduced into the nation a new concept of life.
He brought no proposition save that of getting rich, and thus it was natural for Argentines to become contaminated by an overriding obsession
with material considerations. . . .

Ours is a brave struggle. We must wage it gloriously—in books, newspapers, universities, everywhere—against materialistic interests. We must
preach love of our country, of our scenery, of our authors and national
heroes; we must bring to life the idealism and originality of the past and
teach how these romantic qualities can redeem without discrediting our
material greatness.

.   .   .

Two political tendencies exist in our country. The first, conservative and
in a certain sense traditional and regressive, laments the loss of our old
moral and material physiognomy; it wants to curtail immigration, particularly that which is not Latin, and it seeks to restore the fervent
nationalism of the past. The second tendency is cosmopolitan and liberal;
it dislikes our romantic past and perhaps our Spanish origin; it desires
progress at any price and totally ignores the fact that the country has
its own unique soul. Recently, this second tendency has been called "pro-

SOURCE: "The Spiritualization of Argentina" translated from Manuel Gálvez, *El
solar de la raza*, 2nd ed. (Madrid: Editorial Saturnino Calleja, 1920), pp. 13–14, 16–
17, 19, 21, 52, 55–56, 59–60. The first edition of this work was published in Buenos
Aires in 1913.

gressive nationalism." The first, which is our true nationalism, has lately been referred to as "historic."

I believe both tendencies should unite in one. The modern Argentina, constructed through immigration—in other words, the cosmopolitan Argentina—must conserve a basis of true Argentineness. The precise object of the eclectic nationalism that I urge would be to accept inevitable transformations but at the same time to maintain Argentineness. This would require that all foreigners who enter Argentina be absorbed and modified by the spirit of the nation. Whether our nation is to have character and spirituality will depend upon how much of the Spanish and creole tendencies endures in the final mixture.

.   .   .

The concrete and primary purpose of this book is to enkindle in those who read it sympathy with the spirit of admiration that I feel for Spain . . . where there still dwells the soul of our race and the remains of spiritual greatness. I intend to arouse a love for Spain out of which will result a love for our own race. I want to combat the snobbishness of today, which leads so many to disparage our race as they praise that of the Anglo-Saxon. . . .

During the final third of the preceding century, Hispanophobia came into vogue. Sarmiento, Alberdi, and others directed insults, sarcasm, and abuse against Spain. . . . The normal schools founded in that era, instead of being centers for inculcating patriotism, were centers for the dissemination of those evil Hispanophobic sentiments. . . . There still remain in our midst many enemies of Spain, particularly among the normal school teachers, the anticlericals, the mulattos, and the sons of Italians. The hatred of the mulatto for Spain is the hatred of the dark for the white. The anticlericals see in Spain a country of friars and fanatics, while the Italians and their children see in Spain a rival of their own country and resent the Spanish predominance in Argentina. Hispanophobia will endure in Argentina as long as our sick snobbishness persists. . . .

Today, Argentine nationalism seeks to react against foolish fashion, against the foreign influence that deprives us of our character. The appearance of this noble sentiment is happy and opportune. This is a sentiment that urges us to abandon exotic tendencies and invites us to look toward Spain and Spain in America. We do not hate the Saxon people, to whom Argentina owes much of its progress; we do not hate suave and delicate France, whose elegant and harmonious spirit has greatly influenced our life; we do not hate passionate Italy, which has imparted to us some of her energies. But the moment has arrived in which we should feel Argentine and American and, in the final analysis, Spanish, for that is the race to which we belong. . . . We are and shall eternally be of the Spanish race. Immigrants, in their unconscious efforts to rob us of our character, have failed to tear us from the Spanish family. Castile created us in her image and likeness. She is our womb, the origin of the race that will be born of amalgamation and fusion. . . .

We possess a source of energy. But ours shall not be a barbaric and mechanistic energy such as that which bubbles incessantly in the United States of America. Ours is and shall be a harmonious energy, tempered by Latin elegance and spiritualism, an intelligent force in which action has not been allowed to destroy dreams.

4. *Authoritarianism and Traditions*

Leopoldo Lugones (1874–1938) carried to their full extremes some of the prejudices of Gálvez, blaming all the ills of Argentina upon immigration and the acceptance of exotic models of liberal democracy. Because for a time Lugones was perhaps Argentina's most widely admired poet and man of letters, his plea for military authoritarianism exercised considerable influence. Something of a political-ideological chameleon, Lugones was at one time a leftist. The excerpt below is representative of his writings during his later, conservative period.

This book is an act of faith in the country. In addition, it seeks to offer a diagnosis of the nation's present infirmity. With this as its objective, it points out what can be done to eliminate from the national character those foreign elements that, as their inadequacies become progressively apparent, retard and perturb the nation on the road to its destiny. I refer to the foreign institutions that the nation adopted with erroneous enthusiasm and to the liberal ideology, which, with excessive faith, the nation mistook for liberty itself. . . .

The liberal doctrine in Argentina [with its encouragement of immigration] has plagued us with foreign maniacs, incompetents, and delinquents, whose return to their native countries has become an urgent necessity in the interest of public health. . . . To understand the gravity of the problem, it should be pointed out that foreigners make up more than sixty per cent of those demented souls presently in our insane asylums. It is owing to the infirmities of foreigners that we are falsely regarded by the outside world as a country with one of the worst problems of mental health. . . .

More than half of those in our jails are foreigners. . . . The great

SOURCE: "Authoritarianism and Traditions" translated from Leopoldo Lugones, *La grande Argentina*, 2nd ed. (Buenos Aires: Editorial Huemul, 1962), pp. 177–80, 201, 211. The first edition of this work was published in Buenos Aires in 1930.

majority of city delinquents are foreigners. The beggars, those who abandon and exploit children, the pimps, the peddlers of dangerous drugs and pornographic materials, the alcoholics, the vagrants, and the professional agitators are, in their great majority, foreigners. There is reason to believe that their native countries purposely exported them to our land. Yet the protection that the liberal creed affords foreigners impedes the taking of adequate measures against their menace. . . .

Foreign liberalism is producing another fatal result among us. There abound in large numbers the sons of foreigners, especially writers and university students, who manifest their contempt toward the country of their elders, breaking the historical bonds of our national existence. Actual civil war looms on the horizon, and this fact constitutes the crowning failure of liberalism. . . .

The liberal ideologues assured us, with their infallible logic, that when everyone was politicized—that is, received the right to vote—government would improve. It is now 1929, seventeen years since the secret ballot and obligatory suffrage for literate males were established. And government is getting worse. Democratic government is a success in some lands, a failure in others. Here it is a failure. . . . It has created the crisis of discipline. . . .

Executive power . . . should be placed in the hands of the military. The government could then be technically organized. It is scarcely necessary to point out that because of their scientific and administrative training, their spirit of sacrifice, their disciplined lives, and their devotion to honor, military officials constitute the best conceivable governing body.

5. *Catholicism and Traditions*

Julio Meinvielle (1905–   ), a secular priest who has been publishing prolifically since the early 1930's, saw in the Catholic Church rather than the Army the instrument for protecting true Argentine traditions against the contamination of immigrant-introduced values.

The harmonious equilibrium that during long centuries prevailed in medieval social relations was destroyed when the Protestant Reformation gave free rein to the spirit of greed, to the old sin of avarice, until then firmly held in check within the moral order of Christianity. . . . The liberal bourgeois world was installed in our country, in a definitive manner, beginning around 1853. It was an insertion into our old creole

SOURCE: "Catholicism and Traditions" translated from Julio Meinvielle, *Política argentina, 1943–1956* (Buenos Aires: Editorial Trafac, 1956), pp. 15, 35, 43, 324.

crucible of the liberal optimism of the nineteenth century, which proclaimed that the era of human happiness had arrived. . . .

The evils of our national reality are profound and intimately connected with the crisis of intelligence that the modern Western world now suffers. Thus, we can seek a remedy to our evils only by going to the root of the problem and restoring the traditional principles of intelligence and wisdom that the Catholic Church proclaims. . . .

Our solution must be Catholic. Our historical traditions demand this. The country as a human reality must be informed by a doctrine and spirit. In our country, this is either the laicism of liberalism and socialism, which leads to Communism, or Catholicism . . . a sane, healthy spiritualism, which is the Latin-Hispanic tradition. . . . The liberal-socialist current has only divided the country and weakened its unifying fabric. Catholicism, on the other hand, has strengthened its men and the fundamental institutions of family, property, and state.

A CONTEMPORARY ANALYSIS OF THE PROBLEM OF IDENTITY AND NATIONAL REALIZATION

6. *Immigration and the Molding of Argentine Character*

Julio Mafud, a young professor of sociology at several Buenos Aires institutions, has written a discerning study of the identity problem that continues to render Argentina a divided land.

In the origins of Argentina's constitutional life there coexisted the indigenous element, the gaucho, and the immigrant. In short, there coexisted three opposing beings with three differing and antagonistic personalities and styles of life. When a country has only one basic personality element, it can be anticipated that it will be integrated and well structured socially and culturally. But when various personalities struggle to set the style of national existence, the country tends to disintegrate and to lack sociocultural continuity. . . .

SOURCE: "Immigation and the Molding of Argentine Character" translated from Julio Mafud, *Psicología de la viveza criolla: contribución para una interpretación de la realidad social Argentina y Americana* (Buenos Aires: Editorial Americalée, 1965), pp. 33, 89, 112–15, 118–19, 231, 233–34, 247, 358–59, 374–75.

As the result of a fundamental clash, an "intrusion complex" has existed since the origins of our social experience. The "other" is not viewed as a person with a legitimate claim within the social existence of the country, but rather as a "rival," as an antagonist. . . . From the conqueror, who regarded the Indian as less than human because he allegedly lacked a soul, to the citizen of Buenos Aires, who regarded the gaucho as a "barbarian" opposed to his civilization, and finally to the creole of Spanish origins, who viewed the immigrant as a "usurper" and plunderer of the resources of the land, all Argentines have been cast in the character mold of opposition and exclusion.

.   .   .

Upon migrating to the "civilized" society [of Buenos Aires], the native, creole Argentine found himself at a tremendous disadvantage. Argentine society was being restructured upon European models. The immigrant came . . . to see what he could accumulate, and if he did not succeed he left. These attitudes helped give rise to a new style of life from which the native creole was largely alienated. . . . All of the creole's historic and psychological values were antithetical to purely economic goals. Time for him was not gold; rather, it was infinite. His soul had not yet been disciplined by mechanistic forces. . . . Relaxed, loose, and unstructured in his psychic makeup, he enjoyed a style of life that was the exact opposite of that required by the new scheduled, diagramed, asphalt mode of existence. The newly dominant social norms clashed violently with the old creole style of life.

Faced with the oppression of a new social and economic milieu, the creole man had to react in some manner, and he did it through *viveza*.[1] Unable to make his way in the new era of competition, the creole resorted to viveza, adopting it as a weapon in his struggle with those who had just arrived from beyond the sea. This explains why the creole's psychological reaction was particularly manifest in Buenos Aires, where the new way of life was more completely established and the creole's struggle for existence was most acute. The proof of this is that evidences of creole viveza do not exist in gaucho literature. In the interior, viveza would have been considered a departure from dignity. . . .

Immigrants, after a long or a short stay, themselves . . . assimilated viveza. The sons of immigrants, already partly "creolized," learned about viveza at a dizzy pace because of the psychological impulses of both revenge and compensation. Perhaps they acquired it to gain vengeance against their parents, who in the new environment were always laughed

---

[1] [Viveza refers to a style of life in which one makes his way not by effort and plodding labor but by his wits, by guile and astuteness, by duplicity, deception, cunning, connivance, and craftiness. The person who has mastered this style of life is referred to in Argentina as a *vivo*.]

at and deceived. Perhaps—and this may be the fundamental reason—they assimilated viveza so that they would not be the objects of ridicule and jest. The son of the immigrant preferred anything to being taken for a sucker, a rube, a hick. Scoffed at throughout his early youth, he had responded by becoming a vivo. . . .

Moreover, there unquestionably existed a rupture between immigrant fathers and their sons. Invariably, the fathers united in small and confined groups so as to preserve their original life styles. Through their circles, clubs, and colonies they continued their country of origin within the new land. But the children were torn between two extremes. On the one side was the world of their fathers, from which they were increasingly alienated; on the other, the inhospitable outside world, which they must somehow inhabit and conquer. . . . Viveza was always the road that led them most quickly toward this end. In the final instance, it put them on an equal footing with others, enabling them apparently to rise above a status of inferiority. To manifest viveza was the best way to become creole, to gain acceptance and prestige.

.   .   .

For the intellectuals of our independence period, our country was to be formed by European culture. But Spain was not considered Europe. Spain was barbaric. To gain emancipation from Spain was to emerge from a nonculture so as to enter into civilization and progress. What impelled the generation of our independence period was the desire to plunge America and specifically our country into European culture. . . . What most infatuated our founding fathers was the idea of progress, which then dominated all Europe. . . .

Above all else, this generation [of the independence period] was obsessed with acquiring the spirit that then gave impulse to European culture and civilization. . . . This obsession gave rise to our complex of self-denigration. For America remained outside of the European process of progress. Somehow it did not incorporate itself into the European civilization, which was regarded as the salvation of humanity. Our intellectuals had wanted this to be accomplished quickly, in one blow, and never envisaged a slow and gradual process. Thus, they began to complain and lament that America was remaining outside the stream of new desires and ideas. . . .

Looked at through the lenses of a booming and progressive European civilization, America and Argentina seemed uncultured and barbaric. . . . The progressive culture had all virtue, the other none at all. . . . It came to be no longer a question of American assimilation of European culture; rather, the desire was totally to substitute the European style for the American, to bring Europe in its entirety to America. This desire was the origin of some of the harsh phrases that Sarmiento and Alberdi directed against the gaucho, who was the most specific ethnic-cultural type that this country had produced. . . . The influence of the ideas [of Sarmiento and Alberdi] led to a . . . flood of immigration; their final consequence was the conviction that the American material and human element had to be replaced by the European material and human element. . . .

European culture, when introduced into Argentina, resulted in the predominance of economic values over all others. . . . The pragmatic and economic orientation dominated intellectual circles. The generation of 1880 affords a spectacular example of this. "No other Argentine generation," observes [Argentine philosopher] Alejandro Korn [1860–1936], "was so lacking in spiritual impulses." This generation was too absorbed by the ideas of the positivists to be able to observe the economically inspired divisiveness that was emerging in the country. . . .

Argentine thinkers demanded that all men produce as though they were machines. . . . They considered that one Argentine laborer should produce the same as one English counterpart. No differences in styles of living or in the general social environment in which production was carried on were taken into account. It was forgotten that the industrial revolution was born in England. The fact that the English and European laborers were better conditioned to this system of production, both socially and psychologically, was totally ignored. No one in Argentina bothered to remember that the ancestors of the English and European laborers had worked in shops and factories and through their surroundings, their general environment, had already acquired the habits and standards that led to the successful functioning of their system of production. . . .

The creoles sought a way to link themselves to the new world being born within the social womb of their country. But they had no true ties with the new structure. Hence, they fluctuated wildly amid the crosscurrents of a newly emerging world. They lacked the means and the aptitudes to gain material goods. Their ancestors had not felt the need for these goods. But upon entering the new social cosmos, creoles encountered the absolute dominance of modern values: money, wealth, disciplined labor, and hectic schedules, all opposed to the wide, unstructured, and free world in which they had once lived. Behind them, they saw closed off the possibility of returning to the world they had left; ahead, they saw a world of values opposed to all of their innermost inclinations. They rejected, in almost all of its demands, the world of the lust for profit. They were a people who could not accept the absolutism of money, the voracious psychology of having to have.

When the creole entered, however peripherally, into the new society, created and structured by material interests, he proceeded to some degree to tear himself away from his origins, from the vast pampas of interior

Argentina. With the substance of his old world gone, he found himself in a state of interior emptiness. A lack of vitality, commonly referred to as "the classic laziness of the creole," was the result of his violent uprooting. The creole, due to his uprooting, became passive and lazy. The immigrant, due to his uprooting, became active and dynamic. One removed himself from society, the other advanced it. The first was cut off from his profound roots; the second, without roots and permanent connections, threw himself with all his might into the outer world in order to search for roots. . . . The creole . . . had to decide either to plunge into a utilitarian style of life, seeking only wealth, or to renounce social life. The immigrant abandoned himself to the new style of life and tried to fill an inner void with material goods. Social existence lost all moral and spiritual concern. . . .

All the while, the creole did not lack viveza as the means of gaining what he desired. Neither did the immigrant. . . . The Argentine man, native and immigrant, ended by becoming a piece of metal existing among other pieces of metal, which he sought to manipulate and to make his own. . . .

[Argentina must find a new] style of life with common national goals that will not exclude and negate our old and traditional styles. It must work toward creating a pluralistic social organization that will end the struggle of one style of life to impose itself in totality and that will permit institutional development from the bottom to the top and result at last in social integration. . . . It remains to be seen whether progress toward this type of national society demands a social revolution or can be achieved within an evolutionary social process.

CONCLUSION

In 1956, Peruvian intellectuals appeared on the whole to agree that their country's future did not lie in holding exclusively to either Indian or Spanish traditions. Taking advantage of the prevailing moderate climate of opinion, Fernando Belaúnde Terry founded a new political party, Acción Popular. The ensuing seven years witnessed a rapid growth in the party's membership. In the 1963 presidential campaign, Belaúnde and his Acción Popular partisans encouraged the Andean Indians to utilize the semicollectivist labor and land-ownership customs of the Inca past in undertaking the modernization and politicization of their communities. At the same time, they praised the achievements of Peru's westernized, coastal capitalism that rested upon the individualism and sanctity of private property associated with classical liberalism and also upon Iberian monopolistic and state interventionist policies. The Acción Popular program, envisioning a pluralistic Peru in which Indian and Western, Hispanic traditions could coexist, appealed to the electorate and contributed to Belaúnde's election to the presidency for a six-year term.[1]

According to critics on the left, many of whom despite their professed belief in mestizaje harked back to indigenista positions, Belaúnde's program was simply delaying an inevitable confrontation between participating and unassimilated Peruvians. If their analysis is correct, ethnic tensions are likely gradually to mount to the explosive level as Peru struggles to become a modern nation state.

Historically, ethnic prejudice, especially as nourished by hispanistas, has been one of many factors contributing to the preservation of a rigidly stratified class society. In addition to prejudice, actual discrimination, geographic segregation, and lack of educational and employment opportunities have served to keep the Indian masses in their lowly place within the social order. Now, as more and more Indians crowd into cities, as educational facilities expand, and as employment opportunities increase in the wake of an impressive industrialization process along the coast, some of the old social barriers are being eroded. As a result, ethnic discrimination is apt to become more exclusively the means of maintaining the Indian-origin masses at the lower level of the social pyramid, unless or until the existing sociopolitical order is destroyed. In short, before mestizaje becomes so nearly complete that it begins to resolve tensions, the passions that historically have been associated with the identity problem could touch off class warfare.

---

[1] Belaúnde was overthrown by a military coup on October 3, 1968, in the last year of his presidency.

Like their Peruvian counterparts, the majority of politicized and economically participating Argentines are obsessed with maintaining a class society. As a result, in recent decades, and especially during the Perón era (1946–55), the Argentine identity problem was complicated by class issues. Still further, it was complicated by the appearance of a new nationalism among the creoles and by profound disagreement over Argentine policy toward the United States. These developments accompanied the unprecedented migration of provincial masses from rural Argentina into Buenos Aires, a demographic shift that began before and continued during Perón's period of rule.

Glorified by Juan and Eva Perón as their beloved *descamisados*, these masses from the provinces gradually acquired some degree of self-awareness; and as they did so, they developed a creole style of nationalism. Poets who emerged from the ranks of the descamisados and tried to capture the spirit of their companions pictured the newly arrived masses as the uncorrupted representatives of the only true, authentic, and Hispanic Argentina, the rural provinces. The descamisados also responded enthusiastically to and helped to nourish a new type of antiforeign prejudice in Argentina. Their ire was directed not against those of immigrant background—not, at least, against working-class immigrants—but rather against the United States, which Perón in the early days of his administration depicted as seeking to corrupt and degrade Argentina and to deflect it from its true national destiny. And the affluent citizens of Buenos Aires who had allowed and even encouraged the United States to pursue its nefarious aims became another object of descamisado scorn. Porteños who had reached an accommodation with the United States were reviled as *vendepatrias*, men who had sold out their own fatherland.[2]

Perón in his early days of Yankee baiting perhaps hoped to guide Argentina out of its morass of divisiveness by holding up the United States as a villain against whose menace all previously contending national groups could unite. But the porteños of the upper and middle sectors, priding themselves upon their cosmopolitan attitudes, found it easier to identify with foreign interests, including the United States, than with the provincial masses, whom they referred to disdainfully as *cabecitas negras*—little black heads. Porteños who participated in the uprising that

[2] Poetry composed by *peronistas* who emerged from the ranks of the descamisados and reflecting creole-style nationalism associated with anti-United States and anti-vendepatrias attitudes includes: Juan Carlos Clemente, "El corazón en la cigarra"; Raúl Ezeyza Monasterio, "Marcha triunfal de los descamisados"; Luis Porosito Heredia, "Romance de Perón el conductor"; A. López Torres, "Romance del 17 de octubre"; Zoe Martínez, "Serás justicialista"; and Rodolfo I. Tundera, "Navíos al sur"; all published in *Antología poética de la revolución justicialista*, edited by Antonio Monti (Buenos Aires: Librería Perlado, 1954).

toppled Perón tended to regard their actions as necessary to keep inferior, provincial people in a subordinate position.[3]

In post-Perón days, Argentines have continued to be as seriously divided as at any time in their history over issues that reflect various aspects of an identity problem. And Argentine intellectuals have increasingly begun to concur in the pessimistic view that the passage of at least two generations will be required before these issues can be even partially resolved. Meantime, even as in Peru, the multifaceted and changing problem of identity will continue to impede the march toward modernization and development. It may also continue to foster military dictatorship as an operating consensus eludes civilian intellectuals and politicians.

---

[3] Short works of contemporary Argentine literature depicting the disdain for the cabecitas negras felt by the well-born of Buenos Aires and revealing the extent to which these middle- and upper-sector proteños regarded their campaign against Perón as necessary to preserve their dominance in a class-structured society include: Beatriz Guido, "Occupación," in *Crónicas de la burguesía* (Buenos Aires: Editorial Jorge Álvarez, 1965); Julio Cortazar, "Las puertas del cielo," in *Bestiario* (Buenos Aires: Editorial Sudamericana, 1964); Bernardo Kordón, "Fuimos a la ciudad," in *Crónicas de Buenos Aires* (Buenos Aires: Editorial Jorge Álvarez, 1965); Marta Lynch, "Justitia parvi hominis," in *Crónicas de la burguesía* (Buenos Aires: Editorial Jorge Álvarez, 1965); and David Viñas, *Dar la cara* (Buenos Aires: Editorial Jancana, 1962).

BIBLIOGRAPHY

Peru

Fredrick B. Pike, *The Modern History of Peru* (New York: Frederick A. Praeger, 1967), Chapter 1, devotes considerable attention to the identity problem and cites numerous Peruvian sources. Magnus Mörner, *Race Mixture in the History of Latin America* (Boston: Little, Brown, 1967), presents a perceptive analysis of race relations, based on most recent scholarly investigation, and includes considerable material relevant to the identity problem in Peru. The distinguished Peruvian periodical *Revista Histórica* devoted Vol. 27 (1965) to a summary of a Lima conference on mestizaje in which leading scholars considered the topic and the intimately related issues of national identity and destiny.

Three eloquent Peruvian works envisioning mestizaje as the ultimate national destiny and criticizing extremist hispanistas and indigenistas are Jorge Basadre, *Meditaciones sobre el destino histórico del Perú* (Lima: Ediciones Huascarán, 1947), Aurelio Miró Quesada Sosa, *Costa, sierra y montaña* (Lima: Editorial Cultura Antártica, 1947), and Raúl Porras Barrenechea, *Mito, tradición e historia del Perú* (Lima: Imprenta Santa María, 1951). Peruvian journalist Eudocio Ravines, in *La gran promesa* (Madrid, 1963), suggests that ethnic tensions will only be reduced through a long-range process of mestizaje, which will result in all Peruvians having virtually the same skin color. Peruvian philosopher Antenor Orrego, in *El pueblo continente: ensayos para una interpretación de América Latina* (Santiago de Chile: Ediciones Ercilla, 1939), sees the future of the continent in the revitalized Indian, purportedly closer in his values to the still dynamic Eastern culture than to crumbling Western civilization.

Ciro Alegría, in his celebrated indigenista novel, *Broad and Alien Is the World*, translated from the Spanish by Harriet de Onís (Philadelphia: Dufour Editions, 1962), extols the Indian's simple, communal way of life and excoriates the white–mestizo landowners of the sierra. Henry Dobyns, *The Social Matrix of Peruvian Indigenous Communities* (Ithaca, N.Y.: Cornell University Press, 1964), challenges a central indigenista thesis that Indians still maintain their collectivist, socialist values and attitudes.

Harry Kantor, *The Ideology and Character of the Peruvian Aprista Movement*, rev. ed. (Washington, D.C.: Savile Book Shop, 1966), offers a simplistic, highly favorable treatment of the APRA and attributes exaggerated importance to its indigenista stance.

Thomas R. Ford, *Man and Land in Peru* (Gainesville: University of Florida Press, 1955), presents a valuable survey of rural Peru, emphasizing the tremendous gulf between the worlds of the coast and of the sierra.

Baltazar Caravedo, Humberto Rotondo and Javier Mariátegui, in their careful psychiatric-sociological study, *Estudios de psiquiatría social en el Perú* (Lima: Ediciones del Sol, 1963), stress the sense of alienation prevalent among serranos newly arrived in the Lima slums (*barriadas*). They also comment upon the strong anti-Indian prejudice that is found among virtually all social sectors of coastal Peru.

Argentina

Valuable bibliographical surveys that contain many references to works that touch upon the identity problem are Joseph R. Barager, "The Historiography of the Rio de la Plata Since 1830," in *Hispanic American Historical Review*, 39 (1959), pp. 588–624, and Fritz Hoffman, "Perón and After," in *ibid.*, 36 (1956), pp. 510–28, and 39 (1959), pp. 212–33.

W. Rex Crawford, *A Century of Latin American Thought*, rev. ed. (New York: Frederick A. Praeger, 1966), pp. 12–51, 95–169, provides good analyses of the thought of Alberdi, Sarmiento, and other Argentine intellectuals who have pondered the issues of nationalism, identity, and destiny. Sarmiento's classic work *Civilización i barbarie* was translated by Mrs. Horace Mann and published in 1868 as *Life in the Argentine Republic in the Days of the Tyrants* (New York: Hafner, 1960), paperback. A good biography is Allison Bunkley's *The Life of Sarmiento* (Princeton, N.J.: Princeton University Press, 1952).

The José Hernández masterpiece, *Martín Fierro*, has been translated into English by Henry Alfred Holmes (New York: The Hispanic Institute, 1948). An excellent critique of *Martín Fierro*, arguing that it glorifies a lost cause, is Angel Rosenblatt, *Las generaciones argentinas del siglo XIX ante el problema de la lengua* (Buenos Aires, 1961).

Earl T. Glauert, "Ricardo Rojas and the Emergence of Argentine Cultural Nationalism," in *Hispanic American Historical Review*, 43 (1963), pp. 1–13, makes a thoughtful analysis of the competing types of nationalism that have produced widespread divisiveness. Arthur P. Whitaker and David C. Jordan, *Nationalism in Contemporary Latin America* (New York: Free Press, 1966), Chapter 4, provides a brilliant treatment of Argentine nationalism. M. Navarro Gerassi, *Argentine Nationalism on the Right*, Vol. 1 in the Washington University Social Science Institute's *Studies in Contemporary International Development* (St. Louis: Washington University Press, 1965), gives a good insight into the views of rightists on questions of identity and destiny. Carlos Ibarguren, *La historia que he vivido* (Buenos Aires: Ediciones Peuser, 1955), furnishes the fascinating reminiscences of an important conservative intellectual and politician. An altogether different vision of identity and destiny, from the leftist point of view, is Juan José Hernández Arregui, *La formación de la conciencia nacional, 1930–1960* (Buenos Aires: Ediciones Hachea, 1960).

Gino Germani, *Política y sociedad en una época de transición* (Buenos Aires: Editorial Paidos, 1962), is a solid sociological survey that deals with many of the issues intimately related to the identity problem. Two of the better recent studies dealing specifically with Argentina's lack of a sense of identity are Dardo Cúneo, *El desencuentro argentino, 1930–1955* (Buenos Aires: Editorial Pleamar, 1965), and Julio Mafud, *El desarraigo argentino* (Buenos Aires: Editorial Americalée, 1965).

Two poets, Ramón Plaza in *El libro de las fragas* (Buenos Aires: Ediciones Cuaderno del Alfarero, 1963) and Horacio Salas in *El caudillo* (Buenos Aires: Editorial Losada, 1960), manifest the disillusionment of many intellectuals with Argentina's inertia and stagnation since the overthrow of Perón. Both express admiration for the heavy-handed caudillos of the past and for the rural, provincial environment that produced them.

Additional sources that touch upon the identity problem are listed in the Bibliography for Chapter X. See in particular the books by Samuel H. Baily, John J. Kennedy, Thomas F. McGann, José Luis Romero, James R. Scobie, and Arthur P. Whitaker.

VII

The Problem of Liberalism
Versus Conservatism
in Colombia: 1849–85

J. León Helguera

CHRONOLOGY

1819 Battle of Bovacá begins the effective liberation of Colombian heartland from Spanish rule

1832 Republic of New Granada (present-day Colombia and Panamá) established; Francisco de Paula Santander elected president

1839 Initial phase of Civil War of the Supremos begins

1840 Santander dies; Civil War of the Supremos spreads

1841 Supremos War ends with defeat of federalist faction of the elite and establishment of Ministerials in power

1847 First of several artisans' societies organized to protest low tariffs on imported consumer goods

1848 Ideological impact of the February Revolution in France spurs revival of federalist and egalitarian doctrines in New Granada

1849 José Hilario López elected to presidency; Liberal and Conservative parties founded; purge of Ministerial officeholders from government

1850 Expulsion of Jesuits from New Granada

1851 Ecclesiastical *fuero* (special legal status) abolished; absolute freedom of the press declared; slavery abolished, effective January 1, 1852; abortive Conservative revolt crushed

1853 Church and State separated; adoption of libertarian and federalist Constitution; rising artisan resentment against Liberal leadership

1854 Artisans and military, led by General José María Melo, seize Bogotá; Liberal and Conservative elites join to crush Melo by December 4

1858 New Granada becomes Granadine Confederation; proliferation of semisovereign states ensues

1860 President Mariano Ospina's partisan interference in state politics sparks massive Federalist revolt

1861 Federal forces, led by General Tomás C. de Mosquera, triumph over Ospina's Confederation; Church's landed properties confiscated

1863 Federalist Constitution of Rionegro adopted; United States of Colombia established

1867 Liberal leadership eliminates Mosquera's last bid for national primacy; a decade of Liberal rule, marked by harassment of Conservatives and the Church, keeps the nation in almost constant turmoil

1877 Liberal regime defeats Conservative revolt, but ruling party's unity shattered

1880   Rafael Núñez elected to presidency

1882–84   Final doctrinaire Liberal presidency fails to unify party

1884   Núñez again president, fashions alliance with Conservatives

1885   Liberal revolt against Núñez crushed

1886   Adoption of centralist Constitution; country renamed the Republic of Colombia

1887   Concordat negotiated, placing education in hands of Church

INTRODUCTION

The roots of the bitter rivalry between the Conservative and Liberal parties in Colombia that formally began in 1849 lie buried in the very bedrock of Colombian historical experience. No single geographical, social, or economic factor can be said to have caused the rivalry; rather, family feuds, personal antagonisms, regional animosities, and economic and social frictions reaching back at least to the middle of the eighteenth century all combined to form the partisan antipathies that suddenly became discernible with the inception of the struggle for independence in 1810.

The absence of effective Spanish authority in the mountainous center of the viceroyalty of New Granada opened the way for the proliferation of dozens of new town and provincial units, many soon engaged in virulent contention and rivalry, once the struggle for independence had begun. And this self-perpetuating fragmentation among the patriots permitted their swift and relatively simple reconquest by the Spanish in 1815 and 1816.

The rancors that developed in the 1810–16 period did not vanish with the success of Simón Bolívar's army at the Battle of Boyacá on August 7, 1819. For a few years they were partially sublimated in the grandeur of the Liberator's Republic of Gran Colombia, and they took on new guises, but after 1826 the fashionable new labels became more and more identified with the older dissidences. Five years of strife ensued before the Republic of New Granada (the core of present-day Colombia) emerged from the wreckage of the Gran Colombian Republic in 1832.

The next five years (1832–37) were dominated by the personality and policies of one of the great figures of the Independence struggle, General Francisco de Paula Santander, whose presidency was directed toward internal reconstruction and economic solvency. The political consensus that Santander strove to maintain gradually disappeared, and when in 1836 he tried to impose his personal candidate, the controversial General José María Obando, on the country as the next president, he was defeated, and factions within the elite solidified. Santander's prestige eroded further over the next two years, and in the power vacuum that ensued, regional rivalries revived and coalesced with personal ambitions. Polemics multiplied over the questions of federalism versus centralism in government and the role of the Church in society. The passions that these issues aroused were violently satiated in the bloody War of the Supremos, 1839–41.

As a result of that conflict, many of the more articulate men of property, many of the higher clergy, the triumphant faction of the Army leadership, and the bulk of the Santander-trained bureaucracy banded together in an attempt to restore order. Calling themselves *Ministeriales*, they managed to mold a more centralized state, and they opted for a more religiously orthodox educational system, imported Jesuits from Europe, and for a time (1841–43) managed to keep the most vocal of their opponents silent or in exile.

In 1845, the pugnacious General Tomás Cipriano de Mosquera was elected president as a Ministerial guarantee for peace, but his policies soon began to splinter the ruling elite. His appointment of the doctrinaire economic liberal Florentino González as Finance Minister was followed in 1847 by legislation that reduced import duties on many items, including consumer goods, by an average of thirty per cent. This measure adversely affected the interests of the artisan class scattered throughout the country's cities and towns. The discontented artisans coalesced with the opposition groups of the previous decade, which had been reactivated by the disintegration of Ministerial unity, and a new opposition leadership emerged. This process was influenced by the libertarian example of France, whose republican February Revolution in 1848 served as a catalyst and inspiration for what would become the Colombian Liberal party and its progressive "Generation of 1849." [1]

The election of the Liberal presidential candidate, General José Hilario López, on March 7, 1849, truly began a new era in the country's history. Before 1849, politics in Colombia was a struggle within the leadership elite, but the election of 1849 symbolized the mobilization of the middle classes (the artisans and junior officers in the Army) and a shift (occurring mainly between 1849 and 1854) toward a broader political base. The demoralized and divided Ministerials sought to reunite their ranks as the Conservative party. Mariano Ospina Rodríguez articulated a formal party program in August 1849, but the fissures in the former ruling group were too deep for it to gain complete acceptance. Furthermore, in November of the same year, Mosquera attempted to form his own centrist Progressive party, and this succeeded only in widening the rifts among the ex-Ministerials. This weakness of the Conservative opposition gave the Liberal Administration a chance to initiate some genuinely new policies.

Grouped around the weak figurehead of General López was an inner circle, a part of what would be called the Generation of 1849, dominated

---

[1] The Generation of 1849 was principally composed of young advocates of change, most of them lawyers, who were deeply imbued with British economic liberalism and French political libertarianism and who would emerge over the next decade (1849–60) as the leaders of the Liberal party.

by the libertarian ideologist Manuel Murillo. A brilliant journalist and polemicist, Murillo not only lacked executive governing experience but rid the Administration of most of its competent bureaucrats (mainly Ministerial holdovers) during the first six months of the new regime. To make matters worse, the López Administration, uncertain of its own viability, attempted to rush its program of political and social innovations and indulged in violent attacks on its opponents. The spate of legislation produced between 1850 and 1853 included the abolition of slavery, the separation of Church and State (that is, the end of official subvention, not interference), the legalization of civil marriage, the abolition of all academic degree requirements for the exercise of the professions, and many more provisions in the same egalitarian vein.

In desperation, the more aggressive elements within the divided Conservative opposition sought to overturn the Administration. The revolt that followed (May–September 1851) was quickly smothered, and its effect was exactly the opposite of what the rebels intended, for it revealed the absence of popular support for the Conservative elite in even the most tradition-bound and religion-oriented provinces of Pasto, Antioquia, Tunja, and Pamplona. What is more, for several years it eliminated any chance for the Conservatives to unite and form a "loyal opposition." In effect, it gave the Liberals a free hand to govern as they thought best, subject only to the limits of the economic viability of the Administration.

Ironically, the economic restraints on the Liberals were soon tightened by one of their own measures. Agitation against the colonial tobacco monopoly had gained momentum in the late 1840's, and in 1848 a law providing for its abolition by 1850 was enacted in response to Liberal pressures, causing a severe drop in official revenues. Another effect of the new law was the rise of a small number of tycoons, who were for the most part politically affiliated with the Liberals, with whom they identified their prosperity.

The Generation of 1849 seemed bent upon an immediate destruction of the entire colonial heritage. Not surprisingly, their efforts severely rent the Colombian social fabric, especially in the caste-ridden southern provinces of Buenaventura and Cauca.[2] However, social tensions were hardly less serious by the early 1850's in the cities and in many of the towns, where, especially in Bogotá, the artisan pressure groups (organized by the Liberal intellectuals into Democratic Societies in 1849 and 1850) grew increasingly impatient with unfulfilled political promises. Indeed, the economic position of the artisan class had actually worsened under Liberal rule. The wealth arising from the new private tobacco enterprises went into im-

---

[2] The southern region is emphasized in this chapter (see Documents 3, 4, and 5) because events there illustrate most graphically the clash between Liberal ideals and the social realities of the times.

ported consumer goods, which could successfully compete with wares produced by native craftsmen. The economic position of the artisans continued to deteriorate in the 1860's and 1870's. Their lot was made worse
by official efforts to convert the collectively held Indian lands into individually held property. Much of the communal farming land of the
Indians was purchased cheaply by local magnates and turned into
pasturage. This changeover led directly to food shortages in the cities and
an intensification of the price spiral.

By early 1854, the Liberal intellectuals had hobbled or weakened all
the institutions that they considered stumbling blocks to national progress
—all, that is, save one: the Army. Shrunken government revenues made
the survival of the relatively expensive military establishment all the more
odious to the headstrong theorists. The military in Bogotá became ex-
ceedingly nervous, and on April 17, 1854, under the leadership of General José María Melo, it rose up against the Government. This action was
applauded and joined by the disgruntled and now violently anti-Liberal
artisans of the capital.

What began as a barracks coup showed ominous signs of ending the
dominant role of the upper classes (both Liberal and Conservative) in
political and social life.[3] The members of the elite speedily buried ancient
grudges and personal animosities, and after several false starts, they fielded
armies which finally fought their way into Bogotá and overwhelmed a
force led by Melo on December 4, 1854. A sobered and less dogmatic
Liberal leadership agreed to share office with the more moderate among
the Conservatives, and two years of peace and bipartisan tolerance ensued
(1855–57).[4] The political voice of the artisans was effectively stilled.

The absence of a common danger brought a revival of partisanship.
The elections of 1856 saw the failure of General Mosquera's second effort
to create a third party, this time the National party (intrinsically,
moderately Liberal in orientation). They also witnessed the defeat of the
Liberal candidate, Manuel Murillo, and the victory of the dedicated Conservative candidate, Mariano Ospina. The period of Ospina's presidency
coincided with an insistent demand for an even greater extension of
federalist principles than that which characterized the barely tried Con-

[3] It should be noted that most elite families, whether Conservative or Liberal, were
related by blood or marriage. This, of course, did not prevent bitter partisan antagonisms
from developing once a common danger passed.

[4] The bipartisanship of 1855–57 was to be repeated on several occasions. The most
recent was the agreement reached at Sitges, Spain, on July 20, 1957, by the leadership
of the Conservative and Liberal parties. The Sitges Pact provided for the creation of
the National Front once the dictatorship of General Gustavo Rojas Pinilla was overthrown. The National Front is a system whereby for four presidencies, starting in
1958 and scheduled to end in 1974, the presidency alternately falls to one of the two
traditional parties (with ministerial parity shared by the other) every four years.

stitution of 1853. As a result, in 1858 New Granada became the Granadine Confederation, six nearly sovereign states loosely joined to a central government at Bogotá. Ospina's genuine gifts as an administrator were dissipated by his involvement in the internal politics of the states. His intolerance of political dissent and his espousal of clerical interests combined to rekindle the political aspirations of the Liberals.

The twin issues of effective federalism and destruction of the economic power of the Church, together with the highly personal antagonisms associated with Ospina, set off the Civil War of 1860–61. The Liberals, led militarily by General Mosquera (who by then had abandoned his National party and openly embraced the Liberal cause) and ideologically by Murillo, finally won.

A Constitution giving formal effect to the Liberal Revolution of 1861 was issued in May 1863. It sanctioned the massive confiscations of the Church's income-producing properties and reinstituted, with a vengeance, the federal system of sovereign states contained in the Granadine Confederation. A total of nine states made up what was then called the United States of Colombia. The president of the general government was limited to a two-year term and was elected by a majority of the votes of the states (usually by their legislatures), not by direct popular ballot.

For the next decade the Liberals retained power, but the Liberal elite, by excluding its defeated Conservative enemies from an effective political role, sowed the seeds of its own dissolution. The fragmentation of power and its dispersal into the hands of the state governors, legislatures, and local bosses made for a situation of almost constant turmoil. The repressive anticlerical measures greatly handicapped the most deeply rooted social institution, the Church, in fulfilling its minimal spiritual tasks and very nearly destroyed its ability to perform badly needed social services. With certain regional exceptions (mainly the states of Antioquia and Santander), after 1863 the plight of the masses went from bad to worse. A plethora of constitutional and legal rights were enacted but not implemented. The insecurity of political tenure that characterized the period of "Liberal hegemony," as the years 1867–77 might be called, brought demands for change and a return to stability.

The intransigent exclusivism of the Liberal directorate, its unwillingness to compromise even with other Liberal elements, much less with the Conservative opposition, plunged the nation into still another civil war, that of 1876–77. Although defeated on the battlefields, the Conservatives gained from the political disarray among the Liberals that plagued the subsequent presidency of General Julián Trujillo (1878–80), a moderate Liberal and the commander in chief of the victorious armies of the 1876–77 war. The real benefactor of Liberal disorganization, however, was Rafael Núñez, once a doctrinaire Liberal and a prominent member of the Generation of 1849. Núñez was excluded from the inner councils of the Liberal party by its titular head, Manuel Murillo, for his independence of mind in general and more specifically for his failure to take a definite anti-Church stand as a presidential candidate in 1876. By 1880, Núñez had forged a third political party, the Independents, and in that year, with the support of most political moderates, he was elected president (1880–82).

It can be argued that Núñez's Independents derived their strength and managed their political survival by articulating moderate political, social, and economic demands, both Liberal and Conservative. But Núñez was legally ineligible to succeed himself, and in 1882 the doctrinaire Liberals, taking full advantage of the Conservative party's postwar weakness and the Independent party's indecision, again gained the presidency (their last) by supporting the distinguished and nationally respected jurist Francisco Javier Zaldúa in a virtually uncontested election. Zaldúa was hindered in realizing any fundamental progress for either his nation or his party by an unsympathetic and often antipathetic Independent majority in Congress. A victim of both political and physical disabilities, Zaldúa died in December 1882, nine months after taking office. The acting Chief Executive, José Eusebio Otálora, was as impeded as his predecessor in effecting a program of political consolidation that would benefit his Liberal colleagues. Having refused the acting presidency upon Zaldúa's death, Rafael Núñez was constitutionally eligible for reelection and returned to the presidency in 1884.

Faced by a volatile political situation in the nation, complex personal problems, and the real prospect that his entry into Bogotá might trigger a violent reaction among the opposition, Núñez chose to absent himself from the Presidential Palace for over four months while his designate, General Ezequiel Hurtado, exercised that office. In September 1885, five months after Núñez assumed his presidential duties, the long-feared Liberal revolt flared in the northern state of Santander and spread rapidly throughout the Republic. Confronted by the possibility of a long and bloody war, Núñez acquiesced to the offer of help made by the Conservative party, which by 1885 had built a remarkably efficient political and military organization. Within eight months the revolt was crushed, but Núñez's dream of transforming his nation into a politically stable republic remained unrealized; and with Conservative influence at a new height, Núñez found he was no longer complete master of the situation. Together with his old Independent following and his new Conservative allies, Núñez addressed himself to the perennial question of constitutional reform, which had been bitterly debated since the implementation of the doctrinaire Liberal Constitution of 1863. As a result of their combined efforts, a new and strongly centralist Constitution was adopted in 1886 and remains in effect today. From that date also, and until 1930, the Conservatives alone directed the destiny of their nation. The radical Generation of 1849, which had initiated this turbulent phase in Colombian history, saw it brought to a close by one of its renegades.

In retrospect, the years from 1849 to 1886 are among the most interesting in Colombia's history. Determined to free themselves from what they considered the "shackles" of their Hispanic past, the members of the Generation of 1849 adopted most of the great humanitarian ideals of their European counterparts. They doubtless sincerely believed in the principles they proclaimed. When the time came for them to apply these principles to the broad mass of their countrymen, however, inbred or assumed class biases asserted themselves, and the transition from the ideal to the real did not take place.

This tension between conscious principles and unconscious bias may well have been at the base of the increased role of personalities in politics after 1854. It may also account for the great emphasis on abstract political goals, such as the extreme versions of federalism adopted in 1858 and 1863. An unconscious abdication of social responsibility may have lain at the heart of the performance of the Liberals after 1854. Such an evaluation, if correct, naturally does not imply that Conservatives felt any greater degree of social responsibility or had more imaginative solutions for Colombia's problems.

The Generation of 1849 must, however, be considered in its own historical context, not in that of later years. The very European ideals that they sought to adapt had, of course, been the result of centuries of maturation on the Continent and in England. The human misery that resulted from the application of economic liberalism in nineteenth-century Europe was certainly not less than that suffered by the hapless artisans or landless Indians of Colombia. The difference lay in the final results. In Europe, an economic base for political liberalism was laid by the 1880's, whereas none had been created in Colombia. Only a return to a strong, centralized system of political authority could begin the painful process of laying a solid basis—more consistent with Colombian historical tradition—for the governmental stability so desperately needed for economic development.

READINGS

1. The Liberals' Self-Image and View of Colombian History to 1852

The heady idealism of the Liberal Generation of 1849, its ebullient optimism and vitality, are very much in evidence in José María Samper's *Apuntamientos para la historia política i social de la Nueva Granada desde 1810, i especialmente de la Administración del 7 de Marzo*. Selections from this book follow.

There are high points in the history of nations that merit preferential attention.

New Granada, although a youthful nation, has had six such peaks . . . 1810, 1821, 1828, 1830 and 1831, 1837, and 1849.

The first of these was our glorious epoch: the epoch of the independence of an entire continent, of conquests for liberty, of heroism and battles, of self-sacrifice, of patriotism, and of radical change.

The second peak was one of truce and momentary rest, of organization, of triumph, and of hard work to create a free and sovereign nation where only a tribute-paying and abject people had existed.

The third period was a time of popular ferment, of traitorous ambitions alongside of generous sacrifices, of shame for Colombia, and of ephemeral victories for arbitrary rule—an ignominious time of the sovereignty of the sword.

The fourth peak was a time of usurpation by brutal force and of restoration by the sovereignty of the people. Shameful in its beginning, it was glorious in its prompt resolution.

The fifth peak began the reign of the oligarchy, with its deception of the people, and the . . . power of a depraved theocracy as obscurantist as it was humiliating; the government of privilege, and the somber rule of a political gallows. This was the epoch of absolutist terror.

The sixth period, beginning March 7, 1849, involved the resurrection of liberty, the development of national prosperity, the progress of republican

SOURCE: "The Liberals' Self-Image and View of Colombian History to 1852" translated from José María Samper, *Apuntamientos para la historia política i social de la Nueva Granada desde 1810, i especialmente de la Administración del 7 de Marzo* (Bogotá: Imprenta del Neo-Granadino, 1853), pp. 12–13, 433–35, 458–59, 483–85, 512–13, 515. All the readings in this chapter were translated by the chapter editor.

233

civilization influencing the entire South American continent, and the true foundation of democracy as the government of the [nineteenth] century. . . .

       .   .   .

The revolution of ideas [in nineteenth-century France] was taking a course that seriously threatened the constitutional monarchy of the Bourbons. Writers of fecund genius . . . had established France as the universal tribunal of liberty and had created a current of ideas and of hopes that, extending itself throughout the world, provoked the oppressed peoples of all races into taking part in the conquest for liberty and progress. . . .

Events of such magnitude [the 1848 overthrow of the Orleans monarchy in France] could not help exerting a powerful influence on politics [in Colombia] and greatly favor the efforts of the Democratic [Liberal] party. To this end, the Democratic party proclaimed the lofty principles that would carry it to immense popularity. The Democrats promised reform of the Constitution; abolition of slavery, the death penalty, the tithe, the ecclesiastical *fuero*, the tobacco monopoly, and other odious monopolies; a gradual reduction in the size of the regular Army until it was eliminated; absolute freedom of the press and of education; expulsion of the Jesuits; a general reform of public finance; adoption of strong municipal government; issuance of a civil code; trial by jury in criminal cases; and a host of other great and useful reforms in all branches of public administration. . . .

The defeat of the Conservatives was inevitable, for the people, who are always enthusiastic about the great and the unknown, love frankness, and esteem the courage of those who defend their cause, would of necessity feel themselves inclined toward liberal ideas and would give their support to those who profess them.

       .   .   .

A great revolution seemed about to emerge from the popular victory of the Seventh of March: a revolution in political behavior, in ideas, in institutions, and in the existence and social physiognomy of the Republic. . . .

The error of . . . colonial traditions, of a standstill society, had ended; the grand epoch of social development could begin.

The noble will of the people would substitute itself for the dominance of the three oligarchies: the clergy, the military, and the monopolists. Truth would defeat sophistry; freedom would occupy the place of oppression.

In place of traditional empiricism, the light of science would illumine . . . . Where hitherto inertia reigned . . . the movement of ideas, work, riches, and the popular masses would rule.

. . .

How great and beautiful was the mandate that General López held! . . . To found a republic in the heart of a people that had for so many years been swaying between absolutism and anarchy, a people continually victimized by . . . deception . . . was the colossal mission of the President of the Seventh of March!

. . .

The press and the forum . . . became a battleground for the two great political parties. Pamphlets multiplied . . . . In Bogotá and in the provinces, new printing presses and newspapers were established . . . increasing the agitation of the disturbed spirits. Democratic Societies, modeled on the imposing Society of Artisans of Bogotá, appeared successively, full of energy and enthusiasm and with large memberships, in Cali and Popayán, in Buga and Cartago, in Medellín and Ríonegro, in Mompós and Cartagena, in Santamarta and Pamplona, and in almost all the most important towns of the Republic. They were the centers of the movement, the focuses of the revolution that was taking place in ideas, in customs, and in the social life of the masses.

. . .

Everyone participated in politics: statesmen, the old, the young, women, artisans, priests, soldiers, children. Each individual meant something, because the sovereignty of the masses had begun to make itself felt.

. . .

Until 1848, Bogotá had been held in almost complete subjection by the clergy. The Jesuits and the other friars and clerics dominated most of the families with the power of superstitution, and they had been able to fanaticize the masses and make them into blind instruments of absolutistic propaganda. . . .

But suddenly some patriots conceived the idea of creating in Bogotá a Democratic Society, composed primarily of artisans and designed to be an electoral nucleus. In a few months, the Society's membership, originally drawn from the oppressed classes and numbering only eight or ten at the outset . . . grew to more than four thousand, among whom were found congressmen, the educated youth, and the most eminent republicans.

. . .

But revolutions require various elements. They need to be born, to spread, and to triumph . . . . The Revolution begun in 1848 had found a nucleus . . . in the Democratic Society, but it needed another great focal point of light, of enthusiasm, of spirit, of eloquence, and of gigantic inspiration that could make it take a powerful and sublime direction. The

Republican School,[1] that Gironde [2] of the New Granadan democracy, appeared to fulfill this glorious mission.

.   .   .

2. *The Conservative Response*

> In 1850, after the Liberals had been in power for fourteen months, Mariano Ospina Rodríguez published a meticulous indictment of their regime. His pamphlet, written by a pen seemingly dipped in vitriol, illustrates the passionate indignation felt by leading Conservatives over the behavior of the López Administration. Ospina eventually became President of the Republic (1857–61).

WHAT SHALL WE DO?   Fourteen months have passed since General José Hilario López took up the reins of the Government of New Granada, and in this time enough has been accomplished, both good and and bad, to serve as a basis upon which to judge the Administration.

.   .   .

THE PARTIES . . . The party called . . . Liberal Red has different shades, but we can divide it into three major parts. The first, what is now called in Europe the Red party, is composed of hotheaded men who uphold violence as a principle and who profess the ideas of old-fashioned French Jacobinism; this is the portion that has imposed itself today on the Republic . . . . The second is made up of men who basically accept conservative principles . . . who are affiliated with the Red flag because of family ties, because of regional attachment, [or] because of personal sympathies or antipathies . . . this portion rejects violence and sincerely desires liberty and security . . . . The third portion consists of a great mass of simple men who do not know the principles of the parties or the ideas that divide them; they believe that they belong in the Liberal Red party because they were involved in the rebellion of 1840, because

---

[1] [The Republican School, a political club, was the sounding board of the Generation of 1849. Founded in the capital in September 1850, it lasted until 1853. It was a vocally powerful pressure group that helped shape the policies adopted by the López Administration.]

[2] [The Girondins were a faction of French Revolutionary politicians, many from the department of Gironde (the Bordeaux area), prominent as exponents of republicanism in 1791–93 in the National Assembly and Convention. In July 1793, they were displaced by the Jacobins under Robespierre as the ruling force of the Revolution.]

SOURCE: "The Conservative Response" translated from Mariano Ospina Rodríguez, *Ojeada sobre los primeros catorce meses de la Administración del 7 de Marzo, dedicada a los hombres imparciales i justos* (Bogotá: Imprenta de El Día por José Ayarza, 1850), pp. 1, 7–8, 9–10, 11–14, 17–18, 62.

they have voted for the candidates of that party before, or because they follow a man affiliated with it. These men are usually religious, and if they ever saw clearly what the ideas were that divided the [Liberal and Conservative] parties, they would be singularly surprised to learn that they had been Red Liberals.

. . .

THE RELIGIOUS QUESTION   In Europe, particularly in France, Christianity and materialistic socialism are struggling face to face . . . . Those who in France proclaim the democratic and social Republic and call themselves socialists assume that . . . all religion is no more than a transitional stage of humanity that social progress should erase and that religion and government should be replaced with another order of ideas and formulas, which they call socialism; and they maintain that the time has come for this singular transformation. These socialists . . . clothe themselves with the names of democrats, liberals, and progressives and assert that those who want religion and reject the distribution of wealth . . . are absolutists, aristocrats, reactionaries, and the enemies of the people. . . .

These same nomenclatures and labels are used here, but there is an essential difference in the way the sect operates in France and the way it operates here. In France, the anarchic and antireligious sect has thrown off the veil of hypocrisy . . . and proclaims in a loud voice that it wants to subvert the social order and that it wants no more religion of any sort. Here the sect still wears a mask; and although this mask is transparent for anyone who knows the history of the changes of the sect, it nevertheless succeeds in hiding the face of the sect from the eyes of the people.

The New Granadans, like other Spanish Americans, receive all their opinions and ideas from French books . . . . All the nonsense, all the absurdities . . . propagated there by deeply perverted reason and by depraved and corrupted hearts . . . germinate and are reproduced here.

. . .

Thus, in the opinion of the Administration of the Seventh of March, Catholicism is the cause of fanaticism, ignorance, and the backwardness of New Granada; that is, the religion of the New Granadans is for the Administration the greatest of the calamities of the country.

. . .

Number 98 [of the semiofficial newspaper, *El Neo-Granadino*], after reprinting the violent diatribe directed against the Catholic Church by Victor Hugo in the French Assembly . . . [printed] an article entitled "Jesuitism" that is a direct and violent attack on the Church and on the Catholic religion . . . .

This piece contains a capital truth that the impious hypocrites who appeal to the Catholics in this country have tried to conceal—that the Jesuits are a phalanx of the Catholic Church created to battle heresy and impiety. This is the very reason why the enemies of Catholicism detest and persecute them.

. . .

The Governor of the province of Bogotá, General [José María] Mantilla, officially expostulated with Sr. Lino Peña, director of the provincial prison, because he had visited the Archbishop [Manuel José Mosquera] . . . and gave him to understand that if he maintained relations with the prelate, he would be removed from his post. This was taken to mean that the public servants in the Administration of the Seventh of March should sever relations with the prelates of their faith.

Last January [1849] in the Church of the Enseñanza of this city [Bogotá], a young Red committed certain insolent and irreverent acts against the Holy Eucharist that a respectable priest held in his hands. This action, subject to severe penalties . . . under the penal code, was reported to the authorities . . . but they took no steps, and the crime remained unpunished.

IMMORALITY   The Opposition has repeatedly demonstrated the tendency of the ruling Red extremist faction to undermine moral principles and to pervert and demoralize the people, and for this reason its writings published in the last twelve months deserve to be read by all those who can. . . .

One of the first acts of immorality of the agents of the new Administration . . . was violation of the mails. . . . Efforts to deny the accusation were in vain, because men of the greatest respectability raised their voices in different parts of the country to confirm it. Highly placed officials in the Secretariat of Finance had the cynicism to make this celebrated confession in one of the Government newspapers: "We examine the correspondence that the Conservatives send to the provinces through all the mails."

. . .

FREEDOM OF THE PRESS   Much has been said about freedom of the press in these times, and on this subject the liberalism of the Government can be tested.

. . .

[On May 21, 1850,] the Governor of Bogotá published an order decreeing that authors of stories that make the Government appear odious to the public shall be immediately arrested . . . fined, and jailed from three to twenty days, without advantage of judicial judgment and punishment. That is, all who censure an act of the Government shall suffer fine and arrest imposed by the Governor, although the jury declare them innocent. This order silenced the independent press . . . . Never has the freedom of the press guaranteed by the Constitution been attacked in such a direct and arbitrary manner in this country.

. . .

CONCLUSION   From all that has been shown, one deduces correctly that the conduct and principles of the violent circle that dominates the Republic tend directly to fight the Catholic religion and to demoralize and corrupt the Republic. With its unpublished and repeated violations of the Constitution and the laws, [the Government] is moving toward the exercise of absolute power and the nullification of all types of rights and freedoms. The ruling circle lacks the sincerity and good faith to make one trust its promises; no one can believe what they say or place any faith in what they offer. In such a deplorable situation, all good men have a duty to unite their efforts in order to maintain their institutions and preserve liberty, working through all legal means with firmness and perseverance.

3. *Social Tensions and Class Conflict in the South:* 1

In his *Memorias*, Ramón Mercado attempted to justify his actions as Liberal governor of the province of Buenaventura (the southern portion of today's department of Valle) in 1850–52. His book offers priceless insight into the social and political history of the Cali area from 1848 to 1852.

[THE SOUTH OF THE REPUBLIC BEFORE 1849]

. . . As a colony of Spain, New Granada inherited a part, and no small one, of all the bad traditions that have chained the human spirit since Constantine. For her, liberty was only a dream; when independence broke the chain that connected her to the overseas tyrants, her Moorish-Catholic beliefs, colonial customs, interests foreign to the progress of humanity, and laws set down in barbaric centuries for oppressed and abject peoples all combined, like a vine clinging to an exuberant young tree, to maintain the reactionary character of her society.

In one way, however, the cause of liberty in New Granada was indeed advanced, not because of the institutions that ruled her until 1849 but because of the character and temper of some of the provinces of the

SOURCE: "Social Tensions and Class Conflict in the South: 1" translated from Ramón Mercado, *Memorias sobre los acontecimientos del Sur de la Nueva Granada durante la Administración del 7 de Marzo de 1849* (Bogotá: Imprenta Imparcial, 1853), pp. vii–viii, xxv, xxx–xxxi, xli–xlii.

North of the Republic. This special phenomenon was little known; its beneficent influence did not manage to reach the center of the state, but remained unhappily lost in the territory between the Suárez and Táchira Rivers, like the melody of the goldfinch which does not leave the thick borders of the jungle. Ordinarily, if the echo of the North was perceived at all in the legislature or by the press, the still more robust echoes of the Coast, the Center, the West, and the South drowned out the cry of liberty, and the Republic remained stagnant.

.   .   .

Before the French Revolution of February 1848 and the revolutionary program of the Seventh of March, 1849, the South of the Republic, especially the provinces of Buenaventura and Caucà, presented such a picture of Spanishness and colonialism that an impartial observer would not have found much difference between its civilization and that of four-teenth-century Spain—the Spain of the military orders, holy miracles and infernal spirits, privileges for the few, oppression of the majority, and the fatal rule of the nobles and the friars.

.   .   .

The thirsty and hopeful people looked for freedom; the political party that had risen to power in their name had been master for fifteen months, and still the heaviest chains had not been broken . . . . The decree ex-pelling the Jesuits, which the entire Liberal party considered urgent, [had never been promulgated,] and all circumstances indicated that it would not be promulgated in the future. For the same reason, once the Government became indecisive and fearful, there was no hope of abolishing slavery, nor did the Congress of 1850 give any signs of doing so.

Thus, up to the end of May, the Liberal party of Cali, composed almost entirely of the despised masses, felt the fury of despair—a despair height-ened by the press; and the oligarchy was filled with insolence and the pride of a man who believes himself so great that fear of his power will ensure that his rights will be respected.

The decree of May 18 [1850, expelling the Jesuits] restored the hopes and faith of the despairing, but instead of ending the boldness and tenacity of the aristocracy, it exacerbated them. The decree was a death blow for the *beatos* [religious fanatics] and a formidable threat to the vested in-terests created in the shadow of plunder; the former cried tears of pain, while the privileged classes prepared to do battle.

The projected law of decentralization promised much social progress . . . but municipal power was in the hands of the Conservatives, and this was an obstacle against which the people would fight in vain, because the existing electoral assemblies had three more years to serve in office. The Buenaventura legislature of 1849, ignoring pressing petitions, maintained the *aguardiente* [spirits] monopoly; and the elections of deputies for the session of 1850, held early in August [1849], had seen persons hostile to the popular will selected.

.   .   .

Thus, the political situation of the people of the South was ominous at the end of 1850. The doctrines preached in the Center and North of the Republic had made themselves felt; young men of spirit had presented themselves . . . and preached the most liberal doctrines, those that most corresponded to the tendencies of the people. These were young men saturated with the ideas that would regenerate the masses, men who openly fought fanaticism and reaction of all types, but they were also men too inexperienced to see that conquests by the masses are always achieved by deeds and demand sacrifices. And there [in the province of Buenaventura], like the place where most resistance was found to the impetus of the republican movement [that is, the Liberal party], the clash was most violent, the fight was most demanding, and the results were to be most disastrous.

.   .   .

Aside from the actions of the Buenaventura legislature . . . the main reasons for the discontent of the masses were as follows:

1. The behavior of some landlords regarding the disputed land of the *ejidos* [that is, communal property];

2. The vexatious practices employed by the contractors of the aguardiente monopoly: burdening the daily lives of the poor, searching private houses, imprisoning unfortunate women, auctioning off their insignificant possessions, and molesting them in every sense; [1]

3. The anger produced among the slaveowners by the publication of the decree stipulating the treatment that should be given them [the slaves] and by the faithful enforcement of the manumission law . . . ; [2]

4. The anxiety in which the Negroes were put by the Liberal party's

---

[1] [The aguardiente monopoly operated through a system of government contracts with large distillers, who paid to the treasury an annual sum based on their production. Persons without contracts caught manufacturing liquor were liable to severe legal sanctions. Since the poorer classes could rarely afford the higher-priced legal aguardiente and since their demand for alcohol was high, stills outside the law were widespread. Bootlegging had become almost a cottage industry in the Cali area.]

[2] [This refers to the law passed by the Congress in Bogotá in June 1850, reminding slaveholders that they should observe the Royal Decree of May 31, 1789, which provided for the humane treatment of slaves. Furthermore, the 1850 law strove to hasten the pace of the manumission of slaves born before 1821. In the latter year, the Congress of Cúcuta passed legislation to manumit slave children from bondage after they had reached the age of eighteen and to provide means to accumulate funds to purchase the freedom of the remaining slaves. In practice, however, especially in the southern provinces of New Granada, these humanitarian provisions had been inconsistently enforced. Partly because this social fact of life was recognized and partly because the Liberals wished to punish major slaveowning Conservatives, slavery was definitively abolished by law on May 21, 1851.]

promise to abolish slavery, on the one hand, and by the efforts and determination of the masters that this measure not take place, on the other;

5. The worry caused by several letters from the capital of the Republic, especially those written by the man who was Secretary of the Interior in December of 1850 [Manuel D. Camacho], which told the slaveowners that they could sleep peacefully, because while he was in the Ministry abolition would not be carried out;

6. The distrust and desperation that this produced in the Liberals who sponsored the Negro cause;

7. The effects of the onerous taxes decreed by the Provincial Chamber;

8. The insults, calumnies, and abuses spewed forth by Conservative newspapers such as *El Ariete, La Esfinje, El Día,* and *La Civilización* and by a multitude of broadsides . . . ;

9. The frequent tumults [of the people], which gave [the oligarchy] an excuse for judicial indictments;

10. *The ancient resentments between the aristocracy and the people;*

11. The election struggle over Cabildo [town council] seats . . . and the ire of the oligarchs on seeing the people's candidates filling those positions;

12. *The proclamation of equality;*

13. *The struggle with fanaticism;*

14. The cruelty of certain wealthy men and landlords toward their tenants or debtors;

15. The vision of a future of freedom—a not very distant future, in the avid eyes of the multitude—in place of the old system of oppression.

These factors deeply moved the masses and prevented them from heeding the exaggerated charges of crimes and assaults launched by the oligarchy as it was swept aside by its powerful antagonist [the force of popular opinion].

4. The South as Observed
by a Yankee Traveler

The best nineteenth-century travel account in English about Colombia was written by a sympathetic American observer, Isaac Fenton Holton. This selection from Holton's book gives some of his own views, those of a Conservative from the South, and those of a Bogotá Liberal.

SOURCE: "The South as Observed by a Yankee Traveler" from Isaac Fenton Holton, *New Granada: Twenty Months in the Andes* (New York: Harper & Brothers, 1857), p. 527.

I have reserved till now the mention of a sight that met my eyes frequently between Buga and Palmira. I saw many fields that had once been fenced, of which the fence was destroyed. I think I have known a mile, I might say miles together, destroyed. They tell me that a thousand men have been employed in this work of devastation at once. I applied to the authorities for an explanation of the matter, but for a long time received none, but then received too much. I was never able to read it all.

"No man can dispute or explain away," says Señor [Miguel] Cáldas, "the chief facts. Your own eyes, Señor, have seen the devastation of once flourishing properties; but that is little. The men who did it called themselves Perreristas. Perrero means dog-whip, the heaviest whip known here, with handle of guayacan and lash of raw-hide. The owners of these fields were whipped with them whenever they caught them. Many suffered this ignominy. Many left their property to ruin, and lived in the large towns in poverty and want, and not even then in safety. Houses, too, were damaged, as the Señor has also seen. Women were violated. And all this was done by the secret orders of President López and his more infamous successor Obando."

"I can not deny the crimes," replies [José] Triana; "but there are extenuating circumstances that you do not mention; and as to their origin, I cannot agree with you in attributing them to even the gobernadores, and still less to the President. There has always been a ferocity in the politics on this side of the Quindio. More blood has been shed in this valley than in all the rest of the republic. Pasto has always been an active or dormant volcano. The property of this central part of the valley has been all in the hands of rich holders of slaves and mines in the Chocó. They have no sympathy with the poor. They have been the owners of a large part of the inhabitants of this valley also, till the law made them loose their grasp on the 1st of January, 1852.

5. *Social Tensions and Class Conflict in the South: 2*

Miguel Wenceslao Carvajal's *Escenas democráticas de Bugalagrande i Folleco* is a defense of his tenure as *fiscal* (prosecuting attorney) and as governor of Cauca Province, in 1851 and 1854 respectively. The document included here was a report submitted by Carvajal in June

SOURCE: "Social Tensions and Class Conflict in the South: 2" translated from Miguel Wenceslao Carvajal, *Escenas democráticas de Bugalagrande i Folleco* (Bogotá: Imprenta del Neo-Granadino, 1856), pp. 40–41.

1851 on an assault case of the kind that had become common in Cauca Province (the northern half of what is now the department of Valle) during the López presidency.

Vista fiscal [district attorney's report] in the case against Santiago Cruz, resident of Tuluá.

Señor Circuit Judge:

On the night of the twentieth of April last [1851], at about ten o'clock, Santiago Cruz, walking toward his store in the company of José Antonio Lozano, met up with a group of three or four men, who made a gesture as if to recognize Cruz; but when they stood aside so that [Cruz and Lozano] could pass them, Lozano said to them, "Boys, what's new?" And Cruz shot a pistol at the figures, wounding one of them named Eugenio Pérez. At the sound of the pistol shot and the cries of Pérez's companions, many people appeared and began to pursue the offending individual. Cruz ran and took refuge in the house of Señora Dionisia Escovar, but this was not sufficient to save him from the fury of the mob; despite the presence of the public authorities and the urgings of several prestigious and socially respectable persons, Cruz was the victim of the fury of the mob, which threw itself upon him and manhandled him atrociously.

This is the evidence from the summary investigation, in virtue of which he was charged with assault. In rendering my opinion, I have considered the trial proceedings and compared them with the record of the summary investigation. The witnesses' allegations are not duly proved except in the case of the victim, and . . . his testimony [is legally] irrelevant. Even though [one set of] five witnesses state that they clearly and distinctly *heard* the sound of blows at the indicated time, before the shot rang out, nonetheless the testimony of the [other set of] witnesses in the summary remains in all its vigor: These *saw*, they were eyewitnesses of the event, and they are in agreement as to the manner, time, place, and essential circumstances, so that the affair can be viewed under another aspect.

It is an undeniable and well-known fact that the valley of the Cauca is teeming with bands that, invoking the Seventh of March and the President of the Republic, give themselves over to all kinds of excesses. Their barbarism has reached the extreme of murder—cruelly whipping to death those against whom they bear old grudges. And woe to him who calls himself a Conservative, for then the bands lose all feeling of Christian charity.

Santiago Cruz has proved that at the time of his misfortune the tensions among political parties were at a peak. Cruz has also proved that in Tuluá, all those of his particular political persuasion were persecuted with the ignominious weapon of the whip and that he was one of the candidates for whipping, since [his enemies] had waylaid him several times and had even broken into his house.

Consequently, gripped as he was by fear and panic, it was natural that on leaving a political meeting on a dark night and meeting men who were observing him and trying to identify him, he would persuade himself that they were laying a trap for him, even more so since he was accompanied by a person of whom he was suspicious and who exchanged words with them. Here then, out of cowardice (according to the victim [Pérez] and other witnesses who testified against him) and out of indiscretion, he shot without thinking, believing that he would thus repel the unjust attack that in that moment his overactive imagination convinced him would descend on him.

On the other hand, it is on record that Cruz is an honest young man, of irreproachable conduct and mild temperament, and that, furthermore, he had no contacts with the victim that might have given rise to vengeance.

From all of which I deduce that Santiago Cruz is . . . subject to the fourth part of the minimum penalty assigned . . . for having committed the imprudent or indiscreet act alluded to in Article 627 of the [penal] code.

The District Attorney, *Manuel W. Carvajal*
Buga, June 23, 1851

6. The Confrontation Between Artisan and Intellectual: Bogotá, 1853

Another perceptive visitor to Colombia was the wealthy and conservative Brazilian diplomat Miguel Maria Lisbôa. His *Relação de uma Viagem a Venezuela, Nova Granada e Equador* comments on the widening gap between Liberal intellectuals and their artisan clients.

There are recent and very significant proofs of the good nature of the lower class. During the last part of López's Administration and the first part of Obando's,[1] a group of imprudent Frankensteins created a

---

[1] [General José María Obando won election to the presidency in 1852. His term began on April 1, 1853, and was to have ended on March 31, 1857. He was, of course, deposed by the Melo revolt of April 17, 1854. His strange passivity during the Melo interlude brought him under suspicion of complicity, and he was removed from office by the Senate in 1855.]

SOURCE: "The Confrontation Between Artisan and Intellectual: Bogotá, 1853" translated from Miguel Maria Lisbôa, *Relação de uma Viagem a Venezuela, Nova Granada e Equador* (Bruxellas: A. Lacroix, Verboeckhoven e Cia., 1866), pp. 244–45.

monster that in any part of Europe would have devoured them instantly. Addressing themselves to an uneducated people accustomed only to the dominance of the clergy, they preached the most extreme communist and socialist doctrines. They organized the people into democratic societies, and, foolishly believing that they marched at the head of world civilization and that all other nations were deplorably backward, they brought the Republic to the brink of the abyss. This rash policy engendered unrealistic hopes and ideas, and it divided the classes into two groups—differentiated by their street clothes—called *cachacos* (cassocks) and *ruanas* (ponchos). The cachacos of Bogotá were young men full of fire; acting, no doubt, in good faith and with good intentions, but carried away by the absurd theory that mature men are by their decrepitude and attachment to routine incapable of ruling society, they were the first to set an example of anarchy in the halls of Congress, shouting and taking part in the legislative discussions from the galleries and stigmatizing those whose political opinions differed from their own. This example was shortly followed by the ruanas (on June 8 and 9, 1853), who made a menacing appearance of their own in Congress, demanding a reform of the tariffs *in a protectionist vein,* and who carried their audacity to the extreme of provoking a battle in the streets of Bogotá. But a little energy on the part of the Government and a single rigorous example were enough to bring these men [the ruanas] back to order and obedience, so that on August 11 of that same year, when I left Bogotá, it enjoyed the most complete tranquility.

Cachacos and Ruanas: Bogotá, 1850. From Isaac F. Holton's *New Granada: Twenty Months in the Andes.* New York: Harper & Bros., 1857.

7. The Cleavage Within the Liberal Party (1853–54)

Aníbal Galindo's *Recuerdos históricos* are memoirs written with half a century's perspective by a member of the Liberal Generation of 1849. Like so many of his contemporaries, Galindo tries to ignore the social issues of the 1850's and offers a political explanation for the events of April 17, 1854.

In 1853, the ascendant movement of Liberalism was clashing not with the Conservative party, which now seemed more in agreement with than in opposition to the liberal reforms culminating in the splendid Constitution of 1853 . . . but with another faction of the Liberal party that was motivated more by passion than by ideas—men of action ranged against the ideologists, men who generally preferred the solutions of force to those of liberty. In the religious question, men of this faction have always favored keeping the Church subject to and dependent upon the civil power (with the *patronato*[1] or a system of civil inspections in religious matters) rather than maintaining an absolute separation of the two powers under the principle of "a free Church in a free State." In economic matters, they demand a system of protection for national products and oppose the principle of absolute free trade. In the purely political sphere, they advocate a strong executive power endowed with all the attributes necessary to repress its opponents and to preserve public order. During the debate over the Constitution of 1853, they did all they could to resist the popular election of provincial governors, not only as a matter of principle and because they believed that the national executive power, were it to be thus shorn of its appointive power, would be reduced to impotence and the Administration disorganized, but because they felt that the measure was being advanced out of personal animus against the President of the Republic, General José María Obando. The *Obandistas*, as we may call this faction, christened the university youth, the bubbling spring and nucleus of reform, the *Gólgotas*, using that nickname, derived from the hill where the Savior's cross was raised, to ridicule

---

[1] [The patronato was a legacy from the colonial period. It had been assumed by the republican governments since 1824. In practice, the successive Colombian regimes had collected the tithes, supervised ecclesiastical affairs, and exercised the significant power of nominating churchmen to benefices.]

SOURCE: "The Cleavage Within the Liberal Party (1853–54)" translated from Aníbal Galindo, *Recuerdos históricos* (Bogotá: Imprenta de la Luz, 1900), pp. 74–76.

the absurd idealism of their doctrines. The Gólgotas, in turn, baptized their adversaries with the hateful sobriquet of *Draconianos*. With these names, the division between the two Liberal factions worsened and deepened until it turned into mutual hatred.

In these circumstances, a personal misfortune . . . touched off the [final] clash. General José María Melo, one of the most distinguished officers of the War of Independence, professional soldier . . . proven Liberal, a man against whom there had never been imputed the commission of a criminal act, had recently returned from Venezuela, where he had remained since 1830, and was serving as the Commandant General of the Army. On the night of December 31, 1853, upon entering the cavalry barracks where he had his quarters, he had the misfortune to . . . fatally wound a corporal named [Ramón] Quiros, whom he had found drunk on the stairway. . . .

The radicals [Gólgotas], who controlled the legislative houses and the press and who bitterly hated Melo because of his military command, gave him no quarter; they snatched the case out of the jurisdiction of the military tribunals . . . and threatened to give Melo a public hanging.

Here we have the political environment in which was produced the military coup of April 17, 1854.

8. *A Glimpse at the Events of April 17, 1854*

The collapse of the alliance between Liberal intellectuals, artisans, and the Liberal military that Melo's coup symbolized is aptly sketched in the following lines from Isaac Holton's *New Granada*.

The government itself was desperate. It had yielded to Red Republican (Gólgota) theories too far. These speculators had adopted the belief that universal suffrage and a free constitution were a remedy for all human evils. They had, as their expositor Samper says, "*a blind faith in principles.*" They had made their changes too rapidly, and were bent on trying all kinds of experiments; and especially they had a fanatical hatred to a standing army. That of New Granada did, in fact, strike me rather as a nuisance, but it was small and diminishing, and all attempts at a militia had failed.

SOURCE: "A Glimpse at the Events of April 17, 1854" from Isaac Fenton Holton, *New Granada: Twenty Months in the Andes* (New York: Harper & Brothers, 1857), pp. 556–57, 558, 560.

General Melo . . . seemed to have become particularly obnoxious to the Gólgotas. They hated him. An ex-gobernador said to me one day, "Melo's troop rode furiously past me just now; they had as lief ride over one as not. If I had had a pistol, I would have fired after them."

. . .

A large number of the lower class [were] enemies to coats and gentility . . . .

. . .

Coarse shirts and ruanas were in great request. Few coats were seen in the streets, and those were worn by foreigners. Sudden friendships were formed by old political antagonists, now in common danger. . . . I see too, that my good landlady Margarita is rather prejudiced against cachacos, but has ordered the *cajera* [cashier] to give moderate credit to any wearers of ruanas.

9. Regroupment: A Liberal Reappraisal of the Period 1855–60

In 1877, Enrique Cortés issued a pamphlet, signed with the pseudonym "Ignotus," pleading for progress in Colombia through mass education. The pamphlet was also an acidulous examination of the performance of the author's own Liberal party after 1854.

Doctrinaire liberalism, having reached its apogee in that year [1854], slowed down and began to decline. This loss of momentum was caused by the infusion of conservative elements after the Melo revolt was suppressed.

The purely doctrinaire spirit of the party . . . began to focus on the federalist ideal. All that remained from the recent period of agitation was antimilitarism. This feeling, reinforced by the fresh memory of the Melo revolt, was so strong that in 1856 a standing army of only five hundred men was authorized, the smallest in the country's history.

The federalist idea, now supported by both parties, matured with the rapidity that our national character finds so attractive, and the legislation passed from 1855 to 1857, especially the successive laws creating the eight original states, is permeated with it.

From 1854 to 1858, a slow retrograde movement was seen, more so

SOURCE: "Regroupment: A Liberal Reappraisal of the Period 1855–60" translated from [Enrique Cortés,] *La lección del pasado: Ensayo sobre la verdadera misión del partido liberal* (Bogotá: Imprenta de Medardo Rivas, 1877), pp. 11–12.

in the supplementary legislation than in the new basic laws. Thus, the 1858 Constitution, the creation of an overwhelmingly Conservative Congress, organized the federation already established by previous legislative action, recognized all the conquests achieved by the efforts of the Liberal party, did not reestablish any of the colonial abuses, enshrined federalism, and can in sum be considered a highly liberal document. The reactionary movement of the period was noticeable . . . in the 1854 law of religious freedom that delivered the cemeteries to the Catholics (that is, to the priests); the law of 1856 prohibiting divorce; and the penal laws of 1858 and 1860, which reflect the repressive spirit of the theocratic party. The law of 1859 governing elections should also be mentioned, since, along with the law of the same year spelling out the organization and inspection of the armed forces of the states, it was the direct cause of the Liberal rebellion. . . .

The tempest of 1860–63 had as its doctrinal focus freedom from mortmain [1] of the Church's properties; once it was over, the untrammeled Liberal Party reorganized the country to its taste in the [Constitutional] Convention of Rionegro. The document that emerged [the 1863 Constitution] makes it appear that a double viewpoint prevailed in the councils of the members of the Convention.

On the one hand, the spirit of reform, frustrated since 1854–57 . . . reawakened in the breast of the party, which completed the development of its theories.

On the other hand, the spirit of federalism, inflamed and strengthened by the attacks of President [Mariano] Ospina, was absolutely dominant in the creation of the Constitution.

The Constitution of Rionegro represented the complete development of these two viewpoints—or, more accurately, feelings—that prevailed in the councils of the party. It extended the list of individual rights, adding to those already existing absolute freedom of speech, suppression of the death penalty, and freedom of commerce in arms and munitions. A loose federation was established, and nine *sovereign* states were created.

The movement begun in 1849 thus found itself completed in the Charter of Rionegro, and the federalist idea, put into practice for the first time in 1855, reached its most ample extension.

[1] [Mortmain comes from Old French and means "dead hand." It signifies possession of real estate held in perpetuity by a corporation—usually the Church.]

10. *Some Social Consequences*

of the Second Wave of Liberalism (1867)

The Liberal principles evident in José María Samper's history (see Document 1) can also be seen in the works of his brother Miguel, although the latter is a more reflective and deliberate writer. In a series of essays originally published in 1867 and now collectively entitled "La Miseria en Bogotá," Miguel paints a somber portrait of the fruits of Liberal anticlericalism and federalism.

Let us see how Bogotá appears:

Beggars fill its streets and squares, displaying not only their poverty but also an insolence that is a cause for wonder, for alms are *demanded,* and he who refuses to distribute them is exposed to insults that no one thinks to curb. That mendicancy should develop in a country that is fertile, whose climate is benign, and where industry has hardly begun to exploit the resources that nature's bounty offers; in a land whose institutions open the doors for every attempt to acquire wealth; and where, according to *written* law, all men have equal rights and no man can be deprived of them . . . that mendicancy should develop here, on a great scale and with special characteristics, is an alarming fact in more than one sense.

But not all the beggars are seen in the streets. The majority of the poor of the city . . . hide their misery; they shut themselves up with their children in dilapidated rooms and there suffer the agonies of hunger and nakedness. If it were possible to take a census of all the beggars . . . in Bogotá . . . the number would be terrifying and the danger of the situation would be more visible . . . .

The law and the new political situation have augmented the number of beggars. The nuns who were thrown out on the street in 1863, after having been stripped of all they possessed; the regular clergy and those clerics who served benefices or foundations endowed with incomes from the Church's mortmain properties; the sick, more than two hundred of whom could receive care in the hospital of this city, who now cannot find the means to be cured, cannot work and so are turned with their families into beggars; finally, the host of fired officials, civil as well as military, whom the partisan spirit has torn without pity from their posts—all these needy classes have become greater or lesser burdens on society as a whole.

. . .

SOURCE: "Some Social Consequences of the Second Wave of Liberalism (1867)" translated from Miguel Samper, *Escritos político-económicos de Miguel Samper,* 4 vols. (Bogotá: Editorial de Cromos, 1925–27), 1, pp. 8–10, 56.

The Constitution of 1863, which in the eyes of many is truly a riddle, institutionalizes anarchy. The states are subjected . . . to the same influences as the nation; and if the moral level of the men who are politically influential on the national level has visibly declined in recent years, on the state level it has approached zero. In each one of the states, enthralled or corrupt chieftains dispute power with each other, keeping society in a perpetual upheaval and wracked by the most unrestrained vandalism.

11. *The Contrast Between Promise and Fulfillment: Colombia in 1877*

The bitter harvest of the Liberal hegemony (1876–77) is examined in this additional selection from Enrique Cortés's *La lección del pasado.*

From 1863 to the present [1877], a backward trend has been apparent in the soul of the Liberal party.

Of course, the Constitution of Rionegro itself . . . shows a reaction against the absolute separation of Church and State that had been considered one of the cardinal points of the [Liberal] program in the period from 1849 to 1854. The feeling in favor of subjecting the clergy [to the State] has since then grown increasingly strong . . . .

Opposition to a permanent army [1] and to the military in general, which fourteen years before had served as the party's strongest bond and which had had so much generous blood shed in its behalf in 1854, was to weaken and disappear in the victorious fields of the Civil War of 1860. From 1863 to our own day, that sentiment has not reappeared in our political debates, except in 1871 when the Rojas Garrido Law [which aimed to secure the extinction of the regular Army] was passed. The adoption of that law was unenthusiastic, however, and the proposal to abolish it easily won unanimous approval of the Liberal party in 1876.

Direct, universal [male], and secret suffrage had been a major Liberal

---

[1] [Proposals to replace the regular Army with a citizen militia were deeply rooted in the Liberal credo. Originally created in 1840, the militia was in 1850 given parity of ranks with that of the regular Army. Deliberate efforts to employ it instead of the professional soldiery were made in 1855–56, and in 1862 an ambitious training program for the militia was designed. Although a lack of funds and economic and political instability effectively prevented the formation of a national militia, under the 1863 Constitution the semisovereign states were empowered to, and often did, raise their own militias.]

SOURCE: "The Contrast Between Promise and Fulfillment: Colombia in 1877" translated from [Enrique Cortés,] *La lección del pasado: Ensayo sobre la verdadera misión del partido liberal* (Bogotá: Imprenta de Medardo Rivas, 1877), pp. 13, 25–26.

demand from 1849 to 1854. The old enthusiasm for the measure was notably dampened in the breast of the Rionegro Convention, however. Considered so fundamental in 1853 that it was guaranteed in the Constitution of that year, the principle was not even mentioned in the Charter of Rionegro. From 1863 to the present, suffrage and the radical theories that dealt with it have in practice experienced noticeable alterations. In many states, suffrage has been restricted to those individuals who can read and write. The frauds and abuses to which this keystone of the Republic is subject have discouraged and alienated from it the support of a large number of good Liberals.

. . .

A bird's-eye view of what has happened since the War of Independence will confirm the truth of what I state.

It is understandable why universal [male] suffrage will not work among a people whose general state of ignorance makes a conscientious use of the vote impossible and offers the clergy, the landowners, and factions of the educated class the greatest incentive to defraud and exploit them. If the masses thought and acted [according to reason], then manipulation of the ballot could not be the exclusive domain of the curate, the rich landlord, or the influential local political boss.

. . .

The abolition of the Army is impossible in a country in which an influential individual can, by force or by his influence, head uprisings and sponsor continuous rebellions.

. . .

Municipal autonomy must be a joke in a nation in which a small group in each state can change governments and undo Constitutions by means of that rifle-firing machine, the people. The incentive is too tempting, and the means [are] too easy; so the small number that finds itself in the apex of the pyramid will [always] tear itself to pieces in the perpetual struggle for dominance. . . .

And is it not true that the history of the past thirteen years in Boyacá, Cundinamarca, Tolima, Magdalena, and Panamá has been one of the strife of rival factions? Do we not see here reproduced on a small scale the history of the Italian Republics, divided as we are into small groups dominated by ambitious and small upper classes?

The truth is that all the guarantees and freedoms our Constitution establishes are benefits for the educated class, for the aristocracy, for the insignificant minority. They are not enjoyed by the great bulk of the population.

Of what use is the ballot to a people who do not understand it, who live submissive [to the will of] the landlord or the priest? Of what use is the right of assembly to a people who do not know how to assemble nor have any reason or time to do so after the hard labor of the day? Of what use is the freedom of the press to a people who cannot read or write? Of what use is freedom of commerce to a people who lack capital, credit . . . ?

12. *A Parish Priest Surveys a Decade of Labors, 1865–75*

A sharp insight into the problems confronting the clergy in the field and the plight of the Indians half a century after independence is given in a report written in 1875 by Padre Juan Nepomuceno Rueda, a curate serving in the parish of Sogamoso. Located some 130 miles northeast of Bogotá in the department of Boyacá, Sogamoso had been a major Indian population center before the Spanish conquest.

Forty curates had served in the two centuries of the existence of the parish [but no special altar was ever built for the Holy Week celebrations], despite the fact that Sogamoso had been a rich curacy during the time of the Viceroyalty and in the first years of the Republic, when the Indians still held their common lands and the flatlands were planted with grain and yielded abundant harvests. Today the savanna has only cattle ranches, which produce nothing of benefit to the church or the curate.

The natives, having sold their lands at ridiculously low prices, repaired to the mountain range, where the scarcity of rains and the lack of water for irrigation cause the loss of a greater part of their crops each year. The fact that they sold their land to persons who have not devoted it to agriculture but turned it into beautiful pastures has reduced them to pauperism, and almost all the religious feasts that they celebrated fell into oblivion. The curacy declined, and today it is hardly adequate; it can be said that it is only an eloquent remnant of what it was. The truth is, by virtue of this change, good or bad as it might be from the standpoint of industrial or economic development, the income of the curate has diminished by half, in proportion to the growth of his task due to the increased population and to the distance [he must travel] to reach the natives, who no longer can live in the bountiful fields where they were born and which they owned half a century ago.

SOURCE: "A Parish Priest Surveys a Decade of Labors, 1865–75" translated from Padre Juan Nepomuceno Rueda, *Informe que el Cura de Sogamoso dirije al Ilustrísimo i Reverendísimo Señor Arzobispo en el año de 1875* (Bogotá: Impreso por Cándido Pontón, 1875), p. 18.

13. *Rafael Núñez and His Regeneration:*
Reconstruction or Reaction?

In *Núñez y la regeneración* (1895), Carlos Calderón Reyes describes the sense of national malaise that Colombia felt by 1880. He also reveals the factors that convinced Rafael Núñez that only a return to order with a centralized Constitution would save his country.

A storm was in the offing, and the events that had unsettled the country during the preceding few years were . . . symptoms of the upheaval that was to burst forth—undoubtedly the prologue to the history of the new Constitution. . . . [T]he failings of the current institutions were . . . obvious to everybody except those who from a sort of habit proclaimed the perfections of the system. The frequency of elections and the organization of the vote had created diverse party alignments in the states. The radical Liberal party, spurred by its electoral gains, believed that its chance to recapture power by means of force had arrived, ignoring the fact that it could gain power sooner by employing more subtle means. The Conservative party had lent its votes and its support to the Independent [Núñez] party to defeat the radicals, on occasion sacrificing principle for discipline. The Independent party, although it maintained its power in the states, had been weakened by . . . the struggle and shattered by desertions, and at times it had to use force to retain its position. . . . The result of the political system for the country was intense suffering—unrest, disorder, constant alarm, disorganization, and the demoralization of the parties. . . .

Public funds were dissipated in subsidies to the states and in military expenditures. The country's exports diminished because of competition in the foreign markets. The budget deficit reflected the demands of the political system and the economic illness from which the nation suffered. It is true that for twenty-two years prosperity had kept Santander State peaceful, like a palace that escapes a fire that burns the city around it, but the people of Santander, virtuous, austere, and as republican as the Swiss, threw themselves into the Civil War on the day Java and Ceylon overcame our quinine exporters in the London market. The steel hatchet turned into . . . a murderous weapon . . . men who had searched the forests for the valuable [quinine] bark became soldiers of the rebellion.

SOURCE: "Rafael Núñez and His Regeneration: Reconstruction or Reaction?" translated from Carlos Calderón Reyes, *Núñez y la regeneración* (Sevilla: Imprenta de Izquierdo y Cía., 1895), pp. 63–66, 71–72, 80–85, 108–10.

CONCLUSION

The period of Liberal preponderance in government, lasting from 1849 until the 1880's, was characterized by the wholesale attempt to reject the corporate nature of the Spanish colonial system, which had survived the wars for independence and had been incorporated into the governmental structure of New Granada. The years after 1849 saw the main parts of the Liberal program progressively enacted into laws which were gathered together into coherent form by their partisans in the Constitution of Rionegro in 1863. The removal of obstacles to the realization of republican democracy involved the destruction of centralized government, which was closely identified with oligarchy, and its replacement by a federal form. The Liberals abolished restrictive economic institutions of colonial origin, such as monopolies, high tariffs, slavery, and communal Indian lands. Colombia became a free trade nation. Moreover, the Liberals viewed the corporations of Church and Army as the main supports of oligarchy and sought, therefore, to destroy the Church and replace the professional Army with a citizen militia.

But the results of Liberal legislation were almost entirely negative. Decentralized government resulted in regional bossism; anticlericalism, economic impoverishment of the masses, and recurrent civil war provided the basis for a Conservative reaction within the Colombian political spectrum. The Constitution of 1886 essentially reestablished the Spanish form of corporate government: centralized political control, the maintenance of a standing army, the protection and subsidization of the Church, and high protective tariffs, which provided revenues for government and shielded Colombian industry from foreign competition. Perhaps the only accomplishment of the Liberal era was the intellectual effervescence that the optimism of the early years and the disillusionments of the 1860's and 1870's generated. The best of Colombian creative literature came into being during the Liberal era. It served to console Colombians for their failure to enter the Promised Land of nineteenth-century liberalism.

BIBLIOGRAPHY

As the reader will have noticed, no selections have been taken from any general history of Colombia. The reasons for this are twofold: First, no adequate history of Colombia in the nineteenth century exists; second, it was felt that the pamphlets and books chosen would present the flavor and spirit of the times covered.

The English-language reader will in the main find his choices limited to a handful of journal articles:

Robert L. Gilmore's "New Granada's Socialist Mirage," in *Hispanic American Historical Review* (hereinafter cited as *HAHR*), 36:2 (May 1956), pp. 190–210, is a fine study of the impact of European ideas on the Generation of 1849. Based on official U.S. diplomatic dispatches is Carey Shaw's "Church and State in Colombia as Observed by American Diplomats, 1834–1906," in *HAHR*, 21:4 (November 1941), pp. 577–613. An important segment of economic history is examined in John P. Harrison's succinct "The Evolution of the Colombian Tobacco Trade to 1875," in *HAHR*, 32:2 (May 1952), pp. 163–74. An able contribution is Frank Safford's "Foreign and National Enterprise in Nineteenth-Century Colombia," in *The Business History Review*, 39:4 (Winter 1965), pp. 503–26. Also valuable is "Two Stages in Colombian Tariff Policy: The Radical Era and the Return to Protection (1861–1885)" by David Bushnell, in *Inter-American Economic Affairs*, 9:4 (Spring 1956), pp. 3–23.

For those who can read Spanish, the choices are greater:

The best short general history (with a heavy emphasis on the political narrative of the nineteenth century) is the too-often ignored *Manual de historia de Colombia* by Gustavo Arboleda (Cali: Imprenta Departmental, 1934). The same author's *Historia contemporánea de Colombia*, 6 vols. (Bogotá, Popayán, and Cali: Casa Editorial de Arboleda y Valencia & Others, 1918–35) treats the years 1830 to 1860 in considerable detail. Antonio Pérez Aguirre, *25 años de historia colombiana: 1853 a 1878; del centralismo a la federación*, Biblioteca Eduardo Santos, Vol. 18 (Bogotá: Editorial Sucre, 1959), while it ignores social and economic factors, is almost the only study of this period, though Eduardo Rodriguez Piñeres' *El olimpo radical* (Bogotá: Librería Voluntad, 1950) sympathetically narrates the internal history of the Liberal party from 1864 to 1884.

There is still no general economic history of Colombia, but Eduardo Nieto Arteta's *Economía y cultura en la historia de Colombia*, 2nd ed. (Bogotá: Ediciones Tercer Mundo, 1962), is both stimulating and informative. Broader in scope is Abel Cruz Santos' *Economía y hacienda pública*, Historia Extensa de Colombia, 15:1 (Bogotá: Ediciones Lerner, 1965), which traces the country's fiscal development from preconquest times to 1885. More specialized is Luis Ospina Vázquez's

Industria y protección en Colombia 1810–1930 (Bogotá: Editorial Santafé, 1955), which deals with both industrialization and protection.

Unlike the Church in other Latin American countries, the Church in Colombia has yet to receive the study its paramount role merits, but Juan Pablo Restrepo's partisan account, *La Iglesia y el Estado en Colombia* (London: Emiliano Isaza, 1885), remains the best despite its termination at 1880. An overview of the intricacies of Liberal and Conservative thinking during the nineteenth century is Jaime Jaramillo Uribe's *El pensamiento colombiano en el siglo XIX* (Bogotá: Editorial Temis, 1964).

Definitive biographies of major figures like Obando, López, Murillo, Mosquera, Ospina, and Núñez have yet to appear. For Mosquera, some documentary insight into the man and his times can be found in J. León Helguera and Robert H. Davis, eds., *Archivo epistolar del General Mosquera: Correspondencia con el General Ramón Espina, 1835–1866*, Biblioteca de Historia Nacional, Vol. 108 (Bogotá: Editorial Kelly, 1966). Estanislao Gómez Barrientos' *Don Mariano Ospina y su época*, 2 vols. (Medellín: Imprenta Editorial & Others, 1913–15) is overly worshipful but still the only biography extant. A good although somewhat intuitive study, Indalecio Liévano Aguirre's *Rafael Núñez*, 3rd ed. (Bogotá: Editorial Cromos, 1946), is an incisive appraisal of that complex personality.

VIII

The Continuing Problem of Brazilian Integration: The Monarchical and Republican Periods

Alfred C. Stepan

CHRONOLOGY

1822   Brazil declares herself independent from Portugal

1831   Pedro I is forced to abdicate and the Regency is established to rule until Pedro's five-year-old son reaches his legal majority

1831–48   A period of regionalist revolts and near-disintegration

1841   Pedro II is crowned early as a force for unity

1870   The Republican Manifesto is issued, attacking both the Monarchy and centralization

1889   Monarchy is overthrown

1894–1930   The classic period of the Old Republic, characterized by decentralization; power lies with the state oligarchies

1930   The Revolution of 1930 destroys the Old Republic; Vargas initiates his centralizing policies

1932   São Paulo's unsuccessful counterrevolution against Vargas

1937   Getúlio Vargas imposes his authoritarian, populist *Estado Novo* (New State) by a coup; the New State, he says, is necessary to forge national unity

1945   Vargas is overthrown

1964   The government of João Goulart is overthrown, and the first military regime in twentieth-century Brazil is established

INTRODUCTION

Brazil is the world's fifth largest country in area and the eighth largest in population. From independence in 1822 until the present, a major question has been the country's ability to integrate economically and politically this huge expanse into a single great nation. The challenge of integration has many interacting and overlapping aspects; three will be given special attention in this chapter.

The first aspect is the problem of national unity and physical integration, posed most sharply from 1824 to 1849: How could Brazil remain one country despite great regional centrifugal forces? The second aspect is the question of political integration: What form of government could reconcile the tension between the need to recognize the individuality of the states of the Union and the need to give the Central Government the coordinating power necessary for national development and integration? The third aspect is the problem of social and economic integration: How could the threats posed by the vast social and economic differences between the diverse groups and regions in the country be removed?

Let us turn to the first or *physical* aspect of Brazilian integration, the problems created by geographical size. Brazil is so large that centrifugal forces are inevitably present, yet it survived as one country while Spanish America was fragmenting. Brazilian cohesion clearly cannot be ascribed to the peculiar peacefulness of the Brazilian people or to any absence of local issues, for bloody regional rebellions shook every corner of the country in the first twenty-five years after independence. In the Northeast, the most important revolts were the rebellion centered in Pernambuco, which called itself the Confederação do Equador, in 1824; the Cabanagem in Pará and Amazonas in 1833–36; the Sabinada revolt in Bahia in 1837; and the Revolução Praieira in Pernambuco, 1848–49. The Center-south region was shaken by the 1842 revolt of Minas Gerais and São Paulo. In the South, the Province of Rio Grande do Sul suffered a republican and federalist civil war during the ten years between 1835 and 1845.

What, then, were the underlying sources of unity present in Brazil and apparently absent in Spanish America? Richard Morse, the author of Reading 1, argues convincingly that the very looseness of the colonial Portuguese structure in Brazil, compared with the more formal control of the Spanish Empire, was an important factor in allowing Brazil to develop organic rather than mechanical relationships between the component parts of the country. These organic relationships, particularly the system of extended families in the vast expanse of rural Brazil, had greater survival capacity, once the coordinating force of the colonial power was removed, than the mechanical imperial bureaucracy clustered in the few great cities of the Spanish territories. In addition, Morse argues, the regional economies in Brazil were interdependent and functionally linked by a series of crisscrossing trading routes that physically helped bind the country together.

The organic and functional unity of Brazil that had evolved during the colonial period might have been eroded had Brazil had to fight a long war of independence. In much of Spanish America, the wars of independence split the population into loyalist or patriot groups and into regional, racial, and personalistic factions. These various divisions left a political legitimacy vacuum. When the Portuguese crown prince, Dom Pedro I, declared Brazil independent from Portugal (and from the rule of his father, Dom João VI, the Portuguese king), the country's rural-oriented social structure and the political institution of the monarchy were not disturbed. Later some Brazilian nationalists were to lament the fact that the early unity of their country owed so much to the continuation of the conservative rural colonial structure. Nestor Duarte, for example, has written:

> It is thus of little importance to consider Independence as the beginning of the Brazilian state. A date is not an event if it does not mark a profound revolution or general and intense modification of the social structure.
>
> The political scenes that passed between Dom João VI and Dom Pedro I are the same as the transfer of power, without clash, from father to son. . . .
>
> The prestige of rural society was to become even greater in the century of independence. . . .
>
> In this intellectual climate, the new Brazilian state, without invoking economic interventionism, came to sustain the status quo of the colonial situation of dominance by private landed estates.[1]

Perhaps what Duarte regards as regrettable economically and socially was nevertheless the price the country had to pay for the preservation of physical integration. The monarchical system stabilized and helped maintain the unity of Brazil's far-flung regions, not by its mere existence but because it was congruent with the socioeconomic system of the country and so represented an acceptable legitimacy formula. By the Constitution of 1824, the Emperor became the "Poder Moderador, the key to the entire political organization" and was given wide powers with which to watch the political life of the entire country.[2]

[1] Nestor Duarte, *A Ordem Privada e a Organização Política Nacional*, 2nd ed. (São Paulo: Companhia Editora Nacional, 1966), pp. 94, 95. (Except where noted otherwise, the translations in this chapter are by the chapter editor.)

[2] In addition to the legitimacy it acquired through its mutually supportive relationship with the dominant rurally-oriented social and economic structure, the Monarchy, Hélio

After Dom Pedro I was forced to abdicate and returned to Portugal in 1831, leaving behind his five-year-old son, Brazil was ruled by a regency. During this period, disintegrative forces were increasingly felt; civil war raged in several provinces, and a major decentralization of political power was attempted. A new group calling themselves the Maioristas (after the word *maioridade*, or majority) began to demand the early declaration of the young prince's majority as a counterbalance to the drift toward division and anarchy. This *maiorista* movement ended in the "coup" of the early crowning of Dom Pedro II in 1841, thus ratifying the monarchy as a perceived source of physical and political integration.

The legitimacy of the Crown helped maintain the loyalty of the armed forces. This had a twin effect on integration. First, it avoided the disintegrative and anarchic dynamic involved in the cycle of military coups found in many of the Spanish American republics. Second, it increased the capacity of the Government to enforce integration and prevent provincial civilian *caudillo* coups of the Spanish American type, because the armed forces could be used by the central authority to crush them.

With the suppression of the Pernambuco revolt in 1849, the physical aspect of Brazilian integration was decided. Forty years later, when the monarchy fell in 1889, a new set of problems arose, and the second, *political* aspect of integration became the dominant challenge. What formula of political integration could harmonize the conflicting demands of the component states with the need of the Central Government for a coordinating power? For half a century following the fall of the monarchy, this question of political integration was argued almost dialectically between one group favoring states' rights and another group favoring a strong central government.

The thesis of strong states' rights, put forward in a Republican manifesto in 1870 and incorporated in the Republican Constitution of 1891, was dominant in Brazil throughout the period of the Old Republic, 1889–1930. When the monarchy fell in 1889, Brazil was left without any national governmental institutions except the armed forces. There was only one real political party in the nation, but it consisted of a loose coalition of state oligarchies and was dominated by the three most powerful states, Minas Gerais, São Paulo, and Rio Grande do Sul. Actual power lay with the states, whose cooperation with each other was minimal. States taxed imports from other states, raised militias (in São Paulo and Minas Gerais these forces at times outnumbered the locally garrisoned federal troops by

Jaguaribe has argued, had a further claim to a "plebiscitary" legitimacy. This second source of legitimacy was expressed first in the participation of Dom Pedro I in the declaration of independence. See Hélio Jaguaribe, *Desenvolvimento Econômico e Desenvolvimento Político* (Rio de Janeiro: Editora Fundo da Cultura, 1962), pp. 132–54.

ten to one), and individually contracted foreign loans. Like the monarchical system, this system of state politics was stable and kept Brazil together, but for these benefits the nation had to pay a price in the form of a low governmental capacity to implement national programs and a low mobilization of physical and human resources. Industrialization, unionization, and university education would make significant gains in Brazil only after the triumph of centralist ideas in 1930.

Political behavior in Brazil during the forty-one years of the Old Republic is probably best described by saying that two patterns or paradigms of political action existed simultaneously and were linked vertically in a system of reciprocal obligations and patronage. The upper paradigm, sometimes called the "politics of governors," involved a special form of cooperation between the President and the state governors. In essence, the governors gave the President the minimal support he needed for a national program in return for the freedom to act as they wished within their own states. The President was selected by the most powerful states after a period of negotiation between the governors and other leaders. Their "indicated" choice (in all cases but two, the man indicated came from the important states of Minas Gerais or São Paulo) was then ratified in a virtually uncontested election. On the average, the candidate received over ninety per cent of the votes cast.[3] With slight variations, this paradigm held true for the "elections" of 1894, 1898, 1902, 1906, 1918, and 1926.[4] The proper working of the system required the outgoing president successfully to oversee, but not dictate, the "indication" and election of his successor. The reader will find an interesting account of the process, when it was working "normally," in the selection from the memoirs of President Campos Salles (Reading 5).

Supporting the state-national political system, or upper paradigm, was a second paradigm, the state-local political system, called *coronelismo*. In the typical state, the ruling state political machine gave almost complete autonomy in the municipal sphere to the local rural bosses, called *coronéis* (colonels), whose power originally was based on ownership of land and was often augmented by small private armies. The "colonels" in turn delivered the rural vote to the ruling state party.

The political system based on the thesis of states' rights broke down in 1930. In that year, the election of the "indicated" candidate touched off a revolt, and Getúlio Vargas assumed power as Chief Executive. In the years that followed, he tried to introduce a strong national government into the political system of Brazil, to speed the integration of the national

[3] This near unanimity must be interpreted in light of the fact that overall participation in the pre-1930 elections never surpassed 3½ per cent of the population.

[4] For a summary of the statistics of the presidential elections, see Guerreirro Ramos, *A Crise do Poder no Brasil* (Rio de Janeiro: Zahar Editôres, 1961), p. 32.

economy, and to root out what he called the decadent liberalism of the Old Republic. In 1932, São Paulo mounted a counterrevolution against the political order that Vargas seemed to be constructing and that implicitly challenged its strong position in the federation. This two-month revolt, the last major armed struggle of regionalism in Brazil, had for its rationale a demand for a return to constitutional democracy and to states' rights. The great strength of the São Paulo rebels lay in their appeal to Paulista "nationalism." This appeal also proved their greatest weakness, however, for it smothered the enthusiasm for their cause that they had initially been able to arouse in other states.

In 1937, through a bloodless coup supported by some key military officials, Vargas established his Estado Novo (New State). The Estado Novo was the antithesis of the Old Republic. Vargas justified its strong, centralized, authoritarian character as the necessary solution to the weakness and fragmentation caused by Brazil's federal system.

With the fall of the Estado Novo in 1945, some of the authoritarian aspects of the Vargas period were eliminated, and some of the states' rights and privileges from the period of the Old Republic reappeared. A synthesis of states' rights and centralized government at a higher level of national political integration had been achieved.

But the challenge of integration has yet to be solved. The functioning of the political system continues to be threatened by problems associated with *social* and *economic* integration, the third and last aspect of integration to be considered here. These problems are generally described collectively as the problem of the "two Brazils": groups and regions so separated socially and economically that their effective cooperation within one democratic political system is very difficult.

A turn-of-the-century perception of the two Brazils and an implicit proposal for integrating them may be found in Euclydes da Cunha's classic novel *Os Sertões*, which describes the guerrilla revolt in the backland town of Canudos in 1897 and the yearlong federal counterinsurgency campaign against it. Da Cunha's work is particularly interesting in that it reveals the immense psychological distance and alienation that separate both Da Cunha himself and the federal troops he is writing about from the backland people. It further reveals Da Cunha's belief that the integration problem would be solved by the extinction of the "backward races." But too large a part of Brazil is a backland for it to be left behind in the process of evolution or to be invaded by troops and destroyed. The backlands were, and are, part of Brazil.[5] A more realistic program was needed than that suggested by Da Cunha's pessimistic positivism.

[5] See Ralph della Cava, "Brazilian Messianism and National Institutions: A Comparison of Canudos and Joaceiro," paper delivered to the Annual Meeting of the

In the 1950's, the problem of regional inequalities had become so acute that Brazil began to experience serious social unrest and an exodus from the impoverished interior. A system of differential exchange rates and tariffs had had the effect of partially subsidizing the industrial growth of the Center-south at the expense of a rising cost of consumer goods in the Northeast, thus raising the cry of "internal colonization." [6] A special government agency, SUDENE, was called into being as an emergency measure to develop the Northeast and reverse the increasingly dangerous inequalities.

The heart of the current threat to the social and economic integration of Brazil is not the difference between regions, however; it is a function of the national developmental process itself. In the 1960's, Brazil simultaneously underwent a slowdown in economic development and a radicalization in politics. The combination led to a breakdown of the democratic process in 1964 and the first military government in seventy years. Factors of personality and political history were certainly important in this crisis, but a more fundamental cause was that a major group of political figures perceived the country's unhappy condition as having profound structural origins whose solution called for basic reforms.

The economic crisis of poverty, inflation, and recession was attributed largely to the coexistence of a developed and an underdeveloped economy in Brazil. The industrialization slowdown was explained in terms of the decline of new possibilities for profitable investment created by excluding imports from the national market (the import-substitution mechanism), and further growth was said to depend upon the integration of the large, rural, illiterate, subsistence farming sector into the national consumer economy.[7] It was also argued that a major engine of inflation was the archaic structure of Brazilian agriculture, whose output of some commodities was lagging behind the demands made by the growing urban population, and which was thus both driving up domestic prices and weak-

American Historical Association in New York, September 28–30, 1966, for an analysis of the Canudos revolt and its definite links with national society.

[6] For statistics illustrating the wide disparities of income and growth rates in the different states, and for an analysis of how the Northeast was adversely affected by São Paulo's industrialization, see Werner Baer, "Regional Inequality and Economic Growth in Brazil," in *Economic Development and Cultural Change*, XII (April 1964), pp. 268–85.

[7] For a careful statement of this technical problem, see Maria Conceição Tavares *et al.*, "The Growth and Decline of Import Substitution in Brazil," in *Economic Bulletin for Latin America*, IX, No. 1 (March 1964), pp. 1–59.

Brazil, showing the state boundaries in 1968.

VENEZUELA
GUYANA
SURINAM
FR. GUIANA
ATLANTIC OCEAN
COLOMBIA
Boa Vista
RIO BRANCO
AMAPÁ
EQUATOR
Macapá
Negro
Branco
Belém
São Luís
Fortaleza
Manaus
MARANHÃO
CEARÁ
RIO GRANDE DO NORTE
Amazonas
AMAZONAS
Madeira
PARÁ
Teresina
Natal
PARAÍBA João Pessoa
Jurua
Tapajós
PIAUÍ
PERNAMBUCO
Recife
Purus
Xingu
ALAGOAS
Maceió
ACRÉ
Pôrto Velho
Aracaju
SERGIPE
Rio Branco
RONDÔNIA (GUAPORÉ)
Tocantins
Araguaia
São Salvador (Bahia)
PERU
BAHIA
São Francisco
Guaporé
MATO GROSSO
GOIÁS
BOLIVIA
Cuiabá
FEDERAL DISTRICT
Brasília
Goiânia
MINAS GERAIS
Belo Horizonte
ESPÍRITO SANTO
Vitória
Paraná
Juiz de Fora
SÃO PAULO
RIO DE JANEIRO
PARAGUAY
São Paulo
Niterói
Rio de Janeiro
Sorocaba
GUANABARA
TROPIC OF CAPRICORN
Santos
CHILE
PARANÁ
Curitiba
SANTA CATARINA
Florianópolis
ATLANTIC OCEAN
Uruguay
RIO GRANDE DO SUL
Pôrto Alegre
ARGENTINA
URUGUAY

0   300   600
Miles

BRAZIL

ening the cruzeiro internationally by forcing the nation to deplete its small supply of foreign exchange in buying wheat abroad to make up the deficit in the food supply. Changes in the social and economic spheres could thus be brought about only by political action that would authorize and implement "Basic Reforms," as the desired social, intersectoral, and agricultural changes came to be called.

How and when fundamental steps will be taken to meet the challenges to Brazil's economic and social integration is not clear. In 1963, Celso Furtado, a minister of the overthrown Goulart government (1961–64) and the first director of SUDENE, argued that Brazil's dual economies (one developed and one underdeveloped) had generated a dual system of political power that since the 1950's had been incapable of implementing the Basic Reforms. A conservative Congress based upon the underdeveloped rural social structure, and a Populist presidency responsive to a mass urban society frustrated in its hopes of development, immobilized each other. The result was "a void in power which foreshadowed a change in the conventional methods of political conduct" and an attempt at "forcing an unconventional way out" of the impasse (see Reading 12). The 1964 revolution led by the military was in part a result of both this political immobility and the generalized methods of agitation and radicalization that were being utilized to construct a new political order.

READINGS

1. *Some Sources of Brazilian Unity*

Richard M. Morse is a professor of history at Yale University and author of *From Community to Metropolis: A Biography of São Paulo, Brazil.* In the following selection, he analyzes why postindependence Portuguese America showed greater cohesion than Spanish America.

Why did Portuguese America—roughly a third of modern Latin America in size and population—remain single while Spanish America split into what are now eighteen republics? . . . Only three points will be made here, in an effort to suggest the complexion of Brazilian unity rather than to set forth an exhaustive causal analysis.

.   .   .

[First, the] point is not that the settlers of Brazil harbored a sense of national unity, inherited from the mother country, but rather that their collective life was less dominated by the emblems, codifications, and hierarchical officialdom of imperial, metropolitan Europe. Brazilian institutions developed more freely in response to their New World setting—and interacted more freely with each other. It has become a commonplace in Brazilian history and sociology to say that until well into the nineteenth century the dominant institution was the self-sufficient extended family of rural Brazil, sometimes called the clan. This was much less true of Spanish America, where, except in outlying regions, one feels the paramount institution to have been the Spanish crown, and the various lines of civil and ecclesiastical offices through which its powers were somewhat hesitantly delegated. Upon the crown, ultimately, depended the cohesion of the realm.

.   .   .

A second source of national cohesion lies in the economy of the New World rather than the institutional inheritance from the Old. We have said that the axis of the colonial Brazilian economy was the export to Europe of tropical agricultural products and, in the eighteenth century, precious minerals—these in return for manufactures and African slaves. Complementing and making possible this commerce, however, was an internal movement of jerked beef and other foodstuffs, hides, and cash

SOURCE: "Some Sources of Brazilian Unity" from Richard M. Morse, "Some Themes of Brazilian History," in *The South Atlantic Quarterly*, LXI (Spring 1962), pp. 166, 167, 168, 169, 170, 173–75. Copyright *The South Atlantic Quarterly*. Reprinted by permission.

commodities in transshipment which has only a modest place in colonial statistics, yet which inconspicuously served to articulate those very regions which production for export appeared to isolate one from another. Here again, the point is not that internal trade was wholly lacking in Spanish America, but that in Brazil it did not center, cartwheel fashion, upon a principal city, nor was it funneled through a few principal ports.

Internal Brazilian trade was contained within four main systems. In the north, the vast Amazon river system. In the northeast, a system of routes, often making use of riverbanks, which spread out from the modern state of Piauí. Essentially, this system made possible overland transit between Maranhão and Ceará, north of the "bulge," and Bahia, under the shoulder of it. The component routes brought cattle from scattered backlands areas to the coastal markets. Their more historic function was to articulate the backlands and interconnect their settlements. [According to Caio Prado, Jr.:]

> They permitted those mass displacements and migrations, so common during the periodic droughts. . . . The routes of communication described contributed to melt and intermix all the disparate elements which make up the composition of the backlands population, who, coming from diverse and greatly distant points, were little by little entering into communication and contact.

In the south-central area there were a number of subsystems leading inland to Minas Gerais, Goiás, and Mato Grosso. And finally, there were the southern routes, which had as their axis the highroad from São Paulo south to Rio Grande do Sul. Because of the difficult access to Rio Grande by sea, it was in large measure this highroad that made possible the colonization of southernmost Brazil in the second half of the eighteenth century and its eventual absorption into Portuguese America. . . . [T]he point may be made that by the time of its independence in 1822, Brazil's principal regions of settlement—the coast, the backlands, the mining area, and the cattle plains in the south—were achieving complementariness in the exchange of the products of farm, ranch, and mine, an exchange made possible by a growing tissue of land and river routes.

. . .

A third factor contributing to the cohesion of the nation, the last to be discussed, was the nature of the leadership under which Brazil made the transition to independence and eventually to republican government. At the risk of a severely narrowed focus, we shift from the plane of institutions to that of persons, where the fate of emergent Latin-American nations so often balances precariously. . . . In Brazil, as in any Latin-American country after independence, a government had to meet four specifications if the society were not to fall upon the rocks of despotic or oligarchical caudillismo, or the shoals of disintegrated authority and anarchic factionalism. These specifications were legitimacy, constitutionalism, nationalism, and personalism. That is, a new government, coming on the heels of three centuries of Catholic monarchical rule, the ultimate authority of which had never been questioned, needed that very aura of legitimacy which Metternich was then preaching in Europe. Second, it had to be constitutional, given the example set by the United States, and given a penetration of Enlightenment ideas that was deeper than that in many corners of Europe. Third, it had to embody a popular aspiration toward democratic national sovereignty. And finally, given a situation of political inexperience and incipient social chaos, a new government could be institutionalized only by the astute intervention of strong personalist leadership.

Needless to say, these four elements were difficult to orchestrate. Legitimacy generally meant a European prince (except to those who envisioned a restoration of the Incas), yet this was hard to square with nationalism, or with the need for shrewd personalistic leadership. Personalism and constitutionalism were of course uneasy bedfellows—for, as Machiavelli long ago observed in his *Discourses on Livy*, the charismatic leader who establishes a constitutional regime must, like the old soldier, be willing to fade away.

In Brazil all of the four requirements were met. To the legitimacy of his Bragança lineage Dom Pedro gave popular, nationalist sanction by consulting with local leaders on the eve of independence; by acting under the advice of José Bonifácio, who was rabidly anti-Portuguese; and by declaring Brazil an empire in something of Napoleon's spirit. Then, at the critical moment, when factionalism threatened to impede the process of constitution-making, Pedro packed the Andrada brothers off to Portugal and—in personalistic style that would have pleased Machiavelli—promulgated a constitution. From then on his leadership faltered. His democratic convictions could never be reconciled with his authoritarian temperament, and in 1831 he abdicated in obedience to pressure for responsible government from the soldiery and the populace. Luckily, exile was made palatable by the fact that there awaited him in Portugal the task of rescuing the crown from his usurping brother. As his successor, Pedro left in Brazil his five-year-old son, who came under the tutelage of José Bonifácio, now returned. The decade of the regency which followed placed the fate of the nation, the further elaboration of its constitution, and the handling of separatist revolts squarely in Brazilian hands. When Pedro II assumed power in 1840, he did so as an eminently Brazilian monarch. This retelling of Brazilian independence is neither fresh nor complete. Its object is simply to draw attention to the complex and delicate balance of elements that was necessary to produce stable, constitutional government in nineteenth-century Latin America, and to suggest that the transplantation of the Bragança line to Rio de Janeiro was but one of these ingredients.

2. *The Political Constitution*
of the Empire: March 25, 1824

From 1824 until 1889, Brazil was governed by a monarchy as an imperial empire. The Constitution of 1824 assigned to the Emperor a "moderating power" within the political system. The character of this power, which proved to be an important one, is described in the Constitution as follows.

Title V
Of the Emperor

Chapter I
Of the Moderating Power

Art. 98. The moderating power is the key to the entire political organization and is delegated exclusively to the Emperor as supreme chief of the nation and its first representative, so that he may constantly watch over the maintenance of the independence, stability and harmony of the other political powers.

Art. 99. The person of the Emperor is inviolable and sacred; he is not subject to any responsibility.

Art. 100. His titles are "Constitutional Emperor and Perpetual Defender of Brazil," and he should be addressed as His Imperial Majesty.

Art. 101. The Emperor exercises the moderating power:

1. By naming the senators. . . .
2. By convoking an Extraordinary General Assembly when the General Assembly is recessed and the good of the State requires it.
3. By sanctioning the decrees and resolutions of the General Assembly so that they have the force of law. . . .
4. By approving and suspending provisionally the resolutions of the Provincial Councils. . . .
5. By proroguing or postponing the General Assembly and dissolving the Chamber of Deputies in cases where the safety of the State demands it, convoking another immediately to substitute it.

SOURCE: "The Political Constitution of the Empire: March 25, 1824" translated from *Constituição política do Império do Brasil*, Tomo Primeiro do Manual do Cidadão Brasileiro (Rio de Janeiro: Eduardo e Henrique Laemmert, 1855), pp. 45–47.

6. By naming and dismissing freely the ministers of state.
7. By suspending the magistrates in [specified] cases. . . .
8. By pardoning or modifying the penalties imposed on criminals condemned by sentence.
9. By granting amnesty in urgent cases or when humanity or the good of the State counsels it.

3. *The Maiorista Movement*

The following is a sympathetic contemporary account of the Maioristas' attempts in July 1840 to have the Chamber of Deputies declare the majority (and so the governing authority) of the young Prince Pedro, in the hope that this would help reintegrate the nation. The selection also describes the "plebiscitary" agitation in the streets that followed the Government's move to block the Maioristas by reading an act to prorogue the Chamber. The agitation resulted in the 1841 "coup" consisting of the early crowning of the fourteen-year-old Dom Pedro II.

July 10, 1840

Deputy Andrade Machado: What has actually happened is that the Government has reached such a point of weakness that the country is threatened with dissolution; the provinces are separating themselves from the Union bit by bit; lawlessness reigns everywhere; no one pays attention to the law, no one pays attention to the Government.

Can this state of affairs continue? No, it cannot, and it is with this in mind that the noble senators are going to propose in the Senate the annulment of the minimum age required for the crowning of Dom Pedro, as the only remedy; since one cannot give prestige to the Government, one must bring to the Government something that already has its own prestige. No one disputes that the monarchy has such prestige, that in Brazil the name of the monarchy alone is respected, that the monarchy can even make the use of force unnecessary—because force is only necessary when there is resistance, and no one wishes to resist the King; they only wish to resist other governments. To those of you who do not wish to remedy the ills of society, who do not wish to save the country from revolution, I say time is drawing short; the day will come when you will wish to act, but then it will be too late, the evil will be beyond remedy; you will be lost, dying in the terrors and agonies of revolution and public turmoil.

SOURCE: "The Maiorista Movement" translated from José Antonio Maurinho, *A Declaração da Maioridade* (Rio de Janeiro: Associação do Despertador, 1840), pp. 20, 55–56, 93–94.

July 16, 1840

Deputy Ribeiro de Andrade: I want the Monarch on the throne because I am convinced that he will be the angel of peace that will save us from the abyss that threatens. (Cheers.) I want the Monarch on the throne because I deem that it is the only measure that can remedy our ills.

July 22, 1840

Deputy Cunha Azevedo: Mr. President, either the Government understands that the proclamation of His Majesty the Emperor's majority is a measure demanded by public necessity, or not. In the first case, the Government should be the first to submit to the wisdom and patriotism of the General Assembly. Not having done this, the Government appears as an enemy of the public. . . .

Deputy Rego Monteiro: The act which has been read [to prorogue the Chamber] is an act of conspiracy against public liberty and against the constitutional throne of Dom Pedro II. Therefore, while the Government conspires, it is legal for us to conspire against a monstrous and conspiring Government. (Numerous cheers.)

Deputy Coelho Bastos (with force): The Government conspires against the monarchy. The friends of the Monarch will place him on the throne! (Explosion of cheers.)

Deputy Andrade Machado (heatedly): He who is a patriot and a Brazilian, come with me to the Senate. Let us abandon this prostituted Chamber! (Thundering cheers, uncontrolled shouting, extraordinary agitation.)

This scene of great confusion, which we can but poorly describe, ends with the exit from the Chamber of the deputies advocating the majority of the King, who go to reunite in the Senate to deliberate in joint permanent session the means to resolve the crisis. A crowd of people accompanies them and grows as individuals in the street are informed of what has happened and come along to take part in the dangers of resistance; arriving at the Senate, the deputies resolve with the members of this house to send a delegation to His Imperial Majesty to explain to him the dangers shaking the country, and to ask him to take the reins of government. The delegation leaves, and while waiting for its return, various senators try to calm the crowd of more than three thousand citizens who roam the building, showing signs of intense restlessness and discontent. The crowd continues to grow, and all the students from the Military Academy come with arms to join the people and defend the monarchy.

But then the delegation returns, bringing the news that His Imperial Majesty agrees to govern and has ordered the Regent to revoke the fatal decree and to convoke again the two Chambers for the next morning. The enthusiasm of the crowd can barely be restrained. . . . The Commander of the Army, the Commander of the National Guard, and the magistrates of the country rush to fraternize with the people, who receive them warmly.

At last the delegation enters the Chamber, order is reestablished, and the most notable discussion that the legislative body of Brazil has ever seen begins.

4. *The Republican Manifesto of 1870*

The argument of the late 1830's that the monarchy was the necessary integrating bulwark against centrifugal forces lost much of its validity in the years of internal peace and conciliation after 1850. The problem was no longer seen as one of physical integration, in which the monarchy played a crucial part, but as one of economic development and political participation. In 1870, disaffected Republicans issued a manifesto condemning the monarchy as a stagnating, overcentralized force. Their ideas achieved acceptance in 1889, when the monarchy fell and the extremely decentralized political system of the Old Republic was established. Parts of the Manifesto of 1870 follow.

In Brazil, the principle of federalism existed even before the idea of democracy. The topography of our territory, the diverse zones into which it is divided, the variety of our climates and our different products, the mountains and the rivers, all suggested the need to conform with and respect the particular divisions created by nature and imposed by the immensity of our land.

· · ·

The democratic idea expressed in the first Brazilian Constituent Assembly attempted, it is true, to interpret federalism in the widest sense it could bear. But the dissolution of the Assembly suffocated democratic aspirations and restricted and diluted the federative principle; the Constitution of 1824, though maintaining the existence of territorial divisions, enlarged the scope of the central authority by placing the provinces and their administration in a position of dependence on the intrusive and absorbing monarchical power, the key to the system, which stifled all breath of liberty and reduced the provinces to feudal fiefdoms of the court, the seat of the only sovereign power to survive the ruin of democracy.

· · ·

From 1824 until 1848, from the Federation of the Equator until the Revolution of Pernambuco, one can say that the electric current that ran

SOURCE: "The Republican Manifesto of 1870" translated from Américo Brasiliense, *Os Programos dos Partidos e o 2 ? Império* (São Paulo: Typographia de Jorqe Seckler, 1878), pp. 76–80.

through the provinces, shaking the whole social framework, had one single
source—the desire for local independence, the idea of federation, the belief
in provincial autonomy. . . . The centralism that now exists represents
despotism, the force of personal power that subjugates, spoils, and corrupts character, perverts and makes anarchic the spirit, crushes liberty,
constricts the citizen, subordinates the rights of every man to the arbitrary
rule of one man, nullifies in fact national sovereignty, kills the initiative of
local advancement, sucks in the wealth special to each province and makes
them beholden satellites of the great star of the court—the absorbing and
stifling center that corrupts and concentrates everything into itself—in the
moral and political order, as in the economic and administrative order.

.   .   .

For us Republicans, then, provincial autonomy is more than an interest
created by provincial rights and relations; it is a solemn and cardinal
principle that we inscribe on our banner.

Federalism, based on the reciprocal independence of the provinces,
which are elevated to the category of states and which are linked solely by
the ties of shared nationality and the solidarity of interests of representation and external defense, is what we adopt for our program, as the only
means of maintaining the community of the Brazilian family.

If we had to choose a slogan to explain to the Brazilian conscience the
difference between the two kinds of regimes, we would summarize it thus:
Centralization = Dismemberment, Decentralization = Unity.

5. *National Politics*
in the Old Republic

In his memoirs, published in 1908, Manoel de Campos Salles, president of Brazil between 1898 and 1902 and a son of the powerful state
of São Paulo, gives a frank account of two aspects of the "politics of
governors": the complete absence of any real national political parties,
and the noncompetitive way in which the governors of the major states
and the outgoing President pick the new President.

People accused me of having dissolved the political parties. There
were others, however, who defended me with the formula, "what doesn't
exist can't be dissolved." . . .

 SOURCE: "National Politics in the Old Republic" translated from Manoel de Campos
Salles, *Da Propaganda à Presidência* (São Paulo: Typographia A Editora, 1908), pp. 225,
227, 229, 230, 365, 367, 370–72. Reprinted by permission of the Campos Salles
family.

In Brazil, the only group that emerged with aspirations to influence the National Government called itself the Federal Republican party. But this party, of uncertain direction and indefinite ideas, was not endowed with any of the qualities needed to achieve the high goals that are the destiny of a well-constructed party. . . .

Above all, it lacked purpose in its direction. It is true that it appeared to have a leader with all the trappings of command, but he never managed to instill discipline among the members of the party. In the last analysis, what there was in the top ranks of the party was a group of political caudillos, all equally sovereign and each jealous of his own personal influence. In the absence of ideas that could establish the necessary cohesion, the country witnessed the extraordinary spectacle of uncoordinated actions that these antagonistic groups imposed on the body politic. . . .

It was clear that this party could not give to politics a national form consonant with the essentially conservative character of the classes that made up a preponderant part of the country. Nonetheless—and one must not lose sight of this important fact—it was the debris of this political aberration that made up the groups in the National Assembly, a National Assembly that I found divided when I came into office.

. . .

The election of the President of the Republic is the grand axis around which national politics turns. . . .

I thought . . . that the spirit of my government should be continued by whoever succeeded me. If this were not to happen, if there were to be a reversal of the political and administrative order, then I would have to consider my efforts to have been useless and the ground we had gained to have been lost. . . .

It was under the influence of these thoughts and in observance of the caution that befitted my delicate situation that I determined to take the first step in favor of a candidate whose selection seemed right according to the republicanism and patriotism of my conscience. On November 7, 1900, after a long conference with Olyntho de Magalhães, Minister of Foreign Relations and son of the state of Minas Gerais, I charged him to go to Belo Horizonte and present personally to Dr. Silviano Brandão, president of the state, the reasons why I would be grateful to know whether he and his political friends would accept the candidacy of Rodrigues Alves for the presidency of the Republic. On the fifteenth, Olyntho de Magalhães reported to me the results of his mission, informing me that Dr. Silviano Brandão would accept the indication with the greatest enthusiasm; but, in the interest of guarding against future difficulties, it would be convenient if a vice-presidential candidate could also be presented who would be from Minas Gerais, in order to remove any doubts about a contrary selection; thus reasoning, he brought forward the name of one of the sons of the state. The name suggested by Dr. Silviano was that of one of the state's most illustrious patriots.

Upon receiving this information, I immediately sent the following telegram, in code, to Severino Vieira, the governor of Bahia: "It seems opportune to discuss the choice of my successor, so that I may come to an understanding with certain members of Congress before the closing of the session. I know that Rodrigues Alves has your support, and I am in full accord with the indication of this person, whom I consider competent from both the political as well as the administrative point of view; I give him my strong backing, knowing that other esteemed figures think likewise, including Silviano Brandão; but I have reason to believe that Minas will only accept the agreement if a Mineiro is included, and to avoid entanglements, I think it advisable to indicate Silviano himself for Vicepresident, thereby assuring the decisive support of his great state. If this arrangement seems acceptable, please let me know with great speed, as I am only awaiting your decision before reaching an agreement with Silviano. Given an agreement between Bahia, Minas and São Paulo, I do not expect to find strong obstacles from the other states, which I will consult with due caution, observing the necessary secrecy."

Severino Vieira's reply was received shortly afterward in the following telegram, which was also in code:

"I have just received telegram. Thank you for demonstration of generous trust. With firmness and enthusiasm I accept the arrangement, which I consider patriotically inspired. I think, however, there should be great caution in order to avoid hidden maneuvers. The jealous still have time to act against Minas. Cordial regards."

I will not reproduce the correspondence exchanged with almost all the governors of the states, so as not to prolong the exposition too greatly. I encountered no difficulties, except the natural need to clarify the political ideas and tendencies of the candidates.

6. *Coronelismo: Local and State*
Politics in the Old Republic

The following is a classic account of the working arrangement between the local rural bosses (the coronéis) and the dominant state party. Though the author is writing in 1948, his analysis is especially appli-

SOURCE: "Coronelismo: Local and State Politics in the Old Republic" translated from Victor Nunes Leal, *Coronelismo, Enxada e Voto: O Município e o Regime Representativo no Brasil* (Rio de Janeiro: Revista Forense, 1948), pp. 25–27, 30. Copyright 1948 by Victor Nunes Leal. Reprinted with permission of the author.

cable to the system as it existed in the Old Republic. The compromise ruled out any effective integrated reforms of policy or administration at a national level.

Coronelismo is not a simple phenomenon but a complex one, involving a whole range of factors arising out of municipal politics. . . .

The majority of the Brazilian electorate resides and votes in the municipalities of the interior, and in the interior the rural vote dominates over the urban vote. This rural vote . . . is impoverished. It is, then, the landowners and the local leaders who pay for the expenses of registration and the election. Without money and without direct interest, the peasant would make no effort in this regard. Documents, transportation, lodging, meals, work days lost, and even clothes, trousers, and a hat for the day of the election—everything is paid for by the political agents charged with getting the peasant to register and vote. . . .

Thus, because of a rural structure that maintains the dependency of the rural vote on the landowner and that prevents direct contact between the political parties and the largest sector of the electorate, the state political party cannot do without the intermediary services of the landowner. Despite the fact that the state political party would not submit to the landlord if it were not essential for the control of state politics, the state political party is nonetheless crucial to the coronel in the sphere of his municipality. The coronel realizes that impertinence on his part will only be to his disadvantage, while good relations between his private area of power and the institutional state power sectors can only increase, without fear of challenge, his parcel of public authority. And in this way appears the most important aspect of coronelismo, namely the reciprocal nature of the system: On one side are the municipal chiefs and coronels, who drive the rural electorate like a herd of mules, and on the other side is the dominant political party at the state level, which controls the treasury, employment, political influence, and political favors—which possesses, in short, the power to reward or to punish.

It is obvious, therefore, that these two aspects of coronelismo—the individual prestige of the coronel and the prestige he gains through public office—are mutually dependent and function as both determining and determined factors. Without the leadership of the coronel, whose strength derives from the agrarian structure of the country, the state government would not feel obliged to make a political exchange; without this exchange, the leadership of the coronels would be greatly reduced. . . .

It is with the local chief, if he is a friend, that the state government comes to an understanding in everything that concerns the interests of the municipality. Even the state employees serving in the area are chosen by the coronel: primary school teachers, tax collectors, tax department officials, justice department officials, the public prosecutor, primary school inspectors, public health workers, and so on. . . .

The list of favors does not end here, at the level of personnel. It is well known that public services in the interior are deficient because municipalities lack the funds to carry out their services. Without state help, the municipality would have great difficulty in carrying out even the most necessary public works, such as roads, bridges, schools, hospitals, water, sewage, and electricity. . . . The most logical criterion for state assistance, from the perspective of electoral consequences, is to give help to municipalities that are friends of the state government. Thus, the financial weakness of the municipalities helps to maintain coronelismo in its governmental aspect. . . .

Thus, the essence of the coronelista compromise . . . is this: on the part of the local chiefs, unconditional support for the official candidates in the state and federal elections; on the part of the state government, carte blanche to the local chief supporting the government (preferably the leader of the major local leading faction) in all matters concerning the municipality, including the nomination of the state functionaries in the area.

7. *Vargas on the Need*
for Stronger Government

The following excerpts are from two speeches made by Getúlio Vargas after the Revolution of 1930 had destroyed the Old Republic. They contain two of his proposals for increasing national integration: an expansion of the Central Government's activities and power, particularly in the economic sphere; and a restriction of the economic autonomy of the states, partly in order to restrict the political dominance of the nation by a few of the most economically powerful states.

The great dominating and renovating force in contemporary social life is, principally, economic in character. The edifice of the new law to be erected, remodeled from top to bottom in order to acquire solidity and efficiency, must have as its binding force economic reality, its origins

SOURCE: "Vargas on the Need for Stronger Government" translated from Getúlio Vargas, A *Nova Política do Brasil*, 11 vols. (Rio de Janeiro: Livraria José Olympio Editôra, 1938), 1, pp. 114–15, 120, 122, from a speech before the Legislative Commission, May 4, 1931; and pp. 98–99, from a speech in Belo Horizonte on February 23, 1931. Reprinted by permission of the publisher.

understood, its march and ascension anticipated, its ends foreseen. The juridical order must, then, reflect the economic order, guarantee it, and strengthen it.

In this respect, let us rapidly pass an eye over the past, making a swift analysis of the most important points in Western political development in recent times.

The revolutions that occurred at the dawn of the last century, destroying class privileges, freeing property from feudalism, and making triumphant the rights of man, assured through free competition the access of all men to all positions in life, according to the abilities of each.

This conquest—characteristic of the philosophy of liberalism—had repercussions in the constitutional organization of civilized countries. Classical constitutionalism was born, giving a stamp to the nineteenth century, as a natural reaction against absolutism, which had dominated until then— a constitutionalism that confined the power of the State to the minimum possible, reducing it almost exclusively to the maintenance of order and the distribution of justice.

But the rapid development of the present times, the many moral and social problems provoked by the complexity of modern life, naturally enlarged the power of the State to act far beyond the limits traced by the romantic politics of parliamentary rule.

Referring to these changes in the concept of the State, in view of historical circumstances, [Woodrow] Wilson rightly claims: "A large part of the transformations imposed on the concept of the State consist in a simple modification of the method and extension in the inherent functions of the government." In effect, the State, which is society organized, directed and impelled by the public interest, can have its functions limited only to the extent that it is in the public interest. . . .

I believe that this chance to cancel old formulas and create new ones is opportune. The old political formula, patron of the rights of man, appears to be decadent. In place of individualism, synonymous with the excess of liberty, or communism, a new form of slavery, there must prevail a perfect coordination of all the enterprises lying within the orbit of the State, and the admission of class organizations as collaborators in public administration. . . .

We have at our disposal great possibilities for economic expansion. We are a country rich in unexplored primary resources and unusual products, and simultaneously we have a vast consumer market. Given this, the Brazilian political economy must, in part, orient itself toward defending the possession and exploration of our permanent stores of energy and riches, as though they were precious falls of water or veins of mineral ore. I even judge advisable the nationalization of some industries and the progressive socialization of others, this being feasible through the rigorous control of public utilities and the gradual penetration of the management of private enterprises, whose development should be dependent on official approval.

.   .   .

The time is propitious to announce an important change that I hope to put in effect, benefiting from the sum of powers that the nation conferred on the provisional government and that allows it to effect with relative ease radical reforms that would be impossible to execute in times of constitutional normality. We hope, shortly, finally to resolve two old questions that cannot be left unattended in this period of political and administrative reconstruction we are going through. The opinions of the interested states having been heard previously, we impose on them two economic and financial measures of the widest scope. The first refers to interstate taxes, which, in some cases, resembled a real tariff war between certain federal units, a great evil, perhaps the worst, following from the accumulation of errors, a burdensome legacy from the past that we must confront and extinguish. The other reform concerns the export tax, which the Constitution provides as a source of revenue for the states, but which is uneconomical and has been repudiated by the majority of the producer nations, who agree it should be reduced to the minimum possible. The taxing function will pass into the charge of the Union, the only way to make taxes uniform, permitting the Union at the same time to attend to a grave problem of our economy—the complex question of the foreign debts of the states.

The problem of the states' foreign debts demands an urgent solution, since it reflects adversely on our credit abroad. Some states undertook commitments far larger than their capacity to pay, and their defaulting . . . on interest and amortization shakes the good name of Brazil in European and American financial circles, with grave prejudice to the economy and national finance.

It becomes imperative, as a wise and unpostponable precaution, that the Union, responsible morally and in fact for these debts, assume effective responsibility for them. . . .

8. *The 1932 São Paulo Counterrevolutionary Attempt*

The most powerful reaction against Vargas's new philosophy of strong central government came, predictably enough, from São Paulo, the

SOURCE: "The 1932 São Paulo Counterrevolution." The first manifesto is translated from "The Manifesto of the League for Paulista Defense," which appeared on the

strongest state in the Union. The following two readings are manifestos directed to the people of São Paulo during the revolt of 1932. The first is a typical appeal to São Paulo nationalism. The second is an extreme example of how great regional inequality can breed a threat to national integration; the manifesto expresses São Paulo's aggressive feelings of social and economic superiority.

The Three Factors of Victory

There are three factors necessary for victory: military power, moral force and economic organization.

We have all three in abundance.

Our military power is represented not only by the troops that fight on the front lines, composed of units made up of the elite of our glorious national Army, but also by the entire dedicated state militia and the battalions of volunteers now entering battle, in which people from all walks of life in São Paulo are incorporated. This military power is augmented by the great reservoirs of men in all corners of the state who are ready, when the sound of arms calls, to enlist in the Army instruction camps and to prepare themselves to march. It is these reserves that assure the continuity of action on the front line, maintain the constant and unflagging pressure against the enemy forces, and will proclaim the growing strength of our soldiers until the battle ends. These reserves increase day by day, minute by minute.

The moral force of men who fight for an ideal against those who defend a poor cause cannot be greater. Throughout human history, there has never existed a morale higher than that of those who are fighting for their liberty.

As to material equipment, the capacity for work and organization that characterizes the people of São Paulo is well known. Here is concentrated the greatest industrial center of South America; it was here that the most extensive and efficient transport system was developed in the whole of Brazil; it was here that the most powerful social institutions of the Republic were born and flourished. Today all these resources are mobilized for war. Each man is absorbed in what he has to do; he has no time to look and see what is happening around him. But anyone who will take a look at our state will see a marvelous phenomenon. All the immense and superabundant energy of the Paulista economic complex, the fullness of

editorial page of the leading São Paulo newspaper, *O Estado de São Paulo*, July 29, 1932. The second, translated from "The Manifesto of J. B. Monteiro Lobato," August 10, 1932, was reprinted in Hélio Silva, *1932: A Guerra Paulista* (O Ciclo de Vargas), 6 vols. (Rio de Janeiro: Civilização Brasileira, 1964–   ), 5 (1967), pp. 279, 281–83. Reprinted by permission of Hélio Silva.

its resources and the dynamism of its production, is mobilized for the fight, galvanized by a single idea: to win!

In Defense of the Victory of São Paulo

São Paulo must organize its defense, its legitimate defense. It will not abandon the wealth that it has just created and that it will continue to create to a systematic and growing pillaging by the Central Government and the rest of the federation. . . .

After the victory of São Paulo in the campaign now launched, its leaders must not be lulled by sentimental ideas of Brazilianness, by brotherhood, or by other sweet-sounding phrases. The entire North is our natural enemy. Rio Grande is no friend. Minas Gerais looks after its own ends. *The fact that we are brothers does not imply friendship and support. We must watch out for these brothers.* If Abel had done this, he would not have fallen victim to the mule's jaw with which his brother Cain slew him. We should consider them enemies until proved otherwise; if they are proved to be enemies, we are prepared for it.

The only possible attitude that the instinct of self-preservation imposes on São Paulo after the victory will be expressed in this formula: Hegemony or Separation. Either São Paulo assumes political hegemony, a hegemony already achieved by virture of its contributions in the fields of industry and culture, or it separates itself from the Union. There is no way it could stay in the position in which it finds itself. . . . This would be suicide.

To effect this conquest there is no need for negotiation. It will be imposed with arms. An obvious elementary measure following victory will be, with the absolute disregard of the relevant federal laws (laws on the whole made against us) the transference to São Paulo of the best equipment in the arsenals of Rio—planes, artillery, ammunition, and so on. Instead of arming ourselves to match the enemy, it is cheaper to disarm the enemy and keep his arms intact for ourselves. Disarming him in this manner, we can give federal militarism its first resounding blow. The Federal Government will remain with the bluffs and the arrogance—we will remain with the gunpowder and the grenades.

The dilemma is serious. Either São Paulo disarms the Union and arms itself to direct henceforth national politics through its talents and for its own good, or it separates. To continue like this, contributing to maintain the monstrous bureaucratic and militaristic parasite of Rio de Janeiro—whose primary function is to assault and sabotage São Paulo—is to commit suicide through stupidity.

Let us put aside the grotesque romanticism with which we delude

ourselves. Let us confront reality as it is—as do the strong. Let us realize
. . . that Hobbes will always be right: Man is the wolf of man. Let us
know that never, at any time, will the fact of being a brother take away
from a wolf the wolf's ferocity. Let us accept Hobbes. Let us be wolf
against wolf. Fat wolf against starving wolf. Let us organize our defense.

9. *The Estado Novo of 1937*

> In the first of these excerpts from speeches made after the 1937 Estado
> Novo coup, President Vargas argues to a military audience that the
> coup was necessary in order to impose unity on the "twenty fiefdoms"
> of the Union. In the second, he outlines the authoritarian structural
> changes brought about by the Estado Novo.

The Estado Novo remodeled the structure of Brazil. . . .
What existed before? In what direction was Brazil going? Who fought
against a state of affairs revealing almost incurable ills and for the defense
and preservation of national unity? Unfortunately, Brazil was marching
toward disintegration with quickening steps. The twenty states into which
our territory was chopped up were transformed into twenty fiefdoms, so
that the paramount interests of the country were assailed by regional interests. Budgets, of which eighty per cent was spent on personnel and
barely twenty per cent on public services and material enterprises, were
consumed by those same regional interests, which the conditions and
exigencies of politics made preeminent over the Federal Government,
whose authority was reduced and whose freedom of action was paralyzed
by the influence of local and unintegrated forces. The income of the
Union remained at the mercy of prodigal legislation, which embezzled the
money in favor of factional and private interests.
Crowning this confusion and dissipation were the regional bosses, who
demanded the right to settle national questions by the threat of force and
by the imposition of the disturbing influences and ambitions of local
chieftains.
The armed forces, which were and continue to be the only force
organized at the national level, felt, in the depths of their nationalistic
and patriotic hearts, that in order to save the country it was necessary to
take extreme action against a state of affairs that was drawing us dizzily
toward the loss of our national existence.

.   .   .

SOURCE: "The Estado Novo of 1937" translated from Getúlio Vargas, *A Nova Política do Brasil*, 11 vols. (Rio de Janeiro: Livraria José Olympio Editôra, 1938 and
1940), 5, pp. 242–43, and 6, pp. 154–55. Reprinted by permission of the publisher.

Though the Statute of November 10[1] preserved the traditional lines of organic federation and what existed of substance in the system of free opinion, such as the autonomy of the states, the democratic form, and the representative process, it nonetheless created a new legal structure. Among the profound changes brought about by the new regime are: the limitation of direct, universal suffrage to specific questions accessible to all citizens, thus creating a truer kind of representation; the basing of the nucleus of the political system in the municipality; the replacement of the principle of the independence of powers by the supremacy of the Executive; the strengthening of the power of the Union; the effective and efficient participation of the economy, through its own organizations, in the integration and constructive work of the Government.[2]

The new system sanctions a government of authority, instituting as law the legislative decree and giving the President of the Republic powers to expedite decree-laws when Congress is not in session by giving him, in addition, the prerogative to dissolve Congress in special cases and by taking from the Judiciary the privilege of final interpretation of the constitutionality or unconstitutionality of laws that involve public interest of great consequence. The public interest, guarded by the Government, will always take precedence over private interest.

Profoundly nationalist, the regime insures and consolidates national unity and makes formal restrictions on the autonomy of the states, suppressing regional symbols and expanding the possibilities of intervention by establishing the supremacy of federal laws over local laws in cases of legislative dispute and by giving to the central authority the power to requisition, at any moment, the state militias . . . .

10. *The Canudos Revolt of 1897*

This selection is from Euclides da Cunha's *Rebellion in the Backlands* (*Os Sertões*), considered one of Brazil's literary masterpieces. The excerpts are interesting for what they show of the psychological distance separating the author and the federal troops from the backland rebels.

Backward races today, tomorrow these types will be wholly extinguished. Civilization is destined to continue its advance in the back-

---

[1] The date of the coup of the Estado Novo.

[2] Vargas is describing the move toward a corporate state based upon functional-interest-group representation in Congress.

SOURCE: "The Canudos Revolt of 1897" from Euclides da Cunha, *Rebellion in the Backlands* (*Os Sertões*), translated by Samuel Putnam (Chicago: University of Chicago Press, 1944), pp. xxix–xxx, 161, 405–06. Copyright 1944 by the University of Chicago Press. Reprinted by permission of the publisher.

lands, impelled by that implacable "motive force of history" which Gumplowicz, better than Hobbes, with a stroke of genius, descried in the inevitable crushing of weak races by the strong.

The Canudos Campaign has, therefore, the undeniable significance of a first assault in a struggle that may be a long one. Nor is there any reason to modify this assertion in view of the fact that it was we, the sons of the same soil, who staged this campaign; inasmuch as, being ethnologically undefined, without uniform national traditions, living parasitically on the brink of the Atlantic in accordance with those principles of civilization which have been elaborated in Europe, and fitted out by German industry, we played in this action the singular role of unconscious mercenaries. What is more, these extraordinary native sons, living in a prevalent disunity upon a land that was in part unknown to them, are wholly separated from us by a co-ordinate of history—time.

.   .   .

We must insist upon this point: the war of Canudos marked an ebb, a backward flow, in our history. What we had to face here was the unlooked-for resurrection, under arms, of an old society, a dead society, galvanized into life by a madman. We were not acquainted with this society; it was not possible for us to have been acquainted with it.

.   .   .

After having lived for four hundred years on a vast stretch of seaboard, where we enjoyed the reflections of civilized life, we suddenly came into an unlooked-for inheritance in the form of the Republic. Caught up in the sweep of modern ideas, we abruptly mounted the ladder, leaving behind us in their centuries-old semidarkness a third of our people in the heart of our country. Deluded by a civilization which came to us second hand; rejecting, blind copyists that we were, all that was best in the organic codes of other nations, and shunning, in our revolutionary zeal, the slightest compromise with the exigencies of our own national interests, we merely succeeded in deepening the contrast between our mode of life and that of our rude native sons, who were more alien to us in this land of ours than were the immigrants who came from Europe. For it was not an ocean which separated us from them but three whole centuries.

.   .   .

It was here, along an imperceptible slope, that the Monte Santo Road began—that narrow, ill-famed trail down which three successive expeditions, filled with high hopes, had gone, while down that same road now, bound in the opposite direction, came bands of wretched fugitives. Having forded the shallow, stagnant waters of the Jacuricy, the trail bends and threads its way across the plains that lie beyond, flanked at the beginning by another road marked by the posts of the recently strung telegraph line.

A Geographic Fiction

The railway line runs along the other side. This mark of modern progress is, however, meaningless here and does not in the least alter the genuinely rustic character of the place. One alights from the train, walks a few hundred yards between rows of squat houses, and forthwith finds himself, at the edge of the village square—in the backlands.

For this is in reality the point where two societies meet, each one wholly alien to the other. The leather-clad vaquero will emerge from the caatinga,[1] make his way into the ugly-looking settlement, and halt his nag beside the rails where natives of the seaboard pass, unaware of his existence.

Beyond the Bounds of the Fatherland

The new expeditionaries, upon reaching Queimadas, were aware of this violent transition. Here was an absolute and radical break between the coastal cities and the clay huts of the interior, one that so disturbed the rhythm of our evolutionary development and which was so deplorable a stumbling-block to national unity. They were in a strange country now, with other customs, other scenes, a different kind of people. Another language even, spoken with an original and picturesque drawl. They had, precisely, the feeling of going to war in another land. They felt that they were outside Brazil. A complete social separation expanded the geographic distance, giving rise to the nostalgic sensation of being very far from home. The mission which had brought them there merely served to deepen the antagonism. There was the enemy, out there to the east and to the north, hidden away in those endless highland plains; and far, far away, beyond the plains, a terrible drama was being unfolded.

It was, surely, a paradoxical kind of fatherland whose own sons had to invade it, armed to the teeth, with martial tread, ripping out its very entrails with their Krupp cannon. And, all the while, they knew nothing whatever about it; they had never seen it before but viewed with amazement the arid earth, rugged and brutal, bristling with thorns, tumultuously littered with stone heaps and pulverized mountains, torn asunder with caverns and ravines, while all about were the parched and barren tablelands, great, rolling, steppe-like plains.

What they were being called upon to do now was what other troops had done—to stage an invasion of foreign territory. For it was all a geographic fiction. This other was the reality, plain for all to see from what had gone

[1] A vaquero is a cowboy from the arid northeastern backlands, who normally dresses completely in leather to protect himself from the prickly scrub vegetation of the region. The region is known as the *caatinga*.

before. The soldiers felt this and were obsessed by the thought. Here were those unknown woodsmen sending back to them, day by day, mutilated and defeated, their comrades who, a few months previously, had gone down that same road, strong of body and proud in spirit. As a result, there was no heart left in them; they had not the courage to strike out, unconcerned with what might happen, into the depths of those mysterious and formidable backlands.

11. *The Chronic Problems of the Northeast*
and the Creation of SUDENE

In the 1950's, the Center-south of Brazil was expanding at one of the fastest rates of industrial growth in the world, while the Northeast was becoming increasingly impoverished. The document below, issued by SUDENE, the government development agency set up in the Northeast to correct the regional imbalance, explains the problems the agency faced in trying to integrate the Northeast with the rest of Brazil.

1. The Northeast of Brazil, with an area of 1.6 million square kilometers and a population approaching 25 million, stands out as the major underdevelopment problem of the Western Hemisphere. The average yearly per capita income of this population barely reaches one hundred dollars, and is therefore similar to that of South-East Asia and Africa. As is customary in regions of so low an income level, the degree of concentration of wealth is very considerable, whereas a large part of the urban and rural population lives under extremely poor conditions, which are reflected in high infantile mortality rates and short life expectancy. Besides being extremely weak due to low average productivity, the economy of the Northeast is subject to periodical crises caused by droughts which devastate extensive areas. When this happens, the entire region is afflicted by serious economic disturbances, with repercussions of various types, which are becoming more and more acute as the population increases.

. . .

3. The population of the Northeast is mainly concentrated in the humid eastern area, traditionally a sugar producing region. The labor surpluses move to the coastal cities, of which Recife, with a population of 800,000, is the largest. Agricultural specialization, due to the land-holding system

source: "The Chronic Problems of the Northeast and the Creation of SUDENE" reprinted from Brasil, SUDENE (Superintêndencia do Desenvolvimento do Nordeste), *The Bases of the Development Policy for the Northeast of Brazil and Scheme of SUDENE's Five-Year Plan* (Recife, 1961), n.p., Section I, paragraphs 1, 3, 5, 6, and 7.

which prevails under the sugar economy, subjects the coastal cities to a chronic shortage of staple food items and this in turn puts a brake on possibilities of industrialization. Forced as they are to obtain their food supplies from distant regions, the cities in the humid regions of the Northeast have been faced from the start with the defeat of their prospects of industrialization. Within the humid rural area itself, specialized in sugar production, there is a permanent shortage of food in view of the complete inadequacy of local production.

.   .   .

5. Only by taking a comprehensive view of the situation can one comprehend the debility of the economic system of the Northeast. The growth of urban areas is a mere consequence of the inability of the humid agricultural area to absorb the expanding population. But since the humid area is deficitary as to foodstuff production, the growth of population causes a rise in the relative prices of food products in the sugar zone itself, endangering the profitability of sugar production.

On the other hand, the agricultural growth of the semi-arid zone renders its economy more and more unsuitable to the prevailing ecological conditions. Finally, the urban populations are to an increasing extent dependent on food production surpluses from the drought-affected areas. To sum up: the entire region depends on increasingly expensive food and increasingly unstable supplies.

6. The Northeast problem has been aggravated in the past two decades as a result of measures taken for the industrialization of the South-Central region of Brazil. When the relative prices of manufactured products went up as a result of the protection granted to expanding national industry, the poorer region, traditionally a source of supply of raw materials, was subject to substantial income drainage. The contribution of the Northeast to the financing of industrialization was, relatively speaking, a very high one, even though that industrialization took place outside the region. Furthermore, as the Northeast exports twice as much as it imports and has a much higher export rate than the South-Central region, the policy of low exchange rates for the exporter and high rates for the importer, which prevailed until recently, caused a permanent leaching away of real income from the Northeast to the South-central economy.

7. The increasing vulnerability of the economy of the Northeast to drought and the progressive spread between living standards of the Northeast population and those prevailing in the South-Central region of Brazil were bound to give rise to increasing social tensions. Awareness of the existence of an internal process of "colonization," growing in extent, has aroused reactions which have tended to ripen into the formulation of a policy specifically aimed at the development of the region. This new policy

is to be implanted by the Superintendency for the Development of the Northeast (SUDENE), established . . . December 15, 1959.

12. *The Structural Origins*
of the 1964 Crisis

Celso Furtado, one of Brazil's best-known economists and a minister in the Goulart government, had his political rights taken away after the Government was overthrown by the military in 1964. In the following excerpts from a recent book, he attempts to analyze the structural origins of the events leading to the 1964 crisis.

The present book was written before the military coup d'état that altered the Brazilian political scene during the last few days of March, 1964. To be more precise, it was prepared between October and December of the previous year, a critical period for the recent political evolution of Brazil. Toward the end of September the Goulart government had made an unsuccessful attempt to declare a state of emergency. This abortive attempt was evidence of the government's awareness of the gravity of the situation. On the other hand, the entire nation was conscious of the fact that the government did not possess the means for coping with a crisis that was daily becoming more acute. Thus a situation arose in which there was a void in power which foreshadowed a change in the conventional methods of political conduct.

· · ·

Stagnation in the export agricultural sector, concentration of investments in manufacturing activities, and finally the growth of state activities have brought about important changes in the country's social structure over the last three decades. The principal manifestation of change was a process of rapid urbanization. In effect, the Brazilian population, which in 1920 was about 30 million, with about 7 million living in the cities, is today more than 80 million, of whom more than 35 million are concentrated in urban areas, with a much greater proportional growth in medium and large cities. As the urban population represents a much higher coefficient of literacy than the rural, it is natural that political activity should have undergone an important shift in its center of gravity, at least insofar as the electoral process is concerned.

SOURCE: "The Structural Origins of the 1964 Crisis" from Celso Furtado, *Diagnosis of the Brazilian Crisis*, translated by Suzette Macedo (Berkeley: University of California Press, 1965), pp. xiii, xv–xx, xxiii–xxiv. Copyright by the Regents of the University of California. Reprinted by permission of the publisher.

These changes in the social structure did not, however, find any adequate correspondence in the framework of political institutions.

. . .

The present federal system, in providing considerable power for the Senate, in which the small agricultural states of the most backward areas have a decisive influence, places the legislative power under the control of a minority of the population living in areas where the interests of the great estates hold undisputed sway. On the other hand, as representation of the individual states in the Chamber is proportional to population, illiterates are represented by literate fellow-citizens. Thus, the vote of a citizen living in a state where eighty per cent of the population is illiterate is worth five times as much as the vote of a citizen living in a state with one hundred per cent literacy. Since the traditional oligarchy is most powerful in the most illiterate areas, the electoral system contributes toward the maintenance of this oligarchy, which finds in illiteracy one of its props. This fact is not without bearing on the strong reaction shown by many local authorities in the more backward regions against the introduction of techniques for simplifying the spread of literacy.

Control of the principal centers of a power system is not a sufficient reason, however, for the majority of the population to accept as legitimate the authority emanating from this control. And it is because this legitimacy has been increasingly lacking in Brazil that the exercise of power by the ruling class has become increasingly difficult. In effect, the relative growth of the urban electorate has offered a permanent challenge to the control of the electoral system by the parties based on the oligarchy. Experience has already shown that, if the creation of new parties is possible, a movement based on the urban centers can decide the results of a major election. In fact, elections of the President of the Republic and State Governors in the more urbanized states have been increasingly influenced by forces that evade control by the oligarchy. Thus conditions had arisen in which the Executive Power represented emergent political forces that defied the control of the Establishment, which concentrates its forces in Congress. Tensions between the two power centers had increased over the last fifteen years, and had on occasion even led to hindrance of government action.

. . .

In view of this rupture in the basis of the power system, the very principle of legitimacy has been seriously compromised. In order to make itself legitimate, the government must act within the framework of constitutional principles and at the same time fulfill the expectations of the majority responsible for its election. However, in attempting to carry out the substantive mandate of the masses who elected him, the President of the Republic necessarily came into conflict with Congress, and was faced with the alternative of betraying his program or forcing an unconventional way out. In ten years this unconventional way out has included one suicide, one resignation, and one violent deposition. It could be argued that the Presidential candidate could offer a realistic program, taking into account the power of those who control both Congress and a considerable part of the state apparatus. But this moderate candidate would find it difficult to get himself elected, since another candidate would readily be forthcoming who was prepared to come to terms with the demands of the masses.

The emergence of a mass society, paving the way for Populism, without the formation of new ruling groups able to work out a plan for national development as an alternative to the traditionalist ideology, has been the chief characteristic of the Brazilian historical process in its most recent phase. The Populist leaders, conscious of the psychological state of the masses, called for the country's rapid modernization through "basic reforms" and "structural changes." Control of the principal political power centers, however, continued to be in the hands of the traditional ruling class, who have known how to use Populist pressure as a bogey for bringing to heel the new emergent forces connected with industry and foreign capital. These circumstances, responsible for the growing political instability, favored military intervention and indeed this did in effect take place in March, 1964. The intervention, however, did not eliminate the roots of conflict. . . .

CONCLUSION

We have seen that Brazil has endured as a single nation, despite great pressures on its cohesion. In comparison with many of the newly developing countries of Africa and Asia, Brazil has been fortunate in that its people shared a religion and a language, and that racial intermixing has been so widespread that racial conflict has been muted. The cleavages have been serious, but they stem from political, social, and economic factors and thus have normally been open to negotiation or at worst have resulted in only brief uses of force. In contrast, the splits that sever different groups and communities in countries such as prepartition India and postindependent Nigeria have been compounded by the presence of sentiments with a high "emotional coefficient" of divisiveness. Thus, the initial debate in Nigeria over the federal balance of power was greatly aggravated by the fact that the three major regions were divided from each other by differences of tribe, religion, and language. Brazil has been spared these compounding cleavages.

Nonetheless, the problem of national integration was and still is a serious one in Brazil. The country's difficulties are systematically interrelated: A crisis in one area leads to a crisis in another. We have seen, for example, how the question of political integration in the 1930's temporarily reawakened the apparently solved question of physical unity, resulting in the 1932 counterrevolution of São Paulo. The social and economic crises of the 1960's similarly reawakened the question of Brazil's political structure, resulting in the Revolution of 1964.

The military regime that took power in the 1964 Revolution abolished the old political parties, banned many prominent political figures from political activity, and established indirect elections for the office of the presidency in an attempt to place a moratorium on political agitation and eliminate divisive factors in Brazilian society. This imposed an artificial unity on Brazil. Although the symptoms of political, social, and economic divisiveness lie dormant, the structural causes of that divisiveness to a great extent still remain. This means that the challenge of integrating the dynamism of Brazil into a coherent plan of democratic development still remains.

BIBLIOGRAPHY

Bastos, Tavares. *A Provincia: Estudo sobre a Descentralização no Brasil,* 2nd ed. (São Paulo: Companhia Editora Nacional, 1937). An influential nineteenth century argument for greater decentralization; first edition published in 1870.

Burns, E. Bradford. "Working Bibliography for the Study of Brazilian History," in *Americas,* XXII (July 1965), pp. 54–88. A general bibliographical introduction.

Deutsch, Karl W. *Nationalism and Social Communication: An Inquiry into the Foundations of Nationality,* 2nd ed. (Cambridge, Mass.: M.I.T. Press, 1966). The basic book and bibliographic guide to the general field of integration theory.

Dulles, John W. F. *Vargas of Brazil: A Political Biography* (Austin: University of Texas Press, 1966). A biography of the major twentieth century Brazilian political figure.

Furtado, Celso. *Diagnosis of the Brazilian Crisis,* translated by Suzette Macedo (Berkeley: University of California Press, 1965).
————. *The Economic Growth of Brazil: A Survey from Colonial to Modern Times,* translated by Ricardo W. de Aguiar and Eric Charles Drysdale (Berkeley: University of California Press, 1965). An economic history by one of Brazil's most famous economists.

Hahner, June E. "The Paulistas' Rise to Power: A Civilian Group Ends Military Rule," in *Hispanic American Historical Review,* XLVII (May 1967), pp. 149–65. A good account of the role of São Paulo politicians and their state militia in the creation of civilian rule in the Old Republic.

Haring, C. H. *Empire in Brazil* (Cambridge, Mass.: Harvard University Press, 1958). The best synthesis of the history of the Empire in English.

Hirschman, Albert O. "Brazil's Northeast," in *Journeys Toward Progress: Studies of Economic Policy-Making in Latin America* (New York: The Twentieth Century Fund, 1963), pp. 11–91. An excellent analysis of the events leading to the creation of SUDENE.

Jaguaribe, Hélio. *Economic and Political Development* (Cambridge, Mass.: Harvard University Press, 1968). A Brazilian political scientist analyzes the historical problem of nation building and contemporary models of development.

Lambert, Jacques. *Os Dois Brasis,* 2nd ed. (São Paulo: Companhia Editora Nacional, 1967). A major discussion of the problem of the "two Brazils."

Leal, Victor Nunes. *Coronelismo, Enxada e Voto: O Município e o Regime Representativo no Brasil* (Rio de Janeiro: Revista Forense, 1948). The classic study of coronelismo.

Love, Joseph LeRoy. *Rio Grande do Sul as a Source of Political Instability in Brazil's Old Republic, 1909–1932* (New York: Ph.D. thesis,

Columbia University, 1967). This is the best account of regionalism and the functioning of the Old Republic.

Martin, Percy Alvin. "Federalism in Brazil," in *The Hispanic American Historical Review*, XVIII (May 1938), pp. 143–63.

Morse, Richard M. "Some Themes of Brazilian History," in *The South Atlantic Quarterly*, LXI (Spring 1962), pp. 159–82.

Palmer, Thomas W., Jr. "A Momentous Decade in Brazilian Administrative History, 1831–1840," in *Hispanic American Historical Review*, XXX (May 1950), pp. 209–17. A discussion of the movement toward decentralization and then back to centralization in the Regency period.

———. "The Locomotive and Twenty Empty Freight Cars," in *Inter-American Economic Affairs*, IV (Autumn 1950), pp. 53–94. An analysis of the strains on integration created by São Paulo's dominant economic position in the Union.

Prado Junior, Caio. *The Colonial Background of Modern Brazil*, translated by Suzette Macedo (Berkeley: University of California Press, 1967). Describes the internal migration, interdependent trade routes, and racial mixing that contributed a sense of unity of colonial Portuguese America.

Skidmore, Thomas E. *Politics in Brazil, 1930–1964: An Experiment in Democracy* (New York: Oxford University Press, 1967).

Soares, Gláucio Ary Dillon. "The Political Sociology of Uneven Development in Brazil," in Irving Louis Horowitz, ed., *Revolution in Brazil: Politics and Society in a Developing Nation* (New York: Dutton, 1964), pp. 164–95.

Stein, Stanley J. "The Historiography of Brazil, 1808–1889," in *The Hispanic American Historical Review*, XL (May 1960), pp. 234–78. An indispensable critical evaluation of the literature on the Empire and an excellent guide to the literature on regional revolts.

Wagley, Charles. *An Introduction to Brazil* (New York: Columbia University Press, 1963). Especially good in its descriptions of Brazil's unity within diversity.

IX

The Mexican Revolution, 1910–40: Genesis of a Modern State

John Womack, Jr.

CHRONOLOGY

1910   Díaz reelected president against Madero's challenge; Madero revolts

1911   Díaz resigns, Madero elected president, agrarians revolt and remain in action

1912   Other chiefs revolt but fail

1913   In coup Madero falls, Huerta named provisional president; popular revolts lead to civil war, with Carranza and Zapata against Huerta

1914   Huerta falls; Revolutionary Convention of delegates from Carranza, Villa, and Zapata; schism as Carranza's delegates withdraw

1915   New civil war, with Villa and Zapata against Carranza

1916   Carranza's lieutenants victorious over Villa and Zapata

1917   Carranza's lieutenants frame new Constitution, Carranza elected president

1920   Carranza maneuvers to impose successor, revolutionary chiefs revolt; Carranza falls, Obregón elected president; truce with the agrarians

1923   Chiefs revolt but fail

1924   Obregón retires, Calles elected president

1926   Cristeros revolt and remain in action

1927   Chiefs plot to revolt but fail

1928   Obregón reelected president, then assassinated before taking office; Calles retires, Portes Gil named provisional president

1929   Official National Revolutionary party organized under Calles's direction; Vasconcelos protests, chiefs revolt but fail; truce with Cristeros; official party elects Ortiz Rubio president

1932   Ortiz Rubio resigns, official party names Rodríguez provisional president

1934   Rodríguez retires, official party elects Cárdenas president

1935   Cárdenas exiles Calles, exercises power directly

1936   Cárdenas coordinates unions in Confederation of Mexican Workers

1938   Cárdenas expropriates foreign oil companies, coordinates agrarian leagues in National Country Confederation, reorganizes official party as Party of the Mexican Revolution

1940   Cárdenas retires, new official party elects his chosen successor president

1942   Mexico enters World War II against Axis

298

INTRODUCTION

The past was the proper topic for a public review in Mexico in 1910, the centennial year of national independence. And that September in Mexico City, the pageantry was dazzling—majestic parades featuring Aztec knights, Moctezuma, Cortés, conquistadors, viceroys, inquisitors, and heroes of independence; the consecration of a monumental column to the first martyrs of the nation; the dedication of a grand hemicycle in honor of Benito Juárez, who had saved the Republic in its grimmest trial fifty years before. But curiously, though elegant, modest, and shabby Mexicans celebrated together, they did not celebrate in the same spirit. Among the modest and the shabby, the official homage to history provoked solemn reflection on Mexico's populist traditions. But it inspired the elegant to imagine the country's future.

An ecstasy of triumph pulsed through the commemorations where Mexican gentry, nabobs, and brokers bore the palm. They rejoiced not as if they had inherited the past but as if they had finally outgrown it. Their prime reason for relief was the tremendous economic progress of the last thirty years. From a feeble assemblage of slow provincial markets in the 1870's, Mexico had boomed into a dynamic system of concessions, investments, monopolies, and profits. Its progress was clearest in the favorite statistics: Railroad mileage was up from 400 in 1876 to 12,000 currently; the value of foreign trade had soared from 89.5 million pesos in 1877 to 502 million; mining production of industrial metals had quintupled since 1891. Though still overwhelmingly rural, the country was now knit closely into world economic patterns.

The guarantee of this peace and progress was the Federal Government, which President Porfirio Díaz had directed firmly and adroitly for the last thirty-four years. Into his administration he had recruited a clever troop of intellectuals, nicknamed the *científicos*, who argued persuasively that the rich were a superior race. With científico management Díaz had just won his seventh straight presidential election. This plutocracy was the famous *Porfiriato*.

The plutocrats still had problems—erratic inflation, the grumbling of millions of dispossessed and dislocated villagers declining into peonage, the ugliness of the urban poor, impudence among artisans and the small but useful class of factory workers, an oppressive foreign debt, scattered anarchists, the clamor of petty entrepreneurs ravenous for bigger contracts, heavy dependence on the United States for trade and capital, public agitation for freer politics, and (most troubling) palace rivalries over the aging President's succession. But solutions now seemed inevitable. Content and keen, Mexico's established centennial celebrants looked forward to continuing order and progress. The highest sages of international finance and enterprise confirmed their happy prospects.

Startling changes soon occurred, however, right in the ruling circles that seemed most secure. The breach in the system was a naive revolt in November 1910 by the loser of the recent presidential election, a wealthy young idealist, Francisco I. Madero. Surprised and already divided internally over succession, the Government dawdled in crushing the insurrection. New rebels then arose around the country—grumbling villagers, impudent workingmen, anarchists, and clamorous petty entrepreneurs. Despite American sympathies and British and French suspicions, the contest remained Mexican. In May 1911, after rebels captured the city of Juárez, the científicos agreed to dump Díaz and to hold a new election for Madero to win, on the implicit condition that they retain control over national affairs. The result was an armistice, Díaz's prompt exile, the organization of several political parties, Madero's electoral victory and inauguration as president in November 1911, and the formation of a liberal, almost parliamentary regime.

The científicos remained most powerful, and their domestic and foreign policies still prevailed. But to their dismay, they could no longer dictate deals; they had to logroll them. As the old restraints slackened, villagers, workingmen, and petty entrepreneurs again voiced their claims to justice. A violent agrarian rebellion exploded in several southern states. Strikes broke out, even in the nation's capital. Elsewhere, local braves conned malcontent neighbors into revolt. Alarming debates resounded in federal and state executive offices and, after congressional elections in September 1912, in Congress too, about new laws to defend modest and shabby and even ragged citizens. So far the challenges to the established order were not serious, but who could tell where liberal eccentricities might lead? As Madero's regime took shape in early 1913, it became expensive and dangerous—and sorely annoying to the American and European ambassadors.

To correct this trend, certain plutocrats and generals executed a coup d'état in February 1913. In the confusion, other officers under General Victoriano Huerta seized the initiative, and, after resigning, Madero and his vice-president were murdered. An impressive coalition then formed, representing the científicos, the nabobs, professional Catholics, and the military. The plan was for Huerta to preside provisionally until the científicos could elect and install their own candidate. The Army upheld the deal. Congress acquiesced. European and Asian sovereigns granted recognition. The old regime seemed back in business.

But what ensued was its collapse, much to the shock and bewilderment of contemporaries. The catch was that Huerta held on to the presidency and hobbled his collaborators, which sapped the substance of his authority. And to consolidate power he did not yet have, he cracked down ruthlessly on the populace—which provoked indifferent folk into opposition and drove oppositionists into revolt. His failure to get recognition from the United States crucially weakened him. When the revolts multiplied and strengthened and Congress protested his repressions, he set up a dictatorship to crack down harder—which aroused still more antagonists. A bitter civil war spread through the country. Local communities dissolved into refugee masses. The economy decayed and retracted from world patterns. By the spring of 1914, Huerta's force had run down. To help rout him, the United States Navy occupied Veracruz. From every direction, revolutionary armies pressed into the strategic center of the country. In July 1914, Huerta left for Europe. The old regime was in crisis, but its principal worthies could not rally. In August, they surrendered to the main revolutionary force. They lost all offices and many contracts, and the Army mustered out. Thus the class that had dominated Mexico for a generation disintegrated into ruins. The plutocrats fled into exile.

The whole country now hung in suspense. To reorganize it, neither Great Britain nor the United States would intervene directly, because war had just begun in Europe. Responsibility for a new order therefore weighed on the Mexicans themselves, specifically on three revolutionary factions. These were alike in their popular origins, their fresh national pride, their democratic assumptions, and their ideological crudity. But in their visions of their task they were quite distinct. The strongest faction, which had taken authority in the capital, was essentially entrepreneurial. Its chiefs were tough young Northerners who had resented the Porfiriato for its monopolies and who wanted to make Mexico a land of opportunity for all, where any man of gumption and talent could succeed. They had the best connections with workingmen's unions. Ironically, their First Chief was an old Porfirian politico, Venustiano Carranza, whom they did not like but for tactical reasons respected. Another faction, almost as strong and also Northern, had for its hero Francisco Villa, once a bandit, then a rebel chief under Carranza's orders, but now independent. The Villistas had no definite interests. The Mexico they dreamed of was simply a place where buddies could prosper and carouse. And into their headquarters crept remnants of the old regime angling for restoration. The third faction was Southern, forged in the agrarian rebellion that had raged continually in the South since 1911. Its chief was Emiliano Zapata, a determined countryman. Though the Zapatistas were a small and amateurish force, they probably represented the inarticulate hopes of the majority of the nation. The Mexico they foresaw was basically a traditional commonwealth of market towns and villages.

At issue in 1914 was whether these three factions could work together to refound their country. And in a solemn Revolutionary Convention they tried—and failed. The Villistas then wormed the Zapatistas into an alliance to destroy the Carrancistas. The Carrancista chiefs reconcentrated their forces and counterattacked. Organized workingmen enlisted in their ranks. For two years an immense, bloody civil war blasted Mexico. Swarms of refugees registered its terrible cost. Twice the United States intervened, indirectly in 1915 to recognize Carranza's claim to govern and directly in 1916 to send troops over the border on a wild-goose chase after Villa. But the struggle continued. Though at times it seemed that the rival revolutionaries would tear the country apart, that Mexico was less a nation now than ever before, Mexicans were learning in their common pain and courage a new lesson—their identity as a people.

The Carrancista entrepreneurs emerged victorious. The organized workingmen tagged along. By late 1916, though Villa and Zapata still had raiders in the field, Carranza was able to start building a regular regime. In an exclusively Carrancista convention, his lieutenants ratified their victory and proclaimed their own radical plans in a new Constitution on February 5, 1917. They promptly rigged elections to put themselves in authority. Congress opened. Carranza became president, incorporated his legions as a National Army, and appointed a Cabinet. Governments soon

Zapitista troops. *Casasola Archive. Reprinted with permission.*

formed in most states. After seven years of profound instability and change, the Republic was back in business again.

It often wobbled, however. The economy was a shambles, the populace miserable yet militant. Usually the jolts came from natural mistakes in fabricating the new political system. But the real rub was Carranza, who hardly fit in the regime he presided over. He held his post almost by leave of the Army, and he would not sponsor reforms to gain popular support. In fact, he only superintended while his lieutenants negotiated among themselves over who would succeed him.

Just before elections in 1920 they finally acted. When Carranza balked at their claims, they dumped him (and accidentally allowed his murder), subsumed into their party the rebel remnants still in the field, and carried their toughest and canniest colleague, Álvaro Obregón, into the presidency. Evidently the true masters were now in control, and Mexico was on its true course—bereft through the last decade of hundreds of thousands of lives and poorer by billions of pesos, but somehow heading home. That fall, for the first time, officials commemorated the anniversary of Madero's revolt ten years before. As it began, so the Revolution ended—a thoroughly native operation.

It took Mexicans the next twenty years to make sense of this awful experience. They did so not deliberately, not even in terms of their radical new Constitution, though it survived, but rather in working out troubles as they went along. They could do so because they had already destroyed the class that might have obstructed them. And in their search they still proceeded on their own: Despite the confusion of the world in the 1920's and 1930's, despite appeals and threats from the United States, and despite the tempting models of Soviet Russia, Fascist Italy, and Nazi Germany, the Mexicans went their independent way. And for all their ideological rhetoric, which they often believed, they remained pragmatic in practice.

Initially, they saw themselves awake from a nightmare and prayed for a return to normalcy, assuming that there was a normalcy and that they could return. With the European war ended, world economic patterns would supposedly reform. Mexico would knit back into them. If its new chiefs kept order and balanced the budget, the country would "develop"— which then meant only that foreign investment would resume, mining, trade, and light manufactures would recover, enterprising Mexicans would do better business, and others would at least make a settled living. The force of private energies would again result in individual success and national progress.

Many Mexicans also thought of the grief they had suffered as a sacrifice, however, that had endowed them with rights to a decent existence. Sons of the new Mexico, they assumed, not only could but should live well there, cooperate to a purpose, and feel meaning in their efforts. But because no official organization bound them together into the regime and no official ideology provided a standard vocabulary and certified goals, they disagreed in their definitions of what a decent existence was. As their circumstances varied, they had various interests and committed themselves to various creeds. Far from having solved the great national problems, the Revolution had complicated them.

So while the economy mended, grave social conflicts strained the country. Was Mexico basically a place to make money? A stage for a dictatorship of the proletariat? A fabric of rural communities, villages nestled around their market towns? Was it essentially Indian? Hybrid? Catholic? Liberal? Latin American? Unique? Was order the key to its needs? Education? Prohibition? Foreign investment? Native investment? Medicine? Immigration? Psychoanalysis? Free elections? Safely rigged elections? Sports? Electricity? Free love? Fidelity? Highways? Dams? It seemed that everyone had an opinion, available on request. In advocacy of these views men and women agitated, and groups formed—all engaging devout commitments, all attempting to give Mexico its true shape and spirit. And though conciliation was often the watchword among rival groups, more dramatically often they were at war. When the economy slipped into the Depression after 1929, they became even more combative. Still, Mexicans were learning who they were through fighting each other.

The worst blood ran between professional Catholics (taking the name *Cristero*) and certain fanatic unions, parties, teachers' corps, and ideologues acting on official cues. In 1926, Cristero revolts broke out in several states. And though they formally ceased in 1929, skirmishes recurred off and on into the mid-1930's. Contention in politics was also fierce, as civilian and military aspirants to power connived incorrigibly. Major revolts occurred. Though they failed, sedition continued. In 1928, a crisis flashed when a Catholic assassinated Álvaro Obregón (just elected president again after four years out of office), reopening the issue of succession. The outcome might well have been disastrous, if the departing president, Plutarco Elías Calles, had not affiliated the state political machines into the National Revolutionary party (PNR). Through this agency, Calles and his partisans directed the Government without staying in office. The reform helped, but the three presidents who came and went in the next five years, Emilio Portes Gil, Pascual Ortiz Rubio, and Abelardo Rodríguez, were in constant difficulty. Meanwhile, labor and capital carried on vicious hostilities in a contest for economic control of the Republic. Despite state and federal codes regulating their relations, they clashed repeatedly in strikes, lockouts, and shooting frays. Almost as violent was the wrangling within labor among the three or four main confederations.

To vent their disgust with current failings and their hope for authentic answers, even normally disorganized Mexicans massed in a national crusade in 1929. This was the presidential campaign of José Vasconcelos, the ingenious Minister of Education in 1921–24, now returning from exile as the prophet of free debate, civil respect, and public idealism. What people wanted through him was what an unknown man cried out in a rally early in the campaign: *"Baraja nueva!"*—a new deal. Though Vasconcelos had practically no funds or machine and stood against the Government, thousands cheered him around the country. Of course he lost, but the longing for a new deal grew more acute. It took on a special urgency as the Depression deepened.

The highest authorities persevered in similar confusion, revealing despite their power their popular origins and vision. They figured that Mexico's trouble was essentially a problem of balance and that once they fixed the Republic in the correct shape and place, it would function more or less automatically and sooner or later for the general welfare. But however they ruled, they could not find a satisfactory solution. Back and forth they shifted the thrust of their policies—to favor organized labor, then to disrupt it; to flatter capitalists, foreign and domestic, then to distinguish one from the other, then to scare them both; to discount country people's demands for land, then to gush titles, then to announce the close of agrarian agencies; to persecute priests, then to ignore them; to reproach the United States and aid its enemies, then to oblige it. At least the authorities kept the regime intact and going, a titanic achievement. But since they could hardly claim more, even consistency, they could only assure the public that they were "revolutionary," which was to stress their popular origins and to swear that they were still sincerely trying. After Vasconcelos embarrassed them, they did manage two new nostrums for the next administration (1934–40), a radical Six-Year Plan and an exciting presidential candidate, Lázaro Cárdenas. But though Cárdenas quickly proved to be a soul-stirring president, the Mexico he agitated seemed basically the same frustrated country. Aching for consensus, Mexicans could not yet agree on their priorities or purpose.

During 1935 a clear change finally set in. It still was not deliberate, though various ideologues believed that they had caused it. Nor did it derive from a social or economic emergency, though this was its context. Rather, as in 1910, 1914, and 1920, it came obscurely out of a political struggle that required the mobilization of new support. The struggle was Cárdenas's effort to control his sponsors, rivals, and foes (Calles and the PNR, labor, Communists, the Army, new nabobs, a burgeoning Fascist movement, foreign creditors and investors) and to consolidate his own power. By 1935 he had already gained much popular sympathy; and now he went out to arouse more, touring widely, encouraging strikers, calming Catholics and anticlerics, distributing deeds and credit to thousands of country people. When Calles objected, Cárdenas exiled him without a hitch and appointed a new Cabinet. To hold the aroused masses, he had them organized—labor in 1936 in the Confederation of Mexican Workers (CTM) and country people in agrarian leagues and then in 1938 in the National Country Confederation (CNC), coordinating them separately so that he could rein them like a team. It was an expensive venture, which the Government financed; and it mortified allies and outraged opponents pining still for a classically balanced budget. But Cárdenas, ignorant of the classics, pressed on to reframe federal expenditures and markedly increase deficit spending. Actually, the effect was stabilizing: Country people stayed on the land, outside the cities where there were no jobs for them, and the economy adjusted to the new world patterns of autarky. In effect, Cárdenas had created the instruments of national patronage, the key to national order. But to contemporaries the Government seemed wildly radical.

Cárdenas's boldest act was to expropriate the major British and American oil companies on March 18, 1938, when they defied an adverse verdict from the Mexican Supreme Court. Before, few Mexicans knew about the oil case, and none expected expropriation. Afterward, millions heard of it, and all exulted in defense of the nation—Catholics prayed, workers forfeited pay, the Army paraded, women offered wedding rings, farmers sent in turkeys and pigs. To take advantage of the momentary surge of national unity and to secure control, Cárdenas reorganized the shaky PNR into the Party of the Mexican Revolution (PRM), affiliating the CTM, the agrarian leagues, the Army, and the civil service in a massive political combine. Now he had a modern ruling agency to gear the great majority of citizens into national concerns. The expropriation caused an international crisis, but consciously, steadily, the country pulled through it. By 1940 an epoch seemed over.

The changes in Mexico since 1910 had been manifold and perplexing. Had they been revolutionary? After all, most Mexicans remained rural and very poor. Serious conflicts continued—between capital and labor, moderate nationalists and militant nationalists, union officials and union members, landlords and squatters. Workingmen and villagers did not enjoy much "development" or "democracy." They did not eat much better than in 1910, dress much better, dwell in much better shelters, vote more freely. Mexicans still discriminated cruelly against each other by class, age, sex, regional origin, education, language, religion. All but a few assumed that the world was basically a place of limits and permanent shortage, that progress and welfare were only different dispensations of scarce rations; the idea of economic growth would not start sinking in for another two decades. And yet by 1940, in contrast with 1910, the prevailing political and economic system was an open system, the essential strength of which was that other entrepreneurs than those who ran it could enter into it. More significantly, also in contrast with 1910, most Mexicans now recognized each other as compatriots. And institutionally and emotionally most fit into the new regime. Despite failures in practice, most Mexicans felt that all citizens had rights and responsibilities in the country's career, that only native citizens could have its interests at heart, that social justice was patriotism. In these terms most Mexicans had learned to take their bearings not from a tradition, a local chief, a union, a movement, a bank, a party, the Church, a company, or the "civilized nations" of Europe and the United States, but rather from the federal executive. By 1940, the sense they had made of their ordeal was simple: that as one people they depended on their Government and that it could count on them. But this sense was vital in the world they were about to rejoin for good.

READINGS

1. *The Porfiriato's Success*

Publishers released several deluxe books for the centennial in 1910. In one, the editor told in Spanish, French, and English what Mexicans thought foreign interest in their country meant. Here is his English version.

There are relentless laws!

The individual who rises up and triumphantly dominates adversity encounters friends, sees everybody smile at him, hears applauses and flatteries, and leads a merry life.

The humble, the weak, or the slow, who vacillates and bends, encounters but stern looks, shirkings, haughty hatreds, and rapacious enemies eager to dispute his remains.

The same experience is suffered by societies.

A nation virile, powerful, and progressive has friends and allies; under different conditions they are watching from the frontiers for an opening to conquer it.

Leaving aside generalities, let us proceed with our real subject.

Mexico was in gala dressed! Men of actuality, of fame, veterans of many wars and of universal fame, titles of nobility, a reproduction of the old courts of Europe, a glimpse of the marvelous East, and the cream of the new American democracies came traversing lands and seas in order to offer to our country at the celebration of the first Centennial of its Independence the homage of a friendship under all aspects most appreciable.

What significance shall we give this visit?

The sanction of our entering the nucleus of civilized nations.

We have friends because we belong to the class that succeeds.

. . . [T]he idea of the foreign nations that this is a country of traditional uprisings and revolutions is not a thing to be erased in a day.

But when, still under the influence of this pessimistic opinion, the Delegates encountered a peace-loving nation, a nation that under the sane influence and restraint of the last thirty years has recovered what revolutions had snatched away, has developed its mining resources, has established the foundations of its agriculture and its industries, has en-

SOURCE: "The Porfiriato's Success" from *México en su primer siglo de independencia*, edited by Gonzalo G. Travesi (Mexico City: El Diario, 1910), pp. 133–37.

larged its commerce, built telegraph lines up to its most remote limits and its smallest cities, accredited its solvency, balanced its finances, and accustomed itself to ideas of order, culture and morality, they must have wondered like one who, ready to sacrifice himself in visiting ruins and destruction, finds himself unexpectedly in the midst of a nation enlightened, polished, entirely modern, that seems to have risen as from the magic touch of a fairy. . . .

Have we not conquered the difficulties of more than three-quarters of a century passed in civil and international wars through the malediction of the pessimism that led us to be considered as hopeless?

This in itself guarantees that, having recovered from this most serious ailment, we shall conquer all the other inconveniences placed in our way, either of time or of any other form.

2. *Change in the Old Regime*

President Madero's first report to Congress, April 1, 1912, bore the trademarks of the new notables in the Government, a cautious bent for reform and a trust in political liberty.

I have already referred . . . to the agrarian problem, which has taken on acute forms among us in various regions of the country in different periods of our history. [My] Revolutionary Plan . . . announced that through juridical procedures of review, the cases would be determined in which small proprietors, especially Indians, had been unduly despoiled of their lands, in order to restore these [lands] in kind or to oblige the party responsible for the despoliation to pay an indemnity. In [Díaz's] Presidential Message of April 1, 1911, effective measures were promised for the subdivision of great rural properties, and, as a consequence of this promise, things went as far as a proposal for a law aimed at realizing it.

It is incontrovertible that the promises of [my] Plan and those of [Díaz's] Message . . . exploited as political weapons by agitators without conscience, have contributed to the revival of our age-old agrarian question; but these promises, whose intent is perfectly justifiable, can be fulfilled only after a series of studies and operations, which the Government I preside over has not been able to finish, precisely because those who are

SOURCE: "Change in the Old Regime" translated from "Informe del Sr. Francisco I. Madero, al abrir las sesiones ordinarias el 1 ° de abril de 1912," in *Los presidentes de México ante la nación, 1821–1966,* edited by Luis González y González, 5 vols. (Mexico City: Cámara de Diputados, 1966), 3, pp. 8, 15. Except where noted otherwise, the translations in this chapter are by the chapter editor.

impatient or who aspire to get in on the promises prevent their realization with violent acts. . . . When peace is reestablished, the Government, with the cooperation of Congress, will find the way not only of solving the problem but also of preventing its ever presenting itself again in a violent form. . . .

To conclude this report, I must let you know the opinion of the Executive on the political condition of the country.

The Government I preside over, a genuine emanation of the citizens' votes, as you yourselves recognized in a solemn official declaration, represents the saving principle that all power flows from the people, a principle that we good Mexicans must try hard to sustain, because if it fails, with it the supreme democratic conquest that we have realized would fail, and perhaps also our nationality itself.

When the November Revolution broke out, many believed that the movement was exclusively personalist. No one has a right to think this way now, since the Revolution . . . channeled itself in the path of the law, thus demonstrating the purity of its intentions. The most furious enemies of the November Revolution, those who battle it in the field of politics, must confess that, thanks to this movement which today they condemn, they can exercise rights consecrated by the Constitution that in previous times they could rarely exercise.

3. *The Resentful Reaction*

A rich socialite, formerly Díaz's chief of staff, ex-governor of the southern state of Morelos, and in 1912 still heir to large sugar plantations there, Pablo Escandón was typical of the nabobs angry over the turbulence of freedom. This is the lament he wrote in 1912 to his political mentor, Pablo Macedo, then in exile.

My dear namesake,

I am certain that it will cause you satisfaction to get news from this country of ours, even though what I can communicate to you is not precisely agreeable. . . .

A true test for our country is this epoch of Maderista "LIBERTY AND DEMOCRACY," which is leading us to ruin. Everything our country had earned with so much work, in credit, in wealth, in advances, has been lost or is on the point of being lost. After having managed with so much

SOURCE: "The Resentful Reaction" translated from "El Archivo de la Reacción," in *El Universal* (Mexico City daily), October 12, 1917.

effort to have ourselves classified among THE CIVILIZED AND CUL-TURED NATIONS, if things go on as they are going, surely we will degenerate to our old position as a NATION OF THE LAST ORDER, A TRUE NIGGERDOM.[1] Although you surely read whatever news the European press publishes about us, it will hardly give you an idea of everything that is happening, which is unheard of.

The enthusiasm, the true popular intoxication in the midst of which Madero arrived in the presidency, vanished as rapidly as it came. And after that intoxication, which, IT APPEARS, HAS PERSISTED ONLY IN THE BRAIN OF MADERO, came disenchantment, the greatest disappointment that has afflicted this people, who very quickly realized that THEIR IDOL WAS OF NO VALUE, AND NEITHER WERE THE DISTEMPERED CRIES WITH WHICH THEY HAD CHEERED HIM. . . .

The Government, in my opinion, is at the edge of the abyss, and ONLY AN UNFORESEEN EVENT ABSOLUTELY OUTSIDE ITS CONTROL CAN SAVE IT. Madero has said that he will not retire (IT IS CLEAR HE DOES NOT HAVE THE PATRIOTISM OF GENERAL DÍAZ), and that he will die in the defense of "LEGITIMACY." . . . Anyhow, awaiting us is an epoch even more painful than that which we have already experienced; and God grant that the country have enough vitality to come out of its crisis, although it be battered. . . .

4. *The Failure*
of the Established Order

Helpless woe at the old regime's collapse is frankly detailed in the memoir of a young planter on the scene in Morelos in April 1914.

Like lightning the news spread through the whole town that the Americans had disembarked in Veracruz and that the intervention was a fact. I do not know how to explain the sensation this produced in me. After so many and such deep emotions, the receipt of this news was a blow that, though not unexpected, left me astounded. . . . I understood that the gravity of the case was great and that this circumstance would unavoidably create a new, more anguished and terrible phase in our al-

[1] ["*Cafrería.*"]
SOURCE: "The Failure of the Established Order" translated from Luis García Pimentel, Jr., "Memorias" (MS, dated Mexico City, 1914, used by permission of José García Pimentel), pp. 65–66, 70–72.

ready difficult situation. Taking hold of me was a deep feeling of impotent rage against so many elements that seemed to unite and conspire against me, a great indignation at the thought that, not content with having incited and exploited the banditry and the lack of patriotism of the Mexicans, the Americans in Veracruz were aggravating with their action—as violent as it was unjustified—the already very bad conditions in Morelos. There was no doubt that Huerta's government, with the object or on the pretext of repelling the invasion, would withdraw the federal forces from the state, and it would remain again in the power of the bandits. . . .

[I returned to our Hacienda Santa Clara to evacuate it.] Before mounting my horse [to leave for the last time], I went to the [hacienda's] church to hide the little of value that was still there. When I felt myself alone under the immense vault, and when I thought of the abandon in which all this was going to remain, I could not keep from getting down on my knees and crying like someone who has made a supreme decision, who no longer has to waver and who can freely relieve himself of his pain. . . . Passing around the hacienda grounds, a few people were still tenderly saying goodbye—which again made me feel an indescribable emotion, and despite all my efforts I did no more than weep along the road, and only on arriving in Jonacatepec was I able to control myself and enter the town calmly.

5. *The Populist Revolutionaries*

On December 4, 1914, in a little town just south of Mexico City, Francisco Villa and Emiliano Zapata met to seal their alliance against Carranza. Some of their comments that day are striking evidence of the general disgust with official procedure and the faith in direct action.

Villa: As Carranza is a man so, so, so high and mighty, I realized that [he and his crowd] were going along getting control of the Republic, and me just waiting.

Zapata: All the fellows have already told you: I always said so, I always told them, that Carranza is a son of a bitch.

Villa: [He and his crowd] are men who have slept on downy pillows. How are they going to be friends of people who have spent their whole lives in pure suffering?

SOURCE: "The Populist Revolutionaries" translated from "Pacto de Xochimilco," in *Fuentes para la historia de la revolución mexicana, I: Planes políticos y otros documentos,* edited by Manuel González Ramírez (Mexico City: Fondo de Cultura Económica, 1954), pp. 113, 116–17.

Zapata: The other way around, they have been used to being the scourge of the people. . . . [The people] have lots of love for the land. They still don't believe it when you tell them, "This land is yours." They think it's a dream. But as soon as they see others are getting crops from these lands, they'll say, "I'm going to ask for my land, and I'm going to plant." Above all, that's the love people have for the land. As a rule they never lose it.

Villa: The [politicians] will soon see that it's the people who give the orders and that the people are going to see who are their friends.

Zapata: [People know] if somebody wants to take their lands away, they know all by themselves that they have to defend themselves. But they kill before they turn loose of the land.

Villa: They no more than get the taste, and then we bring them the party [of politicians] to take it away. Our people have never had justice, not even liberty. The rich have all the prime fields, and the people, the raggedy little poor man, working from sunup to sundown. I think that in the future it's going to be another life, and if not, we won't turn loose of those Mausers we have now. . . .

Zapata: Those son-of-a-bitch politicians, as soon as they see a little chance to get in, then quick they want to make their way, and they take off to brown-nose the next big shot on the rise, like a son of a bitch. That's why I've busted all those sons of bitches. I can't stand them. In a jiffy they change and take off, now with Carranza or now with another one farther on. They're all a bunch of bastards. I'd just like to run into them some other time.

6. *The Regular Revolutionaries*

During the war with the Villistas and Zapatistas, this is the style in which Carrancista chiefs paid to have their enemies and themselves caricatured—their enemies as wild animals, themselves as sober stewards of the nation.

The history of Zapatismo is a long, terrifying criminal farce.

. . . How can there be partisans of Zapatismo among people who boast of being civilized?

How can the father of a family feel sympathy for a bestial mob capable of killing his own sons?

. . . If two and a half miles outside Puebla a Zapatista band seizes

SOURCE: "The Regular Revolutionaries" translated from Gonzalo de la Parra, *De cómo se hizo revolucionario un hombre de buena fe* (Mexico City: no publisher given, 1915), pp. 98, 114–16, 122–24.

women and outrages them, abandoning them full of shame and disgrace at the side of the road, how can you be sure, snooty Mrs. Zapatista . . . that tomorrow, for all your devotion, you and your daughter, coming from her first communion, pure in spirit and flesh, may not be victims of the criminal concupiscence of those bandits?

. . . The Zapatistas do not cost their chiefs much money. It is true, the Zapatista does not need clothes or comforts. He feeds on blood. . . .

Francisco Villa has a head full of rocks. He can see no farther than his nose. He detests politicians, but they surround him on all sides, manage him, make him ridiculous; he does not even know what politicians look like. If they were distinguished by some special sign, a pimple on the forehead, one foot bigger than the other, or the tone of their voice, fine; but they are like all other men, they dress and speak like everyone else. Francisco Villa would like to crush the politicians; but . . . he goes through the same labors as an ignorant animal-collector, who, painstakingly in search of scorpions, finds himself in the middle of a jungle before a crocodile and wonders, "Maybe this is the scorpion I'm looking for?"

. . . Those who follow [Villa] are mercenary soldiers, as mercenary and barbarous as those who besieged Carthage. For their complicity they demand payment in gold, in liberty to commit crimes, in authority to rob, rape, and kill with impunity. This bestial, primitive, blind, and foolish mob is called an army because it consists of many men, but truthfully it is only a gang of bandits. For them the Republic is a stagecoach loaded with gold and women; what you do is hold it up.

. . . Obregón's triumph over [Villa's] black hosts is the triumph of military expertise, calculation, calmness, and wisdom. Obregón takes no step that is not calculated, meditated, considered. His advance has been slow but sure, firm, definitive.

. . . Mothers, you can sleep in peace. The rapists are fleeing. Bourgeoisie, don't worry so much now over your coffers. The robbers are dead. Hypocritical neutrals, your hope has gone out. Eternal reactionaries, the Revolution triumphs over all your selfishness. Privileges crumble, and the lights of Liberty go on!

7. The Constitutional Convention

An impressive theme in the 1916–17 Constitutional Convention was the call to disregard native and foreign precedent and write into the

SOURCE: "The Constitutional Convention" translated from *Diario de los debates del congreso constituyente*, 1916–1917, 2 vols. (Mexico City: Talleres Gráficos de la Nación, 1960), 1, pp. 983–84.

charter articles spelling out ordinary people's economic stake in the country. Here is how Jorge E. Von Versen, an obscure workers' delegate, argued for the inclusion of a detailed version of Article 5, on labor. Though the final version of Article 5 was simple, the details did enter the Constitution later in Article 123.

I come to censure the [detailed] recommendation for what's wrong with it, and I come to applaud it for what's good in it, and I come to say also to the gentlemen of the Committee that they not be afraid of what Attorney [Fernando] Lizardi said, that this article [put in the Constitution] was going to look like a pair of pistols hanging on Holy Christ. I'd like the gentlemen of the Committee not to have this fear, because if it's necessary to guarantee the liberties of the people, let this Holy Christ have army leggings and a .30-30, so there! (Applause.) . . . These millions of workers who formed the majority of the fatherland, these millions of men who've assured our independence, this majority of men who must be the base on which our independence and our nationality rest, they must have the greatest number of guarantees, they must have their future assured. Because if we let the capitalists tie them up tight again, then also, gentlemen, refuse them the right to a home just as we have refused them the right to a fatherland; refuse them the right to protect themselves against capitalists, just as we have refused them the right to rest their bones in peace in the soil of the fatherland without paying a cent. . . . I dissent also from the opinion of friend [Dionisio] Zavala and friend [Héctor] Victoria; I don't want to vote in parts on the article which the Committee presents. I ask that it be thrown back and that they reconsider it, that they put army leggings on it, that they put pistols on it, that they hang a .30-30 on Christ, but that they save our humble class, our class which represents the . . . colors of our flag and our future and our national greatness. (Applause.)

8. *Article 27: The Nation*
as Monopolist

The longest and most important article in the new Constitution was number 27, which declared that property was no longer a natural right but a social responsibility.

SOURCE: "Article 27: The Nation as Monopolist" adapted from "The Mexican Constitution of 1917 Compared with the Constitution of 1857," translated and edited by H. N. Branch, in *Supplement to the Annals of the American Academy of Political and Social Science* (May 1917), pp. 15–19.

Article 27. The ownership of lands and waters comprised within the limits of the national territory is vested originally in the Nation, which has had and has the right to transmit title thereof to private persons, thereby constituting private property.

Private property shall not be expropriated except for reasons of public utility and by means of indemnification.

The Nation shall have at all times the right to impose on private property such limitations as the public interest may demand as well as the right to regulate the development of natural resources, which are susceptible of appropriation, in order to conserve them and equitably to distribute the public wealth. For this purpose necessary measures shall be taken to divide large landed estates; to develop small landed holdings; to establish new centers of agricultural population, with such lands and waters as may be indispensable to them; to encourage agriculture, to prevent the destruction of natural resources, and to protect property from damage detrimental to society. The villages, hamlets situated on private property, and communities that lack lands and water or do not possess them in sufficient quantities for their needs shall have the right to be provided with them from the adjoining properties, always having due regard for small landed holdings. . . . Private property acquired for the said purposes shall be considered as taken for public utility.

In the Nation is vested direct ownership of all minerals or substances that in veins, layers, masses, or beds constitute deposits whose nature is different from the components of the land, such as minerals from which metals and metalloids used for industrial purposes are extracted; beds of precious stones, rock salt, and salt lakes formed directly by marine waters; products derived from the decomposition of rocks, when their exploitation requires underground work; phosphates that may be used for fertilizers; solid mineral fuels; petroleum and all hydrocarbons—solid, liquid, or gaseous.

. . . [T]he ownership of the Nation is inalienable and may not be lost by prescription; concessions shall be granted by the Federal Government to private parties or civil or commercial corporations organized under the laws of Mexico, only on condition that the said resources be regularly developed, and on the further condition that the legal provisions be observed.

Legal capacity to acquire ownership of lands and waters of the Nation shall be governed by the following provisions:

I. Only Mexicans by birth or naturalization and Mexican companies have the right to acquire ownership in lands, waters, and their appurtenances, or to obtain concessions to develop mines, waters, or mineral fuels in the Republic of Mexico. The Nation may grant the same right to foreigners, provided they agree before the Ministry of Foreign Relations to be considered Mexicans in respect to such property, and accordingly not to invoke the protection of their Governments in respect to the same, under penalty, in case of breach, of forfeiture to the Nation of property so acquired.

Within a zōne of one hundred kilometers from the frontiers, and of fifty kilometers from the seacoast, no foreigner shall under any conditions acquire direct ownership of lands and waters.

9. *Carranza in Ridicule*

Carranza's presidential faults had no greedier publicist than Vicente Blasco Ibáñez, a liberal Spanish writer in Mexico collecting gossip for a novel.

What man of prominence in Mexico has not been accused of graft? The Mexican people [are] fond of broad generalizations. To save [themselves] the annoyance of making nice distinctions, [they] include everybody in one sweeping judgment and call "thief" after all the people ever connected with the Government.

The venerable Carranza has not escaped such charges by any means. They call him the "First Chief . . . of those who come in the night." Long ago the wags of the capital began to use a new verb, "to carranza," the exact humor of which may not appear in English. "To carranza," in the cafés and vaudeville theaters of Mexico City, means "to steal," and you can hear people conjugating it on every hand: "I carranza, thou carranzest, he carranzas—they all carranza."

10. *The Call to Reunion*

The yearning for a real settlement among all revolutionaries, in or out of government, even those currently outside the law, received shrewd expression in Obregón's announcement of his presidential candidacy on June 1, 1919. He asked a series of questions and gave his answers.

SOURCE: "Carranza in Ridicule" from Vicente Blasco Ibáñez, *Mexico in Revolution,* translated by Arthur Livingston and José Padin (New York: E. P. Dutton, 1920), pp. 83–84.

SOURCE: "The Call to Reunion" translated from "Manifiesto del Ciudadano Álvaro Obregón," in *Campaña política del C. Álvaro Obregón, candidato a la presidencia de la república, 1920–1924,* 5 vols., edited by Luis N. Ruvalcaba (Mexico City: no publisher given, 1923), 1, pp. 40–59.

How many political parties are there presently in the country and what are their tendencies?

There is presently only one political party, and its tendencies are advanced, but it is divided into an infinity of groups which differ among themselves only in details and which can best be considered as variants that obey the character of their organizers.

How many parties have existed in the country?

Only two: the Conservative party and the Liberal party, of tendencies diametrically opposed.

How were these two political parties defined?

As soon as the first libertarian movement began in our country, the Mexican family stood divided in two political parties, one formed by the oppressors and the other by the oppressed, the first taking the name of conservatives and the second that of liberals. Rich grandees, high clergy, and privileged foreigners composed the first, and all the laboring classes the second—day laborers, workers, professionals, farmers, ranchers, and small manufacturers, this latter group constituting a true majority of the Mexican family whose strength was fully demonstrated in armed contests, out of which it invariably issued victorious. . . .

Why does the Liberal party fail in the political contests that follow its armed victories, despite the fact that this party stands for a great majority of the country?

Because when the political struggle begins, it always goes on within the party itself, [which] disintegrates. The divisions that arise take on two aspects: national and local. . . .

What is the present situation of the Liberal party?

Disastrous.

The Liberal party has practically disintegrated because all the phenomena . . . determining its previous failures have been repeated this time. Divisions have been produced in all their aspects, degenerating in many states of the Republic from political divisions to armed contests. . . .

Conscious of the dangers that I have noted and that threaten to extinguish our rights as citizens . . . I am breaking the bonds of tranquility and well-being and opening a parenthesis of anxieties, responsibilities, and dangers in order to offer to my fellow citizens all my energies and all my good will. [Let them accept my offer to help,] if they believe that [it] might mean in these moments a factor of union for all good citizens who without political or moral slackness want to unify their efforts in defense of the national interests.

11. *Wish for a Peaceful Tortilla*

The general feeling that Carranza's fall closed a time for war and heroics and introduced a time for repair—this echoed even in contemporary street songs. The topic of the following song is Carranza's evacuation and Obregón's occupation of Mexico City in May 1920.

The People are very calm
As they watch this fuss and mess.
They say very calmly,
"It's family business."

The scramble to be president
Is one of our oldest haunts,
But to eat a peaceful tortilla
Is all the poor man wants.

Now the case is heated,
As we all can understand.
They're various the candidates
Who're trying to lead the band.

They've all got their program,
So that they can govern.
But what they promise us,
They'd better not give up on.

Let them remember that they've said
When they get in office at last.
Let them do right by the fatherland,
As so many swore to in the past.

Because the People have suffered enough,
And they want some consolation.
Today they ask for peace and work
And a president of reputation.

SOURCE: "Wish for a Peaceful Tortilla" abridged and translated from "La evacuación de México, 1920," in *Corridos de la revolución mexicana,* edited by Jesús Romero Flores (Mexico City: El Nacional, 1941), pp. 200–02.

12. *The Ideal of Getting Ahead*

During the 1920's, many town and city folk imagined that Mexico would now become a system of avenues for individual advancement, open especially to their children. Witness for them is an editor of a boys' and girls' magazine.

It is very consoling to see how modern ideas are making their way into our fatherland, after conquering innumerable prejudices and destroying stale preoccupations.

The youth of today are accepting the new ideas and are entertaining designs more just, more humane, and more practical, which will permit them to progress rapidly and to get ahead in the world, create a good position for themselves, build a magnificent future, and contribute with their effort to make great, prosperous, and respectable this blessed Mexican fatherland, whose greatness depends entirely on what its sons are worth.

Before, most boys were educated to be lawyers, doctors, actors, writers, or employees, who always lived at the expense of others, like octopuses sucking the vital fluid from other organisms, without producing anything, without contributing to the progress of the country with an effective job and with real work and seriousness in their professions.

Girls were taught the chores of the house, the work of maids, seamstresses, or cooks, not on scientific bases but by blindly following the customs of their mothers and grandmothers, finishing their education with a lacquer of music or painting, which they never learned well, much less applied to any useful purpose. This made them believe that for their sustenance they would always have to depend on their poor father, long-suffering brother, resigned husband, or loving son, without having the slightest obligation to help them earn the support of the family.

But now all youth, whatever their sex, are convinced that the greatest obligation they have in life is to be sufficient unto themselves, to earn their living by themselves alone, not to constitute a charge on others, to work, to produce, to contribute to the progress of all, to form some capital by dint of struggle.

SOURCE: "The Ideal of Getting Ahead" translated from *Pinocho, Semanario Ilustrado para los niños* (Mexico City weekly), January 8, 1925.

13. *The Syndical Ideal*

At the same time, many organized workers supposed that Mexico was properly their domain, that unions would exercise authority instead of the Government. For them, balladeers sang ditties like this.

The day when the Workers
Formed their Unions in the plants,
The rich from pure fright
Jumped right out of their pants.

For all the little rich guys,
Who talked so much of fun,
When they saw the Union,
From fear they fell mum.

Will they say they have a conscience?
They don't even know where it might perch.
What they've got is a talent
For leaving us in the lurch.

Down with that crazy rich man,
Who wants to grind up the poor!
Long live the Unions,
Which will defend us for sure!

14. *The Sacramental Ideal*

Other, pious Mexicans wanted a Catholic social order, which many believed the Cristeros would finally impose. For them, hope glimmered in reports like this, on rebel concentrations in Michoacán and Jalisco.

Some of these nuclei have their military chaplain. During a campaign, Masses are said almost daily, the sacraments are given frequently,

SOURCE: "The Syndical Ideal" abridged and translated from "El Pericón de la Huasteca," in Merle E. Simmons, *The Mexican Corrido as a Source for Interpretive Study of Modern Mexico, 1870–1950*, Indiana University Publications, Humanities Series, No. 38 (Bloomington: Indiana University Press, 1957), pp. 364–66.
SOURCE: "The Sacramental Ideal" translated from "Situación Militar de la Defensa Armada en 1927," in Alicia Olivera Sedano, *Aspectos del conflicto religioso de 1926 a 1929, sus antecedentes y consecuencias* (Mexico City: Instituto Nacional de Antropología e Historia, 1966), pp. 185–86.

and it is not unusual to see groups of combatants, as many as six or seven hundred, receiving Holy Communion. These "Liberators" have to suffer hunger and grave privations often and repeatedly, because of the [Government's] campaign . . . of destroying and relocating villages [to eradicate rebel bases] and because of the exhaustion of certain regions in the Center [of the country]. They say that they are having a banquet when they have occasion to take a little nourishment twice a day. Never, or almost never, do they receive spending money, and many of them go around almost naked. Despite this and the lack of a [supreme] chief, the morale of the "Liberators" is magnificent. They never complain of hunger or cold. They only complain about not having enough ammunition. . . .

From groups so idealistic, so generous, so valiant as these, it is inevitable that the true National Mexican Army will surge forth, filled with the spirit of order and patriotism that inspires the nation. Among the youths who lead them, who have already abundantly shed their blood and offered their lives, a body of officers is forming who will be the "elite," that genuine aristocracy, that nobility, which is wholly indispensable for the salvation of peoples.

15. *The Moral Ideal*

Yet other Mexicans believed that personal good will would put the nation in order. For them, Vasconcelos's first campaign speech was delicious.

I return to the fatherland after [a] painful absence, and what should surprise me on my arirval but the happy fortune of finding revealed the strength that throbs in the people, of hearing from my compatriots here assembled and from many other brothers elsewhere that the hour of destiny is coming again to offer us an occasion for salvation. But there is reason for us all to take great pains in considering whether the occasion is going to pass again in vain. . . .

The first thing it is urgent to change is our disposition toward life, substituting for rancor a generous disposition. Only love is understanding, and therefore only love corrects. He who is not moved by love will see that for him justice itself turns into vengeance. Only by getting out of this circle, this circle of hate, only by initiating a new disposition of concord, will we be able to take on situations like religion, which for years now has

SOURCE: "The Moral Ideal" translated from "Discurso en Nogales, Noviembre de 1928," in José Vasconcelos, *Discursos, 1920–1950* (Mexico City: Botas, 1950), pp. 119–22.

been tearing at the heart of the fatherland. To begin, we will proclaim that you fight fanaticism with books, not with machine guns, that it is the State's business to mediate in conflicts among all fanaticisms instead of embracing one of them as its own. Then, and as an indispensable condition for treating the affair, it is necessary that we remember—that we feel— that the Catholics are our brothers and that it is treason to the fatherland to go on exterminating them. . . .

The danger, the only danger, is that the people may not finally feel the call, that the people may not finally move. But I have faith in the people, which is why I trust—I know—that the people are going to stand up now to give us a free and Mexican government.

16. *Reason Confounded*

Reflective Mexicans recognized the confusion and guessed wisely about its causes, but they were at a loss to tell how the country would come out of it. Here is the director of the National Preparatory School carefully replying to an inquiry that the Parisian *Cahiers de L'Étoile* conducted among "all the intellectuals of the world . . . to determine if there exists a special inquietude in our epoch."

We live after the destruction that the nineteenth century produced in spiritual matters. We find ourselves among ruined religious and philosophical systems, but we do not know what it is necessary to construct or what the ideal, the directing line of creative activity in the twentieth century, will be like.

The nineteenth century built only science and its derivative, industry, on firm bases. But it failed in its attempt to found Morality on Science, and the old faith has been lost forever among many of us. . . .

In SOCIAL LIFE, inquietude is expressed by a need to change all religious, moral, esthetic, and political values.

One has the intuition that it is necessary to create something new, something that might be the expression of the modern world, and this change is attempted in the highest activities of the spirit.

INQUIETUDE IS THEREFORE MANIFEST AS A CONFRONTATION WITH SOCIETY, as a rebellion against the mass that has not yet received the shock of the new life. But this rebellion is at times exaggerated, and the rebel mistakes his role, for in most cases he is not very sure of his message. . . .

AND IN SEXUAL LIFE?

SOURCE: "Reason Confounded" translated from *El Universal*, May 10, 1929.

Progress in the domination of human passions being infinitely small if you compare it with the plans reason has had, the sexual question has varied less than what is generally thought. There are men and women who believe they are *modern* for the sole reason that they act the way everyone did before them. . . .

I do not doubt that a new consciousness—that is, a new form of culture—is about to appear in the modern world; but I do not believe that we can yet indicate in what that new consciousness consists or what its characteristics are.

17. *Official Experiments*

> At its second convention in December 1933, the National Revolutionary party announced a Six-Year Plan to give new directions for national development.

Foremost importance attaches, among the tasks that the change of Administration in 1934 brings up, to the drafting of a program for the incoming Administration.—a program that shall be a pledge to the Nation that a social, economic and administrative policy shall be followed, through which the principles proclaimed when armed strife prevailed are to materialize. Through this policy also, direction shall be given to those currents of reconstruction engendered both at home and abroad by the desire of the masses of the people to readjust human relations on a basis of justice.

2. The National Revolutionary Party has now fulfilled its initial mission, which was to bring together all the heretofore scattered groups of the Revolution and to direct them toward definite aims pursued in common. It now declares that the time is come when its political activities and its economic and social endeavors are to reach a higher stage, productive of more fruitful results for the Mexican commonwealth.

3. This evolution entails the systematic framing of the Party's policies in programs painstakingly studied, drafted with a dispassionate knowledge of the real facts which the Nation faces, and made as extensive as the powers of the Administration, on the one hand, may allow, and as demanded, on the other hand, by the purposes that inspire the members of the Party and by the means at their disposal.

4. In our country the determination to maintain the National Revolu-

SOURCE: "Official Experiments" from Gilberto Bosques, *The National Revolutionary Party of Mexico and the Six-Year Plan* (Mexico City: Bureau of Foreign Information of the National Revolutionary Party, 1937), pp. 129–31, 163.

tionary Party in power springs from the constant impulsion of the people toward social and economic changes designed to establish ever higher and more ample living standards for the entire Nation. So long as there is a revolutionary party in power safeguarding the government for the people, the Revolution shall carry on peacefully and constructively through political action. But when such a party is lacking, then the Revolution shall manifest itself through violence, in civil war.

5. Now then, a basic program is vital to every good administration. Such a program fixes the obligations to the people assumed by the party in power, and the responsibilities of the rulers to the Nation and to their party. These obligations become bonds of solidarity, points of cooperation, when, as in the case of the National Revolutionary Party, the men in charge of the various organs of the administration use public office to satisfy the great aspirations of the masses.

6. The foregoing considerations explain why foremost importance was given in the agenda of the Second National Convention of the National Revolutionary Party, to the study and adoption of this First Six-Year Government Plan.

7. From the study which the Convention's Reporting Committee made of the draft for the Six-Year Plan drawn by the Program Committee of the National Revolutionary Party; from the examination of the draft proposed to the Party by its Technical Commission of Cooperation with the Federal Executive; and from the survey of the numerous propositions, suggestions and initiatives, referring to questions of varying importance, submitted to the Program Committee by various public officials, institutions, and private citizens, a thesis was arrived at which commands unanimous recommendation. Upon this thesis the Government Plan that has been drawn is based. It is the thesis that the Mexican State assume and maintain a policy regulatory of the economic activities of the Nation. That is to say, it is openly and definitely declared that in the Mexican revolutionary concept the State is an active agent moving and controlling the vital processes of the country, not a mere custodian of the national integrity and keeper of the public peace and order.

. . .

93. The need to reorganize our country under a well-coordinated economic system of its own that shall guarantee enough supplies for all its inhabitants, does not spring from a merely sentimental nationalistic impulse, but results from transformations that have taken place in the economic structure, and in the trade relations, of all countries.

94. The National Revolutionary Party is certain that could an international agreement be reached to coordinate the economic activities of all countries, and determine the obligation to produce in accordance with the needs of all and with the natural and technological capacities of each,

organizing the world under a system of regional economic units to be not only non-competitive among themselves but designed to complement one another, it would be conducive to economic peace and the welfare of mankind. But having to meet a world-wide attitude characterized by the tendency of planning for national economic self-sufficiency, the National Revolutionary Party considers that Mexico is compelled, on its part, to adopt a policy of economic nationalism, as a measure of legitimate self-defense, without thereby incurring any historical responsibility.

18. *The Limits of Official Dreams*

When President Cárdenas's Director General of Statistics addressed the Institute of Public Affairs at the University of Virginia on July 4, 1935, his remarks revealed that the dimensions of official projects in Mexico were still modest.

Some of us . . . believe that Mexico finds herself in a privileged position to determine her destiny. By being in a pre-capitalistic state with some of her people even in a pre-pecuniary economy and at the same time by observing the effects of the last crisis of the capitalistic world, we think that we should be able to use the advantages of the industrial era without having to suffer from its well-known short-comings. We think that we should attempt to industrialize Mexico consciously, intelligently avoiding the avoidable evils of industrialism, such as urbanism, exploitation of man by man, production for sale instead of production for the satisfaction of human needs, economic insecurity, waste, shabby goods and the mechanization of the workmen. This is not an impossible dream. We are convinced that the evils of capitalism are not to be found in the application of machinery to the productive process, but rather are due to a merely legal question: who is the owner of the machinery. We want the land and its necessary equipment to be at the disposal of those who till it, rather than be the means of exploiting these men. Some of us believe, furthermore, that profit making is not the only incentive of human endeavour, but rather a motive that happens to have been chosen and over-developed in the capitalistic regime.

There is nothing fatal in the mistakes of the system, or at least so we hope. We have dreamt [of] a Mexico of "ejidos" [agricultural cooperatives] and small industrial communities, electrified, with sanitation, in which

SOURCE: "The Limits of Official Dreams" from *Economic and Social Program of Mexico: A Controversy,* translated and edited by Ramón Beteta (Mexico City: no publisher given, 1935), pp. 44–46.

goods will be produced for the purpose of satisfying the needs of the people; in which machinery will be employed to relieve man from heavy toil, and not for so-called over-production. In these communities machine-made goods may still be beautiful, for they will be made by the same people whose artistic sense is now expressed by the work of their hands, and there is no reason to believe that the changing of the tools will per se make them different. What mechanizes men is not the use of machinery, it is the pressure brought to bear upon them to produce at the highest speed the largest amount possible.

In short, we have chosen the "ejido" as the center of our rural economy. Within its limits "land belongs to him who works it with his hands" as our Indian poet expressed it. New methods of production, machinery and new technique will be introduced without having to make rugged individualists out of the "ejidatarios" [the cooperative farmers] and at the same time without killing the human desire of progress in those communities. Then, and only then, could national economy be planned, not by directing the conflicting interests of the various individuals, but by conceiving the country as a unit whose needs are to be satisfied by the harmonious working of these villages, agricultural or industrial, in an effort to make the whole country secure and prosperous.

19. *A Case of Depression*

> Many contemporary observers, in despair over the evidently permanent nature of Mexico's difficulties, found morbid pleasure in a book published in 1934. The author, Samuel Ramos, a young philosopher who had studied Jung and Adler, concluded that the nation's trouble inhered in the Mexican soul.

The most striking aspect of Mexican character, at first sight, is distrust. This attitude underlies all contact with men and things. It is present whether or not there is motivation for it. It is not a question of distrust on principle, because generally speaking the Mexican lacks principles. It is rather a matter of irrational distrust that emanates from the depths of his being. It is almost his primordial sense of life. Whether or not circumstances justify it, there is nothing in the universe which the Mexican does not see and evaluate through his distrust. It is like an a priori form of his oversensitivity. The Mexican does not distrust any

SOURCE: "A Case of Depression" from Samuel Ramos, *Profile of Man and Culture in Mexico*, translated by Peter G. Earle (Austin: University of Texas Press, 1962), pp. 64–65.

man or woman in particular; he distrusts all men and all women. His distrust is not limited to the human race; it embraces all that exists and happens. If he is a businessman he doesn't believe in business; if he is a professional he doesn't believe in his profession; if he is a politician he doesn't believe in politics. It is the Mexican's view that ideas make no sense, and he scornfully calls them "theories." He judges the knowledge of scientific principles as useless. He seems very confident of his practical insight, but as a man of action he is awkward and ultimately gives little credit to the efficacy of facts. He has no religion and professes no social or political creed. He is the least "idealistic" person imaginable. He unreasonably negates everything, because he is negation personified.

What then does the Mexican live for? He would perhaps reply that it is not necessary to have ideas and beliefs in order to live—provided that one does not think. And indeed, this is the situation. In its totality, Mexican life gives the impression of being an unreflecting activity, entirely without plan. In Mexico each man concerns himself only with immediate issues. He works for today and tomorrow but never for later on. The future is a preoccupation which he has banished from his conscience. He is incapable of adventure in projects that offer only remote results. He has therefore suppressed from his life one of its most important dimensions— the future. Such are the effects of Mexican distrust.

In a life limited to the present, only instinct can function. Intelligent reflection can intervene only in those pauses when one is able to suspend one's activity. It is impossible to think and act simultaneously. Thought presupposes that we are capable of expectation, and one who expects is receptive to the future. Obviously, a life without future can have no norms. Mexican life is accordingly at the mercy of the four winds; instead of sailing, it drifts. Men say that they live as God wills. With neither discipline nor organization, Mexican society not unnaturally finds itself in a chaos in which individual beings move unpredictably like dispersed atoms.

20. *The Mobile President*

The change coming suddenly from the new contacts between the Federal Government and local populations was most spectacular when the contact was directly between high officials and individual citizens —like this meeting in 1936 between Cárdenas and farmers who had just opened a road from their village to the state capital.

SOURCE: "The Mobile President" from Oscar Lewis, *Pedro Martínez: A Mexican Peasant and His Family* (New York: Random House, 1964), pp. 266–69.

Shortly after the clearing was finished, we were in the center of town, near where the saloon now is, sitting and talking, when this fellow comes by and says, "The President of the Republic is coming!"

"What would he be coming here for? Where is he coming?"

"He is coming through here."

"You're crazy. There are no signs of preparations. We haven't received any official notice. It's not true. That old man is *loco*," we said.

Well, a few minutes later, Chico comes rushing by like crazy. "Hurry, hurry, the President of the Republic is coming!" And there he went, running and running. Now, Chico is no fool, he has a good head. By that time I was running too. Where was the President? He had to come through the dirt road on horseback. Well, we saw a mob of people there and it was really he, it was President Lázaro Cárdenas, and we came running up.

But what a shame! no preparations, no nothing! Rodolfo was our president at the time and he rushed someone out to buy at least a dozen rockets to shoot off. But President Cárdenas was already there and while he was speaking they shot off the rockets. Then he went to the *palacio* and all the people crowded around there. Afterward, automobiles arrived and some motorcyclists. They came through the road we had cut. Then Cárdenas said, "This is fine but it is only a clearing. We could pass through, yes, but it is not a highway. Do you have any buses here?"

"Just one. We bought only one. It is a co-operative bus."

"Well," he says, "I am going to give you another bus, so you will have a pair."

Fine, we hoped he would. But this Chico put his foot into it by saying, "No, no. They will kill each other over the buses. No, better not send it."

So then Cárdenas gave other things . . . not to me, though. He gave a huge pedigreed bull, and a great big pure-bred pig, and a little light-colored *burro* that was still nursing. Everything went to the cattle raisers and that was all. He gave Víctor Conde a pair of beautiful tall horses. No one else got a thing. They got the gifts because they were the flatterers who knew how to talk. They got next to him so they could soft-soap him.

Then President Cárdenas said that the next week or the following one, the highway would be started. "Don't worry," he said, "I am going to build the highway for you." And immediately everyone drank to that. Well, the municipal president didn't know what to give him. What was he going to give him when he was taken by surprise like that? So he sent for some rolls, filled them with sausage meat, and offered them to the visitors. "Go ahead, Mr. President," he said. "This is all we could improvise."

"It doesn't matter. This is fine," Cárdenas said. "I am a peasant myself." And he picked up one of the rolls with sausage and ate it. But he ate only one.

Then, after that, I don't know why they took him to the churchyard. While we were keeping him busy, the teachers prepared a dinner for him there. They fixed it right out in the open air near the fence of the atrium. They served him dinner there under the trees. The teachers organized everything and then they collected from all of us.

That was the only time Lázaro Cárdenas came to the village.

21. *The Embrace of the Unions*

> More important than presidential tours were the massive regular contacts between the Government and the people through new, officially sponsored organizations like the Confederation of Mexican Workers, the CTM. Here is a report from a waspish but perceptive English visitor in Mexico City.

Questions I often asked myself during my stay in Mexico were: if one were not looking for signs of it, how much would one be aware of the very singular social and political conditions surrounding one? How far would it be possible to lead what in other parts of the world would be considered a normal life? The answer to the last question is that for a Mexican or for anyone doing business of any kind in Mexico, it would be quite impossible. The distressed condition of the country and its uncertain future affect every hour of his day. I think, too, that only a very incurious visitor could be unaware of some of the underlying confusion. Many years ago now, there was a delicious film in which Harold Lloyd, as a convalescent millionaire, arrived in a South American republic in the middle of a revolution and progressed placidly down the main street, bowing left and right, while a battle was raging around him. A few happy visitors no doubt travel through the country engrossed in the antiquities or the natural history of the place, completely oblivious of its condition; but they must be very few. For it is impossible to talk to any inhabitant for five minutes without feeling the obsession of politics. For anyone who troubles to enquire, the oddest information is constantly cropping up.

On the first day of my visit traffic leading to the Cathedral square was paralysed at midday. My companion advised leaving our taxi and walking. After passing an enormous block of cars, some drivers hooting furiously, others resigned to an indefinite wait, others causing further confusion by attempting to back out in the side streets, we came upon the cause of the trouble; a huge procession of schoolchildren, of all ages, themselves

SOURCE: "The Embrace of the Unions" from Evelyn Waugh, *Robbery Under Law: The Mexican Object-Lesson* (London: Chapman and Hall, Ltd., 1939), pp. 59–60.

halted and standing wistfully among their banners. Many of the groups wore distinguishing ribbons and uniforms; the banners seemed merely to state the localities from which they came. I asked, "Is it some football match?"

"No, it is just a demonstration of the children. They are always having them."

"What about?"

"I'll ask." My companion asked one or two spectators who shrugged indifferently, saying it was just a demonstration. Finally he obtained the information. "It is a children's strike."

"What about?"

"They do not like one of their teachers. They have come to protest to the President."

"They seem very well organized."

"Yes, the children's committees do that. The Ministry of Education teach them to organize like the C.T.M."

"What will happen?"

"The teacher will be dismissed. They are always changing their teachers in that way."

Next day the newspapers had a story of a brawl between the schoolboys and some chauffeurs from an omnibus garage.

Strikes are a topic of general discussion, like the weather in England, and like it, the habitual excuse for any failure of plans.

22. *The Crisis of* 1938

When Cárdenas seized foreign oil companies in the spring of 1938, Mexicans quickly and consciously merged in national loyalty to the State—and inspired the American Ambassador in Mexico City to pen the following account.

With the expropriation of foreign oil properties, a wave of delirious enthusiasm swept over Mexico, heightened by bitter denunciations from other countries, as the people felt that a day of deliverance had come. On March 22, upon the call of the Confederation of Mexican workers, some two hundred thousand people passed in compact files before the National Palace acclaiming President Cárdenas and carrying banners such as: "They shall not scoff at Mexican laws." Old inhabitants said there had never been such manifestations of the unity of the Mexican people in

SOURCE: "The Crisis of 1938" from Josephus Daniels, *Shirt-Sleeve Diplomat* (Chapel Hill: University of North Carolina Press, 1947), pp. 246–48.

the history of Mexico as followed the appeals to the people to uphold the Constitution and the sovereignty of Mexico. It was shared by people who lost sight of oil in their belief that Mexicans must present a united and solid front.

Closing his address to the multitude, Cárdenas told labor men they deserved the support of their government, and counselled them to discipline their ranks, increase production, and avoid insolent attacks—"to prove there is a real, individual liberty justly demanded by the Mexican people."

Many thousands of students in the Mexican University organized an enthusiastic parade. Its Rector, speaking to President Cárdenas, said: "The University offers you its solid support in this moment when the fatherland requires the unity of its sons. It comes to offer the youth of Mexico to be with you as you are with the honor of Mexico."

Noticeable was the enthusiasm of Catholics, many of whom had been critical of the Cárdenas government, in raising funds to support his expropriation move. On Sunday, April 30, the Archbishop of Guadalajara advised from the pulpit that it was a "patriotic duty to contribute to this national fund." It was announced (April 3) that Archbishop Martínez had promised a "letter on the oil controversy during Holy Week." On May 3, a circular, approved by archbishops and bishops, was published, exhorting Catholics to send contributions. All over the country in churches collections were taken to help pay for the seized oil properties.

Women in Mexico have generally followed an old slogan: "The place of woman is in the home." That was the attitude of women in the early part of April, 1938. Then, as by a miracle, suddenly they became vocal in their patriotism. Cárdenas had made approval of the expropriation of oil a sort of national religion. The people believed—and had grounds for their opinion—that their patrimony had been given for a song to foreigners who refused to pay living wages to the men who worked in the oil fields. When the men gathered by the hundred thousands to show allegiance to Cárdenas after the oil expropriation, the women poured out of their homes by the thousands to voice their ardent support of the leaders who had somehow made the people feel that the oil exploiters were the enemies of their country. What could they do? President Cárdenas had given his word to me on the day after the expropriation that payment would be made. The people were zealous to see that his pledge was kept. What could the women do? . . .

Something the like of which has rarely been seen in any country occurred on the twelfth day of April. By the thousands, women crowded the Zócalo and other parks and in companies marched to the Palace of Fine Arts to give of their all to the call of their country's honor. It was a scene never to be forgotten. Led by Señora Amalia Solórzano de Cárdenas, the

President's young and handsome wife, old and young, well-to-do and poor—mainly the latter—as at a religious festival gathered to make, what was to many, an unheard-of sacrifice. They took off wedding rings, bracelets, earrings, and put them, as it seemed to them, on a national altar. All day long, until the receptacles were full and running over, these Mexican women gave and gave. When night came crowds still waited to deposit their offerings, which comprised everything from gold and silver to animals and corn.

What was the value in money of the outpouring of possessions to meet the goal of millions of pesos? Pitiably small—not more than 100,000 pesos—little to pay millions—but the outpouring of women, stripping themselves of what was dear to them, was the result of a great fervor of patriotism the like of which I had never seen or dreamed. It was of little value for the goal. It was inestimable in cementing the spirit of Mexico, where there was a feeling that the Cárdenas move was the symbol of national unity.

23. *The Lesson of Life*

In 1938, in the preface to a third edition of his book, the young philosopher-psychologist Samuel Ramos amended his earlier conclusions on the Mexican soul.

Mexico is a young country, and youth is an ascendant force. I see in this fact the assurance that our will strives for the elevation of man's station, for the betterment of his life, and, generally speaking, for the development of all our national capacities. I have enumerated the vices and defects of Mexican psychology, but I am nevertheless convinced that more favorable destinies await us, and that the future is ours. Possibly our errors are errors of youth, which maturity will correct. Our psychology is that of a race in its age of fantasy and illusion; it is therefore fated to failure until it achieves a positive sense of reality. I have faith in the salvation of Mexico because our race lacks neither intelligence nor vitality; it needs only to learn. However, the necessary wisdom is not of the kind that one learns in school. It is rather the kind that only experience can offer. I refer to that knowledge of living which is not to be found in books and which can be learned only in life itself. Up to now, Mexicans have known only how to die; it is time that they learned how to live.

SOURCE: "The Lesson of Life" from Samuel Ramos, *Profile of Man and Culture in Mexico*, translated by Peter G. Earle (Austin: University of Texas Press, 1962), pp. 10–11.

24. *The Signs of Consolidation*

By 1940, one of the closest and most astute observers of his country was Salvador Novo, a poet who for the past three years had produced an anonymous column for the popular weekly *Hoy*. This is how he articulated the general sense that as Cárdenas prepared to elect his successor and retire himself, Mexicans lived in irrevocably new terms.

It is true, as [the President] has never denied, that the Republic suffers still from profound problems of an economic character. With absolute sincerity [he has] told the people that in various regions of the country the conditions of life of large groups of country people are difficult, because of the poverty that prevails, because of the lack of water, roads, and schools or the scourge of plagues or endemic diseases. But not even the most obstinate fools can ask that in a single period of government one correct and achieve what in several centuries of national history it has not been possible to correct or achieve. One does what one can, and in our way we go along plowing so that future generations will enjoy the fruits of it. And if the Government admits its limitations and confesses its deficiencies, which are not to its liking, it has a right to ask [its] certainly disorganized opposition what it would do if it got hold of the skillet. For example, nullify the conquests of the workers? They would not tolerate such a thing; they would insist on defending their closed shop clause, their gratifying right to march, and so forth. Nullify the transfer of land to the country people, their [rights to credit] from government banks, their [claims on the new systems of] irrigation? The country people would not allow this either. Nullify freedom of thought? Article 27? Mexico's skillful international policy? All these are conquests that the people consider their own and that they would not let anyone snatch away.

SOURCE: "The Signs of Consolidation" translated from Salvador Novo, "La Semana Pasada," in *Hoy* (Mexico City weekly), No. 188 (September 28, 1940), p. 21.

CONCLUSION

On May 30, 1942, Mexico declared war on the Axis. The world it thus wholly rejoined was in convulsions of violence until 1945 and in the turmoil of massive, dense, and dangerous change thereafter. The pressures on the country were immense; likewise the opportunities it came into. Around the globe, old and new states maneuvered for advantages in a strange struggle both to accelerate change and to direct it. The favorite strategy was to produce industrial wares, immediately or as soon as possible. A few states thrived, several collapsed, most faltered and languished. Mexico, because of its shape and spirit when it entered the competition, did remarkably well.

The basic reason for Mexico's success was that, before it started competing, its people possessed a deeply ingrained sense of unity and common destiny. As Samuel Ramos had hoped, Mexicans were learning how to live—which was to say, how to live together. Life in the same national household made some conflicts more bitter than ever, but it was also for the time being an experience of security and trust. Thanks to their long revolutionary ordeal, Mexicans had rare social and psychological resources to reinforce them in the new, global struggle. Change would hardly rend this society. Indeed, change was the condition of its strength.

Native ministers of change were already there too, again thanks to the Revolution, in the persons of the nationalist entrepreneurs established in power. Having long ago dispersed the only class that might have opposed industrialization (the old nabobs), they now had control over other classes that might complicate the process (workers through the CTM and country people through the CNC). Enjoying legitimacy, they did not have to destroy in order to rule. They had organized themselves cohesively as directors of the official Party of the Mexican Revolution. And they controlled their main source of industrial energy, oil. Leading a loyal population still mostly rural and used to sacrifice, they could drive native factors into a regular development. Confident at home, they could take foreign investment on their own terms. Inadvertently, the obscure and painful ordeal of 1910–40 had prepared Mexicans for economic growth. This they actually carried out in the subsequent twenty-five years.

In the new boom Mexican authorities went on counting on the people, which amounted to taking them for granted. And at times embarrassing popular protests erupted. Among analysts of the country, it became a galling question whether official control of politics was still a necessity or by now a vicious luxury. But most Mexicans worried more about living decently than about voting, the Revolution having interested them more in welfare than in liberalism. Freedom in modern Mexico was a forced issue, not a heritage, and conflicts remained social, not political.

BIBLIOGRAPHY

Ashby, Joe C. *Organized Labor and the Mexican Revolution under Lázaro Cárdenas* (Chapel Hill: University of North Carolina Press, 1967). Theory and practice of Cárdenas's support of the CTM, with special studies of organized labor's role in affairs like the oil expropriation.

Brandenburg, Frank R. *The Making of Modern Mexico* (Englewood Cliffs, N.J.: Prentice-Hall, 1964). Realistic analysis of politics since 1910; weak on economics.

Clark, Marjorie R. *Organized Labor in Mexico* (Chapel Hill: University of North Carolina Press, 1934). History of unions formed during the revolution and their main confederations during the 1920's.

Clendenen, Clarence C. *The United States and Pancho Villa: A Study in Unconventional Diplomacy* (Ithaca, N.Y.: Cornell University Press, 1961). Origins of American interest in Villa, mutual frustration, and American disengagement.

Cline, Howard F. *Mexico: Revolution to Evolution, 1940–1960* (New York: Oxford University Press, 1963), paperback. Topical analysis of Mexico since Cárdenas, with several statistical tables.

————. *The United States and Mexico*, rev. ed. (New York: Atheneum, 1963), paperback. Historical analysis of American response to developments in Mexico, mainly from 1910 to 1952.

Daniels, Josephus. *Shirt-Sleeve Diplomat* (Chapel Hill: University of North Carolina Press, 1947). Memoirs of his ambassadorial years in Mexico City, 1933–42.

Dulles, John W. F. *Yesterday in Mexico: A Chronicle of the Revolution, 1919–1936* (Austin: University of Texas Press, 1961). Anecdotes about selected political episodes and figures, from the rise of Obregón to the fall of Calles.

Glade, William P., Jr., and Charles W. Anderson. *The Political Economy of Mexico: Two Studies* (Madison: University of Wisconsin Press, 1968), paperback. One general study of the relationship between Mexico's revolution and its economic development, another specific study of Mexican banking since 1917.

González Navarro, Moisés. "Social Aspects of the Mexican Revolution," in *Journal of World History*, VIII, 2 (1964), pp. 281–89. Summary analysis of Porfirian society, revolutionary forces, and rise of the contemporary bourgeoisie.

Greene, Graham. *Another Mexico* (New York: Viking Press, 1964), paperback. A Catholic skeptic traveling through the country in 1938, mainly in the provinces.

Lewis, Oscar. *The Children of Sánchez: Autobiography of a Mexican Family* (New York: Random House, 1961), paperback. The lives of Jesús Sánchez, age 50, and his four grown children, denizens of a Mexico City slum.

————. *Pedro Martínez: A Mexican Peasant and His Family* (New York: Random House, 1964), paperback. The lives of an old villager from Morelos who fought in the Revolution, his wife, and his eldest son.

Lieuwen, Edwin. *Mexican Militarism: The Political Rise and Fall of the Revolutionary Army, 1910–1940* (Albuquerque: University of New Mexico Press, 1968). Political and military history, because revolutionary chiefs were both generals and politicians.

Padgett, L. Vincent. *The Mexican Political System* (Boston: Houghton Mifflin, 1966), paperback. Thoughtful study of modern Mexico's politics, focused in terms of official party's domination.

Pletcher, David M. "The Fall of Silver in Mexico, 1870–1910, and Its Effect on American Investments," in *The Journal of Economic History*, XVIII, 1 (March 1958), pp. 33–55. Declining world price of silver lowered value of Mexican peso, which reduced and disordered American dividends from investments in Mexico.

Quirk, Robert E. *The Mexican Revolution, 1914–1915: The Convention of Aguascalientes* (New York: Citadel Press, 1963), paperback. Account of the Villistas' attempt to control the revolutionary alliance that had defeated Huerta.

Ross, Stanley R. *Francisco I. Madero, Apostle of Mexican Democracy* (New York: Columbia University Press, 1955). Biography of the idealist who led the revolt against Díaz in 1910–11 and became president himself.

Ruiz, Ramón E. *Mexico: The Challenge of Poverty and Illiteracy* (San Marino, Calif.: Huntington Library, 1963). History of the official campaigns to educate Mexico, mainly since 1920.

Schmitt, Karl M. *Communism in Mexico: A Study in Political Frustration* (Austin: University of Texas Press, 1965). Political history of the Communist movement in Mexico; weak on social analysis.

Scott, Robert E. *Mexican Government in Transition*, rev. ed. (Urbana: University of Illinois Press, 1964), paperback. A theory that Mexican government, as it has developed since 1910, is really a function of the official party.

Simmons, Merle E. *The Mexican Corrido as a Source for Interpretive Study of Modern Mexico, 1870–1950*, Indiana University Publications, Humanities Series, No. 38 (Bloomington: Indiana University Press, 1957). Study of street songs, to determine popular interests in the old and new regimes.

Simpson, Eyler N. *The Ejido: Mexico's Way Out* (Chapel Hill: University of North Carolina Press, 1937). Report on agrarian reform and its cooperative farms, written just before Cárdenas revived the program.

Stocking, George W., and Jesús Silva Herzog. "Mexican Expropriation: The Mexican Oil Problem, Mexico's Case in the Oil Controversy, Correspondence Between the United States and Mexico," in *International Conciliation*, 345 (December 1938), pp. 491–558. Official American and Mexican arguments in the case.

Tannenbaum, Frank. *The Mexican Agrarian Revolution* (Washington, D.C.: Brookings Institution, 1929). Detailed analysis of rural society before 1910, the changes during the revolution, and the constitutional reforms afterward.

Vernon, Raymond. *The Dilemma of Mexico's Development: The Roles of the Private and Public Sectors* (Cambridge, Mass.: Harvard University Press, 1963). Sketch of Mexican economic growth since the 1870's, with analysis of contemporary problems and conflicting interests involved in their solution.

Whetten, Nathan L. *Rural Mexico* (Chicago: University of Chicago Press, 1948). Analytic survey of country Mexicans in 1940—villagers, hired hands, Indians, independent farmers, and so on.

Whitaker, Arthur P., ed. "Mexico Today," in *The Annals of the American Academy of Political and Social Science*, 208 (March 1940). Seventeen articles, plus introduction and bibliography, on various aspects of Cárdenas's Mexico.

Wilkie, James W. *The Mexican Revolution: Federal Expenditure and Social Change Since 1910* (Berkeley: University of California Press, 1967). Analysis of projected federal budgets and actual federal spending, to determine moments of real change in federal policy and its ramifications in society.

Womack, John, Jr. *Zapata and the Mexican Revolution* (New York: Alfred A. Knopf, 1969). History of the agrarian rebellion in southern Mexico, 1910–20.

X

Peronism in Argentina: A Rightist Reaction to the Social Problem of Latin America

Kalman H. Silvert

CHRONOLOGY

1930   Army coup overthrows constitutional government for first time in modern Argentine history

1931–43   Conservative restoration: a period of "oligarchical" rightist politics

1943   Pro-Axis military coup prepares the way for the emergence of Juan Domingo Perón and the neo-Fascist "United Officers' Group" (June 4)
Perón appointed Secretary of Labor and Social Security (October 27)

1944   President Pedro Ramírez forced to retire because of foreign policy difficulties in reconciling pro-Axis military feelings with U.S. pressure; Edelmiro Farrell becomes president; Perón becomes minister of war, then also (five months later) vice-president

1945   Argentina declares war on Germany and Japan in exchange for post-hoc participation in Act of Chapultepec and invitation to UN Conference in San Francisco (March 27)
Military discord in Argentina; Perón arrested and stripped of his posts; popular demonstrations lead to Perón's return on October 17, thereafter celebrated as the principal *peronista* holiday
Perón marries Eva Duarte (October 21)

1946   Perón inaugurated president after national elections; Argentine national universities stripped of their autonomy and Supreme Court justices impeached

1949   Argentina's Constitution of 1853 revamped to fit the Peronist political ideology

1951   *La Prensa*, a leading Argentine newspaper, taken over by regime, symbolizing end of freedom of press (March 20)
First military revolt (the Menéndez revolt) against Perón, quickly suppressed (September 28)
Eva Perón undergoes first cancer operation (November 5)
Perón reelected to the presidency, but Eva refused vice-presidency by the military (November 11)

1952   Eva Perón dies (July 26)

1953   Growing peronista violence, including the burning of the Jockey Club and various party headquarters

1955   Perón excommunicated for expelling two Catholic prelates; military revolts begin and are beaten back (June 16)
Opposition organizes and confusion mounts; military revolt again, and Perón falls (September 19)
Caretaker regime of General Eduardo Lonardi is replaced by the administration of General Pedro Eugenio Aramburu, a classical liberal (November 13)

INTRODUCTION

Peronism is a complex phenomenon to analyze, because foreign observers and the Argentines themselves have perceived the movement in radically different ways. The passage of time has not stylized and simplified the conflicting interpretations, but rather has served to confound them even more. For example, when Juan Domingo Perón was at the height of his political power from 1945 to 1955, liberals and leftists the world over, and most conservatives as well, viewed his rule as rightist in ideology and effect. Liberals still tend to see it so, but most Marxists and many conservatives now interpret it as having been leftist in ultimate meaning. For Perón himself, however, his movement was a "third" way, a rejection both of capitalism and Communism, of classical right and left. The Peronist Argentine workers saw the regime as their passport to social dignity and economic justice. The Socialist and Anarchist workers, for their part, despised Perón as a Fascist intent on making the trade union movement safe for the Argentine aristocracy.

This ideological confusion is in part a manifestation of a general ignorance of the politics of the Ibero-American culture world. But it is also —and perhaps more importantly—a result of partial interpretation, of labeling the whole on the basis of the appearance or the operation of a part. Some elements of the economic policies of Peronist Argentina, for example, can be interpreted as laissez faire, others as interventionist, some as nationalistic, still others as subservient to foreign economic interests. Particular aspects of the regime's Church–State policies favored the Catholic Church, and others at differing times opposed its interests. Parts of the Peronist politics of class favoritism can be and have been interpreted as prolabor, but from another point of view the very same elements can be labeled as antilabor. Peronism is thus too complex to fit neatly into any of our traditional descriptive categories. This does not mean, of course, that the phenomenon is impossible to describe, but only that caution and precision are necessary.

The title of this chapter advances the thesis that Peronism was essentially rightist and that it was a reaction to certain critical social issues in an Argentina beset by rapid social and political change in an environment of internal political schism and international war, uncertainty, and ideological dispute. The purpose of the following analysis and the selection of documentary material is to refine and qualify that thesis, justifying it only in terms of explicit definitions and indicating reasons for counterviews.

First, let us consider the historical context within which *peronismo* and

its critics and commentators were formed. Post–World War I Europe
witnessed the development of many variants of what has popularly become known as Fascism, a term that still awaits a coherent, widely accepted, rigorous, academic definition. The trend was begun with the
taking of power by Mussolini in Italy, Primo de Rivera in Spain, and
Salazar in Portugal. Then came the victory of Hitler in Germany, the
Austrian corporate state, the emergence of strong totalitarian movements
of the right in France, and various manifestations of authoritarianism in
Eastern Europe, some before the outbreak of World War II and more, of
course, under the guns of the occupying Axis powers. A partial explanation
of the rise of this kind of authoritarianism is that it was a reaction to the
threat of Communism; for despite the failure of a "workers' international"
to appear and break the nationalism of the warring capitalisms during
World War I, as the theorists of class consciousness and worker solidarity
had predicted would happen, the emergence of international Communist
alliances and the abortive attempts at Communist revolt in Western and
Central Europe were deeply alarming to the leaders of the Liberal as well
as the Catholic countries of the world.[1] Rightist authoritarianism in
Europe was not simply a response to the Communist menace, however;
it had strong domestic political motivations as well, and these are its
aspects that are of particular relevance to the study of Peronism. In both
cases, strong political urges toward reform and social betterment were
channeled into solutions that would leave the social order as little changed
as possible, that would preserve the pecking order of the social classes,
and yet would give some satisfactions to deprived groups.

The struggle and the tensions over how to industrialize efficaciously the
emergent new and old states of the "third world" have constituted one of
the major political-economic crises of the post–World War II scene. Little
attention was paid to this matter between the two world wars; then the
chief world crisis was that of the industrialized states themselves, beset by
economic depression and chronic underemployment as well as unemployment, their agricultural sectors in turmoil, and their traditional ideologies
under attack from authoritarianisms of both right and left. With respect
to these industrialized societies in disarray, the Iberian Peninsula, Italy,
and Latin America—with internal differences, of course—occupied a special

---

[1] This terminology is employed in its Latin Europe as well as Latin American sense.
Essentially, the "Liberal" countries (meaning Manchesterian Liberal ones—those
adhering to Lockean political thought, having essentially free-enterprise-type capitalistic
systems, and being by and large Protestant in religious belief) are the Anglo-Saxon
nations, while the Catholic countries are viewed as those cultures holding to a more
traditional Thomist view of proper human values and social organization. This distinction is crucial to a proper understanding of much of the ideological dispute revolving
around such phenomena as Peronism. See K. H. Silvert, "The Costs of Anti-National-
ism: Argentina," in *Expectant Peoples* (New York: Random House, 1963), pp. 347–72.

place. Lagging economically, they were then, as they are still, the most urbanized, literate, and economically and socially complex lands of the nonindustrialized world. Included in their active political sectors were persons from many walks of life: members of the landed and industrial elites, professionals, white-collar employees and subprofessionals, and some elements of the skilled worker groups. Semiskilled workers also occasionally had a political voice, though peasants almost never did. Most of the very poor in the cities were undoubtedly excluded from political participation, like the rural peasants, but it is well to remember that the vast new urban slums created by the post-1945 industrialization did not exist.

Liberal market capitalism had little appeal in these countries. Certainly their private-ownership systems were never informed by the ethics of a competitive market; [2] certainly their polities were not designed to permit competition on a different level through political organizations. In the face of economic uncertainty everywhere in the world and desiring industrialization at home, political groups in these countries opted for collectivistic solutions: the left for one form or another of socialism, the right for one form or another of corporativism.

This set of ideas, then, made up the ideological *Zeitgeist* of the late 1930's, the spirit of the times as Argentina began to face a massive crisis engendered by its economic organization, its social structure, the international economic effects of war and depression, the nature of its population, and its relatively high degree of development. In a sense, the Argentine nation fell victim to its own modernity and had to choose either to build a broader national community or to relapse into a politics of privilege and irrationality.

By 1930, Argentina was one of the dozen most economically advanced countries in the world. There were even more automobiles per capita in Argentina than in either Great Britain or Sweden. Half the population was urbanized, the country had the world's seventh largest rail system, the population was almost exclusively European, the literacy rate was climbing to ninety per cent, and the consumption of food was among the highest in the world. An Argentine economist has written of this period:

> From 1860 to 1930 the Argentine Republic experienced one of the most spectacular developmental processes in world history. . . .
> All economic indices of that period . . . indicate the prodigious

---

[2] Although the reality of free-enterprise competition has always been distant from the ideal, the existence of the ideal affected law and practice in no inconsiderable way: witness the checkered history of the Sherman Antitrust Act in the United States. In the Latin world, muckrakers of the Lincoln Steffens stripe, concerned with outrages against the workings of a self-adjusting free-enterprise market, never had a reason for being.

growth . . . as much in what are called "basic" or "social" investments (level of public literacy and of cultural and technical progress,
public health, communications and transportation systems, organization of the public administration, public services and the police power
of the state) as in the realm of private economic activity (foreign
and domestic commerce; agricultural, industrial, mineral and fisheries
production; systems of commercialization and credit institutions, etc.).
And to this generalized progress there contributed in obvious fashion
the extraordinary stream to the country of foreign investments, which
climbed to around four billion dollars in 1930. . . .[3]

Despite this material advance, political power was unevenly distributed.
When the world depression of 1929–37 broke out, unorganized workers
could do little to defend themselves. The middle classes struggled to
maintain their standards as best they could through individual effort, and
the upper groups broke into competing sectors—the Argentines against
the European, and the Argentines divided against themselves. This political process is traced below.

The Perón era formally began on June 4, 1943, when a military revolt
permitted the United Officers' Group, a rightist military clique of which
Perón was a member, to take charge of the national government; it formally ended in September 1955, when another military revolt otherthrew
Perón. In between are several important landmarks. On October 17, 1945
(the *peronista* Loyalty Day), an uprising among laboring groups allowed
Perón to emerge from military arrest and have his supremacy among the
military affirmed. In 1946, in a somewhat violent but reasonably honest election for the presidency, Perón took fifty-six per cent of the votes even though
he was opposed by all the standard political parties. The year 1949 saw
the classically liberal Constitution of 1853 rewritten to fit the eclectically
evolving Peronist doctrine somewhat better. The first serious revolt against
Perón—which was handily beaten back—broke out in 1951. In the same
year, Perón won reelection in electoral proceedings that could no longer
be described as even remotely free.[4]

These calendar dates do not indicate the full extent of Peronism's real
impact on Argentina. The movement's functional roots can be traced back
at least to 1930, the year in which President Hipólito Irigoyen was ousted
by the first military revolt of Argentina's truly modern period. Irigoyen was
the leader of the Radical party, a middleclass-based, secularist, mildly nationalist, professional political organization that had first assumed power in
1916. Among the many reasons for the coup are that both Irigoyen and

---

[3] Walter Beveraggi Allende, "Economía y finanzas," in *Argentina 1930–1960* (Buenos
Aires: Editorial Sur, 1961), pp. 243–44.

[4] For an excellent and timely account of these happenings, see George I. Blanksten,
Perón's Argentina (Chicago: University of Chicago Press, 1953), Chapters 3 and 4.

his party had run out of political ideas at the very time the military were being inspired by European military adventurism, and the Catholic Church by Austrian and Italian Fascism. General José F. Uriburu replaced him as president and soon began vacillating between a policy of favoring the old conservative elites in traditional style and propounding an avowedly corporate organization of the state.[5] The General was overthrown in turn

[5] The corporate state favored by the ideology known as corporativism, corporate pluralism, or—the Spanish variant—Falangism is an attempt to gain the institutional differentiation and specialization demanded by industrialization and urbanization by establishing many parallel corporations, or falanges. These pillars of public life are linked at the top by a collegiate management of their chief executives. This social

Evita Peron speaks to a crowd during May Day Ceremonies in Buenos Aires, 1951. Beside her, partially blocked by a microphone, is General Peron. *Keystone.*

within two years, however, and the die was clearly cast in favor of traditional elitism. This situation prevailed until 1943, when the emergence of strongly pro-Axis military elements provided a springboard for Perón's formal ascent to the presidency. An appropriate concluding date for a functional examination of Peronism is still a matter of speculation, for peronista politics continue to be a critically important element in the Argentine scene.

When Perón was deposed in 1955, he was replaced by General Eduardo Lonardi, who ruled but two months before bowing to General Pedro Aramburu. Lonardi's policies had shown traces of a lingering conservatism and corporativism ("Peronism without Perón"), but Aramburu espoused a program that coupled strong anti-Peronism with attempts to return to classical liberal political procedures. In early 1958, constitutional regularity was reinstituted with the inauguration of Arturo Frondizi as president, the first legally and honestly elected civilian (a Radical Intransigent) [6] to take office since Irigoyen's second term began in 1928. Frondizi was removed by the military in 1962, however; his administration was followed by yet another military interregnum; by a new election (1964), won by Arturo Illia, a People's Radical; by Illia's subsequent overthrow (1966); and then by the administration of one more conservative-corporativist, General Juan Carlos Onganía. Throughout this period of coups and countercoups, of elections and counterelections, the Peronists divided and subdivided and regrouped. The fundamental split within the movement was between the *abstencionistas*—those who retained a personalistic loyalty to their exiled leader and showed it by casting blank ballots in every election—and the *concurrencistas*, those who accepted an ideological residue of Peronism without personal adherence to the chief and favored using coalition electoral tactics to attain national advantage. The two groups divided the Peronist vote almost equally, winning between them something over a third of all the votes cast in the Republic.

It is in the interpretation of these events that observers and actors alike make history, for their differing perceptions become one of the manifold causal elements in change. Only the most unsophisticated

---

design is intended to permit economic growth without disturbing the existing class rankings of society; it reflects the ideal of an "organic" state, a society in which every man knows his place and thus the "life chances" of his children. As Latin Americans say, it is an attempt "to change without changing anything."

[6] The Radical party, which became a regular part of Argentina's party constellation in the 1890's, has long been split between an Intransigent wing (UCRI), whose members early in the century believed in intransigently refusing to go along with participation in the then-restrictive governing practices, and a People's wing (UCRP). There have been other splits, but this division has taken on lasting ideological color. The Intransigents are somewhat more populist, leaning a bit to the left of center. The People's Radicals tend to the right of center and make common cause with industrial groups of liberal persuasion.

propose single-cause explanations of Peronism, of course, but political discussion has never lacked for such monistic views. There follows a brief discussion of some of the leading interpretations, with reference made to their principal adherents and influence in Argentine politics.

One school of thought holds that Argentines are inherently unable to govern themselves, that there is something in the Argentine "character" inviting to instability and a lack of rigor, honesty, and self-denial. This dim view of the Argentines as a people is usually propped up by references to the recent record of the Argentine economy. According to economic determinists and certain researchers wedded to the analysis of social indicators, Argentina's level of economic development prior to the Perón era was appropriate to a country already well past the "takeoff" stage of economic growth and in the range of sustained flight. In terms of per capita income, for example, Argentina in 1930 was one of the ten most developed countries in the world.[7] And in the late 1960's, with a third of its population concentrated in the single city of Buenos Aires and a total of two-thirds urbanized, with a literacy rate of almost ninety per cent and a far-flung and complex university structure, a European population, at least forty per cent of its working population in middle-income and middle-occupational brackets, an elaborate communications system, and an active artistic life, Argentina certainly appeared, though it had slipped somewhat in the rankings of relative development, to have all the "preconditions" for a successful national life. Given the fact that Argentina has achieved so much, the argument goes, the current period of economic stagnation and political instability—of which Peronism is a part—can be attributed only to a character flaw *ab initio:* to the Italianate character of the culture of Buenos Aires and other areas through which it has spread, or perhaps to the cosmopolitan character of the national elites.

Another explanation for Peronism emphasizes the role of pressures from abroad. The backers of this theory contend that Argentina, because it is a "peripheral" economic unit exporting raw materials to the developed nations and importing their industrial goods, and also because its population

---

[7] Aldo Ferrer, a leading Argentine economist, writes: "Contemporary observers have been puzzled by the fact that Argentina's relatively diversified social and economic structure more closely resembles that of the developed dynamic countries than that of the underdeveloped stagnant countries. . . . Even after fifteen years of stagnating, per capita income in Argentina is still almost twice the average for Latin America. . . .

"The above conditions have led some observers, such as Professor W. W. Rostow, to place Argentina among the countries having autonomous development possibilities. Rostow, in fact, considers that Argentina has already 'taken off' into sustained growth. However, with the exception of special cases like Haiti, Bolivia, and Paraguay, Argentina is the only country in Latin America to have remained at a standstill during the last fifteen years. . . ." (From Aldo Ferrer, *The Argentine Economy: An Economic History of Argentina* [Berkeley: University of California Press, 1967], pp. 205–10.)

is an ethnic mosaic heavily influenced by immigration,[8] is especially vulnerable to the intromission of foreign powers and their ideologies and is
not free to find its own national "genius." The unhappy course of recent
events, then, and particularly the direction taken by Peronism, can be attributed to foreign intervention, mainly that of the United States. The
United States first opposed Perón, but then it supported him as he bowed
to foreign demands, symbolically rejected the British by forcefully purchasing the Argentine rail system from its British owners, and embraced
American interests by signing agreements with U.S. companies for the
development of Argentina's petroleum resources. This interpretation was
later fortified when the United States suspended its foreign aid to Argentina after President Illia had cancelled another set of agreements with
U.S. oil companies signed by the Frondizi Administration.

A third explanation for Peronism is that the Argentine upper classes,
in a desperate attempt to preserve their privileges against the encroachment of organized labor, enlisted the support of the armed forces and by
so doing turned them into a Frankenstein's monster that has since pursued its own interests to the exclusion of all others. The Argentine armed
forces, professionalized with German assistance after 1910, have acted
with ever-greater willfulness since their initial adventure of 1930. Even
though the military exhibits ideological differentiation in reflection of the
general political spectrum, it is capable of acting against the Government at any time, and the inability of any civilian regime to be assured
that the armed forces will remain in the barracks has been in itself a
perturbing influence in Argentine politics. Colonel Perón, in this explanation, was essentially a natural product of an institutional fact of Argentine
public life.

Class conflict theory provides a fourth view of Peronism. At the time
Perón took power, when Argentina's population numbered about 15,-
000,000, some 2,500,000 adults were in organized labor. The efforts of
workers to gain regularized access to the national institutions had been
hampered since the 1890's. Labor, especially its semiskilled sectors, thus
formed a mobilized mass, but a politically unintegrated one, a body of
persons easily recruitable to the banner of anyone promising them a voice
in the decisions affecting not only their roles as workmen but also their
status as national citizens. Perón appeared with a banner and a wealth of
promises, according to this interpretation, and the Peronist movement was
born.

The last view of Peronism to be mentioned here depends on a theory of
social values that holds that in times of crisis, the ultimate norms or
ideals of a people strongly shape its political behavior. Thus, because

---

[8] See Gino Germani, *Estructura social de la Argentina* (Buenos Aires: Editorial
Raigal, 1955), Chapter 6.

Argentina is in the Mediterranean cultural world and because that world often seeks corporate or falangist solutions to its organizational problems, Peronism can be seen as a culturally acceptable response to a social crisis. A similar theory, involving the values not of a particular culture but of the times, tries to explain Peronism in terms of the contemporary *Zeitgeist* described above; the fact that radical social experimentation was being attempted in the European countries most admired by the Argentines made them more receptive to Peronist experimentation at home.

It is banal but probably valid to say that the correct interpretation of Peronism is probably some combination of the partial explanations listed here. The movement raised its edifice on the mass base of newly organized labor, and thus it followed a populist policy.[9] Under the Peronist regime, laborers were made to feel participant; their status and dignity were increased by important measures, including verbal recognition, real wage increases, and extended social security benefits; and they were psychologically pampered by the Government. But Peronism was not simply a political arm of organized labor; it had its origins in the military, it will be recalled, and besides, members of other civilian groups—including many new industrialists and white-collar workers—also sympathized and worked actively for the Administration. If Peronism had a mass laboring base, it also had a considerable upper- and middleclass following and drew much of its leadership from these groups.

Certainly foreign attachments also affected the development of Peronism. The currents of international ideological competition played upon the movement from the start, for the military elements led by Perón identified strongly with Falangism and Fascism. Furthermore, the destruction of the Axis powers, the weakening of British influence in the southern cone countries,[10] and the quickening of North American interest there required changes in Argentina's political and economic relations, and they implied some shift in ideological alliance patterns as well.

Peronism was undoubtedly influenced by Fascism, but the two phenomena are by no means identical. Insofar as Fascism implies an all-powerful totalitarian state in complete control of the economy, a primary dedication to the protection of middleclass interests, political repression involving racism, concentration camps, and killing, and the militarization of life styles, Peronist Argentina was not Fascist. The Peronist political apparatus as such was not all-powerful; on the contrary, it acted as one "pillar" of power among many, including the Catholic Church (which for at least ten years was a staunch supporter of Perón), the military, segments of the agrarian and industrial elites, and finally, the newly

[9] For an important analysis of labor and Peronism, see Samuel L. Baily, *Labor, Nationalism, and Politics in Argentina* (New Brunswick, N.J.: Rutgers University Press, 1967).

[10] The countries of the "southern cone" are Argentina, Chile, Uruguay, and Paraguay.

organized labor groups. Because Peronism was not revolutionary, middle-class interests could be specifically preserved; through status and income redistribution, the Perón administration tended to lessen the social distance between disparate groups, but it did not pretend to change their relative position or ordering. As for the movement's techniques of political repression, racism died out as an element of Peronism after the first few months. The other methods of political coercion employed by the regime were within the sphere of traditional Latin American authoritarian practice—that is, some torture, no concentration camps, exilings but few killings. A leadership cult of Juan Perón and his wife, Eva, flourished, of course, and civil liberties were suppressed, the opposition was cowed, and the passive acceptance of leadership initiative was promoted as official ideology. Despite these outrages of civil procedures, the country never became militaristic, nor did it go beyond the verbal level in applying pressure against neighboring states.

Peronism in practice was not Fascism, but it was corporativism as we have defined that concept. It attempted to modernize Argentina "without changing anything" by setting up parallel corporations linked at the top and using them to maintain existing class rankings. The labor institutions set up by the Perón government, for example, were designed not to create an independent labor movement but rather to add another parallel power structure to an emergent falangist organization of the whole society. Both as ideology and as attempted practice, then, Peronism, although it adopted a kind of "black populism" for the purposes of initial organization, was ultimately an attempt at a "progressive traditional" and thus essentially rightist solution of the problem of modernization.

Peronism has not died out of Argentine politics. But, true to its confused nature, it remains many things. Some Peronists are simply following trade union interests. Others dream of the return of their leader and the old days of personalistic leadership. Still others have distilled their views and propose truly Fascist solutions to Argentina's ills. Perhaps the principal reason for the continuation of this confusion of neo-Peronist strands, however, is the continued weakness of the general political structure of Argentina. Military leaders continue to rule; the traditional parties are broken; civil liberties are uncertain and under threat of constant governmental violation; and politics is run as though its primary function is the protection of economic interest. Peronism will continue to be attractive to many Argentines as long as major groups remain without proper representation in Argentine society and as long as the ruling groups continue to be unable to provide a viable and stable system of national political organization.

READINGS

1. *Peronism and Labor*

Gino Germani received his higher education in economics at the universities of Rome and Buenos Aires. He organized and for a decade directed the Institute of Sociology of the University of Buenos Aires and is now a professor of sociology at Harvard University. In the following selection, Germani begins by examining the general proposition that Perón's demagoguery is the reason the working classes supported his regime.

The dictator gave the workers a few material advantages in exchange for their liberty; the people sold their liberty for a plate of beans. This interpretation, we believe, should be rejected. The dictator was demagogic, certainly, but the success of his demagoguery depended not on material advantages but on his having given the people the experience (fictitious or real) of having achieved certain rights and of exercising them. The workers who supported the dictatorship, far from feeling deprived of liberty, were convinced that they had gained it. The word "liberty" here obviously refers to two different things. The liberty the workers lost was a liberty they had never possessed, political liberty to act on the level of higher politics, of distant and abstract politics. The liberty they thought they had gained was the concrete, immediate liberty to affirm their rights against foremen and bosses, to elect delegates, to win hearings before labor tribunals, to feel more their own masters. These effects were felt by the laborer—by workers in general—as an affirmation of personal dignity.

It has been said that [by allowing laborers to affirm their rights at work] indiscipline and resentment were fomented. This interpretation, we believe, constitutes an error as grave as the theory of the "plate of beans." Excesses and abuses did occur, the counterpart of the same or worse conduct on the other side but with a different meaning. To understand the significance of these actions, one must remember the state of inferiority and insecurity in which the worker finds himself. This state has been eloquently described by Simone Weil in her impressive work *La Condition Ouvrière.* On the job, says Weil, the worker feels as though people were

SOURCE: "Peronism and Labor" translated from Gino Germani, *Política y sociedad en una época de transición* (Buenos Aires: Editorial Paidós, 1962), pp. 244–52. Except where noted otherwise, the translations in this chapter are by the chapter editor.

continuously saying into his ear, "You are nothing here. You don't count. You are here to obey, to accept, to shut up." Such repetition is irresistible. One comes to admit, from the depths of one's being, that in truth one is nobody. All factory workers, or almost all, says this writer (who shared that type of life for many years), have something subtle in their movements, in their glances, and above all in the expression of their lips, which indicates that they have been obliged to count for nothing. With Argentina's workers in a psychic state of this kind, the affirmation of certain rights in the immediate area of their work, in the very place which had come to be considered a place of humiliation, signified a partial liberation from their sentiments of inferiority, an affirmation of themselves as beings equal to everybody else.

Another fact that should be taken into account is that the experience of liberation was new for a large number of workers. . . . In the first place, let us remember that in Argentina, for more than a decade before, formal democracy did not exist; with few exceptions there had not been free elections, union activity was persecuted, and parties carried out their work with difficulty. In the second place, the process of rapid industrialization initiated at the beginning of the 30's had produced a shift to the cities and particularly to Buenos Aires of large rural masses with neither political nor union experience. For these masses, this pseudo-liberty of the dictatorship was the only direct experience of affirmation of their own rights.

The irrationality of the masses in Nazi-Fascism and in Peronism. In order to compare the Peronist attitudes of the popular classes in Argentina with the Fascist attitudes of the petit bourgeoisie in Europe, we must bear in mind three elements of essential importance:

a. The *real* interests of the two social groups in their respective historical situations;

b. The extent to which each of the two totalitarian regimes effectively satisfied those interests, and the extent of the differences between the "real" satisfaction and the "substitute" and "unreal" satisfactions which Fascism and Peronism could make their followers feel by means of the "myths" of their respective ideologies (nationalism and racism in the ideology of Fascism, "social justice" in the ideology of Peronism);

c. The media of information and methods for the comprehension of the historico-social situation that the two social groups possessed, taking into account their educational level, their degree of participation in national life, and their previous political experience.

When we compare the attitudes of the two groups as a function of the elements noted, we reach the conclusion that the "irrationality" of the European middle class was without doubt greater than that of the popular classes [1] in Argentina. Let us examine what, in effect, was the origin of the deep frustrations to which the former saw themselves subject. . . . The "objective" problem facing them we find in the historico-social changes that tended to proletarianize them. On the one hand their intellectual training, their life styles and plans, and, consequently, their expectations were attuned to a situation which was assuring them—on the average and as a group—satisfaction (in economic affairs—their income level; in vocational matters—their type of occupation and its prestige; and, by the same tokens, in the psychological dimension). But, on the other hand, the possibility of seeing such expectations realized was destroyed by a series of profound changes:

The transformation of the economic structure as it entered a phase of monopolistic and highly concentrated capitalism;

The upsurge of a proletariat that not only exercised an increasing and dangerous power in politics but also now threatened to equal or surpass the traditional positions of small privileges (at the economic and prestige level) until then quietly enjoyed by the lower levels of the middle classes (this also by virtue of the technological changes that increased professional capacity and the social significance of traditionally "proletarian" occupations);

Military defeat; and above all,

An extreme inflation, with its consequences: the destruction of savings and . . . savings' function as a "standard of living" (of "expectation" in life plan), and uncontrolled competition in the liberal professions or the disappearance of these professions as a result of their reduction to bureaucratic "posts."

These are some of the aspects of the crisis that the German and Italian middle classes (and those of other European countries) had to confront in a lapse of time shorter than a generation; that is to say, in a time period so short that they could not adjust gradually in the usual way, through the mechanism of successive generational replacement. . . . Faced with this crisis, the petit bourgeoisie did not perceive the "true" significance of the changes being produced about them, not to mention how these changes would affect them in particular. They remained wedded to their ideas of "prestige" and the "proper life," their (largely illusory) class privileges, and their social "superiority" over the "manual workers." In short, they maintained their traditional identification with the mentality of the upper bourgeoisie. To sustain these attitudes, they had not only to reject any possibility of aligning themselves with the workers . . . to fight for a program of moderate reforms that might better their situation but also

---

[1] ["Popular classes," here used interchangeably with "popular masses," refers to the *urban* proletariat.]

to *differentiate themselves absolutely* from the proletariat and therefore to adopt a political orientation opposite to theirs (which meant opposite to the moderate positions of democratic socialism as well), without taking into account at all the possible coincidences that might exist (and which in fact did exist) between their own "real" interests and those being defended by groups expressing the political positions of the "socially inferior" classes. It is true that the ideology they embraced—the contradictory and incoherent programs of the Nazi-Fascist parties—included some "points" that could be interpreted as directly reflecting problems of the middle class; the theme of the struggle against big business and monopolies (especially big commercial businesses with chains of branches, and so on) was typical and by no means unique. But even in these attacks, the objectives were significantly twisted because of a peculiar nationalist and racist interpretation; it was not "big business" that was attacked, but "foreign" or "Jewish" big business. The defects and contradictions of the socioeconomic structure were thus interpreted as the work of persons really alien to the national community, against whom were projected the hatred and resentment of the "little people" of the middle classes. In addition, as has already been said, Fascist antibourgeois attitudes were limited to opposing proletarian *nations* to bourgeois *nations*.

In this fashion, the frustration of the middle classes was successfully channeled, and at the same time their attitudes were differentiated from the classical "proletarian" positions.

Because of this "blindness," the Italian and German middle classes did not adopt the strategies that, according to a "rational" analysis of their situation, had higher probabilities of rescuing them economically and spiritually (though naturally not of restoring them to precisely the same social situation that was theirs at the end of the nineteenth century). Instead, they projected their problems and their social hopes in terms of nationalism, racism, and imperialism, and they thus became a mass subject to manipulation by elites—elites whose political victories were to place them in much worse situations "objectively" than those from which they were trying to escape. . . .

The triumph of totalitarianism, far from modifying the objective situation and the structural causes that had ruined the middle classes, tended to worsen them (for example, it increased monopolistic concentration and controls). The middle classes were simply given certain "substitute" satisfactions—the affirmation of national pride, military conquest, legal discrimination, hierarchy, and, particularly, racism—which, as we have already seen, could placate the irrational subjective expression of the crisis through which they were passing.

Let us now recall what the objective situation of the Argentine popular masses was. Recently urbanized and industrialized, without union ex-

perience and with very limited means of getting it, with a union movement disorganized by internal conflict and police repression, with social
legislation clearly inadequate for the level of industrialization achieved
(and, in addition, largely a dead letter), they had to confront an employing class no less recent, with all the improvisation and defects of specu-
lative and adventuristic capitalism and with no consciousness of the social problems of labor. This same lack of knowledge existed, in addition,
among the majority of leadership groups, including among them no small
number who sincerely considered themselves democratic. . . . In such a
situation, the popular classes needed, first, to acquire an awareness of
their power and to incorporate themselves into national life as a group
of fundamental importance in all respects. Second, it was (and still is)
within the range of their interests to achieve structural changes capable
of assuring fuller and more harmonious development of the country's
economy as well as a more adequate participation for themselves in the
results of that development. Third, it was essential for them to achieve
a clear recognition of their individual rights in labor matters, rights which
should be sanctioned not only by law and contract but also by the daily
comportment and the consciousness of entrepreneurs and their agents,
representatives of the State—the bureaucracy, police, courts, and so on—
as well as in general by the middle and leadership classes and the press
and other media of communications.

To what extent did the dictatorship achieve these three objectives of
the popular classes? Certainly it did nothing in the area of structural reforms; on the contrary, it provoked a worsening of the existing situation,
and with its mistakes, stealing, and corruption it put into serious danger
the economic stability of the country. Measured in terms of this second
objective, then, popular support for the dictator produced consequences
contrary to popular interests. But a different balance is presented to us
with respect to the first and third objectives. As regards the first, there
is no doubt that the popular masses achieved with Peronism an awareness of their own significance as a group of great importance in national
life, one that was capable of exerting a certain influence. And this happened largely because the popular classes felt that the regime's ability to
take and hold power depended on their support and active participation.
. . . The entire upward career of the dictator until he assumed constitutional power and even his first years as president were marked by numerous strikes; that is to say, many of the workers' conquests of a general nature as well as those improvements gained with respect to specific private enterprises (which have a psychological significance equal to or
greater than the rights sanctioned by law or agreements of a general
character) were gained through labor conflict, although this time the
power of the State was found behind the workers instead of being op-

posed to them. Let us remember here what a strike means to a worker as an affirmation of his autonomy and of his worth as a social being. The experience of having participated in some victorious strikes under the sign of Peronism would suffice in itself (especially for a mass not accustomed to exercising its union rights) to give it the sense of its power and of its significance and role in the political changes of the country.

[This sense of participation was reinforced by the demonstration of support that saved Perón on October 17, 1945], the crucial experience of October 17, which was very soon transformed into myth and in which popular participation, although it had to be organized, was experienced as absolutely spontaneous by the participants. In this connection, it is worth the effort to clarify a rather widely propagated error. The 17th of October is often compared with the March on Rome (1922) or with analogous actions in Germany. Nothing could be more mistaken. The March on Rome, like the (different) actions the Nazis used to take power in Germany, was the work of perfectly militarized formations that were also mostly professional or semiprofessional in character. The permanent cadres of Fascism were made up not of citizens normally exercising their occupations who in addition dedicated their free time to political activity but rather of persons who had been professionalizing themselves in those little private armies that were the Fascist or Nazi bands. This was not true of all the members, of course, but it was true of the men who habitually participated in those activities. Contrast this picture with what we observe in Peronism. Its partisans were workers, and although there were many professional agents (the men who were able to organize the march of October 17, for example), characteristically their participation was spontaneous and improvised, and they were without training or discipline, let alone militarized organization. These signs of spontaneity and immediacy in popular participation were repeated in many episodes that undoubtedly left profound marks on the soul of the people. . . .

All these experiences contributed to forming in the lower classes a clear awareness of their power and significance. Their attitude was not, as many would like to believe, one of gratitude to the dictator for little gifts or "tips" (although, of course, this type of sentiment was not lacking in many) but rather of pride for having . . . imposed . . . their rights against the employing class and of having "conquered power," as the slogans of official propaganda phrased it. Not only did the popular classes acquire a consciousness of their power at this time, but they also achieved that unity never gained by parties authentically proletarian in their tradition and programs. [A study of election results shows that the] electorate polarized itself according to the line of class division, something that had never previously happened in the country. Whether or not this development seems a good one depends on one's particular political philosophy, but the simple fact that it happened testifies to a significant homogeneity in the popular masses and [shows their] new self-awareness as an essential part of Argentine society.

The third objective of the popular classes was also, at least in part, achieved. Evidence of an increased awareness of workers' rights on the part of entrepreneurs and employers, the leadership class, the press, and the general public can be found by comparing the attention given labor questions in the years prior to 1943 and after the September 1955 revolution. It will be said that we are here dealing with a political problem stemming from the heritage left by the deposed regime and its totalitarian union organization. But, even if this were so, the fact remains that in marked contrast to the period before 1943, the problem of workers' rights and the social problem of labor in general were important to the political leadership of the country, and their adequate solution constituted one of the prime tasks of the Government. Contrary to what is usually thought, the principal gains of the workers during the decade were not—we repeat —material (their advances in this realm were largely canceled by the inflationary process); more important was the recognition of their rights, the capital circumstance that now the masses *must* be taken into account, that now they impose themselves on the consideration of even the so-called backers of law and order, the very people who used to regard labor leaders as "professional agitators."

If we strike a balance, then, with respect to the real objectives gained by the popular classes during the dictatorship, we must recognize that, even though they completely failed to win the structural changes they wanted, they were successful in affirming themselves in their own eyes and in those of other social groups. These achievements—unlike those of the German and Italian middle classes—were not simply a matter of "substitute satisfactions," [2] for although they were of a psychosocial and not structural type, they corresponded to the "real" objective of the lower classes in their historico-social situation. It could be argued, of course, and quite rightly, that both self-awareness and recognition by the other classes could have been achieved in some other way. *In truth, not institutional, moral, or economic subversion, much less a totalitarian regime, would have been necessary to achieve both things. The appearance on the political scene of the popular masses and their recognition by the Argentine society could have been realized through the path of democratic education and through the means of expression such education provides.*

---

[2] Although, of course, there is no lack of them. In reality, in [Perón's] second presidential period [1951–55] they were frequent: purely verbal attacks on the "oligarchy," the burning of the Jockey Club, and other similar acts.

From this point of view, there is no doubt that the path taken by the working class must be considered *irrational*; the rational way would have been the democratic way. But at this point it is necessary to ask ourselves whether such a democratic path was possible, given the condition in which the country found itself after the Revolution of 1930. The answer is clearly negative. Therefore, if we take into account the subjective characteristics of the popular classes at the beginning of the decade of the 1940's . . . we must conclude that their transforming themselves into the human base of a totalitarian movement destined absolutely to serve interests alien to them cannot be considered as blind irrationality within the conjunction of given historical conditions.

A very different judgment can be formulated, on the other hand, as we have seen, with respect to the German middle classes, whose educational level, political tradition, and access to information made them capable of realistic political action—action which, again, was also much more viable from the point of view of the objective conditions.

This different level of irrationality expresses certain important differences between the two forms of totalitarian pseudo-solution we have been comparing. In Nazi-Fascism, the greater irrationality implies a particular *impermeability to experience,* and in this respect it is worth remembering that there has been very frequently described and studied a "structure of authoritarian character" in the lower orders of the European middle classes. . . .

One cannot speak of the Argentine popular classes in terms of their "impermeability to experience"; but the opportunity for a positive experience should be *really* placed within the limits of their present possibilities. And this depends not only on the social policy of the Government but also on the orientation of the political parties and, in addition (and very especially), on the comportment of the entrepreneurial class and of its agents.

The Argentine political tragedy resides in the fact that the political integration of the popular masses was initiated under the sign of a totalitarianism that succeeded in providing, in its manner, a certain experience of political and social participation in the immediate and personal aspects of the life of the worker, at the same time annulling the political organization and the basic rights that constitute the irreplaceable pillars of all genuine democracy. The immense task to be carried out consists of achieving that same experience, but *relating it in an indissoluble manner to the theory and practice of democracy and liberty.*

2. *Peronism and Authoritarian Ideology*

José Luis Romero, former rector of the University of Buenos Aires and dean of the Faculty of Philosophy and Letters, is of a distinguished Argentine academic family. One of Argentina's foremost social historians, he has also been an active participant in the political life of his country. He has taught in the United States and Europe as well as in Argentina.

The Alluvial Era

The propaganda and activities of the philo-Nazis were intensified soon after the war began. Periodicals and magazines were published in order to serve the German cause; the information services and espionage and counterespionage organizations sought sympathizers to collaborate in their tasks. Nationalists of all shades seemed most suitable for such jobs, although some of them, out of a sense of honor, refused to collaborate, whereas others accepted, on the principle of uniting for a cause. The nationalists, a great majority of whom were members of the oligarchy, attacked the imperialist powers from the outset, particularly Great Britain. German sources contained abundant materials for ascertaining the character and measuring the rate of penetration of British capital into Argentina, and there was no lack of investigators to study the data, and thus feed the anti-imperialist zeal of the nationalist groups. With that material, and with less substantial data, nationalism forged the belief that it was necessary to shake off the English yoke. To accomplish this, Great Britain and the entire democratic world would have to be smashed by the German forces. These ideas had unity, and nationalism was pro-Nazi by virtue of these beliefs.

The international policy of President [Roberto M.] Ortiz leaned toward a neutrality that was faintly benevolent for the democratic powers and seemed to be a serious obstacle to the nationalists. But beginning in 1940, when Vice-President Ramón S. Castillo succeeded Ortiz, that orientation began to change slowly. Castillo, who was certainly favorably disposed to the nationalists' point of view, began to feel the pressure from the pro-Nazi groups, and the government switched its course. The neutralists, who scarcely concealed their totalitarian sympathies, redoubled

SOURCE: "Peronism and Authoritarian Ideology" from José Luis Romero, A *History of Argentine Political Thought*, translated by Thomas F. McGann (Stanford, Calif.: Stanford University Press, 1963), pp. 240–45. Reprinted by permission of Thomas F. McGann.

their activities, despite evidence that public opinion—even anti-British opinion—was by no means favorable to the Germans. Soon the entire apparatus of public power came to be an instrument of pro-Nazi policy, which in foreign affairs favored the Axis and in internal affairs led to decided gains for totalitarianism. The then Colonel Juan D. Perón was counted in the ranks of those who served the Nazi cause. Faced with the drive toward internal totalitarianism, which now was prudently cloaking the fraudulent old framework of our democracy, the political skepticism and despair of the masses grew deeper. Thus the country moved down strange roads toward the triumph of fascism.

The Revolution of June 1943

In spite of his sympathy for the Axis, President Castillo at heart continued to be a typical representative of fraudulent democracy, which became more and more corrupt with the passage of time, and was increasingly committed to defending its own privileges. Here is the way in which Carlos Ibarguren described the social situation in a letter to Robustiano Patrón Costas, the oligarchy's nominee for president:

> As an Argentine and as your sincere friend, I strongly hope that you may have the greatest success in your government, and that you will clear the public scene of the present actors, who are nothing but a gang of professional politicians striving to hold onto their jobs and their private interests. May you win the complete economic independence of our fatherland, liberating it from monopolies and from the pressure of international capitalism that now choke many of its vital organs. May you bring morality into the public administration, which today, in spite of the personal rectitude of Doctor Castillo, presents such a lamentable spectacle of venality that any part that is examined spurts out the pus of corruption, staining even the highest officials. I am confident that in our foreign relations you will know how to manage effectively Argentina's needs and interests, and that you will defend proudly and valiantly our sovereignty and our traditional honor.

Caught between the need to defend the interests of those who supported his policies and the claims of the pro-Nazis and nationalists who demanded that he support the Axis countries (with the corollary of promoting internal totalitarianism), President Castillo was obliged to juggle his decisions. The year 1943 brought indications of the weakening of the Nazi-Fascist offensive. The president turned again toward his faithful followers, who preferred to resort to the illegitimate tranquillity of fraudulent democracy and sacrifice the glad hope of being part of Germany's Lebensraum. It was then that Patrón Costas was nominated as the conservative candidate for the presidency, but he did not satisfy the toughest

and boldest defenders of the Axis. Out of the barracks emerged the mysterious GOU—the Group of United Officers—a collection of pro-Nazi military men who, one way or another, had to perpetuate the existing situation because of their commitments.

The traditional political parties that opposed fraudulent democracy—
the Radicals, the Socialists, and the Progressive Democrats—continued
to confront the suspected pro-Nazi plotters and the reactionary forces who
were trying to establish in Argentina a totalitarian regime or a hybrid
government made up of a German-type totalitarianism and North American capitalism. At the same time, the GOU went on working in the
greatest secrecy to prevent the country from escaping a system that would
guarantee the security of the groups that were heavily involved with the
Reich. A committee set up by congress to investigate Nazi penetration
found substantial reasons for alarm, and public opinion was put on the
alert, but the administration responded with increased pressure to prevent its own situation from becoming critical.

Meanwhile, the GOU was closing its ranks and preparing to use force;
at the same time, it was trying to present its views as though they were
ideals for the government of Argentina. From the secret document that
Carlos Ibarguren said he possesses and that appears in his book *La historia
que he vivido* (*The History That I Have Lived*), one may extract some
suggestive paragraphs that define the characteristics of the GOU:

> The Work of Unification seeks to bind together the officers of the
> Army, in spirit and in fact, understanding that in such a fusion lies
> the true solidarity of all the ranks, from which is born unity of
> action, the basis of all national, collective effort. The order of the
> day is to create a single body animated by one ideology and possessing
> a single will. It is impossible to protect the Army against all its
> internal and external enemies if one does not place its interest above
> all personal gain and if all of us do not feel the same holy pride in
> being its servants.
>
> We face the danger of war at a time when our home-front is in
> complete collapse. Two enemy courses of action may be clearly seen:
> to bring to bear powerful pressure by the United States or by its
> agents, or to threaten a communist revolution of the Popular Front
> type. . . . Confronted by these hostile political forces, the nation
> shows only a dispersion and division of the elements of order.
>
> In international matters, we follow the orientation of our govern-
> ment. We choose to fight for our country and to die for it, if
> necessary, doing so in defense of its honor and its interests, no matter
> who may try to compromise them. . . . Internally, political instability
> may soon lead either to the victory of existing tendencies (but only
> with a change in the present international situation and, as a result,
> in the war), or to the triumph of the Popular Front, disguised as a
> Democratic Union, which will immediately seek to make a communist
> revolution, as in the case of Spain. . . . The Popular Front must be

destroyed in order that we may avoid a civil war, which we do not fear but which we have the patriotic duty to shun.

Today it is necessary not only to grasp the political problems that in the end may occasion the serious disturbances with which we are familiar, but also to prepare the Army so that it may in good time avoid those problems. That objective will be achieved only when military men are guided by a single ideal and share a single doctrine and, resolved to labor with the greatest unity of action, find each other resolute to impose order, from the moment when stability is first threatened. In our country we have long upheld the concept of exaggerated respect for the Law, which puts us above any suspicion of political activity. This will serve us as a shield when the time is ripe for us to set to work. If that moment arrives, it will be necessary to proceed rationally to do our job: the Chief of the Army will make the decisions and we will execute them.

Evidently this plan aimed at reducing the civil life of Argentina to its narrowest bounds and enclosing it within rigid military limits. This attitude was incomprehensible unless one assumed that the military leaders were trying to justify something in which the public ought not to share, and about which the public should know nothing. Indeed there was something hidden behind the plot that broke out in revolution on June 4, 1943, which in itself was only a salvage operation by the group involved with Nazi infiltration, and which also sought to prevent the Castillo government from swinging toward the United States.

The revolution began as a profoundly unpopular military dictatorship, and it laid the basis for a totalitarian regime, especially after the elimination of the last moderate revolutionists in mid-October 1943. Its methods were unequivocal: the activities of the political parties, of the unions, and of the universities were hobbled; simultaneously, obligatory religious instruction was established by the minister of public instruction, Martínez Zuviría. Perhaps in order to strengthen its weak position, the government turned for support to groups of workers who collaborated with the police. In a vast attempt to compromise the free consciences of the workers, the sub-secretary of war, Perón, was named director of the department of labor. Fully committed to its organizational tasks, fascism was on the march.

The Course of "Peronismo"

This entire process was nothing less than the genesis of a fascist regime, but, as events developed, certain pecularities appeared that derived from the personality of the principal proponent of the movement. There can be no doubt that Perón was the most active leader among the pro-Nazis in the revolutionary government, and he began to utilize methods typical of those counseled by Nazi-Fascist tradition and by the political views prevailing in military circles. The tenets of the military men are summarized in a proclamation issued to the army by pro-Nazi officers shortly before the revolution of June 4. The last paragraphs of the proclamation referred to the manner of using power after it had been seized:

> Once we have conquered power, it will be our mission to be strong—stronger than all the other (South American) countries together. We must arm ourselves and remain armed always, triumphing over difficulties, battling against internal and external conditions. Hitler's struggle in peace and in war will be our guide.
>
> Alliances will be the first step. We already have Paraguay; we shall have Bolivia and Chile, and it will be easy for us to put pressure on Uruguay. Then the five united nations will easily draw in Brazil, because of its form of government and its great nuclei of Germans. The South American continent will be ours when Brazil falls. Our tutelage will become a fact, a grandiose and unprecedented fact, achieved by the genius and heroism of the Argentine Army.
>
> Mirages! Utopia! people will say. Nevertheless, we turn our eyes once more toward Germany. Conquered, she was forced in 1919 to sign the Treaty of Versailles, which would have kept her under the Allied yoke as a second-class power for at least fifty years. In less than twenty years she traveled an amazing road. Before 1939 she was armed as was no other nation, and in the midst of peace had annexed Austria and Czechoslovakia. Later, in war, all Europe was bent to her will. But this was accomplished only by hard sacrifice. An iron dictatorship was necessary, to impose upon the people the renunciation essential to that formidable program.
>
> So it will be in Argentina. Our government will be an inflexible dictatorship, although at the beginning we will make the concessions needed to put it on a solid basis. The people will be attracted to the cause, but they must work, deprive themselves, and obey—work more and deprive themselves more than any other people. Only thus will it be possible to effect the armaments program that is indispensable for the conquest of the continent. Following the example of Germany, we will inculcate into the people by radio, by the controlled press, by films, by books, by the church, and by education a spirit receptive to understanding of the heroic road that must be followed. Only thus will the people succeed in renouncing the pleasant life they now lead. Our generation will be a generation sacrificed on the altar of the highest good—the Argentine fatherland, which will shine with unequaled light for the greater benefit of the continent and of all humanity.

To reach this goal, Perón used a tool of inestimable value—his ability as an orator capable of employing the tone, the vocabulary, and the ideas most appropriate for swaying the Argentine masses, especially the people of the urban working districts. This factor, whose value was multiplied by the use of the radio, came to have immeasurable significance in Argentine politics.

Little by little, this unpopular revolution began to become popular, although the politicians and the middle class did not notice what was happening. A natural orator, who had a monopoly of the radio, Perón began to gather around him more or less dissatisfied labor leaders and worker organizations that were justifiably disenchanted by the conservative policies which had prevailed since 1930. . . .

3. *Peronism and the United States*

Sergio Bagú is a leading Argentine social historian best known for his work on migration. He has long been a professor in the Faculty of Philosophy and Letters of the University of Buenos Aires and is now connected with the Di Tella Institute in Buenos Aires. He has worked and lectured in many of the countries of the southern cone.

Juan Perón, one of the organizers of the 1943 mutiny, began a few months later to organize, with great ability and no little good fortune, the regime that will inevitably be linked to his name throughout history. Pushing aside the aristocratic nationalism of the middle class military and a handful of civilian acolytes of the old oligarchy, Perón passed to a regime that was strongly inspired by Italian Fascism, appealed to a mass much more proletarian than the latter's, and had the substantial objective of preserving intact the archaic economic and social structure of Argentina. What he did was to cover that archaic structure with an autocratic political superstructure sustained by a state-controlled labor organization, with a fervent multitude without any freedom of action, and with the Army.

The new regime extended palpable economic compensation—higher salaries and social security—to the masses entering the national scene. The costs of these benefits could be met during the first years of the regime without any effort by an economy that, without violating in any way its essential pattern of income distribution, was benefited by the extraordinary conjunction of World War II and the postwar period. In effect, the country found itself in 1945 with great reserves of gold and foreign exchange accumulated during the years of the conflict because of the very favorable balance of trade. Later, when these reserves were exhausted, the country ate up its capital, but the regime, in a heroic defense of tradition, did not leave behind even a sketch of a preliminary plan for structural change.

SOURCE: "Peronism and the United States" translated from Sergio Bagú, *La Argentina en el mundo* (México: Fondo de Cultura Económica, 1962), pp. 100–10.

As in the case of Italian Fascism, the regime set up an apparatus of repression and propaganda. . . . What the chief taught his masses had nothing to do with reality. He could therefore dare to use, vociferously and one by one, all the banners that socialism, Communism, and syndicalism had waved in the country for decades, giving them official status and unheard-of propagation, although quietly reserving for himself the right of applying only those of them that could be reconciled with the inherited economic structure.

In the international sphere, the regime left two completely different types of documentation as evidence of its double nature: one, the speeches to the masses and the quasi-official "articles"; [1] the other, the treaties and conventions signed by the Government of the nation during that period, those they were at the point of signing, and their total action in the international sphere.

Ambiguities and mirages. The regime's double nature, reflected in its great verbal audacity and secrecy in the solution of national problems, combined with various internal and external circumstances to wrap all its existence in a characteristic halo of equivocation and an atmosphere of systematized fraud on an enormous scale. No serious resistance could be offered by the opposition groups, which were organically weak and ideologically timid as a result of the persistence of archaic national structures and of the repressive mechanism of the state, which was set up in 1930 and continued to function without any interruption during the entire Peronist regime. Similarly, the large sectors of the masses that were never won over by official propaganda were completely unable to organize, act, or obtain information. In international affairs, the opening of new fronts in the cold war so modified positions and objectives that some great powers, in particular the United States, began to apply a scale of values totally opposed to those they had sustained during the war. In Latin America, the oldest allies of the United States against the Axis came to be enemies of the United States, and vice versa. This sudden turnabout enveloped relations within the inter-American bloc in the most confused terminology for fifteen years.

The new requirements of the cold war had immediate implications for relations between the United States and Latin America. The logic of the new world strategy required that the State Department transform the old and creaky pan-American system . . . into a concrete military alliance and an economic system completely dominated by the United States.

[1] [*50 artículos de Descartes: Política y estrategia* (*No ataco, critico*) (Buenos Aires: no publisher given, 1951). It reprints the articles on international politics signed "Descartes" that appeared in the daily *Democracia* and that, in the opinion of diplomatic circles and the masses, were personally written by Perón.]

Conditions within the Latin American countries were favorable for these objectives. Many of the Latin American countries lived stifled under dictatorial regimes which prolonged their lives, as [John Foster] Dulles said, using military might supplied by the U.S. Department of Defense. And where this type of *ancien régime* was not being suffered, an economic mythology flourished that characterizes the recent history of this part of the world. The representatives of economic and political power in these countries conceived the hope of rapid industrialization using the reserves accumulated during the war and the active collaboration of the United States. All of that, without introducing any substantial reform in the traditional economic and social structures. In order to succeed, it seemed adequate to transform the pan-American system into a sort of protective shield that would safeguard them from the vicissitudes they saw in the world order that were doubtless going to manifest themselves in the much more ample site of the United Nations.

The strategic and economic objectives of the United States coincided with this self-delusion of the representatives of power in Latin America. From this coincidence came the Act of Chapultepec [2] in 1945, support for including the principle of the autonomy of regional systems (eventually Article 52) in the Charter of the United Nations, the Treaty of Continental Defense signed in Rio de Janeiro in 1947, and the orientation within the United Nations of the Latin American bloc, which on fundamental political questions delivered its votes to the United States. . . .

The crass materialism behind the position taken in the post-1945 international order by the representatives of power in the Latin American countries became depressingly manifest in the scarcely concealed satisfaction with which they viewed the prospect that a third world war would grow out of the Korean conflict in 1950. They supposed that once again in the twentieth century the great powers were going to bleed themselves and pay high prices for Latin American raw materials, treating the countries of this continent to another wave of prosperity unearned by any reform of their archaic national structures. They were unable to perceive what was by then a reality known in all diplomatic circles outside Latin America, that there could be no third world war until the powers heading each one of the two great blocs had completed a system of military, political, and economic vassalage within their own spheres. . . .

    [2] [The reference is to the final document of the Inter-American Conference on Problems of War and Peace held at Chapultepec in Mexico City from February 21 to March 8, 1945. The meeting was held to decide how the American republics would approach the forthcoming organization of the United Nations. Argentina was the only American republic not represented, for she had not as yet broken ties with the Axis powers. Shortly after, Argentina did join the Allied powers and was allowed to participate in the San Francisco conference establishing the United Nations, thus becoming a charter member of the international organization.]

From verbal grossness to the practical. The Argentine state introduced no innovations in these propositions formulated by the other Latin American countries. It adhered, tacitly or explicitly, to all their principles and accepted all the practical consequences. The only variation it succeeded in introducing into its international conduct had to do with some attitudes of vacillation or delay, magnified by the characteristic diplomatic looseness with which the State Department has always acted in the Latin American zone.

In 1945, when Perón was elected and when the new stage in the international order that we are analyzing began, the State Department began to utilize new instruments in its dealings. Formally, there were fluctuations between all the extremes, from the greatest personal obsequiousness of American ambassadors with respect to the persons of the Argentine president and his wife [3] to the grossest pyrotechnics of the chief of the shirtless ones, whose victim was and came again to be, with the perseverence that indicates the presence of a popular conviction, the United States. . . .

But if we maintain some distance from these violent fluctuations in what we can call the external history of the relations between Argentina and the United States during that period, we shall see that in that other [internal] history there is an appreciable continuity of conduct by both parties.

A very few days after taking office, President Perón had the Act of Chapultepec ratified and aligned himself with the international policy of the United States. The Argentine delegation to the Rio de Janeiro Conference of 1947 introduced no substantial change in the treaty there elaborated and, in 1950, the Argentine Congress—obviously under the strict orders of the President—ratified the treaty.

In the United Nations: a model of diplomatic indigency. In the United Nations—where, because of the vastness of the scene any small power, no matter how impotent it is against a neighboring power, finds some chance of emancipating itself from immediate tutelage—the conduct of the delegation of the Peronist regime maintained an intrinsic coherence and an ideological definition of the same firmness as that manifested by the chief of state, although without his stridencies and his episodic spectacularity.

Its legacy is a model of indigence in political and ideological matters. It refused to help the cause of the Republic of Indonesia in the Security Council in 1946, and it failed to formulate a single criticism of the aggression, in the old colonial style, that the Dutch Empire perpetrated

[3] Perón, we were assured by James Bruce, Ambassador of the United States in Buenos Aires, was "the great leader of a great nation." . . .

there. It did not state its approval of the emancipation of the Jewish population of Palestine nor, by the same token, the creation of the State of Israel in the conflict that ended in 1948. India was not supported when it accused the South African Union of racial persecution of the population of Indian origin (the first, third, fifth, sixth, and eighth sessions of the General Assembly). Votes were registered against all moves that tended to oblige the Government of the Union of South Africa to give up the Territory of Southwest Africa, the old mandate of the League of Nations which the former illegally incorporated into its national territory (second, fourth, and seventh sessions of the General Assembly). . . . In all fundamental votes on the grave problem of the Korean War, support was never given to the powers that were attempting to limit the effects of the conflict; on the contrary, adherence was indiscriminately given to the proposals and attitudes of the United States (fifth, sixth, seventh, eighth, and ninth sessions of the General Assembly).

The most audacious levels of political autonomy that the Argentine delegation managed to reach in the General Assembly were translated into attitudes of a characteristic pusillanimity. In the fifth session, it abstained from the draft resolution denominated "Uniting for Peace," which implied the transfer to the General Assembly of some powers of the Security Council, an idea advanced by the United States to avoid the Soviet veto on matters related to the Korean War. In the eighth period, it abstained when the Assembly had to decide if Puerto Rico had reached the condition of self-government envisioned in the Charter. In the tenth, it abstained when the same question was raised with respect to two Dutch colonies, the Dutch Antilles and Surinam.[4]

This behavior of reiterated subordination and ideological pauperism in the field of diplomacy represented with the highest degree of fidelity the real objectives of the international policy of the Peronist regime, for as the action of its delegates in the United Nations was totally unknown within the country because of censorship or was presented in a totally different light, the regime could proceed on the international scene with absolute spontaneity.

The only plausible posture of the Argentine representation in the world body during that period was registered in 1948 when Juan Atilio Bramuglia, president by rotation of the Security Council, acted as a mediator between the Soviet Union and the Western bloc in the attempt to find a pacific solution to the blockade imposed by the Soviets on the city of Berlin.

There should also be mentioned, as well, the abstention registered by

[4] See the careful work of John A. Houston, *Latin America in the United Nations,* Carnegie Endowment for International Peace, New York, 1956.

the Argentine delegation during the Tenth Interamerican Conference held at Caracas when dealing with the declaration that, a few months later, was to serve the State Department as justification for overthrowing the Arbenz government in Guatemala.

In economic matters. In economic affairs, the orientation of the regime was similar. Two petroleum contracts that it proposed to sign with United States firms—the Atlas Corporation in 1954 and California Argentina de Petróleo, a subsidiary of Standard Oil, in 1955—were sunk because of the opposition they aroused in national politics. The declared value of private American investment in Argentina rose from $202 million in 1946 to $447 million in 1955. These were businesses of high earnings whose total declared sales in 1955 were $571 million.[5] The percentages of Argentina's foreign trade accounted for by the United States increased. Of the country's total imports, 15.7 per cent came from the U.S. in 1935–39; in the period 1950–54, the figure fluctuated between 14.1 and 21 per cent. Of the country's total exports, 11.7 per cent went to the U.S. in 1935–39; in the period 1950–54, the figure fluctuated between 13.7 and 25.4 per cent.[6]

No one of the facts mentioned in the previous paragraph implies anything sensational. The Peronist regime in economic matters was decidedly conservative and innovated only when an innovation was imposed on it by international circumstances. It bought the French- and British-owned railroads with blocked currency that it had been unable to free, paying notoriously inflated prices for decapitalized enterprises whose sale to the Argentine state was already being counselled in Paris and London themselves. Argentine foreign trade underwent greater diversification because the demand on the international market had suffered important modifications. This change, as well as the greater participation of the United States in Argentine foreign commercial affairs, was simply a logical consequence of the new tendencies in the international economy. The Argentine state reacted passively to the new tendencies and did not introduce any substantial alteration in the national economic structure or in the traditional capacity of Argentina to place in the market an array of raw materials greater than that of other Latin American countries.

The doubling of private American capital invested in Argentine businesses signified no turn in favor of Argentina on the part of private American investors. Their declared total investment in Argentina—less, no doubt, than its market value—which we have mentioned is relatively modest compared to the total of $6,233,000,000 that they had invested in

[5] These figures on private American investment in Argentina were taken from the volume, *Investments in the Latin American Economy,* published by the Department of Commerce of the United States, Washington, 1957.

[6] These data are from A. H. Tandy, *Argentina: Economic and Commercial Conditions in the Argentine Republic,* London, Her Majesty's Stationery Office, 1956, p. 105.

all of Latin America by 1955. Furthermore, the approximately $250 million of declared value added during the Peronist period came in large part from profits obtained by the already established companies and reinvested in their own businesses.

Synthesis. The synthesis forced on us by the Perón decade, then, is not a very difficult one. As regards Argentina's relationships with the United Kingdom and the other European countries, the line inherited from the regime going from 1930 to 1943 was changed only in the measure imposed by extranational circumstances. As for relationships with the United States, behind the verbal pyrotechnics there lies an unquestionable truth. Despite its actions in the United Nations and especially its adherence to the Rio pact of 1947, the Perón regime—it should be recognized—did various things for the first time in Argentine history. In effect, from no Argentine government had the United States previously received such verbal dirty treatment. From none had it received greater concessions. To none, either, had the United States dedicated more enthusiastic eulogies.

4. *Peronism and the Spirit of Evita*

Until her death from cancer in 1952, Eva (Evita) Duarte de Perón was one of the ablest and most dedicated apologists for her husband's cause. Students of peronismo may never agree as to how much of Eva's spoken and written message must be regarded as the disingenuous propaganda of a cunning, opportunistic, power-mad woman, and how much as the sincere testimony of a simple, humanitarian seeker of social justice and national regeneration. Nor do they seem likely to agree who performed the task of ghostwriting if, as seems most probable, Eva did not herself write the book that bears her name and from which the following passages are selected.

Many people are unable to explain what it is that has touched my life.

I myself, many times, have thought about this and about what my life now is.

Some of my contemporaries attribute it all to chance, that strange and incomprehensible thing that no one has ever explained.

No. It isn't chance that has brought me to this position that I hold, to this life that I lead.

SOURCE: "Peronism and the Spirit of Evita" translated by Fredrick B. Pike from Eva Perón, *La razón de mi vida* (Buenos Aires: Ediciones Peuser, 1951), pp. 13–39, 310–15.

Obviously, all that I'm saying would be as absurd as chance itself if my "supercritics" were right when they say that I am only "a superficial woman, lacking preparation, removed from the interests of her country, unfeeling toward the sorrows of her people, indifferent to social justice, and with nothing serious in her head, who was suddenly transformed into a fanatic in the struggle for the cause of the people and who, making this cause her own, decided to lead a life of incomprehensible sacrifice."

I want to explain myself.

That is why I have decided to write these pages.

I profess that I do not do so in order to contradict or refute anyone.

What I truly desire is that the men and women of my country know how I feel and how I think!

I want them to feel with me the great things that my heart experiences.

Of course, many of the things that I will say are lessons that I have received gratuitously from Perón and that I have no right to guard as secrets.

I have had to look backward in the course of my life in order to find the first reason for all that is happening to me now.

Perhaps I am saying it wrong by speaking of "the first reason"; because the truth is that throughout my life I have always acted on impulse and been guided by my feelings.

Even today, amid this torrent of events that I must keep track of, I often, almost always, let myself be guided more by what I feel than by other motives.

In me, much of the time, at least, reason is what explains what I feel; and so, in order to explain my life today . . . I had to seek out in my early years the first feelings which, when rationalized or explained, could make understandable what for my "supercritics" is an "incomprehensible sacrifice" but for me is neither a sacrifice nor incomprehensible.

I have found in my heart a fundamental feeling that absolutely dominates my spirit and my life; this feeling is my indignation against injustice.

For as long as I can remember, every injustice has brought sorrow to my soul, as if something were piercing it. . . .

I remember very well that I was sad for many days when it dawned on me that there were poor and rich in the world; and the strange thing is that the existence of the poor didn't upset me so much as the knowledge that at the same time there were rich people.

The theme of the rich and the poor was, from that time on, the theme of my solitude. I don't believe that I ever spoke about it with other persons, not even with my mother, but I thought about it frequently.

It still remained for me, though, to take another step ahead on the road of my discoveries.

I knew that there were poor and that there were rich persons; and I knew that everywhere there were more poor than rich.

I still did not understand the third dimension of injustice.

Up to eleven years of age, I believed that there were poor people, just as there was grass, and that there were rich people, just as there were trees.

One day, from the lips of a laborer, I heard for the first time that some people were poor because the rich were too rich; and that revelation produced a very strong impression on me.

I related that opinion to all the other things that I had been thinking about this subject, and almost in a flash I understood that that laborer was right. More than believing what he said through a rationalization, I felt that it was true.

And here is something else. Even in those times, I believed more in what the poor said than in what the rich said, because the poor seemed more sincere, more frank, and also more virtuous.

With this last step, I had come to understand the third dimension of social injustice.

Many people undoubtedly take this last step of discovering life and the social problem. The majority of men and women know that there are poor people because there are rich people; but they learn this without really feeling it, and maybe this is why it seems natural and logical to them.

I recognize that I learned this almost in a flash and that in learning it I suffered; and I insist that it never seemed logical or natural to me.

I felt then, within my heart, something that I now recognize as the feeling of indignation. I didn't understand why there had to be poor people and rich people, or why the lust for wealth on the part of the rich had to be the cause for the poverty of so many people.

Since then I have never been able to think about this injustice without becoming indignant; and thinking about it has always produced in me an odd sensation of asphyxiation, as if by not being able to remedy the evil that I saw I was deprived of the air necessary to breathe.

I now think that people become accustomed to social injustice in the first years of life. This reaches the point where the poor themselves believe that the misery they suffer is natural and logical. They become accustomed to seeing it or suffering it, just as it is possible for one to accustom himself to a powerful poison.

Since I was eleven I have not been able to accustom myself to poison, to regard social injustice as natural and logical.

Perhaps this is the only thing that is inexplicable about my life, the only thing that very definitely appears in me without any cause.

I believe that just as some persons are spiritually predisposed to feel beauty more intensely than others do and therefore become poets or painters or musicians, I have a particular disposition of the spirit, born with me, that makes me feel injustice in a special way, with a rare intensity of sorrow.

Can a painter say why he sees and feels colors as he does? Can a poet explain why he is a poet?

Maybe this is why I never say why I "feel" injustice with pain and why I will never accept it as natural, as the majority of men do.

But, although I couldn't explain it even to myself, it is certain that my feeling of indignation against social injustice is the force that has taken me by the hand from the first moments that I can remember up to the present time; this is the ultimate reason that explains how a woman sometimes viewed by various persons as "superficial, vulgar, and indifferent" can decide to lead a life of "incomprehensible sacrifice."

I never thought, though, that I was going to have so direct a participation in the struggle of my people for social justice.

Weak woman that I am, I never imagined that the grave problem of the poor and the rich was someday going to knock so forcefully on the doors of my heart as to require my humble efforts in finding a solution within my Fatherland.

As I grew older, however, the problem enveloped me more and more. Perhaps this was why I tried to hide from myself, to forget this insistent theme; and I surrendered myself fully to my unusual and profound artistic vocation.

Even as a little girl, I remember that I always wanted to declaim. It was as if I always wanted to say something to others, something great and beautiful that I felt in the depths of my heart.

When I speak now to the men and women of my country, I feel that I am expressing that "something" that I wanted to say when I declaimed during functions at my school.

My artistic vocation made me aware of other aspects of life. No longer concerned just with ordinary, everyday injustices, I began to sense and then to know about the greater, more basic injustices; I saw them not only in the fiction that I acted out but in the reality of my new life as well.

I wished not to see, not to take account of, not to look at tragedy, misfortune, and misery; but the more I wanted to forget it, the more injustice surrounded me.

The symptoms of the social injustice in which our country was living then appeared to me at every step . . . ; every day and everywhere they overwhelmed me.

Little by little my fundamental feeling of indignation against injustice filled the cup of my soul to the limits of my silence, and I began to become involved in a few conflicts.

I was gaining nothing for myself out of this, nor was I accomplishing anything by becoming involved in these conflicts in the hope of resolving them. All that I accomplished was to grow increasingly outraged against those who, as I saw it, were mercilessly exploiting weakness. This outrage grew progressively beyond my powers to control it; and my best intentions of keeping quiet, of "not getting involved," would collapse on the first occasion.

I recognize that sometimes my reactions were not suitable and that my words and actions were exaggerated in relation to the particular injustice that provoked them. But, rather than reacting against the particular injustice involved, I was reacting against all injustice. . . .

Once, in one of these reactions of mine, I remember having said: "Someday all of this will change." And I don't know if this was a supplication or a curse or the two together. . . .

Perhaps I believed even then that truly everything would someday be different; but, understandably, I didn't know how or when; and even less did I suspect that destiny would give me a place, a very humble place but a place nevertheless, in the work of redemption. . . .

One day I was driven, by a curiosity that derived from my inclination, to investigate what is referred to as the press of the people.

I was seeking companionship. Isn't it true that almost always in the books and newspapers that we read we seek companionship rather than courses to follow or a guide to lead us?

Probably because of this I read the leftist press of our country. But I found in it neither companionship nor a course of action nor even less a person to guide me.

The "newspapers of the people," it is true, condemned capital and certain wealthy individuals with strong and harsh language, pointing out the defects of the opprobrious social system that the country endured.

But in the details and even in the substance of the preaching that they advanced, one could easily see the influence of foreign ideas, very far removed from everything that was Argentine: the alien systems and formulas of men who were strangers to our land and our feelings.

It was plain to see that what they desired for the Argentine people would not come from the people themselves. And this fact put me on guard at once.

At the same time, I found something else that was repugnant: the formula for the solution of social injustice was a system that was the same for all countries and for all peoples; and I could not conceive that in order to destroy so great an evil it was necessary at the same time to attack and annihilate something so natural and so great as the Fatherland.

At this point I wish to make it clear that until only a few years ago, many working-class "leaders" in this country regarded the Fatherland and its symbols as symbols of capitalism; and they dismissed Religion in the same manner. . . .

Reading the publications that they circulated carried me—this much it did do—to the conclusion that the social injustice of my Fatherland could only be overcome by a revolution; but I found it impossible to accept an international revolution coming from outside and created by men who were strangers to our way of being and thinking. . . .

Why, I said to myself, add to the misery of those who suffer injustice by depriving them, in this world that they are accustomed to contemplate, of the vision of the Fatherland and Religion?

I said to myself that this was like removing the sky from a landscape.

Why, instead of constantly attacking the Fatherland and Religion, didn't the "leaders of the people" try to place these moral forces at the service of the cause of the redemption of the people?

I suspected that those "leaders" worked not for the welfare of the laborers but rather to weaken the Nation and its moral forces.

I didn't like the remedy that was proposed for the sickness.

I knew little, but my heart and my common sense guided me, and I returned to my previous thoughts . . . convinced that I would have nothing to do with that sort of struggle.

I resigned myself to living inwardly the rebellion of my indignation.

From that time on, my natural indignation against social injustice was accompanied by the indignation that had arisen in my heart when I became acquainted with the proposed solutions and disloyalty of the presumed "leaders of the people."

I resigned myself to being a victim. . . . More than that, I had resigned myself to leading a commonplace, monotonous life that seemed sterile but that I considered inevitable. I didn't see any hope of escaping from it. But in the depths of my soul I could not resign myself to what seemed inescapable.

At last my "wonderful day" arrived!

All of us, or almost all of us, have in life a "wonderful day."

For me, this was the day when my life began to coincide with the life of Perón.

I know now that men are divided into two groups. The one, large and infinitely numerous, is made up of those who lust for vulgar and common things; who move only over well-known paths that others have already traveled; who are content to desire simply to be successful. The other group is small, very small; it is made up of men who recognize the extraordinary value of whatever it is that must be done. These men will commit themselves to nothing less than the quest for glory. Already they breathe the air of the future century that will sing their glory; they live almost in eternity.

These are men for whom a new road always exercises an irresistible attraction. For Alexander this was the road to Persia and for Columbus the road to the Indies; for Napoleon the road led toward control of the world, and for San Martín it led to the liberty of America.

The man whom I met belongs to this second class of men. . . .

I placed myself at his side and, summoning my best words, declared: "If, as you say, the cause of the people is your own cause, however far we have to go in sacrifice I will never leave your side until death."

He accepted my offer.

That was my "wonderful day." . . .

Why did the humble men, the laborers of my country, not react [to Perón] in the same manner as the common and the vulgar? Why, on the contrary, did they understand and believe in him?

The explanation is simple. It is enough to see Perón to believe in him, in his sincerity, his loyalty, his honesty.

They saw him and they believed.

Here what occurred in Bethlehem two thousand years ago was repeated; the first to believe were the humble, not the rich, the learned, the powerful.

It is as if the rich and learned and powerful must always have their souls sealed shut by selfishness and avarice.

In contrast, the poor, even as in Bethlehem, live and sleep in the open air, and the windows of their simple souls are almost always open to the breezes from outside. . . .

Happily, Perón won. Otherwise he would have lost everything, including even his life.

I, meantime, fulfilled my promise of "being at his side."

I sustained the lamp that lighted his nights; in whatever way I could and knew, I strengthened his zeal, enveloping him in my love and my faith. . . .

The old anguish of my heart began to disappear, just as snow disappears beneath the rays of the sun. And I said to myself with ever greater conviction: "Yes, this is the man of my people. No one is comparable to him."

.   .   .

I am nothing more than a humble woman typical of a great people (as indeed all the peoples of the earth are great!).

A woman like millions and millions of others in the world. God chose me from among all of them and put me in this place, next to a leader of a new world: Perón.

Why was I chosen instead of another?

I don't know. . . .

I feel myself to be nothing more than the humble representative of all the women of all the world's peoples.

I feel that I, like them, am someone who runs a household; a household that is much larger, it is true, than those that others have created, but a household nonetheless: the great and fortunate household of my Fatherland, which Perón leads towards its highest destinies.

Thanks to him, the household that at the beginning was poor and run-down is now just, free, and sovereign!

He did it all. His marvelous hands transformed each hope of our people into a thousand realities. . . .

In this great household of the Fatherland, I am like any other woman of the infinite number of households in my country.

I too am womanly, just as they are.

I like the same things that they like: jewels and furs, clothes and shoes. . . . Like them, like all of them, I sometimes wish I were free to travel about and enjoy myself. But, as they are, I am bound by household duties, which no one else is obligated to fulfill for me. . . .

Like all the women of all the households in my country, my happy days are those when all the children gather around the head of the house, loving and joyful.

Like other women, I know what the children of this great household, my Fatherland, require of me and my husband, and I try to do what is proper.

Like other women, I try to appear more beautiful before my own family than before strangers; and this is why I put on my finest adornments when attending to the descamisados.

Many times I think, as other women do, about going on a vacation, about traveling all over the world. But on the doorstep of my house a thought detains me: "If I go, who will do my work?" And I remain.

The truth is that I feel myself actually to be the mother of my people! . . . My loves are their loves.

This is why I now love Perón in a different manner, not as I loved him before. Once I loved him for himself. Now I love him also because my people love him!

Because of all of this, because I feel like any other woman who seeks the happiness of her household and because I have achieved this happiness, I want it for each and every woman in my country.

I want them to be as happy in their homes as I am in this great household of mine, my Fatherland. . . .

To the very last day of my life, I want my task to be the opening of new horizons and destinies to my descamisados, my workers, my women.

Like any other woman of the people, I know that I have greater strength than I appear to have and better health than my doctors believe.

Like other women, like each and every one of them, I am resolved to persevere in my struggle for the constant happiness of my great household.

I aspire to no other honor; I only desire that happiness.

This is my vocation and my destiny.

This is my mission. . . .

Perhaps someday when I am gone, someone will say of me what so many children are accustomed to saying when their mothers have departed from this life: "Only now do we understand how much she loved us."

5. *Peronism and the Economy*

While Perón was utilizing political methods and encouraging a type of propaganda that appalled many, he was also employing economic policies that have been widely criticized. In 1959, the Economic Commission for Latin America of the United Nations published a survey stressing the degree to which economic problems had worsened during the Perón decade. The essentially conservative and traditional nature of Perón's fiscal approach is suggested by his unwillingness to take steps toward capturing for national development programs the capital of affluent and relatively tax-free sectors.

The Structural Crisis of the Argentine Economy

The salient features of the crisis. The ills that afflict the Argentine economy result from more than merely incidental events. The great world depression of the early thirties marked the termination of an epoch. New factors have conditioned economic development since then, and the country has not yet fully succeeded in adjusting to them so as to establish for its economy an accelerated rhythm of growth corresponding to its potential.

That rhythm has been slack since the early thirties, scarcely half of what it had been in other times. Between the beginning of the century and the Great Depression, the average per-capita gross domestic product rose at an annual average of 1.2 per cent; since then the rate has been

SOURCE: "Peronism and the Economy" translated by Fredrick B. Pike from *Análisis y proyecciones del desarrollo económico, V, El desarrollo económico de Argentina, I: Los problemas y perspectivas del crecimiento económico argentino*, estudio realizado en 1957 por la Secretaría de la Comisión Económica para América Latina, Naciones Unidas, Departamento de Asuntos Económicos y Sociales (Mexico, 1959), pp. 3–4.

only around .6 per cent.[1] Furthermore, this weak growth rate has been irregular, since it corresponds only to that part of the period which ended with the strong impulse of the postwar years. After 1948, the per-capita product declined, and although afterward it did recuperate some of the loss, it has not risen in the last four years. . . .

The manifestations [of a sick Argentine economy] are well known. The country at present lacks foreign exchange reserves to import not only the most indispensable capital goods but also the primary goods and the intermediary products that are increasingly necessary for the development of its industry. Moreover, the condition of transportation is precarious, and the lack of electrical energy is considerable.

At the base of this process of strangulation of the Argentine economy is the phenomenon of insufficient capital accumulation, notoriously evident in the basic services, in industry, and in petroleum. Production has not increased as it should have because the necessary investments have not been made; at the same time, agricultural-livestock production has declined owing to lack of incentives and resources to correct the deficiencies of investment that have been aggravated since the great world depression.

Because industrial development has not been much more ample, the country now finds itself lacking machinery and equipment, iron and steel, chemicals and petrochemical products, paper and celluloid, as well as other intermediary products, all of which—even a large part of the automobiles, for which the need is so serious—could be produced domestically under conditions of relative economic efficiency. Nor do the possibilities exist for importing the means of production in the necessary quantities. In effect, the ever-growing imports of petroleum and the decline of exports, which are down both in volume and in value as a result of deterioration in exchange prices, have seriously compromised the foreign-exchange resources that Argentina requires to obtain from abroad those capital goods and intermediary products that cannot be produced domestically under conditions of economic efficiency.

The insufficient accumulation of capital was first the result of adverse foreign conditions; more recently, though, domestic factors have prevented the capacity for the self-generation of national savings from developing at the pace required for an accelerated rhythm of development. Thus, in the period when investable resources were relatively abundant during the postwar years, a great part of them was diverted from the sectors of the production and transportation of goods and applied to ends

---

[1] [The contrast in per-capita product figures is all the more striking when it is recalled that the Argentine population was increasing dramatically during the 1900–1930 period, while its annual gains have been relatively small since 1930. Immigration by that year had declined noticeably. Unlike most Latin American countries, moreover, Argentina has not confronted a post–World War II population explosion.]

that did not contribute toward broadening the productive capacity nor toward correcting the deficiencies of the past that have been carried over into the present. These deficiencies, in fact, were aggravated all the more, to the point where they have resulted in the profound structural crisis that now threatens the Argentine economy.

The insufficient capitalization in the sectors of the production and transportation of goods has had, moreover, serious consequences in the distribution of human potential. A very high proportion of the increment of the active population has been diverted from those sectors and into others that are not directly productive. Furthermore, even within those sectors of the production and transportation of goods there have been very serious imbalances in the distribution of the labor increment. Agricultural and livestock production suffered a scarcity of workers that did not result in a transfer of labor into industry. On the contrary, industry in the last twelve years has absorbed a relatively small quantity of additional laborers, precisely because capital investment was insufficient.

Construction and railroad transportation were the sectors, above all others, that absorbed exaggerated proportions of laborers, with a corresponding decline in productivity, either because of the superfluousness of workers or because the decline itself resulted in the need for a greater number of people to perform the same task. Thus, there developed within the very heart of the Argentine economy an observable discrepancy in levels of productivity. While productivity increased firmly and persistently in many parts of industry, it was weakened in those sectors concerned with the production of goods and transportation, and it also declined in those activities [2] that siphoned off an abnormal and exaggerated part of the human potential increment. This process neutralized the beneficial consequences of increased industrial productivity and contributed to the freezing of average per-capita production during the last four years.

These developments have intensified the inflationary pressure upon the economy; for not only has per-capita production not grown, it has been detained at a point lower than that of 1948, the great postwar boom year. The various social groups struggle to regain what they previously had, or what they then or subsequently have lost; and thus inflationary pressures shift constantly from one group to another, without producing any lasting effect so long as per-capita production fails to resume its growth.

[2] [Mainly construction and services.]

6. *Peronism Without Perón*

An analysis of Peronismo since the fall of Perón is presented by
Peter Ranis, an associate professor of political science at the State
University of New York at Stony Brook. Ranis has studied in Argentina as well as other Latin American countries and is developing a
specialization in party politics in Latin America.

The persistence of peronista political power remains the essential
political concern of post-Perón Argentina. This dilemma has never been
resolved and its presence affects any approximation of social and political
integration. As contemporary peronismo responds to an apparent psychosocial void that has not been filled by any other party or movement, the
alternatives today are as they were ten years ago: to allow the peronistas
legal political status, to integrate them into existing political parties, or
to permanently isolate them. The astounding peronista successes in the
March 1965 Congressional elections favor the first solution to this now
historical problem. . . .

Peronismo's historical chronology has been mainly that of a proscribed
party. In 1958, after two years of political suppression under General
Aramburu's Provisional Government, it chose, as a second best alternative,
the support of Arturo Frondizi. In 1960, it returned to its 1957 posture
of opposition and cast blank protest ballots. In 1962 the Unión Popular,
the party most closely representing peronismo, was allowed to run, though
its subsequent victory was later nullified. In 1963, the peronistas again
chose abstention. By 1965, the Unión Popular was finally allowed to compete in Congressional elections and to take its deputy seats. Throughout
these uncertain times, the peronistas have demonstrated a great deal of
self-discipline and moderation. Even in 1962, when overt, and in 1963,
when more subtle means were used to prevent peronista electoral successes,
they retained a sense of presence and calm. They continued to constitute a
party which was certain of its support and political future, and assuredly
unwilling to precipitate a massive campaign aimed at its very existence.
With the legalization of the Unión Popular in the March 1965 elections,
peronismo, by its self-imposed discipline, finally gained its sought-for recognition.

Until the elections of March 1965, post-Perón governments have em-

SOURCE: "Peronism Without Perón" from Peter Ranis, "Peronism Without Perón
Ten Years After the Fall (1955–1965)," in *Journal of Inter-American Studies*, 8, No. 1
(January 1966), pp. 112–26.

phasized electoral gimmicks, political suppression and psychological warfare vis-à-vis peronismo. Though governmental methods have had temporary successes in terms of denying peronismo any policy voice in the last decade, the real failure has been in neither allowing the peronistas a share in the political process nor absorbing them within more acceptable parties. Thus the limits, to date, of government behavior have ranged from the entire proscription of peronista and neo-peronista parties (those parties that are not directly beholden to Perón's choice of electoral policy) to the acceptance in 1965 of peronista candidates for deputy seats in the National Congress. . . .

Argentine governments, under military pressures, have . . . viewed peronismo as a vengeful force to be treated with the greatest caution. When the Unión Popular scored impressive legislative and gubernatorial victories in March 1962, the military intervened and eventually forced the nullification of the elections. With their electoral successes nullified, on December 28, 1962, two leaders of the peronista movement's trade union and political sections spoke. Andrés Framini, who had won the governorship of Buenos Aires province before the army intervention, stated:

> There will be a revolution . . . If blood flows—too bad . . . we must all be agreed that the leaders must stay united and make that clear to all our enemies. . . . This is why I say we must be prepared for anything. It might look as if they are going to let us go to the polls but I don't believe it. The way out for the people must be found—in whatsoever field it may be.

Raúl Matera, who until the March nullification had stood for a moderate approach, said:

> There is no longer a hard line and a soft line with the Peronist movement. We are all Justicialists; [1] we are all companions mobilized for combat. Anyone who does not understand this does not understand the times in which we are living, nor the movement to which we belong. We want a way out by means of elections.
>   We do not want the country to pay the price in blood or destruction. We want a peaceful way out through elections and we are fighting for that. We say this in all seriousness and with responsibility. Then nobody will be able to say that Justicialism repudiated or rejected elections or sought to be proscribed.

Thus not only does repudiation of the peronista vote drive the movement to extremes but it appears to unify it as well.

As the result of an army coup in September 1962, a more liberal "legalist" faction of the military gained ascendancy over the "interventionist"

---

[1] [Justicialists are supporters of Peronism. Used to designate the ideology of Perón's program, the term *Justicialismo* came to be nearly synonymous with *peronismo*.]

faction which opposed an eventual return to civilian government. Therefore when smaller neo-peronista provincial parties achieved representation in 1963 (including two governorships), there was no observable reaction from the military. Having tasted electoral victory without government intervention, the neo-peronista parties have found it increasingly difficult to give up their political autonomy for the uncertainties of a provocative, Perón-directed movement that invites military resistance. The Unión Popular, on the other hand, as the representative of peronismo, had not sufficiently demonstrated that it was no longer under Perón's control and thus was allowed to present candidates for national deputy seats and provincial legislative and municipal offices only. In the presidential and gubernatorial elections, the peronistas were obliged to vote for electors representing the newly formed Frente Nacional y Popular in which the Unión Popular participated along with several other parties. An accumulation of government electoral restrictions during the last month prior to the July 1963 elections eventually forced the Frente to withdraw its candidate list and advocate a policy of abstention. . . .

Generally it can be said that between 1955 and 1965, peronismo as a political force has gradually become more moderate and conciliatory. It has, however, solidified and flourished in opposition and has received consistent support from a great sector of the masses. A general aura has developed around it as peronismo remained at first persecuted, later branded as illegitimate, and finally (by 1965) permitted to compete only under strict and confined conditions. Throughout the past decade a strong mythology has emerged concerning the downtrodden, "benighted" peronista spokesman of the peoples' will. Because of the accumulation of the shortcomings of the Aramburu (1955–1958) and Frondizi (1958–1962) administrations, the peronistas have received growing solid support and general compassion from many persons in academic and intellectual circles. Also Perón in exile has continued to wield his influence successfully. His political posture fed on the illegality of his movement which has made of him a martyr in his role as an effective charismatic leader. . . .

As the March 1965 Congressional elections approached, the UCRP government centered its electoral campaign in the political arena. Its members emphasized that they had brought domestic peace and political democracy to Argentina. The former referred to the absence of military interventions, state-of-siege conditions and popular general strikes. The latter concerned the right granted the Unión Popular and many neo-peronista parties to participate in the March elections and the absence of political and labor prisoners.

Contrary to what might have been expected, the failure of Perón's attempt to return to Argentina in December 1964 succeeded in the calming of the pre-election atmosphere. The peronista anti-government fervor was surprisingly short-lived as the peronistas made an all-out effort to achieve legal recognition and thus sought to avoid antagonizing the government. Before the 1965 Congressional elections, the movement had shown signs of an increasing neo-peronista tendency, to which in the 1962 election Perón himself gave credence by supporting, after the fact, the most peronista-oriented of all the neo-peronista parties, the Unión Popular. By 1963, the other neo-peronistas had reached a momentum of their own which resulted in a disobedience to Perón's call for blank votes and a new-fledged neo-peronista representation in Congress. . . .

The peronistas, now legitimized as the Unión Popular, campaigned vaguely on several issues concerning labor and nationalization of public services, but mainly they hankered after the "good old days," decried present conditions and demanded a universal amnesty for all former peronista leaders and all those who had been politically exiled. This amnesty should cover all Argentines from the fall of Perón through the inauguration of Illia in October 1963. . . .

The March 1965 elections, which had at stake ninety-nine Chamber of Deputy seats, more than half of that lower but all-important Chamber, demonstrated a polarization of votes unknown since the days of the Perón and anti-Perón vote of 1946–1955. The figures [in the table below] represent support of the UCRP as the only alternative to a huge peronista vote. Both parties benefited from the presence of the other, though in ideology they are not polar opposites.

March 1965 Congressional Elections

Parties	Votes	Per Cent (rounded)	Seats Won	Total Seats
Unión Popular (peronista)	2,828,698	31%	36	36
Unión Cívica Radical del Pueblo (UCRP)	2,676,853	30	34	69
Neo-peronistas	620,225	7	8	16
Movimiento Intransigente Reformista (MIR) (Frondizi)	587,790	7	7	16
Federation of Center Parties	476,009	5	4	10
Unión Cívica Radical del Intransigente (UCRI)	411,827	5	1	10
Partido Demócrata Progresista (PDP)	288,568	3	3	9
Partido Demócrata Cristiano (PDC)	248,868	3	0	4
Unión del Pueblo Argentino (UDELPA)	183,863	2	0	5
Partido Socialista Argentino (PSA)	181,034	2	1	4
Partido Socialista Democratico (PSD)	172,295	2	0	2
Provincial and local parties	269,724	3	5	11
			99	192

The Unión Popular received 31% of the vote, which was the most outstanding example of peronista popular support since the dictatorship of Perón. It did notably well in Buenos Aires Province, the Federal Capital and Córdoba Province, the three most heavily populated electoral districts. The neo-peronistas continued their inroads on the national electorate and demonstrated a consistency by receiving 7% of the vote (as they did in 1963). Thus the combined peronista–neo-peronista vote hovers about 38%. The governing UCRP received 30% of the vote and Frondizi's MIR 7%. All other parties reached new lows of 5% or less. . . .

The 1965 elections again reiterated the inescapable fact that peronismo is not only a force completely in its own right but that neither the Radical nor the Socialist groupings can begin to absorb the peronista masses. Thus the peronista "presence" continues to influence the political picture overwhelmingly not only in the area of party tactics and political feasibility but in policy changes and in institutional engineering.

Since the 1965 elections the peronistas have been extremely careful to maintain a sense of harmony within Argentina's political structure. The party has co-operated in the Chamber of Deputies, it has conferred informally with the military hierarchy, and it has tried to convince various business groups and diplomatic circles of its non-revolutionary character. Moreover, to ease political tensions, the peronistas have tentatively decided to adopt the denomination of Unión Popular as the exclusive and only organization to represent peronismo in the country. Thus they would reject, for an indefinite period, any attempts to compete under the doctrinaire Justicialista label which has continuously been outlawed since 1955. What this has amounted to has been the loss of a skirmish over a name but the winning of a major political battle which has left intact the fundamental criteria of peronismo.

The peronistas have three visible factions. The first and most important is the syndicalist section, which is dominated by leaders of the powerful metallurgical and textile unions. This gives the party great mass support at its command as well as vast resources from the funds of the General Confederation of Labor (CGT) whose leadership is completely in peronista hands. It is the richest, largest, and most influential of the sectors. Its members are the "hard-line" peronistas within the movement, men who would like to recover for themselves the benefits of the peronista decade and who, as individuals, suffered under the post-Perón military repressions and interventions into the CGT. These are, by and large, unswerving, die-hard peronistas. The basis for this group's strength unquestionably lies in the Greater Buenos Aires belt of industrial towns just outside the Capital and within the province of Buenos Aires.

The second group is made up of the so-called political peronistas, or those politicians whose grass-roots support comes from such urban areas as the Capital and the cities of Córdoba and Rosario (Santa Fe province). These are generally not trade unionists but usually middle-class professionals, essentially lawyers, who constitute the preponderance of intellectual leadership between the syndicalists and neo-peronistas. This sector

counts as well on the support of disenchanted former international socialists, academicians, and idealists of one or another variety.

The third and most controversial group has given rise to the movement known as neo-peronismo. It is essentially a rural, provincially based,
moderate, nationalistically-oriented grouping of peronistas. They constitute that element of peronismo that is not ideologically well anchored
and that could move in a variety of directions—running the gamut of
the political spectrum. They certainly are the least class-conscious part of
the movement and have received the blessings of some traditionally anti-
peronista sectors of society. Their leadership encompasses middle-class elements and even includes many an aristocratic name. This group has
achieved preponderant positions of strength in the provinces of Mendoza,
Tucumán, Chaco, Jujuy, Salta, Neuquén and San Juan. . . .

The syndicalist wing subscribes to an economic policy that advocates
nationalization of the banking system, a greater preponderance of the CGT
within officialdom, a freeze on prices and rents, a mammoth urban renewal
program, and a large-scale land reform. In the political arena it proposes a
universal amnesty for all exiled or "retired" political and military leaders—
which, of course, includes Juan Perón. The other two factions find this
program in consonance with their general views. They, however, will probably have to wield their influence in restraining possible syndicalist parliamentary walkouts, personality assaults on other deputies and inflammatory
statements that could only create tension among the military under whose
watchful eye all must serve. After years in opposition, the staunchly rigid
syndicalists may find that they functioned better in that atmosphere. The
neo-peronistas with some limited parliamentary experience are, however,
making their influence felt. Meanwhile the political peronistas provide the
cement for this larger commitment to parliamentary solutions. Thus each
one of these three identifiable sectors has potentialities of aggregating
other political party nuclei. For example there is evidence that in the 1965
elections the peronistas attracted Argentine Socialists, Christian Democratic and UCRI votes, no doubt because of the particular political appeal of the syndicalists, political peronistas and neo-peronistas respectively.
Of course, as a party, the Unión Popular has given indication of an ag-
gregative nature when in 1963 it represented the essential bloc within the
conglomeration of parties that made up the Frente Nacional y Popular.

Juan Perón still represents the single most important cog within the
peronista movement. He remains *de jure* leader if not in *de facto* control
of the movement's day-to-day policies and decisions. Should a peronista-
sponsored amnesty law be passed, the way would be open for Perón's return to Argentina. All things being equal, it is unlikely that Perón will
want to return to the country and more unlikely that he relishes the
thought of taking over direct command of the movement he . . . founded.

CONCLUSION

Peronism, despite its name, is not merely a personalistic political aberration. It is a standard political response to a particular kind of crisis of change to which only certain countries are susceptible. The Germani selection included here discusses the social class and social psychological aspects of the growth of Peronism in a comparative frame and concludes that the experience reflected particular Argentine problems of class relations and could not be directly compared with the Italian and German totalitarian experiences. The Romero analysis accents the ideological content of the movement, specifically relating the verbiage of Peronism to its counterparts in European ideology. The description by Bagú of the international relations of the Perón government sarcastically but effectively underscores the distance between words and action. And the last selection, that by Ranis, written when Italian Fascism and German Nazism had become historical specters, studies the lasting political importance of the Peronist kind of politics within Argentina even after the personalistic dictator was exiled. Our concluding question is whether this particular political happening has relevance for other Latin American countries, or perhaps even for lands at a far cultural and geographical remove that find themselves with roughly the same kinds of developmental problems.

Perhaps the closest parallel to Peronism in Argentina that has appeared thus far is not any Latin American phenomenon but Nasserism in Egypt. Nasserism is a populist, developmentalist, militarily supported collectivist ideology that has attraction for many Latin American army officers. Like Peronism, Nasserism promotes unionism, social security, industrialization, and other elements of social and economic development in such a way as not to disturb the social structure. Both movements narrow the social distance between groups but do not upset their rank order. In short, Nasserism and Peronism are closely related political phenomena, despite differences stemming from dissimilar national conditions. And the fact that such similar responses have already occurred in two countries suggests that other countries may undergo the same sort of experience in the future.

In Latin America, Brazil, Mexico, Venezuela, Chile, and Colombia have, like Argentina, large urban complexes, rapidly increasing literacy, expanding populations, fairly large industrial and service occupational groups, powerful military establishments, and difficulties of economic development. Brazil, of all these countries the one that politically most closely resembles Argentina, may already have had an experience with Peronism; the regime of Getúlio Vargas and the military coups of the post–World

War II era have many of the earmarks of the Argentine events. Mexico, on the other hand, seems to have avoided the Peronist response in recent decades and seems unlikely to turn to it in the near future; although it is employing some corporativist organizational devices and manages to contain labor as effectively as the Perón government, its ideology and self-perception remain different and its economic development healthy. Chile has continued to resist authoritarian solutions to its problems and has been little stained by Falangist thought or practice. Colombia and Venezuela are as yet insufficiently urbanized or economically developed to have a free-floating and thus "available" labor mass recruitable to neo-Peronist banners. These countries all differ from Argentina in too many ways for anyone to predict flatly that a corporate state supported by military and clerical authority of the Peronist type is for them a historically necessary future development. However, they resemble Argentina enough so that the Peronist response distinctly seems like one of the available alternatives to democratic national cohesion as they follow the difficult path toward modernization.

As Germani indicates, the alternative to the authoritarian nationalism of Peronism in Latin America is a democratic procedure for the integration of labor. He argues for meaningful education and public freedom to assure societal cohesion about the disagreeable facts of class differentiation. Social cohesion of this kind in Latin America may also demand the creation of a truly national society in which individual merit is allowed to operate to permit the weakening of class lines and the broad sharing of national political power. In the 1960's, respect for this kind of democratic solution was at a low ebb in Latin America. The left became increasingly dedicated to guerrilla activity or Stalinist or Maoist teachings; liberals and conservatives were ever more frequently acquiescing in or openly encouraging military coups; and the center parties almost everywhere had lost influence and self-confidence. Rather than living in a continent of small Soviet states— the future often predicted for them in the 1950's—most Latin Americans in the late 1960's lived under avowedly authoritarian military regimes of the right. It is a sobering and saddening thought that compared with these traditional military dictatorships of Latin America, Peronism can be considered a "progressive" authoritarianism.

BIBLIOGRAPHY

Alexander, Robert J. *The Perón Era* (New York: Russell & Russell, 1951). An early and impassioned study written journalistically. Useful for showing how Perón at the height of his political power looked to a liberal American.

Baily, Samuel H. *Labor, Nationalism, and Politics in Argentina* (New Brunswick, N.J.: Rutgers University Press, 1967). A scholarly study particularly useful for its general treatment of Argentine political history. Includes up-to-date interpretations.

Barager, Joseph R., ed. *Why Perón Came to Power: The Background to Peronism in Argentina* (New York: Alfred A. Knopf, 1967). Most of the materials in this useful collection have been translated from Argentine sources.

Blanksten, George I. *Perón's Argentina* (New York: Russell & Russell, 1953). Written in semipopular style, this book is perhaps the most important study written by a political scientist of the Perón period while that government was still in power.

Di Tella, Torcuato S. *El sistema político argentino y la clase obrera* (Buenos Aires: EUDEBA, 1964). A leading Argentine sociologist traces the relationship between political power and the working classes, with an emphasis on contemporary Argentina. The study is theoretical as well as factual, including much important information on Argentine social structure.

Fayt, Carlos S., ed. *La naturaleza del peronismo* (Buenos Aires: Abelardo Perrot, 1967). A collection of attitudes and scholarly opinions on Peronism from its inception to the present. This collection is extraordinarily useful and presents Argentine as well as North American and other Latin American opinions on Peronism.

Ferrer, Aldo. *The Argentine Economy* (Berkeley: University of California Press, 1967). An analytical study of the Argentine economy written by one of that country's leading economists. A scholarly work, with polemical strains.

Flores, María. *Woman with a Whip* (Garden City, N.Y.: Doubleday, 1952). Another contemporary account, biased, sarcastic, and journalistic in its attacks against Eva Perón.

Kennedy, John J. *Catholicism, Nationalism, and Democracy in Argentina* (Notre Dame, Ind.: University of Notre Dame Press, 1958). An attempt to show that the Catholic Church and Perón were not close partners in his rise to power. The book is also useful for political history.

McGann, Thomas F. *Argentina: The Divided Land* (Princeton, N.J.: Princeton University Press, 1966). A short history of the country, easy to use, emphasizing the difference between the capital city and provinces of the interior.

Romero, José Luis. *A History of Argentine Political Thought* (Stanford, Calif.: Stanford University Press, 1963), translated by Thomas F. McGann. A standard treatment of social thought in Argentina. The author is a former rector of the University of Buenos Aires, a Democratic Socialist leader, and an internationally recognized social historian.

Scobie, James R. *Argentina: A City and a Nation* (New York: Oxford University Press, 1964). A valuable interpretation of the general history of Argentina.

Snow, Peter G. *Argentine Radicalism* (Iowa City: University of Iowa Press, 1965). A monographic history of the Radical Civic Union in its many incarnations. The book comes almost up to date and is very useful.

Whitaker, Arthur P. *The United States and Argentina* (Cambridge, Mass.: Harvard University Press, 1955). Professor Whitaker is the best-known American historian specializing in Argentine materials. This book is his standard short history of the country.

————. *Argentine Upheaval: Perón's Fall and the New Regime* (New York: Frederick A. Praeger, 1956). A brief account of how Perón was overthrown and the immediate consequences. Written soon after the events themselves, the book is fresh but of course lacks the perspective afforded by later developments.

————. *Argentina* (Englewood Cliffs, N.J.: Prentice-Hall, 1964). A general history updating the 1955 work mentioned above.

XI

The Cuban Revolution:
A Leftist Reaction
to the Social Problems
of Latin America

Robert Freeman Smith

CHRONOLOGY

1952   March 10: General Fulgencio Batista takes power

1953   July 26: Fidel Castro leads attack on Moncada Barracks

1956   December 2: Castro and members of the 26th of July Movement land in Cuba

1957   March 13: Student and political groups attack the presidential palace; July 12: Castro issues the "Manifesto of the Sierra Maestra" and calls for the unity of anti-Batista forces

1958   February: The "Second Front of Escambray" established in central Cuba by the Directorio Revolucionario; March: United States places an embargo on arms shipments to Batista government; July 20: United front of revolutionary groups created; December 31: Batista flees Cuba

1959   January 8: Castro enters Havana; February 16: Castro becomes Prime Minister; March–April: First reform enactments; May 17: First Agrarian Reform Law signed; July: President Manuel Urrutia replaced by Osvaldo Dorticós Torrado; November: Ché Guevara replaces Felipe Pazos as head of the National Bank

1960   February: Trade agreement with the Soviet Union after visit by Anastas Mikoyan; June: U.S. oil refineries nationalized after they refuse to handle Soviet oil; July 6: U.S. drastically cuts unfilled portion of the 1960 Cuban sugar quota; July–September: Nationalization of many foreign-owned companies; September 17: U.S.-owned banks nationalized; October: U.S. places an export embargo on trade with Cuba, with food and medical supplies exempted; Cuba nationalizes almost all other U.S. concerns

1961   January: U.S. breaks relations with Cuba; April 16–19: Bay of Pigs invasion; May: Castro proclaims the socialist nature of the Revolution; July: Organization of the new national party (ORI)

1962   January: Cuba "expelled" from OAS; March: Castro denounces sectarian activities of the old-guard Communists; October: U.S.–Soviet confrontation over missiles in Cuba

1963   August: Reversal of economic policy, with re-emphasis on sugar; October: Second Agrarian Reform Law proclaimed; November: Compulsory military service instituted

1964   March: Trial and execution of old-guard Communist Marcos Rodríguez Alfonso for betrayal of student rebels in 1957; May: U.S. curbs shipments of food and drugs to Cuba

1965   February: Castro removes Carlos Rafael Rodríguez from leadership of the National Institute of Agrarian Reform and assumes the post himself; April: Ché Guevara disappears from public view; November: Refugee agreement between U.S. and Cuba; airlift begins

1966   February: Castro attacks Chinese meddling in Cuban affairs

1967   March: Castro criticizes Soviet Union for holding trade talks with other Latin American countries and declares Cuban support for guerrilla wars

INTRODUCTION

The origins and development of a revolution are a subject hardly less complex than a period of human history as a whole. To understand them is not an easy task for historians, even when the revolution they are studying is as remote as the English or the French. The contemporary Castro Revolution in Cuba, which is still in its active phase, presents problems of sources of information, perspective, and objectivity that are particularly difficult—especially because this revolution is still involved emotionally in international and domestic controversies. Analysts of the Castro Revolution must accordingly strive to present their interpretations in a nondogmatic way, and they must also keep in mind the fact that revolutions are historical developments rather than freakish occurrences to be explained in terms of demonology or dialectical "theology."

The term "revolution" has been given to historical developments that produce basic changes in the economic, social, political, and ideological structures of various areas. The term has been applied to the results of long-range changes—the "Industrial Revolution," for example—but it more aptly describes extreme accelerations of change that involve a definite shift in the power structure of a country. Revolution in this sense is a phase in the evolution of a society, but a phase characterized by turmoil, upheaval, and the compression of the historical process of change.

Prerevolutionary conditions exist in many societies. Usually, a mixture of problems has produced a pattern of instability and disunity in almost all aspects of the society. The differences between the inefficient wealthy and the resentful poor are often extreme, and severe economic fluctuation and instability, intellectual alienation, and sharp (often violent) antagonism within and between groups characteristically prevail. Revolutionary upheaval is an ever-present threat in such societies.

Any analysis of a revolution must consider the reasons why some men become active revolutionary leaders and why other men are willing to accept the leaders' version of the "brave new world." The specific problems of a society and the ways various groups interpret and react to them are the basis of all social phenomena, but a revolution actually develops when a problem-ridden society is shaken by a crisis (such as war, depression, or insurrection) and the moral authority of the political leadership declines to the point where a catalytic, revolutionary-oriented leadership can mobilize a following from among those who have lost faith—or have had no stake—in the status quo. Radical changes in the social, economic, and political structures of a country are then possible.

394

Since the turn of the century, Cuban society has exhibited symptoms of a prerevolutionary condition. The Race War of 1912 revealed that Cuba's Negroes were fundamentally antagonistic to the prevailing social system, and this was apparent again during the Revolution of 1933.[1] The latter upheaval also demonstrated that a spirit of nationalism and radical reform had developed that identified the socioeconomic problems of the country with the economic and political influence of the United States. The young men and women most responsible for the Revolution —the "Generation of '33"—had grown up in an intellectual atmosphere that emphasized national regeneration and that assumed a revolutionary orientation as a result of the economic depression of the late 1920's and the corruption and repression of President Gerardo Machado's administration (1925–33).

The triumph of the reform nationalists was short-lived. Fulgencio Batista, a former sergeant, took over the Army in September 1933 and for a time cooperated with the other groups in the revolutionary government of Ramón Grau San Martín; but he soon became convinced that his ambitions for power could better be served by reaching an accommodation with U.S. interests and the old-line, conservative politicians. In January 1934, he overthrew the Grau San Martín government, although intermittent conflict continued until the last activist groups were smashed during the General Strike of 1935.

As the central political figure for the next decade, Batista, the "Cinderella Colonel," did promote some limited reforms. He also sponsored the drafting of a new constitution in 1940, which provided the legal basis for land reform, for national control of mineral resources, and for a guaranteed annual income for all citizens. The fresh promise of reform in every area of Cuban life and the prosperity of the World War II years seemed to create a kind of stability. In 1944 Batista permitted unregulated elections, and Grau San Martín was returned to power.

Expectations of change surged as a result of Grau's election, but the "tired reformers" and "tamed revolutionaries" of his Auténtico party (Party of the Authentic Revolution) did relatively little during his administration (1944–48) or that of his successor, Carlos Prío Socarrás (1948–52), to implement the reform provisions of the Constitution of 1940. Some privileged labor unions received government support for their wage and job-security demands, but very little was done about land reform or the problems of the underemployed and unemployed (who comprised nine per cent of the population, even in prosperous years). While the cause of

---

[1] The 1953 census classified 12.4 per cent of the population (5,829,029 total) as Negro and 14.5 per cent as mixed. The term "nigger" had by then become part of the vocabulary of white Cubans, reflecting the impact of U.S. racial concepts.

reform languished, official corruption increased between 1944 and 1952.

The two Auténtico administrations devoted considerable effort to waging the Cold War inside Cuba. This activity had little to do with the revolutionary nature of the Cuban Communists, since the party (known as the Popular Socialist party, or PSP) was not pursuing revolutionary tactics. The PSP had actually formed part of Batista's political coalition, and through control of several important labor unions it helped to mobilize support for the Colonel's candidates. After 1944 the PSP declined in strength, but it continued to work through the legislative branch to advance proposals to improve the conditions of organized labor and to secularize education. The main element in the Auténtico–PSP struggle was not Communism but the ambition of the Auténticos to control the labor movement for their own political advantage. The Auténticos were generally successful in this endeavor, although the Communists did retain some influence in several unions.

A significant development during the Auténtico period was the growing alienation of young nationalistic intellectuals. Under the leadership of Eduardo Chibás, a group broke with the Auténticos and formed the Ortodoxo party. The frustration of this group with traditional Cuban politics was symbolized by the dramatic suicide of Chibás in 1951. Fidel Castro entered Cuban politics through the Ortodoxo party and was one of the party's congressional candidates in the election that Batista canceled when he returned to power in the quick, bloodless coup of March 1952.

Cuban social unity became even weaker during the postwar years. Conflict within and between groups grew in intensity. Rival cliques in the universities, the police, and the labor movement fought each other for power, and some politicians even maintained private armies. Assassination and other forms of violence were in evidence at all levels of political life. Batista's decision to seize power in 1952 was due at least in part to his belief that he alone could save Cuba from chaos and the threat of radicalism. Numerous Cubans agreed with him, and some business publications welcomed Batista's new and dictatorial regime as a way to save Cuba from socialism.

Initially, Batista's authoritarian rule seemed to provide more social stability in Cuba, but it also served as a stimulus and a clearcut focal point for violent activities by the country's alienated intellectuals. Batista became the symbol for all the problems of Cuba, and the ensuing campaign to overthrow his regime directed the activities of the intellectuals into revolutionary channels. The first sign of this development came on July 26, 1953, when Fidel Castro and 160 "compadres" attacked the Moncada Barracks in Santiago. In the proclamation that was to have been read after the victory, Castro declared that the youth of the revolutionary vanguard wanted a "new Cuba" based on the ideals of José Martí, Antonio Guiteras, and Eduardo Chibás.[2] The attack, however, was a complete failure. Several participants were killed—some later, by torture. Castro and a number of other survivors were sent to prison.

The Batista regime did not feel threatened by these early difficulties. In a mood of supreme confidence, Batista declared a general amnesty in May 1955. Castro went to Mexico and began to organize a revolutionary group, which he named the 26th of July Movement in honor of the attack on the Moncada Barracks. Other symptoms of discontent began to appear in Cuba itself during 1956. An army conspiracy led by Colonel Ramón Barquín was uncovered and aborted in April. Student demonstrations broke out in Santiago and were suppressed violently; another group staged a futile attack on the Giocuria Barracks in Matanzas.

Late in November, Fidel Castro and eighty-two dedicated revolutionaries sailed from Mexico in the *Granma*. Their landing in Cuba was supposed to have coincided with uprisings in various towns of eastern Cuba, but weather conditions delayed them. The 26th of July Movement forces in Santiago, led by Frank País, did manage to take control of the city for a brief time, but this and uprisings elsewhere were quickly crushed. Castro's seaborne expedition was almost wiped out; only thirteen survivors finally reached the safety of the Sierra Maestra.

During 1957, Castro and his small band of guerrilla fighters in the mountains became the dramatic symbol of the growing opposition to the Batista regime. Several other groups actively fought Batista. The Federación Estudiantil Universitaria (Federation of University Students) and the Directorio Revolucionario were the most important; in conjunction with a group of Auténticos, these two groups attacked the presidential palace on March 13, 1957. The rebels hoped to assassinate Batista, but the details of the plot had been betrayed, and more than fifty of the rebels were killed.[3] In February 1958, the Directorio landed a small group of rebels in central Cuba and established the "Second Front of Escambray."

The prestige of the Batista regime rapidly declined during 1958 as the secret police tried to intimidate the opposition through terrorism. Various elements in Cuban society either withdrew support from Batista or retreated to a position of calculated neutrality. The Government faced a crisis of confidence, and this was increasingly reflected in sagging morale in the Army. During the fall of 1958, the Army virtually evaporated

---

[2] José Martí (1853–95) was a great writer and the hero of Cuban Independence. Antonio Guiteras was the leader of the Young Cuba Movement, which participated in the 1933 Revolution. He was killed during the General Strike of 1935. Chibás, as we have seen, was the founder of the Ortodoxo party.

[3] The plot was betrayed by members of the Communist youth group. In 1964, this incident was resurrected and served as a focal point for the conflict between old-guard Communists and other factions in the Cuban Government, and a former leader of the youth group, Marcos Rodríguez Alfonso, was tried and executed.

through desertion and the surrender of entire units by their officers to Castro's guerrilla forces, which now were moving out of the Sierra Maestra.

Opposition to Batista provided a unity among Cubans that was more apparent than real. The motivations and objectives of the dictator's enemies varied widely. Some Cubans became opponents of Batista because he had lost his efficiency and had become a symbolic target for organized revolutionary activity; their objective was simply the elimination of the military symbol and the restoration of the pre-1952 situation. Other Cubans wanted some political reforms mixed with some orthodox economic measures that hopefully would promote development. Still other groups had very specific objectives; the Roman Catholic hierarchy, for example, wanted state support for church schools, and some labor unions wanted a substantial increase in wages.

The active revolutionary groups placed more emphasis on socioeconomic reform. In reality, they were divided over the question of how extensively the economic and political systems of the island would have to be changed in order to promote development and improve the conditions of the lower class. Such a basic divergence of views concerning the nature and extent of future reforms hampered attempts to form a united front of opposition organizations.[4]

Cuba's active revolutionaries can be separated into three general factions, although this separation was relatively obscure until mid-1959. These factions cut across organizational lines.[5] One faction believed that socioeconomic reform could be promoted within the institutional framework of republican government and private-enterprise capitalism (or a modified version thereof). In addition, this faction would not accept any cooperation with the Communists. A second faction believed that substantial reform required a radical change in Cuba's political and economic systems and regarded cooperation with the Communists as a necessity. The third faction wanted radical reform but had less clear-cut ideas about the institutional changes required. As for cooperation with the Communists, this third group was flexible and tended to see the issue in terms of whether or not the Communists would cooperate with them.

---

[4] In Miami, Florida, in July 1957, a unity program was adopted, but Castro repudiated it. A kind of united front finally was proclaimed by the "Pact of Caracas" in July 1958, but the program outlined by the Pact was quite ill defined.

[5] The most important *organizations* (as opposed to factions) were the 26th of July Movement, the Directorio Revolucionario, the Civic Resistance Movement, and the Student Federation.

An aged *guajiro* tells Premier Castro that he wants a pension so he can start a cocoa business.

On January 1, 1959, the Batista government fell, and on February 16, Fidel Castro became Prime Minister. In the year that followed, the issue of Communist cooperation became the touchstone of a widening gulf separating Cuba's active revolutionaries. Political conflict (internal and external) stemming from the reform program produced a rapid metamorphosis in the three revolutionary factions. By early 1960, two clear-cut positions stood forth, and these were labeled pro- and anti-Castro. The Communists themselves, who were divided over many of the same general issues as the revolutionaries, were also torn by the question of collaboration and whether or not to subordinate the party to the leadership of the revolutionaries. Some old-line party members feared that the young rebels were too radical and impatient.

This internal political factionalism and conflict, in combination with a climate of aroused hope—sharpened by past frustration—and the revolutionary mystique surrounding Fidel Castro and his *barbudos*, or bearded followers, provided an important dynamic for the still ill-defined Revolution. Far-reaching reforms generated by the inner core of dedicated revolutionaries were instituted, producing opposition and a polarization of Cuban politics. These developments also led to increased external conflict with the United States. Some of the revolutionaries had feared that the U.S. would react in a hostile manner to basic reforms. The U.S. response to the Agrarian Reform Law was a curt note demanding "prompt, adequate, and effective compensation" for any properties of North Americans expropriated by the Cuban Government. This reaction and the effective efforts of the State Department in blocking arms purchases by the Cuban Government after counterrevolutionary attacks had begun seemed to confirm these fears. Anti-imperialist sentiments were thus soon added to the growing mystique of revolutionary nationalism.

During the latter half of 1959, the revolutionaries began to develop a movement of ideological and programmatic unity, with Fidel Castro as the symbolic—and actual—center of revolutionary loyalty. Dissenting groups either dropped out or were eliminated from positions of power in the political and economic life of the country. This process continued throughout 1960 and 1961 and into 1962. At the same time, the Revolution moved from vague social-reformism (with a wide diversity of orientations) to the pursuit of a completely changed socioeconomic system. Disagreement began to take place within a generally Marxist framework (with all of its Cuban variations). But while the nature and techniques of group conflict changed, conflict itself did not disappear; it still exists within the new framework and concerns the policies and orientation of the revolutionary government. Some questions—such as the fundamental alteration of the economic system—have been settled, but many new questions have arisen, and the resulting disagreement continues to shape the nature of the Revolution.

READINGS

Cuban Views
of the Castro Revolution

1. An Exile Interpretation, 1960

The major themes found in most of the Cuban exiles' interpretations of Castro's revolution are present in a book by Fermín Peinado, the former Dean of the Law School of the University of Oriente. Fidel Castro is portrayed as a gangster turned Communist conspirator solely for reasons of power or status—hence the aside in the following selection about the circumstances of Castro's birth.

At no time did the regime really want American aid. The anti-American propaganda campaign started in the Sierra. We cannot forget the kidnap of American citizens, some of whom were helping Castro, by order of the rebel commander. Anti-Americanism was evident from the start with the persecution of anticommunism. In the "Second Front of Frank País" anticommunist leaders like Major Nino Díaz were taken prisoner and barely escaped death. Anticommunist leaders were always placed in dangerous positions to die, like Frank País in Santiago de Cuba. From the Sierra the stage was set for anti-American propaganda and "counterrevolutionary" suspicions were hurled against "noncommunists." And in January 1959 official communistic indoctrination courses were deliberately started with mimeographed textbooks, placing emphasis on anti-Yankeeism. The United States could do nothing to win over a regime that had no other *raison d'être* but to serve as an instrument of the Soviet Union. Anyone who says otherwise does not know what he is talking about.

. . .

Fidel Castro belonged to groups of university "gangsters" in his student days, having been a member of the Revolutionary Insurrectionist Union. In the adventure at Cayo Confites against Dictator Trujillo, he was a subordinate of the notorious Rolando Masferrer, former communist and

source: "An Exile Interpretation, 1960" from Fermín Peinado, *Beware, Yankee: The Revolution in Cuba* (Miami, Fla.: Frente Revolucionario Democrático, 1961), pp. 12–13.

later a supporter of Dictator Batista.[1] He took part in the famous "bogotazo" (Bogotá riots of 1948) hand in hand with the Communist Party. His social position, for reasons I do not feel it necessary to mention, "was not good."[2] Because Castro was little known and Dictator Batista was wholly repudiated, after Castro came into the public limelight at the time of the attack on Moncada Barracks in 1953, his shady background did not prevent his deification by the Cuban people.

2. Ché Guevara Discusses the Problems and Potential Struggles of the Revolution, 1959

Until his departure from Cuba in 1965, the late Marxist Ernesto "Ché" Guevara generally was considered to be the chief theoretician of the Revolution. A native of Argentina and one of the thirteen survivors of the 1957 expedition, he had been converted into a revolutionary by his experience in Guatemala during the U.S.-backed coup which deposed the Jacobo Arbenz government in 1954.

The first difficulty is that our new actions must be engaged in on the old foundations. Cuba's antipeople regime and army are already destroyed, but the dictatorial social system and economic foundations have not yet been abolished. Some of the old people are still working within the national structure. In order to protect the fruits of the revolutionary victory and to enable the unending development of the revolution we need to take another step forward in our work to rectify and strengthen the government. Second, what the new government took over was a rundown mess. When Batista fled he cleaned out the national treasury, leaving serious difficulties in the national finances. We must work very hard in order to keep intact the balance of foreign exchange, otherwise our national currency will be depreciated. Third, Cuba's land system is one in which *latifundistas*[1] hold large amounts of land, while

[1] [The Cayo Confites episode was a 1947 plot by a group of Cubans to overthrow President Rafael Trujillo of the Dominican Republic. The Cuban Government broke up the expedition, but Castro managed to escape.]
[2] [This is a reference to Castro's illegitimate birth.]

[1] [Owners of large estates.]
SOURCE: "Ché Guevara Discusses the Problems and Potential Struggles of the Revolution, 1959" from "A New Old Ché Guevara Interview," translated by William E. Ratliff, in *Hispanic American Historical Review*, 46, No. 3 (August 1966), pp. 294–97. Reprinted by permission of Duke University Press.

at the same time many people are unemployed. We cannot process our underground ore reserves ourselves, but must depend upon foreign companies to ship the reserves abroad for processing. Ours is a monocultural economy in which it is essential for us to grow sugar cane. Our foreign trade is also monocultural. The United States controls Cuban trade; consequently, national industries are smothered because of United States competition. Smuggling is very serious. Commodity prices are very high. Fourth, there is still racial discrimination in our society which is not beneficial to efforts to achieve the internal unification of the people. Fifth, our house rents are the highest in the world; a family frequently has to pay over a third of its income for rent. To sum up, the reform of the foundations of the economy of the Cuban society is very difficult and will take a long time.

. . .

We must work for national industrialization without neglecting any of the problems that arise therefrom. Industrialization requires the adoption of protective measures for new industries, and an internal market of consumers for the new products. For instance, if we do not open the main door of the market to the *guajiros* [2] who have consumer needs but no buying power, there is no way to expand the internal market.

Events do not entirely depend on us; we will meet with the opposition of the people who control over seventy-five percent of our national trade. Facing this kind of danger, we must prepare to adopt countermeasures, like a doubly enlarged foreign market. We will need to establish a merchant marine fleet, to transport sugar, tobacco, and other products, because transportation expenses of a merchant marine fleet in a large degree affect the progress of backward nations like Cuba.

What is the most important thing if we want to carry out our industrialization successfully? It is raw materials. Because of Batista's dictatorial government, the country's raw materials are all delivered over to the hands of his foreign co-plotters. We cannot fail to redeem our country's raw materials, our ore reserves. Another element of industrialization is electric power. We pledge that electrical power will be returned to the people.

. . .

The Cuban Revolution is not a class revolution, but a liberation movement that has overthrown a dictatorial, tyrannical government. The people detested the American-supported Batista dictatorial government from the bottoms of their hearts and so rose up and overthrew it. The revolutionary government has received the broad support of all strata of people because its economic measures have taken care of the requirements of all and have

[2] [Guajiro: the highland peasant who subsisted on a small amount of land; in recent usage, the term has been applied to all marginal rural inhabitants.]

gradually improved the livelihood of the people. The only enemies remaining in the country are the latifundistas and the reactionary bourgeoisie. They oppose the land reform that goes against their own interests. These internal reactionary forces may get in league with the developing provocations of the foreign reactionary forces and attack the revolutionary government.

The only foreign enemies who oppose the Cuban Revolution are the people who monopolize capital and who have representatives in the United States State Department. The victory and continuous development of the Cuban revolution has caused these people to panic. They do not willingly accept defeat and are doing everything possible to maintain their control over the Cuban government and economy and to block the great influence of the Cuban Revolution on the people's struggles in the other Latin American countries.

3. *Fidel Castro's Concept*
of the Goals of the Revolution
and the Threat from Abroad, 1960

> One major theme in this speech flows from Castro's socioeconomic, rather than political, interpretation of democracy. Castro believed that the system of republican government was a major impediment to basic reform; as he told a *New York Times* correspondent, Tad Szulc, the growing opposition to reform convinced him that elections would provide the status-quo groups with a tool to divide and confuse the people over the question of reform. A second theme in the speech is Castro's belief that the U.S. was determined to destroy the Revolution.

This is democracy, where you, farmer, are given the land that we have recovered from usurious foreign hands that used to exploit it. Democracy is *this*, where you, the sugar plantation workers, receive 80,000 *caballerías* of land in order that you shall not have to live in *guardarrayas*.[1]

This is democracy, where you, worker, are guaranteed the right to work, so that you cannot be thrown out on the streets to go hungry.

---

[1] [Caballería: approximately 33.16 acres. Guardarrayas: strips of idle land that separate the cane fields of a plantation.]

SOURCE: "Fidel Castro's Concept of the Goals of the Revolution and the Threat from Abroad, 1960" from Fidel Castro, *Labor Day Address About the Destiny of Cuba, May 1, 1960* (Havana: Cooperativa Obrera de Publicidad, 1960), pp. 9–10, 14, 16–17, 21.

Democracy is *this*, where you, students, have the opportunity to win a university degree if you are intelligent, even though you may not be rich.

Democracy is *this*, where you, whether you are the son of a worker, the son of a farmer, or the son of any other humble family, have a teacher to educate you and a school where you can be taught.

Democracy is *this*, where you, old man, have your sustenance guaranteed after you can no longer depend on your own effort.

Democracy is *this*, where you, Cuban Negro, have the right to work without anybody being able to deprive you of that right because of stupid prejudice.

Democracy is *this*, where the women acquire rights equal to those of all other citizens and have a right even to bear arms alongside the men to defend their country.

Democracy is *this*, in which a government converts its fortresses into schools, and in which a government wants to build a house for every family so that every family can have a roof of their own over their heads.

Democracy is *this*—a government that wants every invalid to have a doctor's care.

.   .   .

Democracy is *this*, that which gives a gun to the farmers, gives a gun to the workers, gives a gun to the students, gives a gun to the women, gives a gun to the Negroes, gives a gun to the poor, and gives a gun to any other citizen who is willing to defend a just cause.

.   .   .

But [all] this does not mean that the rights of others are not taken into account. The rights of others count just as the rights of the majority count, in proportion to the extent to which the rights of the majority count, but the *rights* of the majority should prevail above the *privileges* of minorities.

.   .   .

Why does our government have to be anathematized, isolated, and threatened by destruction and death? Why does a government that has done only good for its people have to be anathematized, and why do all the diplomatic big brass of a powerful nation move to destroy it? Why do they mobilize thousands of intrigues of the reactionary press and the reactionary news agencies and spread them all over the world?

Why did they not concern themselves with us before? Why did they not concern themselves with the Cuban people while hundreds of thousands of families here were living in miserable huts? Why did they not concern themselves with our people when there was such poverty here, when the *guajiros* lived in guardarrayas, subsisting by planting a yucca plant and a malanga plant and a plant of boniato?

Why did they not concern themselves with the affairs of Cuba, why did they not worry about the problems of Cuba, when in our country young men were found assassinated in the streets and when the police stations and the prisons were torture chambers and farmers were assassinated *en masse?* Why did they not concern themselves with Cuba while there was so much injustice and so much abuse committed? Why did all this merit not a line in any of those newspapers that today so attack our revolution? Why?

.   .   .

They want, simply, to destroy our revolution in order to continue exploiting the other nations of Latin America.

In that way they want our Cuban people to "pay the freight" on the crimes that are being committed against other peoples. They want us to pay the price for them to be able to exploit other peoples. That is to say, they want to destroy us, because we have had the desire to liberate ourselves economically. They want to destroy us because we have desired to do justice. They want to destroy us because we have concerned ourselves with the humble of our land, because we have cast our lot with the poor of our country, because we have remembered the guajiro who had no land, because we have remembered the child who had no school, because we have remembered the worker who had no job, because we have remembered the family who lived in a hut, because we have remembered the sick who had no doctor, because we have remembered the student who had no books and no resources. Because we have remembered justice.

As though certain people of the world were obliged to live in wretchedness, backwardness, and exploitation! As though certain nations were obliged to wear a yoke over their shoulders and around their necks! As though certain nations were obliged to be slaves of others!

.   .   .

The most reasonable, the most sane, the most intelligent thing that could be done by those who do not want to resign themselves to this revolution would be exactly to resign themselves, because this revolution is a reality. It would be intelligent for them to leave us in peace. Otherwise, in the senseless attempt to destroy the revolution, they will lose much more than they have already lost.

Realities do not arise in the world through someone's whim. Revolutions, real revolutions, do not arise by the will of one man or one group. Revolutions are realities that obey other realities. Revolutions are remedies —bitter remedies, yes. But at times revolution is the only remedy that can be applied to evils even more bitter. The Cuban revolution is a reality in the world. The Cuban revolution is already a reality for the history of the world.

4. The Internal Struggle for Influence Between the Old-Guard Communists and the Fidelistas, 1962

During 1961 and early 1962, some of the old-guard Communists (former members of the PSP) had begun to take over key posts in various government agencies and the ORI (the official party). After several months of silence, Castro struck at those he felt to be responsible for this development, accusing them of fomenting disunity in the name of ideological purity and Marxist legitimacy.

[Castro's Speech of March 26, 1962]

One of the fundamental problems produced in the struggle against reactionary ideas, against conservative ideas, against the deserters, against those who wavered, against those with negative attitudes, was sectarianism. It may be said that it was the fundamental error produced by that struggle of an ideological nature which was being waged.

That type of error was produced by the conditions in which the revolutionary process developed, and by the serious and fundamental struggle which revolutionary ideas had to wage against conservative elements and against reactionary ideas.

What tendency was manifesting itself? An opposite tendency began to manifest itself. The tendency to mistrust everybody, the tendency to mistrust everyone who could not claim a long record of revolutionary militancy, who had not been an old Marxist militant.

.   .   .

We believe that *compañero* Aníbal Escalante [1] has had a lot to do with the conversion of sectarianism into a system, with the conversion of sectarianism into a virus, into a veritable sickness during this process.

.   .   .

[1] [Compañero (Comrade) Aníbal Escalante was a member of the Communist party prior to 1959 and became the Secretary in Charge of Organization of the ORI. In this capacity, he gave the important posts to his PSP colleagues and downgraded many of those who had fought actively against Batista. Castro was especially concerned over these demotions; hence his later remarks about Guillermo García, Sergio del Valle, and Haydée Santamaría. The ORI (Organizaciones Revolucionarias Integradas, inte-

source: "Castro's Speech of March 26, 1962" from Fidel Castro, *Fidel Castro Denounces Bureaucracy and Sectarianism* (New York: Fair Play for Cuba Committee, 1962), pp. 7–8, 14–15, 21–22, 36–37. Reprinted by permission of Merit Publishers.

Compañero Aníbal Escalante had schemed to make himself the ORI. How? By the use of a very simple contrivance. Working from his post as Secretary in Charge of Organization he would give instructions to all revolutionary cells and to the whole apparatus as if these instructions had come from the National Directorate.

.   .   .

Because of this there developed from top to bottom—don't imagine that this happened in a matter of weeks, it took months to develop—a truly abnormal, truly absurd, intolerable, chaotic, anarchic process; people were possessed of a mania for giving orders, of an eagerness to decide all problems.

.   .   .

I am going to cite some examples, I am going to cite an example from Oriente Province of a certain gentleman who is Secretary, or was Secretary of the Sectional Committee of Bayamo and who was later appointed ORI Secretary of no less than of a group of peoples' farms of El Cauto. . . .

When the list of compañeros who had been appointed to the National Directorate appeared, this gentleman . . . took the liberty of making comments like the following when he saw the list: "What is this filthy fat man doing here?"—he was referring to compañero Aragonés. He also used another word which I don't want to repeat in public. "And who is this Guillermo García?" he said. "Where did this person come from?" "And this Sergio del Valle, who is he?" "And this Haydée Santamaría, what is she doing here?" Those were the observations made by this individual.

Who was this individual? Why didn't he know Haydée Santamaría? Why didn't he know Guillermo García? Why didn't he know Sergio del Valle? Why didn't he know anybody? Simply because when the people were fighting here, he was under the bed.

.   .   .

From the Cauto River this gentleman was only a day's march from the Sierra Maestra. It shouldn't have been too much for him to grab a knapsack, when Cowley[2] was murdering workers and *campesinos;*[3] when Cowley murdered Loynas Echevarría and so many other militant revolutionists whom he killed in a cowardly and cruel manner in a single night;

grated revolutionary organizations) was an attempt to bring what were currently the three major revolutionary groups together into one national party. These were the Directorio Revolucionario, the PSP (Communist party), and the 26th of July Movement. ORI was reorganized into the PURS (United Party of the Socialist Revolution), and this was later renamed simply the Communist party of Cuba.]

[2] [Cowley was the head of Batista's secret police.]

[3] [Campesinos: peasants.]

when the workers, the campesinos, the students were being murdered by the thousands, and he had only to walk one day in order to join the revolutionary forces.

• • •

Those are the consequences of anti-communism, of harrassment; they engender sectarianism. Once anti-communism is wiped out, if extreme sectarianism still remains, it will once again give rise to anti-communism and to confusion. Because many people will ask: "Is this communism? Is this Marxism? Is this socialism?—This arbitrariness, this abuse, this privilege, all this, is this communism?"

"If this is communism," they will say along with the Indian Hatuey, "then. . . ." When the Indian Hatuey was being burned at the stake, a priest came up to him to ask him if he wanted to go to heaven, and he said, "No, I don't want to go to heaven if heaven is all of this." Do you understand me? I have to speak clearly.[4]

• • •

But, gentlemen, what is the revolution? The revolution is superior to what each of us may have done. It is superior and it is more important than each of the organizations that were here: the 26th [of July Movement], the Partido Socialista Popular, the Directorio—than all of them. The revolution by itself is much more important than all that.

What is the revolution? It is a great trunk which has its roots. Those roots, coming from different directions, were united in the trunk. The trunk begins to grow. The roots are important, but what begins to grow is the trunk of a great tree, of a very tall tree, whose roots came together and were joined in the trunk. All of us together made the trunk. The growing of the trunk is all that remains for us to foster and together we will continue to make it grow.

[Castro's Speech of March 13, 1962]

Compañeros, could we be so cowardly, and could we be so intellectually warped, as to come here to read the political testament of José Antonio Echevarría and be so cowardly, so morally wretched, as to suppress three lines? Just because these three lines are an idiomatic expression

[4] [Hatuey was a prominent chief who came to Cuba during the Spanish conquest to help lead the Indian resistance. The incident referred to happened when the Spaniards were preparing to execute Hatuey. The priest was trying to convert the chief, but Hatuey preferred to die with uncertainty rather than risk a heaven peopled with Spanish Christians.]

SOURCE: "Castro's Speech of March 13, 1962" from Fidel Castro, *The Revolution Must be a School of Unfettered Thought* (New York: Fair Play for Cuba Committee, 1962), pp. 6–9. Reprinted by permission of Merit Publishers.

or José Antonio Echevarría's way of thinking which we have no business analyzing? [1]

Are we going to mutilate what he wrote? Are we going to mutilate what he believed? And are we going to feel crushed merely by what he believed or thought in the matter of religion?

.   .   .

If we followed that line of thinking we would have to destroy the concept of the revolutionist from Spartacus to Martí. As a result of that short-sighted, sectarian, stupid, and warped concept, which denies history and denies Marxism, we would be forced to deny all values, all history. We would be forced to deny our very roots. . . .

.   .   .

It is known that a revolutionist may hold a religious belief. He may hold it. The revolution does not force anyone. It does not go into his heart of hearts. It does not exclude the men who love their country, the men who want justice to exist in their country, justice which will put an end to exploitation, abuse and odious imperialist domination. It does not force them. Nor does it hold them in disgrace simply because they may have in their heart of hearts some religious belief.

.   .   .

We say that in the struggle for national liberation, in the struggle against imperialism, all progressive elements, all patriotic elements, should be united and that in that front there should be not only the sincere Catholic, who has nothing to do with imperialism or with *latifundismo*, but also the old Marxist fighter.

5. Guevara Discusses the Internal Conflict over Economic Policy, 1964

As Minister of Industry from 1961 to 1965, Ché Guevara was always noted for his frank analysis of the economic problems of the country and the policy errors of the Government. The mixed results of the regime's first economic measures produced sharp disagreement among government officials and provided the background for the 1963 de-

[1] [Castro's defense of José Antonio Echevarría (killed in the 1957 attempt to assassinate Batista) was provoked when the man who was reading Echevarría's political testament deliberately omitted the lines concerning faith in God. Castro emphasized the idea that social unity must be built around loyalty to the Revolution rather than around a set of dogmatic propositions.]

SOURCE: "Guevara Discusses the Internal Conflict over Economic Policy, 1964" from Ernesto "Ché" Guevara, "The Cuban Economy: Its Past, and Its Future," in *International Affairs* (London), 40, No. 4 (October 1964), pp. 592–95, 598. Reprinted by permission of the publishers.

cision, probably influenced by the Soviet Union, to reemphasize sugar production and to concentrate on industries that required less importation of raw materials.

. . .

The two main economic problems of the Cuban Revolution during its first months were unemployment and a shortage of foreign currencies. The first was an acute political problem, but the second was more dangerous, given the enormous dependence of Cuba on foreign trade.

. . .

Our first error was the way in which we carried out diversification. Instead of embarking on diversification by degrees we attempted too much at once. The sugar cane areas were reduced and the land thus made available was used for cultivation of new crops. But this meant a general decline in agricultural production. The entire economic history of Cuba had demonstrated that no other agricultural activity would give such returns as those yielded by the cultivation of the sugar cane. At the outset of the Revolution many of us were not aware of this basic economic fact, because a fetishistic idea connected sugar with our dependence on imperialism and with the misery in the rural areas, without analysing the real causes: the relation to the uneven trade balance.

Unfortunately, whatever measures are taken in agriculture, the results do not become apparent until months, sometimes years, afterwards. This is particularly true as regards sugar cane production. That is why the reduction of the sugar cane areas made between the middle of 1960 and the end of 1961—and, let us not forget the two years of drought—has resulted in lower sugar cane harvests during 1962 and 1963.

. . .

Diversification on a smaller scale could have been achieved by utilising the reserves of productivity existing in the resources assigned to the various traditional types of cultivation. This would have permitted the partial use of idle resources for a small number of new products. At the same time, we could have taken measures to introduce more modern and complex techniques requiring a longer period of assimilation. After these new technical methods had begun to bear fruit in the traditional fields, particularly in those related to exports, it would have been practicable to transfer resources from these fields to the areas of diversification without prejudice to the former.

. . .

The second mistake made was, in our opinion, that of dispersing our resources over a great number of agricultural products, all in the name of diversification. This dispersal was made not only on a national scale but also within each of the agricultural productive units.

Immediately after the Revolution the explosive increase of demand permitted a higher degree of utilisation of our industrial capacity, and nationally produced articles accounted for a greater share of total consumption. This industrial growth, however, aggravated the problem of the balance of payments, for an extraordinarily high percentage of the costs of our industry—which was nationally integrated only to a small degree—was represented by the importation of fuel, raw materials, spare parts and equipment for replacement.

The problem of the balance of payments, and that of urban unemployment, made us follow a policy aimed at an industrial development which would eliminate these defects. Here, too, we both achieved successes and committed errors. Already during the first years of the Revolution we ensured the country's supply of electric power, acquiring from the socialist countries new plant-capacities which will meet our needs until 1970. New industries have been created, and many small and medium-sized production units in the mechanical field have been re-equipped. One result of these measures was that our industry could be kept running when the American embargo on spare parts hit us hardest. Some textile factories, some extractive and chemical installations, and a new and vigorous search for fresh mineral resources have all contributed to successes in the more efficient use of native natural resources and raw materials.

.   .   .

I have spoken of certain achievements in the industrial field during the first years, but it is only just that I should also mention the errors made. Fundamentally, these were caused by a lack of precise understanding of the technological and economic elements necessary in the new industries installed during those years. Influenced by existing unemployment and by the pressure exerted by the problems in our foreign trade, we acquired a great number of factories with the dual purpose of substituting imports and providing employment for an appreciable number of urban workers. Later we found that in many of these plants the technical efficiency was insufficient when measured by international standards, and that the net result of the substitution of imports was very limited, because the necessary raw materials were not nationally produced.

.   .   .

As the dependent countries of America and other regions of the world cast off the monopolistic chains, and establish more equitable systems and more just relations with all the countries of the world, the heavy contributions made by them to the living standard of the imperialist Powers will cease, and of all the capitalist countries the United States will then be the most seriously affected. This will not be the only outcome of an historical process; displaced finance capital will be forced to seek new horizons to make good its losses and, in this struggle, the most wounded, the most powerful and the most aggressive of all the capitalist Powers, the United States, will employ her full strength in a ruthless competition with the others, adopting, perhaps, unexpected methods of violence in her dealings with her "allies" of today.[1]

6. *Castro Discusses*
the Development of a Revolutionary
and the Future of Cuba, 1965

In August 1965, a U.S. journalist, Lee Lockwood, conducted a marathon seven-day interview with Fidel Castro, out of which emerged a detailed picture of the influence of internal and external conflict on the shaping of the Cuban Revolution and revolutionaries. Castro's comments on his own ideological development provide some insight into the intellectual, political, and psychological factors that were melded in this crucible of conflict to form a peculiarly Cuban approach to Marxism.

Castro: . . . I especially am a partisan of the widest possible discussion in the intellectual realm.

Why? Because I believe in the free man, I believe in the well-educated man, I believe in the man able to think, in the man who acts always out of conviction, without fear of any kind. And I believe that ideas must be able to defend themselves. I am opposed to the blacklists of books, prohibited films, and all such things.

·   ·   ·

Lockwood: But such an atmosphere is not possible at the present time?
Castro: It would be an illusion to think so. First on account of the economic problems involved, and second because of the struggle in which we are engaged.

·   ·   ·

[1] [Guevara ended this article with an admonition that the British and French could profit by adapting to revolutionary changes in the developing nations, since an economically wounded United States might adopt policies that would adversely affect their economies.]

SOURCE: "Castro Discusses the Development of a Revolutionary and the Future of Cuba, 1965" reprinted by permission of The Macmillan Company from *Castro's Cuba, Cuba's Fidel* by Lee Lockwood. Copyright © Lee Lockwood, 1967, pp. 127–28, 130, 138–39, 141, 180–81.

Lockwood: What do you think has been responsible for the growth of this atmosphere?

Castro: I believe various circumstances, but fundamentally the situation of emergency and strain under which the country has been living, required to survive by the skin of its teeth. Almost all activities have had to be subordinated to the need for survival.

.   .   .

Lockwood: Are you saying that you were already a Marxist-Leninist when you came to power in 1959, and that if you hadn't been busy defending the Revolution you would have drawn up a socialist constitution at that time?

Castro: Look, often things cannot be understood unless they are analyzed as a process. Nobody can say that he reaches certain political conclusions except through a process. Nobody reaches those convictions in a day, often not in a year. A lot of time has to pass before one reaches reliable political conclusions.

.   .   .

When I graduated from the university I still did not have a very good political training.

Even so, one might say that I had advanced extraordinarily, since I had been a political illiterate when I entered the university. As the son of a landowner, educated in a Jesuit secondary school, I had brought nothing more than a rebellious temperament and the uprightness, the severe character which they had inculcated into me in the Jesuit school.

.   .   .

I have said that when we came to power I was somewhat idealistic and utopian, in the sense that I believed that everything we would do inside our country would have to be respected, both because it was just and because we had the full right to do it. I thought that nobody would dispute that right. But no sooner had we begun to carry out our revolutionary program, for which we had been fighting for years, than the phenomenon of American imperialism and its close connections to the problems of our country began to reveal themselves to us with full clarity. The contempt they felt toward the nation's affairs was manifested in a thousand ways. . . .

The conflicts between all that the Revolution stands for and everything the United States stands for became clear immediately when they gave asylum to the worst criminals, individuals who had murdered hundreds of Cuban people. It was revealed by the campaigns they unleashed against the Revolution, and by their attempts to coerce us by every means.

That process completed my political education. With the passion that I felt for the Revolution, for the need to correct injustice, to eradicate exploitation, to wipe out privileges, with that same passion I collided with those who were opposed to all that, with imperialism and all that it represented.

. . .

Very honestly, I can say that nothing satisfies me more than seeing that every day things depend less and less on me, and more and more upon a collective spirit grounded in institutions.

One question must be asked: What importance can what a man accomplishes have if those accomplishments are going to last only as long as he lasts? If we really do love the Revolution, if we hope that the Revolution will always continue upon its road, and if we wish for our people the great happiness in their future, what value would all our good intentions have if we didn't take steps to ensure that they would not depend wholly on the will of only one man? If we didn't take steps to make it depend on the collective will of the nation?

We love the Revolution as a labor. We love it just as a painter, a sculptor, or a writer may love his work. And, like him, we want our work to have a perennial value.

. . .

Lockwood: Under the new constitution which you say will be promulgated soon, will the people have any electoral voice in determining who the collective leadership will be?

Castro: We will have a system of permanent participation of the mass of workers in the formation of the party, in the election of its members, and in the replacement of such members of the party who do not deserve the trust of the masses.

That is, there will be a continuous election, a continuous participation of the masses in the formation of the political apparatus. The representatives of the working masses will be the members of the party. The party will be something like a combined parliament of the workers and interpreter of their will.

Lockwood: And will that "parliament" in turn choose the directorate of the party?

Castro: It will be chosen by assemblies of delegates who in turn are elected by the mass membership of the party.

. . .

Lockwood: What role do you expect to play in your government in the future, once the party is fully established and the constitution is in effect?

Castro: I think that for a few more years I will figure as the leader of the party. If I were to say that I didn't want that, people would think I was crazy. But you want me to speak sincerely? I will try to make it the least time possible. You know me very well, and you have seen how many other things I am attracted to which are not official activities.

I believe that all of us ought to retire relatively young. I don't propose this as a duty, but as something more—as a right.

7. The Crisis Mentality
in Revolutionary Music

These verses are from "La llama" ("The Flame"), a song by Manuel Navarro Luna glorifying the Cuban defense at Playa Girón (Bay of Pigs) and comparing President John F. Kennedy to Hitler and Mussolini. The theme of successful struggle against the strong forces of imperialism characterizes the entire song.

La llama

¡El imperio del Norte tiene los días contados,
como los tienen todos los imperios podridos!
¡El socialismo avanza! ¡Y serán sacudidos,
exterminados
y barridos
por huracanes desencadenados!

¡Cuba será un crucero de heridas! ¡Lo sabemos!
Pero clavados en nuestra trinchera,
sin dar un paso atrás, resistiremos;
sin dar un paso atrás, defenderemos,
hasta la última gota de sangre, la bandera.

The Flame

The days of the empire of the North are numbered,
like those of all rotten empires!
Socialism advances! And they will be beaten,
exterminated
and swept away
by unleashed hurricanes!

SOURCE: "La llama" from Richard R. Fagan, "Mass Mobilization in Cuba: The Symbolism of Struggle," in *Journal of International Affairs*, 20, No. 2 (1966), p. 255. Reprinted by permission of the publishers. Professor Fagan also provided the original Spanish version of the song.

Cuba will be a crossroad of wounds! That we know!
But nailed in our trench,
without taking a step backward, we will resist;
without taking a step backward, we will defend
the flag to the last drop of blood.

Interpretations of the Castro
Revolution by Outside Observers

8. North American Influence on Cuba

William Appleman Williams, professor of history at the University
of Wisconsin, has analyzed the historical role of the United States
in Cuba and its effect on the island's economy, society, and thought.
His studies show that a subtle anti-Yankee feeling characterized the
pre-1959 nationalism of numerous Cuban intellectuals and also that
among the lower classes, though they were much less articulate, evidence of the same sentiments could be found.

[N]ot only had the Cuban upper class increasingly abandoned its
own traditional guidelines under the pressure for Americanization, but
the Cuban middle class had done likewise. By the mid-1950's, at any
rate, Cuban upper-class leaders trying to adapt and act upon a corporate
program would have met serious opposition from within their own class
as well as from the middle class and from Cuban radicals.

This underlying, distorted kind of Americanization became the short-
run factor which plagued the Castro revolution from the moment of
victory in January 1959. Its power and persuasiveness is nowhere better
dramatized than in Castro's own ambivalence.[1] On the one hand, he
realized that any real change in Cuba depended upon breaking the traditional pattern of American control. In this sense, at any rate, no Cuban

[1] In the significant opening sentences of this selection, Professor Williams hints at
the fact that Cuban animosity against the United States rested at least in part on an
internal crisis of identity. However much they might accept at least the outer trappings
of U.S. culture and values, many Cubans were deeply upset that the island populace
was being "depersonalized," robbed of its true nature, and pressured into adopting
alien attitudes and life patterns. This feeling, long present in many Cuban circles, helps
explain the strength of anti-Yankee sentiment in the Cuban Revolution.—FBP

SOURCE: "North American Influence on Cuba" from William Appleman Williams,
"Cuba: Issues and Alternatives," in The Annals of the American Academy of Political
and Social Sciences, 351 (January 1964), p. 78. Reprinted by permission of the author.

could be a social revolutionary without being anti-American. On the other hand, and as Castro understood—and admitted many times—any program of development would be much easier and cheaper if it was undertaken within a broad framework of co-operation with—or at least acquiescence by—the United States. This was true not only because the Cuban economy had been built as part of the American system—as illustrated by the spare-parts crises—but also because breaking the American tie would politically antagonize those who had been partially Americanized even though they favored extensive changes in Cuba. This interaction was intensified by the depression which existed when Castro came to power.

Any social revolutionary movement in Cuba would thus have faced—and would face tomorrow—the same difficult choice among three alternatives. Either the United States had to modify its policy and evolve a new and basically different relationship with Cuba, the social revolutionaries had to give up the essence of their own program, or the revolution had to be carried through with the assistance of other support and at great cost to the Cuban people. The heart of the Cuban issue is simply and essentially defined by the refusal of either American policy-makers or Castro to abandon their existing commitments. Everything that has happened since the spring of 1959 flows from that confrontation.

It can be argued, of course, that the impasse was inevitable. Even if one accepts that formulation, which I do not, there is still a vital purpose in understanding why it was unavoidable. It is possible, that is to say, to conclude that one event was inevitable and still seek ways and means of avoiding an unending sequence of similar difficulties. American power was the overwhelmingly most significant factor in Cuban development since 1895, that power was developed and used within a unilaterally determined framework of interest and ideas, and the refusal of the United States to modify its policy was the central cause of any inevitability. This is so not only in the direct sense but in the sense that Cuban radicalism in general—and Castro's social revolutionary leadership in particular—evolved within that American framework.

9. *Internal Support*
for Revolutionary Policies

Boris Goldenberg participated in various Communist and radical socialist groups in Germany until he fled the country during the 1930's.

SOURCE: "Internal Support for Revolutionary Policies" from Boris Goldenberg, *The Cuban Revolution and Latin America* (New York: Frederick A. Praeger, 1965), pp. 293, 296–98, 301–02. Reprinted by permission of the publishers.

He went to Cuba in 1941, gave up politics, and lived as a Cuban citizen until his departure for England in 1960. Goldenberg contends that the Cuban Revolution cannot be understood in classical Marxist or Leninist terms and stresses conflict, noting that "a revolution passes through various phases and changes its character because the seeds of later stages exist already at the beginning and develop under the pressure of conflicting tendencies."

The Cuban revolution had certain distinctive features, both in the first democratic phase of the struggle against the Batista dictatorship, and in the two subsequent socialist phases, the transitional phase of "revolutionary humanism" and the "socialist totalitarian" phase.

. . .

The transition from the democratic to the socialist phase took place without civil war and without a change of leadership. It was not directed by a Marxist-Leninist party but by a charismatic leader. It contradicted not only the fundamental ideas of Marx, but also one of the main tenets of Leninism.

In the first "humanist" phase the leadership was willing and, by sacrificing the interests of the immediate future, able to provide the lower sections of the population with a rapid improvement of their living conditions. The ensuing mass enthusiasm made it possible for the revolution to dispense, at first, with a well organized political apparatus and to do without terror. The bureaucratic transformation of the charisma into a commonplace (as Max Weber called it), the totalitarian normalization of the revolution, its "bolshevization," was not completed even by the end of 1962.

The development towards socialism was not based on a clearly conceived plan but resulted from the interplay of spontaneous personal decisions of the leader and the consequences of those decisions, which crystallize the ideas of the leadership.

The transition to the "revolutionary humanist" phase and from there to the "socialist totalitarian" phase was possible because Cuba was economically more highly developed than other countries in which Marxist-Leninist revolutions had taken place, and because the revolution was able to take over a running economy which had at its disposal unused factors of production—land, labour, and capital equipment.

Politically the transition was possible because the masses were enthusiastic and there were no organized forces inside the country which could act as a brake. International considerations deterred the USA from intervention and the Cuban revolution could rely on the sympathy of the Latin American masses and on help from the Eastern bloc.

. . .

Although it is impossible to answer the question about the "class character" of the Cuban revolution, there were nevertheless some social groups which were more or less predisposed to favour the revolution and could hope to benefit from a fundamental change. The two most important of these groups were the young intellectuals and the unemployed or rather the underemployed, particularly in the towns. . . .

Because the unemployed and underemployed were numerous in Cuba and, together with the underpaid, formed a majority of the population, the national revolution can be regarded as a "revolution of the rootless." Its "anarchistic radicalism" can be used against capitalism but can also be an obstacle to social change.

The frustrated young intellectuals naturally played a leading role. Impatient, influenced by radical ideologies rather than by facts, they doubted their own economic future and prospects of advancement. They stood for national independence, social justice, and quick modernization of the country. Their impatience led them to favour rapid changes carried out from above and to reject compromises, while their inexperience made them under-estimate the difficulties.

There were various factors which made the socialist transformation in Cuba easier and others which made it more difficult than in other countries where Marxist-Leninist revolutions have taken place.

The favourable factors included the objective need for planning; sound, rapid development was impossible while there was a relatively free market economy. Secondly, Cuba was more developed than other countries which had had Marxist-Leninist revolutions. Its economy was intact and its potential unexploited. Thirdly, the majority of the agricultural population consisted of proletarians working in large enterprises. There was, therefore, little opposition to collectivization. Finally, Cuba was not isolated and could count on economic and political help from the Eastern bloc.

Against this there were several unfavourable factors. Because of its size, its lack of fuel and raw materials, and its concentration on sugar and tobacco, Cuba was very much tied to the world market and was much less capable of autarchy than the other countries had been at the beginning of their revolutions. . . .

The character of the Cuban people, their inclination towards individualism and materialism, the absence of a collectivist tradition in agriculture, the fact that some of them were accustomed to a certain standard of comfort which the lower classes also longed for, the anti-revolutionary, trade unionist attitude of the workers, all this has made the change to socialism more difficult and was bound to cause problems as soon as sacrifices were required.

In spite of its utter dependence on the Soviet bloc, Cuba did not become a satellite but a new centre speaking a new kind of Marxist-Leninist dialectic in the polycentric world of post-Stalinist communism. Hence its attraction for other Latin American countries in search of a future.

. . .

The picture is full of contradictions. The whole experiment may fail, but many of the radical changes made can hardly be undone or còuld be undone only by a foreign invasion and the imposition of a new and probably reactionary dictatorship. Unless, of course, the Cuban masses rise; but this is not a likely prospect.

10. *The Cuban Revolutionary Tradition*

The revolutionary tradition in Cuba has its roots in the 1890's, when the effects of radical European thought were demonstrated at the First National Worker's Congress in Havana. From that time on, Marxism remained an influential element in the intellectual milieu of the country, since it offered an explanation for the island's problems and emphasized their connection to Cuba's relationships with the developed countries. The distinguished British historian Hugh Thomas succinctly describes the interplay between this intellectual background and the progress of the Cuban Revolution.

Although Castro did not come to power with a real party organization, or even a real political plan, he nevertheless did have behind him a real revolutionary tradition, a tradition which was firmly rooted in the previous sixty years of Cuban politics, almost the whole of which had been passed in perpetual crisis. This tradition had been most recently expressed among the Ortodoxo Party founded by Eddy Chibás and to which Castro himself had belonged until about 1955. Before the ortodoxos there had been the auténticos, who had provided the Governments of Grau and Prío from 1944 to 1952, and who also had promised many things when they were young, before they had come to power—in the "heroic" days of the students' Directorate, fighting first against Machado and then latterly against Batista. Batista himself had come in in September 1933, promising everything and perhaps even meaning it for a while. Before him Machado had been thought of at first as the man the young republic had been waiting for—"almost 'Apollo-like,'" someone had writ-

SOURCE: "The Cuban Revolutionary Tradition" from Hugh Thomas, "The Origins of the Cuban Revolution," in *The World Today*, 19, No. 10 (October 1963), pp. 459–60. Reprinted by permission of the author.

ten in a French review. And long before that, in 1895–8, during the War
of Liberation, the promises had been extremely full and glowing. To these
recurrent waves of enthusiasm, most of them nationalistic and anti-
American, most of them radical, each one of them more vigorous, more
extreme than the last, Castro was the logical heir.

In 1959 the enthusiasm and the hopes for the revolution were greater
than ever before, specifically because they had been deceived so often
before. The pattern of elation and betrayal is a familiar one in Cuba (it
is to be found even in Miami today), though it is surprising that so many
betrayals should not provoke cynicism. All the time between 1902 and
1959, Cubans were trying to prove themselves worthy of the heroic figures
of the War of Independence—Martí, Gómez, or Maceo. Efforts were
made, understandably, necessarily perhaps, by Castro to make himself,
Camilo Cienfuegos, and others the equals of the heroes of the past.[1] The
men of 1959 were undoubtedly in many cases the real sons of the men
who made the revolution in 1933. Castro was to do the things that many
people had been talking about before. Many moderately middle-class
Cubans suspected, without much economic knowledge, that the only
way out of the chronic sugar crisis, the only way to diversify agriculture,
was to embark on very radical measures: to nationalize American property
and to force a break in commercial relations with the United States.

Amateur Marxism was a strong force on the left wing of the Ortodoxo
Party in the early 1950s, though it is now proving an illusion to suppose
that even Marxist-Leninism can bring a swift diversification of agriculture.
One can see how the illusion nevertheless became widespread, how anyone
who seemed likely to realize it was certain of backing, regardless of
whether he trampled on formal democracy. There can be only one reason
why the moderates in the Cuban Cabinet of 1959—the admirable professional and liberal persons who now perhaps back Manuel Ray[2] and
argue that Castro has betrayed the revolution—failed to unite and resist
Castro, backed by the considerable strength of the Cuban middle class:
the reason is surely that they half felt all the time that, given the betrayal
of so many previous revolutions, Castro was right. Many moderates after
all did stay in Cuba, and many are still there.

[1] [Máximo Gómez and Antonio Maceo were leading generals in the Cuban struggle against Spanish rule (1858–98). Maceo, a Negro, was killed in 1896. Cienfuegos
was one of the survivors of the 1957 landing; he died in a plane crash in 1959.]
[2] [Manuel (Manolo) Ray directed the sabotage section of the 26th of July Movement during the battle against Batista. He served as Minister of Public Works until
November 1959. Later he left Cuba and became the leader of the People's Revolutionary Movement in Florida. The CIA disliked Ray because he espoused "Fidelismo
without Fidel." He was captured while trying to land in Cuba.]

11. Conflict in the Agricultural Sector and Revolutionary Unity

At each of the several stages in the evolution of the Cuban Revolution's agrarian policy, the amount of land to be left in the hands of private farmers has been a critical question. But the reduction of the private sector has gone forward, and this has produced conflict. Adolfo Gilly, an Argentine socialist, analyzed this conflict and attacked the elitist interpretation of the Revolution, arguing that group pressures have an effect on the leadership.

The refuge of the counter-revolution in the countryside was the rich agricultural sector of the population which continued to exist after the agrarian reform nationalizing all lands down to thirty caballerías. Farmers who possess less than five caballerías are considered small farmers and belong to the National Association of Small Farmers through which they obtain credits and regulate their relations with the state. Until recently, those owning from five to thirty caballerías made up the category of middle and rich farmers.[1]

There were more than six thousand of these, and they were, in the main, landlords who lived in the cities and had their lands worked for them; some were farmers whose past or present position gave them a certain influence with poor farmers of the region who were a species of "clientele." Owing to their economic and social situation, many of these middle and rich farmers opposed the Revolution, for it had closed off their chance of becoming a farming bourgeoisie and of increasing their holdings.

In a country with a more solid and widespread industrial structure it would perhaps have been easier for a socialist regime to use this category of farmers and if not to win them over at least to neutralize them. . . . But under Cuban conditions, the natural hostility to socialism of the rich farmer—prevented from further enriching himself and acquiring more land—was bound to turn into enmity. It was also inevitable that he would try to drag with him a class of middle and even small farmers who were

[1] [By the end of 1966, approximately thirty per cent of Cuban land was still held by private farmers. The Second Agrarian Reform Law limited private holdings to 150 acres, but exceptions are made (a few 900-acre farms are still operating).]

SOURCE: "Conflict in the Agricultural Sector and Revolutionary Unity" from Adolfo Gilly, "Inside the Cuban Revolution," in *Monthly Review*, 16, No. 6 (October 1964), pp. 21–23, 26–27, 30. Reprinted by permission of the publishers.

disgusted with the difficulties of revolution; for while the city worker understands these difficulties and endures them because he sees socialism as his future, the farmer does not see anything beyond the boundaries of his own piece of land.

. . .

As for the small farmers, the revolutionary government has pursued a steady policy designed to keep them as allies. Even with this class, success has not always been achieved: the farmer first sees his piece of land, then the country and the Revolution. Nevertheless, the majority do support the Revolution. What has been done in the countryside is certainly great enough to compensate for scarcities and other difficulties in the farmer's books.

. . .

[M]ost commentators still have not discarded an old formula which has long since been transcended by reality: to divide the leadership of the Cuban Revolution between Fidelistas and Communists and to search frantically in every episode where differences of opinion come into the open for the line of the "Communists" (the former members of the PSP) and that of the "non-Communists" (the old team of the Sierra). Other commentators believe that in Cuba the leadership is always united and that everything is decided by Fidel Castro according to his own whims and fancies. . . . In each of these interpretations, the word "masses" has a pejorative meaning, the masses being those who support the ideas of this or that leader. It is never the other way around—that the masses oblige this or that leader to adopt these ideas.

. . .

A good case in point is the way the foreign press saw in the expulsion of Aníbal Escalante an action exclusively and independently taken by Fidel Castro as soon as he "learned what was happening." What this overlooks is that Fidel Castro himself said publicly a few weeks after the fact that for months the masses had been seeing what was happening and that "if we didn't take this measure now, in a short time we would all be dragged down."

. . .

This is not said to negate, whittle down, or dilute the roles that the leaders play but to explain why and how they can undertake them, which forces they lean on, the pressures which drive them forward and permit them to act with more or less rapidity, decisiveness, and firmness.

. . .

You cannot gauge what happens in Cuba nor judge the internal play of social pressures by what happens in a capitalist country. . . .

In Cuba all that is over. There is only the palpable feeling, the collective conviction, that to save yourself you have to do so together; that to live better, all have to live better together. . . .

Then who, why, and how is, anyone to resist a social pressure which demands in a thousand different but unanimous manifestations that the Revolution take one particular road and not another?

The Cuban leadership, even if it believed the contrary, could not oppose such pressure frontally, nor would it have the means to do so. (As a matter of fact, of course, it does not in general believe the contrary.)

12. *Unity and Mass Mobilization*

One of the basic problems confronting revolutionaries in power is that of building social unity and support for governmental policies through the development of a national mystique. Richard R. Fagan, of the political science faculty of Stanford University, discusses the Cuban attempts to accomplish this through the symbolism of struggle.

The conditions for a mobilization system [1]—the presence of a charismatic leader and the semicolonial relationship with the United States—existed in 1959 when Castro came to power. But the real development of the present regime did not begin until sometime later in the year. The suppression of opposition, reform of education, control and exploitation of the communication media, creation of the mass organizations, the felt need for a functioning Leninist party and the open antagonism with the United States all followed in the early 1960's. Furthermore, these changes, although massive, were only the structural outcroppings of the leadership's more fundamental drive for unanimity, control and the total utilization of human resources. *It is this elite commitment to total exploitation of human resources in the service of revolutionary goals which both indexed and motivated the transformation of Cuba in less than five years from a standard repressive dictatorship under Batista to a mobilization regime under Castro.*

Thus, the dominant ideal of political development in Cuba today is what Pye has called the model of mass mobilization and participation. Every Cuban a revolutionary and every revolutionary a militant is the goal. To accomplish this, an impressive new institutional order has been

[1] [A mobilization system is designed to achieve complete harmony, or "oneness," in the political life of a country; see Lucian W. Pye, *Aspects of Political Development* (Boston: Little, Brown, 1966), pp. 39–40.]

SOURCE: "Unity and Mass Mobilization" from Richard R. Fagan, "Mass Mobilization in Cuba: The Symbolism of Struggle," in *Journal of International Affairs*, 20, No. 2 (1966), pp. 257, 269–71. Reprinted by permission of the publishers.

fashioned, and it is through these institutions that the symbolism of struggle is carried to the masses in the hope that they too will be mobilized in the service of the Revolution.

.   .   .

The Cuban leaders are well aware that wide-spread popular participation cannot be achieved by appeals to nineteenth or even twentieth century abstractions. On the other hand, for both political and ideological reasons, they are committed to a mobilization strategy that includes the use of ideas as well as the use of the carrot and the stick. Thus, in common with all politicians who seek to move the masses with some mixture of ideology, threats, bribes, promises, and rewards, the Cuban leaders must translate the great issues into language easily understood by the common man. The elite definition of the Revolution as a continuing struggle against a never-ending series of adversaries represents a first attempt at translation.

.   .   .

Because Cuban history, culture, and political practice do not suggest a clear picture of what the new Cuba will look like, the Revolution needs models. As we have seen, these models are of two basic types. The first type derives directly from the negative evaluation of the United States and its imperialist friends and allies. This is what we called "moralizing by counter-example." The Revolution is in part defined as the antithesis of its enemies. A second type of model is more positive. The Soviet Union and its allies have come to be presented as good, powerful, and worthy of imitation. The Revolution is now also defined by its friends.

This shift in identification is rooted in and responds to international developments, but it signifies more than new political alignments. The embrace of the Soviet Union opens up new possibilities for the guidance and the education of the masses. To understand these possibilities, it is necessary to appreciate the new demands placed on the Cuban people. The transformation of the Cuban polity, society, and economy cannot be accomplished by enthusiastic but untutored citizens. It is no longer sufficient to gather in the plaza and shout *Patria o Muerte, Venceremos* (Fatherland or Death, We Will Win). This does not put bread on the table or tractors in the field. What is needed, the regime argues, is a technological revolution which will support and continue, but *not* supersede, the political revolution. The technological revolution must produce the cadres of specialists who will lead in constructing the new socioeconomic order. These cadres will combine both material and political expertise, and through them the masses will eventually grow in political and technological sophistication. The models for this new man and the society he is to create have been, in large part, taken over from East European theory and practice.

.   .   .

Lacking studies of the attitudes and political behavior of the Cuban population, we cannot evaluate in detail the successes and failures of the extensive mobilization campaigns. In any event, such evaluation is in part premature, for no generation of Cubans has yet grown to political maturity exclusively under the tutelage of the present regime. The leaders have reaped certain short-term benefits from increased public participation in revolutionary activities, but the long-term consequences of the drive for total participation and commitment are not yet known.

13. The Problem of Unity
and Organization

In 1966, Irving Louis Horowitz, professor of sociology at Washington University (St. Louis), argued that the Cuban Revolution had entered its own version of the "Stalinist" period. In part, this development was based upon the continuing conflict within the leadership structure over the nature of the Revolution and over the problem of maintaining its emotional drive.

Within the first months of 1966 there have been three proclamations issued by Fidel Castro which, I submit, bear out my contention that Fidel Castro has become a Stalinist. Given the ideological assumptions of the leading players in the international power game, Castro perhaps had little alternative than to become what he became: as Stalin himself claimed, must is must. But whether the deterministic framework out of which Castro operates is a consequence of social forces or personal ideology is at issue. For the assumptions he now makes about the condition of the world deserve further scrutiny.

First, there is the stated need for rapid development and the internal obstacles to such development—the counter-insurgency forces operating with United States support in Camaguey, Matanzas and Las Villas provinces, the rise of absenteeism and slower work schedules developing among even the loyal workers. These require military effort in the first instance and repressive legal measures in the second. Second, there is the belief that Cuba is surrounded by hostile forces, led by the United States. And that this ring of bases makes impossible the normalization of trade and aid agreements with the capitalist bloc generally or with other "captive"

SOURCE: "The Problem of Unity and Organization" from Irving Louis Horowitz, "The Stalinization of Fidel Castro," in New Politics, 4, No. 4 (Fall 1965), pp. 62–63, 67–69. Reprinted by permission of the publishers.

Latin American nations. Third is the growing dissatisfaction with any other "roads to socialism," particularly those of the more extreme variety such as China; hence the continued emphasis on independent forms of political expression invariably creates the base for leadership ideology derived from within rather than from international Communist leaders such as Mao Tse Tung. In other words, the "socialism in one country" slogan is not so much a cause as a consequence of Stalinization.

.   .   .

The decline of internationalist pretensions, meshed as it is with the growth of a tight-knit political party bureaucracy, characterizes the new Castro regime just as assuredly as it did the pre-war Stalin period between 1929 and 1941.

What do we find in Cuba leading to this conclusion, and what are the unique conditions of the Cuban situation which give its form of Stalinism special properties? Most important is that Cuba is a small nation dependent on the world economy, dependent on a single group and above all simply dependent. By contrast, Russia in 1918 was relatively advanced industrially as well as being a politically sophisticated nation. Geographically, Russia dominates Europe while Cuba is dominated by the Americas. Given these conditions plus the fact that Cuba is engaged not in forced industrialization but in forced collectivization, the possibilities of liberalism in the Cuban situation are minimized.

.   .   .

A special characteristic of Castro is his growing reliance on nepotism, on familial contacts as political leaders. The steady rise in position of his brother Raúl Castro, the influence of other members of his extended family, all serve to surround Fidel with non-threatening figures. Personalism in Latin America has traditionally served to enhance the direct link of the Leader to the People. In the case of Fidel it enables him when necessary to bypass the only stable party apparatus remaining in the country—the Communist Party. By this tactic he is striving to make the image of the party his own.

.   .   .

Related to this emergent nepotism is the increased demand for proletarian puritanism. First, in 1965 there was a concerted attack on alleged examples of homosexuality among government officials (featured by a "parade" of deviants in Havana); and in 1966 this was widened to include all those engaged in "antisocial activities." The dismissal of Efigenio Almeijeiras as Armed Forces Vice Minister, and his pending court martial along with several dozen others in government life "for activities contrary to revolutionary morals," indicates that such puritanism has the dimensions of a full-scale purge. The fusion, or rather fudging, of personal and political aspects of behavior has served to justify an increased politicalization of the military and, no less, of the diplomatic corps. Changes in the Army Chief of Staff, Commander of the Navy, and of leading posts in the Foreign Ministry, represent not simply a tightening of the political net, but an increased penetration by the Maximum Leader into middle echelons of power. For with each series of dismissals the actual power lodged in both civil and military agencies seems to become correspondingly weaker; the replacements are less able (or willing) to make decisions independently.

What do we make of this Cuban position at the Tri-Continental Conference meetings? [1] The most important thing is that it announces that Castro is no longer a significant threat to the United States. Any government bent on national redemption, on the national road to salvation, on national socialism, on a concentration upon internal problems, can hardly threaten the international position of the United States. The meetings of the Tri-Continental Conference, far from announcing a new stage of struggle against the "imperialists," in fact announce that a condition of national sovereignty now prevails.

. . .

This is not to deny in any way that the Cuban Revolution is an authentic revolution; only that it has little chance of becoming hemispheric in character. The Cuban Revolution is of such major consequence that no leader can capture it, not even a man as powerful as Castro or the whole Castro family. The restoration of the Cuban bourgeoisie is neither warranted nor possible. It is inconceivable that there can be a restoration of Cuban barracks revolutionists, since democracy of arms still exists. The Cuban Revolution represents a total rupture with the past. There is no gainsaying that. Castro led as complete a revolution as ever took place in Europe. What is at stake is the character and purpose of that revolution; the strategy of Stalinism versus that of Trotskyism. What we are observing is the consolidation of a socialist Cuba and an indefinite postponement of a socialist Latin America.

14. *The Conflict*
over Revolutionary Motivation

In an article published in 1966, Sol Argüedas, a prominent Latin American political analyst, discussed the issue of motivation in a

---

[1] [Cuba has periodically been host to meetings of revolutionary leaders from Asia, Africa, and Latin America.]

SOURCE: "The Conflict over Revolutionary Motivation" from Sol Argüedas, "Where Is Ché Guevara?" in *CIF Report*, 5, No. 17 (September 1, 1966), pp. 129–30, 132–35;

revolutionary society. He sided with those who argue that economic success can overcome a multitude of psychological difficulties—especially the difficulty of motivating Cubans who are less than true believers. Like other, more orthodox Marxists, Argüedas believed that Cuba should concentrate on building a "socialist" example rather than on trying to lead revolutions in the hemisphere.

To "come down from the mountains" meant that the Cuban Revolution was about to begin. For its leaders it meant that they were about to transform and accelerate that revolution. Both terms—"begin" and "transform"—mean the growing identification of the revolutionary movement with the working classes which had been fighting for the things the revolution promised. This "identification" means that the revolutionary leaders had to discover and synthesize the proletarian ideology at its very core: the philosophical concept. It is an error to believe that the "class struggle"—which sometimes is very violent and other times seems to be drowsing—disappears when forces which tend to be socialistic triumph. Disappear nothing! It only changes form, as does everything. It evolves from its fossilized causes in the political and economic areas, and explodes in an ideological crisis which will not end until the appearance of that "new man," to which all revolutionaries aspire (even Ché).

.   .   .

Ché Guevara explained his path in the now-famous article written for a Uruguayan magazine, and reprinted in Mexico. It might be considered the revolutionary "ideary" of Ché Guevara.[1]

He wrote: "The need for the creation of the 'new man' is not sufficiently understood. This 'new man' is not the one represented by nineteenth-century ideals, nor can he be found in our century's decadent and morbid ideals. We must create the man of the twenty-first century, even if this is still an unsystematized aspiration. . . ." Referring to the first, heroic stage of the Revolution, he added: ". . . to find a formula for perpetuating this heroic attitude in everyday life is one of our basic tasks, from the ideological point of view." And later he explained: ". . . thus it is so important to correctly choose the instrument for the mobilization of the masses. *This instrument must be an essentially moral one, without forgetting the correct use of material incentives,* especially those of a social nature. . . ."

originally published in *Cuadernos Americanos*, No. 3 (May–June 1966). Reprinted by permission of both publishers. Translated by the staff of the Center for Intercultural Documentation.
    [1] ["Ideary" is a fanciful translation of the Spanish *ideario* (or of the Latin *idearium*, used in Spanish), signifying a collection of the principal thoughts of an author, doctrine, or party.]

Fidel Castro points out another path, if not in his statements, at least in the tendencies which are shaping the Cuban Revolution. We might define those tendencies in the following way: *"Create constant change in man's material conditions. This change, since it will be a product of man himself, parallels the concomitant modification of his spirit and leads to the formation of the 'new man.'"*

. . .

To increase production, work productivity must first be increased, and to increase work productivity, the worker must be stimulated. How?

Motorcycles, vacations on the beaches, and other recreation centers were the prizes which Fidel promised and delivered to the best cane cutters during the last season, which was so successful.

"Direct material rewards and the conscience are, in our mind, contradictory terms"—stated Ché.

And those who agreed with "moral" stimulation for the workers clung to Ché's every word, and they made a great effort to apply and to keep alive the spirit of sacrifice characteristic of the "conscious" revolutionaries. But to judge by the results, Fidel Castro sees man as he *is*, and Ché Guevara sees him as he *ought to be.*

Moral stimulation (understood as Ché understood it, and applied it to the organization of industry, and probably as Fidel understood it at first) in this sense means the attempt to prolong the heroism of the Revolution's most difficult moments (Sierra Maestra, October of 1962, or Hurricane Flora) in everyday life. Unless I am badly mistaken, this solution didn't work (or so it would seem given the social class of those who recently "skipped out" to the United States). Many of those people were workers, and they left for economic and political reasons. And this is not only true of those who fled, but also of those who stayed behind physically, but have "skipped out" in their attitude toward their work.

. . .

These people would have stayed in Cuba if they had been given economic encouragement and sufficient ideological enlightenment to understand where their interests lay, and who was defending them.

. . .

Given the differences in intellectual training of the various social layers, and the lack of capable intermediate leadership, there are inevitable conflicts of an ideological nature. These disputes have visible manifestations which can confuse anyone who tries to explain them psychologically, sociologically, or ethnologically. . . .

Scientific leadership of society—the goal of all socialist construction— would mean the solution of the current ideological dispute. The proportionally greater cultural background of the ex-petite-bourgeoisie undergoing ideological transformation and the ideological orientation of the

working classes toward intellectual training would merge into one movement. But this goal is a long way off for Cuba. The scientific leadership
of society has not been undertaken (or even decreed) by the nation's
leaders. Society itself will force such a measure once it reaches a certain
degree of complexity and scientific, technological development. In other
words, when the social system itself regulates and develops the material
processes.

. . .

Cuba can offer two things to Latin Americans. The first is an example,
endorsed by increasing future success as she builds socialism. This will
prove to the doubters that socialism is the only road to the development
of all nations in the Southern Hemisphere. The second contribution will
be material and ideological aid to the movements of liberation now under-
way. . . .

Could it be possible that we will have to choose between the two?

CONCLUSION

In spite of external pressures and internal conflicts, the Cuban Revolution has now survived for one decade. While it has not proved to be the immediate wave of the future, as some feared in the early 1960's, it still poses questions concerning the nature of reform in Latin America. Some authorities believe that the best hope for reform resides in the so-called democratic left, as personified by Eduardo Frei (Chile) and Rómulo Betancourt (Venezuela). But a fundamental question is still to be answered: Can a leftist government provide effective, far-reaching reforms and still remain democratic? Many observers insist that Latin American countries must choose between a vastly moderated reform program carried out within the existing socioeconomic structure and a drastic, immediate program that can be carried out only by eliminating the power of those groups that are relatively satisfied with the status quo. Can reforms that will affect the conditions of the lower class immediately and effectively in fact be instituted without first changing the existing power relationships through social revolution?

In Cuba during the first half of 1959, the options seem to have been open. But the rising tide of militant opposition to reform confronted Castro and the revolutionaries with a choice between circumscribing the reform program in order to maintain power in the existing political system and eliminating the power of the opposition in order to carry out effective reforms. In the Dominican Republic, Juan Bosch was faced with a similar choice but did not make a decision and was deposed in 1963. The fear that as a result of this experience Bosch would choose to follow Castro's example were he to regain power was a factor in the massive U.S. intervention that aborted the pro-Bosch Dominican Revolution of 1965. The internal situation varies from country to country, of course, and the Cuban example does not neatly and automatically apply elsewhere. Currently, Venezuela and Chile are test cases to see whether in some Latin American contexts effective reform can be combined with republican government.

How successful has the Cuban Revolution been in solving the socioeconomic problems of its people? The answers vary widely, depending upon the source consulted and the indicators used. Production in some areas has declined, and various aspects of free expression have been curbed. The sociologist Oscar Lewis has indicated at least one area of novel success. He revisited a slum in Havana and noted that while the people were still poor, the atmosphere of despair and apathy (produced by the culture of poverty) was gone. He concluded, "The people have found a new sense of power and importance in a doctrine that glorified the lower class as the hope of humanity, and they were armed." [1]

Whatever the verdict of historians concerning the Cuban Revolution (and it will be mixed), some things are clear. The Cuban experience has forced the nations of Latin America to face some basic issues of human society. Fidel Castro is the not-so-silent Banquo's ghost present at every meeting of the Alliance for Progress, the OAS, and the various committees concerned with reform and development. Attempts to remedy the social crisis in Latin America and the entire role of the political left have been influenced decisively by the Cuban Revolution.

[1] Oscar Lewis, "The Culture of Poverty," in *Scientific American*, 215, No. 4 (October 1966), p. 23.

BIBLIOGRAPHY

Barnett, Clifford R., and Wyatt MacGaffey. *Cuba: Its People, Its Society, Its Culture* (New Haven, Conn.: HRAF Press, 1962). Good survey of Cuban history in the twentieth century, giving some attention to cultural factors.

Batista, Fulgencio. *Cuba Betrayed* (New York: Devin-Adair, 1962). The former dictator's version of why he lost power; places much emphasis on the treason of his military leaders.

Casuso, Teresa. *Cuba and Castro* (New York: Random House, 1962). One of the best personal accounts by a participant in the Castro movement (to mid-1960). Valuable for the ideas and feelings of the "Generation of '33."

Cuban Economic Research Project. *Cuba: Agriculture and Planning, 1963–1964* (Miami, Fla.: Editorial AIP, 1965). Exile economists present an enormous quantity of statistics; a useful work, but the text is characterized by a completely anti-Revolution point of view.

Dewart, Leslie. *Christianity and Revolution: The Lessons of Cuba* (New York: Herder & Herder, 1963). Liberal, Roman Catholic analysis of the role of the Church in Cuba, before and during the Revolution; basic theme is the dilemma of a conservative religious body in a rapidly changing social order.

Draper, Theodore. *Castro's Revolution: Myths and Realities* (New York: Frederick A. Praeger, 1962). Collection of articles on Castro's relationship with the Communists and on the Bay of Pigs invasion; strong tendency toward the "revolution betrayed" thesis.

————. *Castroism: Theory and Practice* (New York: Frederick A. Praeger, 1965). Rational, conservative analysis of the Cuban Revolution, with emphasis on the period from 1960 to 1965 and on the development of the "new Communists." The best presentation of the strictly anti-Castro school.

Du Bois, Jules. *Fidel Castro* (New York: Bobbs-Merrill, 1959). Sympathetic and dramatic account of the struggle to overthrow Batista.

Goldenberg, Boris. *The Cuban Revolution and Latin America* (New York: Frederick A. Praeger, 1965). Especially good for placing the Revolution in its historical and cultural context and analyzing its relationship to basic trends in Latin America.

Guerra y Sánchez, Ramiro. *Sugar and Society in the Caribbean: An Economic History of Cuban Agriculture* (New Haven, Conn.: Yale University Press, 1964). Excellent background on the development and problems of the plantation economy.

Huberman, Leo, and Paul M. Sweezy. *Cuba: Anatomy of a Revolution* (New York: Monthly Review Press, 1960). A socialist interpretation, stressing the peasant base of the Castro movement.

Lockwood, Lee. *Castro's Cuba, Cuba's Fidel* (New York: Macmillan, 1967). Indispensable for any understanding of Fidel Castro and the development of the Revolution; the verbatim report of the author's lengthy conversation with Castro is valuable.

López-Fresquet, Rufo. *My Fourteen Months With Castro* (Cleveland: World, 1966). Useful description of the author's relationship with the Castro government as Minister of the Treasury.

Matthews, Herbert. *The Cuban Story* (New York: George Braziller, 1961). A sympathetic and intelligent appraisal of the Revolution, with stress on the influence of U.S. policy; good account of the author's famous February 1957 interview with Castro.

———. *Return to Cuba* (Stanford, Calif.: Hispanic-American Society, 1964). Perceptive analysis of the changes that had taken place since 1960.

Miller, Warren. *90 Miles From Home: The Face of Cuba Today* (New York: Fawcett, 1961). Much human-interest material; conversations in Cuba and Miami Beach provide a fascinating dimension of social history.

Nelson, Lowry. *Rural Cuba* (Minneapolis: University of Minnesota Press, 1950). This significant sociological study provides basic background information and analysis.

Morray, J. P. *The Second Revolution in Cuba* (New York: Monthly Review Press, 1962). Marxist interpretation of the 1959–60 ideological shift in the Revolution; emphasizes role of the workers.

Suárez, Andrés. *Castroism and Communism, 1959–1966* (Cambridge, Mass.: M.I.T. Press, 1967). The most scholarly version of the "one-man revolution" thesis; good discussion of the dilemma of the old PSP as it tried to keep pace with Castro.

Sears, Dudley, *et al. Cuba: The Economic and Social Revolution* (Chapel Hill: University of North Carolina Press, 1964). Economists from Chile and England present one of the best analyses of the economic and social developments of the Revolution; the historical background is also presented.

Smith, Robert Freeman. *Background to Revolution: The Development of Modern Cuba* (New York: Alfred A. Knopf, 1966). A collection of essays describing and analyzing the many facets of Cuban culture since the early nineteenth century.

———. *The United States and Cuba: Business and Diplomacy, 1917–1960* (New York: Bookman Associates, 1960). The role of economic ideas and interests, and their impact on U.S. policy and Cuban nationalism.

Szulc, Tad, and Karl E. Meyer. *The Cuban Invasion: The Chronicle of a Disaster* (New York: Frederick A. Praeger, 1962). Good account of the Bay of Pigs invasion, especially for the political rivalries between the exile groups and the involvement of the Kennedy administration.

Wallich, Henry C. *Monetary Problems of an Export Economy: The Cuban Experience, 1914–1947* (Cambridge, Mass.: Harvard University Press, 1950). Necessary background for an understanding of the prerevolutionary economy, especially the problems of the sugar trade.

Williams, William Appleman. *The United States, Cuba, and Castro* (New York: Monthly Review Press, 1962). Basically, a confrontation with the views of Theodore Draper; also, one of the best analyses of the Constitution of 1940.

Zeitlin, Maurice. *Revolutionary Politics and the Cuban Working Class* (Princeton, N.J.: Princeton University Press, 1967). A systematic inquiry into the differing responses of workers to the Revolution, which concludes that the Revolution is now based upon the working class; a significant contribution to an understanding of the labor movement in Cuba.

XII

The Problem
of Population Growth
in Latin America

William V. D'Antonio

INTRODUCTION

Between 220 million and 250 million people lived in Latin America in the summer of 1967. Figure 1 shows the growth of this population from 1900 through the present to a projected figure for the year 2000. Growth lines of this type should be familiar to the reader; much the same line can be drawn for the world as a whole, which explains why the phrase "population explosion" has become as common in the 1960's as "atomic explosion" was in the 1940's and 1950's.

At its present rate of growth, the current population of Latin America will more than double by the end of the century. Figure 2 shows that the rate of population growth—which is obtained by subtracting the annual number of deaths per thousand population from the annual number of births per thousand population in a given country or region—is considerably greater in the underdeveloped areas of the world than in developed areas. Latin America in particular currently has the highest growth rate in the world (see Figure 3). The former president of Colombia, Alberto Lleras Camargo, observes that Latin America achieved this dubious distinction by dramatically cutting its death rate while birth rates remained the same. It took more than one hundred years for most of the developed countries of the world to lower their death rates as much as Latin America has done in the past two decades by improving its practice of preventive medicine and sanitation procedures. Indeed, this author can well remember that when he began studying Latin America just twenty-five years ago, population growth was seen as one of the necessary conditions for the continent's development. Today, the fact that this very prerequisite has become a reality appears to threaten the continent with what may be the gravest crisis in its history.

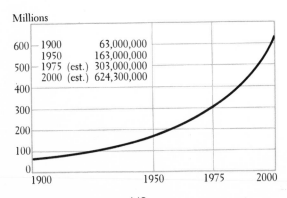

Millions

1900	63,000,000
1950	163,000,000
1975 (est.)	303,000,000
2000 (est.)	624,300,000

Figure 1. Population in Latin America: Historical and Projected. Reprinted from Report No. 3 of the Victor Fund for the International Planned Parenthood Federation, September 1966, by permission of the International Planned Parenthood Federation. *Sources: Chase Manhattan Bank; United Nations.*

Population growth is a problem not only because it touches on the pragmatic question of whether there will be enough food to feed those who are being born but also because it raises fundamental questions of human values and beliefs, especially ones involving principles of freedom and control. One school holds that married couples alone have the right to decide when and how many children they will have and, further, that

Figure 2. Components of Population Growth in Major World Regions, 1960 Estimate. From A. Y. Boyarsky, "A Contribution to the Problem of World Population in the Year 2000," in *Proceedings*, World Population Conference, 1965, 2, p. 12. The demographic characteristics for the areas included must be regarded as only approximations, due to different levels of reliability of national censuses and the use of estimates for areas where these are not even available. The chapter editor appreciates the generous help of Professor Fabio DaSilva in the preparation of this bar graph.

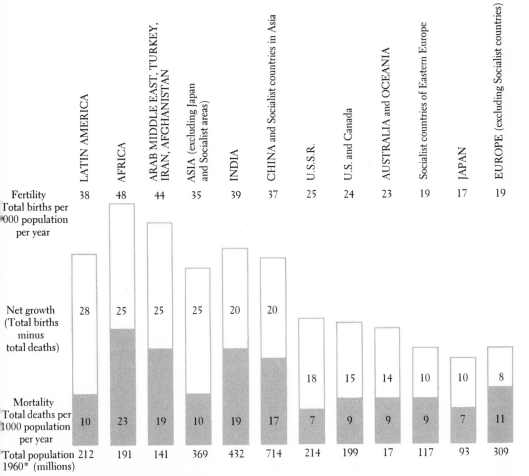

	LATIN AMERICA	AFRICA	ARAB MIDDLE EAST, TURKEY, IRAN, AFGHANISTAN	ASIA (excluding Japan and Socialist areas)	INDIA	CHINA and Socialist countries in Asia	U.S.S.R.	U.S. and Canada	AUSTRALIA and OCEANIA	Socialist countries of Eastern Europe	JAPAN	EUROPE (excluding Socialist countries)
Fertility Total births per 1000 population per year	38	48	44	35	39	37	25	24	23	19	17	19
Net growth (Total births minus total deaths)	28	25	25	25	20	20	18	15	14	10	10	8
Mortality Total deaths per 1000 population per year	10	23	19	10	19	17	7	9	9	9	7	11
Total population 1960* (millions)	212	191	141	369	432	714	214	199	17	117	93	309

*United Nations, *Demographic Yearbook*, 1962

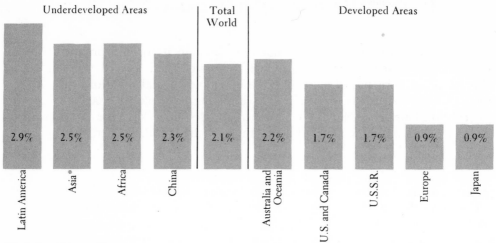

Underdeveloped Areas   Total World   Developed Areas

Latin America	Asia*	Africa	China		Australia and Oceania	U.S. and Canada	U.S.S.R.	Europe	Japan
2.9%	2.5%	2.5%	2.3%	2.1%	2.2%	1.7%	1.7%	0.9%	0.9%

*Excluding China and Japan.
Note: Growth rates are estimated from an analysis of 1920-62 growth rates.

Figure 3. Projected Population Growth Rates for Selected Areas, Through 1980. Reprinted from Raymond Ewell, "Famine and Fertilizer," in *Chemical and Engineering News*, 42 (December 14, 1964), p. 114, by permission of the publisher and the author. *Source: United Nations Demographic Yearbook, 1963.*

they cannot be considered free unless they have access to information about effective ways to limit and space childbirths and also have access to the necessary facilities for doing so.[1] This school believes that freedom necessarily implies a knowledge about human choices and their consequences. For the Latin American couple the question must be, What are the differential consequences of having more or fewer children? The consequences that they must consider involve the education and rearing of their children, fulfillment in job and career, the mysteries and joys of sexual pleasure and love, and a range of other matters.

Another school argues that since private marital acts that lead to the begetting of children have societal consequences, society has a right to influence a couple's decision about the number of children they will have. If a society has the right to self-preservation, does it not follow that this right extends even to matters of procreation? When uncontrolled procreation is seen as threatening society's ability to survive, can societal control and marital freedom be congruent? These questions, perhaps the most essential value questions raised by the present rate of population growth in Latin America, will be examined here in relation to four crucial aspects of society: government, religion, the family, and the economy. The readings have also been selected with these four aspects of society in mind.

[1] For a fuller discussion of this point, see W. V. D'Antonio, "Birth Control and Coercion" in *Commonweal*, 85, No. 9 (December 2, 1966), pp. 247–49.

Traditional Inaction

The role of government in the population problem. When Latin American political leaders were concerned about population at all in the past, their concern was generally that their countries were underpopulated, not overpopulated. The strong reaction of many Brazilian opposition leaders to the announcement made in August 1966 that their government was accepting birth control help from the United States may be taken as typical of traditional Latin American thinking on this subject.

The claim that a country is underpopulated often is valid from certain points of view, but the ideal relationship of population size to land mass is a more complex subject than leaders of the developing nations make it out to be. No one denies that there is a lot of land in Latin America. But how much of it is cultivable by the technology that is currently available? How much is livable? Why are not masses of people now moving out to the open spaces, into the highlands, into the jungles, instead of moving into the new forms of jungle on the peripheries of ancient cities? The fact of the matter is that Latin America's cities are growing in population much more rapidly than its rural areas, and its slums most rapidly of all. Bolivia may be as large as Germany in land area, but it does not necessarily follow that it can support sixty million people.

In judging the ideal relationship between land area and population, the quality of the people involved is no less relevant than the quality of the land. In terms of skilled laborers, teachers, engineers, managerial talent, and literate farmers with know-how about machinery, Latin America is indeed an underpopulated area. It is overpopulated with starving, illiterate, unskilled people who have little or no opportunity to live in a manner more dignified than that of their ancestors, to live in some degree of freedom.

The possibility that world population might be growing more rapidly than was desirable for the achievement of higher living standards became a concern to a few western scientists and government leaders only during the 1950's, and they did not really begin to understand the full significance of the population explosion for several more years. This is the main reason that most Latin American governments were not at all interested in population growth as a problem until recently. Another reason is that many governments in the area were controlled either by dictators who did not choose to think about the future or by democratic leaders struggling with more immediate problems who were unable to do so. A third reason is that accurate census data was usually unavailable. In societies with subsistence economies and an average life expectancy of only thirty-five or forty years, census data can seem slightly irrelevant. When death rates decline and there is population growth at all age levels, however, and when governments and peoples commit themselves to raising living standards, accurate data becomes vital for effective planning.

A fourth reason that Latin American governments have been slow to concern themselves with the problem or to take any action has been their fear of the Roman Catholic hierarchy's reaction. "What will the Archbishop say?" has been bandied about as a typical reaction of a government leader approached on this subject. Until recently, government leaders could not have expected support from Church leaders for any birth control projects.

Two other factors must be taken into account to complete the picture of traditional inaction by government leaders, one involving a desire to emulate the developed world and the other involving fear. The belief is widespread that urbanization and industrialization will automatically lead to rising levels of living and smaller families in Latin America, as they had done before in the United States and Western Europe; hence, no action by government officials is required. The fact that patterns of growth in Latin America today are distinct from those of the industrial revolution elsewhere has been overlooked, however. Not least important is the difference in the speed at which the death rate has been cut. One important result has been that in most of Latin America today, a majority of the people are less than twenty years old. It is a tremendous burden for the economy to provide education and housing for this age group, to say nothing of job opportunities. Urbanization is taking place more rapidly than industrialization. The resulting masses of young people in urban areas with no stable life patterns make good fodder for political demagogues.

The fear that keeps some Latin American governments from acting is part of an old problem of national identity and hemispheric suspicions. Many Latin Americans believe that *people* are equated with national power; others suspect that the United States, which has stolen everything else, now "wants to steal our children." Thus, government officials should look favorably on population increase as a matter of political strategy. However, India and the Arab world should demonstrate that numbers of people alone do not equal political or economic power. The suspicion about the United States may be more difficult to dispel wherever Yankee-phobia is strong, although it should be possible to point out that most of the Communist countries of Europe have lower growth rates than does the United States, whose own rate is significantly below that of Latin America.

The Roman Catholic Church and population. The readings in this chapter include official statements of Catholic Church leaders, setting forth their traditional views on the question of birth control. These theoretical points should be seen in the context of traditional Church practices and beliefs in Latin America.

The rigid hierarchical structure of the Church produced a belief system in which God was visualized as being on his throne in heaven, a *patrón* in charge of the hacienda, a father in charge of the family. Hierarchy, order, and discipline were the keynotes of this system, and reverence for and obedience to authority were the consequences. The Church provided a model for the Latin American family structure and easy justifications for authoritarian political structures. These, once established, tended to perpetuate all aspects of social life, including the desirability of a large family.

Pastoral teaching traditionally emphasized that children were a blessing from God. Children were born by God's will, not by man's. This being the case, how could one dare to interfere with God's work?

The Latin American Church, perhaps showing how much a part of general Latin American culture it is, has traditionally acquiesced in the double standard of sexual morality, which in its extreme form is characterized by *machismo* and the *casa chica*.[2] In part, this acquiescence went back to the early days of the Christian Church and to the formulations of St. Augustine. Augustine and other early writers taught that sex in marriage is for procreation, but also that man is human, is fundamentally a sinner, and must be expected to express himself sexually. This dichotomy was continued as the Church emphasized Mary, virgin and mother, pure and undefiled, as a symbol of good, while also reminding the faithful that the temptress Eve was the cause of man's fall. In many cases, wives were seen only as objects for procreation, not as partners in sexual love. (More recent Church teachings, which stand in sharp contrast to these attitudes, are discussed on pages 472–73.)

The Latin American family. In Latin America, the large family was the good family; extended kinship ties were an important resource, and in many countries they continue to be valuable. However, it must be remembered that for the average man, a large family and extended kinship ties were mainly an ideal, not an actuality. High death rates used to keep the population in balance; while seven or eight children might be born to a couple, only two or three survived. Probably only in the upper classes did the ideal of the large family and extensive kinship ties ever come close to realization until recent decades.

The Latin American family pattern has obviously been influenced by

[2] The word *macho* in Spanish refers to male virility as measured primarily but not exclusively by sexual power. Thus, a man who is called "macho" is one who has demonstrated his sexual prowess through many conquests, through the number of children (especially sons) he has fathered, or through both. His machismo may also be manifested in his physical power, his ability to face death with courage, and even his ability to achieve distinction in his professional career. In "Neurosis and the Psychological Structure of the Mexican family" (excerpted here as Reading 7), Rogelio Díaz Guerrero argues that in Mexico, at least, cultural patterns continue to support the machismo syndrome. Casa chica (small house) refers to the male custom of establishing a mistress in a separate household.

the machismo and casa chica syndrome, if only psychologically. To be macho is to be virile, brave, able to produce children. It is not yet possible to prove or disprove the hypothesis that machismo itself is positively correlated with family size, nor to say that extramarital affairs have added significantly to population growth, but it is already clear that these patterns are in conflict with emerging teachings on sex in marriage, the role of women, and birth control.

Another aspect of the traditional family pattern is expressed by the aphorism that "a woman's place is in the home." A woman was worshipped as a mother but not loved as a wife in the sexual sense. As Díaz Guerrero points out, there was a fear of arousing in the wife the same emotions expected from a mistress or a prostitute. The mother found her emotional outlets through her children, especially her sons. These ideas perhaps subtly fostered pronatalist sentiments in the mother.[3]

Food and people. Every student of Latin America knows that one of the region's main problems has been defined as the need for land reform. The *latifundio* and the *minifundio* are traditional obstacles to progress in Latin America, and land reform still remains part of the rhetoric of political life. In many countries, the traditional hacienda system had combined with a rigid Church structure, a strong sense of familism, and often a corrupt, weak, and authoritarian government to foster a way of life that no longer satisfied the aspirations of either leaders or followers. But there are no quick and easy solutions, as the struggles for thoroughgoing reform in Cuba, Bolivia, and Mexico demonstrate.

Social Change

The last two decades in Latin America have seen an increasingly rapid breakdown of the hacienda system, and with it a questioning of traditional values and beliefs. Urbanism, incipient industrialism, the growth of commercial bureaucracies, and pentecostal Protestantism have become important factors in effecting this change.[4] Discussions regarding population growth and family planning are one of the manifestations of this change. The remainder of this introduction will attempt to indicate briefly how the governments, the Catholic Church, married couples, and agriculturists are reacting to these tides of change.

[3] For a suggestive commentary on other consequences of this family pattern, see Bernard C. Rosen, "Socialization and Achievement Motivation in Brazil," in *American Sociological Review*, 27 (October 1962), pp. 612–24.

[4] See Emilio Willems, "Protestantism in Brazil and Chile," in *Religion, Revolution and Reform: New Forces for Change in Latin America*, edited by W. V. D'Antonio and F. B. Pike (New York: Frederick A. Praeger, 1964), for a careful analysis of the relationship between the growth of Protestantism and the decay of the traditional system.

Changing government attitudes and plans for action. The position of several Latin American governments regarding birth control has changed dramatically in recent years. Chile was the first to draw hemispheric attention. In 1960, as a result of studies on abortion dating back to 1950, the Chilean Government, through its National Health Service, allowed privately supported birth control clinics to be established on an experimental basis. Chile is no longer alone, however; a majority of countries are now fostering demographic studies, and in several countries the government has itself decided to sponsor birth control clinics. Colombia, long considered a citadel of conservative Catholicism in Latin America, was the only Latin American nation among the twelve nations to sign the United Nations Human Rights Day Declaration of December 10, 1966, in support of population control. Under the leadership of President Carlos Lleras Restrepo, Colombia opened the first of a projected 1200 birth control clinics throughout the nation as part of a program aimed to put it in the forefront of Latin American nations in facing up to population problems. By 1967, Colombia already ranked fourth in the world in the number of birth control pills sold per thousand fertile women, behind the United States, Australia, and Belgium.[5]

How greatly the attitudes of Latin American governments toward population control had changed was made evident to the world in April 1967, when the Eighth International Conference of Planned Parenthood was held in Santiago, Chile. The Conference, attended by more people from more countries than ever before in the movement's history, was addressed by President Eduardo Frei of Chile and by his Health Minister. This writer attended the Conference and came away with the conviction that most Latin American governments were now ready to confront the problem, through either public or private agencies. Rising abortion rates were clearly one of the main motivating factors in this decision to act.

The Catholic Church in the face of change. The Catholic Church continues to have more influence in Latin America than the numbers of practicing Catholics or consciously committed Catholics would suggest. But the Church cannot be said to be directly responsible for the rapid rate of population growth. It would seem most accurate to say that the Catholic Church can hasten or hinder the process of change but cannot stop it. For example, in March 1967, the Cardinal Archbishop of Bogotá violently condemned the Colombian Government's plans to establish birth control clinics offering all forms of contraceptives, but this did not alter the Government's plans.

The views of the Colombian cardinal are not necessarily typical of Latin American Church leaders, many of whom have been profoundly

[5] See "Advances in Fertility Control," in *Excerpta Medical Foundation*, 2, No. 1 (March 1967), p. 1.

affected by Schema XIII in the document "The Church in the Modern World," issued by the Second Vatican Council and accepted by Pope Paul VI in 1965. This document places new emphasis on autonomy, personal responsibility, and individual conscience. It recognizes conjugal love as a good in itself, praises responsible parenthood (meaning that couples should have no more children than they can hope to bring up in at least simple dignity), and states that couples alone are responsible for deciding when and how many children they will have. Another influential document is Pope Paul's encyclical "On the Development of Peoples" (1967), in which he acknowledged the right of governments to act to check too rapid demographic increases. The encyclical was interpreted in Santiago by almost all leaders as justifying their planning activities.

When U.S. aid to Brazil's population control program was announced in 1966, the comments of the Brazilian Church hierarchy seemed more restrained than those of many government officials. It may be too much to expect that a majority of the members of the Church hierarchy in Latin America will forcefully preach the progressive ideas contained in the Vatican II documents issued in 1965, but the winds of change have clearly touched the Church.[6]

Changing family patterns. Although population growth is a national and hemispheric problem, in another perspective it is still basically a family problem. Were there no explosion of population at all, the facts of

[6] The July 1968 papal encyclical, *Populae vitae*, added a new factor to the problem discussed in this chapter. In this encyclical, Pope Paul VI confirmed the traditional ban of the Roman Catholic Church on all methods of birth control other than the rhythm system. Widely challenged by many eminent Catholic theologians, this encyclical, which does not fall within the realm of pronouncements for which papal infallibility is claimed by the Church, seems likely to have little impact in Latin America. In most of the republics, scarcely more than twenty to thirty percent of the population are *practicing* Catholics. Historically, moreover, the admonitions of ecclesiastical leaders have been ignored even by the practicing faithful.

In the nineteenth century, despite clerical insistence that God's precepts and all the traditions of Christendom were being challenged, despite massive excommunications and countless threats of eternal damnation to all the allegedly atheistic advocates of liberal legislation, most Latin American republics enacted the condemned measures: religious toleration, secularization of cemeteries, state-supported educational systems, civil marriage, separation of Church and State, abolition of private ecclesiastical law courts, and state collection of tithes. Papal condemnations of various political constitutions were also ignored. Eventually, the Vatican and the churchmen of Latin America came to accept the situations and conditions that they had so intransigently denounced as contrary to natural law and divine positive law.

In many instances, then, the Church has eventually brought itself into conformity with changing conditions. Many observers expect this pattern to be repeated in the present controversy over birth control. In the meantime, many Latin American women —probably a majority of them—will take advantage of the decision-making role that "the pill" and other devices have provided for them. They will thus continue to advance toward greater equality with the male, even though this equality is contrary to the traditions of Latin America and, indeed, to some of the early teachings of the Catholic religion.—FBP

modern life—particularly the greater mobility and economic instability associated with urbanization and industrialization—would justify a reevaluation of procreation, family size, and sexuality. Perhaps for this reason, the people of Latin America have in fact reevaluated their ideas about these matters without waiting for encouragement or instruction from their governments or for alterations of the Church's position.

The most startling evidence of the difference between popular and official attitudes is found in the astounding abortion rates that have been reported for almost every country of Latin America. At the Santiago Conference, abortion rates were said to vary between one in three and one in four live births. The great majority of husbands apparently approve of abortion, and economic reasons were given as the primary motivating factor. Both abortion and the desire for family limitation preceded actual birth control propaganda by the governments.[7]

Sociologist J. Mayone Stycos reports that studies from various parts of Latin America consistently show that between sixty per cent and eighty per cent of the couples surveyed desire to limit their families and consider two to four children to be an ideal family size. Father Gustavo Pérez Ramírez reports that in three cities studied, at least fifty per cent of all women were using contraceptives; the differences between churchgoing Catholics and nonchurchgoers in this respect were very small.

The family pattern in Latin America is clearly changing, but the extent of the change should not be exaggerated. First, it must be remembered that abortion and contraception are not practiced by the majority of fertile women in the area at present, nor are they likely to be in the immediate future. Second, even assuming that all Latin American couples were to limit themselves to the currently popular ideal of four children per family, the population of the area would still grow rapidly. With the prevailing low mortality rates, any standard beyond two children per family assures that.

Food and people. With the population of Latin America certain to continue to grow at a fairly rapid rate for at least ten or fifteen years, what are the prospects for feeding the people? Most experts feel that it ought to be possible to double the food supply during the next twenty-five years. If the food supply is doubled, while the population is also doubling, this would simply mean that twice as many people will be living at the same level of poverty. Reading 13, on "famine and fertilizer," provides a sober reminder of the immensity of the task of feeding the population of Latin America during the years immediately ahead. There is little cause for optimism in this report.

[7] See "Epidemiology of Provoked Abortion in Santiago, Chile," by R. Armijo and J. Monreal, a paper presented at the Fourth International Conference of Planned Parenthood, for the most up-to-date findings on the abortion studies made in Chile during the past fifteen years.

READINGS

1. Lleras Camargo on Birth Control
in Latin America

Dr. Alberto Lleras Camargo is a former president of Colombia and one of Latin America's most distinguished statesmen. He is chairman of the board of *Visión* magazine and was a prime mover and chairman of the First Pan American Assembly on Population, held in Cali, Colombia, in August 1965. The following extracts from an article originally published in 1966 constitute a broad survey of population problems in Latin America.

Until a relatively short time ago, discussion of the problem of over-population was taboo in Latin America. But recent studies and growth estimates in relation to uncontrolled fertility have stunned the world. This is particularly true in Latin America, where the growth rate is higher than anywhere else in the world. The result is that discussion has forced itself to the foreground of public interest.

Ever since the days of the prehistoric era and until the beginning of our own time, diseases, periodic famines, genocide, the great plagues and epidemics accounted for a steady drain in demographic growth. War helped to boost mortality.

In the second decade of this century, things began to change rapidly. With endless patience and resourcefulness, means were developed to curb the rule of death over mankind.

. . .

It is not surprising, therefore, that today we are faced with a totally new social phenomenon. The problem of our era is, in its simplest terms, that we have boldly and effectively fought the causes of death, but we have not yet mastered the art of controlling the source of life.

When the global population attained one billion, the Protestant clergyman Thomas Robert Malthus published a book entitled, "An Essay on the Principle of Population." This study was prophetic. But the Malthusian thesis was distorted and maliciously oversimplified. Malthus

SOURCE: "Lleras Camargo on Birth Control" from Alberto Lleras Camargo, "The Key Issue in Latin America: Birth Control—the Sooner the Better," in Report No. 3 of the Victor Fund for the International Planned Parenthood Federation, September 1966, pp. 7–11. Reprinted by permission of the International Planned Parenthood Federation.

thought that food production would not keep pace with population growth and that a great famine was threatening the civilization of his time. When this reasoning was contradicted by the formidable increase in agricultural productivity, people lost interest in the population problem. There would always be food, they said, for any number of people, even if it meant obtaining it from the sea, or, if necessary, creating it synthetically.

As the Chilean demographer Carmen Miró points out, the essential element in population trends in Latin America is the speed of growth. At the beginning of this century, Latin America's population was estimated at 60 million. By 1960 it had already exceeded 207 million. In other words, the population had multiplied by almost three and a half times in the span of sixty years. The population of 1900 took forty years to double, but that of 1950 will double in twenty-five years.

Latin America today is an underdeveloped region without sufficient capital, and facing tremendous problems of development. It must become industrialized and make fundamental changes in its way of life if it is to provide work for all its people and if it is to reach a level of development at which a reduced birth rate and natural adaptation to prevailing conditions can make an impact. The trouble is that, at the current rate of its population growth, Latin America is headed for a serious crisis.

It was Julian Huxley, the writer and biologist, who reduced the problem to its essential terms when he wrote: "In some parts of Asia and in most of Central and South America, the population is growing so rapidly that it will double in a little over twenty years. If the production of food and manufactured articles, houses, schools and teachers could reach the same growth rate as that of the population, it would be possible to ameliorate the disastrous plight of these underdeveloped, overpopulated countries."

Our countries are continuing their programs of preventive hygiene, which further speed up the population spiral. The steep, though still inadequate drop in infant mortality, combined with the high birth rate is leading to a gradual reduction in the average age of the whole area.

In many countries, especially in the tropical zone, fifty-five per cent of the population is now below the age of twenty. In any normal situation these young people would be dependent and non-productive. Most of them would be in school. But in Latin America, it means that millions of teenagers are looking for work and are unable to find it.

Under the pressure of overpopulation and growing unemployment in the rural areas, millions of men and women have been migrating from the countryside to the cities. These people are in the lowest economic and cultural strata. The majority are illiterate and not equipped for work that requires at least some technical schooling. Generally, they are families with a large number of children who have not gone to school. The largest number has flocked to the most heavily populated urban centers. But the cities already suffer from unemployment and overpopulation, just as the rural areas. The migrants crowd together outside the workers' suburbs, and within just a few hours they build the unbelievable slums which have ruined and blackened the image of Latin American cities. . . .

Conflicts soon began to develop between the newly arrived refugees from the land and the organized workers of the cities. The migrants came into contact with the underworld, who sought to use them. This situation has led to a number of complicated social phenomena. Quite a few political movements which have destroyed—or aim to destroy—the beginnings of democratic government, as well as some violent and crude dictatorships, can be traced to these social tensions. The urban salary level is constantly threatened by the added supply of manpower from the rural areas, and irresponsible demagogues haunt the slums in their quest for easy gains. Here in this huge mass of eroded and desperate humanity lie the seeds of Latin America's gravest hazard.

Latin America's traditional political systems are not equipped to deal with the problem of overpopulation. The excessive drain on capital resources which virtually neutralizes the influx of new funds; the frustrated attempts at economic development, economies over-burdened by an inordinately high percentage of dependent children and youths; the continuing migration of hopeless rural masses; urban and rural unemployment—all these problems require ever higher levels of administrative capability.

But with each passing day, the range of action narrows. For more and more resources are needed to ward off an endless string of emergencies. . . .

There is a shortage of capital to finance the urgent needs of economic development. The ratio of new capital investment made to attain an added income flow in developing nations runs at something like three to one. In other words, three units of investment must be made in productive facilities in order to return, in the future, one new unit of per capita income.

Therefore it requires a nine per cent increase in capital investment annually in order to sustain a three per cent increase in per capita income—sizable investments that only hold the status quo in a country where the population is expanding by three per cent each year.

This is how we consume our scarce reserves. We need more schools, more colleges and more universities. Our needs for hospitals, for health services, better food and housing, for gainful employment, for expansion and strengthening of our weak economic structure exceeds our financial capacity. In underdeveloped countries where the population is exploding, a twelve to fifteen per cent increase in capital investment must be attained each year. We also must carry out agrarian reforms and decentralize the administration of rural communities so as to extend to the rural areas some of the benefits that are available in the cities. We must introduce modern farming methods and provide decent living conditions for our present population.

But neither land reform nor revenue-boosting tax reforms represent solutions as long as wave after wave of people pile misery on misery—people who are illiterate, half civilized, in bad health, undernourished, poorly dressed and shod and without a roof over their heads. These people do not contribute to production and hardly figure in consumption. Constantly growing in number, and jammed into their slums, they are becoming aware of their capacity for trouble. This is why the professional agents of world revolution dog their footsteps.

Up to now the population problem has been side-stepped. The politicians and even some orthodox economists have skipped over it with noncommittal phrases.

The truth is that nobody sounded the warning in time, and that all of us—clergymen and military, politicians and sociologists, psychologists and demographers—have been caught by surprise.

Now that we are asking ourselves why the cozy world of twenty or thirty years ago has suddenly become so violent and unmanageable—now that our hopes for an economic and social "take-off" have been frustrated over and over again—we are finally putting our finger on the root of the problem.

. . .

We cannot allow mankind to suffocate in an abyss of its own making—least of all our own people here in the Americas. The humane, Christian, economic and political solution is birth control. And the sooner the better.

2. *The Brazilian*

Birth Control "Bomb" of 1966

Dr. J. Mayone Stycos, one of the leading authorities on population growth in Latin America and author of *The Control of Human Fertility in Jamaica*, is professor of sociology and director of the International Population Program at Cornell University. Dr. Stycos has instituted a service that reviews newspaper articles on population and family planning published in all parts of Latin America. His first

SOURCE: "The Brazilian Birth Control 'Bomb' of 1966" from Cornell University International Population Program, "Latin American Newspaper Coverage of Population and Family Planning," Bulletin No. 1 (January 1967), pp. 1–4. Reprinted by permission of the author.

bulletin, from which the following excerpts are drawn, included nearly 4000 items, all originally published in the second six months of 1966. They reveal an increasing popular concern about the population problem in Latin America and show that small but significant percentages in all countries (eleven to twenty-eight per cent) favor birth control.

On August 4, 1966, Brazilian newspapers contained such headlines as: The Government Wants to Control Births; Brazil Asks for Aid to Control Progeny; Brazil Limits Births with Yankee Aid; etc. These statements headed articles from Washington telling of Secretary of State Dean Rusk's announcement to the Subcommittee on Foreign Operations of the U.S. House of Representatives that the United States had granted financial aid to five Latin American countries which had requested it, among them Brazil.

Subcommittee Chairman Otto Passman was noted to have said that aid for studies leading to a birth control program might turn out to be as explosive as the atomic bomb in case the offer met with the opposition of religious authorities.

The "bomb" exploded immediately in the form of headlines and articles in the next day's papers expressing the shock, disapproval and anger of numerous Brazilians prominent in the fields of politics, religion and education. Reactions to what the editor of *La Folha de S. Paulo* called "this story of birth control with dollars nobody asked for" continued occupying a considerable amount of space in the papers for the next ten days.

Politicians state views. Political figures expressed their views in press and TV interviews and in speeches in the Legislative Assembly.

Deputy Gilberto Azevedo, Vice President of the Foreign Affairs Commission, announced that the Commission was going to ask the Itamarati [the Ministry of Foreign Affairs] on what authority aid had been requested. In addition, he would ask for the official text of the petition so that the Diplomatic Commission of the Chamber of Deputies could express its opinion. "This seems to me like the work of the Planning Ministry, which is planning everything now, even births," he said, concluding by stating that as a Catholic he was opposed to birth control in Brazil.

Deputy Jader Albergaria of the ARENA of Minas Gerais requested the Health Commission to make a declaration, terming it an outrage that, before informing its Congress, the Brazilian government should communicate with the United States on such a matter.

During a meeting of the Education Commission, Deputy Brito Velho said, "Before seeking to limit births, our authorities might better have asked the United States for a contraceptive for the Institutional Acts." [1]

---

[1] [The Institutional Acts replaced the Brazilian Constitution in 1964.]

In the August 5 session of the Chamber, Deputy Alfonso Arinos, Jr. argued that "those who want birth control are certain classes of the economic-financial oligarchy and servants of national and foreign capitalism, for whom it is necessary to keep population down to the low rate of productivity of the present economic-financial system." [He continued:] "We cannot have a growth of productivity, occasioned by social and agrarian reforms (the latter a joke at present), unless we have a substantial population growth. This is the hidden interest of many who are now planning to control the increase of births in Brazil."

Arinos said he was anxiously waiting for the irony of fate to make Minister Roberto Campos, perhaps for the first time, contradict North American Secretary of State Dean Rusk, author of the declaration in respect to Brazil's being interested in birth control. He added that the Brazilian government is having difficulties introducing to the public a project of that sort which deservedly meets with strong objections by the Church.

On August 17 Deputy Getúlio Moura, member of the opposition party from Rio [de Janeiro], told the Chamber that the Government and American technicians were making the final review of their birth control project. He added that they should not believe the Government would send the proposition to the Congress, "having to institute birth control by decree. It is not admissible that the Chamber should accept this limitation which is imposed on us by a country which, with the same dimensions as ours, has 300 million [sic] inhabitants, because the impression is that the American people with their land already overpopulated is concerning itself with our empty spaces and intends to occupy our territory."

Deputy Tufi Nassif stated that the Government is mistaken in supporting a birth control program when the problem is not one of birth but of infant mortality. Birth control may be useful to the United States but not to Brazil which is not sufficiently populated.

Deputy Noronha, Jr. called for the evidence demonstrating that the country's geographic area and potential riches were insufficient for a population greater than the present. Instead of trying to cut down on the population, it would be more constructive to increase the productivity of Brazilian manpower.

Deputy Pereira Pinto attributed the United States announcement to groups involved in the manufacture of birth control pills. He offered to get up on the platform of the Legislative Assembly as many times as necessary to defend the right to be born. "It is absurd to think of birth control by the government in a country as big as ours. What we need is better living conditions."

Adauri Fernandes, a Deputy from Rio, terms birth control for a country the size of Brazil absurd and calls upon the authorities to abandon their "poetry" and turn their attention to the "drama" of infant mortality.

Deputy Pedro Braga, saying that he considered the denials of the Government on the birth control aid matter weak and unconvincing, asserted that carrying out such a measure would represent "the ultimate in betrayal and an iniquitous example of servility." He said the Brazilian government ought not to hand out contraceptive pills and protested in the name of future generations this "attempt against the security of the nation." [2]

A least one strong defense of attention to population problems was reported. In a speech before the Assembly, Deputy Moab Callas criticized his fellow parliamentarians for manifesting opposition to the American offer of aid to Brazil. He painted a dramatic picture of the hunger which will occur within the next twenty or fifty years unless the world's birth rate declines and declared that such a decrease is necessary to avert famine and an atomic war.

Announcing his opposition to abortion and sterilization, Moab Callas said he felt that birth control merited serious thought since he dared to hope that the Pope was going to decide in favor of it. [He continued:] Birth control cannot be accomplished by compulsory governmental measures but by education of the people so that they will exercise voluntary control. Such a program of education in keeping with the customs and religious beliefs of the people would be of immediate benefit in cutting down on abortion.

This view was supported by the remarks of two other Deputies, Larry Faria and Siegfried Heuser. The former said that when he was town councillor he had asked the Welfare Secretary to create posts in the poorer towns where the idea of birth control could be explained.

.   .   .

Replies of government officials. José Maria Vilar de Queirós, adviser on international affairs of the Planning Ministry, hastened to deny on August 5 that Brazil had made any request for North American aid for birth control.

He said that the studies made so far by the Demographic Center of the Planning Ministry only referred to the economic implications of the matter, such as the composition of the Brazilian populace, its growth and

[2] The reaction of many Latin American men, particularly those of conservative persuasions, against birth control rests in part on their understanding of national identity. Traditionally, they have sought a national identity characterized by a hierarchical, disciplined society, by the authority of those at the top and the submission of those below. In the basic social unit (the family), men held the position as head, regarded themselves as the natural wielders of authority, and assigned to women the role of submission. They felt that domestic harmony depended on this arrangement. Many men now fear that birth control will liberate women by placing them on a basis of equality with males in matters of family planning and sex habits, and thus disrupt at its very roots the hierarchical organization of society; it would threaten to lead ultimately to the destruction of the entire corporate order to which K. H. Silvert refers in his introduction to Chapter X, and would initiate a leveling process that could only result in the twisting and distorting of the nation's true and proper identity.—FBP

participation in economic activity, without going into the problem of birth control in any way.

The Itamarati announced that Brazil had not made any official request of the U.S. government for financial aid to control births in the country. Press Secretary Orlando Carbonar declared, "There must have been some confusion in the news transmitted." [He continued:] Certainly the Center of Demographic Studies of the Planning Ministry would be interested in receiving North American financial aid and technical assistance for demographic studies—and not specifically for birth control—so as to better fulfill its mission as an auxiliary organ of economic planning.

In a television press interview on August 23 Planning Minister Roberto Campos said, "To say that the problem does not exist is absurd. The problem is not to control, but to know if we ought to put at the disposal of the people the means and information necessary for this measure. Therefore the Government will create a Demographic Center in order to study the problem more deeply, awaiting the official word of the Church before making a definitive decision on birth control."

[Campos explained that] the unprecedented population growth causes great difficulties in planning. In Brazil barely 38 per cent of the population is of the age to produce; the major part are at the pre-productive age which will cause difficulties in the future with the lack of a market for so many working people. Half of the population is less than 20 years old, more than 40 per cent below 14. Each worker has 3.3 dependents.

A recent survey [reported Campos] reveals that more than 40 per cent of married couples in Brazil use brutal contraceptive practices such as abortion. [He] quoted the Chilean Jesuit priest, the Rev. Roger Vekemans, who said, "The statistics on abortions in Latin America constitute the best plebiscite in favor of birth control."

3. *Controversy in Honduras*

> Just before the "population bomb" exploded in Brazil, a smaller commotion arose in Tegucigalpa, as described in the following newspaper article.

Promotion of Birth Control Policy Gets Health Minister in "Hot Water"

Tegucigalpa, Honduras—Archbishop Héctor Santos Hernández of Tegucigalpa has asked for the removal of Dr. José Antonio Peraza as min-

SOURCE: "Controversy in Honduras" from the *Philadelphia Catholic Standard and Times* (official newspaper of the Philadelphia Archdiocese), August 5, 1966, p. 13.

ister of public health on grounds that he is trying to implement a birth control program that is detrimental to the real interests of Honduras.

A conference on birth control organized by the International Planned Parenthood Federation was held here at the beginning of June with the cooperation of Peraza.

The archbishop accused Peraza of being responsible also for a secret agreement signed with the U.S. Agency for International Development (AID) to promote birth control measures in Honduras.

The archbishop had threatened to excommunicate 16 civic officials who attended the birth control conference, and decried the use of Honduras as a "guinea pig" in birth control experiments.

Peraza at that time denied that the archbishop's criticism of the conference indicated that there is a serious church-state conflict over the government's policy on birth control.

In calling for Peraza's removal as minister of public health, the archbishop claimed that the policy of favoring limitation of population growth is politically misguided.

Archbishop Santos warned that larger nations, including Latin American nations such as Mexico, Brazil, and Argentina, want only a small population in Honduras and Central America in order to further their own expansive political programs.

We are a people poor in human resources, the archbishop said, and government officials without a patriotic vision will never lead us out of our present dependent and defenseless condition.

He demanded that the government of President Oswaldo López Arellano name another minister of public health, one who is more aware of national problems and who has more love for Honduras.

4. *Population and Economic Growth in Brazil*

> Ing. Glycon de Paiva was formerly president of the National Bank of Economic Development and also president of the National Confederation of Commerce of Brazil. The following excerpts are from a speech Mr. de Paiva delivered in 1964, showing the effect of population growth on economic development in Brazil.

SOURCE: "Population and Economic Growth in Brazil" from Ing. Glycon de Paiva, "Relations Between Population and Economic Growth in Brazil," an address delivered at the Fourth Conference of the International Planned Parenthood Federation, San Juán, Puerto Rico, April 1964. Reprinted by permission of the International Planned Parenthood Federation.

Brazilian population grows at the annual rate of 3.4%. This means it will reach 100 million in 1970, in about seven years, and 150 million in 1982; 200 million in 1990 and and 225 million in the year 2000, that is, 36 years from now. At present, with nearly 80 million inhabitants, the country faces a shortage of almost all items needed to carry on life: houses, hospitals, schools, universities, means of communication, power, water, drainage, wheat, petroleum, coal, steel, and the majority of the metals. It is easy to imagine what may happen from now on.

The deficits of goods and services are translated, financially, in structural inflation: excessive expansion of currency with no corresponding increase of goods produced or services. There is everywhere the intention of tentatively doing what is normally necessary to keep social life going by utilizing currency without corresponding factors of production. This attempt results in a financial toxicosis: uncontrolled inflation [and other serious social, economic, and educational effects].

.   .   .

It is amazing to see how difficult it is for people to locate the real origin of social problems of the nature here briefly described. Causes are put everywhere except on the real source of social troubles which is the fast widening gap between economy and population.

The following are two sets of false explanations and consequent remedies for the Brazilian crisis frequently advanced in the press, radio, television or political parties.

a. Capitalist spoliation of Brazilian economy, principally foreign spoliation and especially American spoliation. . . . If the State would own everything and if it would substitute private initiative by the sole governmental initiative, the crisis would be solved in the long run and quietness would return permanently to our souls under the maximum social justice possible in the circumstances.

b. Others imagine that the cause of the chronic crisis is the financial disorder resulting from bad governmental management of public finance, from the corruption that grows in governmental circles. It would suffice to reestablish good public order. . . .

[The explanation offered here] proclaims the excess of population over economy as responsible for the structural situation of a crisis unavoidable and insoluble, either by communist surgery or by democratic clinics.

According to this point of view, the great spoliative agent of Brazilian economy is not the yankee, nor the native businessman, nor even the bad manager of the public [treasury], but the undesired child, the adolescent that invades our lives in a number geometrically growing, repressing the development and exhausting the Nation. . . .

5. The Official Views
of Pius XI and Pius XII on Birth Control

Early in 1967, Milton Meier carefully reexamined the major policy statements on birth control, conjugal love, and responsible parenthood made by the Popes in recent years. He also examined in detail the deliberations of the special Papal Commission on Birth Control and concluded that Pope Paul VI would reaffirm the traditional teaching against "artificial birth control." In July 1968 the Pope did confirm the traditional ban, as Meier foresaw (see footnote 6, page 448). Excerpts from Meier's survey article follow.

December 31, 1930: In answer to a widely-publicized statement of the Anglican Church condoning contraception in certain cases, Pope Pius XI issued *Casti Connubii*, an encyclical explicitly stating the official Catholic doctrine on marriage and its abuses. It contained his famous condemnation of contraception:

> Others plead that they can neither observe continence, nor, for personal reasons or for reasons affecting the mother, or on account of economic difficulties, can they consent to have children. But no reason whatever, even the gravest, can make what is intrinsically against nature become conformable with nature and morally good. The conjugal act is of its very nature designed for the procreation of offspring; and therefore those who in performing it deliberately deprive it of its natural power and efficacy, act against nature and do something which is shameful and intrinsically immoral. . . . [A]ny use of matrimony whatsoever in the exercise of which the act is deprived, by human interference, of its natural power to procreate life, is an offense against the Law of God and of nature, and . . . those who commit it are guilty of a grave sin.

April 1, 1944: A few Catholic theologians had begun to teach and write that the Church overemphasized the "biological integrity" of the sexual act, that the marriage act as an expression and source of mutual love between the spouses is equally important.

The Sacred Congregation of the Holy Office, the chief Vatican arbiter of dogmatic and moral matters, did not agree. On this date, it answered a question submitted to it by several anxious bishops with a decree that was approved by Pope Pius XII:

SOURCE: "The Official Views of Pius XI and Pius XII on Birth Control" from Milton Meier, "No Comment," in *Report* (February 1967). Reprinted by permission of the publishers.

To the query: "Is it possible to admit the opinion of some authors who deny that the primary end of matrimony is the procreation and education of the offspring, or teach that the secondary ends are not essentially subordinated to the primary ends, but are with them parellel (*aeque principales*) and independent?" the Holy Office decrees: "It cannot be admitted."

October 29, 1951: Addressing the Italian Association of Midwives, Pope Pius XII made a major re-statement of the two doctrinal points mentioned above, plus the first authoritative declaration on the morality of periodic partial abstinence, practiced to avoid conception by limiting sexual expression to the periods of natural sterility (the so-called "rhythm" method). He said:

> The moral lawfulness of such conduct of husband and wife should be affirmed or denied according as their intention to observe constantly those periods is or is not based on sufficiently morally sure motives. The mere fact that husband and wife do not offend the nature of the act and are even ready to accept and bring up the child, who, notwithstanding their precautions, might be born, would not be itself sufficient to guarantee the rectitude of their intention and the unobjectionable morality of their motives.
>
> From this it follows that the observance of the natural sterile periods may be lawful, from the moral viewpoint: and it is lawful in the conditions mentioned (serious motives, such as those which not rarely arise from medical, eugenic, economic and social so-called "indications"). If, however, according to a reasonable and equitable judgment, there are no such grave reasons either personal or deriving from exterior circumstances, the will to avoid the fecundity of their union, while continuing to satisfy to the full their sensuality, can only be the result of a false appreciation of life and of motives foreign to sound ethical principles.

6. The Double Standard
in Venezuela (1965)

Adultery Bill Riles Women

Caracas, Venezuela (AP)—Venezuelan husbands who kill two-timing wives would get a legal break under a bill approved by the Senate this week.

They no longer would be charged with homicide, like 280 men whose

SOURCE: "The Double Standard in Venezuela" from the *South Bend Tribune*, October 29, 1965, p. 14. Reprinted by permission of the publisher.

cases are pending. Conviction might mean only six months in jail instead of the 30 years that is the maximum under present law.

Now Venezuelan women are demanding equal shooting rights.

"If they can shoot us in an act of adultery and go almost unpunished by law, why can't we do the same?" a woman lawyer, Rosa Brunstein, indignantly asked the lawmakers.

The bill still is subject to approval by the Chamber of Deputies. Perhaps the Chamber will pass it, but the pressure of women's groups suggests it may be pigeonholed.

As drawn up in the Senate, the bill says:

"He will not be guilty of homicide or injury who, finding his wife in the actual act of adultery, kills or injures her or her accomplice or both. Sentence in this case would be no more than three years and not less than six months."

The same applies to a brother or other male relative who, in his own home, finds a woman in sexual intercourse with a man.

"This amounts to legalizing the death penalty in Venezuela," was the comment of another woman lawyer, Mercedes Omana.

A prominent woman politician vowed to mobilize her party's "female masses in defense of the rights of women which this government has taken away."

A woman deputy of the Democratic Popular Front, Petra de Aranguren, said, "This law is a violation of our rights."

Lawyer Brunstein said the easiest solution is divorce. She said divorces would even reduce the conceivable number of murders should women be given the right to avenge the family honor with a .45.

"The law always condemns women, but all men are adulterers," she said.

Miss Haydee Rangel, a law student, said: "What happens is that in the case of women, adultery has more serious repercussions because of the possibility of pregnancy."

And that is the whole point, according to Sen. Mejias Salvatierra of the government Democratic Action Party.

The senator argued that in the case of adultery by a woman her husband's paternity is always in jeopardy.

"Besides," he said, "one must always remember that man is the head of the family and when he commits adultery he usually does it outside the house and always in circumstances which are not offensive to conjugal and social relationship, whereas when a woman commits adultery she jeopardizes paternity and relaxes moral authority."

7. Aspects of the Psychology of Sex in Mexico

Dr. Rogelio Díaz-Guerrero is chief of psychological research at the National University of Mexico, president-elect of the Interamerican Psychological Society, and one of Mexico's leading psychiatrists. He has long been a leader in cross-cultural research, with particular interest in family structural and identity problems. The following passages from a paper by Dr. Díaz-Guerrero discuss the Mexican male's understanding of virility and related matters.

The Mexican family is founded upon two fundamental propositions: (1) the unquestioned and absolute supremacy of the father and (2) the necessary and absolute self-sacrifice of the mother.

The mother's role has from times unknown acquired an adequate qualification in the term "abnegation," which means the denial of any and all possible selfish aims.

.   .   .

Even before a Mexican child is born, a set of expectations is already at work. Although in many societies there is a preference for boy babies, in Mexico the stress is greater—it must be a boy!

During the entire childhood the sign of virility in the male is courage to temerity, aggressiveness, and not to run away from a fight or break a deal (no rajarse). But both the boy and the girl must be obedient within the family. Paradoxically a father will feel proud of the child who did not run from a fight in the street, but at home may punish him severely for having disobeyed his orders regarding street fights. This appears to mean that the child must be masculine but not as much as his father.

During adolescence the sign of virility in the male is to talk about or act in the sexual sphere. He who possesses information and/or experience regarding sexual matters is inevitably the leader of the group. The prepubescent boys are coldly discriminated from the "seances" of adolescents on the basis that they are not sufficiently male-like to participate. Girls, now instead of being avoided, are the alluring goal of the males. During adolescence there comes into being a peculiar phenomenon. The pursuit of the female unfolds into two aspects. In one the adolescent searches for the ideal woman—the one he would like to convert into his

SOURCE: "Aspects of the Psychology of Sex in Mexico" from Rogelio Díaz-Guerrero, "Neurosis and the Psychological Structure of the Mexican Family," in American Journal of Psychiatry (December 1955), pp. 411–14.

wife. This one must have all the attributes of the perfect feminine role. She must be chaste, delicate, homey (*hogareña*), sweet, maternal, dreamy, religious, and must not smoke or cross her legs. Her face must be beautiful, especially her eyes—but not necessarily her body. Sexuality takes a very secondary role. In the other aspect the adolescent searches for the sexualized female and with the clear purpose in mind of sexual intercourse. Here the roundness of the lines, and their quantity [are] determinant [factors]. The male Mexican's female ideal implies breasts and hips, particularly hips, far broader and far more quivering than is considered proper in this country. It is even more interesting to note that in every case as soon as the individual has found the woman he may idealize, *ipso facto*, all other women become objects for the sexualized search, and tempting objects of seduction.

As adolescence advances into youth and adulthood the extreme differentiation among feminine objects loses some of its momentum. And although the entire expression of sexuality is still only open to lovers or prostitutes, it is also true that the youth or the adult who looks for a woman with matrimonial intentions will, before making his decisions, attend a little more to the quality and quantity of the secondary sexual characteristics of the female. It is well to repeat, however, that even in this case chastity and the other factors of femininity continue to weigh heavily.

From adolescence on and through the entire life of the male, virility will be measured by the sexual potential, and only secondarily in terms of physical strength, courage, or audacity. So much so, that even these other characteristics of behavior as well as still other subtler ones, are believed to be dependent upon the sexual capacity. The accent falls upon the sexual organs and their functions. The size of the penis has its importance. The size of the testicles has more, but more important than the physical size is the "functional" size. It is assumed they are in good functioning when: (1) the individual acts efficiently in sexual activity or speaks or brags convincingly of his multiple seductive successes; (2) when he speaks or actually shows that he is not afraid of death; (3) when the individual is very successful in the fields of intellectuality, science, etc.

But it is during adolescence and youth that the Mexican women are going to experience their happiest period. In effect, they will sooner or later be converted into the ideal woman for a given male. Then they will be placed on a pedestal and be highly overevaluated. The girl in this period will receive poems, songs, gallantries, serenades, and all the tenderness of which the Mexican male is capable. Such tokens are numerous, for the male has learned very well in his infancy, through relations with his mother, a very intensive and extensive repertoire for the expression of affection; and, as a part of the maternal ideals, romanticism and idealism dig deep into the mental structure of the Mexican. At any rate, our Cinderella, who has heretofore given all and received nothing in exchange, enters into an ecstatic state as a result of this veneration, this incredible submission—as a slave to a queen—of the imposing, proud, dictatorial and conceited male.

Soon after the termination of the honeymoon, the husband passes from slave to master and the woman enters the hardest test of her life. The idealism of the male rapidly drops away toward the mother. To make matters worse, the wife cannot be considered as a sexual object in a broad sense. Mexican husbands repeatedly indicate that sex must be practiced in one way with the wife and in another with the lover. The most common statement refers to the fear that the wife might become too interested in sex if he introduces her into the subtilities of [sexual] pleasure. At other times this fear is expressed in a clearer fashion by saying that the wife might become a prostitute.

8. Increasing the Output
of Mexican Agriculture

The following excerpts from a bulletin written under the direction of Dr. Robert C. Cook of the Population Reference Bureau give some indication of the profound effect Mexico's rapid population growth will have on its efforts to raise living standards.

With a total land area of 487 million acres, Mexico is about one-quarter the size of the contiguous United States. Only 74 million acres are suitable for agriculture. In 1963, only 40 per cent (31 million acres) was actually under cultivation. Thus less than one acre per capita was available for food production. In the United States, where yield per acre is much higher than in Mexico, there are two and one-half acres of crop-land per capita.

Almost half of Mexico's territory lends itself only to grazing. One-sixth is forest, which is being depleted, as Mexican forests have been for centuries, by uncontrolled exploitation.

If it comes to pass that there are indeed about 70 million Mexicans in 1980, the ratio of arable land to man will be almost halved unless more

SOURCE: "Increasing the Output of Mexican Agriculture" from "Mexico: The Problem of People," in *Population Bulletin*, 20, No. 7 (November 1964), pp. 183–89. Reprinted by permission of Population Reference Bureau, Inc.

land can be brought into production. This is not a very probable solution because the supply of suitable land is shrinking.

.   .   .

Augmenting food production to provide for 70 million people will be a considerable feat. In order to raise consumption to a satisfactory level for all, annual food production must increase much more rapidly than population growth. Between 1958 and 1962, food production increased at an annual rate of about 3.8 per cent. Theoretically, if this rate is maintained, there will be enough food for everyone. However, improvement in the quantity and quality of the average Mexican's diet is unlikely in the near future.

.   .   .

According to the *Hispanic American Report*, February 1959:

> Since one hectare (2.47 acres) per person is required to feed the population, Vasques de la Parra figured that Mexico has a deficit of 18 million hectares (44.5 million acres) of arable land. As if to emphasize this statement, Dr. Frederico Gómez, director of the Children's Hospital in Mexico City, said that malnutrition was responsible for from 40 to 60 per cent of deaths of children aged one to four.

.   .   .

Scarcity of land, as well as the prevailing pattern of landholding in Mexico, severely handicaps increased food production. Some land is privately owned, but the most typical form of landholding is the *ejido* system, a series of farming communities established under Mexico's agrarian reform program in 1915.

Since the Revolution, land has been expropriated from the owners of vast haciendas and redistributed among the peasants. The ejido system has satisfied the peasants' hunger for land ownership, but because much of this land is poor, it fails to satisfy their physical hunger or to improve their economic status.

Ejidos are land-owning villages in which the land may be worked cooperatively or by each family on its own plot. Each group decides which system to use.

Although the *ejidatario* may pass his land on to his heirs, he is prohibited from renting or selling it.

. . . In 1963, approximately 50 per cent of the land in cultivation was held by ejidatarios. While it is very difficult to state accurately the average size of the ejidatario's holdings, certainly few exceed 10 acres and many contain less. "Farms" of such small size produce unsatisfactory yields because they are unsuitable for mechanized farming methods.

Since the ejido is an accepted institution, plans have been made to overcome its disadvantages by integrating ejidal lands into an organization of cooperative production units. By bringing together land units large enough for mechanical farming and the utilization of other modern farming techniques, the Department of Agrarian Affairs and Land Settlement expects to increase both production per unit and farm income.

9. *The Situation in Chile*

> In the following selection, Dr. Hernán Romero, professor of preventive and social medicine at the National University of Chile, describes the problems he and his colleagues encountered in Chile and the program they developed as a response, which put their country in the forefront among Latin American nations in dealing with family planning.

Latin America enjoys the dubious distinction of having the most rapidly growing population in the world, unprecedented in the history of mankind. At the current rate, Latin America's population should double in twenty-three years and triple before the end of the century. The substantial drop in the death rate, coupled with a steady birth rate, has resulted in an unbalanced distribution of age groups. Persons under fifteen years of age account for forty and, in some areas, even fifty per cent of the population, compared with twenty-five per cent for Europe and thirty per cent for North America.

This has placed a heavy burden on people in the working and producing years who have to support and educate many non-producers. They are thus forced to devote a major part of their income to current consumption. Neither families nor states are able to practice the economies and make the savings that the formation of capital requires.

Until 1950 Latin America was a leading exporter of grain to world markets. Until recently, Spanish America, excluding Brazil, sold more grain abroad than North America and Oceania combined. Today we are importers, with considerable strain on our national economies. Some governments have even had to impose rationing systems.

Notwithstanding the growing appropriations for education, there are nine to twelve million children who still cannot attend school, and we have made no real progress against illiteracy. Our schools and colleges cannot cope with the demand.

Chile has a population of nine million inhabitants of whom over one-

SOURCE: "The Situation in Chile" from Hernán Romero, "Responsible Parenthood: A Human Right and Duty," in Report No. 3 of the Victor Fund for the International Planned Parenthood Federation, September 1966, pp. 16–18. Reprinted by permission of the International Planned Parenthood Federation.

third are clustered in Santiago. The same situation prevails in Argentina. Montevideo has almost half of Uruguay's total population. If this same ratio were to prevail in the United States, Washington would have ninety million inhabitants.

The trend toward urbanization all over the world displays certain peculiar features on our continent. The flow toward cities is particularly intense. It is out of step with the industrialization process, and the attraction is usually exercised by the capital city rather than by cities in general.

This double mechanism—internal migration and the insufficient development of industries—has led to widespread unemployment and the formation of slums which are known as "villas miserias" in Buenos Aires, as "favelas" in Rio de Janeiro, and as "callampas" here in Chile.

These slums have no social coherence, and their populations include great percentages of people under fifteen years of age. There is much illiteracy and unemployment. They constitute one of the most frightening social menaces of our time.

One of the distinguishing features of modern times is the vehement drive for self-improvement. The flight from the countryside is largely due to the attraction exerted by the mirage of the city. The city is believed to offer more regular and better paid employment, social services and insurance, the possibility of acquiring education and of rising to a higher status. As disillusion comes, resignation and asquiescence are everywhere gradually giving way to real rebelliousness.

.   .   .

The Chilean woman has learned from experience that she need not bear three children to keep one, and that too many offspring can become a truly agonizing burden.

Chile is one of the few countries where a serious study has been made of abortions over a period of more than fifteen years. As part of extensive research on human reproduction, the Department of Preventive and Social Medicine, which I have the honor of heading, established the frequency of abortions, in 1950, in a sample of more than 3,000 women who had had 10,612 pregnancies. Of these 26.5 per cent were voluntarily aborted, with a large number of cases requiring hospitalization.

Abortion is induced in one of every two or three pregnancies; it is contemplated in one of every five pregnancies ending in birth. The frequency is greater among married women or common-law wives and among persons who attempt to practice birth control by more or less absurd procedures. In ten out of fifteen cases, the husband approved the decision to abort and in one out of eight the abortion was performed by the patient herself. As everywhere, abortion is the cruelest and most reprehensible procedure for the prevention of unwanted pregnancies. One group of fifteen women in the Armijo-Monreal inquiry provoked it 187 times.

In the National Health Service, abortions account for more than eight per cent of total patient admissions. They tie up twenty per cent of the beds in maternity and gynecology wards; necessitate thirty-five per cent of the surgical interventions, require seventeen per cent of the transfusions and close to twenty-seven per cent of the blood supply administered in emergency wards. . . .

The professional people who were alarmed by the swelling tide of abortions and the other repercussions of excessive fertility resolved to organize the Chilean Family Protection Association, which eventually joined the International Planned Parenthood Federation. . . .

There are now birth control clinics or wards in every public hospital in Santiago and in many provinces, and also in some private institutions. They are ordinarily filled to capacity, and the enormous demand cannot be fully met. The public is offered various methods of demonstrated effectiveness from which to choose. Experience has shown that our women ordinarily reject the rhythm method and express a clear preference for pills and intra-uterine devices. . . .

10. Demographic Research
in Latin America

Father Gustavo Pérez Ramírez, who has a Ph.D. in sociology, is director of the Colombian Institute for Social Development in Bogotá. He has courageously and publicly defended the thesis that the Church today is not pronatalist and does not necessarily favor large families. In the following selections, he describes some of the new demographic research institutions at work in Latin America and presents a sample of the data these institutions are beginning to produce.

The study of population has been, until recently, inadequate or nonexistent in most Latin American countries, not only because of inadequate vital statistics, but also because of the lack of persons trained in the methods of demographic analysis.

Nevertheless, much improvement has been achieved in the last decade and we hope that as a result of the program "Census of the Americas 1960" more and better demographic data will be available in the future.

With the purpose of finding a solution to this situation (which is not restricted to Latin America) the Economic and Social Council of the

SOURCE: "Demographic Research in Latin America" from Rev. Gustavo Pérez Ramírez, "Family Planning Policies and Research in Latin America," in The Problem of Population (Notre Dame, Ind.: University of Notre Dame Press, 1965), Vol. 3, pp. 171–83. Reprinted by permission of the publisher.

United Nations adopted, in May 1955, a resolution to explore the possibilities of establishing in underdeveloped areas of the world centers for the study of the problems of population and for the training of personnel in the field of demographic analysis.

A general consensus of the need for one of these centers in Latin America was manifested at the first Seminar on Demographic Problems in Latin America held in Rio de Janeiro, December 1955, sponsored by the United Nations. Two years later an agreement was signed between Chile and the United Nations for the creation of the Latin American Demographic Center, CELADE.

It organizes programs of professional training for individuals from all Latin American countries and Puerto Rico and provides instruction in demography at other international centers operating in Santiago and at the University of Chile.

It promotes and develops demographic research either in given countries or regions and, on request, furnishes technical assistance to the countries. Finally, it also actively supports and assists ECLA (Economic Commission for Latin America) and the Latin American Institute of Economic and Social Planning in work related to population problems in Latin America.

Under the auspices of the United Nations and of the University of Chile, and in collaboration with the Department of Sociology of Cornell University, CELADE is directing a comparative research on seven studies on fertility in Latin America, based on previous studies made in Puerto Rico (1951), Santiago de Chile (1959), and Lima, Peru (1961). . . .

The purpose is not to formulate a population policy, but to observe and analyze the facts in order to improve knowledge of such vital problems as the relationship between population and factors influencing ways of life and production. . . .

Another institution dealing with population research in Latin America at the continental level is the recently established Latin American Center for Family and Population, CELAP (January 1965) with headquarters in Santiago (Chile). It will play an important role in Latin America, if it really operates on a continental scale, avoiding "Chileanization."

There is general consensus that, if Catholic programs for research, diffusion of information and instruction on family limitation are to be put into practice, Catholic public opinion must be mobilized.

·   ·   ·

I agree with Carmen Miró, Director of the Latin American Demographer Center, CELADE, who says: "It seems justified to state that the doctrinal position of the Catholic Church is not an obstacle to family planning. The persistence of a very high rate of fertility in Latin America is not to be attributed to the predominantly Catholic conditions of the population but to the backwardness, both economic and social, in which it exists." . . .

Yet, causation with respect to values and norms is one of the most controversial issues in the social sciences today.

"No one can doubt that norms exercise some influence on behavior, but the question of how much influence they exercise is highly debatable." There is some evidence of discrepancy between religious values and behavior, according to the comparative study on fertility in Latin America, directed by CELADE (Santiago, Chile).

Thanks to the director of CELADE, I had access in Santiago last February to the preliminary results of the first tabulations. The distribution in three Latin American cities (for which data were available) of married women using contraceptives in relation to their church attendance is shown in the following table.

Percentage Using Contraceptives

Regularity of Church Attendance	Panama	Rio de Janeiro	San José (Costa Rica)
Once a week or more	59.3	57.9	65.2
One or two times a month	64.4	47.1	54.2
A few times a year	—	51.1	53.2
Only once a year	58.2	59.7	62.4
Only once over several years	—	64.0	78.0
Never attend	50.0	58.0	71.9

These figures show in general the percentage in favor of the use of contraceptives. Paradoxically, with only one exception, there is a significant majority among church-going married women who use contraceptives.

Once all the CELADE data are available, it will be important to do further research on the motivations and knowledge of the women whose behavior seems deviant in relation to Church norms. . . .

The institutionalization of a permanent dialogue with the secular world is needed to assist Catholic natural and social scientists and theologians to approach, in an interdisciplinary effort, one of the most urgent, complex and challenging problems faced by Latin America.

11. *Modern Statements of the Position of the Roman Catholic Church*

The first of the following passages reflects the thinking of the bishops of the Roman Catholic Church as expressed in *The Pastoral Constitution on the Church in the Modern World.* This Constitution was adopted by the bishops and accepted by Pope Paul VI in December 1965. The final paragraph in this section is taken from the encyclical letter of Paul VI, *On the Development of Peoples,* delivered March 29, 1967.

[Fostering the Nobility of Marriage and the Family]

The biblical Word of God several times urges the betrothed and the married to nourish and develop their wedlock by pure conjugal love and undivided affection. Many men of our own age also highly regard true love between husband and wife as it manifests itself in a variety of ways depending on the worthy customs of various peoples and times.

This love is an eminently human one since it is directed from one person to another through an affection of the will; it involves the good of the whole person, and therefore can enrich the expressions of body and mind with a unique dignity, ennobling these expressions as special ingredients and signs of the friendship distinctive of marriage. This love God has judged worthy of special gifts, healing, perfecting, and exalting gifts of grace and of charity. Such love, merging the human with the divine, leads the spouses to a free and mutual gift of themselves, a gift providing itself by gentle affection and by deed; such love pervades the whole of their lives: indeed by its busy generosity it grows better and grows greater. Therefore it far excels mere erotic inclination, which, selfishly pursued, soon enough fades wretchedly away. . . .

Marriage and conjugal love are by their nature ordained toward the begetting and education of children. Children are really the supreme gift of marriage and contribute very substantially to the welfare of their parents. The God Himself Who said, "it is not good for man to be alone" (Gen. 2:18) and "Who made man from the beginning male and female" (Int. 19:14), wishing to share with man a certain special participation in His own creative work, blessed male and female, saying: "Increase and multi-

source: "Fostering the Nobility of Marriage and the Family" from "The Church in the Modern World," Part II, Chapter 1, as reprinted in the *National Catholic Reporter,* February 16, 1966.

ply" (Gen. 1:28). Hence, while not making the other purposes of matrimony of less account, the true practice of conjugal love, and the whole meaning of the family life which results from it, have this aim: that the couple be ready with stout hearts to cooperate with the love of the Creator and the Savior, who through them will enlarge and enrich His own family day by day.

Parents should regard as their proper mission the task of transmitting human life and educating those to whom it has been transmitted. They should realize that they are thereby cooperators with the love of God the Creator, and are, so to speak, the interpreters of that love. Thus they will fulfill their task with human and Christian responsibility, and, with docile reverence toward God, will make decisions by common counsel and effort. Let them thoughtfully take into account both their own welfare and that of their children, those already born and those which the future may bring. For this accounting they need to reckon with both the material and the spiritual conditions of the times as well as of their state in life. Finally, they should consult the interests of the family group, of temporal society, and of the Church herself. The parents themselves and no one else would ultimately make this judgment in the sight of God.

.   .   .

The sexual characteristics of man and the human faculty of reproduction wonderfully exceed the dispositions of lower forms of life. Hence the acts themselves which are proper to conjugal love and which are exercised in accord with genuine human dignity must be honored with great reverence. Hence when there is question of harmonizing conjugal love with the responsible transmission of life, the moral aspect of any procedure does not depend solely on sincere intentions or on an evaluation of motives, but must be determined by objective standards. . . .

Relying on these principles, sons of the Church may not undertake methods of birth control which are found blameworthy by the teaching authority of the Church in its unfolding of the divine law. . . .

[DEMOGRAPHIC INCREASE]

It is true that too frequently an accelerated demographic increase adds its own difficulties to the problems of development: the size of the population increases more rapidly than available resources, and things are found to have reached apparently an impasse. From that moment the temptation is great to check the demographic increase by means of radical

SOURCE: "Demographic Increase" from the encyclical of Paul VI, *On the Development of Peoples,* paragraph 37, as reprinted in *The New York Times,* March 29, 1967.

measures. It is certain that public authorities can intervene, within the limit of their competence, by favoring the availability of appropriate information and by adopting suitable measures, provided that these be in conformity with the moral law and that they respect the rightful freedom of married couples. Where the inalienable right to marriage and procreation is lacking, human dignity has ceased to exist. Finally, it is for the parents to decide, with full knowledge of the matter, on the number of their children, taking into account their responsibilities toward God, themselves, the children they have already brought into the world, and the community to which they belong. In all this they must follow the demands of their own conscience, enlightened by God's law authentically interpreted, and sustained by confidence in Him.

12. *Changing Attitudes Toward Family Planning in Latin America*

> In a paper delivered in 1967, Dr. J. Mayone Stycos (the author of Reading 2 in this chapter) captured the sense of rapidly changing attitudes toward the family and birth control in contemporary Latin America. The following passages are from his paper.

In Latin America, a series of systematic surveys has recently been conducted in major Latin American cities by the United Nations Latin American Demographic Center (CELADE) in collaboration with Cornell University. Carefully trained local staffs interviewed representative samples of approximately 2,000 women of childbearing age in each of the following cities: Bogotá, Caracas, Lima, Mexico City, Panama City, Rio de Janeiro, San José and San Salvador. In all instances women were asked the following question: "If you were to start a family now, how many children would you want?" The number desired ranged from an average of 2.4 in Rio de Janeiro to 4.1 in Mexico City, or from a quarter to half the number of the average North American Catholic Woman of the Year.[1] We then classi-

[1] [A Catholic Woman of the Year has traditionally been named in the United States. Stycos found that the women selected invariably had brought forth eight or more children during their married lives.]

source: "Changing Attitudes Toward Family Planning in Latin America" from J. Mayone Stycos, "Catholicism and Birth Control in the Western Hemisphere," a paper delivered at the Fourth Annual Meeting of the Catholic Inter-American Cooperation Program, Boston, January 1967, printed (with the simpler title "Birth Control") in *Integration of Man and Society in Latin America*, edited by Samuel Shapiro (Notre Dame, Ind.: University of Notre Dame Press, 1968), pp. 17–21. Reprinted by permission of the author and the publisher.

fied the women in each city according to the frequency with which they receive Communion. In no city did the difference in ideal number of children vary by as much as one child between those who receive Communion less than once per year, and those who receive twice or more per year. Another kind of datum is provided by a recent public opinion survey conducted in seven Brazilian cities. While the average family in these cities had only between three and four living children, only about a quarter of the couples planned to have more children.

But this is what people *want*. Are such desires based on selfishness, on hedonism, on irresponsibility? Are the lower income populations of Latin America capable of reaching "correct judgments" in the light of their low levels of education? I believe that we often underestimate both the intelligence and responsibility of the uneducated. To illustrate what I mean, let me give you some examples of what poorly educated Latin Americans say when questioned in this area. My first illustrations are from Mexican women interviewed by Father Alfonso Orozco Contreras in a family planning clinic in Mexico City. For example, a 29-year-old woman with five children:

> I came to the clinic because, since I am not able to support them, I no longer want to have more children. I now have five, why more when with these I already have too many? Two or three would be enough. I know that the Church says we should not try to avoid having children, but I believe that it is a greater sin to have them and not educate them. The point is not only to bring them into the world but to educate them also. I am not in accord with those families who have ten or twelve children but can only half dress and feed them, turning them into beggars and delinquents. Many say that pills are used so as to keep a slim figure but these people do not know that what we want is something much more important: our home, children and husband.

Another 35-year-old patient of the clinic said:

> Religion says that we should accept the children that God sends but my personal opinion is that it is a much greater sin to have children one can't educate. Of course, I would not discuss this with any priest because it is my own personal feeling. I believe in confession and all but I have not confessed this. Also, I do not feel I am living in sin because I believe it to be good. I have seen many children who are almost in misery and never go to Church. On the other hand, if you ask the families why they have so many children they answer, "because it is a sin to prevent them." They are not faithful Church attenders but resort to the Church to justify a large family. I really believe that if they were better Church members they wouldn't have so many children. They consider it a sin to avoid having children but on the other hand they find it very normal not to fulfill their obligations as parents. Doesn't this seem like a contradiction?

Another said:

> I know that according to my religion I am doing wrong because I
> have not gone to confession and I have not wanted to confess, but
> I would like to see them with nine children and begging bread and
> milk with not enough to go around, or walking without shoes or with
> torn clothes because they do not have means to buy them. Also, if I
> have not gone to confess and do not go, they will not be charged
> with my sin.

It might be thought that the desperation of poverty drives such women
to desire to limit the size of their families, and that if their economic level
were improved they would desire more children. While there may be
some truth to this argument, as the standard of living rises we can also
anticipate comparable increases in the standards for responsible parenthood. In short, the number of children viewed as adequately supportable
may decline. A Puerto Rican mother with some high school education
explained the process with admirable clarity on being interviewed by one
of our students this summer:

> If I have to send my children to school, I have to dress them properly.
> One, two or five is not the same as ten. . . .
>   One lives here as one's neighbors. A poor woman sees her neighbors
> send their children to the *Colegio* nicely dressed and neat, she feels
> sad because she can't have her children the same. She decides, well
> I already have five and I'll have no more.

And what of the males' sense of responsibility: Much has been written,
largely by journalists and pseudo-sociologists, of the Latin American complex of machismo. In my earliest investigations in Puerto Rico I used this
presumed drive to manifest virility as a major hypothesis in accounting
for high birth rates. Research proved me wrong, and proved that lower
income Puerto Rican males had attitudes far more responsible than had
ever been supposed. When we asked them how a man could prove he
was an "hombre completo" or a "macho" they cited the need to prove
one was not sterile, but they added that beyond this point manhood was
demonstrated by being able properly to support one's children. As
phrased by a sugar cane cutter with three years' education: "To be an
hombre completo a man should have a wife and children, and . . . these
should be well fed and have clothes to wear and the necessary things to
live well."

The Bishops noted that "free decision is curtailed when spouses feel
constrained to choose birth limitation because of poverty, inadequate and
inhuman housing, or lack of proper medical services." This may well be,
and it behooves governments to move with all due haste to remove poverty

from the face of the earth. But what can the individual family be expected to do in the meantime? Reprehensible as our social system or our leaders may be, in the face of today's poverty can a poor family's desire for a moderate number of children be considered anything other than responsible parenthood? I would say that such motives, in the face of religious and legal obstacles and almost a conspiracy of silence on the part of our mass media, [are a] magnificent tribute to the "correct judgment" and "conscientious decision-making" of the common man. The fact that he often fails to *achieve* these goals is no reflection on his judgment or responsibility, but a reflection on the forces which deny him adequate knowledge and facilities to realize the dictates of his conscience.

.   .   .

To many intellectuals, the key to freedom is knowledge, and institutions which are viewed as suppressing knowledge are regarded with particular suspicion. In a series of lengthy interviews conducted with Colombian intellectuals this summer, in speaking of the role of the Church and population problems, one of them put it this way:

> To my view all the purposeful hiding of knowledge is immoral, be it political knowledge in a totalitarian state, or birth control in a religious state. The worst example is what happens economically when a selected group keeps a new technology to itself and does not allow other groups in the society to benefit from it. Our higher classes are using birth control quite widely although they would never admit it because they maintain a facade of religiousness to appear as favorites of the Church. But it is these same people who oppose birth control in the general population. It is this kind of double standard that I see as the highest immorality in the world.

13. Agricultural Technology and the Prospect of Famine

Dr. Raymond Ewell, vice-president for research at the State University of New York at Buffalo, has written more than seventy articles on various aspects of chemistry and economics. He concludes this article with the warning that Thomas Malthus "may be proved right after all—unless the world's resources are mobilized soon and effectively."

There is no doubt that agricultural productivity could be raised greatly in any country in the world—if there were time. But time is the

SOURCE: "Agricultural Technology and the Prospect of Famine" from Raymond Ewell, "Famine and Fertilizer," in *Chemical and Engineering News*, 42 (December 14, 1964), pp. 111–16. Reprinted by permission of the author and the publisher.

crux of the problem. The use of improved agricultural methods represents a basic social and cultural change, and social change is a slow process. Most of the farmers of Asia, Africa, and Latin America are totally illiterate —they can't read or write or add numbers, nor do they understand the elements of plant biology. Under these conditions, the introduction of scientific agriculture into Asia, Africa, and Latin America is likely to be a slow process. In fact, the social, cultural, and educational factors, not the technical factors, are the real bottlenecks in improving agriculture in these countries.

If the population would remain constant for 30 or 40 years agriculture could change gradually and begin to supply a more adequate diet. Instead the population of these three continents will probably double in the next 25 to 30 years. Where will the food come from to feed 2 billion more people in Asia, Africa, and Latin America by 1990?

Of the various technical factors, increased use of fertilizer offers the best possibility for a quick increase in agricultural production. Field trials in many countries have established that moderate applications of fertilizer will give large increases in yields even if other technical inputs such as seed varieties and water supply are left unchanged.

. . .

Improved seeds, increased irrigation, pesticides, and all other technical inputs must be utilized to the fullest extent possible, yet it should be recognized that the principal means of raising agricultural productivity in Asia, Africa, and Latin America in the critical next 15 years will have to be fertilizer.

How much fertilizer will it take? What facilities will be needed? How much will it cost? How will the fertilizer be distributed and applied to the soil?

As a minimum goal, let us assume that agricultural production should be increased enough to provide 16 ounces of grain per person per day in Asia, Africa, and Latin America in 1970 and also in 1980. This is the present level of consumption, so the minimum goal suggested is simply maintaining the present nutritional level, inadequate as it is. Everyone with any humanitarian instincts would like to see the diet of the underdeveloped areas improved, but this is virtually impossible until the birth rate is reduced substantially. The underdeveloped countries will be pushed to the limit to maintain the present diet even with maximum help from the developed countries. The people of Asia, Africa, and Latin America ask only for enough rice, wheat, corn, and beans. Foods like meat, fish, eggs, and milk are beyond the reach of most of the people of these lands now and are likely to be even less available in the future as the populations continue to increase.

To provide **16 ounces of grain** per day for the **400 million** additional population of these continents in 1970 would require 15 million tons of plant nutrients, compared with consumption of 3 million tons in 1960–61. Consumption is probably about 4 million tons in 1963–64. To feed the 900 million additional population in 1980, 30 million tons of plant nutrients would be required. These figures were calculated on the basis that one ton of plant nutrient results in 8 tons of additional grain and that two thirds of the fertilizer would be used on grain, one third on all other crops. . . .

To emphasize this point further, I am willing to put myself on record that if Asia, Africa, and Latin America are not using quantities of fertilizer approaching 30 million tons by 1980, they are almost certain to be engulfed in widespread famine.

The consequences of the population explosion have been discussed and analyzed in theoretical terms for a decade now, but the time for theory is nearing an end and the time for action is here. There has been too much talk and theorizing about how to solve the world food crisis in the year 2000 when the beginnings of the crisis are probably only five or six years away.

· · ·

The immediate problem is how can the countries of Asia, Africa, and Latin America obtain a supply of 15 million tons of plant nutrients by 1970 and 30 million tons by 1980. Domestic production of fertilizer in all three continents together is about 1.5 million tons in 1963–64, and a good estimate for 1970 production would be 3 to 4 million tons. Production in 1970 might be increased to 5 to 6 million tons by a new crash program of fertilizer plant construction, but generally speaking it is already too late to increase production greatly by 1970. I believe, therefore, that most of the fertilizer needed by Asia, Africa, and Latin America in 1970 will have to be imported from the industrialized countries. Some countries would have the foreign exchange to buy the fertilizer they need through commercial channels, but most countries would have to rely on foreign aid.

For the longer term in 1980, most countries should plan to become largely self-sufficient in fertilizer production—at least the larger countries. In round numbers, fertilizer plants cost about $1 billion per 6 million tons of annual production of finished fertilizer (on a plant nutrient basis). Therefore, enough fertilizer plants to produce 30 million tons of fertilizer would cost about $5 billion—10% of the cost of putting a man on the moon. If 30 million tons of fertilizer were produced and used in Asia, Africa, and Latin America, it would be a giant step toward solving the world food problem in 1980. Historians of the future may remark on whether it was more important to have devoted our resources during the 1960's to putting a man on the moon or to have devoted our resources toward averting the world famine of the 1970's.

CONCLUSION

At varying rates and in various ways, change is occurring in Latin America. Change is being impelled by several agents: Protestantism, commercial bureaucracies, urbanism, Marxist and Christian Democratic revolutionary governments, Catholic Church leaders and clergy, and, not least, the pressure of population growth now heightened by the introduction of modern preventive medicine and sanitation.

Population growth in particular has forced more and more governments to change their policies with respect to family planning and to take an interest in the most intimate acts of individual citizens. It has apparently helped convince some Catholic Church leaders of the need to reevaluate the meaning of marriage and family. It is probably one of the reasons that more and more married couples act against traditional beliefs and sentiments about the virtues of the large family. Finally, population growth has put a tremendous burden on the economies of every country that has shown concern for the improvement of the living standard of its people.

To reiterate, when death rates are high, high birth rates are needed to guarantee the survival of a family or a society. Religious and familial values (such as "Children are a blessing from God" and "The large family is the good family") sustain and give meaning to these patterns. And, historically at least, this has meant a dependent and low status for women. Increased control over death alters the equation, and high birth rates suddenly threaten survival. The traditional values and beliefs that had sustained Latin American life for so long have suddenly become dysfunctional, and a struggle has ensued on the level of values as they are expressed in beliefs, ideology, and concrete behavior patterns.

Whether the Latin American nations will be able to feed their peoples and give them a higher material standard of living in the remaining years of this century—an aspiration to which most of them are now committed—is a basic question but one that at this stage can receive no confident answer. Several other matters, particularly those touching on husband-wife relations, can in the meantime be considered.

It seems certain that contraceptives will be widely accepted by the upper, middle, and lower classes of Latin America within the next ten years. What consequence will this advance in medical technology have for husbands and wives? How will this fact affect the machismo syndrome where it still persists? Will this medical facility not mean another important step on the way to sexual equality for the woman? Will such equality improve the quality of marital life or be disruptive of it? How may contraception, along with new church teachings on marriage and love and new opportunities for education and for employment outside the home, affect the status and self-image of women? And conversely, how will the men be affected? If we can project from the experience of the United States and Europe, the long-run effect should be beneficial. Beneficial, that is, if a sufficient damper is put on population growth.

The evidence presented strongly supports the argument that, given a knowledge of the choices available to them, the people of Latin America, of all social classes, do opt for a decent life, for education for their children, and for smaller families. Whether that smaller family means two, three, or four children is itself a question that looks less and less like a strictly personal husband-wife matter the more one looks into the social consequences of this decision. Can family life be meaningful for whole societies where two and three children are the limit rather than three and four? Throughout most of history, only two or three children in the average family survived to adulthood. Now that nearly every child born seems likely to survive, perhaps this same number will be found to be satisfying for familial relations—especially given the wide range of human relations that modern urban society itself makes possible.

BIBLIOGRAPHY

Dasilva, Barbosa, J. F. "The Urbanization of Latin America," in L. Cárdenas, ed., *Urbanization of Latin America* (Austin: University of Texas Press, 1967).

Erickson, E. Gordon. "Changing Virility, Virginity Complexes as Related to Fertility Patterns of Middle Strata Wives: Costa Rica," in *Proceedings of the World Population Conference 1965*, 2 (New York: United Nations, 1967).

Freedman, Ronald, ed. *Population: The Vital Revolution* (Chicago: Aldine, 1965).

Hauser, Philip, ed. *The Population Dilemma* (Englewood Cliffs, N.J.: Prentice-Hall, 1963).

Lewis, Oscar. *Five Families* (New York: Basic Books, 1959).

Paddock, William, and Paul Paddock. *Famine, 1975* (Boston: Little, Brown, 1967).

Roberts, Thomas. *Contraception and Holiness* (New York: Herder & Herder, 1964).

Saunders, John V. D. *Social Factors in Latin American Modernization* (Nashville, Tenn.: Nashville Graduate Center for Latin American Studies, 1966).

Shapiro, Samuel, ed. *Integration of Man and Society in Latin America* (Notre Dame, Ind.: University of Notre Dame Press, 1968).

Smith, T. Lynn. "The Growth of Population in Latin America," in *Problems of Population Growth*, 1963 (Washington, D.C.: U.S. Government Printing Office, 1963).

Stycos, J. M., and Jorge Arias, eds. *Population Dilemma in Latin America* (New York: Taplinger, 1966).